Women, Violence,
and English Renaissance Literature

Medieval and Renaissance Texts and Studies

Volume 256

Women, Violence,

and English Renaissance Literature

Essays Honoring Paul Jorgensen

edited by

Linda Woodbridge

&

Sharon Beehler

Arizona Center for Medieval and Renaissance Studies
Tempe, Arizona
2003

Dust jacket image: Reproduced with the permission of
the Pepys Library, Magdalene College, Cambridge.

© Copyright 2003
Arizona Board of Regents for Arizona State University

Library of Congress Cataloging-in-Publication Data

Women, violence, and English Renaissance literature : essays honoring Paul Jorgensen / edited by Linda Woodbridge & Sharon Beehler.
    p. cm. — (Medieval & Renaissance texts & studies ; v. 256)
Includes bibliographical references (p.) and index.
ISBN 0-86698-299-X (acid-free paper)
    1. English literature — Early modern, 1500–1700 — History and criticism.
2. Women and literature — England — History — 16th century. 3. Women
and literature — England — History — 17th century. 4. Violence in literature.
5. Women in literature. 6. Rape in literature. I. Jorgensen, Paul A. II. Woodbridge, Linda, 1945– III. Beehler, Sharon A. IV. Medieval & Renaissance
Texts & Studies (Series) ; v. 256.
PR428.W63W66 2003
820.9'3522'09031—dc22   2003063731

This book is made to last.
It is set in Caslon,
smythe-sewn and printed on acid-free paper
to library specifications.

Printed in the United States of America

For Virginia Jorgensen,

the wind beneath his wings.

Table of Contents

B. Violence and the Interior Subjectivity
of Women

C. Violence toward Women in Shakespeare's *Othello*

PART TWO:
VIOLENCE BY WOMEN

Introduction

"Some have no pleasure but in violence."
— Fletcher and Rowley, *The Maid in the Mill*

WOMEN AND VIOLENCE: PROLEGOMENA

A satisfying Swedish fairy tale features a little goatherd who exceeds even the high standard of good-hearted gentleness expected of the folk-tale hero. His sweetness seems downright feminine. When on his journey he is threatened with violence from a ferocious bear, a ravenous wolf, and a snarling lion, he befriends each with a soft answer and they let him pass upon his way, singing his sweet little song about how kindness wins more friends in this world than does violence. The Renaissance woman did not so lightly escape from the violent claw as does the little goatherd; but in his gentle, soft non-violence this folk-tale hero resembles the ideal Renaissance woman. ("Her voice was ever soft,/ Gentle, and low, an excellent thing in woman": *King Lear* 5.3.277–278.[1]) But let us finish the tale of the gentle goatherd a little later.

The weight of the essays in this volume — ten on women as objects of male violence and four on violence committed by women — reflects the extent to which the Renaissance itself gendered violence mainly as male: men were usually its subjects and women often its objects. Women were the gentle goatherd, and men were the bears, wolves, and lions. Why should this have been so? The age, after all, is known for its violent spectacles: hangings, drawings-and-quarterings,

---

[1] References to Shakespeare in the Introduction are to the *Complete Works*, ed. David Bevington, 4th ed.

burnings at the stake, whipping of beggars and prostitutes naked through the streets, hurling of refuse at offenders confined in the stocks, bear-baitings, cock-fights. Women too were spectators at these theaters of violence, and if the effect was brutalizing, it should have been brutalizing for both genders; and yet violence was most often represented as more typically male. Why?

The obvious starting point in answering this question is the fact that violence was (by long historical precedent) a way to prove masculinity, and although male violence against other males (as in war or sport) was a primary validator of masculinity, the instrumentality of violence in the male ego's self-fashioning is relevant to women too, in several ways. Identity was fashioned against a defining Other, individual male prowess against male adversaries, and masculinity itself against female opposites. In her study of Renaissance male identity formation, *Man's Estate*, Coppélia Kahn shows both sides of this mechanism of identity-forging at work in *Romeo and Juliet*, where the feud allows individual young men to "prove themselves" by violence against each other, but also initiates the whole male gender into patriarchal roles by encouraging men (right down to the scrapping, would-be rapist Sampson) to define masculinity in opposition to femininity and to practice violence against women: "It leads them to scorn women and to associate them with effeminacy and emasculation, while it links sexual intercourse with aggression and violence against women, rather than with pleasure and love" (Kahn, *Man's Estate*, 86–88). According to the essentialist gender theory of the age, males were aggressive by nature, and only men could legitimately commit violence: to commit violence was to be not-female and to be not-female was to commit violence. When women did commit violence, it called forth a rhetoric of exceptionality and unnaturalness, and provoked a special horror that owed much to its being an infringement on male prerogative. And when women were objects of male violence, it graphically established their subjugated state and hence ratified male superiority.

It may be that identity always requires distinguishing oneself against an Other,[2] but the Renaissance seems to have been a time of especially anxious mascul-

---

[2] Piotr Hoffman, in a philosopher's view of violence, sees the formation of identity against a defining other, which has so characterized the thinking of modern centuries, as itself conditioned by the pervasive daily experience of violence in the Renaissance: "The political philosophy with which the modern age begins–the thinking of Machiavelli and Hobbes–focuses upon a constant possibility of violence threatening the life of human communities" (*Violence in Modern Philosophy*, vii). In positing the violent other as a force of equal strength to any given ego, however ("my adversary in violence, the other ... threatens me with annihilation" [10]), Hoffman fails to take into account the unequal power distribution of the gendered form in which most women experienced violence;

inity, to use the term of Mark Breitenberg, who links this special anxiety to a particular moment in the history of patriarchy. To his thoughtful analysis, we want to add recognition of the importance of violence in changing constructions of masculine identity, especially seeing that attitudes toward violence in society's higher echelons were changing — something that Breitenberg and others neglect. This period of crisis for masculinity was also a time which when the discourse of violence came under considerable cultural stress, with inevitable repercussions for masculinity. In his influential account of the changing situation, Norbert Elias reminds us that in late medieval society,

> rapine, battle, hunting of men and animals ... were vital necessities which ... for the mighty and strong, ... formed part of the pleasures of life. "I tell you," says a war hymn attributed to the minstrel Bertran de Born, "that neither eating, drinking, nor sleep has as much savor for me as to hear the cry 'Forwards!' from both sides, and horses without riders shying and whinnying, and the cry 'Help! Help!', and to see the small and the great fall to the grass at the ditches and the dead pierced by the wood of the lances decked with banners." ... A particular pleasure [was] taken in mutilating prisoners. ... The pleasure in killing and torturing others was great, and it was a socially permitted pleasure." (*The Civilizing Process*, 158–59)

Elias, Lawrence Stone, and others have documented the ways in which gunpowder helped change this aesthetics of violence: bullets didn't come decked with banners as lances had, and bullets helped render obsolete the aristocracy which had been a martial, equestrian class as well as a landowning class. Guns and cannons, with their long range and indiscriminate explosive power, were no respecters of persons, and this had a certain effect of social leveling on the battlefield. Though as brutal as ever, war had lost whatever glamor had been conferred on it by charging steeds in colorful battle attire that had almost a festive air, at least in art: the decorative mounted knight was now relegated to nostalgic jousting matches before the ladies of the court. War also encountered principled opposition from the likes of Erasmus and More: in their humanist platform, pacifism constituted an important plank. And finally, England in the sixteenth century enjoyed several long periods of peace. Elias tracks the aristocracy's shift from martial prowess to civility, to increasingly refined manners, as a new mech-

---

thus, while his historicizing of the issue of violence and othering is valuable, his failure to consider the gender dimension of the issue undercuts his philosophizing.

anism for establishing distinction from classes below them. As formerly blood-thirsty bluebloods were reduced to tame courtiers obliged to prove themselves by competitive sonnet-writing rather than by skewering rivals on lances, the psychic transition must have been trying.

Historians have typically seen this changing face of violence as part of a crisis of the aristocracy, neglecting its implications as a crisis for masculinity.[3] Not only the aristocratic identity but also the male identity had been dependent upon martial prowess. It is hard to overemphasize the contrast between establishing one's masculine, aristocratic identity through writing sonnets and establishing it by lopping the noses and ears off captured enemy soldiers. Not surprisingly, alarmists throughout the sixteenth century decried pacifism as effeminate and predicted the eclipse of traditional English manliness and national pride. Paul Jorgensen, in his classic study *Shakespeare's Military World*, discusses Elizabethan and Jacobean unease with peace; moralists often associated it with disease, sloth, softness, and (most important for our purposes) effeminacy. Particularly memorable are Jorgensen's discussions of the many works — from pamphlets by Barnabe Rich to plays by Shakespeare — that juxtapose manly soldiers with effeminate courtiers. Though soldiers were often represented as ungainly figures when they turned up at court, "The soldier's ineptitude in peace is excused by making the courtier's harmony with peace seem blameworthy" (Jorgensen, *Shakespeare's Military World*, 226). The play *A Larum for London* "presented a frightening picture

---

[3] Stone's well-known account of the waning of the aristocracy's status as a military elite, for example, focuses first on the Crown's efforts to curb the power of over-mighty subjects by gradually replacing the old aristocratic military retainers with a national militia. Then a period of peace weakened the aristocracy's link with military pursuits: "During the long period of peace from 1562 to 1588 the nobility lost the habit of military service, and even during the war years of the 1590's only a minority took an active part in military campaigns. Another twenty years of peace after 1604 meant that they were now almost entirely absorbed in private and civilian pursuits, and no longer looked to war as a natural outlet for their energies. The movement of the aristocracy out of the countryside into London and about the Court greatly accelerated this shift by providing alternative fields of competition, intrigue, and pleasure. By 1640 the bellicose instincts of the class had been sublimated in the pursuit of wealth and the cultivation of the arts. . . . The ancient obligation to serve the Prince in war gave way to one of service in government and at Court" (*Crisis of the Aristocracy*, 96–113, 116). Norbert Elias, Richard Helgerson, Arthur Marotti, and others have traced the domestication of a warrior class into a class competing for favor at court. All these writers, however, concentrate more on class issues than on the effect of diminished military preoccupations — diminished violence — on the formation of the Renaissance masculine identity. (One exception is Thomas Laqueur; see *Making Sex*, 125–27.)

of the sack of Antwerp, a prosperous city with peace-loving citizens, 'Their bodies us'd to soft effeminate silks'" (171; see also 216–18, 243). Civility had its
downside for the masculine man: as John Hale summarizes, "From the mid-six-
teenth century the effeminating effect of civility was fairly widely deplored" (*The
Civilization of Europe in the Renaissance*, 369). Though Tudor culture was offi-
cially committed to refined manners, many Tudor subjects harbored a nagging
suspicion that civility was for sissies.

Anxiety about the effeminizing effects of peace helps account for the shift
from the medieval chivalric ideal, in which violently warlike behavior could
coexist with courtly love, to a Renaissance separation between the soldier and the
lover: the one staunchly masculine, the other effeminized. A medieval culture
hero like Sir Lancelot was both a stalwart warrior and an accomplished lady's
man; but when Renaissance writers cast about for a perfect example of polar opposites to illustrate the rhetorical device of antithesis, they thought of the soldier
versus the lover as automatically as they thought of the king versus the beggar.

The older, violent model of macho masculinity runs headlong into a feminized
world of civility in the returning soldier figure, a recurrent type in Renaissance
drama who has a Rip Van Winkle touch, as if his days at the wars have been a-
sleep from which he has awakened to find society utterly changed: no longer
sharing his values, no longer delighting in the rape of enemy women or the severing of enemy noses and ears, but demanding (of all things!) *civility*. The returning soldier character is usually a bitter man, finding his violent contributions
to the nation now undervalued, and from Claudio in *Much Ado About Nothing* to
Jacopo in Beaumont and Fletcher's *The Captain* to Shakespeare's Othello, the
soldier who tries to make a transition to a civilian world experiences real difficulty in adjusting to a realm of civility whose values seem feminine.[4] In some crucial cases, he finds it impossible to give up his violence.

Under the influence of new civilian concepts of manliness and nobility, however, some key texts of this period interrogate traditional notions of violence as
a determinant of masculinity.[5] Castiglione's *The Courtier*, seeking traits of the

---

[4] It is true that Henry V walks off a battlefield and into a courtship with the polished
and mendacious aplomb which marks all his highly-theatricalized roles, but his smooth
role-playing while courting Katherine incorporates an allusion to the conventionally difficult transition from soldier to lover: he wishes he could "win a lady" by "vaulting into my
saddle with my armor on my back," and claims, "I speak to thee plain soldier" (*H5*
5.2.139–151). On the returning soldier figure, see Woodbridge, *Women and the English
Renaissance*, 159–68.

[5] Violence was never of course the sole determinant of masculinity: male identity was
also dependent on such factors as the respect of other males, position in a patriarchal

ideal male courtier, first fixes upon distinction in feats of arms; but Cardinal Bembo, early on in the book, stoutly defends literature as worthier than military violence, and during the course of *The Courtier* martial prowess gradually yields to the virtues of civility as defining marks of the masculine courtier: skill at governing, the exercise of the arts, delicacy in the games of love, the ability to tell a good joke with some finesse. And once violence (a male prerogative) has ceased to define the ideal courtier, the text is free to take up the question of the ideal *female* courtier: women gain more value and acquire some cultural space, once violence and weapons cease to be all-important.[6] In another key text, *Macbeth*, Lady Macbeth manipulates her husband by equating masculinity with murderous violence ("When you durst do it, then you were a man")[7] but Shakespeare also lets Macbeth challenge this equation: "I dare do all that may become a man; who dares do more is none" (1.7.47–50). Macduff is advised to react to the destruction of his family in a traditionally masculine way — that is, by violence: "Dispute it like a man." Although he agrees to inflict violent retribution — "I shall do so" — Macduff significantly adds, "but I must also feel it like a man" (4.3.221–223), admitting "feminine" emotion and sensitivity into the definition of manliness. Male violence, in short, was no longer the norm in this period. Even a soldier like Macbeth, hardened to scenes of brutality, can recognize that violence is often not acceptable in civilized society; and many other Renaissance voices, both male and female, challenged definitions of manliness that were predicated on violence.

Renaissance drama was quite capable of representing as unhealthy — nay, kinky — the male soldiers who get a sexual kick out of war, such as Julianus in Middleton and Rowley's *All's Lost by Lust*, who calls war "a gallant mistress" and "my second nuptials" (1.2.51–52), or Shakespeare's Coriolanus who tells his military rival Aufidius, "I loved the maid I married; never man / Sighed truer breath. But that I see thee here, / Thou noble thing, more dances my rapt heart / Than when I first my wedded mistress saw / Bestride my threshold. Why, thou Mars

---

hierarchy, successful paternity, and (depending on social class) material possessions or occupational skill.

[6] Though the focus of this volume is on England, the inclusion of Castiglione here is a reminder that notions of masculinity, war, and violence were under scrutiny all over Europe.

[7] And as Paul Jorgensen points out in *Our Naked Frailties: Sensational Art and Meaning in "Macbeth,"* "do it" (then as now) was a euphemism for sex, and the Macbeths' employing it to mean "commit murder" ("Why then 'tis time to do 't") [5.1.35; cf. the Witches' "I'll do and I'll do and I'll do," 1.3.10] conflates sex and violence in ways we will also see in other parts of this volume.

. . ." (4.5.119–123). Such characters belonged to a world of sexually-charged male violence that was slowly becoming outmoded.

The Renaissance had its share of physically violent women, in life and literature. Husband-beaters, and their husbands, were punished by humiliating Skimmington rides. Accused witches, the majority of whom were female, were thought to inflict serious physical harm on their victims. Shakespeare's Queen Margaret stabs a child to death on stage. Nobody ever said that women were never violent. But violence was normative for men and abnormal for women, natural for men and unnatural for women. Violence — at least before civility took hold — defined a man's masculinity; but it damaged a woman's femininity.

We can see in literary genres an inverse relation between the status of women and the acceptability of violence: women occupy positions of eminence and sometimes even of power in the genres of non-violence, such as comedy, love lyric, and pastoral, but in genres of violence such as epic, history plays, and to a large extent tragedy, women are demonized, marginalized, or absent. Because such ideology underpinned traditional gender hierarchies and helped create an artificial gulf between male and female behavior, any decline in the cultural acceptability of male violence was bound to have important repercussions for women. The diminished distinction between the sexes when physical violence drops away as a marker of gender difference should ideally allow women more scope in society. The decline in military prowess as a signifier of masculinity, however, could go in a very different direction: rather than creating spaces for female agency by eroding fixed gender boundaries, it could create a backlash against "feminine" values, as happens in alarmist, anti-pacifist texts such as Barnabe Rich's, and even *promote* violence toward women (rape, wife-beating) as an alternative outlet for aggressions formerly directed at enemy soldiers.[8]

So far we have been talking mainly about male violence toward other men, in war, and its indirect effects on women via its implications for the gender system. Before turning to the issue of male violence directly toward women, we want to raise the question of how much violence women suffer in English Renaissance

---

[8] Our own era has debated whether wife-battering has increased as a consequence of our own challenges to gender boundaries during the feminist movement of the last third of the twentieth century. On this issue, the jury is still out: Richard J. Gelles, summarizing studies by social scientists, reports that the question remains untestable: "there are few consistently reliable incidence or prevalence data that can be used to assess the claim that change in gender roles produces men's fear of loss of power and thus increases violence toward women" ("Male Offenders," 45). The situation four centuries ago, offering even fewer reliable data, is obviously even more difficult to test.

literature, compared to men. What exactly are the demographics of Renaissance literary violence? One fairly often encounters the assumption that women are more frequently the victims of violence in Renaissance literature than men are. Take, for example, this statement by Leonard Tennenhouse: "It is difficult to think of a Renaissance tragedy in which at least one woman is not threatened with mutilation, rape, or murder. Her torture and death provide the explicit and exquisite dénouement and centerpiece of the play in question. Yet despite concerted efforts to historicize the literary past, criticism has done little to account either for the pervasiveness of such violence or for the gender of its victims" ("Violence Done to Women on the Renaissance Stage," 79). Isn't it equally true, however, that it is difficult to think of a Renaissance tragedy in which at least one *man* is not threatened with mutilation or murder? How often, in fact, is a woman's death the "centerpiece" of a tragedy? One thinks of the usual small clutch of examples: Cleopatra, the Duchess of Malfi, possibly Evadne in *The Maid's Tragedy*, and a few others; but the "centerpiece" death of a female hero is hardly the overwhelming impression left by the genre of tragedy, as Tennenhouse suggests. Dreary as it would certainly be to count and tabulate poisonings, mutilations, stabbings, and rapes, we think that some statistical analysis might prove quite revealing, and we would like to see someone undertake a study of the proportional representation of the victimized among males and females in this literature, before categorical statements about the heavy victimization of women continue to be made.[9]

We turn now from the indirect effects on women of cultural violence to the question of more direct male violence against women. One can tell a good deal about a culture by looking at its favorite stories; for example, the favorite

---

[9] The essay by Tennenhouse in which that statement occurs, "Violence Done to Women on the Renaissance Stage," should potentially be of great interest given our topic. Tennenhouse argues, for example, that "around the year 1604, dramatists of all sorts suddenly felt it appropriate to torture and murder aristocratic female characters in a shocking and ritualistic manner" (77), and attempts to link theatrical violence against women to political developments and strain between social classes. His argument, however, is problematic in a number of ways: it is reductive in focusing narrowly on how people felt about the monarch; in conflating "aristocratic" with "royal" it ignores the many ways in which royalty and aristocracy represented competing rather than identical interests; it offers no control group that would indicate what dramatists did to *male* characters in the same period; and it ignores the fact that around the year 1604 the drama regularly subjected women of *all* social classes to violence (consider, for example, the abused women in *Patient Grissil, How a Man May Choose a Good Wife from a Bad, The London Prodigal, The Fair Maid of Bristow*, or *The Miseries of Enforced Marriage* — hardly an "aristocratic" assortment).

Renaissance story of Icarus suits a culture anxious about its blossoming worldly aspirations, and the favorite story of the prodigal son suits a culture torn between the legal principle of condign punishment which sought to give everyone exactly what he deserved, and the Christian ideal of unconditional forgiveness. If a culture's taste in stories, then, can provide doors into its cherished preoccupations, it is significant that one of this period's favorite stories was "The Rape of Lucrece." The story itself was the subject of numberless dramatic poems, plays, and paintings, and was alluded to constantly; and beyond the Lucrece story, sexual assault and threatened sexual assault were central plot elements of narrative and dramatic literature of the period. The beauteous Florimell in Spenser's *Faerie Queene* is pursued by so many leering lechers that her story comes to resemble *The Perils of Pauline*, and becomes at times grotesquely comic, as when Florimell, fresh from encounters with a lecherous forester and a malevolently lustful witch's son, escapes (covered in fish scales) from the clutches of a lewd fisherman in a boat only to fall into the sea and find herself pursued by the lascivious sea god Proteus. Fear of rape if a woman travels alone routinely supplies the motive for women to cross-dress for travel in English Renaissance comedy. The shame of rape causes women to commit suicide (Lucrece) or to be murdered by their fathers (Lavinia in *Titus Andronicus*). Even the threat of extorted sex can cause a father to murder his daughter preventively (*Appius and Virginia*). As Jocelyn Catty notes, "debate, the guiding principle of Renaissance education and rhetoric, frequently takes rape stories as its subject" (*Writing Rape, Writing Women*, 2).[10] Such preoccupation, we suggest, stems from the imbrication of rape in the cultural contest over violence and masculinity.

The essays in this volume treat rape primarily not as a fulfillment of sexual desire but as a forceful imposition of the will on an unconsenting victim.[11] This

---

[10] See also Donaldson, *The Rapes of Lucretia*, 40. Considering the fact that in ancient Rome "the legend of Lucretia . . . seems to have been imported with the express purpose of conferring legitimacy upon the new laws and institutions of Republican Rome," Stephanie Jed asks, "If the narrative of Lucretia's rape somehow legitimizes the foundation of Republican Rome, we might wonder if there is some kind of reciprocal relationship: do republican laws and institutions also legitimize the conditions of sexual violence?" (*Chaste Thinking*, 2). The popularity of the violent Lucrece story in humanistic eras such as Roman antiquity and the Renaissance is but one piece of evidence Jed marshals to argue that humanistic studies have been and are now implicated in the violence of the cultures that have sponsored them (see eadem, "The Scene of Tyranny," and Wolfthal's *Images of Rape*).

[11] As Amy J. Marin and Nancy Felipe Russo remind us, over the past several decades it has been feminist thinkers and writers who have led the way in creating a conceptual shift from rape as a matter of individual passion to a matter of systemic cultural violence;

violent atrocity functions, economically enough, to establish a rapist's masculine identity twice over: it allows him at the same moment to subjugate a female and to triumph over male enemies or rivals who are her protectors or possessors. Often an essential feature of war, rape also offers the sadistic pleasures of war in peacetime. Rape is hardly about mutual erotic desire between a man and a woman; but our contributors find that, in text after text, it is mostly not even about erotic desire on the man's part: it is about male power and domination. However, the idea of mutual desire is often bruited about intriguingly in rape scenes. Barbara Mathieson's essay in this volume, treating the many scenes of rape and attempted rape in John Fletcher's plays, uncovers a repeated scenario wherein a woman avoids rape by pretending to desire her assailant. That the rapist recoils at the first sign of a woman's desire shows that the Renaissance clearly understood rape as a demonstration of male ability to subjugate the female, not as a matter of erotic arousal — at least, except for the erotic charge some male characters get from the exercise of power and control in itself.[12] For a woman to rewrite the script, revising rape into mutual desire, is to spoil the whole point of rape, since as Mathieson argues, in order for rape to confer a sense of powerful virility, "power must be wielded over a non-subject, without her consent, in the essential absence of her desire."

Renaissance sexual assault comprised the quintessential exercise of what René Girard calls "mimetic desire": a rapist desired a woman not for herself but as a sign of triumph over a male rival who possessed her, in a patriarchal system which represented women as property. Rape, in Eve Sedgwick's term, was an affair "between men." We may feel that the theory of mimetic desire has been pressed too far in Renaissance studies — so far as to reduce all heterosexual relations to a by-product of homosocial rivalry between men. In his aptly-titled,

---

emphasizing the "gender, power, [and] structural dimensions of violence," feminist writers began in the 1970s to "reconstruct rape and other forms of male violence as forms of power and control" ("Feminist Perspectives," 19). A groundbreaking study which shifted the thinking of a whole generation toward rape as a crime of violence rather than of sexual desire was Susan Brownmiller's *Against our Wills: Men, Women, and Rape*, of 1975. There is no reason, of course, why rape should not be construed as *both* a crime of sexual lust and as a form of power and control ultimately in the service of patriarchy. For an important caveat against desexualizing our concept of rape, see De Lauretis, "The Violence of Rhetoric."

[12] Marin and Russo generalize that in patriarchal societies, "there is a basic heterosexual cultural script that legitimizes male dominance and eroticizes sexual inequality" ("Feminist Perspectives," 33); the erotics of dominance are frequently visible in Renaissance texts.

highly influential essay " 'Love is Not Love': Elizabethan Sonnet Sequences and the Social Order," Arthur Marotti finds all courtly love poetry to be merely a displacement of male careerist strivings in a court dominated by a queen: as in the case of rape, what appears to be heterosexual desire actually turns out to be male competition. Readers may ultimately sense that here is one more method for erasing women from the Renaissance cultural scene altogether, if they happen not to be the Queen. However, though the theory of "mimetic desire" has been taken to extremes, contributors to this volume do regard sexual assault in particular as more an expression of the male power drive and homosocial rivalry with other males than of any real sexual desire by a man for a woman. As an act of power and of competition with other males (as in Tarquin's expressing rivalry with Collatine by raping Collatine's wife in *The Rape of Lucrece*), Renaissance sexual assault required the absence of female agency: to work in the triangulated economy of mimetic desire, sex had to be imposed against the will of the woman and of her male protectors.

The violent exercise of sexuality may have assuaged an anxiety built into beliefs about male sexuality: in the Renaissance, giving in to lust involved a lack of control that — far from establishing male dominance and power — was in itself effeminizing. The crucial distinction between rape as a lustful act and rape as a violent act was that lust was effeminizing while violence allowed a man to maintain a sense of masculine strength and forcefulness. In an age of "anxious masculinity," this must have been one of the attractions of sexual violence for men.

Even rapists will offer at least a perfunctory rationalization for their actions: many a male literary character in the period shifts blame for rape to the woman herself by claiming he was carried away by her beauty. This notion is enshrined in the slippery word "ravishing," which literally meant "raping" but came metaphorically to mean "so beautiful that it carries away (or ravishes) the beholder," a deft shift of responsibility from the violent ravisher to the ravishingly beautiful object (see Kathryn Gravdal, *Ravishing Maidens*, and Catty, *Writing Rape, Writing Women*, 14). This rationalization is straightforward, but another is complex and puzzling: the persistent claim of sexual assailants that women secretly desire to be raped. Typical of such claims is one cited by Mathieson (below in this volume), in Fletcher and Rowley's *The Maid in the Mill*: "Oh force her, force her, Sir, she longs to be ravished, / Some have no pleasure but in violence."[13] Popu-

---

[13] Readily to hand in the Renaissance was Ovid's "Vim licet appelles: grata est vis ista puellis," "Though they apply force, that force is pleasing to girls" (*Ars Amatoria* 1.673). Some vigorous protests against this notion from women writers are extant; for example, Christine de Pisan's report that she was "troubled and grieved when men argue that many

lar belief had it that when women said "no" they really meant "yes": "Play the maid's part — still answer nay, and take it" (*Richard III* 3.7.51); "Maids, in modesty, say 'no' to that / Which they would have the profferer construe 'aye'" (*Two Gentleman of Verona* 1.2.55–56).[14] Although the assertive widow of John Cooke's *Greene's Tu Quoque* succeeds in binding to a post a man who threatens to rape her, she sarcastically acknowledges the existence of a popular view that widows in particular adore the cave-man approach: "Thou art worthy / Of the best widow living ... / Those that will win widows must do thus" (Sig. L). A violent suitor in Nathan Field's *Amends for Ladies* can't believe that "no" really means "no": the woman must merely be testing him. If he doesn't impose sex on her violently, he tells her,

> you'll laugh at me
> Behind my back, publish I wanted [i.e., lacked] spirit,
> And mock me to the ladies, call me child,
> Say you denied me but to try the heat
> And zeal of my affection toward you,
> Then clap 't up with a rime, as for example,
> *He coldly loves, retires, for one vain trial,*
> *For we are yielding, when we make denial.* (4.1.42–51)

The problem here is that if men believe that women *desire* rape though the women declare the contrary, can we still assert that the gratifications of rape depend mainly on the woman's unwillingness?

The plot line Mathieson has isolated suggests that male characters, whatever they say, don't really believe that the women desire rape, since at the first sign of the woman's willingness they back off. But the question remains, why do they say it? Why say that the women are secretly willing, if they do not believe it or would prefer not to believe it, and seem surprised to find it apparently true?

---

women want to be raped and that it does not bother them at all to be raped by men even when they verbally protest" (*Book of the City of Ladies*, trans. Richards, 160–61).

[14] Complicating this issue, Catty reflects that although "stock motifs in the rhetoric of rape, such as the idea that a woman's 'no' means 'yes,' play a significant role in the troping of rape as normative," such a belief "may also reflect a historical contingency, whereby women were obliged by the constraints of ideology to act 'coyly' and say 'no' despite, or as part of, their own erotic agendas" (*Writing Rape, Writing Women*, 11). An example of such strategic coyness or even strategic "rape" appears in the use of the "marrying the rapist" move as a deliberate ploy by young couples wishing to exercise free choice of marital partner against the restrictive wishes of their parents; see Carolyn Sale's essay in this volume.

Saying that the woman really desires rape could be mere hypocrisy or rationalization, a salve to a rapist's conscience; after all, a brutal will to power is not a pretty sight and perhaps not a pleasant thing to acknowledge in oneself. Or it could be that such texts are inviting us to recognize that the brutality of rape is altogether different from the eroticism of sexual desire.[15] The male fantasy was not that women enjoy sex but that women want to be subjugated and brutalized, and therefore what came as a surprise was that what the men thought would be pain and humiliation, the women suggested would be pleasure and fun. This still does not make perfect sense, because even if the woman wanted to be subjugated and brutalized, she would still, if he raped her, be getting what she wanted rather than what he imposed against her will. But it goes at least a little way toward making sense of this rather mysterious phenomenon: the belief and simultaneous disbelief that the woman desires rape.

Here is another possible explanation for statements about women's desire for rape: although it is true that something is lost to the rapist's self-definition in the assumption that women secretly desire rape — that is, the satisfaction of imposing his will without her consent — something may also be gained: a kind of knowledge. He has forced from her the secret of her masochistic desire to be raped. In an obvious sense, such knowledge would gratify a rapist's desire for power and dominance, since masochism is to female subjugation what sadism is to male dominance: a synecdoche of wider gender relations. Female masochism as a sexual taste reinforces the normative gender hierarchy.[16] But more interestingly, the male attempt to prove that women secretly desire rape depends upon the conviction that women harbor deep secret wishes which can be forced from them by violence. Essays in this volume by Ellen Caldwell and Akiko Kusunoki ascribe male violence toward women partly to male anxiety about what they fear

---

[15] As Guido Ruggiero notes of rape prosecutions in Renaissance Venice, "violence played a primary role in the description of the crime, occasionally so major that the records are unclear about whether the rapist actually succeeded" (*Boundaries of Eros*, 89) — a concept of rape as more an act of violence than of desire.

[16] As in, for example, Helena's begging Demetrius, "The more you beat me I will fawn on you. / Use me but as your spaniel, spurn me [i.e., kick me], strike me, / Neglect me, lose me; only give me leave, / Unworthy as I am, to follow you" (*Midsummer Night's Dream* 2.1.204–207). Similarly, the wife in Heywood's *How a Man May Choose A Good Wife from a Bad* grovels before her abusive husband: "If you delight to see me drudge and toil, / I'll be your drudge, because 'tis your delight. / Or if you think me unworthy of the name / Of your chaste wife, I will become your maid, / Your slave, your servant — anything you will, / If for that name of servant and of slave / You will but smile upon me now and then" (1.2).

is an occulted, uncontrollable interiority in the women they have hoped to dominate completely. Because a rapist forces from his victim the secret of her desire
for rape, he is still imposing his will on her; and he is also allaying anxiety about
her possessing an uncontrollable area of secret thought. Here we encounter forms
of male violence toward women other than the unambiguously sexual: Caldwell
and Kusunoki write of physical and mental torture. The itch to "know" a woman's interior — to "know" in the biblical sense of carnal knowledge or to "know"
in the anatomical sense of the torturer or the dissector[17] — seems motivated by
anxieties about women's possibly secret mental life, inaccessible to men. An obviously comforting fantasy for those beset by such anxieties is that if one looks
below the surface of what a woman says, what she really wishes for in that secret
mental life is to be subjugated by a male. The satisfaction of forcing this degrading secret from her is part of the pleasure of rape.

A related disclosure was the secret pleasure even a resistant rape victim might
feel once intercourse was under way. The question of consent was complicated
by the Renaissance belief that pregnancy was a sign that a raped woman had actually consented, since in medical thinking orgasm was necessary to conception.
Whether Lucrece committed suicide out of guilt because she had actually enjoyed the rape had long been debated, and many readers have noticed that
Shakespeare's Lucrece fears that she is pregnant, raising the distinct possibility
that Shakespeare meant us to understand that she experienced orgasm during the
rape. Concluding her thorough, nuanced discussion of Renaissance issues of consent involved in rape ("Effacing Rape," 71–82), Barbara Baines discusses Lucrece's orgasm in terms of violent male disclosure of a female secret: "I believe
Shakespeare could easily have counted upon his gentlemen readers to entertain
this possibility and that it functions as a prurient secret at the heart of this text
— a male fantasy of totalizing phallic power" (88–89).

---

[17] Jonathan Sawday (*The Body Emblazoned*) extensively documents how, in the practice of dissecting cadavers, Renaissance yearning to know what was "inside" a human
being overcame even the revulsion caused by the association of human entrails with mortality, and the widespread taboo against violating dead bodies. This cultural preoccupation
helps explain the popularity of another favorite Renaissance tale, the ghoulish account of
the Roman emperor Nero's ripping open his mother's uterus, to have a look at where he
came from; comparisons were sometimes made between Nero's act and the writing of
antifeminist tracts by misogynists who were thus accused of ingratitude toward their
mothers. Michael Neill (*Issues of Death*) has pointed to Renaissance texts that compare
tragedy as a genre to a dissection of the suffering hero, and has compared the theatre in
which tragedies were enacted to the anatomist's dissection theatre. The dissecting urge is
an issue in essays by Caldwell and Wall in this volume.

Such an interest in women's secret mental lives was hardly new in the Renaissance. Chaucer offered a male glimpse into woman's inner thoughts when he had the Wife of Bath declare that what women really wanted was sovereignty in marriage. Tellingly, she gained the upper hand in her fifth marriage during a scene of serious marital violence: her husband struck her head hard enough to make her permanently deaf and then handed over the marital reins to her out of guilt and terror that the blow might have killed her. But significantly, having achieved dominance in the marriage, the Wife relinquishes dominance and chooses to be obedient to her husband. The violent episode ultimately exposes her little secret: she wants not to dominate but to be dominated.[18] After her autobiographical Prologue, the Wife of Bath tells a tale in which exactly the same pattern recurs. Forced to perform expiation for an act of sexual violence, the rape of a young girl, a knight is ultimately constrained to yield marital dominance to the wife who has saved his skin by providing the answer to the question of what all women want: again, sovereignty in marriage. But again, having gained the driver's seat in her marriage, the wife in the tale voluntarily chooses to be obedient to that convicted rapist, her husband. Both Prologue and Tale are structured as disclosures of women's secret mental lives, of the secret of what women want, sovereignty in marriage. But further unfolding of the plot reveals a yet more deeply buried secret: they don't necessarily want sovereignty in marriage. They want to be dominated. In both cases, the quest to expose women's interiority involves a male act of violence against a woman.

Perhaps because of the strain being put on traditional conceptions of boldly dominant masculinity by shifts away from martial and physical prowess as the markers of manliness, the Renaissance continued to take an interest in scenes wherein men tried to force from women the secret that women really wanted to be forced. Presumably men wanted reassurance that women wanted to be dominated; but there is evidence that men wanted to force from women nearly *any* secret: men wanted to know what women were thinking in their private hearts. Many male-authored texts purport to reveal what women talk about when they are alone together; such texts often situate the author as an eavesdropper on the conversations of women (see Woodbridge, *Women and the English Renaissance*, 235–36). That what women are shown to talk about when alone together usually

---

[18] A further twist in the tale's psychological complexity, however, is that a husband whose wife has freely chosen obedience on her own terms will always be obliged to remember his own indebtedness to that choice, always be haunted by its potential reversibility. A wife who has engineered these circumstances has her own kind of sovereignty.

turns out to be men and sex, often the sexual inadequacy of their husbands,[19] provides a telling glimpse into the male anxieties activating these texts. Though scorn for her husband's erotic equipment might be the worst sort of secret hidden in a woman's heart, any secret seemed threatening. Elizabeth Hanson posits a "Renaissance obsession with the discovery of the heart's secrets" (*Discovering the Subject*, 1). "Let them anatomize Regan; see what breeds about her heart," cries King Lear (3.6.75–76). Renaissance gender theory that sanctioned male control of women was butting up against a growing sense of interior subjectivity, and women's hearts, which should lie open as a flower to the gaze of fathers or husbands, had now become impenetrably dark. If God could still see into a woman's heart, a husband could not. "In Venice they do let God see the pranks / They dare not show their husbands" (*Othello* 3.3.216–17) — perhaps because a husband's violence was more immediately frightening than God's.

The connection between violence and secrecy merits further thought. Did men grow violent toward women in an attempt to break open their wall of secrecy?[20] Did women withdraw into the secret garden of their hearts in response to the threat of male violence? Women were not the only group subjected to violence in order to force secrets from them. Political prisoners were tortured to reveal secrets about seditious plots or networks of hidden Catholic priests. Witches were harshly pressured into confession, and their bodies stripped naked and searched for tokens revealing clandestine consorting with demons. During the reign of Elizabeth I, interrogatory torture seems to have been employed by the state more routinely than in any other period of English history (see Hanson, *Discovering the Subject*, 19–54). Convicted "rogues" were punished by being

---

[19] In the anonymous *A Talk of Ten Wives of Their Husbands' Ware*, a group of women gripe about their husbands' pathetic sexual equipment. Several wives dramatized in Edward Gosynhyll's *The School House of Women* complain about their husbands' impotence. A wife in William Dunbar's "The Two Married Women and the Widow" accuses her husband of having grown impotent through too much wenching, and a wife in Dunbar's "The Twa Cummeris" (The Two Gossips) declares of her husband, "in bed he is nocht wirth a bene" [i.e., not worth a bean]. A group of women on their way to an upsitting in Henry Parrot's *The Gossip's Greeting* plan an extended conversation on their "husbands' powers" (Sig. [B3]v).

[20] Catty thinks anxiety about women's secret lives was abetted even by "the relative invisibility of the female genitals and female sexual pleasure" (*Writing Rape, Writing Women*, 15). Writing of fascination with bodily interiors during this period, Sawday notes that "as an entrance to the 'house' of the body, ... the female genitalia may, indeed, reveal the opening to a strange and secret place which is the body-interior"; Renaissance anatomy books represented the body interior of both men and women "as a feminized (and hence alien) region" (*The Body Emblazoned*, 161, 9).

whipped and pulled through the streets behind carts while naked, the nakedness designed both to increase the pain of the violent physical punishment and to expose to public view the bodies disfigured with whiplashes and criminal brands; stripping also seems to respond obliquely to a popular image of rogues as members of secret societies and speakers of a secret language, thieves' cant. "Rogue literature" represents itself as a kind of extended public service announcement, promising to unmask the impostures of beggars who (for example) seek alms through feigning disability. The promise of disclosure animates the whole genre. Robert Greene and other "cony-catching" writers claim to have infiltrated the criminal underworld to disclose its secrets to a vulnerable, non-streetwise public. In *A Caveat for Common Cursetors*, justice of the peace Thomas Harman reports torturing an alleged dumb man until he broke into speech: the secret of feigned disability was unmasked by physical violence. (Similarly, the tale of Simpcox in Shakespeare's *2 Henry VI* features a phony blind and lame man whose fakery is exposed by the physical violence of whipping.) In rogue literature, the lantern shedding light on dark practices was a controlling image, as in Dekker's *Lantern and Candlelight*. The lantern of truth-seeker Diogenes came to symbolize the rogue writer's relentless spotlight on hidden evils.

That the unmasking of imposture, the shining of a bright light onto occulted identities and hidden practices, is a crucial trope in the period, has much to say about subjectivity. Many theorists have noted in the early modern period a changing subjectivity, a new interiority. Puritans saw God by their own inner light, diary-keeping flourished, household architecture began evolving private rooms. People had secret inner selves to protect, as never before. The new subjectivity seems intimately connected with the age's preoccupation with imposture and with secrecy, and it may help account for various kinds of violence.

People had secret hearts to protect, and the state and many special interest groups arrogated to themselves the privilege of violating such secrecy, opening up the private heart to public view, through domestic spying and judicial torture, often by violence. As Hanson notes, "The struggle to discover the secrets in another's heart, or to resist being the object of such discovery, is rehearsed not only in the drama but in the records of the Privy Council and state trials, and in correspondence, philosophical writing, conduct books, and literature of social description of the period" (*Discovering the Subject*, 1).

As Sharon Beehler notes,[21] the passion to reveal what lay hidden in another's heart is clearly visible in Reformation contexts, such as the interrogation,

---

[21] Personal communication.

imprisonment, and/or torture of women such as Anne Askew and Anna Trapnel for their independent religious thinking. In the late Middle Ages, Margery Kempe had been interrogated for independent religious behavior thought to be tinged with Lollardry, a movement that was proto-Protestant in its personal approach to God. What produced the invasive prying in all these cases was not only fear of religious dissidence in the abstract, but fear of religious experience involving precisely an interior and personal relationship to God rather than a more institutional religious experience mediated by public ritual — fear of religious experience that was ungovernable because hidden.

The case of beggars' supposed impostures offers a phenomenon intriguingly similar to the one Mathieson identifies: just as rapists, professing to believe that women desired rape, were shocked at any evidence that the woman really did desire to have sex with them, so under the influence of rogue literature, many people professed to believe that most beggars' disability was faked, but reports of observers feeling nausea at the sight of beggars' sores reveal that whatever they said, people found the disgusting sores quite real. Both the rapist and the writer of rogue literature avowed determination to unmask the secrets of another's heart, but the determination itself seems a sham: neither the rapist nor the rogue writer was prepared to accept what his violent probings actually revealed. The rapist, the torturer, the dissector harbored secret wishes of their own that we are still digging to unearth. It was an age of private, safeguarded interiority all round, and people seemed routinely to have responded to secretiveness by violent assaults upon each other's bodies.

Intricately overdetermined, Renaissance violence toward women had to do with anxious masculinity, responding to a diminution in its traditionally sanctioned violence with some freelance violence, actual or vicarious. But violence toward women also had to do with new experiences of privacy and secrecy which institutionalized paranoia and called forth violent forms of surveillance and prying.

Annette Kolodny long ago taught us to read the rhetoric of New World exploration through the lens of gender violence: exploration and conquest of new lands was figured as penetration of "virgin territory." Karen Robertson's essay on Pocahontas in this volume shows conquest, colonization, and hostage-taking imaginatively transformed into love and courtship, a colonial version of the assertion that rape is really just giving a woman what she secretly wants.

One area of the general topic of women and violence not very prominently addressed in this volume is wife-beating and husband battering. Our contributors' deëmphasis of such domestic violence points to a revealing erasure within Renaissance literature itself. On the whole, mainstream literature of this period is silent on the topic of wife-beating. A couple of minor pieces take sadistic delight in rehearsing the brutalization and degradation of a wife: in *A Merry Jest of a Shrewd and Curst Wife Lapped in Morel's Skin*, a man beats his wife senseless and wraps her naked, bleeding body in the salted hide of a horse; when the salt in her wounds revives her, she agrees to any number of degrading demonstrations of subservience and masochistic submissions to her husband's sexual practices — he wants the threat of further violence to make her "shrink / And bow when I her bed" (Sig. Eiii); as the title indicates, this is all meant to be funny. In John Dickensen's *Fair Valeria* a husband forces his wife to watch him copulating with whores — she knows that if she objects, he will beat her as he often has before. In Thomas Heywood's didactic play *How a Man May Choose a Good Wife from a Bad*, a young man beats his wife in front of her own father. But these are rather eccentric, out-of-the-way, non-Norton Anthology texts. One looks in vain for wife-beating as a plot element anywhere in Shakespeare. The closest instance is Othello's striking his wife onstage, and the play represents that as so extremely exceptional as to be almost unheard of: Lodovico cries, "My lord, this would not be believed in Venice, / Though I should swear I saw 't," and over thirty lines later Lodovico is still marveling, "What, strike his wife?" as if no husband in the history of the Venetian republic had ever thought of any such thing (4.1.245–246).[22] And Shakespeare is not exceptional in this regard: most of the Renaissance writers we now consider canonical largely avoid scenes of wife-beating. This is odd, given that wife-beating was an important social issue of the day, and *outside* mainstream literature it got talked about rather a lot. Wife-beating was legal,[23] but in that day of a developing ideal of companionate marriage, many sermons and tracts inveighed against it: see, for example, William Whately's marriage sermon *A Bride-Bush*, William Gouge's *Of Domestical Duties*, or William Heale's *Apology for Women*. Such discussions can sound quite enlightened: "The small disparity which . . . is betwixt man and wife, permitteth

---

[22] Lodovico's horror, as Sharon Beehler points out, may owe something to the public nature of the blow, since wife-beating was "one of those private vices that were allowed as long as the public wasn't subjected to them" (personal communication).

[23] We have no reliable statistics on the prevalence of wife-beating from this period, but considering that it was legal, it is sobering to reflect just how pervasive it might have been, given how pervasive it is now even though it is *illegal*: in the United States last year, partner violence was "the most common source of injury to women aged 15 to 44, more frequent than muggings, auto accidents, and cancer deaths combined. . . . Research on national probability samples suggests that 20% to 30% of *all* women will be physically assaulted by a partner or expartner at least once in their lives" (Marin and Russo, "Feminist Perspectives," 18).

not so high a power in a husband, and so low a servitude in a wife, as for him to beat her" (Gouge, *Of Domestical Duties*, 226); but one problem with injunctions against wife-beating was that moralizers often positioned it as the male equivalent of female scolding, and made cessation of wife-beating contingent upon cessation of scolding. Since scolding often turned out to be indistinguishable from the free expression of opinion by wives, even the discourse against husbandly violence became a tool for the silencing of wives. And anti-wife-beating tracts were hardly feminist in a modern sense; as Frances Dolan notes, "Gouge and Whately . . . do not rely on some [arguments] that we might most expect to find. They do not argue that the husband has no right to beat his wife or that doing so is unfair, immoral, or illegal. Instead, they maintain that refraining from violence is more dignified, authoritative, and expedient than resorting to it. In their view domestic violence is counterproductive because it promotes rather than subdues resistance" (*Taming of the Shrew* 221). But at least a discourse critical of husbandly violence existed in polemical texts; in fiction and especially in drama, the issue was downright suppressed. It is difficult to know why this should have been so, and we raise the question in hope of provoking further discussion and research of this topic.[24]

But while wife-beating is erased in mainstream Renaissance literature, *female* domestic violence looms relatively large in late medieval and Renaissance texts, and significantly, it is very often comic. In the mystery plays, Mrs. Noah boxes her husband's ears rather than forego a pleasant afternoon's tippling with her gossips to climb aboard his ridiculous ark. In Lydgate's *Mumming at Hertford*, a group of tradesmen petition the king for relief from regular beatings by their "fierce wives" (l. 12). Even the butcher, slayer of boars and bulls, quakes in his shoes when his wife approaches: "Though his belly were rounded like an oak, / She would not fail to give the first stroke"; her right jab to the jaw "full oft made his cheeks bleed" (99–100, 108). A wife who is a wafer-maker routinely pelts her husband with hot cakes, until his hairs glow red. The king's sympathy for the downtrodden husbands is soon over-ridden when the aggressive wives burst upon the scene to remind him that by ancient precedent wives should rule their husbands at all times, and the king finally agrees to let the wives have their way for another year while he considers the matter, since he acknowledges that their right to rule is confirmed by "custom, nature, and eke [i.e., also] prescription, /

---

[24] For further discussion of wife-beating and other means of controlling "aggressive" wives, see Dolan, *Taming of the Shrew* 218–32; Amussen, " 'Being stirred to much unquietness' "; Boose, "Scolding Brides"; Hunt, "Wife Beating"; Ingram, "Ridings" and " 'Scolding Women' "; Underdown, "The Taming of the Scold."

Statute used by confirmation, / Process and date of time out of mind, / Record of chronicles . . ." (ll. 235–238). In Thomas Ingelend's *The Disobedient Child*, a wife beats her husband into submission and loads him with firewood like a donkey; he can but reply, "I will do your commandments whatsoever" (305). She threatens him, "I will make thy skin to rattle, / And the brains in thy skull more deeply to settle" (305), and stage directions indicate that she makes good on her threats: *Here the Wife must strike her Husband handsomely about the shoulders with something* (303). The husband moans, "Alas, alas! I am almost quite dead! / My wife so pitifully hath broken my head!" (306). A shrew named Strife in the anonymous play *Tom Tyler and His Wife* sits drinking with her gossips in a tavern and is incensed when interrupted by her husband, who has stopped by for a drink after a hard day's work; for his idleness and his interrupting her, she beats him up and then needs another drink, since beating is such thirsty work. A wife in *Johan Johan, the Husband, by John Heywood* (?) threatens to make her husband's blood run about his ears with her distaff or shears; he defends himself with a shovel full of hot coals. A hapless husband in Greene and Lodge's *A Looking-Glass for London and England* complains that his wife calls him "rascal, rogue, runnagate, varlet, vagabond, slave, knave," but that these are "but holiday terms; but if you heard her working-day words, in faith sir they be rattlers like thunder sir, for after the dew follows a storm, for then am I sure either to be well buffetted, my face scratched, or my head broken" (Sig. [C4]). Mistress Otter in Jonson's *Epicoene* threatens to chain her husband up with his bulldogs (3.1.2–4).

These are all comic scenes; the temper of the age ran pretty heavily to slapstick humor. We should not make the mistake, however (as Brian Vickers egregiously does, for example, in the case of misogyny) of assuming that when something is cast in a comic mode in literature, it is a sign that the culture did not take it seriously. Sometimes an issue will be cast comically in order to belittle it, as when beggary was most often treated comically in the Renaissance; and some characters are cast comically in order to keep them in their place, as when the lower orders get restricted to comic subplots in the drama. In the case of husband-beating, we suggest that its comic aura reveals the extent to which it is a World-Upside-Down inversion of expectation: in real life, indications are that wives suffered far more beatings than did husbands. The very topsy-turviness helps to trivialize spouse-beating of any sort as a topic fit for comic treatment. But above all, the fact that male authors ignored wife-beating and focused instead on rather cute and harmless scenes of husband-beating, which they treated with a good-natured comic chagrin, points to the function of such comic scenes as a hand-is-quicker-than-the-eye distraction. While laughing at scenes of husband-abuse, we are invited to forget about wife-abuse as a serious social problem. As sexual assault was a power issue disguised as a matter of sexual desire, wife-beating looks like a power issue disguised as a non-issue.

Frances E. Dolan and Viviana Comensoli have given us excellent studies of domestic violence of various kinds, from spousal murder to the pecking order under which a beaten wife might herself beat servants (see Dolan, *Dangerous Familiars* and "Household Chastisements," and Comensoli, *Household Business*). Dolan theorizes that the lurid depictions of domestic crime that were a prominent feature of the literary landscape "express fears that the home was unsafe and could not be protected against those who would rise against it from within"; and she notes that, tellingly, the law classified as petty treason the murder of a husband by a wife or a master by a servant, underlining the analogy between father and king (*Dangerous Familiars*, 29, 13). We have seen that the drama tended to replace wife-beating with comic husband-beating, and a similar inversion of real life occurs in the case of domestic murder: Dolan notes a "disparity between assize court records, which tend to depict women more often as the victims of domestic murder than its perpetrators, and legal statutes, pamphlets, plays, and ballads, which invert this pattern by depicting women as the dangerous, rather than endangered, murderers of their intimates" ("Household Chastisements," 205). We would like to see further research on the imbalance between male and female domestic violence in mainstream literature, and the disparity between the seriousness of wife-beating and wife-murder in real life and the non-seriousness or absence of treatments of wife-beating and wife-murder in mainstream literature.

As our brief review of husband-beating females shows, though women who were themselves violent were in the minority compared with women victimized by violence, violent women were not altogether absent from the Renaissance scene. Essays by Catherine Thomas and Wendy Wall make the important anti-essentialist point that ideological tenets to the contrary, Renaissance violence was not limited historically to males. Thomas reminds us of criminal documentation on infanticide by mothers, and Wall demonstrates how cooking and medical care — both women's work — often "smacked of licensed violence." Literature too offers physically violent women — not only comically violent but also seriously violent, such as Margaretta in William Rowley's *All's Lost by Lust* (whose prototype in Bandello was aptly named Violenta). Margaretta, foiled (by a masculine use of the conventional bed trick) in her attempt to stab her faithless husband to death in his bed, flies into a violent rage upon discovering that she has killed her husband's friend by mistake and the main job remains to be done. As in the case of representations of spousal violence, literature seems to operate at an oblique angle to life when treating other sorts of female violence: as Thomas shows, even though historically child murder by parents consisted largely of infanticide by lower-class unwed mothers, the drama avoids this theme almost entirely and instead limits female child murder to the killing of adult offspring by queens. Similarly, as Jennifer Low shows in her essay on female sword-fighters, there is little evidence that the swashbuckling female fencers of the drama had any counterparts in real life. Why female violence took such fantastic forms in literature when real-life models of violent women were available in the back streets and even in the kitchen, is a question requiring further thought.

Jennifer Low shows that in literature, weapon-wielding Amazons join a "manly" world through a capacity for brutality. In this world of changing gender roles, literature was not blind (or not always blind) to the possibility that a capacity for brutality was not particularly flattering as a defining characteristic of the male sex. Catherine Thomas's essay traces a rhetoric of unnaturalness deployed to castigate murderous women. But couldn't such language easily boomerang back onto the male sex? The shocking inappropriateness of murder to women just might jar readers and audiences into noticing the shocking inappropriateness of murder to men. The shock effect when violent women ruptured the expected division of labor — violence for men, nurturance for women — exposed the extent to which violence was routinely legitimated under the rubrics of male gender ideology. Low argues that Beaumont and Fletcher's *Love's Cure, or The Martial Maid* exposes male violence as "senseless," through the agency of a female sword-fighter. The shock of counter-cultural female violence holds up to audience scrutiny the normatively male valence of physical brutality.

The editors and some of the contributors to this volume cut their intellectual and political teeth in the days when they were encountering Paul Jorgensen's teaching at UCLA — during the years of protest against the Viet Nam war. Those were exciting years for the University of California, and some of us are committed pacifists to this day. It would be all too easy, when discussing women and violence in the Renaissance, to reflect complacently that, since violence is inherently bad, if women had to be assigned some restrictive subject position by Renaissance ideology, it was just as well that it was preponderantly a non-violent one. But several of the last group of essays in our collection, those on violent women, reveal at least a sneaking delight in some female violence of the period, and even the pacifists among us can understand that mood, and can even laugh a little more heartily than is decorous when a Renaissance shrew lands a good punch. One could explain this cerebrally: we experience intellectual gratification in discovering Renaissance critiques of essentialism: even the Renaissance, we find, did not always believe in its own dogmas about women's passive, non-violent sweetness, did not always judge to be "unnatural" or exceptional women who were physically violent, but occasionally suspected that women and men were both subject to violent urges, shaped by cultural expectations to varyingly successful degrees. Yes, we might just be experiencing a moderate intellectual approval of anti-essentialist evidence; or we might wish to put it in terms of female empowerment: fighting-for-your-rights feminism is more gratifying to us 1970s feminists than is what might be called "victim feminism," the endless rehearsal of female disempowerment in history.

We suspect, however, that our occasional applauding of violent women is something more full-blooded than either of these explanations. To find that women, so relentlessly urged to chastity, silence, and obedience, could occasionally stand up and give some male a sound drubbing (or at least put up a fight for her life, as Edward Pechter thinks Desdemona does) — well, that offers its own peculiar *emotional* satisfactions, even to us pacifists. Though we may never have hired a hit man to get rid of a pesky suitor, or challenged a man to a duel, or stabbed a king for dishonoring us, all of which happens in the plays Naomi Liebler discusses, yet — thinking of Wendy Wall's essay — which of us has not at least taken out a few frustrations with a meat cleaver in the kitchen?

But to return to the story of the little Swedish goatherd. After winning over by kindness the hearts of the violent bear, wolf, and lion, the goatherd encounters as his final adversary a troll who threatens to eat him. The boy replies to the troll with his customary sweetness, pointing out the incivility of murder and cannibalism. But the troll shoves the goatherd rudely into the stone wall of his cave and advances upon him with carving knife slashing. Unabashed, the boy sings a little song about how kindness can do almost anything in this world, but even kindness really can't make any headway against trolls. Then he gives his special magic whistle, which summons the bear, wolf, and lion, now his loyal friends. They hasten to the cave and beat the troll senseless.

The last few essays in our collection, for better or for worse, put a somewhat different spin upon women and violence, and show Renaissance women mobilizing their troll-thumping forces.

The Essays in this Volume

As we have said, ten of our fourteen essays deal with violence *against* women, and four with violence *by* women. Under the former rubric, the first five essays deal with women sexually assaulted, kidnapped, murdered, or threatened with serious violence.

In "Representing Lavinia," Carolyn Sale approaches the rape and subsequent murder of Lavinia in *Titus Andronicus* by way of early modern laws concerning rape and ravishment, largely conceived as property crimes against men. Lavinia, "who can make known what has happened to her only by writing 'stuprum' in the sand becomes a cipher for the actual women who find themselves figuratively 'ravished,' or forcibly unpropertied, by legal operations they do not know how to negotiate." Noting that Lucrece's suicide is made by Shakespeare to appear a refutation of the potentially important judicial principle that a woman's non-consenting mind should erase any taint rape might give her, Sale finds it crucial that Lavinia, in contrast, declines suicide as an acceptable response to rape. Lavinia thus refuses the misogynistic paradigms to which Lucrece and Tamora both subscribe: Lucrece to her own self-destruction, and Tamora, Sale argues, in ways that make her at the very least an accessory to Lavinia's rape.

In the second essay, "Rape and Redemption in *The Spanish Gypsy*," Karen Bamford focuses on another response to rape which is also discussed by Sale: marrying the rapist. In an argument centering on Middleton and Rowley's *The Spanish Gypsy*, Bamford notes that, although rape was a capital offense from 1285 to 1840, its infrequent prosecution suggests that it was commonly regarded as a venial sin, "a sexual act that both parties enjoy, something the woman could have avoided, the subject for a bawdy joke," and shows that women who sought legal redress for rape were regarded as malevolent and disruptive. What Bamford calls "the redemptive rape," in which the love of a good woman reforms the rapist who then marries her, reaches an apex in *The Spanish Gypsy*, but is a feature of many other plays of the period.[25]

After laying the groundwork with material on classical rape narratives in Paleolithic and early Mediterranean art and literature, Michael Hall's essay "Lewd but Familiar Eyes: The Narrative Tradition of Rape and Shakespeare's *The Rape of Lucrece*" compares Shakespeare's poem unfavorably with Livy's and Ovid's treatments of the same story, showing that Shakespeare truckles much more explicitly than do Livy or Ovid to primitive readerly enjoyments of rape. No bardolater, Hall teases out a strain of the downright Paleolithic in Shakespeare's poem. Alone among these three writers, Hall argues, Shakespeare "eroticizes violence in such a way as to legitimize and incite a thrill-of-the-chase response."

Fourth, Karen Robertson, in "The First Captive: The Kidnapping of Pocahontas," shows that even in North America, where England was engaging in

---

[25] In treating legal statute and legal practice, these two essays are entering a vigorous debate on the complexities and implications of early modern rape prosecutions; see, for example, Baines "Effacing Rape"; Ruggiero, "Violence and Sexuality" in *Boundaries of Eros*; Catty, *Writing Rape, Writing Women*; Gossett, "'Best Men'"; Bashar, "Rape in England"; and Chaytor, "Husband(ry)."

conquest and colonization, violence toward a woman was refigured as love and courtship, and a kidnapping represented as a religious conversion. The ambiguous representation of Pocahontas in England Robertson shows to be a product of conflicting interests: the Virginia Company, promoting tobacco and hoping to attract English colonists to North America, depicted Pocahontas as a princess and her father as a sovereign monarch, aiming to attract male colonists hoping to better themselves by marrying princesses as John Rolfe had done; but the Crown was unwilling to recognize royal status in Pocahontas or her father: "The representation of Powhatan as an emperor presented a . . . dilemma to the court, since that attributed national status to the land the English were violently appropriating. If Powhatan was a 'mighty Prince,' then English colonists were engaged in an invasion of national boundaries." And far from being the romantic episode Pocahontas's marriage to an Englishman has come down to us as being, Pocahontas's joining of the English was actually (Robertson shows) a hostage-taking. English justifications for seizing Pocahontas papered over "at least kidnapping, perhaps rape, and possibly bigamy."

And finally, ranging widely over the plays of John Fletcher, who was absorbed with the topic of rape, Barbara Mathieson's essay "Rape, Female Desire, and Sexual Repugnance in John Fletcher's Plays" identifies a pattern of male repugnance in the face of female sexual desire, of a rapist's loss of interest in a woman who actually *wants* sex so that he doesn't have to impose it by force. Identifying this phenomenon sheds light on many other Renaissance representations of rape besides Fletcher's.

In the next sub-section, on violence and the interior subjectivity of women, Akiko Kusunoki, in "Female Selfhood and Male Violence in English Renaissance Drama: A View from Mary Wroth's *Urania*," investigates male characters' violent attempts to open up to view a concealed inner female subjectivity. Focusing on *Urania* and also treating Elizabeth Cary's *Mariam*, Kusunoki shows how female characters perform an outward self in conformity with societal gender expectations, and a husband may torture or even execute a wife to expose the concealed self below the performative façade. Where women authors insist on a woman's right to private selfhood that is not subject to a husband's control, male authors represent female split subjectivity as duplicity. Women who keep sexual secrets are punished by male authors with grotesque tortures such as those inflicted upon the Duchess of Malfi and on Tamora in *Titus Andronicus*, a pattern also visible in several Kabuki plays which also use the grotesquely-tortured body as a visible emblem of violently exposed female selfhood. Ellen Caldwell's "Invasive Procedures in Webster's *The Duchess of Malfi*" posits that the new interior subjectivity of the early modern period in itself prompted attempts to penetrate interiority (by torture or interrogation) or to bridge it so as to diminish the self's sense of aloneness (by dialogue or letter-writing). The Duchess of Malfi's soliloquies are overheard, not answered, and the image in Act IV of the severed hand, no longer capable of letter-writing, is an emblem of failed access to interior subjectivity. Caldwell relates the violent invasiveness of surgery and dissection to the wish for access to a private interior. But unlike Hamlet's posturing soliloquies, the Duchess's colloquies affirm connectedness to others and resistance to the invasive procedures of a torturing state.

The third sub-section, dealing with violence toward women in Shakespeare's *Othello*, takes up a text crucial to the study of women and violence in the Renaissance: in this play with only three female characters, two women are murdered and a third shamefully treated, and the play explores the conditions under which such violence towards women can arise. In "The 'Erring Barbarian' and the 'Maiden Never Bold': Racist and Sexist Representations in *Othello*," Sara Deats demonstrates links between the play's marital violence toward two wives and its xenophobia toward a black outsider. She reads Iago as representing "the largely repressed xenophobia and misogyny of his society, . . . determined to interpellate these two deviants: the Westernized Moor and the unruly woman: into accepted subject positions within a racist and sexist ideology." Edward Pechter's " 'Too Much Violence': Murdering Wives in *Othello*" traces the growth to heroic stature of an initially docile Emilia, and with regard to Desdemona, he takes aim at a venerable critical tradition: "whether celebrating or deploring it, the critical tradition has been remarkably consistent for two centuries in describing Desdemona as silent, submissive and in a sense even complicit in her own murder." Pechter argues, however, that Desdemona does *not* accept abuse and murder with that passivity which nineteenth-century critics such as Coleridge found "adorable": she stands up for herself verbally, and (as the text specifies) also physically puts up a fight for her life. Noting that the view of Desdemona as victim seems to suit the agendas of some feminist critics even now, Pechter argues for a Desdemona who is her own woman and "sings her own song."

Finally in this sub-section on *Othello*, Lynda Boose's essay " 'Let It Be Hid': The Pornographic Aesthetic of Shakespeare's *Othello*" explores elements of voyeurism in *Othello*: "the play holds up a mirror that mercilessly exposes the complicity of the audience's spectatorship."[26] Iago, inviting the audience into his

---

[26] Pechter's essay takes up a different facet of the problem of voyeurism: that inherent in *narrative* representation of sexuality and sexual violence; for further discussion of this issue, see Relihan, *Fashioning Authority*, 69–70.

twisted consciousness, "plays the pander who opens the door to the listener's pornographic imagination," drawing on an obscene, coarsely sexual language introduced into England via Pietro Aretino. Boose links the play's "pornographic imagination" to the violence which culminates in the abuse and murder of women.

The final segment of the collection deals with violence *by* women. In "When Women Fight: Upsetting Gender Assumptions in the Staged Duel," an essay on women sword-fighters in Renaissance plays, Jennifer Low distinguishes these literary representations from social reality, where the wielding of weapons by females was rare. After some discussion of Beaumont and Fletcher's *The Maid's Tragedy*, Heywood's *The Fair Maid of the West*, and Middleton and Dekker's *The Roaring Girl*, Low focuses a more extended discussion on Beaumont and Fletcher's *Love's Cure, or The Martial Maid*, following the career of a girl raised as a boy for sixteen years and then suddenly obliged to become female, and the challenges this poses to essentialist assumptions about gender. Though Clara must give up the soldierly, sword-fighting violence of the male life, she obliges male characters to give up such a violent life too, and the play ultimately calls into question the "senseless violence" of male rituals such as dueling.

In line with the notion that has emerged from so many of the essays in this volume, namely that violence was largely gendered male in early modern culture, Catherine Thomas's essay " 'You make me feel like (un)natural woman': Reconsidering Murderous Mothers in English Renaissance Drama" examines the language of unnaturalness that attaches to violent mothers in the drama. Writing of Fletcher's Queen Bonduca, Thomas notes that there are moments when the Roman soldiers find Bonduca's suicidal and filicidal resolve quite heroic, even Roman: "Her use of violence is more acceptable when viewed through constructed masculine values of honor and militarism." (Jennifer Low's essay suggests that Aspatia's suicide in *The Maid's Tragedy* might also have been regarded in a heroic Roman light.) Thomas shows that one is not allowed to forget, however, that Bonduca is "a woman, a mother, and a queen, and that . . . she has killed herself and her children." Although infanticide by unwed mothers was historically common, the queen who kills her adult children, as in the politically-charged *Gorboduc* and *Bonduca*, is as artificial a construct in the drama as is the sword-fighting female Jennifer Low writes about. Although neither Thomas's nor Low's essay is concerned exclusively with gender issues, it is notable that in both cases the shock effect of "abnormal" female violence serves to highlight and perhaps to challenge the "normality" of male physical brutality.

In "Blood in the Kitchen: Violence and Early Modern Domestic Work," Wendy Wall contemplates the violent imperative verbs in Renaissance cookbooks: "wing," "untack," "unjoint," "disfigure," "dismember," "unbrace," "spoil,"

"unlace," "break," "splat," "splay" — and thinks about the way Lady Elinor Fettiplace records the flaying of cats and hedgehogs and whipping a cock to death.
Wall muses, "When conduct book writers instructed housewives and workers to
remain at home quietly learning subjection, did they have in mind these scenes
of indulgent stabbing and flaying?" Frances Dolan has written of housewives'
abuse of servants ("a person who is the victim of violence ... may strive for
dominance elsewhere" ["Household Chastisements," 204]), and Wall extends this
perception into a housewife's culinary and medical realms, noting that "cooking
and medical care smacked of licensed violence. ... As cookbooks link medicine
and butchery, they invite early modern people to glimpse connections between
eating and the anatomist's dissection theater." And the volume's final essay,
Naomi Liebler's "'A Woman Dipped in Blood': The Violent Femmes of *The
Maid's Tragedy* and *The Changeling*" takes up Beaumont and Fletcher's *Maid's
Tragedy*, with a woman sword-fighter and a female murderer, and Middleton
and Rowley's *The Changeling* with its heroine who evades an arranged marriage
by hiring a hit man to remove the unwanted fiancé. Liebler overcomes generations of sexist belittlement of these characters to put the case for Aspatia,
Evadne, and Beatrice-Joanna as tragic heroes, women who take action — even
violent action — in a world where men lack initiative.

   The essays presented here deal with a range of English Renaissance writers.
Hall, Sale, Pechter, Deats, Boose, Wall, and Low discuss Shakespeare; Caldwell
focuses on Webster; Mathieson and Thomas write on Fletcher; Low and Liebler
take up Beaumont and Fletcher; Thomas writes on Sackville and Norton; Kusunoki discusses Wroth and Cary;[27] Bamford and Liebler write on Middleton and
Rowley; Robertson examines accounts of New World settlement; and Wall
writes of a play by Thomas Heywood and of cookbooks. Though all of our contributors historicize their subjects and are alert to early modern political, legal,
and economic contexts, our interests are in the *literary* representation of such
violent acts as rape and murder. Susanne Kappeler, a scholar of pornography,
declared that the object of her study was "representational practices, rather than

---

[27] The preponderance of male-authored texts in this list reflects more than the large
numerical disparity between surviving texts by men as compared to texts by women in
this period: women authors also tended to avoid explicit scenes of violence toward
women, as compared with male authors who often seem deliberately to have sought these
out. Catty discusses, for example, "the paucity of explicit portrayals of rape in texts by
women, relative to the proliferation of rapes in male-authored literature," but notes that
one important exception is Lady Mary Wroth, who "explicitly and frequently deals with
rape, using it as a narrative and ideological tool which proves an integral part of her portrayal of female identity" (*Writing Rape, Writing Women*, 3).

sexual practices" (*The Pornography of Representation*, 2). Similarly, our quarry is not the "facts" of violence, but the representation of violence as it concerned women of the English Renaissance. It is the literature that interests us, and that makes for continuity, we hope, with the work of the scholar whom this volume honors.

PAUL JORGENSEN:
A CAREER IN RENAISSANCE LITERARY STUDIES

Shakespearean English was a kind of second language to Paul Jorgensen: he appeared to think in it. When a graduate student was devastated at failing his comprehensives, Paul advised, "Let grief convert to anger," and the student rallied and passed on the second attempt. An undergraduate once suggested in class that since that the Fool and Cordelia are never on stage together, perhaps the Fool is really Cordelia in disguise; Paul noted (more in sorrow than in anger), "This way madness lies." A graduate teaching assistant stopped by his office one day lugging a huge sack full of bluebooks, all answers to a question on Falstaff, and Paul observed, "a monstrous deal of sack." When a graduate student who was habitually late to Paul's 8:00 a.m. Shakespeare seminar straggled in at 8:15 yet again one morning, Paul read in a firm voice from his text, "Enter bastard."

Paul was a lifelong sufferer from what the Renaissance called melancholy, which called forth heroic support from his family, but which was somehow of a piece with his serious commitment to his profession. One of his students remembers, "When I think of Paul, I always remember him walking to and from class, shoulders bent, books held high under his arm, a slightly worried look on his face and, in general, looking like a warrior going to do battle with a ferocious enemy: in this case, the ignorance of his students!" His melancholy also gave an especially crisp edge to his Shakespearean wit. In that melancholy voice, witticisms were twice as funny. And his quick wit, even when not Shakespearean in flavor, could sometimes save the day: during the dissertation defense of a student Paul was supervising, the harried candidate was being badgered by a committee member, who demanded, "Don't you think the critics you are refuting here are rather out of date? They're mere straw men! Nobody believes that any more." Paul rescued the student and stopped all conversation on the point by asserting self-sacrificingly and unanswerably, "I believe it."

After Paul Jorgensen died on June 16, 2000, Thomas Wortham, the chair of his department, wrote, "Brilliant, witty, compassionate: a distinguished teacher, a leading Shakespearean scholar of his generation, and a faithful departmental citizen, Paul helped define for many some of the best aspects of life in the department of English at UCLA since his arrival in 1947. He is the author or editor of eleven important books, including *Shakespeare's Military World* (1956), *Redeeming Shakespeare's Words* (1962), *Lear's Self-Discovery* (1967), *Our Naked Frailties: Sensational Art and Meaning in Macbeth* (1971), and several influential classroom anthologies. . . . He was a good mentor, a good friend." Jorgensen was the recipient of a Guggenheim Fellowship and many other honors, but we who have assembled this volume remember him best as a teacher.

Everyone who took Paul Jorgensen's Shakespeare classes remembers them to this day; we find ourselves unconsciously serving up his *bons mots* to our own students, who immediately write them down. As one former student of Paul's remembers, "He also gave a brilliant survey of Renaissance literature, the notes from which I still use in my own teaching. He is one of a small handful of teachers in my life who have had a permanent impact on me." What made Paul Jorgensen's classes so memorable, aside from his great knowledge? He had a good ear for the plays, for what didn't work as well as what worked, for what made some of them great and what showed others up as interesting apprentice work. "Brutus is a first draft of Hamlet," he would suggest, "and in this scene you can see Shakespeare's earlier tragic method: the hero announcing he is pensive." In his undergraduate course, students didn't learn that Professor Jorgensen found King Lear a greater character than Othello — because Lear learns so much more about himself — until after the class had finished *Othello*, perhaps because Jorgensen didn't want to damage students' full participation in the experience of *Othello* itself. When he read aloud in his melancholy voice Othello's words, "But yet, the pity of it, Iago. Oh Iago, the pity of it, Iago," the whole class felt that pity. This excellent historicist scholar never let historical context overwhelm a play. If knowing more about Elizabethan conflictedness over war and peace helped students understand a play, he would talk about that, but the complex economy of each drama far outweighed, for him, the articulation of the drama with its surrounding culture. Nobody knew more about the surrounding culture than Paul Jorgensen did; but for him, the play was the thing.

This literary value system, so visible in his teaching, underpinned his scholarship as well. His early book *Shakespeare's Military World* (1956) was a fine cultural study which brought to life the tensions between hawks and doves which perennially crackled in Elizabethan society. Our understanding of Henry V, of Othello, of Bosola in Webster's *Duchess of Malfi*, of Jacopo in Beaumont and Fletcher's *The Captain*, and a host of other soldiers and ex-soldiers in the drama, would be much the poorer without this book, a book still alive and useful today. But his two greatest books deal with single plays. *Lear's Self-Discovery* (1967) mobilized vast knowledge of Renaissance thinking on identity — the book has much to teach students of Renaissance subjectivity today; and *Our Naked Frail-ties: Sensational Art and Meaning in "Macbeth"* (1971) was informed by Jorgensen's intimate familiarity with Renaissance ideas about bodily sensations, with Elizabethan theories of condign punishment, and with witchcraft lore. But what he cared about was not so much the intellectual milieu, or the theories, or the lore, but the plays themselves. Few books of literary criticism in our time have brought to life those two greatest of Shakespeare's plays with more force and vitality than have *Lear's Self-Discovery* and *Our Naked Frailties*. Placing *Lear* and *Macbeth* ahead of *Hamlet* as "greatest plays" reflects Jorgensen's own estimate: while giving *Hamlet* its full weight when he taught it, he once remarked that after many years of living with the play, he had come to believe that "more than almost any other Shakespeare play, *Hamlet* is shot through with mainly pointless problems." Statements like that gave us confidence to criticize Shakespeare even in his greatest plays, though all the while respecting him, and helped turn us into "resisting readers" who could still enjoy the plays.

And not only in *Our Naked Frailties*, where he writes wonderfully about the Macbeths' euphemisms, but in other books such as *Redeeming Shakespeare's Words* (1962), Paul Jorgensen always had a sensitive and attentive ear for Shakespeare's use of the English language, which he rendered richer and more comprehensible by recovering the historical context of some key words: "nothing," "honour," "noble," and even "pistol." This language to which he was so sensitive finally became part of him, and when occasion offered, he spoke it himself.

He wrote so well. One sometimes thinks that the art of writing with such precision, humaneness, and grace has been lost from the scholarly world. It isn't fashionable any more to write about the way plays move us, the way they get under our skin. Paul Jorgensen did sometimes write about that, in prose so restrained that it made emotion all the more powerful for being curbed: like a generous horse, Jorgensen's prose showed most true mettle when he checked its course. This spring, my mind full of violence from reading the essays in this volume, and especially of torture from reading the essays by Kusunoki and Caldwell, I re-read *Our Naked Frailties* with its memorable discussions of violence and torture, and was moved to take it to class with me on the last day we were discussing *Macbeth*. I read aloud from Chapter X, "Torture of the Mind," a passage crowning Jorgensen's excellent discussion of the "tomorrow, and tomorrow, and tomorrow" soliloquy:

> We must not neglect its meaning for Macbeth's life. Essentially it is a denial of everything in this life which might give meaning or hope. There is surely no God, no hereafter, no possibility of redemption in "lighted

fools / The way to dusty death," in "a tale / Told by an idiot," in "then is heard no more," or in "signifying nothing." Like Cecropia's discourse, Macbeth's is a testament of atheism. Its desperation is dangerous less in its gloomy view of man than in its implicit comment upon any God who might preside over this tragicomic stage spectacle. It is, in substance, the most blasphemous utterance that Shakespeare ever wrote. But it is of course safe in its blasphemy because it is placed so securely in dramatic context. Macbeth is damned, and we are not Macbeth. (*Our Naked Frailties*, 214)

Earlier that hour, students had been maintaining that they couldn't feel pity at the death of a murderer, and I had been trying to persuade them that Shakespeare (by making a murderer the hero) had gone far beyond Aristotle in radically demanding that we pity not only unmerited misfortune but also merited misfortune. Since Jorgensen had also tackled this issue, I read aloud to them the closing words of Chapter X, which were also (except for the Epilogue) the closing words of the book *Our Naked Frailties*:

How much pity we owe a tragic hero who is a "butcher" (V.ix.35) and "this fiend of Scotland" (IV.iii.233) depends perhaps upon each one of us. But we must acknowledge that he takes us upon one of the most profoundly violent, most vividly felt experiences of life that we shall ever know. Through his tortured mind and senses we experience a range of sensation extending through the excited inception of shared ambition and hope, through plausible temptation, through reluctant evil, through hopeless labor, through racked nerves and restless fear, to a blasphemous negation of a life robbed of meaning.

But the whole experience is securely placed for us by dramatic context. Macbeth is damned, and we are not Macbeth. Or are we? (216)

Academic books don't sound like that any more, I was thinking as I read. Recent critics don't often allow themselves to be drawn into emotional participation with a suffering hero, and they don't often write with anything like Jorgensen's quiet eloquence. These students of mine had never encountered the book, which has been out of print for some time, and they were much struck by it. "Wow! Who wrote that?" demanded one, pencil poised over her notebook. Well, Paul Jorgensen wrote it.

We are happy to dedicate this volume to Paul Jorgensen's memory because he taught both of the editors and many of the essayists of this volume, and he also taught the editor of Medieval and Renaissance Texts and Studies, Robert Bjork.

The methodology of the essays reflects the historically-informed methods Jorgensen taught us. I talked with him about the volume as it progressed (it had just been sent off to the Press at the time he died) and he was keenly interested in the topic of violence and women. He had a career-long interest in violence, from the violence of war in *Shakespeare's Military World* to the violence of murder and of tortured senses in *Our Naked Frailties*, the dust jacket of which features a contorted hand dripping with blood. And as for women, Paul was always very fair to us. His most cherished human contacts were the beloved wife and daughters who all rejoice in Tudor names — Virginia, Mary, and Elizabeth — and he gave significant support and encouragement to the legion of women graduate students he supervised. Never much of a believer in feminism, he was perhaps a little chagrined that so many of his former students grew up to be feminists. But he believed in us and supported us anyway, and took our work seriously during years when not everybody did. Paul Jorgensen was a memorable teacher, a fine scholar, an eloquent writer, and a caring human being.

We shall not look upon his like again.

Linda Woodbridge
Pennsylvania State University

Works Cited

Amussen, Susan Dwyer. " 'Being stirred to much unquietness': Violence and Domestic Violence in Early Modern England." *Journal of Women's History* 6 (1994): 70–89.

Baines, Barbara J. "Effacing Rape in Early Modern Representation." *ELH* 65 (1998): 69–98.

Bashar, Nazife. "Rape in England between 1550 and 1700." In *The Sexual Dynamics of History: Men's Power, Women's Resistance*, 28–42. London: Pluto Press, 1983.

Beaumont, Francis, and John Fletcher. *The Captain*. Ed. L. A. Beaurline. In *The Dramatic Works in the Beaumont and Fletcher Canon*, ed. Fredson Bowers, 10 vols., 1:541–670. Cambridge: Cambridge University Press, 1966.

———. *Love's Cure, or The Martial Maid*, ed. Marea Mitchell. Nottingham: Nottingham Drama Texts, 1992.

———. *The Maid's Tragedy*, ed. Andrew Gurr. Berkeley: University of California Press, 1969.

Boose, Lynda E. "Scolding Brides and Bridling Scolds: Taming the Woman's Unruly Member." *Shakespeare Quarterly* 42 (1991): 179–213.

Breitenberg, Mark. *Anxious Masculinity in Early Modern England.* Cambridge: Cambridge University Press, 1996.

Brownmiller, Susan. *Against Our Will: Men, Women, and Rape.* New York: Simon and Schuster, 1975.

Cary, Elizabeth. *The Tragedie of Mariam,* ed. Barry Weller and Margaret Ferguson. Berkeley: University of California Press, 1994.

Castiglione, Baldassare. *The Courtier,* ed. W. E. Henley. London: David Nutt, 1900. (Thomas Hoby translation, first printed 1561.)

Catty, Jocelyn. *Writing Rape, Writing Women in Early Modern England: Unbridled Speech.* London: Macmillan, 1999.

Chaucer, Geoffrey. *The Works of Geoffrey Chaucer,* ed. F. N. Robinson. 2nd ed. Boston: Houghton Mifflin, 1957.

Chaytor, Miranda. "Husband(ry): Narratives of Rape in the Seventeenth Century." *Gender and History* 7 (1995): 378–407.

Comensoli, Viviana. *Household Business: Domestic Plays of Early Modern England.* Toronto: University of Toronto Press, 1996.

Cooke, John. *Greene's Tu Quoque.* Amersham, England: Tudor Facsimile Texts, 1913.

Dekker, Thomas. "Lantern and Candlelight." London: G. Eld, 1608. STC 6485.

De Lauretis, Teresa. "The Violence of Rhetoric: Considerations on Representation and Gender." In eadem, *Technologies of Gender: Essays on Theory, Film, and Fiction,* 31–50. Bloomington: Indiana University Press, 1989.

Dickenson, John. *Greene in Conceit: New Raised from his Grave to Write the Tragic History of Fair Valeria of London.* London: R. Bradocke, 1598. STC 6819.

Dolan, Frances E. *Dangerous Familiars: Representations of Domestic Crime in England 1550–1700.* Ithaca: Cornell University Press, 1994.

———. "Household Chastisements: Gender, Authority, and 'Domestic Violence'." In *Renaissance Culture and the Everyday,* ed. Patricia Fumerton and Simon Hunt, 204–25. Philadelphia: University of Pennsylvania Press, 1999.

———, ed. *William Shakespeare: The Taming of the Shrew, Texts and Contexts.* Boston and New York: St. Martin's Press, 1986.

Donaldson, Ian. *The Rapes of Lucretia: A Myth and its Transformations.* Oxford: Clarendon Press, 1982.

Elias, Norbert. *The Civilizing Process,* trans. Edmund Jephcott. Oxford: Blackwell, 1994. (First published in German as *Über den Prozess der Zivilization* [Basel: Haus zum Falken, 1939].)

Field, Nathan. *Amends for Ladies.* In *The Plays of Nathan Field,* ed. William Peery, 159–236. Austin: University of Texas Press, 1950.

Fletcher, John. *Bonduca*, ed. Cyrus Hoy. In *The Dramatic Works in the Beaumont and Fletcher Canon*, ed. Fredson Bowers, vol. 4: 149–259. Cambridge: Cambridge University Press, 1979.

———, and William Rowley. *The Maid in the Mill*, ed. Fredson Bowers. In *The Dramatic Works in the Beaumont and Fletcher Canon*, ed. idem, vol. 9:569–669. Cambridge: Cambridge University Press, 1994.

Gelles, Richard J. "Male Offenders: Our Understanding from the Data." In *What Causes Men's Violence Against Women?*, ed. Michèle Harway and James M. O'Neil, 36–48. Thousand Oaks, CA: Sage, 1999.

Girard, René. *Deceit, Desire, and the Novel: Self and Other in Literary Structure*, trans. Yvonne Freccero. Baltimore: Johns Hopkins University Press, 1965.

———. *A Theatre of Envy: William Shakespeare*. New York: Oxford University Press, 1991.

Gossett, Suzanne. " 'Best Men are Molded out of Faults': Marrying the Rapist in Jacobean Drama." *English Literary Renaissance* 14 (1984): 305–27.

Gravdal, Kathryn. *Ravishing Maidens: Writing Rape in Medieval French Literature and Law*. Philadelphia: University of Pennsylvania Press, 1991.

Greene, Robert, and Thomas Lodge. *A Looking-Glass for London and England*. Malone Society Reprint. Oxford: Oxford University Press, 1932. First published 1594. STC 15927.

Hale, John. *The Civilization of Europe in the Renaissance*. New York: Atheneum, 1994.

Hanson, Elizabeth. *Discovering the Subject in Renaissance England*. Cambridge: Cambridge University Press, 1998.

Heale, William. *An Apology for Women. Or an opposition to Mr. Dr. G. his assertion that it was lawful for husbands to beat their wives*. Oxford: Joseph Barnes, 1609. STC 13014.

Helgerson, Richard. *Self-Crowned Laureates: Spenser, Jonson, Milton, and the Literary System*. Berkeley: University of California Press, 1983.

Heywood, John (?). *Johan Johan, the Husband, Tyb, His Wife, and Sir Johan, the Priest*. In *Chief Pre-Shakespearean Dramas*, ed. Joseph Quincy Adams, 385–96. Cambridge, MA: Houghton Mifflin, 1924.

Heywood, Thomas (?). *How a Man May Choose a Good Wife from a Bad*. In *A Select Collection of Old English Plays Originally Published by Robert Dodsley*, 15 vols., ed. W. Carew Hazlitt, 9:5–96. London: Reeves and Turner, 1874.

———. *The English Traveller*. In *The Dramatic Works of Thomas Heywood*, ed. John Pearson, 6 vols., 4:6–95. London: J. Pearson, 1874.

Hoffman, Piotr. *Violence in Modern Philosophy*. Chicago and London: University of Chicago Press, 1989.

Hunt, Margaret. "Wife Beating, Domesticity, and Women's Independence in Eighteenth-Century London." *Gender and History* 4 (1992): 10–33.

Ingelend, Thomas. *The Disobedient Child*. In *A Select Collection of Old English Plays*, 15 vols., ed. Hazlitt, 2:265–320.

Ingram, Martin. "Ridings, Rough Music and the 'Reform of Popular Culture' in Early Modern England." *Past and Present* 105 (1984): 79–113.

———. " 'Scolding Women Cucked or Washed': A Crisis in Gender Relations in Early Modern England?" In *Women, Crime, and the Courts in Early Modern England*, ed. Jenny Kermode and Garthine Walker, 48–80. London: University College London Press, 1994.

Jed, Stephanie H. *Chaste Thinking: The Rape of Lucretia and the Birth of Humanism*. Bloomington and Indianapolis: Indiana University Press, 1989.

———. "The Scene of Tyranny: Violence and the Humanistic Tradition." In *The Violence of Representation: Literature and the History of Violence*, ed. Nancy Armstrong and Leonard Tennenhouse, 29–44. London and New York: Routledge, 1989.

Jonson, Ben. *Epicoene*. First acted in 1609. In *Ben Jonson*, ed. C. H. Herford, Percy Simpson, and Evelyn Simpson, 11 vols., 5: 161–272. Oxford: Clarendon Press, 1937.

Jorgensen, Paul A. *Lear's Self-Discovery*. Berkeley: University of California Press, 1967.

———. *Our Naked Frailties: Sensational Art and Meaning in "Macbeth."* Berkeley: University of California Press, 1971.

———. *Redeeming Shakespeare's Words*. Berkeley: University of California Press, 1962.

———. *Shakespeare's Military World*. Berkeley, Los Angeles, and London: University of California Press, 1956.

Kahn, Coppélia. *Man's Estate: Masculine Identity in Shakespeare*. Berkeley: University of California Press, 1981.

Kappeler, Susanne. *The Pornography of Representation*. Cambridge: Policy Press, 1986.

Kolodny, Annette. *The Lay of the Land*. Chapel Hill: University of North Carolina Press, 1984.

Laqueur, Thomas. *Making Sex: Body and Gender from the Greeks to Freud*. Cambridge, MA: Harvard University Press, 1990.

Lydgate, John. *A Mumming at Hertford*. In *Minor Poems of John Lydgate*, ed. Henry Noble MacCracken and Merriam Sherwood, 2 vols., 2:675–83. London: EETS, 1934, repr. 1961.

Marin, Amy J., and Nancy Felipe Russo. "Feminist Perspectives on Male Violence Against Women: Critiquing O'Neil and Harway's Model." In *What
Causes Men's Violence Against Women?*, ed. Harway and O'Neil, 18–35.

Marotti, Arthur F. "'Love is Not Love': Elizabethan Sonnet Sequences and the
Social Order." *ELH* 49 (1982): 396–428.

A Merry Jest of a Shrewd and Curst Wife Lapped in Morel's Skin. (Probably written around 1525.) London: H. Jackson, 1580 (?). STC 14521.

Middleton, Thomas, and William Rowley. *The Changeling.* In *Drama of the
English Renaissance*, ed. M. L. Wine, 601–84. New York: Random House,
1969.

———. *All's Lost by Lust.* In *The Spanish Gipsie, and All's Lost By Lust*, ed. Edgar
C. Morris, 137–252. Boston: Heath, 1908.

———. *The Spanish Gypsy.* In *The Spanish Gipsie, and All's Lost By Lust*, ed.
Edgar C. Morris, 1–126. Boston: Heath, 1908.

Neill, Michael. *Issues of Death: Mortality and Identity in English Renaissance
Tragedy.* Oxford: Clarendon Press, 1997.

Ovid. *Ars Amatoria*, trans. J. H. Mozley. Loeb Classical Library. Cambridge,
MA: Harvard University Press, 1947.

Parker, Patricia. *Shakespeare from the Margins: Language, Culture, Context.* Chicago and London: University of Chicago Press, 1996.

Pisan, Christine de. *The Book of the City of Ladies*, trans. E. J. Richards. New
York: Persea, 1982.

Relihan, Constance C. *Fashioning Authority: The Development of Elizabethan
Novelistic Discourse.* Kent, OH and London: Kent State University Press,
1994.

Ruggiero, Guido. "Violence and Sexuality: Rape." In idem, *The Boundaries of
Eros: Sex Crime and Sexuality in Renaissance Venice*, 89–108. New York: Oxford University Press, 1985.

Sackville, Thomas, and Thomas Norton. *Gorboduc, or Ferrex and Porrex.* In
Drama of the English Renaissance I: The Tudor Period, ed. Russell A. Fraser
and Norman Rabkin, 81–100. New York: Macmillan, 1976.

Sawday, Jonathan. *The Body Emblazoned: Dissection and the Human Body in Renaissance Culture.* London and New York: Routledge, 1995.

Sedgwick, Eve Kosofsky. *Between Men: English Literature and Male Homosocial
Desire.* New York: Columbia University Press, 1992. (First published 1985.)

Shakespeare, William. *Complete Works*, ed. David Bevington. 4th ed. Glenview,
IL: Scott, Foresman, 1992.

Spenser, Edmund. *The Faerie Queene*, ed. A.C. Hamilton. London and New
York: Longman, 1977.

Stone, Lawrence. *The Crisis of the Aristocracy, 1558-1641*. Oxford: Clarendon Press, 1965.

Tennenhouse, Leonard. "Violence Done to Women on the Renaissance Stage." In *The Violence of Representation: Literature and the History of Violence*, ed. Nancy Armstrong and idem, 77–97.

Tom Tyler and His Wife. Malone Society Reprint. London: Chiswick Press, 1910.

Underdown, David. "The Taming of the Scold: The Enforcement of Patriarchal Authority in Early Modern England." In *Order and Disorder in Early Modern England*, ed. Anthony Fletcher and John Stevenson, 116–36. Cambridge: Cambridge University Press, 1985.

Vickers, Brian. *Appropriating Shakespeare: Contemporary Critical Quarrels*. New Haven: Yale University Press, 1993.

Webster, John. *The Duchess of Malfi*, ed. John Russell Brown. London: Methuen, 1964.

Whately, William. *A Bride-Bush, or, A Direction for Married Persons*. London: B. Alsop, 1623. (First printed 1616.) STC 25298.

Wolfthal, Diane. *Images of Rape: The "Heroic" Tradition and its Alternatives*. Cambridge: Cambridge University Press, 1999.

Woodbridge, Linda. *Women and the English Renaissance: Literature and the Nature of Womankind, 1540–1620*. Urbana and Chicago: University of Illinois Press, 1984.

Wroth, Mary. *The First Part of the Countess of Montgomery's Urania*, ed. Josephine A. Roberts. MRTS 140. Binghamton, NY: Medieval and Renaissance Texts and Studies, 1995.

PART ONE:

VIOLENCE AGAINST WOMEN

A.
Women Sexually Assaulted,
Kidnapped, Murdered,
or Threatened with Serious Violence

Representing Lavinia:
The (In)significance of Women's Consent in
Legal Discourses of Rape and Ravishment
and Shakespeare's *Titus Andronicus*

This paper analyzes the relationship between legal and literary discourses of rape and ravishment in sixteenth-century England. I begin, however, not with legal discourse, but with the single most vexing moment in Shakespeare's "The Rape of Lucrece." Shakespeare's poem depicts Lucrece's rape by Tarquin, and then represents Lucrece's attempts to deal with the crime's aftermath. In a reiteration of earlier narratives of Lucrece, Shakespeare's Lucrece believes that there can be only one resolution to the situation in which she finds herself: she must kill herself, and through her suicide demonstrate irrefutably her non-consent to the crime. Just before she stabs herself, however, Lucrece suggests that there is another, non-violent means by which she might be cleared of the "taint" of "accessory yieldings" to Tarquin:

> "O, speak," quoth she,
> "How may this forced stain be wip'd from me?
> What is the quality of my offense,
> Being constrain'd with dreadful circumstance?
> May my pure mind with the foul act dispense,
> My low-declined honor to advance?
> May any terms acquit me from this chance?
> The poisoned fountain clears itself again,
> And why not I from this compelled stain?"[1]

---

[1] William Shakespeare, "The Rape of Lucrece," in *The Riverside Shakespeare*, ed.

Lucrece suggests that "terms" may exist that would "acquit" her from the situation in which she finds herself, but does not seem to know where such "terms"
might be found. It is now that we reach the heart of the problem, the point of
great vexation. For while Lucrece's audience is only too willing to accede to the
rhetorical claim that the "pure mind" ought to be able to "with the foul act dis-
pense," Lucrece herself is not so inclined:

> With this they all at once began to say,
> Her body's stain her mind untainted clears,
> While with a joyless smile she turns away
> The face, that map which deep impression bears
> Of hard misfortune, carv'd [in it] with tears.
>   "No, no," quoth she, "no dame hereafter living
>   By my excuse shall claim excuse's giving."
>   (1709–1717)

Shakespeare represents Lucrece as performing a very particular kind of error. In
a decidedly misogynistic turn, Lucrece negates the political potential of the
moment, her opportunity to perform a legal innovation. That legal innovation
would allow other women to liberate themselves from one discourse, a discourse
that reads the raped woman's body as a document in shame, by making recourse
to another, a discourse through which they might invoke their "minds" as the
entities that remain free from any stain which may attach to their bodies.[2] In a
poem much concerned with questions of representation, Shakespeare rationalizes
Lucrece's self-destructive act by suggesting that it is symptomatic of her collusion
with a certain failure in judicial thinking. Lucrece imagines the potentially negative consequences of her precedent rather than its positive implications. She
imagines, in short, that other women, women who do not deserve to be "excused" of the crime, will gain their excuse by redeploying her rhetoric or citing
her as a precedent. Positing such women as her excuse for not seizing the opportunity of the precedent-setting moment, Shakespeare's Lucrece reiterates the
force of legal operations at their most misogynistic: she denies not just herself

---

G. Blakemore Evans (Boston: Houghton Mifflin, 1974), lines 1700–1708. All further references to "The Rape of Lucrece" are to this edition.

[2] Livy's Lucrece attempts something similar, by claiming that, while her body has
been violated, her "heart is innocent." In Livy's account, this claim is undermined by the
men who gaze upon her dead body, for they claim that "it was the mind that sinned."
See Ian Donaldson, *The Rapes of Lucretia: A Myth and Its Transformations* (Oxford: Clarendon Press, 1982), 31.

but all women the opportunity to make "mind" a legally significant entity. This is a perverse deployment of her powers of consent, born of the very kind of collusion against which the author of *The Lawes Resolutions*, a text I will discuss at some length below, warns his "scholars" to take heed. That perversion finds itself reduplicated in the failed act of writing in which her "will blots [her] wit," making it impossible for her to put in writing to her husband Collatine anything other than his need to hurry home. Refusing to engage with the law in such a way that she might innovate a solution for herself and a precedent for the future, Lucrece finds herself unable to write, and unable to write back against Tarquin's destruction of her "true type," that of "loyal wife." She agrees to a monolithic legal construction that sees no relevance in the intention or subjectivity of the person who is caught up in another's act of violence, and as a result is unable to instantiate the "wit" through which she might liberate herself from the tragic confusion of her own will with the impersonal "will" of discursive networks. This paper will articulate the dynamics through which legal discourse consistently (re)performs Lucrece's error by, like her, asserting the legal insignificance of female will and mind. It will trace the ways in which representatives of the law make strange use of the phantasmatic entity of a woman's "consent," and will culminate with a reading of *Titus Andronicus* that argues that the play criticizes the legal operations that reproduce and magnify Lucrece's mistake.

I. "OF NOTHING WORTH"

Titus Andronicus stages two very different acts defined as rape in England at the end of the sixteenth century. In the opening scene of the play, Lavinia is "ravished," conveyed "out of the possession and against the will of her father" into the possession of another man, and in 2.3 she is "raped," "enforced violently to sustain the fury of [the] brutish concupiscence" of two men, Demetrius and Chiron, the sons of Tamora, Queen of the Goths.[3] In its representation of "ravishment," the play highlights the anxieties generated by the ostensible object of the crime, the ravished woman, who can exert a legally troubling agency by choosing not to speak at one or more moments in the proceedings; and in its representation of "rape," it displays the law's inadequate description of the crime by allotting much of the agency in the rape to a person other than those who commit

---

[3] These definitions of "rape" and "ravishment" are drawn from T.E.'s *The Lawes Resolutions of Womens Rights: or, the Lawes Provision for Woemen* (London, 1632), 377–78. All further references to *The Lawes Resolutions* will be furnished directly in the text. The original spelling and punctuation have been retained.

it. In both cases, the play suggests that the law's beguiling conceptual terms for the acts obliterate the person acted upon at their center; the tongueless and handless Lavinia who can make known what has happened to her only by writing "stuprum" in the sand becomes a cipher for the actual women who find themselves figuratively "ravished," or forcibly unpropertied, by legal operations they do not know how to negotiate. It is those women to whom the anonymous author of *The Lawes Resolutions*, who goes only by the initials T.E., addresses himself.[4]

For T.E., "woman" signifies a position of particular vulnerability under the law. "Women onely women," he writes, "have nothing to do in constituting lawes, or consenting to them, in interpreting of Lawes, or in hearing them interpreted at lectures, leets or charges," yet they are "strictly tied" to whatever the law legislates on their behalf (*Lawes Resolutions*, 2). Not only are women unable to exercise their powers of consent in relation to the writing, interpretation, or application of laws, they are also subject, he contends, to the "concealment" of the law from them in "an uncouth language, clear abstruded from their sex" (403). (Most of English law in the period was written in what is known as "Law French.") Claiming that this "concealment" is "neither, just, nor conscionable," he claims to operate from a moral imperative in writing and publishing his book. "[M]ee thinks it were pitty and impiety any longer to hold from [women] such Customs, lawes, and Statutes, as are in a maner, proper, or principally belonging unto them" (2). He claims that he will therefore provide, "with as little tediousnesse as I can ... that part of the English Lawe, which containeth the immunities, advantages, interests, and duties of women, not regarding so much to satisfie the deep learned or searchers for subtility, as woman kind, to whom I am a thankfull debter by nature" (3).

The situation is gravest, T.E. contends, in relation to matters of rape; for not only does the crime involve a violent deprivation of a woman's powers of consent, the English law makes it possible for men to exploit their literacy against women:

> I can but marvell that when, so damnable a crime as rape, had given so often to the whole Realme such cause of bitter complaint, and men in

---

[4] The British Library catalogue suggests that Thomas Edgar, a justice of the peace for the county of Suffolk, and the author of another legal text, *Two Charges* (1649), is the author. The ESTC, which suggests the same, also notes that the text is sometimes attributed to Sir John Doddridge. A third candidate for the identity of T.E. is Thomas Egerton, a prominent circuit court justice in the period, and later Lord Chancellor.

sundry ages, had beaten their braines so carefully in finding out remedy against it: how it was possible, so long space together, to leave such a privilege to him that could read the blessed Psalme of Miserere, &c., that though hee had ravished the fairest Lady in the Land, hee might almost goe away without touch of breast for it. (401)

T.E. here inveighs against the legal loophole known as "benefit of clergy" through which men convicted of a crime that demanded a penalty of "life or member" might elude punishment by demonstrating their literacy. That literacy might be little more than token, since the proof of it lay in the reading of a verse or two from the Bible, verses which could easily be learned by rote. Rewarding men for their token literacy while making it almost impossible for women to be literate in legal matters, the law in its "ignorance" produces injustices against which T.E. adjures his "scholars" to take heed. He shows them how to take heed in part by providing an abridged history of the legal discourses around the crimes of rape and ravishment.

T.E.'s history suggests that, legally speaking, both Lavinia and the women whom *The Lawes Resolutions* addresses are nothing more than the *loci* at which property interests converge and clash. T.E. traces a decided shift in the history of the crimes, a shift that shows rape or "stuprum" being sidelined as the law expends its efforts on codifying its response to the crime with which it is so intimately related, ravishment. T.E. is particularly concerned with what he construes as the "mitigation" or weakening of the force of the laws against rape, a mitigation that occurs, he suggests, because statutory law increasingly focuses not on the offense against the woman's person but the offense against the man or men for whom she constitutes a valuable commodity. T.E. locates the roots of the attenuation in the "antique law of King Adelstan," which, although it was itself quite hard on the rapist, as it called for judgment upon "life and member," simultaneously introduced a notion of the woman's "consent" to the crime, a notion which was to precipitate the devolution of the crime into a "verie small trespasse" (380). It allows for a woman's exercise of her consent *after* the rape; the raped woman could elect to save the alleged rapist from punishment by claiming that she now consented, after the fact, to what had been done to her. She would signify her consent by agreeing to marry the alleged rapist. This provision, combined with William the Conqueror's ruling that no man shall be executed for the crime of rape, results, according to T.E., in two "enormities": a proliferation of the crime, and the "mitigation" of the law's power to do anything about it.

In the course of this "mitigation," the two crimes come to be defined in ways that increasingly distinguish them from one another. In T.E.'s preliminary definition, as quoted above, the distinction between the two turns on whether the woman "is left where she is found, as in her owne house or bed, as Lucrece was," or whether she is "hurried away" to another place, "as Helen by Paris, or as the Sabine Women were by the Romans" (*Lawes Resolutions*, 377–78). As the law works to define the crime of ravishment more and more precisely, it loses the graduated sense of the crime of rape that Adelstan's law secured by subdividing the crime into several acts, each of which was met with an increasingly severe punishment. Under Adelstan a man could be punished, for example, for simply *touching* a woman "unhonestly," even though this act of touching stopped well short of anything like enforced copulation. If he went further and "threw [the woman] on the ground," he "lost the Kings favour," and if matters escalated further still, and he went so far as to "cast himselfe upon her," he would forfeit all of his possessions (378). T.E.'s argument is that this scheme disappears, inexplicably, in an attenuation of the law's attitude to the crime, an attenuation that is formalized in the first statute that speaks of rape, *West. 1 cap. 14*. *West. 1 cap. 14* "allay[s] the rigour of the former Lawe" by decreeing that any man found guilty of rape shall not lose life and member, as Adelstan required, but simply be imprisoned for two years (380). The statute does, however, account for the crime when it is perpetrated against "*any* damsell within age" [my emphasis], a fact that will be of some importance later in this discussion. It also refuses to make the matter of a woman's "consent" the means through which a rapist might seek exoneration. The crime of rape will be punishable whether or not the man attempts to claim that the woman has consented to the act of copulation.

With *6 Richard 2* the single most dramatic shift in the law's conceptions of the crimes takes place. Construing the crime of ravishment as a property offense, *6 Richard 2* transfers the right to make an appeal of rape from the woman herself to her husband or father. The assumption here is that the "consenting" woman, whose consent may or may not be actual, is forfeiting the right to protect her own interests, a right that others must move to protect on her behalf. But in T.E.'s interpretation, the statute does not seek to *protect* women as much as it seeks to *punish* them. "[A] new Law was made," T.E. writes, "to punish women, which consented to their ravishors":

> It is ordained, [the statute states,] that wheresoever, and whensoever such Ladies, daughters or other women bee ravished, and after rape doe consent to such ravishers, as they which be ravished, bee from henceforth disabled, to have or challenge Heritage, Dower of Joint feoffment after the death of their husbands, and ancestors. (382)

The implications of *6 Richard 2* are clear: English statutory law would no longer permit women to exert agency in the matter of their marriage by orchestrating, along with their lovers, a performance of "ravishment" that was the mere pretense of abduction. Decisively establishing "ravishment" as a matter between men, *6 Richard 2* deprives women of the small but important leverage that their ability to "consent" to the "rape" gave them if they sought to use the "crime" to marry as they chose.

4 & 5 Phi. & Mary makes matters worse still. It confirms that the only form of consent with which the law is concerned in matters of ravishment is that of the ravished woman's father or mother:

> ... yf any pson or psons, above thage of xiiij^{ene} yeres, shall ... unlawfully take or convey or cause to be taken or conveide any Maide or Woman Childe unmaried, being within thage of xvj^{ne} yeres, out of or from the possession and against the will of the Father or Mother of suche Childe ... then every suche pson and psons so offending ... shall have and suffer Imprisonement of his or their Bodies by the Space of Twoo whole yeres without Bayle or Mayneprise.[5]

In fact, by this stage in the legislative history, a woman's "consent" can do only one thing: work *against* her. In a reversal of Adelstan's law, the woman who consents to her ravisher not only does not gain the man's lands, she loses her own; any property which she stands to inherit now goes immediately to the person who stands to inherit after her:

> ... if any Woman Childe or Mayden, being above thage of twelve yeres, and under thage of xvi yeres, doo at any time consent and agree to such pson that so shall make any Contract of Matrimonye contrarye to the fourme and effecte of this Estatute, then the next of the Kinne of the same Woman Childe or Mayde, to whom thinheritance shoulde discende returne or come after the decease of the same Woman Childe and Maide, shall from the time of suche Assent and Agrement have holde and enjoye all suche Landes Tenementes and Hereditamentes, as the same Woman Childe and Mayden had in Possession Reversion or Remainder at the time of suche Consent and Agreament, during the Lyfe of suche persone that so shall contracte Matrymonye.[6]

---

[5] *Statutes of the Realm*, 11 vols. (London: Dawsons of Pall Mall, 1810–1828), 4:329.
[6] *Statutes of the Realm*, 4:329–30.

When *4 & 5 Phi. & Mary* is read within the context of an earlier statute, *3 Henry 7*, it also applies to widows, a fact important to a later aspect of this discussion. *4 & 5 Phi. & Mary* makes its only distinction between ravishment that involves only abduction and ravishment that includes rape in the length of the sentence: the former crime results in imprisonment for two years, the latter, for five.

Sir Henry Hobart's report on the Star Chamber case of *Bruton v. Morris* underscores the ramifications of the sixteenth-century statutes when they are interpreted in conjunction with one another. (Hobart does not date the case, but, since his role in it is that of Attorney General, the case must have been heard during Hobart's tenure as Attorney General, which runs from 1606 to 1613.) Hobart contends that the ravishment of John Bruton's twelve-year-old daughter cannot be construed as a felony because the "daughter was neither heir apparent to her father, nor had lands or goods."[7] Hobart grants that the wording of *3 Henry 7*, which reiterates *6 Richard 2*, may "seem general to all women, taken unlawfully against their wills," but insists that this is in fact not the case: the statute requires not only that the "maids, widows, or wives" who have allegedly been ravished must have "substance in goods or lands" but "that the motive [for the ravishment] should be lucre" (329). Furthermore, *3 Henry 7* and *4 & 5 Phi. & Mary* allow for the prosecution of a man who has forcibly "deflowered" a woman (that is, raped her) only where the crime has been motivated by his *intention* to secure her property as his own. In Hobart's interpretation, law will take account of ravishment only where the woman stands to inherit property. This interpretation contributes to the effacement of the crime when it is performed, to use Hobart's wording, against women who are "nothing worth" — the very circumstance in which the crime is more likely to be rape in the sense of enforced copulation rather than ravishment in the sense of enforced marriage.

The statutory law's failure to make as adequate provisions for the crime of rape as it does for the crime of ravishment — the crime, that is, where real property is at stake — is graphically evident in the trial of James Dyckson, a Scot who is indicted for the rape of a six-year-old girl, Christine Launde, in the 1560s. According to a report of the case by Sir James Dyer, after Dyckson unsuccessfully attempts to elude indictment by claiming that he has a right to be

---

[7] For Hobart's account of *Bruton v. Morris*, see *The English Reports*, vol. 80 (Edinburgh: William Green & Sons, 1907), 329. All further references to Hobart's report will be provided directly in the text.

tried in his native tongue, a jury of matrons reports that, from what the women have seen in their examination of Christine's body, Dyckson must be held guilty of rape.[8] The presiding justices nevertheless refuse to judge Dyckson guilty. Both Dyer and T.E. articulate the sticking point. In T.E.'s words, "the Justices were in doubt whether rape could be of a child of such tender years" (*Lawes Resolutions*, 401). The "doubts" are generated by *4 & 5. Phi. & Mary*, which accounts for the crime only in reference to children of the age of twelve or over. Reading Christine's body according to the strict text of the law, the justices refuse to concede that Christine has been raped because statutory law makes no provision for such a crime.

What we witness, as a result, in Dyer's report of the case is a legal glossing of the body which disregards the principal or primary text, the body itself. In the official record, Christine Launde and her body disappear from the text. The charge is that Dyckson has "violently and feloniously raped her the said Christine against her will, and then and there carnally knew her," but after this Christine vanishes.[9] The bulk of the record is about Dyckson's appearances "in his own person" before the representatives of the Queen. The written form of the law dominates, and the facts it chooses to present have little to do with the body of the plaintiff (which clearly creates a great deal of unease), but everything to do with the body of the defendant and the demonstration of the law's authority over him. The record does register the abstraction that generates the court's doubt, but all other contexts that might have contributed to the court's inability to render judgment are suppressed.

Though Dyer himself does not pursue the ramifications of the judicial failure that we witness here, the owner of a sixteenth-century manuscript edition of Dyer's *Reports* has noted, at the end of Dyer's account of a related case, how William Fleetwood, the most prominent court recorder of Elizabeth's reign, responded with frustration to a similar miscarriage of justice. Fleetwood responds to the miscarriage, which was brought about by the justices' concession to their heuristic impotence in the face of the written law's inadequacy to deal with the rape of a ten-year-old child, with a declaration about the urgent need for a new law. The new law he desires would prevent a person convicted of raping a child from eluding judicial punishment by pleading benefit of clergy.

It is not clear from the marginal annotation, which is reprinted in the Selden

---

[8] *Reports from the Lost Notebooks of Sir James Dyer*, ed. J. H. Baker, vol. 1 (London: Selden Society, 1994), 66–67.

[9] *Reports from the Lost Notebooks*, 1:66.

Society's edition of Dyer's *Reports*, whether the justices in that case found themselves similarly impotent in light of the wording of *4 & 5 Phi. & Mary*; but the annotation records one legal practitioner's determination to do something to rectify the law's general inefficacy in regard to the crime of rape: "Fletewode, recorder, said that the first bill in the next parliament to which he would set his hand would be that ravishers of women should be ousted of their clergy."[10] With Elizabeth's eighteenth statute, Fleetwood secures his end. The statute creates a new law that will stand, T.E. writes, as a "firme bulwarke against all manner of iniurers that possibly might oppresse women" by ordaining that henceforth not only will no "ravishor" be allowed benefit of clergy (*Lawes Resolutions*, 400), but, more importantly, that any abuse or "unlawful and carnal knowledge" of a "woman child under age of ten years" shall be a felony (401). *18 Eliz. 1* thus redirects the statutory law's attention back to the crime where it is enforced copulation that has nothing to do with a "taking" for "lucre," and does so in such a way that no justice can ever again doubt whether "rape could be of a child of . . . tender years." It also reinstates *West. 1*'s guarantee that "consent" can never be deployed *against* any such child by specifying that it "is not material whether she consent or no" (402). But this statute will itself have to be reiterated near the close of Elizabeth's reign, as justices fail to uphold its provisions.

The story so far has been a rather dismal one. Up until Elizabeth's eighteenth statute, statutory legislation in regard to rape has appeared to work against women, rather than for them. But the work of another legal writer suggests that women could, on occasion, still manage to deploy their consent, at least in matters of ravishment, to their advantage. The point is that, even though the law may appear, in some records of its application, not to protect the interests of women, or their powers of consent, some women were capable of, in T.E.'s rhetoric, "shifting it" — that is, finding their own ways to ensure that the law upheld their acts where those acts expressed their agency.

Michael Hawke offers the case of Margaret Keble as an example of one woman's successful deployment of her "consent" in relation to the allegations of one Roger Vernon that it is he, not Keble, who is her rightful husband. When Vernon, claiming that Margaret is already married to him, attempts to "reclaim" her from the house where she is living with Keble, Margaret brings an action of trespass against him in which she contradicts his claims that they were married "according to the lawes of the Church."[11] According to Hawke, she acts ac-

---

[10] *Reports from the Lost Notebooks*, 1:66, n. 1.

[11] Michael Hawke, *The Grounds of the Lawes of England* (London, 1657), 146. Hawke

cording to the legal principle, derived from moral philosophy, that "a marriage enforced, contrary to the will of either party, is unnatural and illegal" (*Grounds of the Lawes of England*, 146). Making use of the legal formula available to her, she argues that the "espousalls [with Vernon] were made by menaces and duresse of imprisonment," and were therefore "against [her] will" (147). The real wedding ceremony, she contends, is that which has taken place between her and Keble, even though that ceremony takes place *after* her marriage to Vernon. She "praye[s] her damages," and the court finds that it is Vernon, not Keble, who is the ravisher (147).

In his variation on the legal problem that Margaret Keble poses, T.E. offers the case of Thomas Haufegl. Haufegl brings a suit of ravishment against Thomas V., who, he claims, has made off with his wife. As the allegedly wronged husband, Haufegl must work within the formal terms provided by *6 Richard 2*; he must claim that his wife has assented to the ravishment in order for him to bring the action. This he fails to do, and when the question of the (nameless) woman's assent arises in the courtroom, the defense contends that she was in fact married to the plaintiff against her will and has come "of her owne accord to the Defendant who had now married her" (*Lawes Resolutions*, 391). This woman claims to have been engaged to the defendant before she was compelled to marry the plaintiff under duress. If the question now is who really is the husband and who the ravisher, the court contends that both Thomas V. and the anonymous woman have made significant errors in failing to bring, in Thomas V.'s case, a suit of ravishment, and in the woman's, either an action of trespass or an appeal of rape. Omitting to tell his readers how the case concludes, or choosing simply to enumerate the case's various problems, T.E. lets his partial account function as a cautionary tale to his female readers about the necessity for pre-emptive legal action. Reading Keble's case in the light of Haufegl's, we see that, unlike the anonymous woman caught in the middle of the legal wrangle between Haufegl and Thomas V., Margaret Keble has had the foresight to *initiate* the legal action through which she persuades a court to uphold the second of two wedding ceremonies as legally binding. Haufegl's case is important to T.E. for precisely the opposite reason, because it testifies to the pitfalls into which the unwary woman may fall if she does not display the kind of savvy that allows her to pre-empt a ravishment suit by bringing her own action of trespass.

---

offers no date for the case in question. All further references to *The Grounds of the Lawes* will be provided directly in the text.

II. "MARK THIS CASE"

T.E.'s cautionary tale deepens when he turns his attention to the case of Elizabeth Venor. Venor's case reveals the complications that arise from the law's various constructions of a woman's "consent" in relation to the crimes of rape and ravishment where more than one construction is deployed at the same time.

After her husband's death, Elizabeth Venor is allegedly ravished by John Worth. Somebody, it is not clear who, secures an indictment of rape against Worth, who takes sanctuary at Westminster along with Venor. T.E.'s account is opaque here on two fronts: not only does it not make clear who secures the indictment of rape, it also does not tell the reader on what basis such a charge is taken seriously. T.E. does suggest, however, that the entire case arises from the conditions that attach to property held in tail by Elizabeth's first husband, William Venor. The property in question is almost certainly descending to Elizabeth from her father, who has designed his will in such a way that the land will pass to any children that his daughter Elizabeth may have before it would be inherited by anyone else. The lands stand to be inherited first by Elizabeth, then by any children from her marriage with William Venor; next by any children Elizabeth may have in any subsequent marriage; then by one Robert Babbington and his heirs; and finally by any other heir of Elizabeth's father. The problem is that Elizabeth has no children by William Venor. As a result, Robert Babbington and his heirs have a vested interest in preventing or invalidating any second marriage on Elizabeth's part. It is therefore of considerable importance to Elizabeth that she help extricate Worth from the charge of rape while validating their marriage. But matters are more complicated still. For, as her counsel warns her, if Venor helps Worth to extricate himself from the charge of rape by assuring the Star Chamber justices that she has married him of her own free will, the person to whom T.E. refers to only as "Babbington's issue" could deploy *6 Richard 2* against her by claiming that she has consented to her "ravishment." At Westminster, Venor is thus "advised to dis-assent, and to part from [Worth] to save her inheritance" (*Lawes Resolutions*, 399). Venor chooses, however, to assert the validity of her marriage to Worth: "[B]eing there demanded if she assented or not, she answered, that John Worth was her husband, and she would not forsake him" (399).

Venor does her best, however, to prevent "Babbington's issue" from using the statutes against her. When her legal adversary brings an Assize suit against Venor, claiming, under the ravishment statutes, that Venor, having consented to her "ravishment," has forfeited her property, she allows her counsel to plead the following on her behalf:

... for Elizabeth it was alleaged, that the espousals and all the assentings were by dures and force, and for feare of the ravisher, which might not be called assenting, for none consenteth but frankly, voluntarily, and sans feare, *Quod videtur Lex ibidem.* (399–400)

Venor's move is a clever one. Since her earlier gambit to clear Worth of rape has not decisively put an end to Babbington's issue's attempt to deprive her of her property, she attempts to foil the subsequent legal action by claiming that the earlier testimony before the Star Chamber must be read as an instance of the fear that resulted in her "consent" to the "ravishment." She is doing her best, in other words, to counter the ways in which the written law may punish her for her choices, which include marrying Venor and then affirming that marriage before the Star Chamber. She will say whatever she must to keep the law from working against her.[12]

The decision that the Assize justices subsequently reach reveals what legal theorist Duncan Kennedy would call the trace of a legal "ground rule," the hint of a largely unspoken ideological basis for the law's operations,[13] or what T.E. refers to as the "ignorance" of the law, which is "not more rigorously penned, than sometime put in execution against [women]" (399). Ignoring the possibility that Venor may indeed have been acting out of fear when she testified before the Star

---

[12] Babbington's issue's actions may seem extraordinary, but unfortunately for widows in the period they were not. T.E. notes a similar abuse of the ravishment statutes in the case of Anne Powes. The problem is that the statutes and those who appear to abuse them as Babbington's issue does are both drawing upon the same double standard, one that holds only women culpable for sexual activity that offends against societal mores. T.E. inveighs vociferously against this standard as he describes how Powes, who has purportedly lived, off and on, with another man during her husband's lifetime, finds herself subject, after her husband's death, to a legal contest precipitated by her opponent's claim that her adulterous activities constitute a felonious exercise of her consent under the ravishment statutes that permits the opponent to claim her lands. Though Powes argues that there has been no "ravishment," voluntary or otherwise, since her husband knew about and tolerated the extra-marital liaison, T.E. bemoans how the law, which "wanteth equality," will punish women like Powes by depriving them of "the third foot of [their] husband[s'] lands when [they] are dead, for all the service [the wife] did him during the accouplement (perhaps a long time and a tedious) ... if she be extravagant with a friend," at the very same time that it permits the husband to make whatever "adulterous sojournings" he will without any legal consequences. For men, he writes, "a thousand out-ridings ... is no forfeiture, but as soon as the good wife is gone, the bad man will have her land," and "not the third," he notes, "but every foot of it" (*Lawes Resolutions*, 146).

[13] See Duncan Kennedy, "The Stakes of Law, or Hales and Foucault," in idem, *Sexy Dressing, Etc.* (Cambridge, MA, and London: Harvard University Press, 1993), 83–125, esp. 90–92.

Chamber, the court holds against her. "[I]n the end," T.E. notes, "because she might have disagreed before the Councell, and did not, her assent was holden voluntarie, and the Assize passed for the Plaintiffe" (400). If Venor is speaking the truth before the Assize justices, the case highlights the injustice of this application of 6 *Richard 2*, which is going to be used to punish her for an enforced statement of assent that is part of the compulsion from which earlier law was designed to protect her; and if she was telling the truth before the Star Chamber, the Assize justices are punishing her for the evidence of her will that it sees as negatively inflected in her refusal to speak out against Worth ("she might have disagreed") even though, as a widow, she is acting entirely within her rights by taking Worth as her husband. In other words, if 6 *Richard 2* is itself motivated, as T.E. claims, by a desire to "punish women which have consented to their ravishers," the Assize court opts to reinscribe the punitive aspects of the statute by rejecting Venor's statement as inauthentic. They do so presumably because in the first evidence of her "will" ("she answered that John Worth was her husband"), Venor has performed a variant on the legally troubling female agency against which 6 *Richard 2* is designed to work; and in the second, her attempt to deploy the notion of her non-consent in order to defeat Babbington's issue's property suit, she asserts her agency in an even more troubling way, by seeking to use particular legal wording to her advantage even though her statement there is a direct contradiction of her statement in the Star Chamber. Either way, the Assize justices' decision draws upon and reinscribes the misogynistic assumptions of 6 *Richard 2*.

The justices in the case attempt to rationalize their decision to punish Venor for the statement she has made before the Star Chamber by citing a case from the time of Henry VI:

> It was remembered in this case, that in former time a woman being ravished, after she had continued seven yeares with the ravisher, and had borne him a childe, escaped from him, and sued in Parliament in the time of H.6. against him, til he was attainted. And being demanded how she could now say that she never assented, having conceived, &c. shee answered, that her flesh consented to him, but her soule and conscience did ever abhorre him, 5 E. 4. fol. 58. (*Lawes Resolutions*, 400)

The anonymous young woman cited here is attempting to counter Adelstan's "antique law," which allows a woman's body to be turned against her; Adelstan's law asserts that "if at the time of rape supposed, the woman conceive child, there is no rape: for none can conceive without consent" (396). The "consent" to which the law refers here depends upon the medical fiction promulgated by the classical anatomist Galen that women as well as men produced a generative seed necessary to conception. This generative seed was released, however, only upon orgasm. A pregnancy that follows upon a rape is thus understood to offer the court decisive proof that the woman in fact consented to the rape.[14] This fiction fallaciously invokes the voluntarism or agency we associate with the word "consent" to read the woman's pregnancy as evidence of her disloyalty to the property systems that uphold the well-ordered patriarchal state. The production of an "illegitimate" child was, after all, one of two things that the laws against ravishment sought to prevent. When presented with an irremediable *fait accompli*, however, the legal regime moves quickly to bring the baby back within the fold of its discursive operations. Appropriating the idea of a woman's consent and using it against her, the law bestows upon the child a form of legitimization by insisting that the woman has consented to the crime that she has cried out against. The Assize justices remember a a young woman who attempted to defeat the invidious use of her alleged "consent" against her by insisting that there was a crucial disjunction between her body and her "soul": she claimed that while her "flesh" may have consented to the rape, the phantasmatic entity called her "soul" did not. This is, of course, the very argument that Shakespeare's Lucrece *refuses* to use because she does not wish her use of it to serve as a precedent for other women. The Assize justices in Venor's case remember the precedent, as well as the wording of *5 Edward 4,* to underscore the availability to Venor of such a precedent to prove her non-assent *if she had chosen to do so.* But they here engage in a grave hypocrisy because this act of "remembering" is simultaneously an act of *forgetting.* The justices do not themselves recall, or "remember," for the court, an important instance in which the very assertion that they are demanding from Venor was deemed ineffectual by another court.

In a 1493 "reading," Littleton cites Lady Butler's case as an instance in which precisely such a claim met with a completely unreceptive judicial audience:

> It was said by the counsel of Bishop Nevill of York that although the body consents nevertheless the mind does not; to which the justices said that their authority extended only to the body and not the mind.[15]

---

[14] For an extended discussion of Galen's theory, see Thomas Laqueur, *Making Sex: Body and Gender from the Greeks to Freud* (Cambridge, MA, and London: Harvard University Press, 1992), esp. 40–47.

[15] *Readings and Moots at the Inns of Court in the Fifteenth Century: Vol. 2, Moots and Readers' Cases,* ed. S. E. Thorne and J. H. Baker (London: Selden Society, 1990), 275.

The maneuver we witness here is a strange one, a bizarre gesture of humility by which the justices claim a limited jurisdiction: "the justices said that their authority extended only to the body and not the mind." The gesture is bizarre because it contradicts legal principles about the mind that are well articulated elsewhere. "The exterior act of the body," Dyer writes in his analysis of *Hales v. Petyt*, "shall be measured and known by the will, intent and purpose of the mind, which is the inner part of man, because the intention and purpose are what distinguish wrongdoing, and in wrongdoing the intention is regarded and not the outcome."[16] Dyer's subject is admittedly quite different (he is trying to determine whether Sir James Hales's suicide was felonious), as is the circumstance in which the principle is derived, but it nevertheless suggests the availability of other discourses about "mind" which might have been deployed in the rape case under discussion here to make female "will" and "mind" legally significant where they might serve to counter the use of a woman's body as evidence against her. The Assize justices who preside over Venor's case restore the notion that a woman's "mind" may have significance within the legal arena, but, in a capricious use of precedent, they do so not to make that use of "mind" available to a woman who might benefit from it, but in order to deploy it against Elizabeth Venor.

Another "reading" from the Inns of Court contributes to the sense that T.E.'s account of Elizabeth Venor's case teases into legibility some of the ideological positions that are silently informing the actions of the Assize justices. That reading, which is located in Harley 1691, addresses itself to the following legal conundrum:

> A husband and wife are divorced; then the wife is raped and brings an appeal; pending the appeal the divorce is revoked, as a result of which the appeal abates. The question is: may the husband or the wife have a new appeal?[17]

The first lawyer to respond (who is not named) argues that they may not. His conclusion depends upon the contention that the woman's status is changed, with the revocation of the divorce, in two ways. First, he claims, she is not the same person; with the revocation, she is subsumed once again into the legal status of a "feme covert." The suit "is abated," he argues, "inasmuch as she has changed her name." He further contends that the husband may not bring an

---

[16] *Reports from the Lost Notebooks*, 73.

[17] *Readings and Moots*, 180. All further references to this case will be provided directly in the text.

appeal because the alleged rape has taken place during the period when "the woman was outside the sovereign power of her husband" (*Readings and Moots*, 180). To give the husband the right to appeal, he argues, would be to bestow upon him an unreasonable "right to punish a thing which was not done in his time" (180). In short, any offense which has been done to the woman during the time when she was out of her husband's care is deemed non-actionable once she returns to it. This lawyer's argument thus performs a (violent) de-propertying of the woman; it effaces not just the legal status that she assumed when she was in theory unmarried, but also all sense of the rape as a crime against her person.

The second lawyer who responds to the question counters both of these erasures. First, Fulwood argues that the woman has in fact never left her husband's care; the revocation of the divorce means that she has retrospectively been married the entire time. This means that both she and her husband are entitled to bring the appeal at any time. More importantly, Fulwood takes aim at the contention that with the change in name the woman somehow loses her right to appeal the crime. "Here," he writes, "the appeal is given solely for the wrong done to the woman's person; and even if she marries afterwards (which I do not concede in this case), she still remains the same person to whom the wrong was done . . . and shall have an appeal" (*Readings and Moots*, 181). This latter contention specifically reasserts a sense of the crime as a crime against the woman's person to which she is *always* able to respond, no matter what her marital status. Fulwood's rationale draws acute attention to the presence of a governing precept in his own argument, the importance of the woman who is at the center of the problem, and the converse lack of that precept in his opponent's. The tension between the two arguments makes visible an effacement which elsewhere may occur invisibly. Fulwood's argument specifically underscores the existence and importance of alternative legal constructions to any process through which a judicial decision is reached. This particular "reading" thus heightens the sense that the only way a woman could possibly counter legal operations that seek to use one precedent or argument against her is to know for herself what other arguments are at her disposal. This is, of course, precisely what T.E.'s book, an extraordinary document in which an agent of the law shows some of its disenfranchised subjects how to speak back to *lex loquens*, is designed to provide. T.E. does not limit the talking back that the book advocates: he suggests how those constituted as powerless under the law might appropriate the words of the law. Any woman who must use the language that T.E. provides in a legal contest would have to invent her own ways of doing so: T.E. provides no scripts or prescripts by which the citational possibilities of the words he reports might be exploited. He leaves both the words he reports and his own words open to the unpredictable and improvisational use that would be essential to their success in the innovative moment of their appropriation.

III. "SEE, . . . , SEE!
NOTE HOW SHE COATES THE LEAVES"

Let us now consider that moment in *Titus Andronicus* in which Lavinia is "coating" (Q) or "quoting" (F) the leaves of her Ovid in her attempt to make known the crime that has been committed against her. In the aftermath of her rape, the handless and tongueless Lavinia, who is in no position to engage in a conventional "hue and cry" against her rapists, chases down her younger brother to wrest from him the copy of Ovid's *Metamorphoses* that has been given to her by her mother. Giving Lavinia a book to read, the play suggests the importance of literacy and the literary to the processes by which women might negotiate their rights within legal arenas in an environment in which the law is increasingly lettered.[18] But what is Lavinia really doing here, with her furious "coating" or "quoting"? "Quoting" may signify the manner of reading to which Wye Saltonstall refers in the preface to his 1637 translation of Ovid's *Heroicall Epistles*, when he asks female readers to "have the lines thereof in reading sweetened by the odor of your breath, while the dead letters form'd into words by your divided lips, may receive new life by your passionate expression"[19] — the process, in short, of reading out loud. If Lavinia is attempting to read out loud, she is engaged in a grotesque dumb show whereby she functions as a metonymic figure for the relationship between women and the law: she speaks but is not heard, or

---

[18] For a quite different reading of the play's engagement with questions of literacy, see Sara Eaton, "A Woman of Letters: Lavinia in *Titus Andronicus*," in *Shakespearean Tragedy and Gender*, ed. Shirley Nelson Garner and Madelon Sprengnether (Bloomington: Indiana University Press, 1996), 54–74. Eaton reads Lavinia as a figure for the violence of humanist education, and the particular violence that humanist education perpetrates on aristocratic ladies. Her argument is thus at odds with my argument here. In my reading, the play presents not the violence of humanist education, but rather the violence of the law, which makes it impossible for women to use their literacy to counter its misogynistic operations, and which punishes exercises of agency on the part of women. Eaton's reading does not pursue the ways in which Lavinia attempts to exercise her agency, or the ways in which her actions (and non-actions) reveal her engagement with legal matters. Eaton believes that Lavinia complies with the will of the men around her, and concludes, for example, that Lavinia, out of "loyal obedience," "will marry either brother as her father or brothers dictate" (65).

[19] Saltonstall as quoted in Suzanne Hull, *Chaste, Silent, and Obedient: English Books for Women 1475–1640* (San Marino, CA: Huntington Library, 1982), 190.

what is "heard" is not necessarily what she speaks. If Lavinia is "coating" —
examining the text and attempting to mark it in such a way that she can demonstrate its significance to her — the dumb show becomes more grotesque (the
physical act of "coating" would have to be performed with her stumps). This vigorous "quoting," or "coating," or "quoting" *and* "coating," continues, we should
note, *after* the crime has been "deciphered," but Titus and Marcus force Lavinia
to quit it (they want her to devote herself to recording the names of her rapists
in the sand). Having "wrest[ed] an alphabet" from Lavinia's signs and gestures,
an alphabet that provides him with what he considers to be the essential information — the name of the crime and the names of her rapists — Titus loses all
further interest in Lavinia herself. He throws himself into the quasi-legal activity
of having her words reinscribed or translated into another form. Calling for
Lavinia's words to be transferred from the sand in which she has written them
into brass, Titus ostensibly seeks to give her words permanent form so that they
can be referred to again as evidence of what has been done to her. But likening
the impermanence of Lavinia's inscription to the vulnerability of the "Sibyl's
leaves," and focusing on compensating for that gendered vulnerability, Titus fa-
cilitates the process through which Lavinia's words are alienated from their auth-
or. The text, produced by Lavinia to speak of the crime done to her body, now
exists materially as a thing apart; as such it can be fetishized, cited, and re-inter-
preted at will by whoever wishes to read or make use of it, without any reference
back to the "text" to which it was intended to be merely ancillary. In the process,
the several acts of violence perpetrated upon Lavinia are reduced to a single
crime, the crime of rape. The suggestion is that only rape is actionable, and that
it is actionable because it is a property crime against the men related to Lavinia
(as, of course, is the ravishment of 1.1, for which Titus goes so far, in his revenge, to slay his own son, Mutius).

The process through which Titus extracts his text from Lavinia thus rapidly
reperforms the history of the law's constructions of rape and ravishment as we
have seen that history articulated in T.E.'s text and readings of statutes and cases
by judicial figures including Sir James Dyer and Sir Henry Hobart. Titus's brass
text cannot authenticate the narrative of Lavinia's choice, even if she could make
that narrative known, because Titus requires it to authenticate another, the obliteration of her "spotless chastity" in a discourse of shame and pollution. To provide what he considers a suitable proof of the words inscribed in the brass, he
will subsequently kill Lavinia in order to authenticate not only the veracity of the
words in brass but the veracity of his particular interpretation of her body. He
believes that the course he pursues constitutes a better one than the writing of
justice directly onto bodies that young Lucius advocates ("... thou'lt do my

message, wilt thou not? / Ay, with my dagger in their bosoms, grandsire"
[4.1.117–118]) because the textual processes in which he engages take inert materials (brass, parchment) rather than human flesh as their media; but the "civilizing" process in which he engages involves the appropriation, decontextualization,
and distortion of the "text" of Lavinia's body to his own ends. He believes in the
abstraction he has authored (the discourse of shame), and the process which figuratively takes place here involves the transference of "letters" (the "wrested alphabet") from Lavinia's body into another medium in redacted form. The process entails a lethal forgetting of all the contexts for the abstracted text that the
body provided. The words that Lavinia has author(iz)ed in pursuit of justice thus
boomerang back at her to her own detriment as forcefully as Elizabeth Venor's
words uttered in one context and abstracted and transferred for use to another
end up working against her. The text in brass proves ineffectual at securing her
judicial recompense against Chiron and Demetrius, who, though they do not
"get" their Horace, might very well, in a late sixteenth-century setting, have
walked away from the rape, even if convicted, with nothing more than a brand
in the hand.

But let us consider what Titus does not, what Lavinia is "coating" the leaves
of her Ovid *for* when she keeps reading for something *else*, something *more* than
the name of the crime. Presumably Lavinia is reading Ovid's narrative of rape,
rather than Livy's version of Lucrece's story, because the Ovidian narrative of
rape and its aftermath offers her something that Livy's Lucrece does not. The
Ovidian narrative is, amongst other things, a tale about the effective and powerful transmission of a text between women. Philomela creates a tapestry for
Procne into which she sews words that tell of the crime that has been done to
her. Another woman, a nameless messenger, carries the text between them. Philomela's text is received by a receptive and trusting reader, her sister, who does
not challenge its central claim, that Philomela has been raped, and does not subsequently demand proofs from the injured body. After Procne, with a "troop of
women," has liberated Philomela from the house in which Tereus has imprisoned her, she not only rejects Philomela's construction of the rape as the source
of her shame, she sacrifices her own son in the name of revenge on her sister's
behalf.

We could argue, then, that what Lavinia finds in the Ovid, that text that has
been given to her by her mother, is an alternative (and feminist) hermeneutic
within which to read what has been done to her body. Her tragedy is that she
may "coate" the Ovidian narrative as furiously as she likes, but cannot establish
or maintain any interpretive control over the text that Titus appropriates from
her and inscribes into brass. She cannot persuade him to adopt her reading of

the Ovid over his own; cannot insist that he read Ovid *rather than* the Livy to which he immediately reverts when he opts for the Lucretian narrative of rape over the Ovidian (4.1.63–64); and thus cannot keep Titus from making her pay the price for the discourse of shame within which he situates her body. It is surely significant that Lavinia does not kill herself — despite the fact that she receives not one but two marked suggestions that that's precisely what she ought to do. But it does not matter how much this refusal may signify her own rejection of the discourse that Titus insists on applying to her body. Titus first figuratively asserts Lavinia's status as an involuntary receptacle for the fluids of men by making her hold up the bowl into which Demetrius and Chiron's blood pours from their slit necks, and then, mistaking matters in an even more dire way than Lucrece does, uses a precedent from Virginius in order to execute her. The veiled Lavinia, figuratively headless and thus without "mind," is executed so that a headless Rome can be re-membered and its broken limbs reknit into a newly functioning state with a fresh "head," Lucius. The "lesson" that Titus learns from the Ovidian narrative is thus limited, and does not extend to using it to resist the Lucretian narrative's construction of the violated female body as the text of the woman's shame, a text which can be expunged only by destroying the medium upon which it is written. The power of *Metamorphoses* as the source of an alternative to the chastity/shame paradigm for rape thus remains largely untapped, and Titus's use of the text that he extracts from Lavinia functions as a corollary for the heuristic practices of the law as we have seen them at work in more than one legal record.[20]

Through Titus's distortion of the precedent from Virginius, the play makes suspect not just texts themselves, which within its fictions are forged, misinterpreted, blown away, and serve as the occasion for an innocent man's execution, but also the particular legal practices through which they are appropriated, redacted, and misapplied to contexts for which they are not apt. The play thus demonstrates an ambivalence towards certain developments in the law, particularly the law's increasing recourse to the written texts through which it constitutes its history and records what will later function as precedent. It is suspicious both of the citation of certain texts as precedents for judgment and of the Roman law as a model for the English law. If we read Lavinia as a metonymical

---

[20] Eaton, who reads Titus as the heroic victim of his relationship with his literacy, strangely underplays the violence that he does to Lavinia. She claims that "Titus's recourse to writing ennobles his actions" and that, over the course of the play, "he sheds the look of the savage patriarch of act 1" ("A Woman of Letters," 60). I contend that he is at his most savage when he executes his daughter.

figure for the English common law, what the play demonstrates through its representation of the means through which a written text is abstracted from her
mutilated body is the process through which the unwritten English common law
would be disfigured if lawyers heeded Francis Bacon's call for an English counterpart to the great written text of the Roman law, Justinian's *Corpus Juris Ci-
vilis*.[21] (My corporeal metaphor, deliberate, echoes the metaphors legal writers
themselves used in the course of this protracted debate.)

T.E. explicitly rejects the application of foreign constructs or narratives to
Englishwomen's bodies in a discussion which extends his already well-articulated
concerns with the violence that women suffer – not just through the crime of
rape, but also in their own homes, at their husbands' hands. Under the subtitle
"That no crime dissolveth marriage," *The Lawes Resolutions* counters Roman and
patristic arguments that a woman may never be permitted to leave her husband,
no matter what violence he does to her:

> Of old time, some Crimes were numbred amongst the Causes of Dissolv-
> ing marriage: but Justinian changed the Law here in part ... So that
> *nodus legitimi matrimonij* is never dissolved but by death, and the wife as
> long as she liveth is subiect to the law of her husband by Saint Paul.
>
> Yet saith Lagus, seeing that in Contracts of Wedlock we regard as well
> what is decent and convenient as well as what is lawfull, I cannot tell why
> we be not bound in dissolving of it to follow the like equitie; and, for
> example, if a Wife cannot dwell with her husband without manifest dan-
> ger of death because he is cruell and bloody why may not shee be separ-
> ated *judicis ordinarij cognitione precedente*. (67)

Justinian, that great codifier of the Roman law, is invoked as having had a disas-
trous effect upon the English common law; legal writers and practitioners who
have made recourse to his text have made what was once flexible and local, rigid
and univocal. Against his perception of the Roman law, which he construes as
requiring strict application even where its refusal to allow for a range of inter-
pretations may result in a woman's death, T.E. opposes local decisions about
what constitutes the "decent and convenient." Consideration of things "decent
and convenient" liberates interpreters of the law from what may be "lawful" but
inimical to women: it liberates T.E., at any rate, who rejects the (Roman) law's

---

[21] For a detailed discussion of this legal debate, see Richard Helgerson, *Forms of Nationhood: The Elizabethan Writing of England* (Chicago and London: University of Chicago Press, 1992), esp. 65–87.

letter in order to furnish his female readers with an opinion through which they may liberate themselves in turn. The negative effects of applying Justinian's law to English subjects might be avoided, he suggests, by turning to a local ecclesiastical authority, the *ordinarius*, for judgments in what constitutes the "decent and convenient." The *ordinarius* will make recourse not to Justinian's written law but to his own sense of what constitutes an ethical decision based on his personal knowledge of the situation. T.E. thus promotes local authority based on personal knowledge of the particular facts of a given case, and the common law way of proceeding, over an interpretation of the law according to an inflexibly written paradigm imposed from without — which is rejected precisely because it cannot take account of the local and the particular, those very things which, under English customary law, would be the most important sources of precedent. For T.E., in 1632, the solution is simple: if Justinian cannot take account of the state of a particular woman's violated body, Justinian must be discounted; but some forty years earlier, *Titus Andronicus* demands that its audience members take account of the damage that Roman letters, both legal and literary, do to women. The play suggests that English law already bears the traces of Roman letters within it, traces revealed in the discourse that Titus applies to Lavinia's body after she is raped. It further suggests that literary discourse is caught up in the law's inscriptions: the story that the play tells is the story of Titus's subscription to legal narratives. But the fact that the play points towards Ovid as the source of an alternative literary narrative within which Lavinia might be read suggests that its writer is not suspicious of precedent in and of itself. The force of the play's critique of legal hermeneutics falls instead on the ways legal practices fail to take account of the unexplored hermeneutic potential of certain *literary* precedents.

The play's ambivalence about texts, occurring as it does in a form that is not exclusively text-based (if we understand "text" in this instance to mean language recorded in the form of either writing or print), may be part and parcel of the theater's vaunting of the play's own much more extensive media resources, resources that allow it to imagine what the law, stymied by its own recourse to a limited form of precedent, cannot: new definitions for crimes and new ways of prosecuting them. It is a fuller "textual" record, one that takes account of as much context as possible, that *Titus Andronicus* seeks to provide. It is important, for example, that Aaron frames Martius and Quintus for the murder of Bassianus by drafting an incriminating document which, when it is read in the *sole* context of the Martius's and Quintus's presence in the pit in which Bassianus's body is found, is sufficient to have them condemned for murder: "Let them not speak a word; the guilt is plain" (2.4.301). Demonstrating the means through which Aaron orchestrates the convergence of these two false pieces of evidence, the play suggests just how inadequate textual and other forms of material evidence may be at the same time that it vaunts its own representational powers — its ability to take "lively bod[ies]" as media for communication, legal and otherwise (the play is strewn with body parts, every one of which functions as a text), in order to create a semiotics of body and gesture from which the audience may "wrest an alphabet." Through that alphabet, it imagines other ways of defining both crimes and precedents.

In this context, let us consider the play's representation of just a single crime, Lavinia's rape. Under sixteenth-century English law, only one man would have been held accountable for the crime as principal because the law could not reconcile itself to the notion that this was a crime for which two could be held equally responsible. Over a 150-year period there is a lot of legal dissension over whether two or more men can be held responsible for felonies like murder and rape, and dissension in particular over whether someone who "procures" a crime, or stands by while it is being committed, can be held accountable as *either* a principal or an accessory. In a fifteenth-century reading, Littleton argues that everyone present at the killing of a man is a principal, but is contradicted by Frowyk, who argues that "no one is principal except the one who gives the blow."[22] But Frowyk himself acknowledges that it is important to trace "the blow" to its original source, or author: "Therefore if someone by my command, on pain of his life, kills someone else, I am the felon and the principal, and the other is no felon, because I am the person who has directed the blow."[23] This line of thinking is regularly reiterated in sixteenth- and seventeenth-century texts, and in books like Bacon's *Maxims* and Hawke's *Grounds* digested into a precept. But in the fifteenth-century reading, Brudenell contradicts Frowyk: "all who set hands on the deceased, even if only one of them gives him the blow, are principals. . . ."[24] Littleton concludes that not only everyone who participates in, but also everyone who is present at a murder may be indicted as principals. Curiously, he notes that "an appeal of rape against two as principals" is a strong ground for exception to this principle because "that act cannot be committed except by one alone." He nevertheless concludes that, despite this possible exception, the general principle "was held good." In the "reading" rape is decisively bracketed off as a crime that poses unique problems, but those problems are not allowed to interfere with the readers' attempts to derive a principle by which the

---

[22] *Readings and Moots*, 273.

[23] *Readings and Moots*, 273.

[24] *Readings and Moots*, 274.

status of principals can be determined in an act of murder. Concluding, as it does, with the rape example, the "reading" suggests some of the ways in which the crime of rape troubles legal discourse.

Titus Andronicus is itself stymied by its own inability to provide a stage representation of rape (it cannot provide us with a representation of one man in the act, never mind two), and is forced to depend upon what it can register in language (we are to understand that Demetrius and Chiron can, will, and do "take turns"). Aaron plots the crime, but in an Elizabethan courtroom would have evaded judgment with ease; the law may concede that the person who plots a crime, even if himself does not actually deliver the "blow," can be held accountable for the crime and moreover can be held accountable as principal, but legal records suggest that it is difficult for someone tenuously connected to the "blow" to be indicted for it. The play appears confident in the force of the proofs it can offer as to Aaron's status as principal, however; it clearly presents Aaron as the "procuror," or author of the crime. It is in fact Tamora's actions which would confront the law with the greatest interpretive challenge here: she does not originate the idea of the crime, and she is not present when it is committed. But there is nevertheless a sense in which Tamora is complicit: she urges Demetrius and Chiron to enact the rape on the family's behalf, promising them affective rewards for helping themselves to "the honey *we* desire" (2.3.131, my emphasis).

Casting Demetrius and Chiron as the instruments through which Tamora perpetrates the crime of rape on Lavinia's body, the play exposes the crime as just one in a series of acts through which men and women battle for the right to wield the power of life and death over others' bodies. Much of that battle focuses on Aaron the Moor and the "illegitimate" baby that he and Tamora produce. In terms of the legal fictions I have discussed herein, that biracial baby is doubly significant: it is the evidence Aaron might present to exonerate himself from an accusation of rape, an accusation to which his previous incarnations are subject in Shakespeare's source texts, but, more importantly, it is his capital or hope, the means by which he might subvert the well-ordered Roman state by substituting for the emperor's supposed son the son of a countryman, a baby that can pass as "white." If Aaron's substitution were successful, the state would, unknown to itself, assign to a body which should, properly speaking, be illegitimate or uncategorizable within its scheme, the power and prerogatives which would accrue to the person who occupies the position of greatest agency under the law. But the play destabilizes not just the law and the property system it upholds, but bodies themselves, and displays that deconstruction most audaciously at the site of the play's central crime, where the two men who function as the play's ostensible rapists are revealed as little more than prosthetic extensions for the person who commissions the rape, their mother. Representing Tamora as something more than merely complicit in Lavinia's rape, the play generates a spectre of female agency that exceeds anything the law might comprehend: if two *men* cannot commit the crime of rape, certainly no *woman* can. The play thus raises the very spectre of female agency that prompts the kind of action we have seen the Assize justices take in the case of Elizabeth Venor. But in its representations, that agency is bifurcated: frustrated in the figure of Lavinia, whose literacy is of little use to her, and demonized in the figure of Tamora, who becomes the pitiless judge presiding over another woman's fate precisely because her own voice, the voice that pleads for the life of a son, goes unheard. Tamora's misogynistic turn may be quite different from Lucrece's, but it produces similar results: by the play's end, both Lavinia's and Tamora's bodies are ritually expunged, and thus co-opted, for the rule of (a new) law. This law depends, as the republic that rises in relation to Lucrece's dead body does, on an obliteration of female identity within a discourse of pollution and shame. Where literature colludes with this foundational legal narrative, it produces tragedy. Titus's tragedy is that he does not consider or explore the liberatory possibilities of literature, and, specifically, the alternative hermeneutic for rape offered by Ovid. Within the play, literature is both the source of precedent that may be invoked to rationalize the violent application of the law to women's bodies, and the source of alternative narratives through which the law might be rewritten. But, in the form of Titus's citation of Virginius, literature is co-opted, along with the bodies of the play's female characters, for the rule of law.

Carolyn Sale
Stanford University

Works Cited

Statutes of the Realm. Vol. 4. London: Dawsons of Pall Mall, 1810–1828.

The English Reports. Vol. 80. Edinburgh: William Green & Sons, 1907.

Baker, J. H., ed. *Reports from the Lost Notebooks of Sir James Dyer*. Vol. 1. London: Selden Society, 1994.

————, and S. E. Thorne, eds. *Readings and Moots at the Inns of Court in the Fifteenth Century: Vol. 2: Moots and Readers' Cases*. London: Selden Society, 1990.

Donaldson, Ian. *The Rapes of Lucretia: A Myth and Its Transformations*. Oxford: Clarendon Press, 1982.

E., T. *The Lawes Resolutions of Womens Rights: or, the Lawes Provision for*

Woemen. London, 1632. (repr. Amsterdam: Theatrum Orbis Terrarum; Norwood, NJ: W.J. Johnson, 1979.)

Eaton, Sara. "A Woman of Letters: Lavinia in *Titus Andronicus*." In *Shakespearean Tragedy and Gender*, ed. Shirley Nelson Garner and Madelon Sprengnether, 54–74. Bloomington: Indiana University Press, 1996.

Hawke, Michael. *The Grounds of the Lawes of England*. London, 1657.

Helgerson, Richard. *Forms of Nationhood: The Elizabethan Writing of England*. Chicago and London: University of Chicago Press, 1992.

Hull, Suzanne. *Chaste, Silent, and Obedient: English Books for Women 1475–1640*. San Marino, CA: Huntington Library, 1982.

Kennedy, Duncan. *Sexy Dressing, Etc.* Cambridge, MA, and London: Harvard University Press, 1993.

Laqueur, Thomas. *Making Sex: Body and Gender from the Greeks to Freud*. Cambridge, MA, and London: Harvard University Press, 1992.

Shakespeare, William. *The Most Lamentable Romaine Tragedie of Titus Andronicus*. London: John Danter, 1594.

———. *The Riverside Shakespeare*, ed. G. Blakemore Evans et al. Boston: Houghton Mifflin, 1974.

Rape and Redemption in
The Spanish Gypsy[1]

In a recent essay, Barbara Baines observes that the task of historicizing rape entails listening to the silences, the evasions of the past ("Effacing Rape," 69). Analyzing legal, medical, and literary texts, Baines demonstrates the way "conceptions of consent" (82) worked to efface rape in the early modern period — in effect by blaming the victim — and to promote a culture which idealized suicide as a woman's appropriate response to her sexual violation. In this essay I examine another and perhaps more surprising strategy for "effacing rape" in early modern drama: it is, paradoxically, a strategy of accommodation, of justification — indeed, of celebration. Instead of killing herself after her rape, the heroine of *The Spanish Gypsy* (1623)[2] survives to marry her assailant with gratitude. The rape is not simply trivialized by this strategy — not merely rendered "inconsequential," as Gossett suggests ("'Best Men'," 326)[3]; rather, it is sanctified as part of

---

[1] The argument of this essay is developed more fully in my book, *Sexual Violence on the Jacobean Stage* (New York: St. Martin's Press, 2000), esp. 123–54. I would like to thank Sharon Beehler and Linda Woodbridge for their comments on my work.

[2] The play was licensed on 9 July 1623 for performance by the Lady Elizabeth's Servants and published in 1653, with a title page ascribing it to Middleton and Rowley (Bentley, *The Jacobean and Caroline Stage*, 4:891–92). Modern scholars have been sceptical of Middleton's involvement in the play. Studies of authorship favour Ford for the main plot and Dekker for the gypsy scenes (Oliphant, *Shakespeare* 2:18; Lake, *Canon*, 218–30). Brittin, however, finds "strong evidence" that Rowley was responsible for the gypsy sub-plot (*Thomas Middleton*, 97), and believes Middleton might have written some of the main plot and songs (98–99). All citations of the play are from Bullen's edition of Middleton's works (6:113–230).

[3] According to Gossett's analysis, marriage as an outcome of rape represents an innovative trend in late Jacobean drama. In contrast to earlier plays, where, like the classical figures of Lucretia and Philomela, the raped woman either commits suicide or is killed as a direct consequence of her violation, the later plays, she argues, "abandon the usual

a providential design. The rape becomes a fortunate fall, through which the forgiving heroine reconciles the erring hero to his righteous parent and judge. In a
paradigm that celebrates the triumph of the patriarchal will over youthful male
lust and the injured female's desire for revenge, rapist and victim are part of a
triangle dominated by an older male: a triangle the dynamics of which ensure the
legitimate continuity of the patriarchal family. In contrast to the triangular
model proposed by René Girard, in which desire is primarily imitative,[4] or, in
Eve Kosofsky Sedgwick's terms, in which male homosocial desire is routed
through the female,[5] in this triangle a son's unruly heterosexual desire, which
threatens to rupture his bond with his father, is contained through an alliance
between the father and the injured female. As a passive partner in the "tragicomic solution" of marriage (Gossett, " 'Best Men'," 326), the heroine is merely the
instrument of the paternal grace that renews the fabric of patriarchal society.
Scrutiny of the rape and marriage plot thus reveals what Rebecca Bach calls "the
homosocial imaginary" that structured the culture of early modern England
("Homosocial Imaginary," 504), an "imaginary" that conceived of all social relations (including rape) "in terms of male-male relationships" (518).

Although Gossett terms the marriage of rapist and victim a "shocking" innovation to "the standard rape plot" (" 'Best Men'," 309) at a time when laws
against rape were severe, I believe it was neither innovative nor shocking. Not
only, as I contend below, were there precedents on the Elizabethan and Jacobean
stage for such a solution, but *The Spanish Gypsy* — along with the other late Jacobean rape plays Gossett discusses — reflects an ambivalence about rape characteristic of both its treatment in the drama generally and in early modern English
culture and society at large. If, in spite of the law, rape is commonly treated as
a venial sin — a forceful seduction prompted by passion, a sexual act that both

---

story in ways which undermine the force in any verbal strictures against rape" (" 'Best
Men'," 305); thus the heroines do *not* commit suicide and, in a "tragicomic solution
which makes rape ultimately inconsequential" (326), three of them actually marry the rapist. Gossett's early plays are Shakespeare's *Titus Andronicus, The Revenger's Tragedy* (attributed to Tourneur), Heywood's *The Rape of Lucrece,* and Fletcher's *Valentinian.* The
late plays are *The Queen of Corinth,* by Fletcher, Massinger, and Field; Rowley's *All's Lost
By Lust*; Middleton's *Women Beware Women*; and *The Spanish Gypsy.*

[4] Put simply, the desiring subject imitates a model, or "mediator," who may thus also
be a rival for the object of desire. In this triangle, the model is more important than the
object of desire itself. As Girard explains, "the mediator's prestige is imparted to the object of desire and confers upon it an illusory value. Triangular desire is the desire which
transfigures its object" (*Deceit, Desire and the Novel,* 17).

[5] See especially Sedgwick's discussion of *The Country Wife* (*Between Men,* 49–82).

parties enjoy, something the woman could have avoided, the subject for a bawdy joke — then the woman who seeks legal redress will appear malevolent and disruptive, especially if, as in early modern England, this effectively means demanding her assailant's life.[6] Surely far more significant than the severity of the punishment for rape in England — where it was a capital offence from 1285 to 1840 — is the infrequency with which legal punishment was exacted.[7]

Although there is no way of determining the actual incidence of rape in Jacobean England, it seems certain that most sexual assaults were not prosecuted in law. In her study of sample records between 1558 and 1700, Bashar found that rape "usually constituted less than 1 percent of all indictments" (" 'Rape in England,' " 34).[8] In addition to the humiliation involved in appealing the crime, the victim would in many cases have been silenced by pressure from, variously, the assailant, his family, her own family and the community.[9] The 1631 case of Margery Evans and Philibert Burghill — discussed in detail by Marcus ("The Milieu of Milton's Comus," 293, 296–313) and more briefly by Gossett (" 'Best Men'," 313) — provides a clear example of a community's reluctance to prose-

---

[6] In her analysis of narratives from early modern law courts, Garthine Walker notes the effect of the strong cultural prejudice against female physical strength. Since only "a discordant, disorderly, dishonourable woman used violence" ("Rereading Rape," 9), declarations of rape had "to deflect notions of female complicity and disorderliness that could undermine them. Consequently . . . physical resistance was underplayed, sometimes in ways which verbally denied agency to the raped woman or girl . . ." (18). The cultural prejudice against females also operated against the credibility of a complainant. As Carolyn Williams observes, "the more modest the victim (and therefore, the more potentially credible), the harder she should find it to state her case" (" 'Silence'," 106).

[7] Commentators on rape law frequently note this striking discrepancy. See, for example, Bashar, "Rape in England," 40–41; Clark and Lewis, *Rape*, 55–57; Toner, *The Facts of Rape*, 85; De Groot, "The Crime of Rape," 324.

[8] In Sussex, for example, during the reign of Elizabeth I "over 1,000 cases of larceny were prosecuted, about 150 burglaries, about 100 homicides and only 14 rapes" ("Rape in England," 33). Since it is unlikely that there were more than seven times as many murders as rapes in Sussex during this period, we may presume that most rapes did not come to trial. Bashar's findings are supported by the work of Cockburn, who found 50 indictments for rape out of 7544 in sample records for 1559–1625 ("Nature and Incidence," 58); Sharpe, who notes "a virtual absence" of indictments for rape (*Crime in Early Modern England*, 170); and Bridenbaugh (2 out of 250 convictions for Middlesex in 1624 [*Vexed and Trouble Englishmen*, 367–88]). Only one of the eight women who told the physician Napier that they had been sexually abused by their masters is known to have prosecuted her employer (MacDonald, *Mystical Bedlam*, 88).

[9] In her study of thirty-four rape accusations from the north of England (1640–1700), Chaytor notes that several of those "who did finally report the rape said that they had hesitated at first because they were afraid of reprisals" ("Husbandry," 402 n. 9).

cute a man accused of rape. According to the evidence presented by Marcus, Burghill and his male servant were almost certainly guilty of raping and robbing the fourteen-year-old Evans. Nevertheless, when she accused them Evans was arrested, physically abused, detained for two days, and soon after imprisoned again at Burghill's suit for almost a month without a charge. The subsequent history of the case reveals the general collusion of the community with the offender. A more blatant instance of intimidation, supported by some part of the community, occurred in 1615 at Malmesbury in Wiltshire:

> A certain John Vizard, on the eve of his examination before the justices for rape and defamation, showed his contempt for the law and terrified the constable of the town by organizing a parade of armed men with rough music and a mock marriage ceremony, proclaiming that the morrow was his wedding day and bidding company to see him married — "which company ... should be none but cuckolds and cuckold makers."[10]

Of those men actually indicted for rape few were found guilty.[11] The very low rate of conviction may have been due in part to the difficulty of proving rape, in part to the reluctance of (male) juries to take the life of the accused.[12] The figures also suggest, however, both a pervasive scepticism about rape accusations and a general tolerance of the offence.[13]

---

[10] Ingram, "Ridings," 91. Without knowing more about the case it is impossible to interpret Vizard's joke accurately. However, given the connection between rape prosecutions and marriage explored in this essay, Vizard's mocking transformation of his trial for rape into a wedding is interesting. For instances of the assailant's friends attempting to silence the victim and her family, see the episodes involving Joseph Parkins reported by Underdown (*Fire*, 67–68).

[11] Of 274 prosecutions for rape between 1558 and 1700, studied by Bashar, only 45 resulted in conviction (31 of the condemned were hanged, 6 were granted benefit of clergy, and 6 were reprieved) ("Rape in England," 34–35). "There was an overall preponderance of child victims in the cases that came to court, and a tendency to convict men accused of raping children and to acquit when the victim was an adult woman" (40).

[12] Bashar points out, however, that juries were quite willing to impose the death penalty for other offenses, like burglary. Thus in Kent between 1558 and 1599 150 people were tried for burglary, 88 were hanged, and 34 granted clergy (an 80 percent rate of conviction); however, of the 26 men tried for rape, 4 were hanged, and 2 granted clergy ("Rape in England," 40).

[13] Medieval studies also show very low rates of appeal for rape: see De Groot. "The Crime of Rape," 330; Kittel, "Rape in Thirteenth-Century England," 104; Hanawalt, *Crime and Conflict*, 66; and Carter, *Rape in Medieval England*, 153. Carter concludes that in the thirteenth century "the legal system itself presented almost insurmountable prob-

Given the deep-rooted, if unacknowledged, reluctance to support the prosecution of rape in Jacobean society, it is not surprising that some plays dramatize the forgiveness of sexual assault rather than its punishment. In both *The Queen of Corinth* and *The Spanish Gypsy*, the rapist is a young man whose sexual sin represents a fall from grace. Each is tricked into confessing and repenting the crime by an older man, who exercises a providential care for the youth's regeneration. Here the male heroism which in the earlier, classically-derived plays expresses itself in a potentially tragic demand for vengeance becomes the benevolent plotting of the male "spiritual director," whose guile ensures the comic outcome of the play. The role of the heroine — like that of the earlier Lucretia figures — is largely confined to passive suffering. Instead of a glorious death, however, she endures an ignominious half-life after the rape; and instead of redeeming her community she performs the more modest task of saving her rapist. Thus, unlike the legendary Lucretia, who demands her ravisher's life,[14] the heroines of the "marriage" plays give up the right to revenge and instead accept their penitent assailants as husbands — a resolution that signifies the salvation of the errant youths.[15]

The departure of Fletcher and his collaborators in *The Queen of Corinth* from the conventional pattern of rape, suicide, and revenge had an important precedent on the Elizabethan stage. George Whetstone had already solved the prob-

---

lems of humiliation for the victim" (153). For the period between 1660 and 1800, Beattie calculates that a rape case "came before the Surrey assizes on average once every year and a half and before the Sussex courts only once every four years"; many of these cases involved attacks on children (*Crime and the Courts*, 126–27). See also Toner, *The Facts of Rape*, 97–98.

[14] According to Livy, Lucretia says to her father, husband and their friends, "Give me your solemn promise that the adulterer shall be punished — he is Sextus Tarquinius. He it is who last night . . . took his pleasure of me. That pleasure will be my death — and his, too, if you are men" (*History*, trans. de Sélincourt, 99).

[15] The anonymous *Dick of Devonshire* (c. 1626) continues this pattern: a callous young man rapes his betrothed but denies the crime in court. A pious fraud practised by his father and the presiding judge prompts the rapist to repent; the victim's willingness to forgive and marry him secures the happy ending. By contrast, in *Women Beware Women* (c. 1621) — Gossett's third "marriage play" — the heroine leaves her husband to live with the tyrant who has raped her, and marries him in the last act. Here the rape is the means of the heroine's corruption rather than the villain's redemption, and the wedding is a blasphemy that precipitates their end. Nevertheless, the motif of the rapist's repentance is parodied in 4.1 when, in response to the Cardinal's stern warning, the Duke vows "never to know her [Bianca] as a strumpet more" (269) and immediately resolves to murder her husband, so they can be lawfully married (270–74 [Revels edition, ed. J. R. Mulryne]).

lem of sexual violation with mercy and marriage in his pious two-part comedy, *Promos and Cassandra* (1578), in which the heroine surrenders her virginity to a lustful magistrate to save her brother's life. When the magistrate fails to keep the bargain, she appeals to the emperor for justice; he first marries her to the villain, and then condemns him to death. In an outstanding act of mercy, the heroine pleads for and obtains the life of her husband-rapist. The outline of this tragic-comic rape plot is more widely known through Shakespeare's adaptation of it in *Measure for Measure.* There the Duke — like Whetstone's Emperor, a father figure — arranges the erring young magistrate's public exposure. After Angelo, like Promos, has been accused of being a "virgin-violator" (5.1.43), his victim intercedes to save his life.[16] *Measure for Measure*, however, differs from *Promos and Cassandra* in that technically no rape occurs: the Duke's substitution of Mariana (the villain's intended bride) for Isabella (his intended victim) means that although Angelo *enacts* a rape, he does not *effect* one. The bed-trick simultaneously satisfies the requirements for lawful intercourse and transforms the victim into the loving wife necessary for the villain's redemption.

In *The Queen of Corinth*, Fletcher, Massinger, and Field develop the tragi-comic solution to rape — marriage and mercy under the direction of a benevolent older male — established by Whetstone and continued by Shakespeare. The play's direct debt to *Measure for Measure* is implicitly acknowledged through the names of the paired heroines. Here, as in Shakespeare's play, the villain's intended bride, Merione (cf. Mariana), substitutes for his intended victim, Beliza (cf. Isabella), and so ensures his salvation. Here too a second man — Euphanes, the play's hero — assumes the role of "spiritual director" to expose the rapist's crimes, threaten him with justice, then theatrically allow his reprieve. Here, as in *Measure for Measure*, the moral stratagem covers its inventor in glory: Euphanes, like Shakespeare's Duke and Whetstone's Emperor, appears wise, benevolent, and forgiving as he enables mercy to season justice. Here too it is the substitute victim who pays for the rapist's redemption and the glory enjoyed by manipulator.

In *The Spanish Gypsy* the motif of the redemptive rape reaches its acme. Here sexual assault is used neither for suspense nor eroticism, as it is in *The Queen of Corinth* and, to a lesser extent, in *Measure for Measure.* It is simply the dramatic starting point: a young man abducts a girl in the opening scene and spends the next four acts dealing with the consequences of his lust. Once again, however, the victim plays a merely passive role in the youth's redemption: his return to grace is achieved primarily by the loving deception of his father — a patriarch

---

[16] I use the Arden edition, ed. J. W. Lever.

who is also judge — and the drama of his repentance strongly recalls the story of the prodigal son.[17]

The play's main plot is based on one of Cervantes' *Exemplary Novels*, "La Fuerza de la Sangre" ("The Force of Blood"), in which a virtuous young noblewoman is assaulted one night by a dissolute young nobleman.[18] He carries her in a faint to his father's house, where he rapes her in darkness: when he releases her neither one knows the identity of the other. Subsequently the youth, Rodolfo, goes off to Italy to complete his education, and the girl, Leocadia, bears his child in secret. Six years later the child, a boy, is injured in front of the house of Rodolfo's father, who carries him inside to recover. Providence thus leads Leocadia back to the very room in which she was raped. She tells her story to Rodolfo's parents, and they immediately recall their son from Italy. Instead of confronting him with his crime, however, Rodolfo's mother tricks him into marrying Leocadia of his own volition. Only then does he learn that she was the girl he raped. After a jubilant wedding feast, everyone lives happily ever after.

Cervantes' story presents a variation on the romance theme of the family reunion: the "force of blood" is so strong that Rodolfo's father is mysteriously drawn to his unknown grandson when the boy is injured. This is *not* a story of spiritual regeneration: Rodolfo shows no sign of penitence or growth. (He never even apologizes to Leocadia.) The happy ending comes about when, by the grace of God, the patience of Leocadia, and the guile of his mother, Rodolfo's sexual desires are directed into a socially responsible contract.

The authors of *The Spanish Gypsy* transform this amoral tale into a moral exemplum. The initial circumstances of the rape are much the same as in the source story: a young man, Roderigo, glimpses a beautiful girl in the street and, with the help of friends, abducts her from her parents (1.1). However, the interaction between rapist and victim after the event differs significantly. When Clara and Roderigo are "*discovered*" in a bedroom at the beginning of 1.3, her first words establish the distinctively homiletic tone of the drama:

> Though the black veil of night hath overclouded
> The world in darkness, yet ere many hours

---

[17] Burelbach distinguishes four separate plots in the play and points out that "all are variations on the theme of the prodigal son" ("Theme and Structure," 38).

[18] Another of the *Exemplary Novels*, "La Gitanilla" ("The Little Gypsy Girl"), is the source of the subplot. According to Bentley, Cervantes' *Novelas Ejemplares* were published in Madrid in 1613 and translated into French within a year. No English translation before 1623 has been discovered (*The Jacobean and Caroline Stage*, 4:895).

> The sun will rise again, and then this act
> Of my dishonour will appear before you
> More black than is the canopy that shrouds it. (1–5)

The imagery of dark and light that Clara initiates here pervades the play, and foreshadows Roderigo's subsequent spiritual awakening.[19]

As a conventionally virtuous victim of rape, Clara asks for death after dishonour ("so with your sword / Let out that blood which is infected now / By your soul-staining lust" [11–13]). Like Fletcher's Merione, however, and unlike Cervantes' Leocadia, she also appeals to her unknown assailant for marriage ("Are you noble? / I know you then will marry me; say!" [13–14]). Roderigo refuses to speak to her, but adds insult to injury by offering her gold (25). While the source heroine just pleads pathetically for anonymity and silence, Clara is aggressive in her despair. As Roderigo leaves the room, she clings to him in a gesture that foreshadows his inability to elude the consequences of his crime (21–31).

Left alone, Clara kneels to invoke "Revenge" (33) and beg the "lady regent of the air, the moon" — Diana, goddess of chastity — to lead her "to some brave vengeance" (36–38). By the light of the heavens she discerns a "goodly" chamber and the garden it overlooks. Her bewildered question, "dwells rape in such a paradise?" (43), suggests the primal nature of the sexual sin Roderigo has just committed.[20] Clara also manages to find a "precious crucifix" which she conceals about her person (50). Her prayers for vengeance, her careful search for clues, the co-operation of the heavens in her efforts, all arouse expectations of a revenge tragedy — expectations which serve to heighten the ensuing comedy of forgiveness.

We do not learn why Roderigo leaves Clara alone, though obviously he must, if she is to steal the crucifix; but when he returns, he is already a changed man: he asks her name (53–54).[21] The question signals a new willingness to see her

---

[19] The Kistners note that "moral darkness, symbolized by the darkened stage, and its opposites, truth and light, are recalled throughout the play in images of night, blackness, sunlight, and moonlight" (*Middleton's Tragic Themes*, 14). Clara's name is itself part of the dark/light motif (cf. Samuel Richardson's Clarissa Harlowe).

[20] We also learn that "Roderigo has into his father's house / A passage through a garden" (1.2.9–10): the garden, with its sexual associations, recalls Angelo's. Roderigo's passage to "his father's house" through the garden suggests the passage to manhood through the garden of sexual sin.

[21] In the source story Rodolfo leaves Leocadia locked in his chamber in order to ask his friends for advice; when he comes back he simply takes her away blindfolded and leaves her in the street (*Exemplary Novels*, 317–18).

as a person. Clara, however, refuses to reveal her identity: "You urge me to a sin / As cruel as your lust ... / Think on the violence of my defame" (54–55). Asking only for an anonymous grave, she renews her appeal for death (65–71). Impressed by the girl's response to her violation, Roderigo apologizes:

> since I find
> Such goodness in an unknown frame of virtue,
> Forgive my foul attempt, which I shall grieve for
> So heartily, that could you be yourself
> Eye-witness to my constant vow'd repentance,
> Trust me, you'd pity me. (74–79)

Clara's exemplary death-wish thus initiates the process of Roderigo's reformation. By contrast, in the source story, Leocadia's virtue only provokes Rodolfo to attempt a second rape (317). With this appeal for Clara's compassion, Roderigo effectively reverses their roles: although she is his victim, he demands her pity. This tactic is successful: she utters no further reproaches.

In spite of his growing remorse, Roderigo refuses to give Clara his name (and thus a means to revenge or reparation). He does, however, say he *would* pursue her honorably if he had not already raped her:

> trust me, fair one,
> Were this ill deed undone, this deed of wickedness,
> I would be proud to court your love like him
> Whom my first birth presented to the world. (83–86)

Roderigo's words imply that his "deed of wickedness" has left him unlike himself (Kistner and Kistner, *Middleton's Tragic Themes,* 15), and hint at his need for regeneration in a second birth. They also provide the first of many suggestions that the two are a well-matched couple, destined for union.

Roderigo concludes by offering to do anything to make amends, short of identifying himself. In addition to an oath of secrecy and her release, Clara demands his reformation:

> Live a new man: if e'er you marry —
> O me, my heart's a-breaking! — but if e'er
> You marry, in a constant love to her
> That shall be then your wife, redeem the fault
> Of my undoing. I am lost for ever. (96–100)

Her tone is extraordinary: it is the voice of a dying woman addressing a lover. Her "heart's a-breaking" because she imagines her unseen, unknown rapist plighting his troth to another (enviable) woman. By implication, then, Clara sees her rape as a *de facto* marriage: any legal marriage Roderigo contracts will be at her expense. He will be plighting a troth that should be hers. Clara, however, demonstrates her selfless virtue by suppressing her desire for reparation and placing the welfare of her rapist (*de facto* husband) above her own. Acknowledging herself "lost for ever," Clara offers her ruin as a sacrifice to his spiritual growth. In less than sixty lines she has moved from her prayer for "some brave vengeance" (38) to self-immolation for the sake of her assailant.

Roderigo leads Clara away closely veiled. As the Kistners point out, the stage image suggests her loss of identity through the rape (*Middleton's Tragic Themes*, 18). It also ironically reverses the action of a wedding, where the husband first unveils his bride, then leads her to bed.

§

In Cervantes' story Rodolfo departs for Italy "with as little thought or concern about what had passed between him and the beautiful Leocadia as though it had never happened" (*Exemplary Novels*, 320). In *The Queen of Corinth*, the vicious prince Theanor is wholly unrepentant until Euphanes arranges his exposure; Angelo regrets Claudio's death rather than Isabella's maidenhead; and none of the tyrant-rapists in the earlier Jacobean plays experiences remorse.[22] The authors of *The Spanish Gypsy* thus depart from both narrative source and known dramatic models in their portrait of the remorseful ravisher. Roderigo pretends to leave Madrid, but returns "*disguised as an Italian*" (3.1 SD) to look for the woman he wronged, and act 3 opens with his lengthy meditation on sin ("A thousand stings are in me: O, what vild prisons / Make we our bodies to our immortal souls! / .... [1–30]).

Clara, meanwhile, is pining ("I have fallen; thoughts with disgraces strive, / And thus I live, and thus I die alive" [2.2.4–5]). Like Fletcher's Merione, she is in a spiritual netherworld. Unlike Merione, however, she has not published her shame. Her doting parents, Pedro and Maria, nurture her and the hope of a "noble" revenge (2.2.19). They also nurture the hopes of her noble suitor, Louis, encouraging him to woo her "hard" (3.2.49). Obviously, they do not see Clara's rape as an obstacle to her marriage with another man. Clara apparently does,

---

[22] Shakespeare's Tarquin, however, "hates himself for his offence" (*Rape of Lucrece*, 738), and leaves Lucrece's bed "a heavy convertite" (743). I use the Arden edition of *Lucrece*, ed. F. T. Prince.

however: she cannot acquiesce to Louis, and I think we are to understand her reluctance as a sign of her virtue. By implication, she feels that she is inseparably bound to her unknown rapist-husband.

The crucial discovery of Roderigo's identity comes swiftly: in 3.2 Clara faints near his father's house and is carried into the very room of her assault (an experience which thus partially repeats that of the rape). 3.3 opens with "CLARA *discovered seated in a chair,* PEDRO *and* MARIA *standing by.*" Grief-stricken, Clara demands to know who owns the house, and learns that it belongs to Don Fernando, the "corregidor" of Madrid.[23] Don Fernando's response when Clara produces the crucifix is appropriately melodramatic:

> You drive me to amazement! 'twas my son's,
> A legacy bequeath'd him from his mother
> Upon her deathbed, dear to him as life;
> On earth there cannot be another treasure
> He values at like rate as he does this. (41–45)

Like the "ancestral ring" of Bertram in *All's Well That Ends Well,* the crucifix is Roderigo's most precious possession, the symbol of the honour he has lost in a dishonourable sexual transaction. In assaulting Clara he has betrayed not only the religious values which the crucifix represents, but the mother who bequeathed it to him. And just as Helena's possession of Bertram's ring proves both the fact of their sexual intercourse and her status as the young Countess, so too Clara's possession of Roderigo's crucifix proves the truth of her story, and her right to succeed his mother.[24]

The playwright spares Clara a narration of the rape. Instead he has her pull from her bosom an account written "in bloody characters"[25] and bid Fernando

---

[23] *Corregidor* is the Spanish term for mayor or chief magistrate. It comes from the verb *corregir,* "to correct," and is thus an appropriate title for Fernando, who undertakes the moral correction of his son. In Cervantes' story Rodolfo's father has no official position.

[24] Cervantes' heroine also corroborates her story with a stolen crucifix, but by contrast, it has no particular significance for Rodolfo: "having returned home, and having missed the crucifix, [he] guessed who had taken it, but gave himself no concern about it. To a person of his wealth such a loss was of no importance . . ." (*Exemplary Novels,* 320).

[25] Clara's use of blood to write her story connects her with Bel-imperia in *The Spanish Tragedy* (3.2.24–31), Tamyra in *Bussy D'Ambois* (5.1.176–78), and Annabella in *'Tis Pity She's a Whore* (5.1.31–47). (If the attribution of *The Spanish Gypsy* to Ford is correct, then the latter connection seems particularly interesting.) However, while Bel-imperia and Annabella write in blood because they are imprisoned, Clara, like Tamyra, *chooses* to write in blood. (Obviously the "bloody characters" are appropriate to her pain.) Nevertheless,

read it. As he does so she invokes his impartial judgement of her wrongs:

> call back the piety
> Of nature to the goodness of a judge,
> An upright judge, not of a partial father;
> .... consider
> What I have suffer'd, what thou ought'st to do,
> Thine own name, fatherhood, and my dishonour:
> Be just as heaven and fate are, that by miracle
> Have in my weakness wrought a strange discovery:
> Truth copied from my heart is texted there:
> Let now my shame be throughly understood;
> Sins are heard farthest when they cry in blood. (52–65)

Clara's appeal calls attention to Fernando's official position as *corregidor*, a magistrate charged with the administration of justice. Like the Queen of Corinth, Fernando has to pass sentence on his own son.[26] His initial response is reassuring ("This is the trumpet of a soul drown'd deep / In the unfathom'd seas of matchless sorrows" [67–68]). Rather abruptly, however, he leaves in order to "lock fast the door" (69), then returns immediately. The obtrusive and unnecessary exit seems designed to evoke a visual echo of 1.3, where Roderigo responds to Clara's pleas by locking her in. The repeated action thus calls attention to the crucial contrast between the two scenes: in 1.3 Clara's request for marriage is denied by the son; in 3.3 it is granted by the father.

The visual echo also points to a parallel between the two scenes. When Roderigo returns to the room in 1.3, the emotional balance shifts, and he begins to plead with Clara. So too, when Fernando returns from locking the door, he becomes the suppliant, urging Clara to sit (71). His appeal suggests that she has been kneeling before him while he read her story; a posture emblematic of his

---

all four women are "unchaste," and the blood seems to signify the punishment they suffer. All four letters are also connected to a revenge motif: Bel-imperia tries to incite revenge, Annabella and Tamyra try to prevent it, and Clara establishes her claim to the revenge she forgoes.

[26] The playwrights have added this dimension to the story. It picks up a theme — the conflicting demands of parental affection and justice — which goes back through *The Queen of Corinth* and *The Revenger's Tragedy* to the narrative sources of the "monstrous ransom" story in which the emperor loves the erring magistrate like a son (in Cinthio's tale, Juriste is "very dear to" the Emperor [378]). Compare too the preference of Euarchus for justice over the lives of his son and nephew at the end of Sidney's *Arcadia* (bk. 5, chap. 8: 842). I use the Penguin edition, ed. Maurice Evans.

status as magistrate and hers as suppliant. Now he dramatically reverses their positions:

> mark me how I kneel
> Before the high tribunal of your injuries.
> Thou too, too-much wrong'd maid, scorn not my tears,
> For these are tears of rage, not tears of love, —
> Thou father of this too, too-much-wrong'd maid, —
> Thou mother of her counsels and her cares,
> I do not plead for pity to a villain;
> O, let him die as he hath liv'd, dishonourably,
> Basely and cursedly! I plead for pity
> To my till now untainted blood and honour:
> Teach me how I may now be just and cruel,
> For henceforth I am childless. (78–89)

Just as in 1.3 Roderigo had rhetorically changed places with Clara, insisting that his future suffering would deserve her pity, so here Fernando rhetorically (and physically) upstages Clara with his demonstration of grief. Clara's protest ("Pray, sir, rise; / You wrong your place and age" [89–90]) emphasizes the startling nature of the role reversal: patriarchs do not kneel to young girls.[27] Fernando, however, continues his theatrical self-immolation: "Point me my grave / In some obscure by-path, where never memory / Nor mention of my name may be found out" (90–92). His plea for an anonymous death echoes Clara's earlier plea to Roderigo ("I must not leave a mention of my wrongs, / The stain of my unspotted birth, to memory; / Let it lie buried with me in the dust" [1.3.65–67]); and this coincidence strengthens the connection between Fernando and Clara which the whole scene is designed to establish: *both* now appear as victims of the rape, victims whose sufferings have an equal claim to pity.

Clara does not protest this absurdity. Just as in 1.3 Roderigo's plea for pity silenced her reproaches, so here Fernando's grief elicits her exemplary compassion:

> My lord, I can weep with you, nay, weep for ye,
> As you for me; your passions are instructions,
> And prompt my faltering tongue to beg at least
> A noble satisfaction, though not revenge. (93–96)

---

[27] Clara is apparently about the same age as Fernando's lost daughter (Constanza/ Pretiosa, the eponymous Spanish gypsy), in her early teens (2.1.82).

Because Fernando has offered to surrender his son to justice (death), Clara dares "with faltering tongue" to ask for much less: a "noble satisfaction" — marriage — instead of "revenge". Fernando clutches at her offer — "Speak that again" — and Clara delicately rephrases her request: "Can you procure no balm / To heal a wounded name?" (97–98). Fernando is transported: "O, thou'rt as fair / In mercy as in beauty! wilt thou live, / And I'll be thy physician?" "I'll be yours," Clara answers (98–100). And so they restore each other: Clara by giving up her right to "revenge," Fernando by giving up his right to negotiate a more advantageous match.[28]

This mutual resurrection of Clara and Fernando is part of a larger romance pattern. The corregidor had two children: the first was Roderigo, the second a daughter whom he lost years ago in a shipwreck (3.3.35–36). By graciously agreeing to marriage, Clara restores to Fernando both his son, whose life was forfeit to the law, and — symbolically — the daughter who drowned at sea.[29] His immediate and passionate adoption of Clara — "This daughter shall be ours" (102) — strengthens the play's depiction of rape-as-marriage. Roderigo's crime seems increasingly like the providentially ordained means of Clara's union with both father and son.

The scene ends with Fernando's paternal benediction of the recumbent girl:

> — Sleep, sleep, young angel,
> My care shall wake about thee. . . .
> Night curtains o'er the world; soft dreams rest with thee!
> The best revenge is to reform our crimes,
> Then time crowns sorrows, sorrows sweeten times. (102–107)

By implication Fernando presents Clara's willingness to marry Roderigo as "the best revenge," the reformation of his crime. Leaving her to sleep, he assumes the burden of active "care."

After her apotheosis as sleeping angel, Clara more or less retires from the play. Like Fletcher's Euphanes and Shakespeare's Duke, Fernando takes center

---

[28] Significantly, however, there is no suggestion in the play that Clara is unequal to Roderigo in wealth or rank: she is an eminently suitable match for him and thus Fernando does really not sacrifice anything in accepting her as a daughter-in-law. By contrast, in Cervantes Leocadia's family, though of noble blood, is impoverished and powerless either to enforce a settlement or exact revenge (*Exemplary Novels*, 317).

[29] Fernando's recovery of a daughter-in-law from the "unfathom'd seas of matchless sorrows" in 3.3 foreshadows the recovery of his own daughter in 5.3. There Fernando's ecstatic response to the revelation of Constanza's identity (41–71) recalls Pericles' response to Marina.

stage to reform the villain, and like them too, he uses craft against vice. Instead
of confronting Roderigo with his crime, Fernando, for no obvious reason, *tricks*
him into the marriage. In this the play partially follows its Spanish source. However, in Cervantes it is Rodolfo's *mother* who, with Leocadia's co-operation, orchestrates the deception: she is a comic Fate, a variation on the "clever woman"
of romance tradition. The wedding is the triumph of female manipulation of male
desire. There is no suggestion of moral judgement for the original sin of rape.

In *The Spanish Gypsy* the scheme is wholly managed by Roderigo's *father* and
is subordinate to a moral framework. The playwright retains the basic device of
Cervantes' story, in which the mother shows her son a portrait of an ugly
woman, designated as his bride. His aversion to the image prompts him to declare his desire for the beautiful heroine instead. In *The Spanish Gypsy*, however,
this deception is introduced through an inset morality play. When he discovers
his son in disguise among the gypsies, Fernando commissions him to write a
play on a prodigal son theme (an angry father demands that his wastrel son marry, his son rejects the chosen bride on the basis of her portrait [4.3.8–143]). This
play-within-the-play does nothing to advance the plot. However, it does allow
Fernando to express his righteous anger at his erring son indirectly; and it also
allows Roderigo, who takes the part of the son, to act out his rebellion against
paternal authority. More importantly, like the "play extempore" between Hal and
Falstaff in the tavern, Fernando's play provides an interpretative key to the larger
action. Like the Boar's Head play, it emphasizes the primary importance of the
father–son bond, and adds a typological resonance to the action. Now the grieving father emerges as the *primary* victim of Roderigo's sin, and the disruption of
their relationship becomes the most serious consequence of the rape.

When the fiction of the inset play dissolves, Fernando springs the trap in earnest. He insists Roderigo must marry the woman of the portrait, and his son
kneels on cue to beg instead for "that young pensive piece of beauty" who
watched the play, the anonymous Clara (4.3.223). Their wedding, indicated simply by a procession "*from church*" (5.1 SD), follows immediately.

At this point the playwright adds another twist to the deception. Instead of
revealing the truth about Clara's identity, Fernando tells Roderigo that his wife
is "a wanton" (11) and demands to know what sin he has committed to deserve
such a fate (12–14). Under the pressure of his father's stern interrogation, Roderigo confesses to the rape, begs forgiveness, and finally repents his refusal to
marry his victim. As soon as he expresses this regret aloud — "O, had I married
her, / I had been then the happiest man alive!" (37–38) — Roderigo finds that
it is miraculously assuaged. Clara and her parents emerge "*from behind the arras*"
(38 SD). Her responsive declaration — "As I the happiest woman, being mar-

ried" (39) — is both an enigmatic identification of herself as the rape victim, and a retrospective declaration of love for her rapist: if only he had married her, she would have been "*the happiest woman [alive]*."

Roderigo does not ask Clara's forgiveness, nor does Clara offer a fresh reproach. Instead she vows that she will endeavour to "deserve" his love (54–55). Roderigo's vow goes to his parents: "Fathers both, and mother, / I will redeem my fault" (56–57). Fernando, Pedro and Maria bless him in unison (57). I think we should imagine Roderigo kneeling here, surrounded by his forgiving wife, father and parents-in-law: a more elaborate version of the prodigal's return, in which the marriage between rapist and victim is wholly subsumed in the (re)-union of the larger family. This tableau all but concludes the main plot of the play. The entrance of Louis, Clara's old suitor and Roderigo's friend, allows Clara to confirm the providential nature of the marriage: "heaven's great hand," she tells Louis, "that on record / Fore-points the equal union of all hearts, / Long since decreed what this day hath been perfected" (59–62). The rape is now explicitly the divinely ordained means to the union of their equal "hearts."

In spite of its melodramatic opening, *The Spanish Gypsy* is not, like *The Queen of Corinth*, a crudely exploitative thriller. Nor is it, like *Measure for Measure*, a problem play. It is a sentimental romance that in its main plot celebrates sexual assault. To the female viewer it offers the comforting fiction that her rape might promote the rapist's redemption, and her suffering have meaning and purpose. To the male viewer it offers the comforting fiction that his victim — if she is worthy of him — will forgive him. To both it offers the prospect of finding true love and a prosperous marriage through sexual violence.

Like the earlier "marriage plays," *Measure for Measure* and *The Queen of Corinth, The Spanish Gypsy* dramatizes the accommodation of sexual assault in a patriarchal society. Gossett observes that the structure of the rape-and-marriage plays "identifies rape with all sexual impulse as it is treated in comedy. . . . Rather than being a tragic crime rape becomes a comic error by being brought into the social order" ("'Best Men'," 324). I would emphasize, however, that while rape may be represented as a "comic error" in *The Spanish Gypsy* and its predecessors, it is not a trivial one; on the contrary, it has marvellous, providential consequences. The comedy it precipitates is neither bawdy nor festive, but the "divine comedy" of Christian salvation. Thus in contrast to most of the earlier, classically-derived plays — like *Titus Andronicus* and Heywood's *The Rape of Lucrece* — where sexual assault is rationalized as the cause of a community's liberation, in these plays it is rationalized as the cause of the assailant's redemption. In each case the crime is mitigated by youth: it is a first fall; and in each case an older man — a benevolent patriarch — engineers the rapist's penitence at the expense of the victim, who literally atones — effects an at-one-ment — for her rape, reconciling the erring youth with his parental judge. All three plays thus offer the modern reader an insight into "the homosocial imaginary" of early modern England, within which the heroine's rape derives its significance from the male bonds it first threatens then finally promotes.

Whetstone's play, a source for Shakespeare's, highlights the miraculous transformation of angry victim into redeeming wife. Shakespeare's bed trick blurs this transformation, dividing the role of angry victim and forgiving wife. Nevertheless, Isabella makes a deliberate and deeply felt choice for forgiveness. It is Shakespeare's Duke, however, who receives credit for the happy ending. In *The Queen of Corinth* Fletcher, Massinger, and Field emphasize the destructive potential of the victim's anger, rather than its justice, and highlight Merione's abasement rather than any ethical choice. There is no scene in which Merione, like Isabella and Epitia, considers the injury she has suffered and decides to forgive her rapist. Theanor secures her consent to the rape trick offstage, and she reappears only to participate in the mock battle with Beliza for Theanor's life. The credit for saving Corinth and penitent prince goes to Euphanes. In *The Spanish Gypsy*, where the heroine's willingness to forgive the hero *is* celebrated, Roderigo's father eclipses Clara as a victim of the rape, and forgiveness is a sentimental rather than an ethical or moral issue. Clara never weighs the claims of just anger against mercy. She understands herself as Roderigo's true wife from act 1, and like a true wife prefers his good to her own. Like Euphanes and the Duke, the patriarch Fernando arranges the happy ending.

The evolution of the marriage plot from *Promos and Cassandra* to *The Spanish Gypsy* represents a progressive softening of the issues the story raises — in Baines's terms, a progressive "effacement" of rape. Cassandra wants revenge against Promos, but Mariana, Merione and Clara are all eager to marry the men who have abused them. Mariana's role as substitute victim palliates the problem. But the authors of *The Queen of Corinth* simply evade it: Merione's forgiveness is assumed, not dramatized. The authors of *The Spanish Gypsy* mystify the issue: Clara's forgiveness springs from her love for her *de facto* husband, and her marriage is represented as the acme of bliss: she is "the happiest woman."

Gossett points out that these plays allow the audience to watch "the fulfilment of a fantasy of rape and yet the guilt attached to the fantasy — and the act — is removed by the final marriage. The fantasy is both permitted and denied, which may account for the appeal of the plot . . ." ("'Best Men'," 324). I think she is right, and the appeal she describes is surely gendered, operating more strongly for males. However, there is another, perhaps less obvious, but more sinister appeal for females, who are invited to enjoy identification with the graciously forgiving victim. That invitation seems particularly strong in *The Spanish Gypsy* where Roderigo's father kneels before Clara, simultaneously empowering her and securing her aid; calls her "as fair / In mercy as in beauty" (3.3.98–99) and promises to look after her: "Sleep, sleep, young angel, / My care shall wake about thee ..." (102–103). What could be more seductive?

At one point in Margaret Atwood's *The Handmaid's Tale*, the narrator, who has endured coerced sexual intercourse repeatedly, tells an imagined male reader: "please remember: you will never be subjected to the temptation of feeling you must forgive, a man, as a woman. It's difficult to resist, believe me" (144). She concludes,

> Maybe none of this is about control. Maybe it isn't really about who can own whom, who can do what to whom and get away with it, even as far as death. Maybe it isn't about who can sit and who has to kneel or stand or lie down, legs spread open. Maybe it's about who can do what to whom and be forgiven for it. Never tell me it amounts to the same thing. (144–45)

The Spanish Gypsy, like the earlier Jacobean "marriage" plays, enshrines the gendered paradigm of sexual sin and absolution that Atwood's narrator recognizes but cannot escape. They are finally about "who can do what to whom and be forgiven for it."

Karen Bamford
Mount Allison University

Works Cited

Atwood, Margaret. *The Handmaid's Tale*. Toronto: McLelland and Stewart, 1985.

Bach, Rebecca Ann. "The Homosocial Imaginary of *A Woman Killed With Kindness*." *Textual Practice* 12 (1998): 503–24.

Baines, Barbara. "Effacing Rape in Early Modern Representation." *ELH* (1998): 69–98.

Bamford, Karen. *Sexual Violence on the Jacobean Stage*. New York: St. Martin's Press, 2000.

Bashar, Nazife. "Rape in England between 1550 and 1700." In *The Sexual Dynamics of History*, 28–42. London: Pluto Press, 1983.

Beattie, J. M. *Crime and the Courts in England 1660–1800*. Princeton: Princeton University Press, 1986.

Bentley, G. E. *The Jacobean and Caroline Stage.* 7 vols. Oxford: Clarendon Press, 1941–1956.

Bridenbaugh, Carl. *Vexed and Troubled Englishmen.* New York: Oxford University Press, 1968.

Brittin, Norma. *Thomas Middleton.* New York: Twayne, 1972.

Burelbach, Frederick M., Jr. "Theme and Structure in *The Spanish Gypsy.*" *The Humanities Association Bulletin* 11 (1968): 37–41.

Carter, John Marshall. *Rape in Medieval England.* Lanham, MD: University Press of America, 1985.

Cervantes Saavedra, Miguel de. *Exemplary Novels*, trans. Walter K. Kelly. London: Bell, 1908.

Chapman, George. *The Tragedy of Bussy D'Ambois*, ed. Nicholas Brooke. Revels Plays. London: Methuen, 1964.

Chaytor, Miranda. "Husband(ry): Narratives of Rape in the Seventeenth Century." *Gender and History* 7 (1995): 378–407.

Clark, Lorenne, and Debra Lewis. *Rape.* Toronto: Women's Press, 1977.

Cockburn, J. S. "The Nature and Incidence of Crime in England 1559–1625: A Preliminary Survey." In *Crime in England*, ed. idem, 49–71. London: Methuen, 1977.

De Groot, Roger D. "The Crime of Rape *temp.* Richard I and John." *Journal of Legal History* 9 (1988): 324–34.

Dick of Devonshire, ed. J. G. McManaway and M. R. McManaway. Malone Society Reprints. Oxford: Oxford University Press, 1955.

Fletcher, John. *The Dramatic Works in the Beaumont and Fletcher Canon*, gen. ed. Fredson Bowers. 10 vols. Cambridge: Cambridge University Press, 1966–1992.

Ford, John. *'Tis Pity She's A Whore*, ed. Brian Morris. New Mermaids. London: Benn, 1968.

Girard, René. *Deceit, Desire and the Novel*, trans. Yvonne Freccero. Baltimore: Johns Hopkins University Press, 1966.

Gossett, Suzanne. " 'Best Men are Molded out of Faults': Marrying the Rapist in Jacobean Drama." *English Literary Renaissance* 14 (1984): 305–27.

Hanawalt, Barbara. *Crime and Conflict in English Communities, 1300–1348.* Cambridge, MA: Harvard University Press, 1979.

Heywood, Thomas. "The Rape of Lucrece" in *The Dramatic Works of Thomas Heywood*, ed. R. H. Shepherd. London: J. Pearson, 1874. 6 vols. 5: 161–257. New York: Russell, 1964.

Heywood, Thomas. *Dramatic Works*, ed. [R. H. Shepherd for] J. Pearson. 6 vols. London: J. Pearson, 1874. New York: Russell, 1964.

Ingram, Martin. "Ridings, Rough Music and the 'Reform of Popular Culture' in Early Modern England." *Past and Present* 105 (1984): 79–113.

Kistner, A. L. and M. K. *Middleton's Tragic Themes*. American University Studies, Series 4: English Language and Literature 10. New York: Peter Lang, 1984.

Kittel, Ruth. "Rape in Thirteenth-Century England: A Study of the Common Law Courts." In *Women and the Law*, ed. D. Kelly Weisberg, 2: 101–15. Cambridge, MA: Schenkman, 1982.

Kyd, Thomas. *The Spanish Tragedy*, ed. Philip Edwards. Revels Plays. London: Methuen, 1959.

Lake, D. J. *The Canon of Thomas Middleton's Plays*. London: Cambridge University Press, 1975.

Livy. *The Early History of Rome*, trans. Aubrey de Sélincourt. Harmondsworth: Penguin, 1960.

MacDonald, Michael. *Mystical Bedlam*. Cambridge: Cambridge University Press, 1981.

Marcus, Leah Sinanoglou. "The Milieu of Milton's *Comus*: Judicial Reform at Ludlow and the Problem of Sexual Assault." *Criticism* 25 (1983): 293–327.

Middleton, Thomas. *Women Beware Women*. Ed. J. R. Mulryne. Revels Plays. London: Methuen, 1975.

———. The Works, ed. A. H. Bullen. 8 vols. London: Nimno, 1885–1886; repr. New York: AMS Press, 1964.

Oliphant, E. H. C. *Shakespeare and His Fellow Dramatists*. 2 vols. New York: Prentice Hall, 1929.

Rowley, William. *The Spanish Gipsie, and All's Lost By Lust, by Thomas Middleton and William Rowley*, ed. Edgar C. Morris. Belles Lettres Series. Boston: Heath, 1908.

Sedgwick, Eve Kosofsky. *Between Men: English Literature and the Homosocial Imagination*. New York: Columbia University Press, 1985.

Shakespeare, William. *Measure For Measure*, ed. J. W. Lever. Arden Shakespeare: University Paperback. London: Methuen, 1967.

———. *Pericles*, ed. Philip Edwards. New Penguin Shakespeare. Harmondsworth: Penguin, 1976.

———. *The Poems*, ed. F. T. Prince. Arden Shakespeare: University Paperback. London: Methuen, 1969.

Sharpe, J. A. *Crime in Early Modern England 1550–1750*. London: Longman, 1984.

Sidney, Sir Philip. *The Countess of Pembroke's Arcadia*, ed. Maurice Evans. Harmondsworth: Penguin, 1977.

Toner, Barbara. *The Facts of Rape*. London: Hutchinson, 1977.

Underdown, David. *Fire From Heaven*. London: HarperCollins-Fontana, 1993.

Walker, Garthine. "Rereading Rape and Sexual Violence in Early Modern England." *Gender and History* 10 (1998): 1–25.

Whetstone, George. *Promos and Cassandra* (1578). In *Narrative and Dramatic Sources of Shakespeare*, ed. Geoffrey Bullough, 2: 442–513. London: Routledge, 1958.

Williams, Carolyn D. "'Silence, like a Lucrece knife': Shakespeare and the Meanings of Rape." *Yearbook of English Studies* 23 (1993): 93–109.

Lewd but Familiar Eyes:
The Narrative Tradition of Rape
and Shakespeare's *The Rape of Lucrece*

Rape stories have been a familiar part of Western culture for well over two millennia, but they carry within them an inherent contradiction. On the one hand, they portray a crime that makes most of us very uncomfortable, not only because of the horror of the act itself, but because rape in various ways threatens to unravel the social fabric that allows men and women to live and work together. Rape is an undeniable expression of male power over women, and as such it serves as a destabilizing metaphor of the many other expressions that we suppress or deny in order to maintain a façade of trust and mutual respect.

On the other hand, rape stories are built on a form that has nothing directly to do with gender relations and that provides pleasure in many other kinds of chase stories. Whether it is a case of a detective tracking down a criminal, a scientist heroically seeking a lifesaving cure, or a high school student attempting to win his or her dream date for the prom, chases are fun because we enjoy the tension created by one character struggling to catch and overcome another. The form itself is pleasurable; that's why it appears so often and in so many ways.

Employing this form helps keep at a distance the horror and danger of sexual violence by making narrative rape seem more like other chases than like the crime, and by focusing attention away from the victim and toward the rapist and the victim's would-be protector. Emphasizing the chase, especially if it involves a contest between the rapist and a hero, pushes readers away from the threatening implications of rape, while any substantial portrayal of the forced intercourse or the victim's response to it has just the opposite effect. The traditional narrative buildup of rape stories, then, is at odds with the representation of the act, for the one effaces the horrors and destabilizing implications of rape while the other always threatens to make them vividly and uncomfortably clear. This essay looks briefly at the historical development of the rape story and then shows how Livy's, Ovid's, and especially Shakespeare's version of the Lucrece story differently balance the menacing tension within the form.

The ancestor of this form started out as a close adjunct to communal hunting and, later, war. Conquest narratives were ways of representing and vicariously experiencing the proof of masculinity and male camaraderie that hunting and war provided, but the stories continued long after the activities ceased to be significant parts of most men's lives.[1] One of the most common subjects in Paleolithic art is groups of men hunting — not surprising given the economic importance of hunting in that period[2] — but the subject was just as important ten millennia later at Çatal Hüyük (Turkey), even though too many men lived there for everyone to participate in hunts or for hunting to be central to the economy.[3] It was even less common an activity in the agricultural and trading cities along the Tigris and Euphrates three millennia after that, but many of the surviving cult vessels nevertheless represent wild animals, hunting scenes involving the priest-king, and hunting-related deities.[4] Representations of lion hunts are almost as prominent as wars on the massive reliefs of the great first-millennium Assyrian palaces. The Greeks loved hunting stories, as did the Romans, who also found thrilling mock hunts and then kills of captured animals in the coliseum. Hunting and especially its representation remained important in all the western medieval cultures.[5]

Warfare has been a common part of life in the western world since the Late Paleolithic,[6] and well before the founding of the first cities in the third millennium B.C., it must have replaced hunting as the communal, masculinity-proving activity in which large numbers of men could actually participate.[7] Even as late as fifth-century Athens, all males were trained to fight and expected to do so. Sophocles fought in at least two major battles, one when he was in his fifties and had long been a famous playwright. From the end of the fourth millennium on,

---

[1] On the relationship of hunting, war, and representation in the ancient world, see Cartmill, *A View to a Death in the Morning*, 28–44.

[2] Mellars, "The Upper Palaeolithic Revolution," in *The Oxford Illustrated Prehistory of Europe*, ed. Cunliffe, 70–75.

[3] Mellaart, *Çatal Hüyük*, 223–24.

[4] Amiet, *Art of the Ancient Near East*, 356–70.

[5] Cartmill, *A View to a Death in the Morning*, 28–91.

[6] Keeley, *War Before Civilization*, 36–39.

[7] On the connection of Neolithic hunting and warfare, see Ferril, *The Origins of War*, 18–26.

representations of war are very common. Notable early examples are the Egyptian Narmer Palette, c. 3100 B.C., on which the founder of the first dynasty is
about to brain a kneeling enemy and throw him into the river with the bodies of
his comrades, and the Sumerian Standard of Ur, c. 2500 B.C., one side of which
portrays a fierce battle in which charioteers trample enemy infantry. As soon as
significant literary works appeared, they too often included war stories, and in
ways that closely tie them back to their hunting ancestry. In the Sumerian-
Akkadian epic *Gilgamesh* (3rd–early 2nd millennium B.C.), for example, Gilgamesh and Enkidu show their friendship by working together to kill the giant
Huwawa, who is sometimes described as an enemy leader (their first contact is
with his lookout) who must be killed in combat and sometimes as an animal that
must be hunted (he roars and breathes fire). A millennium later, the *Iliad* describes battles both as communal activities and as individual contests between
men who are often compared to animals of the hunt.

War directly contributed to the development of rape as a subject for stories,
for while there must always have been cases of men forcing themselves on wom-
en, it was only in war that they could do so as a communal expression of male
and group identity, as in battle itself and, earlier, in communal hunts. Many
texts from the second millennium B.C. on describe the sexual use of women captured in war,[8] and artwork occasionally makes the point in a very public way.
One set of relief panels from the palace of Assurbanipal at Nineveh (668–630
B.C.), for example, portrays the defeat of an Arab army, followed by the destruction of their tent village. The upper register of the last panel (figure 1) shows
Assyrian soldiers stripping the wife of one of the defeated Arabs, while below
the old men who stayed behind have been flayed alive. Placed in a public location along with representations of lion hunts and other battles, these images told
visitors from the far-flung reaches of the Assyrian empire that one of the costs
of rebellion would be the gang rape of their women.

The plot of the *Iliad* centers on a dispute between Achilles and Agamemnon
over the distribution of captured Trojan women, and other accounts of the Trojan War tell with pride of the rapes of the women of Troy at the conclusion of
the siege. Many vases portray these horrific scenes, including the earliest representation of the Trojan Horse, on a large (about four feet tall) Archaic pointed
amphora from about 670 B.C. (figure 2). Photographs of this famous relief are
frequently reprinted, but the twenty smaller ones below it are also important to
the composition, showing the fruits of the victory brought about by the defeat of

---

[8] Lerner, *The Creation of Patriarchy*, 76–89.

Figure 1. Assyrian soldiers attack Arab women:
gypsum, Nineveh, Palace of Assurbanipal, 668–630 B.C.,
British Museum. Author photo.

the Trojans. Nineteen of them are scenes of rape, shown as a soldier seizing a woman preparatory to carrying her off. Several of the reliefs tell the story of a small boy attempting to defend his mother before being skewered by a heavily-armed soldier (figure 3), who then tosses aside the boy's body and grasps the woman. None of the people in these small images is identified by name or attribute; the point is simply that massacring your enemies leads to an equally satisfying exercise of violent domination upon their wives.

The basic form through which hunting, battle, and rape were all represented is both straightforward and familiar: a man or group of men select and attack an object (animal, enemy soldiers, woman), which resists and is eventually defeated. Although we now think of such stories mostly in terms of individuals, the form developed as a way of glorifying the group: the men of a particular tribe or city. Individual men could play out conquest narratives, but the reason the stories needed to be told at all was to establish group identity, and to assert the values — such as strength, cunning, dominance, and teamwork — that came to be associated with masculinity. So even when the stories are about individuals, the point is to reinforce male group identity.

Conquest can make a man seem masculine and dominant only if the object is a worthy adversary, and so it, he, or she must be seen as clever and strong, and often as magical. As a result, hunters since the Paleolithic have defined their objects partly in terms of the qualities they want to assert in themselves, thereby setting the stage for a battle in which these qualities are proven important and the hunters are proven their exemplars. To prove their worthiness, the hunters must accomplish their victory through a combination of intelligence, teamwork, and strength, not through luck or the incompetence of the quarry. Otherwise, the hunt will not have shown anything about the hunters, and they will not be dominant over anything significant.

This need to value themselves through valuing their quarry is behind the frequent identification of men with the animals they hunt. Rituals in primitive societies throughout the world involve men dressing as animals, and numerous examples of ancient western ritual clothing and armor represent animals, and often are partly built with horns or other animal parts. The earliest writing, from third-millennium B.C. Sumer, commonly represents the king as an aggressive, fighting animal: he is a "true offspring engendered by a bull, speckled of head and body," "a fierce-eyed lion born of a dragon," "a fierce panther fed on rich milk," "a thick-horned bull born to a big lion," "a mighty warrior born to a lion."[9] These descriptions reflect a much older tradition of establishing the value

[9] Kramer, *From the Poetry of Sumer*, 60–61.

Figure 2. Trojan Horse and the sack of Troy:
early Archaic, c. 670 B.C., pointed amphora, height: c. 4 ft.,
Municipal Museum, Mykonos. Author photo.

of such qualities as great physical strength, ferocity, and bloodthirstiness by assigning them to animals to which men are then favorably compared.

But at the same time that the animal is given some of the hunter's own desired qualities, it must also be devalued so that its defeat might seem justified and natural. Its death must seem an affirmation of the value of the hunters, as well as the value of the hunt. So at the same time that the animal — and eventually enemy soldiers and women — are portrayed as worthy adversaries they are also mere meat. The same kings who describe themselves as having the qualities of animals also represent themselves as killing them by the dozen. And even though human enemies are habitually described as valiant and strong, there is nevertheless great relish in their slaughter or enslavement. The king climbs to the top of the mountain over the bodies of his victims in the Victory Stele of Naram-Sin (c. 2250 B.C.), and the Stele of Vultures (c. 2450 B.C.) contains a description of the heaping up of thousands of enemy bodies; the much later Assyrian palace walls are covered with similar valuing/devaluing of both hunting and war. All of us are familiar with the unhappy results of applying this double view to sexual relations.

Another aspect of the hunting-based narrative form that has been with us since far back in prehistory is its emphasis on the chase or fight as opposed to the victory. The point of conquest narratives is the hunters' attempt to defeat their prey, for it is only through this attempt that they can prove anything about themselves or about the masculine values through which they are making the proof. The victory is important only as a symbol that this proof has been accomplished. Indeed, while the definition of actual rape is usually based on both penetration and the victim's resistance,[10] in rape stories only the victim's resistance is essential. In the myth of Apollo and Daphne, for example, the chase is the center of the story, but the rape we expect to conclude it is replaced by the victim's metamorphosis into a tree. Apollo's attempt to chase down Daphne is exciting and tense, but the actual act is not an essential element of the plot.

This narrative form and the ideology behind it both long precede their use in rape stories, and in Shakespeare's as well as our own time many other kinds of stories continue to demonstrate masculinity through descendants of this ancient form. I do not mean to imply that rape stories and other versions of this form are all at heart merely hunting stories or that they are all controlled by some

---

[10] See Baines, "Effacing Rape in Early Modern Representation," 71–84; Tomascelli, "Introduction," in *Rape: An Historical and Social Enquiry*, 9–12.

Figure 3. Greek soldier prepares to rape conquered Trojan woman:
detail of an early Archaic (c. 670 B.C.) pointed amphora, height: c. 4 ft.,
Municipal Museum, Mykonos. Author photo.

kind of transcendent narrative structure. All narrative forms are historically bounded, reflecting social and literary changes as well as the experience and knowledge of individual readers. Still, traditions from the oldest versions of conquest narratives continue to impose themselves on the newer ones. This is especially true of rape stories.

Rape stories borrowed their basic plot from the old hunting narrative, and they carry over from that form the idea that masculinity can be demonstrated through violent domination. An even more central legacy of the older form is what might be called the thrill of the chase. A reader's excitement at the pursuit of the object at first seems like the product of successful examples of the form and not a part of the form itself. But it is more properly seen as part of the form in the same way that sympathy for the lovers is essential to love stories. Just as we expect to sympathize with lovers and would have trouble reading a love story if we did not, we expect to find exciting the chase in all narratives that derive from the hunting form. When readers identify a story they are reading with this form they already expect a chase and are disposed to find it exciting, and this is whether the chase concerns a hunt, a battle, a rape, or even a contest of wits. The thrill of the chase in rape stories is the tension readers feel as the rapist threatens his victim; it is not whatever moral or sympathetic response this tension stimulates. Like the basic plot, this tension is both built into the form and extremely old, whereas the resulting response varies depending on the historic period, the reader's gender, her or his individual experiences, and other factors. So while Greek men evidently found pleasurable rape stories that most of us find disturbing or horrifying, all of our responses begin with the thrill of the chase.

The basic plot, the proving of masculinity, and the thrill of the chase were all part of the conquest narrative form long before it was used to represent sexual violence, and in consequence the use of this form to describe an activity quite different from hunting or war created tensions that have remained within portrayals of rape ever since. Hunting and war are group activities, and rape as a proof of masculinity probably developed out of wartime group rapes. But rape stories are almost inevitably about individual rapists and victims. War stories break down into individual conflicts too (as in the *Iliad*), but whereas one armed soldier defeating another in battle plausibly demonstrates strength and other masculine virtues, rape does not easily carry the same meaning. Women in the lower social positions of ancient cultures were so disempowered — especially in terms of sexual relations — that assaulting them could not be used to prove anything. Actual rapes of such women were evidently quite common, but fictional rapes had to be of upper-class women, much as Achilles' battlefield conquests had to be men of class rather than ordinary foot soldiers.

Homer had no problem providing a long list of upper-class victims of Achilles' spear, but because upper-class women — wives and future wives — were responsible for passing property from one male generation to another, their rape was too destabilizing and threatening easily to allow for fictions in which rape proves masculinity. And besides, even in such fiercely patriarchal societies as Classical Greece, men were in frequent contact with women for whom they cared. There were not many Persians in Athens, so it was easy for Athenian men to imagine them as barbarians (the word refers to the supposed babble — the "bar-bar" speech — of non-Greeks): unproblematic to kill both in reality and fiction. But women were and are different. Men live with their wives and are raised by their mothers. They have sisters and daughters, and they live in cultures that in various ways assert the value of women, especially women of class. Rape is a profoundly gendered act that threatens all these relationships by denying the sense of respect and civility (though not necessarily equality) that is essential to them.

Rape is also disturbingly analogous to consensual intercourse, not just physically but because it harshly demonstrates the unequal power that at least until very recently has characterized most sexual relations. Both for us and for people of the ancient world, sex is more fun and respect between the sexes more possible if rape is kept at a considerable distance. "It's no fun for them when it's no fun for you. It's not copulation without cooperation,"[11] says Lysistrata in predicting that the husbands of Greece so need consensual relations with their wives that they will be willing to stop the Peloponnesian War to have them. It is part of a woman's role in patriarchal marriages to submit herself sexually to her husband, but as Lysistrata points out, neither wives nor husbands want this authority made apparent. Rape as both threat and metaphor destabilizes the idea that sex in a patriarchal marriage is about mutual love rather than power.

The ancient Greeks kept the tensions inherent in rape stories under control by mostly restricting them to two categories, both of which justify rape in terms of class. In the first, rape was portrayed as one of the ways an army could show its victory over the men of another city. The main struggle was thus with armed men rather than defenseless women, and their rape showed that the conquered men were all along inferior, deserving to be married to women who could be treated like servants or slaves. A prominent example is the many retellings and pictorial representations of Ajax's rape of Cassandra during the sack of Troy.[12]

---

[11] Aristophanes, *Lysistrata*, trans. Rudal, 18.

[12] Gantz, *Early Greek Myth*, 654–55.

The second kind of story is the rape of high-born or otherwise significant women by gods. The king of the gods, Zeus, was also the champion rapist, with Callisto, Io, Danaë, Europa, and Alcmene just a few of his dozens of victims. The form is so common that on some vases groups of gods are represented as chasing unidentified women who exist only as fleeing victims.[13] These stories avoid the problem of sympathy for the victim by de-emphasizing the rape itself and devoting most of the story to the stratagem and the chase. The story of Danaë, a staple of fifth-century literature and art,[14] centers on Zeus's clever strategy for outwitting her father, who has locked his daughter in a barred cavern. Danaë is represented as sometimes resisting, sometimes not. Her struggle is mostly deflected onto her father, leaving her only barely in the story at all. Logically, of course, Zeus needs no stratagem; he could as easily break apart the passage grates (another projection of Danaë's resistance) as he could compel her or anyone else's submission. But told this way, the story would portray Zeus as brutish rather than clever, and, just as problematic, it would force attention on the actual assault, redirecting attention and sympathy to the victim. Focusing on a clever (if logically unnecessary) strategy and its execution follows the traditional form and thus allows both the demonstration of masculinity and the thrill of the chase that are essential to it.

Both kinds of Greek rape stories assume that the reader will identify with the rapist, which in turn assumes an audience almost exclusively male. Four centuries later, the upper-class women of the Roman world were more respected and more fully integrated into civic life than their classical Greek predecessors had been, and they were also literate and wealthy enough for some of them to be literary patrons. They were part of the audience, as were the men who lived with and among them and who must in many cases have grown uncomfortable with the idea of proving masculinity through rape. Still, Roman men loved Greek stories, including rape stories, and so they were forced to evolve several strategies for enjoying the basic form without the moral inconvenience of having to see themselves as sympathizing with rape.

In the one most important to this study, our sympathy is directed not to the rapist but to a new character: the hero who rescues or avenges the victim and often marries her in the conclusion. It is his masculinity that the narrative proves, but the thrill of the chase still attends the rape or near-rape of the victim. Central to many Hellenistic plays and novels, this form is also used in Livy's

---

[13] Keuls, *The Reign of the Phallus*, 47–64.
[14] Gantz, *Early Greek Myth*, 299–303.

version of the rape of Lucrece, in *The Early History of Rome* (c. 29 B.C.).[15] In it, much more space is given to the opening description of Brutus and to his concluding vengeance than to the rape story itself. His words when he pulls the knife from Lucrece's body made it easy for male readers of the time to identify with Brutus, but now the male group bonding comes from avenging rape rather than participating in it. In addition, the focus is shifted from the individual assault of the younger Tarquin on Lucrece to a more general conflict between the Romans and their Etruscan rulers:[16]

> By this girl's blood — none more chaste till a tyrant wronged her — by the gods, I swear that with sword and fire, and whatever else can lend strength to my arm, I will pursue Lucius Tarquinius the Proud, his wicked wife, and all his children, and never again will I let them or any other man be King in Rome. (1.59)[17]

The framing presence of the avenging Brutus allows us to experience a thrill of the chase without having to understand that excitement as sympathy for the crime. Creating a defender or avenger thus obscures the central tension, at least for men, in all stories based on the Greek model: the problem of being thrilled by a violent assault, not only on a class of people that men need and love, but via an analogue of the act through which that need and love is often shown.[18]

Besides providing the framing avenger, Livy tries to control the sympathies of the reader by providing the reader as few physical details as possible of the rape itself:

> Here he waited till the house was asleep, and then, when all was quiet, he drew his sword and made his way to Lucretia's room determined to rape her. She was asleep. Laying his left hand on her breast, "Lucretia," he whispered, "not a sound! I am Sextus Tarquinius. I am armed — if you utter a word, I will kill you." Lucretia opened her eyes in terror; death was imminent, no help at hand. Sextus urged his love, begged her to submit, pleaded, threatened, used every weapon that might conquer a

---

[15] For an analysis of how Livy manipulated his sources, see Donaldson, *The Rapes of Lucretia*, 3–12.

[16] For an analysis of Brutus's function in Livy's rendition of the story, see Jed, *Chaste Thinking*.

[17] This and other quotations are from Livy, *The Early History of Rome*, trans. de Sélincourt.

[18] On the use of Brutus in Livy's, Ovid's, and Shakespeare's versions of the story, see Patterson, *Reading Between the Lines*, 304–9.

woman's heart. But all in vain; not even the fear of death could bend her
will. "If death will not move you," Sextus cried, "dishonor shall. I will kill
you first, then cut the throat of a slave and lay his naked body by your
side. Will they not believe that you were caught in adultery with a servant
— and paid the price?" Even the most resolute chastity could not have
stood against this dreadful threat.

Lucretia yielded. Sextus enjoyed her, and rode away, proud of his
success. (1.58)

The description of Tarquin's sinister hand on one of Lucrece's breasts invites the
reader to visualize the scene, but this visualization is quickly overwhelmed by the
other elements of Tarquin's speech, followed by less than a line of general allusion to the rape. Lucrece says nothing, nor does she physically resist. It is easy,
of course, to imagine her terror, but Livy is careful not to encourage us to do so
by providing imagery that would be uncomfortable and would take away from
his larger purpose of showing why overthrowing the monarchy was in this case
a noble act.

Ovid's version of the story, in *The Fasti* (c. A.D. 14), is obviously based on
Livy's, but with significant differences.[19] Most importantly, Ovid mostly drops
the frame hero. The long description of Brutus's disguise and clever use of the
oracle is reduced to two lines: so clipped that a person unfamiliar with Livy
would have a hard time understanding why Brutus was even in the story. His
part in the conclusion is also reduced, and where Livy has Brutus and Lucrece's
husband and father jointly swearing to revenge her and overthrow the monarchy,
Ovid gives us the dying Lucrece agreeing with Brutus that the elder Tarquin
should be banished: "As she lay, she turned her glazed eyes toward his voice, and
seemed to shake her head in assent" (*Fasti*, 2.845–846).[20] By emphasizing Lucrece rather than her eventual avengers, Ovid pushes readers to see her as a subject, and hence what happens to her as more personal and more horrible: in
other words, to focus more on the act than on the chase leading up to it. The
form of Livy's story makes Lucrece mostly an object over which men struggle,
but Ovid does not permit such an easy and conventional escape from the brutal
facts of rape. Nor does he allow her rape to prove even the avengers' masculinity.

De-emphasizing the avengers, however, focuses more attention on Tarquin
and his movement toward his victim, which would tend to objectify Lucrece and

---

[19] On the relation of Livy's and Ovid's versions of the story to Shakespeare's, see
Newman, " 'And let mild women to him lose their mildness'," 320–25.

[20] Ovid, *Fasti*, trans. Nagle.

depersonalize what happens to her in a different and older way. Ovid for the most part circumvents this tendency by making the assault seem as little like a hunt as possible, while still staying within the conquest form. Like Ovid's procedure in many places in another work, *Metamorphoses*, Tarquin's desire for Lucrece is described in terms of emotional self-indulgence rather than hunting and other kinds of chase imagery:

> likewise, although that attractive beauty was no longer present,
>   there remained the passion that beauty's presence had caused.
> He burned, and aroused by wicked passion's goading, he planned
>   rape and coercion against that innocent bed.
>
> (*Fasti*, 2.777–780)[21]

Putting it this way enables Ovid not to have to describe Tarquin through traditional images of masculinity, such as intelligence, cunning, and self-control. By having his Lucrece too terrified to speak at this point in the narrative, Ovid avoids a verbal debate that would have extended the tension just before the rape and would also have undercut the brutishness of the actual assault. His one hunting image, in which Lucrece is "a lamb caught away from the fold, / lying beneath a predatory wolf" (*Fasti*, 2.799–800), is of a grossly unequal contest: appropriate for the context, but unlikely to make Tarquin seem heroic. Finally, the description of the rape is even more terse than Livy's and is immediately followed by a line undercutting any sense of Tarquin as heroic or even genuinely a conqueror:

> Fear for her honor triumphed and the girl gave in.
> Why gloat triumphantly? This conquest will be the end of you.
>   A single night has cost you your kingdom!
>
> (*Fasti*, 2.810–812)[22]

Shakespeare also de-emphasizes Brutus and the other avengers in *The Rape of Lucrece*; they don't appear at all in the beginning and have distinct second billing to Lucrece in the conclusion.[23] And even more than Ovid he makes sure that after the rape we see Lucrece as a person with her own subjectivity. But several elements of the narrative before that point are troubling, beginning with the 238

---

[21] Ovid, *Metamorphoses*, trans. Mandelbaum.

[22] On the relation of this passage to ll. 729–735 in Shakespeare's poem, see Donaldson, *The Rapes of Lucretia*, 52.

[23] I use *The Norton Shakespeare*, ed. Stephen Greenblatt.

lines of self-debate as Tarquin creeps toward Lucrece's bedroom. The rhetoric and self-indulgent illogic of his psychomachia have been examined elsewhere.[24] My interest is in how it allows allows male readers both to identify with the moral Tarquin and to be titillated by the actions of the evil. This evil side is described through just the conventionalized masculine qualities that Ovid avoids. For example, Tarquin defends his decision to rape through imagery any young warrior might use:

> Then childish fear avaunt, debating die,
> Respect and reason wait on wrinkled age!
> My heart shall never countermand mine eye,
> Sad pause and deep regard beseems the sage. (274–277)[25]

In other words, careful consideration is for old men; the mark of a virile young man is to act rather than contemplate.

The long description of Tarquin's movement to Lucrece's bedroom is full of martial images and suggestions of stealth, power, and mastery. "The Roman lord marcheth to Lucrece' bed" (301), and on the way "The locks between her chamber and his will, / each one by him enforced, retires his ward" (302–303); "each unwilling portal yields him way" (311) until "with his knee the door he opens wide" (359), sees the "dove" that the "night-owl will catch" (360), and "stalks" (365) into her room. These images ensure that Tarquin's assault will be seen within the traditional conquest-narrative form and that there will be the resulting thrill of the chase. But the frequent references to Tarquin's doubts even as he approaches his quarry enable male readers to experience this thrill at the same time they see themselves as identifying with the "good" Tarquin, the one who like them finds rape revolting. The split Tarquin thus mirrors the two basic ways of experiencing narrative rape: as an exciting chase and as a dangerously disruptive act that needs always to be displaced onto criminal others. Ovid's Tarquin, in contrast, never questions his intention to rape, never says or thinks anything that makes him less unsympathetic, and is never characterized in masculinized terms. Unlike Shakespeare, Ovid does not allow his readers easily to separate the pleasure in the chase from their revulsion at the act.

Ovid's characterization of Lucrece before the assault also points up a significant difference in the way the two narratives approach their subject. His Lucrece

---

[24] Kahn, "*Lucrece*," 143–50; Dubrow, *Captive Victors*, 80–168; Kramer and Kaminsky, " 'These Contraries Such Unity Do Hold'," 149–53.

[25] My text here and elsewhere is from *The Norton Shakespeare*, ed. Greenblatt *et al.*

is a patriarchal fantasy of a good wife, devotedly sewing a "homemade cloak" for
her husband and fretting about his possible harm in battle:

> ". . . that man of mine is so impulsive,
>   rushing all over with his sword at the ready.
> I grow faint and almost die when I imagine him fighting,
>   and a cold chill grips my heart."
> In tears she stopped and let go the thread she'd begun,
>   and looked modestly down in her lap.
>
> (*Fasti*, 2.751–756)

When he returns unexpectedly (with Tarquin), she "hung, a sweet armful, from
her husband's neck" (760). Her physical appeal is noted but de-emphasized:

> Her beauty is attractive, her snowy complexion and golden hair,
>   and a charm which is completely uncontrived.
> Her speech is attractive, and her voice, and her unavailability.
>   The smaller his chances, the greater his desire.
>
> (*Fasti*, 2.763–766)

Shakespeare's characterization is just the opposite. He stresses his Lucrece's
chastity, but none of the other wifely virtues. His heroine seems not to be doing
anything when Tarquin arrives, and her only function once he is there is to be
the object of his attention and secret lust. The focus is so much on her physical
attractiveness that even her virtue is physicalized and eroticized:

> When at Collatium this false lord arrived,
> Well was he welcomed by the Roman dame,
> Within whose face beauty and virtue strived
> Which of them both should underprop her fame.
> When virtue bragged, beauty would blush for shame;
> When beauty boasted blushes, in despite
> Virtue would stain that o'er with silver white. (50–56)

There are a number of problems with this "scopic economy," as Coppélia Kahn
calls it,[26] but one of them is that the denial of any Lucrece except the eroticized
body discourages readers from seeing her as a person with whom they could
sympathize. Shakespeare repeatedly portrays Tarquin's desire as evil during the
approach to the bedroom, but he also declines to humanize his victim. Like

---

[26] Kahn, "*Lucrece*," 145.

many female characters in Greek rape stories, Shakespeare's Lucrece initially exists exclusively to be her attacker's game.

The eroticized descriptions intensify very uncomfortably in Lucrece's bedroom. The two ends of her pillow seem to be "swelling" at their frustration at not touching her lips, and stray strands of hair play with her breath in a dance that mingles innocence and sexuality:

> Her hair like golden threads played with her breath —
> O modest wantons, wanton modesty! (400–401)

"Her breasts like ivory globes circled with blue" excite Tarquin — and increasingly the male reader as well — because as "A pair of maiden worlds unconquered" (407–408) they call out to be taken, like an undefended town or a new world.[27] This relentless sexualizing of Lucrece's body makes clear that she exists only "To be admired of lewd unhallowed eyes" (392).[28] The question is whose eyes that includes.[29]

Ovid alludes to Lucrece's breasts as well: after Tarquin draws his sword and climbs onto Lucrece's bed, "His hands on her breasts were forcing her down, / breasts only her husband had ever touched" (803–804). By suggesting male competition for women, this description plays into the conquest narrative, but it at the same time suggests the violence and immorality of Tarquin's actions. Neither in this passage nor anywhere else does Ovid idealize and thereby eroticize his heroine's body. Shakespeare's opposite approach encourages visualization, draws out the rape scene, and makes his depersonalized victim seem more valuable as a conquest, like a deer with a large rack of antlers.[30] Compared to six hundred ninety-six by Shakespeare, Ovid uses only twenty-six lines to move from Tarquin's arrival at Lucrece's house to the completion of the rape, the same space he allots to his earlier description of Lucrece's devoted housewifery. He is careful that whatever thrill of the chase is induced by the swift movement to Tarquin's assault will be balanced by sympathy for his victim. And while Ovid shows us

---

[27] Woodbridge examines the erotic/military metaphors in terms of the Elizabethan (and earlier) image of the body as the commonwealth: "Palisading the Elizabethan Body Politic"; Vickers examines the same metaphors in " 'The blazon of sweet beauty's best'," 104–8.

[28] Cousins sees the eroticizing rhetoric in the rape scene as a parody of Petrarchism: "Subjectivity, Exemplarity," 45–60.

[29] For a different approach to how Shakespeare makes the reader complicit in the scene, see Wall, *The Imprint of Gender*, 214–20.

[30] Maus, "Taking Tropes Seriously," 76–77.

some of the horror of sexual assault (especially in the image of Tarquin pushing Lucrece down by her breasts), he doesn't dwell on the physical.

Shakespeare's presentation of the same scene is, again, disturbing. His Tarquin also starts his molestation at the breasts:

> His hand, as proud of such a dignity,
> Smoking with pride marched on to make his stand
> On her bare breast, the heart of all her land,
>   Whose ranks of blue veins as his hand did scale
>   Left their round turrets destitute and pale. (437–441)

Ovid's parallel passage describes an act of brutality and terror, but this one, while making the same claim, is erotic rather than violent, or rather eroticizes violence in such a way as to legitimize and incite a thrill-of-the-chase response. Greek rape stories produce what must have been for their original audience exciting and pleasurable chases principally by refusing to portray the necessary violence of rape, thereby blurring the distinction between it and consensual intercourse. The passage above follows its forbears in depersonalizing rape through the use of martial imagery, but it also takes the Greek method one step farther by portraying assault directly in terms of a familiar act of consensual sexual relations: a man erotically touching his lover's breast.[31]

More troubling yet, Tarquin's gagging of Lucrece is described as "Entomb-[ing] her outcry in her lips' sweet fold" (679). The separation of her lips by the gag suggests, of course, the penetration of her other "fold." Such a graphic metaphor invites the reader to visualize both the penetration itself and the place it occurs.[32] But describing it as "sweet" again draws away from the violence and hatred of rape and towards the appreciation of the lover's body in consensual sex. Such images (and I recognize that I am recreating them) legitimize rape in a particularly dishonest way, by portraying it simultaneously as evil and just like sex based on mutual desire. The preceding section of the story incites a thrill-of-the-chase response by showing us a woman being hunted down, but the allusions to the act itself allow the more comforting eroticism of desire for a willing partner's body. The pain and terror of the victim and the disturbing eroticism of sexual violence are both effaced when, at the last moment, Shakespeare portrays the

---

[31] Jed discusses a startling fourteenth-century Florentine version of Tarquin's hand on Lucrece's breast: *Chaste Thinking*, 42–43.

[32] See Kahn, "*Lucrece*," 149–50; Fineman, "Shakespeare's *Will*"; and Patterson, *Reading Between the Lines*, 303–4.

rape through imagery borrowed from consensual sexual relations. Thus much as with Tarquin's psychomachia, the use of consensual images allows us not to have to put in conflict the narrative pleasure of rape stories and our personal revulsion at the act itself.

A necessary adjunct of conflating consensual and forced sex is denying the object a voice, for had she one she would make clear the difference. Shakespeare's version of the story does provide Lucrece a voice: substantial speeches before and especially after the rape. In suddenly giving the victim a voice after a long introduction focused almost exclusively on the rapist, Shakespeare is following Ovid, not in his Lucrece story, but in various *Metamorphoses* rapes, especially "Tereus, Procne, and Philomela" (6.412–679).[33] That story, like Shakespeare's *Lucrece*, gives Philomela a voice just before and then after the rape. But again the differences are striking. First, Ovid's story avoids any images that conflate forced and consensual sex. The character of the voice is different as well. As Kahn has demonstrated, both of Lucrece's speeches are patriarchal in many senses, but especially in their passivity; both continually reinforce Lucrece's acceptance of the rightness of male power and of the inevitability of female victimization:[34]

> If, Collatine, thy honor lay in me,
> From me by strong assault it is bereft;
> My honey lost, and I, a drone-like bee,
> Have no perfection of my summer left,
> Bur robbed and ransacked by injurious theft.
> > In thy weak hive a wandering wasp hath crept,
> > And sucked the honey which thy chaste bee kept. (834–840)

Lucrece here self-objectifies herself as her husband's property, as a bee, and even merely as the beehive. In contrast, Ovid's Philomela responds to her rape by calling Tereus a barbarian and asserting that she will exact a revenge:

> If the gods
> Of heaven see these things, if deities
> still have some power, if my loss of honor
> does not mean all is lost, then you — someday —

---

[33] Newman, "'And let mild women to him lose their mildness'," 304–20; Maus, "Taking Tropes Seriously," 73.

[34] Kahn, "*Lucrece*," 152–57.

will pay. I'll cast aside my shame, proclaim
your crime. If that be possible for me,
I'll tell my tale where people crowd.

(*Metamorphoses*, 6.540–546)

By refusing to accept the passivity that Tereus demands and that is in rape
stories traditional, Philomela reorients our attention from Tereus's desire, which
is portrayed largely within the tradition, to the unmasculine, barbarian savagery
of his attack, which cuts against the tradition and makes Tereus seem weak and
irrational and Philomela strong and defiant. Shakespeare's Lucrece has neither of
these traits, and his Tarquin, while evil, is never made to seem weak. Tarquin's
conquest of a victim who is never allowed to be anything but a victim is ad-
vanced through many images of strength: he has a "dead-killing eye" (540) and
is a griffin holding a "white hind" under his "sharp claws" (543); and he is like
a "night-walking cat" holding in his paw a panting "weak mouse" (554–555).

Associating rape with strength and hence masculinity connects this story to
the oldest elements of the tradition. But even as this association is being made,
The Rape of Lucrece often asserts the wrongness of Tarquin's actions. This conflict makes reading the poem a disturbing process for me and probably for many
other men, for Shakespeare induces us to identify with Tarquin at the same time
we are repelled by him, and to wish he would make what is obviously the moral
choice even as we, like him, find exciting the long approach to his vicious assault. I am not arguing that the condemnations of the rape are insincere; the
poem genuinely and repeatedly denounces Tarquin and his actions. I do argue
that the narrative tradition through which *The Rape of Lucrece* and most rape stories before and since are told carries with it a different, much older, and much
more aggressively patriarchal message.[35]

It is worth noting in conclusion that Shakespeare soon developed more interest in subverting traditional forms, especially as they relate to the representation
of women. Had he not done so, it is hard to imagine that his plays would have
their present appeal, not just because the ideology he employs in *The Rape of Lucrece* is outdated, but because the traditional forms he uses to portray women are
so inherently limiting. Rosalind and Viola control the characters around them
rather than being controlled by them, and while both are described as chaste and
beautiful, these qualities are not the ones that motivate their characters. Whatever Shakespeare thought about women and their position in Elizabethan soci-

---

[35] For a different approach to the use of narrative traditions in Shakespeare's *Lucrece*,
see Hart, "Narratorial Strategies," 59–71.

ety, he certainly came to realize that portraying his heroines as passive, as victims, and as defined by their chastity could not produce interesting plays or the kind of female character for which he is now known. Shakespeare's Lucrece is given little to talk about but her body and its use by men. In contrast, whether it is using legal trickery to rescue a husband's best friend or steeling a husband to regicide, Shakespeare's later women do more than merely reinforce female sexual objectification. As a result the plots they appear in do so as well.

Michael Hall
Virginia Wesleyan College

Works Cited

Amiet, Pierre. *Art of the Ancient Near East*, trans. John Shepley and Claude Choquet. New York: Abrams, 1980.

Aristophanes. *Lysistrata*, trans. Nicholas Rudal. Chicago: Ivan R. Dee, 1991.

Baines, Barbara. "Effacing Rape in Early Modern Representation." *ELH* 65 (1998): 69–98.

Briscoe, John. "Livy." In *The Oxford Classical Dictionary*, eds. Simon Hornblower and Anthony Spawforth. Oxford: Oxford University Press, 1996, 878–79.

Cartmill, Matt. *A View to a Death in the Morning: Hunting and Nature Through History*. Cambridge, MA: Harvard University Press, 1993.

Cousins, A. D. "Subjectivity, exemplarity, and the establishing of characterization in *Lucrece*." *Studies in English Literature, 1500–1900* 38 (1998): 45–60.

Donaldson, Ian. *The Rapes of Lucretia: A Myth and Its Transformations*. Oxford: Clarendon Press, 1982.

Dubrow, Heather. *Captive Victors: Shakespeare's Narrative Poems and Sonnets*. Ithaca: Cornell University Press, 1987.

Ferril, Arthur. *The Origins of War: From the Stone Age to Alexander the Great*. London: Thames and Hudson, 1985.

Fineman, Joel. "Shakespeare's *Will*: The Temporality of Rape." *Representations* 20 (1987): 25–76.

Gantz, Timothy. *Early Greek Myth: A Guide to Literary and Artistic Sources*. Baltimore: Johns Hopkins University Press, 1993.

Hart, Jonathan. "Narratorial Strategies in *The Rape of Lucrece*." *Studies in English Literature, 1500–1900* 32 (1992): 59–77.

Herbert-Brown, Geraldine. *Ovid and the Fasti*. Oxford: Clarendon Press, 1994.

Jed, Stephanie. *Chaste Thinking: The Rape of Lucrece and the Birth of Humanism*. Bloomington: Indiana University Press, 1989.

Kahn, Coppélia. "*Lucrece*: The Sexual Politics of Subjectivity." In Lynn Higgins and Brenda Silver, eds., *Rape and Representation*, 141–59. New York: Columbia University Press, 1991.

Keeley, Lawrence H. *War Before Civilization*. New York: Oxford University Press, 1996.

Keuls, Eva. *The Reign of the Phallus: Sexual Politics in Ancient Athens*. New York: Harper and Row, 1985.

Kramer, Jerome, and Judith Kaminsky. "'These Contraries Such Unity Do Hold': Structure in *The Rape of Lucrece*." *Mosaic* 10 (1977): 143–55.

Kramer, Samuel Noah. *From the Poetry of Sumer: Creation, Glorification, Adoration*. Berkeley: University of California Press, 1979.

Lerner, Gerda. *The Creation of Patriarchy*. New York: Oxford University Press, 1976.

Livy. *The Early History of Rome*, trans. Aubrey de Sélincourt. New York: Penguin Classics, 1960.

Maus, Katherine Eisaman. "Taking Tropes Seriously: Language and Violence in Shakespeare's *Rape of Lucrece*." *Shakespeare Quarterly* 37 (1986): 66–82.

Mellaart, James. *Çatal Hüyük: A Neolithic Town in Anatolia*. New York: McGraw-Hill, 1967.

Mellars, Paul. "The Upper Palaeolithic Revolution." In *The Oxford Illustrated Prehistory of Europe*, ed. Barry Cunliffe, 70–75. New York: Oxford University Press, 1994.

Newman, Jane. "'And let mild women to him lose their mildness': Philomela, female violence, and Shakespeare's *The Rape of Lucrece*." *Shakespeare Quarterly* 45 (1994): 304–26.

Ovid. *Metamorphoses*, trans. Allen Mandelbaum. New York: Harcourt Brace, 1993.

———. *Fasti, trans.* Betty Rose Nagle. Indianapolis: Indiana University Press, 1995.

Patterson, Annabel. *Reading Between the Lines*. London: Routledge, 1993.

Shakespeare, William. *The Norton Shakespeare*, ed. Stephen Greenblatt *et al.* New York: Norton, 1997.

Tomascelli, Sylvana. "Introduction." In *Rape: An Historical and Social Enquiry*, ed. eadem and Roy Porter, 1–15. New York: Basil Blackwell, 1986.

Vickers, Nancy. "'The blazon of sweet beauty's best': Shakespeare's *Lucrece*." In *Shakespeare and the Question of Theory*, ed. Patricia Parker and Geoffrey Hartman, 95–115. New York: Methuen, 1985.

Wall, Wendy. *The Imprint of Gender: Authorship and Publication in the English Renaissance*. Ithaca: Cornell University Press, 1993.

Woodbridge, Linda. "Palisading the Elizabethan Body Politic." *Texas Studies in Language and Literature* 33 (1991): 327–54.

The First Captive:
The Kidnapping of Pocahontas

An engraving of Pocahontas, daughter of Powhatan, wife to John Rolfe, was produced by Simon van de Passe, and circulated in London in 1616 and 1617. This, no doubt, is the print that John Chamberlain sent to his friend Dudley Carleton in the Hague with the comment, "Here is a fine picture of no fayre Lady."[1] The print, the first example of Pocahontas ephemera which crested in the summer of 1995 in a wave of Pocahontas backpacks, balloons, napkins, pillows, nightgowns, cupcake tins, and plastic figurines tied in to the Disney animated feature, was produced in sufficient numbers that it survived. One copy was tipped into the original 1624 edition of John Smith's *Generall Historie of Virginia* and has provided the template for numerous subsequent reproductions.[2] The complex representation of the native American woman's body reveals strains in the enterprise of colonization. Unlike an ordinary portrait that memorializes favor and status,[3] the portrait must also signal a set of transformations: from heathen to Christian, from Indian to English, from princess to gentlewoman. In this essay I explore the disturbances figured in this representation and argue that the justifications asserting the success of the colony particularly embedded in the

---

[1] *Letters of John Chamberlain*, ed. McClure, 2:56–57.

[2] "Tipped in" is a bookbinder's term for material not sewn into the binding of the book, but glued in. The term usually signals an item originally alien to the book (Carter, *ABC for Book Collectors*, 192). The engraving probably served as model for the Booton Hall portrait, the nearest contemporary depiction of Pocahontas. One British Library copy of Smith's *Generall Historie* has two prints of Pocahontas, one a counterfeit engraving tipped in opposite the original. At some time, someone painted the dress in the original print red. For a contemporary rendering of the portrait, see the work of Mary Ellen Howe, widely disseminated in *Life* magazine (July 1995: 65).

[3] "Favour" is the term Nicholas Hilliard uses in *A Treatise Concerning the Art of Limning*, ed. Thornton and Cain, 58, to describe likeness and true proportion (58).

comedic narrative of conversion attempt to mask a narrative of kidnapping that by English law was defined as rape. The essay is titled "The First Captive" in echo of John Demos's *The Unredeemed Captive*, an elegant history of the capture of the seven-year-old Eunice Williams in 1704 from Deerfield, and in deliberate juxtaposition to the tradition of American studies which focuses on the captivity and redemption of whites who cross from the Anglo-American center to the native American margins.[4] I draw on Lynn Hunt's definition of history as the "ongoing tension between stories that have been told and stories that might be told"[5] to present an alternative narrative of kidnapping and coercion that destabilizes the triumphant claims asserted in the engraving.

Such an alternative narrative is made possible because the stories told about the capture of Pocahontas do not succeed in erasing the coercion involved in her capture. By setting the reports of the kidnapping and marriage of Pocahontas which are epitomized in the portrait within the context of English law, as explicated by T.E. in *The Lawes Resolutions of Womens Rights*, the illegality of her seizure becomes clear.[6] The Caroline publication in 1632 of T.E.'s Tudor compilation of case law not only underscores the contested understandings of legal terms, but also signals changes in the position of women that warranted publication of such a summary.[7] Even though martial law had been imposed on the colony, Tudor law would have relevance both for the colonists and for English readers of the reports publicizing the Virginia Company. Even by the martial laws of the settlement, ravishment was forbidden.[8] This essay focuses in particu-

---

[4] Demos, *The Unredeemed Captive*.

[5] "History as Gesture; or, The Scandal of History," in *Consequences of Theory*, ed. Jonathan Arac and Barbara Johnson (Baltimore: Johns Hopkins University Press, 1991), 103; cited in Montrose, *The Purpose of Playing: Shakespeare and the Cultural Politics of Elizabethan Theatre*, 4.

[6] The text, identified in the British Library catalogue as written by Thomas Edwards, and printed in London in 1632 with the running head *The Woman's Lawyer*, is a discussion of English case laws pertaining specifically to women. Organized around the conventional pattern of a woman's life, it traces a woman's legal status from virginity, to marriage, widowhood, remarriage, with attention to murder, revenge, and rape. W. R. Prest in "Law and Women's Rights in Early Modern England," tentatively identifies the final compiler as Thomas Edgar, of Gray's Inn.

[7] In this essay, I consider the difficulties surrounding the status of an exceptional woman. I place my work within the context of analyses such as Howard's *The Stage and Social Struggle in Early Modern England* and Bowen's "Amelia Lanier and the Invention of White Womanhood."

[8] See Strachey, *For the Colony in Virginea Britannia: Lawes Divine, Moral and Martiall, etc.*

lar on the stresses implicit in English judgment of the kidnapping of a woman of Pocahontas's rank.

The rule of English law in newly appropriated land was in dispute. To the English colonists involved in a ruthless struggle for possession, the application of English laws to the indigenous peoples of the Chesapeake Bay hardly obtained, particularly for colonists themselves barely governed by the brutal martial law of the Virginia Company council. Instructions to Sir Thomas Gates by the Virginia Company that urge him to "beget reverence to your authority, and to refresh their mindes that obey the gravity of those lawes under which they were borne"[9] suggest an intensification of standard Tudor and Stuart anxieties over the inculcation of obedience in subjects produced by their distance from the legal center. Supporters who wrote about the colony in the first decade of settlement insisted on ameliorating the brutal particulars of conquest and elevating the status of the participants and the struggle, embellishments which provoked further difficulties. Once the participants in the conflict were represented as subjects of a great nation, an emperor and his daughter, English rules of conduct, law, and national diplomacy became pertinent. The abduction of the princess of a nation, although in a territory technically outside English legal sway, then disturbingly fits English legal prohibitions about the abduction of women of property. T.E.'s discussion of the seizure of an heiress could be applied to the abduction of Pocahontas, whose "innocency and simplicity" were used to engineer her abduction.

Pocahontas is mentioned in John Smith's first pamphlet on the colony, printed in London in 1608, which describes her embassy on behalf of her father Powhatan[10] and her successful negotiation for the return of several captives taken. She then disappears from the record for several years until she is prominently featured in Ralph Hamor's pamphlet, *A True Discourse of the Present Estate of Virginia*, reporting the successful outcome of conflicts with Powhatan.[11]

---

[9] Kingsbury, ed., *Records of the Virginia Company of London* 3:15.

[10] Powhatan, the father of Pocahontas, took the name of his village when he became an Algonkian overlord. His name then was given to the association of a group of tribes that he formed (*Complete Works of Captain John Smith*, ed. Barbour, 1:xlvii; Bridenbaugh, *Jamestown 1544–1699*, 16).

[11] Ralph Hamor's *A True Discourse of the Present Estate of Virginia and the successe of the affaires there till the 18 of June. 1614.* is carefully prefaced with the announcement of the satisfactory outcome of her marriage to John Rolfe: "The Christening of *Powhatans* daughter and her mariage with an English-man" and is published with the groom's letter to Sir Thomas Dale explaining his marriage in April of 1614. The defense, printed in London in 1615 and sold by William Welby the year before Pocahontas's arrival in England, features several justifications for intermarriage.

The accounts of the kidnapping and marriage of Pocahontas bracket a year-long gap in which curiously little information is recorded. Where she lived, who supervised her, when she began to wear English dress, who taught her the catechism, and just how this "princess" was treated while in English hands remain obscure. The silence of the narratives covers the time when, by English law, the men who seized a woman of Pocahontas's alleged status would be subject to the law of *raptus*, a form of rape.

In the spring of 1613, as a stratagem to force her father to a truce, Pocahontas was lured onto an English ship for a meal and was then seized by Captain Argall. Her resistance to her capture is clear in Ralph Hamor's text. The abduction of a high-status woman against both her will and that of her father fits clearly within English prohibitions against the kidnapping of heiresses. While kidnapped and held by the English, she was forced to witness the burning of an Algonkian village. Toward the end of her year of captivity, she consented to baptism and accepted John Rolfe as her husband, their wedding serving the propagandists as triumphant evidence of the success of the colony.[12] The details of her capture, though scarce, are sufficient to expose the coercion involved in her detention and to cast a shadow over the freedom of her consent to baptism and marriage.

Two years after the wedding, Pocahontas and her English husband John Rolfe arrived at Plymouth on 3 June, 1616,[13] and made their way to London, where she was received by the Bishop of London at his palace and attended a masque at court, Ben Jonson's *Vision of Delight*. She was sponsored on her visit by the Virginia Company, which provided £4 weekly for her maintenance. Rolfe's purpose in London was to urge the virtues of colonization and the profits to be earned from tobacco. Pocahontas served as symbol and proof of Virginia Company promises of even worthier profits: the acquisition of new souls for the

---

[12] Kim Hall cites Michael Ragussis on the generic pattern of colonialist discourse: "Conversion, the master trope of this literary form [comedy], represents the institutionalisation — that is, the legitimisation of one group's mastery and absorption of another group. The triumph of one group over another is marked by a festival of incipient conjugals in which propagation and propaganda become one" ("Representation, Conversion, and Literary Form: *Harrington* and the Novel of Jewish Identity," *Critical Inquiry* 16 [1989]: 135, cited in Hall, *Things of Darkness*, 56).

[13] John Chamberlain on 22 June, 1616, reports her arrival in conjunction with the transport of commodities from Virginia: "Sir Thomas Dale is arrived from Virginia and brought with him some ten or twelve old and younge of that countrie, among whom the most remarquable person is Poca-huntas ... I heare not of any other riches or matter of worth, but only some quantitie of sassafras, tobacco, pitch, and clap-board" (*Letters*, ed. McClure, 2:12).

Protestant God. At some point on her visit, Simon van de Passe engraved the portrait, one of several that he executed of participants in the early colonization in Virginia: Sir Walter Ralegh, Captain John Smith, and Sir Thomas Smythe.[14] Baptism and translation are central to the narratives encapsulated in her portrait.

The engraving of Pocahontas is a standard half-length, turned slightly to the left. The Latin words in the lettered oval frame are translated in the four lines below. In Latin she is presented as "*Matoaka Al[ia]s Rebecca Filia Potentiss: Princ: Powhatani Imp: Virginiae.*" The English beneath amplifies and adjusts the Latin of the oval: "Matoaks al[ia]s Rebecka daughter to the mighty Prince Powhatan Emperour of Attanoughkomouck al[ia]s virginia converted and baptized in the Christian faith, and wife to the worth. Mr: Joh: Rolff." Unlike several other portraits by van de Passe, the portrait of Pocahontas relies on words and costume, unembellished by decorative pictures in the corners.[15] The frame is similarly unadorned, though Pocahontas, like Elizabeth of Bohemia, carries an ostrich feather fan in her right hand, the ostrich feathers a signal of royalty.[16]

---

[14] Van de Passe's younger brother, Willem, cut the engraving of Frances Howard, Duchess of Richmond and Lennox, who was the dedicatee of Smith's *Generall Historie*. Simon van de Passe's engraving of Ralegh was used as frontispiece to the third edition of Raleigh's *History of the World* (London, 1617), but there is no record of Ralegh sitting for van de Passe between his release from the Tower on 30 January 1616 and his departure for Guiana in April 1617. Legend persistently arranges a meeting between Ralegh and Pocahontas on her visit to London, but there are no records of such a meeting. Virginia Company supporters may have been reluctant to taint their advertising campaign with a meeting between their trophy and the still condemned traitor, Ralegh. Richard Martin, speaking on 17 May 1614 to the House of Commons urging support for the Virginia Company, called Ralegh "a subject of envy in his greatness, now a mirror of the vanity of all earthly things": Neill, *History of the Virginia Company of London*, 69.

[15] In some of his other English portraits, van de Passe signaled rank and profession not only through details of clothing and the use of names and titles, but also through the addition of descriptive scenes or details drawn in the lower corners. One of the most elaborate is the portrait of Sir Thomas Smyth, "late Embassador from his Majestie to the great Emperour of Russie, Governour of the honorable and famous Societyes of Marchants tradinge to the East Indies, Muscovy, the French and Somer Islands Company; Tresurer for Virginia." Thomas Smyth, to whom Ralph Hamor dedicated his report of the Virginia Colony, wears furs and holds a map. The portrait oval is bordered by a ship in the right-hand corner and a barrel, bale, and sack of gold coins in the left. John King, Bishop of London, wears clerical garb and is depicted before a view of the city of London and the Thames. Women, more difficult to identify through professional interests, at most hold identifying objects in their hands. Mary Sidney, Countess of Pembroke and translator of the Psalms, holds a book of verses; Princess Elizabeth carries an ostrich feather fan. These van de Passe prints are in the British Museum.

[16] The English princess and Virginian colonization were linked through the performance of George Chapman's wedding masque for Princess Elizabeth on 15 February

To demonstrate the comedic conclusion of the process of conversion, Pocahontas is depicted in European dress, for the exposure of the body in non-European clothing was proof of savagery;[17] she wears an elaborate lace collar, above a tightly buttoned bodice under a loose gown with prominent cuffed sleeves with closed tabs.[18] Unlike Uttamatomakkin, Powhatan's ambassador and Pocahontas's companion who traveled through England wearing the standard dress of the Eastern woodland native — a triangular hide, the hair of a *werowance* (chief) — and carrying a stick on which he attempted to count the number of Englishmen, until, overcome by numbers, he abandoned his task,[19] Matoaka (her secret tribal name) or Matoaks has been transformed into Rebecca, a gentlewoman who wears ordinary English clothing.[20] Uttamatomakkin remained a spectacle or wonder from another world, picked out by clothing as distinctive as the turban of a Persian, the fur hat of a Russian, or the red dress of a Venetian courtesan. Pocahontas's presentation in English costume offers a spectacle of another sort. When the savage wears European dress, civility has been achieved. When the heathen becomes a Christian, colonization is legitimized. The origin of the convert must nevertheless be registered in the portrait both to mark the process of change and to increase the marketability of the print. Van de Passe signals the heathen, Indian princess in two ways: through representation of the face and through reiteration of her birth. The strongly marked facial features of the picture, the overbite, and the cleft chin in conjunction with the dark eyes with the heavy eyebrows represent a face unlike those common in van de Passe's portraits of other court ladies of the time. Fair hair and pointed nose and chin emphasize

---

1613, which featured musicians costumed as Virginian priests and masquers dressed as Indians (Neill, *History of the Virginia Company of London*, 61–62).

[17] Alexander Whitaker reported, "They live naked in bodie, as if their shame of their sinne deserved no covering": *Good News from Virginia*, G2v.

[18] The gown most like this one is worn in a portrait of Mary Throckmorton, Lady Scudamore, painted in 1614–1615 by Marcus Gheeraerts the Younger. See Strong, *The English Icon*, Plate 279, 285. The prominent closed tabs on the cuff of the sleeve are unusual in portraits of women.

[19] John Smith records the story: "the King purposely sent him, as they say, to number the people here, and informe him well what wee were and our state. Arriving at Plimoth, according to his directions, he got a long sticke, whereon by notches hee did thinke to have kept the number of all the men hee could see, but he was quickly wearied of that taske": *Generall Historie*, in *Complete Works*, ed. Barbour, 3:261.

[20] Comments were made on her graceful manners, which suggest competent manipulation of her costume. Purchas, who met her in London, reports that she "did not only accustom her selfe to civilitie, but still carried her selfe as the daughter of a King" Purchas, *Hakluytus posthumus or Purchas his Pilgrimes*, 19:118.

MATOAKA ALS REBECCA FILIA POTENTISS · PRINC · POWHATANI IMP · VIRGINIÆ ·

Ætatis suæ 21. A̅.
1616

Matoaks als Rebecka daughter to the mighty Prince
Powhatan Emperour of Attanougskomouck als virginia
converted and baptized in the Christian faith, and
wife to the wor.ᵗᵗ Mr. Joh. Rolff.

Si: Paß: sculp: Compton Holland excud.

Engraving of Pocahontas.
Reproduced with the permission of The British Library.

delicacy in the English ladies.[21] The cross-hatching on Pocahontas's face may attempt to convey high cheekbones or perhaps darker skin tone.

Reiteration of her birth as daughter of the emperor of a great foreign nation creates a further contradiction. In an attribution of a European title to a New World leader, Powhatan is described as an emperor. The imposition of such categories clarifies and regularizes the societies new to Europeans. The impulse to tidy and rectify New World representations can be seen in De Bry's revision of John White's drawings of Indians, in which huts are arrayed on streets like idealized English villages.[22] Even the figures of dancers, although seemingly strange, are regularized and formalized into patterns similar to the dances of the grotesques in court masques or the dances of country folk. Such tendencies to filter New World experiences through the grids of European monarchy appear in John Smith's labeling of Powhatan dances as "masques."[23] Similarly, English commentators imposed the political stratification of their society on the Algonkians. The regularization of Pocahontas's status produces a contradiction that is embedded within the semiotics of the portrait itself. The representation of a foreign princess, a status reiterated in two languages, is confirmed by the ostrich feather fan[24] and the elaborate lace collar, but then made ambiguous by the modesty of her robe. For display to the English population, she does not wear court fashion — unlike van de Passe's other portraits of English aristocratic women — but rather wears a robe that in the print, without the embellishment of color, signals an ambiguous status. Although the fabric of her gown may be brocade and thus a mark of high rank, the extreme propriety of her dress, buttoned to the neck

---

[21] On comparison with the van de Passe portrait of Frances Howard, the eyes may be seen as similar, but the lower half of the face is unlike that of other English court women. Morphing could help this investigation. In my essay, "Pocahontas at the Masque," 560, I argue that racial difference is represented as gender difference. Given the unusually defined bone structure of the face, perhaps Uttamatomakkin sat as a model for the face print. His conversations with curious interlocutors in London are more fully documented than those of Pocahontas.

[22] Compare White's drawing of the Indian village of Secoton, Plate 36, with De Bry's print, Figure 24 in Hulton, *America 1585*. Karen Kupperman makes a similar point in *Roanoke: The Abandoned Colony*, 43. I am grateful to Elihu Pearlman, who first drew my attention to this representational tendency.

[23] See Robertson, "Pocahontas at the Masque" for a longer discussion of this process of infiltration.

[24] Feathers, frequently used to signal New World inhabitants, are confined in the portrait to her fan, the cockade, and perhaps the braid on her hat. For a consideration of gender and feathers later in the seventeenth century, see Ferguson, "Feathers and Flies."

and worn with the high-crowned hat,[25] could signal a woman of the middling sort — not a princess, not even a lady, but a burgher's wife.[26]

The decision to present Pocahontas in dress that suggests less exalted standing, though with high-status accessories, calls into question the meaning of her rank as a princess. The insistence on the imperial status of Pocahontas's father, Powhatan, emperor and mighty prince, is queried by the modesty of her clothing.[27] Furthermore, if she is indeed a princess, then her marriage to an English yeoman involves a loss of status. While elevation of her father's standing concomitantly elevates the successes of the Virginia plantation and amplifies the advertising brochures which promise untold riches to prospective planters, it destabilizes the fixity of the natural order of kingship. If one Englishman can go to the New World and there meet and marry a princess, others may have similar prospects. For an English man, status mobility may be available in foreign lands, Englishness abroad compensating for lesser rank. Yet the Indian princess has suffered a status injury. When an aristocratic woman marries down, her rank is disparaged, an issue of great interest in Jacobean tragedy.[28] Such a loss of status calls into question European notions of natural hierarchy. Conversion presents a further challenge to notions of natural hierarchy, for, if the savage can be educated, then civility and savagery may be the result of nurture, not birth. The failure to receive John Rolfe at court may signal an attempt to maintain distinctions of rank by welcoming a princess and effacing her humbler husband.[29]

The engraving's narrative of an Englishman's marriage to a foreign princess is

---

[25] The hat, though often worn in portraits of men, was a fashion also worn by women. For an example, see the hat worn by Joan Alleyn, the wife of Edward Alleyn (1596), in the Dulwich Picture Gallery portrait. See *Edward Alleyn: Elizabethan Actor, Jacobean Gentleman*, ed. Reid and Maniura, Fig. 4 (15).

[26] See Arnold, *Patterns of Fashion* for illustrations of the kneeling effigies of Magdalen, wife of Edward Lord Bruce of Kinloss in 1610 (Plate 65), and of Elizabeth Suckling in 1611 (Plate 67), 13.

[27] Contradictions in the print are regularized in paintings based on the engraving, when color is used to indicate gold thread and expensive fabric. Consider the decorative color and use of gold in Mary Ellen Howe's modern version of the picture.

[28] See, in particular, John Webster's *The Duchess of Malfi* (1613), 1.2.260–416. Disparagement was prohibited in the Court of Wards.

[29] There is no record that John Rolfe, a simple English gentleman, was received at court. His absence from Chamberlain's description is pointed. Pocahontas's companion Uttamatomakkin did attend the masque, but Rolfe was not noted at the event. His rank as country gentleman did not warrant participation at a court event for which spaces were limited; and furthermore, Rolfe's purpose as propagandist for the tobacco industry ran counter to James I's well-known distaste for tobacco (*Letters*, ed. McClure, 2:57).

a romance narrative used by the Virginia Company to mask the dreadful gamble with death in which any colonist engaged. Like many settlers, John Rolfe had suffered losses: his first wife and their daughter, Bermuda, born on and named after the island on which they were shipwrecked, had both died, Bermuda soon after her baptism. Settlers who survived the first two years of contact with New World malaria and agues, called seasoning, had also to combat casual violence, accident, and starvation.[30] The death rate for the colony in the bad winter of 1609–1610, called the starving time, reduced the population from five hundred and fifty to sixty.[31] The indigenous population suffered dismally on contact with European diseases, as well as from deliberate assault with superior European weapons. The engraving disguises the brutal violence of the early settlement. For one commentator, the imperial claims and costume rang false. John Chamberlain, so particular about rank and income, found her clothing in the portrait a sham: "[A]nd yet with her tricking up and high stile and titles you might thincke her and her worshipfull husband to be sombody."[32]

The imperial claims of the print were not ratified by Pocahontas's reception at the English court. In fact, her presence provoked a dilemma in court protocol and exposed contradictions in the logic of colonization. Factions at court were divided, some resisting colonization, some eager to challenge Spanish New World claims. Since James I was less interested in New World expansion and more eager to solidify his role as European peacemaker, he preferred to placate the Spanish. The representation of Powhatan as an emperor presented a further dilemma to the court, since that attributed national status to the land the English were violently appropriating. If Powhatan was a "mighty Prince," then English colonists were engaged in an invasion of national boundaries. Virginia Company advertising might insist on Pocahontas's imperial status, but English diplomatic protocol could not ratify that claim.[33] Although James I did seat

---

[30] Horn, *Adapting to a New World*, 138.

[31] The story of the husband who killed and salted and ate his wife's body during the starving time is a contested narrative. Leadership in the colony preferred to represent this as an act of domestic violence which the murderer tried to claim was starvation (Neill, *History of the Virginia Company of London*, 33). Smith, on the other hand, reports the incident with relish: "now whether shee was better roasted, boyled or carbonado'd, I know not, but of such a dish as powdered wife I never heard of" (*Generall Historie*, in *Complete Works*, ed. Barbour, 2:232–33). The story bolsters the superiority of his leadership, since the starving time began after he sailed for England.

[32] *Letters*, ed. McClure, 2:57.

[33] I am grateful to an anonymous reader for *Signs* who explained the diplomatic complexities involved in Pocahontas's status as daughter of an emperor.

Pocahontas well at a masque at court and did meet her advisor Uttamatomakkin, he failed to engage in an exchange of gift-giving which, from, Uttamatomakkin's point of view, entirely nullified James's royalty as well as exposing his contempt for the Powhatan delegation, for a king is known by the gifts that he gives. Smith reports that Uttamatomakkin "denied ever to have seene the King till by circumstances he was satisfied he had: Then he replyed very sadly, You gave Powhatan a white Dog, which Powhatan fed as himselfe, but your King gave me nothing, and I am better than your white Dog."[34]

Most prominently, the engraving trumpets the conversion of Pocahontas, a change confirmed by her new identity as the wife of an Englishman. Adult baptism and marriage are two religious ceremonies which assume consent of the subject, though the past participles, "converted and baptized," in the description below the van de Passe print hide the coercion central to the story. That story was told in a book published in London the year before her visit. Ralph Hamor in his *True Discourse* (1615) wrote an account of the colony which was less certain about the status of the Indian princess and more emphatic about the danger of the "salvages." Although Hamor attempts to construct the story of Pocahontas's conversion and marriage as a romance, he inadvertently exposes the dishonorable behavior of the English and their violation of decorum in contact with an Indian princess. By English protocol, the daughters of kings should be treated with immense respect and courtesy, not subject to coercion.[35] Hamor's Englishmen lack chivalry.

Telling that story of Pocahontas's long captivity presented a dilemma for the recorders of the colony. Publication of events in Virginia had been conceptualized as a crucial element in the colonizing project, as one of the earliest Virginia Company documents, "A Justification for Planting Virginia," explains: "that some forme of writing in way of Justification of our plantation might be conceived, and pass, (though not by publique authorytye) into many handes. ... First, that it mought give adventurers, a clearnes and satisfaction, for the Justice of the action, and so encourage them, and draw on others."[36] The early accounts of the settlement follow from this imperative for justification, yet inad-

---

[34] As in so many of Smith's reports of Indian reproaches to English lack of generosity in the *Generall Historie*, Smith may be using the Indian figures to ventriloquize his own resentments (*Complete Works*, ed. Barbour, 2:261).

[35] Contrast the chivalric gesture of Christian of Brunswick who mounted Elizabeth of Bohemia's glove on his helmet and vowed never to lay down arms until she was restored to her throne in Strickland, *Lives of the Queens of Scotland*, 8:125.

[36] Records of the Virginia Company, ed. Kingsbury, 3:1.

vertently expose the enormous stresses of survival, particularly conflicts over food.[37] To encourage further settlement, individual and group behavior must be clarified as both honorable and successful. While the story of her conversion, so central to the colonial prospectus, seems a lost opportunity, it does not fit comfortably into the romance in which Hamor attempts to contain the disturbing particulars of New World settlement. Romance becomes the defining trope for Pocahontas's story because her marriage to John Rolfe handily serves as a metonym for the union of England and Virginia and might possibly appeal to women readers whose participation in the colony as brides was desperately required.[38]

Romance itself is a tricky narrative form, however, since violence and coercion compose its elements. The liminal gap between the seizure and subsequent marriage of a real woman is an interlude when a judicial discourse of *raptus* could describe her. Rape and marriage, closely intertwined, both pivot on consent, the woman's word legitimizing or criminalizing sexual intercourse.[39] The laws of the colony prohibit ravishment — "No man shall ravish or force any woman, maid or Indian, or other, upon pain of death" — a prohibition promulgated within the context of other sexual crimes, sodomy, adultery, and fornication.[40] Yet, within the period, ravishment, like sodomy and even adultery, was a contested term. In Jacobean England the word "rape" signaled both forced coitus and seizure, and legally the concepts were fused. T. E. in *The Lawes Resolution of Women's Rights* attempts to distinguish two categories of crime, *raptus* and *stuprum*, by returning to the Latin derivations of the two terms. For "ravish-

---

[37] Justification provides access to the conflicts, particularly the pressure over food. For example, Wingfield attacks Smith who "in the tyme of our hungar, had spread a rumor in the Collony, that I did feast myself and my servants out of the common stoare. . . . I tould him privately in Mr. Gosnold's tent that indeede I had caused half a pint of pease to be sodden with a peese of pork, of my own provision for a poore old man which in a sickness, whereof he died, he much desired" (Neill, *History of the Virginia Company of London*, 21).

[38] Linton's *The Romance of the New World* is a rich study of the generic interplay between romance and colonial narratives.

[39] For an eloquent examination of this feminist insight, see Elizabeth Robertson's "Public Bodies and Psychic Domains." It is difficult to acknowledge fully the extent of intellectual indebtedness. My awareness of the significance of consent within marriage is the result of long conversations with my sister while discussing her work on female consent in Chaucer. Those conversations alerted me to the significance of Pocahontas's protest when she is trapped, and thus led me to the legal significance of kidnapping and its connection to rape.

[40] Trachey, *Lawes*, 5. Ravishment is the term which appears frequently in seventeenth-century court records in New England. See Norton, *Founding Mothers and Fathers*, 347–57.

ment," the term that seems closest to modern understandings of rape, he substitutes the word *stuprum*, in reference to a crime he abhors. Although he begins firmly, his explanation becomes entangled in the linguistic difficulties he himself is attempting to clarify:

> There are two kindes of Rape, of which though the one be called by the common people, and by the Law itselfe, Ravishment; yet in my conceit it borroweth the name from *rapere*, but unproperly, for it is no more but *Species stupri*, a hideous hatefull kinde of whoredome in him which committeth it, when a woman is enforced violently to sustaine the furie of brutish concupiscence: but she is left where she is found, as in her owne house or bed, as *Lucrece* was, and not hurried away, as *Helen* by *Paris*, or as the Sabine women were by the Romans, for that is both by nature of the word, and definition of the matter. (*Lawes Resolution*, 377–378)

Adjudication of rape, then and now, poses numerous problems, in particular because legal systems have amplified masculine attitudes — most recently applying masculine standards of resistance to aggression — while failing to investigate the problematics of female consent to heterosexual intercourse.[41] For T.E. the definition of rape turns not on the matter of violent sexual enforcement, but on the location of the woman, "hurried away" rather than left where she is found. He slides from the violation of the woman to the injury to the guardians. Yet T.E.'s own example of Helen, a notoriously puzzling figure, makes manifest the issue of consent.[42] Such difficulties in the discernment of consent mark one of the extraordinary provisions of English rape law in the early seventeenth century: that the death penalties for ravishment could be rescinded should the rape victim subsequently marry her rapist. (See Karen Bamford's essay in this volume.)[43] That provision retrospectively erases a felony and demonstrates the way in which rape law was bound to property law, inheritance, and marriage, rather than simple concern for violation of the woman's person.[44]

---

[41] For examination of the problem of consent in modern American rape law, see Estrich, *Real Rape*.

[42] For discussion of this problem as it surfaces in medieval literature, see E. Jane Burns, *Bodytalk* esp. 1–23 and Robertson, "Public Bodies."

[43] Gossett, " 'Man-maid, Begone!': Women in Masques" is the early exploration of this question.

[44] I recognize that rape has consistently formed one aspect of military pacification of enemy populations, yet defenses of soldiers tend to occlude the rapes performed by one's own men. Brownmiller's early feminist study of rape, *Against Our Will* begins with a long analysis of the link between rape and war. The connection between war and rape manifest

T.E. uses a philological argument to support his endeavor to confine concupiscence and sexual violation to the term *stuprum*, arguing that "rape," because etymologically connected to *rapere*, must necessarily involve a component of abduction or seizure. Confirmation of popular awareness and promulgation of the distinction is demonstrated in Shakespeare's *Titus Andronicus*, when Lavinia painfully writes the accusation of her violators and names the crime "*stuprum*."[45] For T.E., *raptus* is a crime of abduction which interferes in paternal adjudication of property and inheritance. "The second and right ravishment, *Cum quis honestae famae foeminam, sive virgo, sive vidua, sive sanctimonialis sit invitis illis in quorum est potestate, abducit. Neque refert, an quis (volente vel nolente rapta) id faciat, nam vis quae Parentibus vel Curatoribus sit, maxime spectat.*" [When anyone carries off a woman of good fame, either an unmarried maid, a widow, or a religious woman, against the will of those to whom that power belongs. Nor is it allowed (whether she is willing or unwilling that he do this) for the violent act which occurs belongs to the kin or guardians.][46] T.E. divides the definition of ravishment, limiting rape to describe women carried away, a distinction not recognized in modern terms, nor even in some sixteenth-century popular understandings.

Unfortunately the clarity of T.E.'s etymological distinction is confounded by English verbal practice, for "rape," not *stuprum*, entered the English language. T.E. himself becomes entangled in translation difficulties: "it seemeth the first kinde of rape [*stuprum*] deserved alwayes death by Gods Lawes." T.E. mitigates the abhorrence directed at *stuprum* by adding the proviso that the felon might avoid death for rape if "the woman ravished were unbetrothed, so that the ravisher might marrie her, as you may read *Deuteronomy, chap. 22, vers 23*" (378).[47] This proviso casts a complicated light on just what hateful act is embedded in

---

in the west since the story of the Sabine women has recently been confirmed by the inclusion of rape in war as a human rights abuse. See also its inclusion in the *Platform for Action at the Fourth World Conference on Women in Beijing*: "Women often are also victims of torture, disappearance and systematic rape as a weapon of war" (Point 5, Platform for Action: Critical Areas of Concern"). In 2001, systematic rape of women was declared a crime against humanity.

[45] Shakespeare, *Titus Andronicus*, 4.2.78, in the Arden Shakespeare, 3rd edition, edited Jonathan Bate. Compare, in this volume, Carolyn Sale on *stuprum* in *Titus Andronicus*.

[46] I thank Margaret Fusco for assistance with this translation.

[47] *Deuteronomy*: "If a man finde a maide that is not betrothed, and take her, and lye with her, & they be founde, Then the man that lay with her, shal give unto the maides father fifty shekels of silver: and she shal be his wife, because he hathe humbled her: he can not put her away all his life" (*Geneva Bible*, Deuteronomy 22: 28–29).

either *stuprum* or *raptus*, for in sixteenth-century English law the violation and coercion of the female victim is of less import than the violation of paternal consent and inheritance.

When the facts of Pocahontas's capture are set within the context of English law, the actions of Captain Samuel Argall and Sir Thomas Dale could be judged as legally suspect, a dilemma narratively resolved by her marriage to John Rolfe. (By a strict reading of English law, she would have had to resolve the *raptus* by marriage to her kidnapper, Samuel Argall). The two texts recounting her capture, Ralph Hamor's report of the colony and John Rolfe's letter explaining his reasons for wedding a savage, are bound together in one volume. Ralph Hamor's comedic history concludes an account of military maneuvers and the manipulation of a hostage with the description of a wedding. John Rolfe's letter justifying his marriage tells of his heroic religious investigation of the erotic attractions of the savage. Ralph Hamor, a secretary to the colony, is justifying settlement in general. John Rolfe is justifying his erotic contact with a heathen woman as legitimized through her baptism and then marriage. Neither narrative is particularly concerned with the consent of the bride. When the two accounts are combined into a sequence that considers the agency of the bride, some insight into the circumstances under which Pocahontas consented to marriage can be gained.

Ralph Hamor's narrative places romance in the foreground. Beginning in war, the narrative moves toward two weddings, one achieved, and one proposed, with descriptions and praises of the land and the settlement threaded through the story. Two rulers are contrasted: Powhatan is presented as a tyrant, Sir Thomas Dale as a benevolent ruler (Hamor, *A True Discourse*, 27). Two courtships punctuate Hamor's account: the marriage of Pocahontas and John Rolfe, and the proposed marriage between Sir Thomas Dale and a second daughter of Powhatan, a sister of Pocahontas younger than twelve. The meaning and status of the marriages are uncertain. Pocahontas's marriage occurs as the result of kidnapping. The second marriage is proposed in the context of sale and bribery.[48] From the English point of view the marriages are used to effect a peace in the feud be-

---

[48] Hamor's suit begins with the presents sent by Dale, "by me sent you a worthie present, vid. two large peeces of copper, five strings of white and blew beades, five wodden combes, ten fish-hookes, and a paire of knives" and the promise of a a grinding stone (Hamor, *A True Discourse* 40). While an ambassador customarily offers gifts, the word 'sale' is used within this context. Powhatan replies that he cannot satisfy Dale's request because he has recently "sould within these few daies to be wife to a great *Weroance* for two bushels of *Roanoake* (a small kinde of beades) made of oystershels" (Hamor, *A True Discourse*, 41).

tween the English and the Powhatans,[49] an attitude seemingly shared by Powhatan himself. The desires and consent of the daughters hardly marks the texts. Despite Hamor's attempts to justify and legitimize the actions of the English, Pocahontas is shown in Hamor's narrative as manipulated by English force.

In recounting the kidnapping, Hamor projects blame onto the Indian agents, Iapazeus and his wife, used to lure Pocahontas onto Captain Argall's ship. In Hamor's account the Indian wife bears the narrative burden of cupidity and deceit. He attributes her skillful counterfeiting to essential feminine qualities, "which sex have ever bin most powerfull in beguiling inticements." As is common in misogynist discourse, the essentializing of femininity also universalizes women. That collapse of all distinctions among members of the group further situates Pocahontas within the bounds of English law.[50]

Pocahontas's seizure is framed within details suggestive of a sexual encounter. She is lured "to a merry banquet" on board the ship by her faithless companions, whose joy is amplified by their success: "[M]erry on all hands, especially *Iapazeus* and his wife, who to expres their joy would ere be treading upon Capt. Argals foot, as who should say tis don, she is your own" (*A True Discourse*, 5). The procurers then convince the maiden to withdraw to an inner room. Lulled to sleep, she wakes full of fear. These elements of betrayal, isolation, sleep, and fear are narrative details well suited to a story of rape.

After she wakes, Pocahontas's request to leave the ship is denied. Argall explains to her:

> that for divers considerations, as for that his father had then eigh [eight] of our English men, many swords, peeces, and other tooles, which he had at severall times by trecherons [treacherous] murdering our men, taken from them which though of no use to him, he would not redeliver, he would reserve Pocahuntas. (*A True Discourse*, 5)

Pocahontas became "exceeding pensive, and discontented" when she understood that she had been betrayed (6). "Much a doe there was to perswade her to be patient, which with extraordinary curteous usage, by little and little was wrought in

---

[49] The exchange of daughters to cement alliances was common practice in Europe as well. Compare James I's attempts to arrange the marriage of his son Charles with the Infanta of Spain. For an anthropological discussion of the use of women to effect peace in a feud, see Black-Michaud, *Cohesive Force*, 92–93, no. 1.

[50] I am grateful for Linda Woodbridge for her insights into this passage, and for her scrupulous editorial care.

her, and so to James towne she was brought" (*A True Discourse*, 6). "Much ado"
reveals the resistance of the captive despite the defensive claim of "extraordinary
curteous usage." However Hamor attempts to modulate the story, the English
captain is revealed as one who violates the honor of hospitality to capture a
woman and hold her by force. Captain Argall's explanation to his prisoner, describing his act as hostage-taking within the context of a formal war, attempts to
obscure that alternative story of *raptus*.

Ostensibly, English rape law had been formulated to prevent any sort of rape
at all. When T.E. traces the long English condemnation of both *raptus* and *stuprum*, from Bracton through the first and second statutes of Westminster, he
mentions the significance of the felony against the persons of all women. The
moderation of penalties for rape in the first statute of Westminster "in a few
yeeres brought forth so many enormities, That at the next Parliament, which
King *Edw.* held ten yeeres after" (*Lawes Resolutions*, 381) the former punishment
of death and loss of member were reinstituted. Contemplating this ferocity of
punishment, T.E. observes, "A Man would have thought, that this Statute
should have repressed for ever, all violence towards the persons of women" (381).
Despite this stated concern for the "persons of women," for T.E. *raptus* pertains
only to women connected to property. In T.E.'s view, because the crime is ad-
judicated by the measure of goods attached to the person of the woman, *raptus*
should be understood less as a sin of concupiscence and more one of avarice.
"And now comes in the second rape by abduction, wherein avarice is as great an
agent as carnality, and something wiser in avoiding of danger, now men turned
themselves for loves sake into Centaures first, and tooke on them the shape of
Buls afterward" (383). The law of *raptus*, reiterated in the thirty-first year of the
reign of Henry VI, significantly legislated at a time of civil war which was destabilizing the conventional structures supporting paternal and familial control of
women, is construed as a law devised to protect women from false seducers. T.E.
explains the necessity of protecting naïve women:

> [D]ivers people of power, moved by insatiable covetousnesse, against all
> right and gentlenesse, had found new inventions, to the danger, trouble,
> and evill intreatings of Ladies, Gentlewomen, and other women sole,
> having substance of land, tenements, or moveable goods, perceiving their
> great innocency and simplicity, willing to take them by force, or other-
> wise come to them, seeming to be their great friends, promising them
> their faithfull loves, and so by great dissimulation, they caught them into
> their possession, conveying them into places where the Offenders were of
> power. (383)

When this definition of rape, emphasizing the significance of property, is applied to Ralph Hamor's account, several questions arise. Certainly "innocency and simplicity" mark her willingness to accept hospitality. She is betrayed, "caught in their possession" through the "great dissimulation" of Iapazeus and his wife, who themselves are motivated by desire for reward — primarily a copper kettle. Captain Argall says that he is holding Pocahontas hostage in exchange for tools, weapons, and men. Just how the English viewed the property claims of Pocahontas as her father's daughter is not entirely clear. Avarice certainly marked the designs of some English in the New World, although English views of the inheritance status of an Indian princess are difficult to assess and Pocahontas's dowry obscure. The recent reign of Elizabeth I clearly demonstrated the importance of a ruler's daughter, as did the claims, though distant, to the English throne of the Infanta of Spain,[51] even though, by Powhatan practice of matrilineal descent, Pocahontas had no claim to her father's kingdom and would not inherit from her father's clan. The extent to which that matrilineal descent pattern was understood in England is unclear.[52] The advertising on the portrait elevates her to a standing comparable to that of Princess Elizabeth, the daughter of James I, who had herself recently become a "foreign" princess.[53] In 1705, Robert Beverley claimed that questions were raised in the Privy Council about John Rolfe's violation of royal prerogative. "In Body, so much that the poor Gentleman her Husband had like to have been call'd to an Account for presuming to marry a Princess Royal without the King's Consent; because it had been suggested that he [Rolfe] had taken Advantage of her being a Prisoner, and forc'd her to marry him."[54] This retrospective story suggests the fluidity of English understandings of Pocahontas's legal position. It appears that some did see

---

[51] Contemporary English pressure against female heirs suggests common beliefs in gender inequity. Compare, for example, Anne Clifford's lengthy struggle against her uncle to inherit her family property (*Diaries of Anne Clifford*, ed. Clifford, 59, 76, 88, 92).

[52] Matrilineal descent was vaguely understood by the early settlers. See John Smith's explanation in *A True Relation*: "For the Crowne, their heyres inherit not, but the first heyres of the Sisters, and so successively the weomens heires: For the Kings have as many weomen as they will, his Subjects two, and most but one" (*Complete Works*, ed. Barbour, 3:61).

[53] In English terms, the daughter of an emperor would command a dowry. The marriage of the Princess Elizabeth to the Elector Palatine, a spectacle fresh in English memory, had cost her father £93,000, including a dowry of £40,000: Akrigg, *Jacobean Pageant*, 156.

[54] Beverley, *History and Present State of Virginia* (1705), cited in Tilton, *Pocahontas*, 16. Tilton's discussion centers on the issues of intermarriage featured in that passage. For intermarriage, see also Hulme, *Colonial Encounters*, 142–47.

Pocahontas as a potential heiress, thus precipitating greater gravity in judgment of her kidnapping.

In Hamor's account the duplicity and veiled threats of Captain Argall precede more violent evidence of English intentions. Captain Argall claimed that she had been taken hostage to force Powhatan to a treaty. When, three months after her capture, Powhatan returned seven English hostages with several unserviceable muskets and offered 500 bushels of corn for the return of his daughter, the transaction was refused by the English, with a veiled threat to her safety encased in a reminder of her status as hostage: "his daughter was very well, and kindely intreated, and so should be howsoever he dealt with us" (*A True Discourse*, 6). The violence escalated. In March, after nearly a year in captivity, Pocahontas was carried by ship toward Powhatan's camp, Werowocomoco. Hamor reports the English "carried with us his daughter, either to move them to fight for her, if such were their courage and boldnesse, as hath been reported, or to restore the residue of our demands, which were our peeces, swords, tooles" (7). When the offer was rejected, the English killed five or six men and burned and pillaged the encampment, a violence witnessed by Pocahontas. These experiences of violence expose the coercion underpinning both her conversion and marriage. Like his daughter's, Powhatan's consent is precipitated by the violent intrusion of the English into his territory: "The bruite of this pretended marriage came soone to *Powhatans* knowledge, a thing acceptable to him, as appeared by his sudden consent thereunto" (11). A continuing suspicion of English motives marks Powhatan's behavior. He sends his sons to see their sister "whom they suspected to be worse intreated, though they had often heard the contrary" (10). Her marriage soon followed the English show of force.[55]

As I noted earlier, except for these details of her manipulation as hostage and lure, there are few details of the circumstances in which Pocahontas was held. Where she lived, who supervised her, and what household trained her in English costume and English manners is not recorded. Alexander Whitaker, minister to the colony, attributes her lessons in Christian catechism to Governor Dale, who "labored mightily in her conversion" (*Good News*) while Dale compliments Whitaker. What women supervised her during her captivity remain unnamed.[56] She

---

[55] Consider Shakespeare's depiction of the choices available to Cressida in the Greek camp, *Troilus and Cressida*, 4.5. and 5.2.107–112. See also Linton who uses the inconstancy topos constructed in *Troilus and Cressida* to read colonial narratives, *Romance of the New World*, 131–43.

[56] The first gentlewoman to arrive in the colony, Mistress Forrest, and her servant, Anne Burras, are featured in the story of the first marriage in the colony, when Anne

enters baptism and marriage accompanied by unnamed women. Her romance with Rolfe is mentioned by Hamor within the context of tobacco cultivation, in a sentence beginning with a commendation to Rolfe for his labors for the colony, particularly in testing the virtues of West Indian tobacco and ending with praise for the gesture of his marriage to Pocahontas, "one of rude education, manners barbarous and cursed generation, meerely for the good and honour of the Plantation" (*A True Discourse*, 24).

Hamor's words are an echo of the description that John Rolfe makes of his bride, "one whose education hath bin rude, her manners barbarous, her generation accursed, and so discrepant in all nurtriture from my selfe"(64).[57] When John Rolfe sets out to explain his decision to marry, he makes no mention of the kidnapping of his wife, deftly splitting her seizure from his wedding. Rolfe, caught in the tangle of presenting his "unspotted soul," justifying his own desires, and affirming his righteousness, is silent on the material circumstances of her captivity. In his letter, his beloved curiously collapses into the diabolical and angelic tempters he describes pulling at his ear. She enters her husband's letter as "an unbelieving creature" (63) who precipitates an extraordinary conflict in his soul. He describes his feelings for this creature in terms that transform him into a Theseus trapped in a labyrinth or a man entangled in a spider's web: "To whom my hartie and best thoughts are, and have a long time bin so intangled, and inthralled in so intricate a laborinth, that I was even awearied to unwinde my selfe thereout" (63). The following paragraphs trace the hero's struggle to wind his way out of the labyrinth, unassisted by Theseus' companion, Ariadne.[58] Frailty, evil propensities, indulgence, and God's displeasure as well as other "inconveniences" lead him to judge his desires diabolical. That resolution is then tested by a voice "pulling me by the eare, and crying: why dost not thou indevour to make her a Christian?" Rolfe finds evidence of God's work in his preoccupation with Pocahontas: "even when she hath bin furthest seperated from me, which in common reason (were it not an undoubted worke of God) might

---

Burras married John Laydon in 1608 (Smith, *Generall Historie*, in *Complete Works*, ed. Barbour, 2:192). Sir Thomas Dale had married Elizabeth Throckmorton, but she seemed not to have followed him to the colony (Barbour, *Pocahontas and Her World*, 153). Women as well as men died in starving time. See the mention of the wife eaten by her husband (above, note 31).

[57] A copy of John Rolfe's letter to Sir Thomas Dale was printed at the end of the Hamor's *True Discourse*, 61–68.

[58] See Linton, *Romance of the New World* for an extensive discussion of the "labyrinth of racial fears" (176).

breede forgetfulnesse of a farre more worthie creature" (65). The voice pulling by the ear, waking him in his sleep, oddly collapses into the woman herself who also provides powerful inducements: "adding hereunto her great apparance of love to me, her desire to be taught and instructed in the knowledge of God, her capablenesse of understanding, her aptnesse and willingnesse to receive anie good impression, and also the spirituall, besides her own incitements stirring me up hereunto" (65–66). Rolfe, describing a kidnapped hostage moved back and forth as a lure in war, witness in Hamor's text to the murder of tribesmen and the burning of villages, represents Pocahontas as the aggressor and agent of seduction, inverting his actions as colonizer in her country as passive, and vesting desire in the woman, who acts at God's behest.

While Pocahontas's motives and agency are scanted in Hamor and Rolfe's texts, John Smith in 1624 retrospectively attributes the motive of love to Pocahontas: "Long before this, Master John Rolfe, an honest Gentleman, and of good behavour, had been in love with Pocahontas, and she with him" (*Generall Historie*, in *Complete Works*, ed. Barbour, 2: 245). A more particular description of Pocahontas's reaction to captivity and the negotiations over her release is provided by Sir Thomas Dale in his letter describing the scene when Pocahontas is carried to her father's camp as a hostage and witnesses the killing of several Indians. She "would not talke to any of them, scarce to them of the best sort, and to them onely, that if her father had loved her, he would not value her lesse then olde swords, peeces, or axes: wherefore she would stil dwel with the English men, who loved her."[59] This scene puts some pressure on the casual use of the word "love." Abandoned by her father, and weighed against the value of metal tools and weapons, Pocahontas acknowledges her isolation and her limited agency.[60] Although Mary Murray's arguments against too easy an evaluation of women simply as property are telling, this scene demonstrates the close approximation of the two, while allowing the woman to voice outrage at her position.[61]

---

[59] *Purchase His Pilgrimes*, 19:104.

[60] The pleas of Elizabeth of Bohemia to her father for assistance at the inception of the Thirty Years War provides an intriguing counterpoint to Powhatan's concern for his daughter. Elizabeth wrote asking Buckingham to persuade her father to help her husband: Plowden, *The Stuart Princesses*, 34.

[61] This question has recently been addressed by Murray, *The Law of the Father?*. Murray contests the feminist view that sees women in the Renaissance simply as property. See in particular Chapter 7, "Women as Property." Her argument provides more precise texture to feminist analyses of legal history. The problem is, as Elizabeth Robertson shows in her analysis of Criseyde in "Public Bodies," that women are slippery, linked to property, at times treated like property, but granted legal status in courts of law, able to

Dale's account, in which Powhatan is upbraided for his failures of paternal love, actually inverts the reality of the situation and elides Powhatan's return of English hostages. The English certainly estimated metal tools and weapons as more valuable than a woman or bargains with heathens. They had kidnapped her and manipulated her to achieve the return of hostages, and then kept her to force the return of tools. Anxiety over the safety of his daughter led Powhatan to agree to a peace treaty: weapons, tools, and men were returned and a truce ensued. (One could call that metal her dowry.) Pocahontas and John Rolfe married around 5 April 1614.

The exchange of women to cement peace in the feud is emphasized as conventional Powhatan practice. Hamor, in his defense of Rolfe, inadvertently exposes the gossip and backbiting that marked the colony, energetic movements of the tongue and pen that coexisted with the desperate exertions for survival:

> the rather to give testimony to the misconstruing and ill censuring multitude of his integritie, in the undertaking a matter of so great a consequent, who in my hearing have not spared to speak their pleasures; his owne letter hits them home, and the better sort, who know to censure judiciously cannot but highly commend and approve so worthy an undertaking. (*A True Discourse*, 25)

Despite Hamor's evaluation of the dubious nature of the bride, marriage between the Englishman and one Powhatan princess was sufficiently successful to lead Sir Thomas Dale to employ Hamor as ambassador seeking a second Powhatan daughter as a bride. The story of this courtship, one that came to nothing, seems included in the text for two reasons: first, because Ralph Hamor was used as ambassador, he can recount his own heroic confrontation with the Indian emperor; second, this courtship can substitute for the uncivil courtship of Pocahontas. Hamor set out on 15 May to seek from Powhatan another bride, a suit conducted this time with formal propriety. He is an exemplary ambassador, filled with compliment:

> The bruite of the exquisite perfection of your yongest daughter, being famous through all your territories, hath come to the hearing of your Brother Sir *Thomas Dale*, who for this purpose hath addressed me hither, to intreate you by that brotherly friendship you make profession of, to

---

hold property, buy wardships, and write wills. Consider, though, Hamor's description of the marriage transaction for Powhatan's younger daughter as a sale (*A True Discourse*, 7), cited above, note 48.

permit her (with me) to returne unto him, partly for the desire which himselfe hath, and partly for the desire her sister hath to see her of whom, if fame hath not bin prodigall, as like enough it hath not, your brother (by your favour) would gadly [gladly] make his neerest companion, wife and bedfellow ... and the reason hereof is, because being now friendly and firmely united together, and made one people (as he supposeth and beleeves) in the band of love, he would make a naturall union betweene us, principally because himselfe hath taken resolution to dwel in your country so long as he liveth, and would therefore not only have the firmest assurance hee may, of perpetuall friendship from you, but also hereby binde himself thereunto. (*A True Discourse*, 40–41)

Hamor ignored Powhatan's numerous attempts to interrupt him, only to discover that the marriage offer could not be accepted, because the girl had been granted to a warrior for "two bushels of *Roanoak* [oystershell beads]" (41). Sir Thomas Dale's wife, living in England at the time, seems not to have constituted an impediment to this marriage proposal.

Powhatan, urged to renege on the bargain made with a warrior and redistribute his daughter, refused. For the English, the daughters of Powhatan are clearly being sought as tokens of peace in the feud. Powhatan's recognition of the political negotiation and meaning is clear. His wariness about kinship with the English is exposed in his refusal to attend Pocahontas's wedding, though he did send two of his sons. The fears and anxieties of the father and the loss he incurs by the marriage of his daughters to English men are revealed by Hamor: "his answere hereunto was, that he loved his daughter as deere as his owne life, and though he had many Children, he delighted in none so much as in her, whom if he should not often beholde, he could not possibly live, which she living with us he knew he could not, having with himselfe resolved upon no termes whatsoever to put himselfe into our hands, or come amongst us" (*A True Discourse*, 42).

This analysis of the narrative dilemmas faced by Hamor reveals the uneasy fit of a romance structure on the particulars of colonization. When a real princess is forcibly held in a camp, her captors transmute from chivalrous knights to men subject to English law. During the time Pocahontas was held against her will in the Jamestown settlement, English legal discourses could describe her as a victim of rape. In T.E.'s analysis, English rape law would have judged not only Captain Argall but also Sir Thomas Dale, the leader of the colony, and Alexander Whitaker, the minister, of complicity in rape: "that whosoever taketh against her will unlawfully, any maid, widdow, or wife, shall together with the procurers, abbetters, and receivers of any such women (knowing her to bee so taken against

her will) bee felons, and every of them beene reputed and judged as felons principall" (*Lawes Resolutions*, 384).

That odd provision in English law, that the marriage of a rape victim to her
kidnappers retrospectively clears her captors of participation in a felony, prolepti-
cally serves as a model for the larger erasures performed by Pocahontas's marriage to John Rolfe in April 1614. Her marriage triumphantly effaces any criminal taint from the colonists for their seizure of land from the ruler of another
nation. Whatever the discursive claims made for the London market, however,
Powhatan remained wary. Sending his sons to check on her treatment and her
consent, he refused to attend the wedding.

One further elision marks this colonial romance. Powhatan marriage customs,
as reported by English colonists, seemed to grant greater sexual agency to
women than was customary for English women. Helen Rountree in her historical ethnography of the Powhatans summarizes the practices from the point of
view of the groom. He would seek a girl, marriageable at puberty, through negotiations of bridewealth. She would then move to her husband's village. Polygyny
was practiced. Divorce was available for men, and possibly for women. "Considerable sexual freedom was permitted to both sexes outside marriage."[62]

English accounts are vague about the age of Pocahontas, her age at the time
of her marriage being given variously from sixteen to twenty. The traditional
date of her birth, 1595, is based on van de Passe's claim on the portrait that she
is twenty-one. John Smith calls her a "child of tenne" early in 1608, which
would make her somewhat younger and her age at marriage sixteen. This later
date of birth is bolstered by Strachey's claim that in the early days of the settlement she cartwheeled through the fort naked, an activity unlikely for a young
woman after puberty. The imprecision about her age is surprising when compared to the precision about the age of her younger sister, which Hamor swiftly
offers as justification for nullification of her marriage contract. Hamor suggests
to Powhatan that he can revoke his consent to the marriage without dishonor:
"the rather because she was not full twelve yeeres old, and therefore not marriageable" (*A True Discourse*, 42). The confusion over Pocahontas's age may relate
to the legal question of rape. As T.E. observes: "Therefore it is ordained, that it
shall not bee lawfull to convey any maid or woman child, unmarried, or under
the age of sixteene yeeres, out of the possession, and against the will of her
father" (*Lawes Resolutions*, 385). If Pocahontas were younger than sixteen at the
time of her kidnapping, as John Smith's evidence seems to suggest, then the

---

[62] Rountree, *The Powhatan Indians of Virginia*, 92.

English had ravished a maiden. If William Strachey's report that Pocahontas had been married in 1610 to "a private captain," Kocoum, were true, then the rape of a minor gives way to a second problem. If the validity of Powhatan marriages were respected, then the English had kidnapped a married woman and thus condoned bigamy. Strachey's 1612 account, unfinished and not published until 1853, could have circulated in London at the time of her visit to the court, although this shadowy marriage is entirely erased in Ralph Hamor's account.

The confident claims of the van de Passe portrait about the imperial rank, conversion, and marriage of the Indian princess are attempts to regularize and justify English activities in the New World. Yet the verbal and visual claims of triumphant possession are contested by the strains embedded in the portrait and in the competing acounts of the colony. The portrait itself and the accounts contemporary with it expose English justifications as papering over at least kidnapping, perhaps rape, and possibly bigamy. Coercion marks the story of Pocahontas's capture before her wedding and coercion also marks the end of her story. According to John Chamberlain, Pocahontas was reluctant to leave England and return to Virginia. He wrote to Dudley Carleton, "She is on her return (though sore against her will) if the wind wold come about to send them away" (*Letters*, ed. McClure, 2:50). The ship she was to sail on was captained by the same man who had tricked her into captivity with his deceptive hospitality, Samuel Argall. On Argall's ship she was carried as hostage toward her father's village. On Argall's ship, she sailed to England. On her final voyage with Captain Argall, who had, after "much ado," "kindely entreated" her, ravished her, and held her hostage, on that last voyage "against her will," Pocahontas died.

Karen Robertson
Vassar College

Works Cited

Akrigg, G. V. K. *Jacobean Pageant: or, the Court of King James I.* Cambridge, MA: Harvard University Press, 1962.

Arnold, Janet. *Patterns of Fashion: The Cut and Construction of Clothes for Men and Women c. 1560–1620.* London: Macmillan, 1985.

Barbour, Philip. *Pocahontas and Her World.* Boston: Houghton Mifflin, 1969.

Beverley, Robert. *History and Present State of Virginia* (1705), ed. Louis B. Wright. Chapel Hill: University of North Carolina Press, 1947.

Bible. *The Geneva Bible: A Facsimile of the 1560 Edition.* Madison, WI: University of Wisconsin Press, 1969.

Black-Michaud, Jacob. *Cohesive Force: Feud in the Mediterranean and Middle East*. New York: St. Martin's Press, 1975.

Bowen, Barbara. "Aemilia Lanyer and the Invention of White Womanhood." In *Maids and Mistresses, Cousins and Queens: Women's Alliances in Early Modern England*, ed. Susan Frye and Karen Robertson, 274–303. New York: Oxford University Press, 1999.

Bridenbaugh, Carl. *Jamestown 1544–1699*. New York: Oxford University Press, 1980.

Brownmiller, Susan. *Against Our Will: Men, Women and Rape*. New York: Simon and Schuster, 1975.

Burns, E. Jane. *Bodytalk: When Women Speak in Old French Literature*. Philadelphia: University of Pennsylvania Press, 1993.

Carter, John. *ABC for Book Collectors*. 3rd ed. London: Rupert Hart-Davis, 1961.

Chamberlain, John. *Letters of John Chamberlain*, ed. Norman Egbert McClure. 2 vols. Philadelphia: American Philosophical Society, 1939.

Clifford, Anne. *The Diaries of Lady Anne Clifford*, ed. D. J. H. Clifford. Stroud, Gloucs: Sutton Publishing, 1990.

Demos, John. *The Unredeemed Captive: A Family Story from Early America*. New York: Knopf, 1994.

E., T. *The Lawes Resolutions of Women's Rights: The Woman's Lawyer*. London: John More, 1632; (STC 7437) repr. Amsterdam: Theatrum Orbis Terrarum, 1979.

Estrich, Susan. *Real Rape*. Cambridge, MA: Harvard University Press, 1988.

Ferguson, Margaret. "Feathers and Flies: Aphra Behn and the Seventeenth-Century Trade in Exotica." *Subject and Object in Renaissance Culture*, ed. Margreta de Grazia, Maureen Quilligan, and Peter Stallybrass, 235–59. Cambridge: Cambridge University Press, 1996.

Gossett, Suzanne. " 'Man-maid, Begone!': Women in Masques." *English Literary Renaissance* 18 (1988): 96–113.

Hall, Kim F. *Things of Darkness: Economies of Race and Gender in Early Modern England*. Ithaca: Cornell University Press, 1995.

Hamor, Ralph. *A True Discourse of the Present Estate of Virginia and the successe of the affaires there till the 18 of June. 1614*. London, 1615; (STC 12736) repr. Amsterdam: Theatrum Orbis Terrarum, 1971.

Hilliard, Nicholas. *A Treatise Concerning the Art of Limning*, ed. R. K. R. Thornton and T. G. S. Cain. Ashington: Carcanet Press, 1981.

Horn, James. *Adapting to a New World: English Society in the Seventeenth-Century Chesapeake*. Chapel Hill: University of North Carolina Press, 1994.

Howard, Jean. *The Stage and Social Struggle in Early Modern England*. New York: Routledge, 1994.

Hulme, Peter. *Colonial Encounters: Europe and the Native Caribbean, 1492–1707*. London: Methuen, 1992.

Hulton, Paul. *America 1585: The Complete Drawings of John White*. London: British Museum Publications, 1984.

Kingsbury, Susan Myra. *Records of the Virginia Company of London*. 4 vols. Washington, DC: Library of Congress, 1933.

Kupperman, Karen. *Roanoke: The Abandoned Colony*. Totowa, NJ: Rowman and Allanheld, 1984.

Linton, Joan Pong. *The Romance of the New World: Gender and the Literary Formation of English Colonialism*. Cambridge University Press, 1998.

Montrose, Louis. *The Purpose of Playing: Shakespeare and the Cultural Politics of Elizabethan Theatre*. Chicago: University of Chicago Press, 1996.

Murray, Mary. *The Law of the Father? Patriarchy in the Transition from Feudalism to Capitalism*. London: Routledge, 1995.

Neill, Edward. *History of the Virginia Company of London*. Albany, NY: J. Munsell, 1869; repr. New York: B. Franklin, 1968.

Norton, Mary Beth. *Founding Mothers and Fathers: Gendered Power and the Forming of American Society*. New York: Knopf, 1996.

Platform for Action at the Fourth World Conference on Women in Beijing. New York: United Nations, 1995.

Plowden, Alison. *The Stuart Princesses*. Stroud, Gloucestershire: Sutton Publishing, 1997.

Prest, W.R. "Law and Women's Rights in Early Modern England." *Sixteenth Century* [GB] 6 (1991): 169–87.

Purchas, Samuel. *Hakluytus posthumus or Purchas his Pilgrimes*. 20 vols. Glasgow: J. Maclehose, 1905–1907.

Reid, Aileen, and Robert Maniura, eds. *Edward Alleyn: Elizabethan Actor, Jacobean Gentleman*. Dulwich: Dulwich Picture Gallery, 1994.

Robertson, Elizabeth. "Public Bodies and Psychic Domains: Rape, Consent, and Female Subjectivity in Geoffrey Chaucer's *Troilus and Criseyde*." In *Representing Rape in Medieval and Early Modern Literature*, ed. *eadem* and Christine Rose, 281–310. New York: Palgrave Press, 2001.

Robertson, Karen. "Pocahontas at the Masque." *Signs* 21 (1996): 551–83.

Rountree, Helen. *The Powhatan Indians of Virginia*. Norman, OK: University of Oklahoma Press, 1989.

Shakespeare, William. *Titus Andronicus*. The Arden Shakespeare, 3rd ser., ed. Jonathan Bate. London: Routledge, 1994.

Smith, John. *The Complete Works of Captain John Smith 1580–1631*, ed. Philip Barbour. 3 vols. Chapel Hill: University of North Carolina Press, 1986.

———. *The Generall Historie of Virginia* (1624). In *The Complete Works*, ed. Barbour, 2:225–488.

———. *A True Relation*. In *The Complete Works*, ed. Barbour, 1:3–117.

Strachey, William. *For the Colony in Virginea Britannia: Lawes Divine, Morall and Martiall, etc.* London, 1612. (STC 23350).

Strickland, Agnes. *Lives of the Queens of Scotland and English Princesses Connected with the Royal Succession of Great Britain*. 8 vols. Edinburgh: W. Blackwood, 1850–59.

Strong, Roy. *The English Icon: Elizabethan and Jacobean Portraiture*. London: Paul Mellon Foundation for British Art, 1969.

Tilton, Robert. *Pocahontas: The Evolution of an American Narrative*. Cambridge: Cambridge University Press, 1994.

Whitaker, Alexander. *Good Newes from Virginia*. London, 1613. (STC 25354).

Rape, Female Desire, and
Sexual Revulsion in John Fletcher's Plays

The threat of rape haunts the plays of John Fletcher, sometimes treated tragic-ally, but more commonly (and often with little visible sensitivity) as a comic plot element. Over the course of his prolific career and of many treatments of rape, Fletcher provides his female characters with three essentially different strategies for dealing with sexual aggression, none of which seems palatable to modern audiences. For the virtuous, tragic rape victims, suicide and marriage to the ag-gressor offer the only two options. His clever women in the comedies, however, repeatedly deflect assault through a third course of action: they pretend to desire and enjoy the proffered attentions. By assuming the voice of a desiring subject and verbally enacting a fantasy of sexual appetite, Fletcher's comic heroines avert sexual threat and establish their own power. In an era noted for its radical trans-formations in the concept of the female subject in both legal and literary treat-ments, Fletcher's plays reveal the anxieties and ambivalence surrounding women who voice desire. At the same time, the swift retreat of Fletcher's sexual preda-tors exposes the fragility of male desire and power when conventional gender roles are disrupted.

Nancy Cotton Pearse, one of the first critics to consider John Fletcher apart from his several collaborators, identified his overriding interest in the trials and valorization of female chastity. Pearse defined the morality-play format of the chastity test as the core of his writing: "an allegorical play in which the opposing forces that contend for the soul are Chastity and Lechery" (*John Fletcher's Chas-tity Plays*, 33). Fletcher continually employed this plotting convention through-out his long career, along with three exemplary female types, Penelope, Susanna, and Lucrece, who defend their chastity against seduction, slander, and rape respectively. Citing examples in Chaucer, Spenser, and other English writers, Pearse argues that Renaissance audiences were familiar with this conventional pattern and would have immediately recognized the use of the exemplum in Fletcher's work. His interests are moralistic, she concludes, tending to create a female heroics of chastity and to reform seducers. Pearse's illuminating study of the chastity test and its repeated use in Fletcher's drama diverts attention from the male assaulter, however, as if he were a mere tool for the valorization of female chastity. The contradiction of desire and revulsion in the psychology of the assaulters seems worth our wonder and exploration in its own right.

In the rape scenario as ordinarily conceived by popular imagination, early modern legal codes, and traditional psychology, gender roles seem clear-cut and firmly divided. A powerful, aggressive male desires and takes by force a female who resists his sexual advances. Male desire is assumed to be stronger, and male strength more powerful, than female. In *Three Contributions to the Theory of Sex*, Sigmund Freud confirms this culturally accepted script by arguing that sexual experience differentiates sharply at puberty. The increase in repression and sexual passivity of young women, Freud claims, "produces a stimulus in the libido of the man and forces him to increase his activities" (*Three Contributions*, 613). Moreover, he suggests, most sexually mature men cannot be completely satisfied by mere possession of the desired object:

> The sexuality of most men shows an admixture of aggression, of a desire to subdue, the biological significance of which lies in the necessity for overcoming the resistance of the sexual object by actions other than mere *courting.* (*Three Contributions*, 569)

Thus Freud proposes the female impulse to resist and masculine need to overcome resistance as universal, biologically determined, and complementary truths. Though in extreme instances masculine aggression takes shape as sadism, a sexual aberration, he cautions that "it is something *which is congenital in all persons; which as a predisposition may fluctuate in intensity, and that it is brought into prominence by influences of life*" (*Three Contributions*, 578). From this perspective and its extremely pessimistic implications for heterosexual relationships, violent rape can be viewed merely as an extreme version of "normal" sexual drives, providing a script for the satisfaction of desire in which a masculine subject forcibly acquires his female sexual "object." This scenario and the gender roles specified historically have formed the basis of most understandings of rape, including that underlying Fletcher's single tragic treatment of the topic.

A number of modern theorists, however, reject Freud's vision of polarized and conflicting sexual drives inevitably spawning aggression. When Nicholas Groth published his seminal 1979 study, *Why Men Rape*, he concluded that rape was a "pseudosexual act" (13). Rejecting Freud's insistence on the sexual energies be-

hind rape, Groth identified the desire for power as a dominant motivator, arguing that the attempt to satisfy this hunger for power compensates for the assailant's own sense of inadequacy and threatened masculinity (25–28). Such rapists
select victims who "symbolize everything the offender dislikes about himself
(being weak, powerless, effeminate, and the like)" in a "desperate need to reas-
sure himself of his virility and sexual competency" (30). Sexual aggression enacts
the need "to protect the centrality of the male subject" by forcing the female into
the role of sexual object (Cameron and Frazer, *The Lust to Kill*, 168). Sexual satisfaction is merely an outward garment disguising the rapist's fear of inadequacy
and clothing his underlying drive for power. Although the Freudian model of
rape provides a satisfactory template for analysis of Fletcher's tragic rape drama,
only Groth's formulation can help explain the comic treatments.

The *Tragedy of Valentinian*[1] (c. 1612) mirrors the plot of Shakespeare's *The
Rape of Lucrece* and the traditional moral exemplum offered to all raped women:
a chaste young Roman matron, Lucina, unhesitatingly responds with suicide to
her violation by the Roman emperor of the title. The shimmering and sensual
poetic tissue of Shakespeare's poem is replaced by Fletcher's familiar forensics, as
debates about honor and the necessity for suicide occupy the long scene before
Lucina's death, and the two acts following it are given over to her husband
Maximus's conflict between personal revenge and the ideal of absolute loyalty to
a vicious monarch who has violated his trust as citizen, soldier, and husband.
Though the rape itself provides the central moment in the plot, the erotics of
sexual passion surface only through the substitute voices of the panders and
bawds who unsuccessfully attempt to bend Lucina toward compliance in seduction. Both the verbal and physical interactions of the main players in the rape,
Lucina and Valentinian, condense into a constrained dialogue of chastity and
honor. Although this is not unexpected on Lucina's part, Valentinian's motivation for rape ultimately emerges as the desire not for sensual pleasure but to
possess and violate her perfect chastity.

A series of panders despairing over Lucina's refusal of all jewels, honors, and
bribes offered by the emperor open the tragedy. Mentioning her beauty only
once in passing with no attempt to conjure up a physical description, the panders
continually emphasize her sexual unavailability. Did you ever, marvels one pander, "discover such a peece of beauty" who was chaste and "honest"?

---

[1] All dates for the plays and ascriptions of authorship follow those suggested in *The
Dramatic Works in the Beaumont and Fletcher Canon*, ed. Bowers.

> Honest against the tide of all temptations,
> Honest to one man, to her husband only,
> And yet not eighteene, not of age to know
> Why she is honest? (1.1.17–21)

The reiteration of "honest" is echoed in the scene by the most frequent descriptions applied to Lucina. "Cold" is used twice in this short scene: "Cold as Christall" (43), "chaster then cold Camphire" (86). Her very blushes offer the "holyest" sight; she is the "purest temple of her sect" (80). This pattern extends throughout the play, which conjures audience identification with Lucina almost entirely upon the strengths of her chastity, virtue, and lack of sexual desire.

Chided in the third scene for licentiousness and excess by his plain-speaking general, Aecius, Valentinian breezily contemplates reform, but his own first mention of the woman who has incited his lust focuses on the seductive quality of her chastity:

> . . . of all
> The sins I covet, but this womans beautie,
> With much repentance, now could I be quit of:
> But she is such a pleasure, being good,
> That though I were a god, she would fire my bloud.
>   (1.3.246–250)

From this first description of his passion, the erotic call of chastity and the attendant compulsion to sully it are evident. The same virtue which must be destroyed in her violation is also the incitement to lust. Anticipating Freud's theory of the biological need to overcome resistance, Valentinian suggests that if Lucina simply surrendered to seduction, the lure would be lost. This double bind plagues many of Fletcher's male characters.

In Act 2, Valentinian entices a mistrustful Lucina to the palace with her husband's wedding ring, lost in a gambling match with the emperor. Valentinian's pander and bawds conduct her through the rooms in a tightening noose of seductive ploys. Erotic suspense and verbal double-play extend the excitement over three scenes, while Lucina parries and resists the bribes, love songs, and innuendoes spun around her. When Valentinian finally arrives to complete the seduction, he provides no corresponding scene of protested love, no blazon of Lucina's beauty, no sensual catalogue of her anatomy or physical attractions. No erotic energy emerges at all except for the malign suspense of predation and a destructive fascination with her moral virtue. When Lucina steadfastly protests her loyalty to her worthy husband, Valentinian pretends that he has been interested only in testing her virtue, and leads her offstage, ostensibly to rejoin her husband.

The next scene, 3.1, opens immediately with a pander's crisp line, "Tis done." None of the erotic language of seduction surfaces for the audience either before or after the offstage rape. When Lucina and Valentinian reappear, her bitter reproaches are met only with his all-too-familiar declaration that she herself caused the rape by enticing him, not only with her "heavenly beauty" but, paradoxically, with her virtue itself:

> If I have done a sin, curse her that drew me,
> Curse the first cause, the witchcraft that abusd me,
> urse those faire eyes, and curse that heavenly beauty,
> And curse your being good too. (3.1.54–57)

Valentinian highlights her goodness as his essential call to pleasure, naming the forceful destruction of that chastity and virtue as the aphrodisiac that lures him: "Ye are so excellent, and made to ravish, / (There were no pleasure in ye else)" (3.1.103–104).

Discovering Lucina weeping, her husband Maximus immediately guesses her history and unswervingly concurs with her decision for suicide. His friend Aecius demurs, wavers, and begs for her to live another year at least in hopes of reforming the emperor with her virtues, but Maximus replies decisively, "she must not" (3.1.208). Bidding her farewell, he reiterates the cold images of crystal and marble that so frustrated the bawds in the opening scene:

> Why wert thou chosen out to make a whore of?
> To me thou wert too chast: fall Christall fountaines,
> And ever feed your streames you rising sorrowes,
> ill you have dropt your mistris into marble.
> Now goe for ever from me. (3.1.182–186)

Most of the major speeches in this scene between the rape and Lucina's death are Maximus's extended arguments for the necessity of her death, the family honor attached to it, and the losses to both their names and reputations if she lives. Unlike Lucrece, who dominates Shakespeare's poem after her rape, Lucina, so eloquent earlier in defending herself and in reproaching Valentinian, barely speaks after her husband returns, completely decided upon suicide. In a six-page discussion of *Valentinian*, Charles Squier devotes only two paragraphs to Lucina herself and the rape, the central event of the first two acts, and the rest of his chapter to the male characters' debates on the necessity of her suicide and the ethics of revenge against an emperor ruling by divine right (*John Fletcher*, 101–6).

Lucina herself accepts without question the position that a woman's value lies in her chastity, and fervently embraces death as the only conceivable response to her chastity's violation.

Coppélia Kahn notes that narrative closure for Shakespeare's *Lucrece* arrives only with the expulsion of the Tarquins and the formation of the Roman republic: "Rape authorizes revenge; revenge comprises revolution; revolution establishes legitimate government" ("*Lucrece*," 141). Fletcher's play, unfortunately, provides no such positive outcome from sexual violence or a heroic public role for Lucina. Although she issues a stirring call for justice and rebellion against Valentinian's tyranny immediately after her rape, the play concludes with the emperor's death but also with a highly pessimistic vision of the value of Lucina's sacrifice: in the final acts her husband Maximus transforms with breathtaking speed into a monster of ambition who attempts to take over both the empire and Valentinian's widow, declaring with chilling calculation that, if he succeeds, his "wife was ravish'd well" (4.3.39).

Commenting upon western culture's long fascination with the Lucretia narrative and her essential act of suicide, Ian Donaldson observes that in a society such as Rome "in which a woman is regarded as a subordinate and property of her husband, her rape, even if she has resisted and detested it, may seem to bring disgrace not merely upon her, but — more importantly — upon her husband" (*The Rapes of Lucretia*, 11). The many versions of the story in early modern Europe suggest a continued affinity for that vision of woman as a prized object of property. Maximus perceives Valentinian's act as a violation of his own honor and value and as the theft of his most prized possession, bewailing the loss to Valentinian of "That cursed Ring, my selfe, and all my fortunes" (3.1.163). Just as a raped woman is described as "crackt i'th' ring" in Fletcher's *Bonduca* (1.2.271), the lost ring here becomes the material symbol of Lucina's chastity.

Ancient law as well as literature, of course, viewed woman as an object of property, rightfully in the possession of husband or father. Barbara Baines traces the connection in early English law between rape and property value: the violent defloration of a virgin was the only form of sexual assault steadfastly prosecuted under medieval and Renaissance law, for such a rape "clearly destroys the worth of a woman" and "renders her worthless to the man who legally possesses her" ("Effacing Rape," 85). Chastity and a woman's value, argues Baines, were discussed by medieval legal authority as if physically located in the objectified body, particularly in the virginal hymen (70–71). Henry de Bracton, to whom is attributed a thirteenth-century legal compendium, recommended as appropriate punishment for a rapist who breaks a virgin's hymen the loss of some of his own members; for the rapist of a wife or widow (whose hymen has previously been broken) "a like punishment will not be imposed for each" (quoted in Baines, "Effacing Rape," 71).[2] Different qualities of female property, then, command different prices.

Aecius argues, in contrast, that not Lucina's body but rather her will, voice, and assent constitute her identity, and that these remain unstained and un-changed despite the rape. Since she was "compeld and forcd with violence / To what ye have done, the deed is none of yours, / No nor the justice neither; ye may live" (3.1.220–222). Lucina herself identifies with her violated body, how-ever, and remains unmoved by Aecius's plea. The literary representation of rape victims such as Lucrece and Lucina "idealizes the suicide of the raped woman as the ultimate consent to patriarchal imperatives" and the acknowledgment of her loss of value (Baines, "Effacing Rape," 89). Although Aecius suggests that Lu-cina is not an object of property but rather a speaking subject, Fletcher's plot and heroine both discount that possibility.

Even beyond his distress at the loss of honor and value in his wife's violation, Maximus is anxious that her continued life might incite onlookers to inquire whether she actually enjoyed being "ravishd, / And make a doubt she lov'd that more then Wedlock? / Therefore she must not live" (3.1.143–145). Ian Donald-son notes similar concern for the victim's feelings of pleasure in a number of ear-lier versions of the Lucrece narrative, including Bandello's, an anxiety which in each case fuels the perceived need for suicide (*The Rapes of Lucretia*, 36–37). Barbara Baines suggests that Shakespeare implicitly opens a similar possibility for his Lucrece by emphasizing her fear of pregnancy as a motivation for suicide. Since the medical and legal codes inherited by the Renaissance argued that with-out a woman's sexual pleasure there could be no conception, and that pleasure implied the consent of the body at least, the "simple equation between concep-tion, sexual pleasure, and consent ... neatly effaces, as far as the law is con-cerned, the reality of rape" (Baines, "Effacing Rape," 80). Thus by the act of suicide Lucrece and her violated sisters also punish their own transgression as subjects who may have dared to experience pleasure.

Fletcher's later tragicomedy, *The Queen of Corinth* (written with Nathan Field and Philip Massinger, c. 1616–17), offers an alternative and supposedly happier outcome of rape. Suzanne Gossett points out that, although all four English plays containing a completed rape which survive from the period 1594–1612

---

[2] See Henry de Bracton, *De Legibus et Consuetudinibus Angliae*, trans. Samuel E. Thorne, ed. George E. Woodbine, 2 vols. (Cambridge, MA: Belknap Press, 1968), 2:414–18.

follow the tragic Lucrece formula, with the chaste, violated wife and her rapist both dying, three of the four plays produced between 1617 and 1623 allow the rape victim to survive and resolve the sexual and legal tensions by actually marrying her to the reformed rapist. In this libertine period corresponding with Buckingham's ascendancy in the Jacobean court, Gossett suggests, audiences flirted with taboo by watching "the fulfillment of a fantasy of rape and yet the guilt attached to the fantasy — and the act — is removed by the final marriage" ("'Best Men'," 324). Since the rapists are reformed and domesticated by marriage, these plays also reevaluate rape as "a natural instinct which must be brought under social control by marriage . . . . Rather than being a tragic crime rape becomes a comic error cured by being brought into the social order" (Gossett, "'Best Men'," 324). Freud might have approved such a correction of the excesses of this "natural instinct" and the reintegration of the conventionally gendered pair — rapist and victim, male and female, subject and object — into the social community.

In *The Queen of Corinth*, Merione, awarded as a political prize to a rival king by Corinth's queen, is raped on the eve of her marriage by her former suitor, the queen's own son, Theanor, who reportedly had loved and wooed her "in the noblest way" (1.1.27). Merione's own response compounds her established status as a political pawn, an object to be disposed of by others. Even before she knows the identity of her masked rapist, Merione laments her "ravisht honour" (2.1.2), berates the deaf and heartless gods who permitted her violation, and immediately demands marriage from the attacker, even as he and his henchmen mock and threaten her: "But one kinde loving look, be what ye will, / So from this hower you will be mine, my Husband" (2.1.25–30). Viewing herself as the property of whatever man first penetrated her sexually, regardless of her own lack of consent, Merione remains adamant in refusing Agenor, the royal bridegroom who persists in wanting to marry her. After Theanor is discovered to be her rapist, he experiences a quick repentance, and the play is resolved by his marriage to Merione. Suzanne Gossett remarks wisely that this "ostensible happy ending retains the notion that a woman is marked as the property of a man who has sexual relations with her, but it does not confront her feelings as she enters the marriage" ("'Best Men'," 324). Like Maximus's friend Aecius, Agenor argues that because Merione's will did not consent, she is unsullied.[3] She herself, however, never acknowledges a standard of will, desire, or personal happiness, whether in submit-

---

[3] Again taken from Livy, *Ab Urbe Condita* 1.58, on Lucretia: "corpus . . . tantum violatum, animus insons."

ting to her first broken engagement, her perceived duty to marry the rapist, or her refusal of Agenor.

Fletcher and his co-authors reworked their source, one of the elder Seneca's *Controversiae* (1.5) concerning a man who raped two women, by substituting the play's two leading women for Seneca's speakers in the final debate over whether the rapist's punishment should be marriage or death. Allowing the two women themselves to stand as the agents shaping the outcome of their lives would seem to acknowledge the women's subjective voices, but ironically theirs are conventional declamations. Merione's speeches throughout the play reveal little perceptible change in the assumptions that guide the traditional rape victim's response or that limit her own ability to speak or desire outside the traditional strictures of patriarchy.

In other social, legal, and literary arenas, however, women in early modern England were increasingly viewed as subjects with agency and the power of consent. Rape, seduction, and elopement were rarely distinguished from one another in laws written during the Middle Ages, since in all three the property inhering in a man's daughter or wife was displaced without his consent by another man's actions. A series of sixteenth-century statutes distinguishing rape (non-consensual penetration) from elopement, however, marked a new recognition of the role of the woman's will. "These laws," Barbara Baines notes, "resulted in, or perhaps contributed to, a shift in the way rape was perceived: no longer as a crime against property but as a crime against the person" ("Effacing Rape," 72). Legal confusion in the transition period, Baines concludes, "reveals a crisis in the Early Modern construction of woman's subjectivity: she is both property or passive object and a person invested with agency, with the will and discernment that define consent" ("Effacing Rape," 72–73). The questions raised by this crisis in female identity, by women's status as subjects and agents, become a field of playful inquiry in Fletcher's comic rape plays. His witty heroines do not merely protest their chastity; they will not wait to be acted upon. Instead, they intervene in their own unfolding rape dramas and take active initiative in their manner of refusing consent. They invent and enact a subjective self who voices open sexual desire, playing with the elements of identity and consent. Most important, by speaking from this subject position, the comic women acquire through their language the power to deflect sexual aggression and to dissolve the dominance of the male attacker into confusion.

When a woman's agency is acknowledged, her ability as a speaking subject to refuse unwanted sexual approaches carries with it the converse possibility, that of choosing to accept those advances or even to seek them herself. Around this distressing possibility converges much of Fletcher's theatrical energy. His plays contain a wide assortment of villainous women who freely indulge their sexual desires outside the legal boundaries of marriage. Most distinctively, however, many of Fletcher's comic heroines share the notable ability to give voice to the language of desire, even a coarse eroticism that would suggest a lewd and promiscuous wench rather than a well-born lady of high virtue, if this language were not clearly assumed in each case as a defense against rape or forceful seduction. Inverting Valentinian's objectification of the rape victim, the comedies place in the foreground the possibility of female sexual desire and make it the instrument of self-preservation. This intriguing defense, employed by a number of Fletcher's besieged women, seems to strike terror into the lusting male heart.

In his monograph *Textual Intercourse*, Jeffrey Masten contemplates Fletcher's own ability to elude our contemporary categories of both authorship and erotic identity. Indeed, Masten might caution, naming "Fletcher" as the subject of the present essay is an act of convenience based on his reputed participation in all of the plays and probable role as sole author of several; whether he in fact originated the rape pattern under discussion cannot be known. The collaborative approach assumed with his fellow playwrights and with the theatrical companies producing his work has prevented the earliest editors of the plays and the most dedicated modern scholars alike from identifying with any certainty the specific passages produced by Fletcher's personal pen. In a parallel manner, Masten notes, Fletcher's erotic life also defied and escaped rigid contemporary divisions. Memorializing Fletcher inseparably with his friend and collaborator Francis Beaumont, John Aubrey wrote that the pair "lived together on the Banke side, not far from the Play-house, both batchelors; lay together ... and had one wench in the house between them" (quoted in Masten, *Textual Intercourse*, 61). After Beaumont's death, Fletcher shared an equally close collaborative friendship with playwright Philip Massinger, who was buried with him in a single grave (1). Despite the patriarchal imperatives that took shape in the seventeenth century to fix both authorial and sexual identities, Masten argues, the indeterminacy of Fletcher's work, friendships, and sexual preferences escape the clear, exclusive categories that our contemporary disposition attempts to impose upon them. How fitting it seems, then, that Fletcher should repeatedly explore the rape plot, the moment of complete gender polarization, and most characteristically examine in that moment the consequences of gender confusion and disruption. In contrast to *Valentinian*, Fletcher's comic rape plays begin with the culturally accepted gender script for rape — strong, lustful male; passive female victim — but, by inverting the roles and allowing the women to voice strong desire, repeatedly suggest that male identity and violent performance depend on the script itself and are rendered vulnerable by its loss.

The virginal Clorin of *The Faithful Shepherdess* (1609), the one early work wholly by Fletcher that preceded his partnership with Francis Beaumont, first enacts this defensive posture and at the same time sums up the erotic predicament of so many of Fletcher's men. Clorin has vowed in memory of her dead lover to remain single and celibate for life, but the shepherd Thenot predicates his passion for her upon that unattainable status. She comments upon the paradox implicit in her suitor's attraction to her and, implicitly, on the erotic economy of so many of Fletcher's male characters, including Valentinian:

> did ever man but hee,
> Love any woeman for her Constancy,
> To her dead lover, which she needs must end,
> Before she can alowe him, for her freind,
> And he himselfe, must needes the cause destroye,
> For which he loves, before he can injoye. (4.5.21–26)

In this earliest of Fletcher's plays, the several elements of his unique configuration of the double bind are already visible. To cure Thenot's destructive passion, Clorin pretends to offer herself to him; Thenot hastily retreats, sputtering with open misogyny, revealing clearly the impossible inner conflict between his own protestations of love and his simultaneous rejection of active female desire:

> Your Sexes Curse, foul falshood, must and shall,
> I see once in your lives light on you all:
> I hate thee now ... (4.5.57–59)

This pattern, the woman's pretense of sexual desire and availability and the concomitant male revulsion, emerges as a staple of Fletcher's dramaturgy. His female characters become increasingly playful as they dexterously manipulate the elements of sexual desire, assent, and female agency to defend themselves in an aggressive male environment and, ultimately, to wrest some measure of control and self-determination within the conventional boundaries of marriage.

In *Monsieur Thomas* (1610–1616), for example, another early solo work by Fletcher, a middle-aged traveler named Valentine returns home from a long journey with his new young friend Francis, to the welcoming arms of Cellide, Valentine's ward and fiancée. Young, lovely, and virtuous, Cellide has been so carefully raised by Valentine that she bends her own will entirely to his, accepting the great difference in their ages without question and meekly deferring to him even on the date of their wedding: "When heaven, and you sir / Shall think it fit: for by your wils I am govern'd" (2.1.12–13). She seems incapable of asserting herself in ways that might contradict her parent-bridegroom. When

Valentine discovers that Francis has fallen in love with Cellide and by repressing his love has fallen gravely ill, he instantly and with remarkable generosity bequeaths Cellide to his friend. Furious at being handed between these men like a piece of property, Cellide vows to take her own form of revenge with actions that will "minister no comfort, no content / To either of ye, but hourely more vexations" (2.5.99–100). The dutiful young woman discovers her own rebellious capacity as a subject.

At Francis's sickbed, Cellide pretends to offer herself to him. At first enraptured by her generosity and her kiss, Francis draws back when he learns that she has come in obedience to Valentine's wish. He moves to actual revulsion, however, when Cellide shifts the terms of discussion to her own sexual satisfaction by intimating that she prefers him to her "old and impotent" fiancé. She argues that life with Valentine would mean "everlasting banishment from that / Our yeares doe only covet to arive at" (3.1.99–100). Unlike the virile young Francis, Valentine could sire no children with her and thus no "art of memory but fruitlesse doating" (3.1.113). To her final, coy suggestion that she "would faine say more / If you would understand" (3.1.111–112), he responds in horror, calling her a "devill": "Me thinks you are not faire now; me thinks more / That modest vertue men delivered of you / Shewes but like shadow to me, thin, and fading" (3.1.115–117). Though dying from desire to possess her, he cannot love her unless she denies him her own desire. A woman cut from the same cloth, Cellide falls completely in love with him when he spurns her, admitting that "Till this minut / I scorn'd, and hated ye, and came to cosen ye" but that "now truely, / Truely, and nobly I doe love ye deerely" (3.1.153–154, 159–160). Fletcher resolves the dilemma with the discovery that Francis is Valentine's son, lost in infancy, and the delighted father joyfully accepts Cellide as a daughter-in-law instead of a wife.

In many of Fletcher's plays, the teasing theatricality of falsified female desire is heightened by its conjunction with a rape threat. Two of the three linked plots of *The Faithful Shepherdess*, for instance, outline the attraction-repulsion pattern, and all three intertwine the threat of rape. As Verna Foster observes, *The Faithful Shepherdess*, like the bulk of Fletcher's work, seems designed "to explore the anxieties and fantasies that exist between desire and its fulfillment, between sexuality and the act of sex" ("Sex Averted or Converted," 312). Just as Thenot recoils from the unattainable Clorin as soon as she suggests that she could actually love him, so in the second of the entwined plots the shepherd Perigot twice stabs his beloved Amoret when a woman impersonating Amoret makes sexual overtures to him. A third and contrasting plot involves a less virtuous shepherdess, Cloe, who unabashedly invites two suitors to meet her in the wood, confident that at least one will assist her in tasting "those rare sweetes, for which I pine" (1.3.153). Cloe, unlike the other two women, is rejected not by her lover but by Fletcher himself, who reforms her into a conventionally monogamous character at the play's conclusion.

In the second plot, Perigot begs Amoret to meet him in the forest at night for an exchange of chaste vows. Another shepherdess, Amarillis, declares her love to Perigot and is rebuffed, but with the aid of a coarse and melancholy Sullen Shepherd transforms herself into a physical replica of Amoret. Taking the true Amoret's place at the moonlight assignation, Amarillis lures Perigot into an erotic embrace. Though Perigot believes at first that his innocent Amoret is merely testing him, Amarillis offers herself in an increasingly explicit manner:

> Still thinkst thou such a thinge as Chastitie,
> Is amongst woemen? *Perigot* thers none,
> That with her love is in a wood alone,
> And wood come home a Mayde: be not abusd,
> With thy fond first beleife, let time be usd. ....
>
> (3.1.296–300)

Like Cloe in the third plot, Amarillis openly feels and speaks desire and attempts to act upon it. Though numerous other playwrights of the period created lustful women, Kathleen McLuskie comments that Fletcher's innovation lies in "transposing the discourses of male lust on to them, making the connections between gender, language and action arbitrary and thus infinitely malleable to the dramatic action" (*Renaissance Dramatists*, 202). Perigot recoils in shock from this "serpent," whose disguise he fails to penetrate. Furiously chasing the elusive Amarillis, he encounters the real Amoret wandering through the dark forest and stabs her. Returned to her true shape, Amarillis reveals her deception to Perigot and offers to prove the trick by once more assuming Amoret's shape. She finds Amoret, cured of her wound by the God of the River, and lures her toward Perigot. Still blind to the truth, Perigot again mistakes the true Amoret for false Amarillis and stabs her a second time. Clorin's ministrations and the sacred power of virginity effect another cure and clarify all mistakes, and the lovers are finally united.

The dark presence of a would-be rapist, the anti-romantic and amoral Sullen Shepherd, threatens all three plots with conventional sexual violence that diverts attention from Perigot's murderous penetrations. Meeting Amoret in the forest, the Sullen Shepherd marvels at her bright beauty and "virgin innocence" (3.1.119) but, at the next moment, regrets that he allowed her to pass unmolested:

Alone, I might have forcd her to have tried
Who had bene stronger: o vaine foole, to let
Such blest occasion passe, Ile follow yet,
My blood is up, I cannot now forbeare. (3.1.129–132)

Only the arrival of the third pair of lovers, Cloe and Alexis in their guilty tryst, saves Amoret, for the Shepherd redirects his rape threat to Cloe: "Now lust is up, alike all women be" (3.1.135). Though he is fortuitously frightened away, Cloe declares in a comic reversal of rape energy that it "is Impossible to Ravish mee, / I am soe willing" (3.1.212–213), and runs off to look for another available lover. In the meantime, the Sullen Shepherd finds Amarillis and claims the sexual favors she promised for his help in the attempted seduction of Perigot. Protesting that Perigot has not yet been won, she refuses and must flee his outright attempt at sexual assault. Thus the Sullen Shepherd threatens with rape the women of all three plots in succession. The chase ends when the Priest of the grove apprehends and banishes the Sullen Shepherd and the sexual violence he embodies, and reforms the moral disposition of Amarillis, while Clorin in her bower similarly purges Cloe and Alexis of all lustful desire. This pastoral, idyllic fantasy successfully eliminates both violent male desire — the energy of rape — and non-marital female desire, while toying with the appearance of two virtuous women's sexual availability.

Several early plays by Fletcher locate the rape motif and the sexual repugnance that greets female desire in entirely separate plots, allowing us to appreciate the repeated conjunction between the two elements in Fletcher's thinking, apart from the exigencies of any particular story line. The main plot of *The Coxcomb*, performed at court in 1612 and written with Francis Beaumont perhaps a few years earlier, mirrors *Monsieur Thomas*: just as Valentine had returned to his fiancée bringing along an eligible male friend, so Antonio, a foolish traveler, returns to his patient wife Maria with his travel companion Mercury, who immediately conceives a passion for Maria. Antonio, like Valentine, tries to give his wife to his friend. Though Maria firmly resists, her husband fakes his own death and comes in a disguise (which she readily sees through) to urge her to accept Mercury. Maria takes revenge by accepting Mercury's suit; uncharacteristically for Fletcher's women, she does not merely pretend. She exhibits no real attraction to Mercury, seemingly acting merely to teach both men a lesson and to take to control of her own body. Thus she enacts her own independence as a sexual agent outside the bonds of marriage. Having enjoyed her for a night, however, Mercury promptly succumbs to guilt and revulsion, losing all desire. The cuckolded husband is easily duped into believing that Maria has been a chaste and loving wife, Mercury is cured of his adulterous passion, and Maria has the doubtful satisfaction of dealing both men their just deserts.

The secondary plot focuses on attempted rape. Sixteen-year-old Viola promises to elope with her suitor Richardo, who gets drunk with friends while waiting for her. When Viola, unrecognized, arrives at the appointed spot, the whole gang, including Richardo, mistakes her for the whore they have been seeking and attempts to rape her (1.6). Reeling away from this threat, she is assailed in the night by a tinker and his vicious trull, who rob and bind her, with suggested threats against her virginity. A passing gentleman rescues her and pretends friendship but harbors his own lewd intents, deserting her far from the city when she refuses his assaults. Though the newly sober and repentant Richardo ultimately finds and rescues her and is reconciled to her, Viola's story turns upon a continuous series of threatened sexual assaults. What is most intriguing about this play is the utter lack of narrative necessity for juxtaposing rape and sexual disgust. Neither story line contains or requires both elements, yet Fletcher and his partner choose to combine in a very loosely connected subplot a recoil from female desire — Mercury's post-coital revulsion — and the reiterated attempts to rape Viola.

The Loyal Subject (1618), another of Fletcher's solo works, provides one of the most playful versions of this pattern. This play alludes briefly to sexual violence, while in an entire series of episodes women (and one man disguised as a woman) fabricate the appearance of lust in order to protect themselves and reform corrupt sexuality. When the old general Archas falls into disfavor with the impulsive young Duke of Muscovy, he is banished to the country, but his daughters Honora and Viola are summoned to the treacherous court. Outspoken Honora mocks the lewd practices and sexual commerce of the court, but marches off "half a souldier" to test her own virtue. Strikingly, Honora clearly assumes the dramatic and verbal offensive, the position of an agent rather than of a victim or object, in her campaign to defend her chastity.

Reluctantly escorting his sisters to court, Archas's blunt soldier son Theodor sets the tone by pretending to pander Honora and Viola to the hungry courtiers who soon cluster around, brashly advertising them as rare sexual goods that he will auction to the highest bidder. Although uncertain of his sisters' ability to withstand temptation, Theodor appears to gamble on the predatory male's aversion to an openly available female body, and his gambit succeeds in frightening away the "flesh-flies" (3.4.67). Here, as in a parallel incident involving a second brother, young Archas, Fletcher's paradoxical dynamics of male lust and repugnance are visible. Since their father's fall, young Archas has been living at court in female disguise for safety, and now he also arrives, unrecognized, to test

Honora and Viola, regaling them with fabricated tales of the delights of court debauchery and sexual opportunism, and of the ways they can "profit / In kissing, kissing sweetly" (3.6.74–75). The girls fail to see through Archas's disguise, and they firmly denounce "her" immorality. "A man made up in lust would loath this in yee," warns Honora, "The rankest Leacher, hate such impudence" (3.6.91–92). The two girls are amazed when this loose-tongued new acquaintance departs, leaving scrolls praising their steadfast virtue. Honora's focus on the disgust felt by a lecher or a lustful man for a sexually willing woman articulates clearly the assumptions visible in Theodor's gambit and in so many of Fletcher's plays. Though Fletcher has left us no separate essay or treatise on male desire, his plots and characters both male and female repeatedly assume the reality of extreme male ambivalence toward the female body, desirable only so long as it has no desires.

Honora echoes her two brothers' satiric style and salacious pretenses when her opportunity arrives to drag the young Duke through a needed sexual reformation. The Duke welcomes the sisters to court, as to a "place created for all sweetnesse" (4.3.27). While covertly suggesting that they "were not made for Cloisters" (36) and can explore their sensual natures here at court, he nonetheless admires in asides their "sweet modestie" and cool restraint, which "like a nipping morne pulls in their blossoms" (39–40). Like Valentinian, he is a sexual aggressor in a power role, enticed by the very chastity he hopes to pervert. Not a girl for polite equivocation or passive resistance, however, Honora boldly takes the offensive, summarizing the Duke's flowery and flattering speech as a seduction attempt: "You would dishonour us; which in your translation / Here at the Court reads thus, your grace would love us" (4.3.53–54). Finding Honora obstinate, he turns to the more timid but equally virtuous Viola, who spurns him as well. The Duke admires the two women precisely for their rejection of his advances. "Lord how she blushes: here are truely faire soules," he marvels with clear respect, but in his frustration he intimates the possibility of sexual violence: "Why doe I stand entreating, where my power . . ." (89). Again he expresses the Fletcherian double bind, desiring women who reject his desire outside of the social regulation of marriage and fantasizing a forcible violation of that purity which he eroticizes.

Honora, however, immediately blocks his assault and assumes the dominant position. First, she interrupts his threat in mid-sentence:

> Duke. Why doe I stand entreating, where my power —
> Honora. You have no power, at least you ought to have none
>   In bad and beastly things. . . . (4.3.89–91)

Then, in a flirtatious reversal, she erotically teases both the Duke and the audience with unveiled sexual energy. She touches and kisses him, declaring provocatively, "I am no coward. / Doe you believe me now? or now? or now sir?" (101–
102). Proclaiming that she "dare doe any thing, / Thus hang about your neck,
and thus doat on yee" (106–107), she encourages Viola to join her in the play of
arousal:

> Sister come hither,
> Come hither, feare not wench: come hither, blush not,
> Come kisse the Prince, the vertuous Prince, the good Prince.
> . . .
> Sit downe, and hug him softly. (4.3.109–113)

Immediately the Duke recoils with the shocked disgust that Honora predicted
earlier a "Leacher" would feel in such circumstances:

> Fie *Honora*,
> Wanton *Honora*; is this the modesty,
> The noble chastity your on-set shew'd me,
> At first charge beaten back? Away. (4.3.113–116)

Disregarding his dismissal, both girls throw off their lascivious posture and celebrate this manifestation of the Duke's true moral nature. He, in return, thanks
them for having "done a cure upon me, counsell could not" (126), and ultimately
marries Honora in gratitude for the moral education she has forced upon him.
Virtue is rewarded, and the efficacy of the strategy of performing desire is once
more confirmed.

The most extended and outrageously comic of Fletcher's treatments of the
rape avoidance pattern provides the main plot of *The Maid in the Mill*, written
with Rowley in 1623. Kidnapped by Otrante, a handsome nobleman, the young
heroine Florimell resists his advances first with argument and then, when that
proves ineffective, with bawdy songs and suggestive speeches that fill her horrified pursuer with revulsion. Count Otrante first enters the play in Act 2 to
hunt in the country, but Florimell, the miller's daughter, is his secret target.
After luring the miller away from home, Otrante incites the miller's clownish
son Bustofa to disobey his father by leaving his work and taking his sister Florimell to a feast day celebration. Once away from home, Florimell is easily ab-
ducted while she portrays Venus during a country enactment of the Judgment of
Paris. The audience of nobles and peasants momentarily believes that her abduction is part of the play but, hearing Florimell's offstage cries for help, eventually
mount a slow and unsuccessful pursuit. Secreting the girl in his castle, Otrante

spends the next three acts alternately attempting to seduce and threatening to rape her.

The initial presentation of Florimell focuses on her extreme youth and inno-cence, for she is even younger than Lucina, who was "yet not eighteene":

> Otrante: If you go, your sister ought to go along with you.
> Bustofa: There I stumble now: shee is not at age.
> Otrante: Why? shee's fifteen, and upwards . . .
> That's womans ripe age; as full as thou art
> At one and twenty: shee's manable, is she not?
> Bustofa: I think not: poor heart, she was never tryde in my
> conscience.
> Tis a coy thing; she will not kisse you a clown, not if he would
> kisse her —
> Otrante: What, man?
> Bustofa: Not if he would kisse her, I say.
> Otrante: Oh, twas cleanlier, then I expected: well sir.
>   (2.1.126–137)

The combination of untouched youth and her aptitude to become "manable" ap-parently serves to fuel Otrante's lust, as he reaches for an obscene joke to launch it. His villainous servant Gerasto leads Florimell and Bustofa off to the feast and her intended site of corruption with suggestive songs that "ravish'd" the brother but leave Florimell unmoved, a first test. After her abduction, Florimell holds off Otrante in his castle with argument and a strong verbal display of virtue, the tra-ditional woman's ineffective strategy for defense. Initially, her would-be lover threatens rape:

> Otrante: I have stolne ye
> To enjoy ye now, not to be fool'd with circumstance,
> Yeeld willingly, or else —
> Florimell: What?
> Otrante: I will force ye. (3.3.63–65)

When Otrante wavers, however, Gerasto berates him for failing to have "handled her as men do unmand Hawks" (3.3.118). Gerasto becomes a spokesman for the prevailing script of rape, counseling the use of force as supremely pleasing to the victim:

> Gerasto: Oh force her, force her, Sir, she longs to be ravishd,
> Some have no pleasure but in violence;

To be torne in pieces is their paradise. . . .

(3.3.124–126)

His point is still audible in some twentieth-century discussions of rape: women secretly long for rape and for the pleasure of being forced to surrender to a powerful man's violent desire.

Gerasto's clichéd assumption rationalizes sexual aggression through a disturbing vision of the masochistic nature of female desire, a vision also implicit in Freud's theories. At the same time, however, a real inconsistency in thinking becomes apparent. On one hand, the potential rapists exclusively desire and want to subjugate women who are remarkable for their own lack of desire. On the other hand, Gerasto suggests that these chaste and resistant women are secretly willing and thus imperfectly chaste, which would seem to undermine their desirability. The behavioral pattern further compounds this contradiction in thought. Why are Fletcher's men so disturbed when an intended victim suggests that "rape" actually will be pleasurable rather than humiliating? If women are secretly willing, their pleasure should be neither a complete surprise nor a deterrent unless the conventional gender roles themselves — male dominance and female submission — are at stake and for the sake of male satisfaction must be maintained in appearance despite any underlying psychic reality. Otrante, fortunately, fails to indulge in such abstract questioning. He simply reveals his aptitude as a redeemable lover rather than a genuine rapist when he cannot perform his part. He delays for a night to allow Florimell to consider his demands and submit voluntarily.

In the morning, Florimell assumes the offensive. She advances upon her horrified suitor with a series of suggestive dances and bawdy country songs:

> *Think me still in my Father's Mill,*
> *   where I have oft been found-a*
> *Thrown on my back, on a well-fill'd sack,*
> *   while the Mill has still gone round-a:*
> *Prethee sirrha try thy skill,*
> *   and again let the mill go round-a.* (5.2.82–87)

Florimell pretends that her prior resistance was a ploy to capture him in marriage and that now she is showing her true face, a woman hungry for pleasure and sexually experienced with "Any that will offer, / All manner of men, and all Religions Sir, /. . . all States and Ages, / We exempt none" (5.2.92–95). Instead of kindling Otrante's passion, this successfully deflates his lust: "I do confesse I freeze now, / I am another thing all over me: / It is my part to wooe, not to be courted" (33–35). The presence of a desiring female subject renders impossible a rape, the ultimate sexual objectification of women.

Seeing her shed a tear under the strain of the imposture, Otrante begins to guess that Florimell's wantonness is a pose, but the king's unexpected arrival interrupts the moment and forces him to lock her up, wondering still whether she is "a damnd divel, or an Angel" (5.2.123). When the king forces open her door, she saves Otrante from royal fury by calmly asserting her continued virginity. Otrante quickly repents and offers her recompense, and she claims him as a husband. All are satisfied — in the space of seventy lines from the king's arrival! Conveniently, the miller's wife quickly reveals Florimell's true birth as the daughter of a nobleman present. Thus Florimell manages to speak for female desire and pleasure while preserving her chastity and her value in the marriage exchange. The "comedy," of course, lies in her actual lack of desire; her status as a subject commanding her own erotic life is illusory and, perhaps as a consequence, her reward is a privileged place in the hierarchy of wealthy aristocrats.

Although *The Maid in the Mill*'s comic form may prevent viewers and readers from inquiring too deeply into the emotional dynamics of this sequence of rape, revulsion, and reconciliation, Otrante's horror reveals the recurring pattern that surfaces in many of the plays associated with John Fletcher through his long career and multiple collaborations. In play after play, sexual aggressors are shocked and successfully repulsed by the potential victim's pretended responsiveness. Female desire disturbs and incapacitates Fletcher's male characters, who depend upon a vision of self as the pursuer rather than the pursued to assure themselves, in Nicholas Groth's terms, of their virility and power and to establish their own centrality as subjects. The erotic performance by the comic women disables the sexual performance of their attackers. In acting out the existence of an autonomous sexual drive, however insincerely, Fletcher's female characters also create themselves as apparent subjects and thus disrupt the assailant's enactment of his own gendered identity. In comic and tragicomic versions of this pattern, such as *The Maid in the Mill*, the assault is not merely deflected; the assaulter also is morally transformed, enabling him to provide a dramatically suitable if somewhat tainted mate for the female.

Ultimately, sexual desire is as slippery and difficult to fix in the plays as are early modern treatments of female subjectivity and the elusive authorial and erotic identity that Jeffrey Masten discovers in Fletcher's own life (in *Textual Intercourse*). The actual nature and presence of sexual desire in the plays remains completely ambiguous. Emasculated by the presence of female desire, aggressive male sexuality is unmasked as a failed quest for power. The women voice a language of lust to which the plays suggest they are complete strangers in experience. No satisfying explanation for the presence of such language can be offered apart from the women's need to establish themselves dramatically as subjects, as agents with will and desire, rather than objects. Like the men, the women exhibit no unalloyed drive for sexual pleasure. Instead, the wanton stance of Fletcher's female characters merely enacts their own subjectivity and their embodiment of power in the hierarchy of desire. Repeatedly, Fletcher depicts male disgust and loss of desire as the women assert their own independent subjective natures and speak the language of physical desire. Just as in Renaissance legal codes the suspicion of female pleasure invalidates the name of rape, so in Fletcher's plays its presence extinguishes the desire of the would-be rapist.

Barbara Mathieson
Southern Oregon University

Works Cited

Baines, Barbara J. "Effacing Rape in Early Modern Representation." *ELH* 65 (1998): 69–98.

Bart, Pauline B., and Patricia H. O'Brien. *Stopping Rape: Successful Survival Strategies*. New York: Pergamon Press, 1985.

Bowers, Fredson, ed. *The Dramatic Works in the Beaumont and Fletcher Canon*. 10 vols. Cambridge: Cambridge University Press, 1966–1996.

Cameron, Deborah, and Elizabeth Frazer. *The Lust to Kill*. New York: New York University Press, 1987.

Donaldson, Ian. *The Rapes of Lucretia: A Myth and its Transformations*. Oxford: Clarendon Press, 1982.

Fletcher, John. *Bonduca*, ed. Cyrus Hoy. In *Dramatic Works*, ed. Bowers, 4: 149–259.

———. *The Faithful Shepherdess*, ed. Cyrus Hoy. In *Dramatic Works*, ed. Bowers, 3: 483–583.

———. *The Loyal Subject*, ed. Fredson Bowers. In *Dramatic Works*, ed. Bowers, 5: 151–288.

———. *Monsieur Thomas*, ed. Hans Walter Gabler. In *Dramatic Works*, ed. Bowers, 4: 415–540.

———. *The Tragedy of Valentinian*, ed. Robert K. Turner, Jr. In *Dramatic Works*, ed. Bowers, 4: 261–414.

———, and Francis Beaumont. *The Coxcomb*, ed. Irby B. Cauthen, Jr. In *Dramatic Works*, ed. Bowers, 1: 261–366.

———, Nathan Field, and Philip Massinger. *The Queen of Corinth*, ed. Robert Kean Turner. In *Dramatic Works*, ed. Bowers, 8: 3–111.

———, and William Rowley. *The Maid in the Mill*, ed. Fredson Bowers. In *Dramatic Works*, ed. Bowers, 9: 569–669.

Foster, Verna A. "Sex Averted or Converted: Sexuality and Tragicomic Genre in the Plays of Fletcher." *Studies in English Literature, 1500–1900* 32 (1992): 311–22.

Freud, Sigmund. *Three Contributions to the Theory of Sex*. In *The Basic Writings of Sigmund Freud*, ed. A. A. Brill, 553–629. New York: Random House, 1938.

Gossett, Suzanne. "'Best Men are Molded out of Faults': Marrying the Rapist in Jacobean Drama." *English Literary Renaissance* 14 (1984): 305–27.

Groth, A. Nicholas. *Men Who Rape: The Psychology of the Offender*. New York: Plenum, 1979.

Kahn, Coppélia. "*Lucrece*: The Sexual Politics of Subjectivity." In *Rape and Representation*, ed. Lynn A. Higgins and Brenda R. Silver, 141–59. New York: Columbia University Press, 1991.

Masten, Jeffrey. *Textual Intercourse: Collaboration, Authorship, and Sexualities in Renaissance Drama*. Cambridge: Cambridge University Press, 1997.

McLuskie, Kathleen. *Renaissance Dramatists*. Atlantic Highlands, NJ: Humanities Press, 1989.

Pearse, Nancy Cotton. *John Fletcher's Chastity Plays: Mirrors of Modesty*. Lewisburg, PA: Bucknell University Press, 1973.

Squier, Charles L. *John Fletcher*. Boston: Twayne, 1986.

B.
Violence and
the Interior Subjectivity
of Women

Female Selfhood and Male Violence
in English Renaissance Drama:
A View from Mary Wroth's *Urania*

The ideology of marriage in Renaissance England, although its effects upon women were depressingly oppressive and its upholders tended to inflict terrible violence upon women who did not submit to its demands, ironically seemed also to offer women the opportunity to construct their sense of self. Faced with the image of female roles in marriage as defined by patriarchal authority, many women in early modern England became conscious of the gap between what they felt they were and what they were supposed to be, even if most of them, however strongly they may have felt the demands of their interior selfhood, probably did not dare to challenge conventional female roles, conforming instead to the passive behavior assigned to them. Nevertheless, historical records do show some cases of aristocratic women who, feeling their sense of self to be in conflict with the notions of femininity assumed in the discourse of marriage in their society, resorted to sexual transgression. Lady Penelope Rich, for instance, who was discontented with her arranged marriage with the wealthy Lord Rich, developed a long-standing adulterous relationship with Lord Mountjoy, later Earl of Devonshire, and, after bearing him five illegitimate children, finally married him, which caused a great scandal at the Court (Rawson, *Penelope Rich*). Similarly, Frances Hatton was forced into an arranged marriage with John Villiers, Buckingham's elder brother, by her father, Edward Coke, despite the strong opposition of her mother, Lady Hatton. Frances sought solace in an extramarital relationship with Robert Howard and bore his child, whom she named Robert Wright (Norsworthy, *The Lady of Bleeding Heart Yard*, 117–45).

Among the women who resisted the contemporary discourse of marriage in order to overcome the gap they felt between their experience of their own selves and the expectations placed upon them, the most remarkable was Lady Mary

Wroth, who had an adulterous relationship with her first cousin, William Herbert, the third Earl of Pembroke, and bore him two children, Katherine and William, in around 1614. Lady Mary Wroth was different from other adulterous women in the period in that she chose to assume the position of author in order to explore the significance of the gap created in female identity by patriarchal society.[1] She was the first English woman to write a pastoral play, *Love's Victory* (c. 1621), and to publish a prose romance, *Urania* (1621) and a sonnet sequence, *Pamphilia to Amphilanthus*, which was appended to *Urania*. In all these works Wroth explores what a female self experienced as autonomous might signify in a society which denies the availability of such experience to women. In particular, *Urania* is filled with descriptions of women whose innermost thoughts are in contradiction with concepts of female identity as defined in the contemporary discourse of marriage.

Another woman writer in the period who investigated female selfhood in terms of the ideology of marriage was Elizabeth Cary, Lady Falkland. Although, unlike Wroth, Cary did not engage in sexual transgression, in *The Tragedy of Mariam* (c. 1603), the first known play written by an English woman, she dramatizes the heroine's way of constructing her sense of self in the process of considering her feeling of incompatibility with the conventional notion of wifehood.[2] Cary also pursues the problem of female sexual transgression in her portrayal of Queen Isabel in *The History of the Life, Reign, and Death of Edward II* (c. 1626), which, if the attribution of this work to her is correct (as seems likely to be the case), is the earliest historical writing by an English woman.[3]

Many male playwrights in the English Renaissance also deal with wives' marital unhappiness and sexual transgression. However, their approaches to this problem are quite different from the approaches of these women writers. Rather than fully exploring the significance of a female sense of contradiction with the ideology of marriage, most male writers present the wife's adultery as caused simply by what they regard as innate female weakness or as monstrous sexual

---

[1] See Marion Wynne-Davies, " 'For *Worth*, Not Weakness, Makes in Use but One': Literary Dialogues in an English Renaissance Family," in *"This Double Voice": Gendered Writing in Early Modern England*, ed. Danielle Clarke and Elizabeth Clarke (London: Macmillan, 2000), 164–84. See also Robyn Bolam, "The Heart of the Labyrinth: Mary Wroth's *Pamphilia to Amphilanthus*," in *A Companion to English Renaissance Literature and Culture*, ed. Hattaway, 257–66.

[2] For Cary's life and the construction of female sense of identity in *The Tragedy of Mariam*, see Lewalski, *Writing Women in Jacobean England*, 178–211.

[3] For a discussion of the uncertain authorship of *The History of the Life, Reign, and Death of Edward II*, see Lewalski, *Writing Women in Jacobean England*, 317–20.

assertiveness, qualities which had been attributed to womanhood in misogynistic writings since medieval times.

Male Renaissance playwrights often portray male characters who consider female identity in terms of consistency and wholeness, as something which can be wholly displayed on the surface and which hides no innermost self (that is, no self which is, to whatever degree, independent of male assumptions about womanhood) underneath; female characters in their plays who do show a discrepancy between appearance and selfhood are usually depicted in terms of female duplicity which harms the men around them. On the other hand, both Wroth and Cary represent female identity as constituted of plural aspects. In their works the gap between female innermost thoughts and female outward appearance is presented as something which women of integrity cannot but experience within themselves, and yet which they are forced to conceal underneath the mask of conventional female behavior in order to avoid their ruin in society.

These innermost thoughts, which the female characters in the works of Wroth and Cary typically try to keep private and prevent men from knowing — especially if the male attempt to gain access to these thoughts is associated with violence — often prove to be unstable in terms both of their self-consciousness and of the way in which their selfhood is constructed; their sense of self is not single or monolithic since it is mediated by social factors. What the female characters consider to be their autonomous selfhood may actually be, as Catherine Belsey in *The Subject of Tragedy* or Judith Butler in *Gender Trouble* have argued,[4] the product of the cultures they live in, even though they are not conscious of this fact; the construction of what they regard as their selfhood thus tends to be deeply affected by the very social assumptions about womanhood from which they are trying to free themselves. And yet, their sense of the discrepancy between what society assumes women to be and what they consider themselves to be is still highly significant in the light of the long-term history of changes in women's self-consciousness and in social concepts of womanhood. Although the construction of women's innermost feelings is greatly influenced by the cultures they live in and thus may be unstable, women's sense that they have autonomous selves which are not constrained by patriarchal society interacts with various elements in their cultures, such as social concepts of gender or contemporary economic conditions, and functions as a factor in instigating a new concept of womanhood in society, a concept which considers womanhood from a perspective different from that of orthodox views.

---

[4] Belsey, *The Subject of Tragedy*; Butler, *Gender Trouble*.

Both in male-authored Renaissance plays and in works by Wroth and Cary, when male characters realize that underneath a woman's outward appearance there exists such an area of inner thought or female self-identification which they cannot dominate, they often inflict physical violence on her by torturing her body, or psychological violence by regarding her as mad. What distinguishes male writers' treatments of this problem from those of Wroth and Cary is their tendency to incorporate grotesque elements in their representations of male characters' infliction of violence. (In this essay the terms "grotesque" and "grotesqueness" are used in the senses defined by the *OED* [s.vv. grotesque B. 2. a. and 3; grotesqueness]; that is, as referring to things or events or artistic works characterized by distortion or unnatural combinations, or by incongruous absurdity.) In contrast to these male writers, both Wroth and Cary present the gap within female identity not through images of grotesqueness, but in terms of theatricality: they demonstrate female identity as constituted of both a woman's performance of her assigned role and what she regards as her innermost autonomous self.[5] In Wroth's and Cary's works both good and bad female performers appear, that is, women who are good or bad at performing their conventional roles, while concealing their inward state successfully.

This essay examines the significance of the representations of female selfhood and male violence in English Renaissance drama in the light of female viewpoints on these problems as expressed in works by women writers, particularly in Mary Wroth's *Urania*. In order to highlight the characteristic features in English Renaissance drama, the essay also briefly examines two well-known Kabuki plays, *Tokaido Yotsuya Kaidan* (*The Ghost Story of Yotsuya*) and *Dojoji*. In these plays female roles are performed by men, as in plays in the English Renaissance, but the representations of female assertive power function in somewhat different ways.

I

Women in *Urania* can be divided largely into two groups, depending on how successful they are in their performance of their theatrical self. The tale of Limena is one of the episodes in which Mary Wroth presents most clearly her notion of the split within female identity, a split between female innermost selfhood and female outward appearance. Limena's husband, Philargus, suspects that after marriage his wife still loves Perissus, with whom she has pledged love

---

[5] My understanding of Wroth's theatrical vision of female selfhood is indebted to Weidemann, "Theatricality and Female Identity in Mary Wroth's *Urania*," 191–209.

before her marriage, and repeatedly tortures her to make her confess her true feelings for her former lover. As Elizabeth Hanson has argued, a torturer assumes the existence of a truth hidden within the body of the tortured, and the torture is an attempt to draw this truth out from the body of the tortured by inflicting violence (Hanson, *Discovering the Subject in Renaissance England*, 24–54). In the case of Philargus, two conflicting issues make his situation complicated: since in the contemporary discourse of marriage his sense of identity as a man and husband depends on his wife's constancy in both a mental and a physical sense, the success of his torture will lead to the loss of his own sense of identity. What is more, to his embarrassment and fury, despite his repeated and increasingly cruel torture of her body, Limena not only rejects Philargus's definition of her as a faithless wife, asserting that she has not betrayed him sexually, but also declares the impossibility of his gaining possession of her inmost self. In her concept of her identity she distinguishes her interior selfhood from her tortured body. In a letter she narrates to Perissus what she said to her husband:

> This wretched, and unfortunate body, is I confesse in your hands, to dispose of to death if you will; but yet it is not unblest with such a mind as will suffer it to end with any such staine, as so wicked a plott, and miserable consent might purchase ... I will with more willingnesse die, then execute your minde; and more happily shall I end, saving him innocent from ill, delivering my soule pure, and I unspotted of the crime you tax me of, or a thought of such dishonour to my selfe ... (Wroth, *Urania*, ed. Roberts, 13)

Later, she and Perissus are able to meet, and her narrative of the torture on that occasion points to her agency in two respects. First, in disclosing the violence which her husband has inflicted upon her body and her defiance of it, she tries to demonstrate an autonomous self which eludes Philargus's authority as a husband. Moreover, she shows her agency even in her dealings with Perissus, by manipulating her narration in such a way as to evoke his admiration for her integrity as well as his attraction to her eroticism:[6]

> ... he [Philargus] opened my breast, and gave me many wounds, the markes you may here yet discerne (letting the Mantle fall againe a little lower, to shew the cruell remembrance of his crueltie) which although they were whole, yet made they newe hurts in the loving heart of

---

[6] For the significance of Wroth's representation of Philargus's sadistic torture of Limena's body, see Hackett, "The Torture of Limena," 93–110.

Perissus, suffering more paine for them, then he had done for all those
himselfe had received in his former adventures ... (Wroth, *Urania*, ed.
Roberts, 87)

Thus, in the episode of Limena, Wroth not only gives Limena victory over
her husband, representing her as able to maintain the agency of her autonomous
self in the face of the physical pain inflicted by him, but also allows her to dominate Perissus through manipulating her narrative of the torture in such a way as
to awake his desire. In her married life, Limena succeeds to a certain extent in
her performance of her theatrical self by concealing her passion for Perissus underneath the appearance of being an obedient wife. Yet her performance is not
entirely successful, since her husband notices that her appearance does not en-
code her whole selfhood. When Philargus starts to torture her, trying to force
her to confess her true feelings, she stops performing her theatrical self by confessing her true feelings of love for Perissus and her hatred for her husband, thus
exposing to him the split which exists within her identity, while rejecting his
claim as husband to her inmost thoughts. Hence Limena is not a totally successful performer, and yet Wroth enables her to obtain happiness in the end; after
having tortured his wife, Philargus dies of remorse, allowing Limena and Perissus to be united after all.

Few women who have a divided self in *Urania* can obtain such happiness,
however. Bellamira, who is generally regarded as a partially autobiographical portrait of Wroth herself, also experiences a divided self,[7] when, despite having a
lover, she is forced to marry Treborius:

> ... the marriage followed: what torture was it to mee, standing betweene
> my love, and Treborius, when I was to give my selfe from my love to
> him? How willingly would I have turned to the other hand: but contrary
> to my soule I gave my selfe to him, my heart to my first love. Thus more
> then equally did I devide my selfe. ... (Wroth, *Urania*, ed. Roberts, 388)

Unlike Limena, Bellamira cannot be united with her lover. Moreover, even while
her husband, Treborius, is alive, she is pursued by the King of Dalmatia, and
after Treborius's death, she is forced to renew her affair with the king. Thus she
is portrayed as a woman who suffers the split within herself endlessly.

The notion of a husband's right to possess his wife's interior self, a notion
deeply rooted in the ideology of marriage in Renaissance England, is one of the

---

[7] For discussions of Wroth's autobiographical narratives in her work, see Wynne-
Davies, "'So Much Work'," 76–93.

main assumptions that women writers in the period, especially Mary Wroth and
Elizabeth Cary, question in their works.[8] In *The Tragedy of Mariam*, Elizabeth
Cary makes the Chorus insist on this male claim and blame Mariam for her re-
fusal to reveal her inmost thoughts to her husband, Herod:

> When to their Husbands they themselues doe bind,
> Doe they not wholy giue themselues away?
> Or giue they but their body not their mind,
> Reseruing that though best, for others pray?
> No sure, their thoughts no more can be their owne,
> And therefore should to none but one be knowne.
>
> Then she vsurpes vpon anothers right,
> That seekes to be by publike language grac't:
> (Cary, *Mariam*, ed. Dunstan, 3.3. 1237–1244)

Cary makes it clear that this articulation by the Chorus of the husband's right
contrasts sharply with Mariam's sense of self. She objects to Herod's treatment
of her as a beautiful object rather than as a person with an autonomous self.
When Sohemus, Herod's trusted servant, tells her that Herod has ordered her
and her mother to be imprisoned while he is away in Rome, and that, if Herod
cannot come back from Rome, he is to murder Mariam in order to prevent her
remarriage, she decides not to welcome her husband on his return home, and
furthermore to refuse to go to bed with him. Her rebellion causes him to suspect
that she has sexually betrayed him with Sohemus, and, egged on by his malicious
sister, Salome, he executes his wife. Faced with her impending execution,
Mariam realizes that her sense of integrity, which has taken no account of the
importance of outward appearances of wifely obedience, has led her to not live
"wisely":

> Had I but with humilitie bene grac'te,
> As well as faire I might haue prou'd me wise:
> But I did thinke because I knew me chaste,
> One vertue for a woman, might suffice.
> That mind for glory of our sexe might stand,
> Wherein humilitie and chastitie

---

[8] See Findlay, "Women and Drama," 7–11; Hodgson-Wright, "Beauty, Chastity and
Wit," 55–59, 66–67.

> Doth march with equall paces hand in hand,
> But one if single seene, who setteth by?
> (Cary, *Mariam*, ed. Dunstan, 4.8. 1833–1840)

Mariam acknowledges that she has not been a good performer of her theatrical self. Nonetheless, she immediately declares that her selfhood is independent of the conventional notion of femininity required from a wife, and takes pride in maintaining her autonomous self, even though it has brought her death:

> ... tis my ioy,
> That I was euer innocent, though sower:
> And therefore can they but my life destroy,
> My Soule is free from aduersaries power.
> (Cary, *Mariam*, ed. Dunstan, 4.8. 1841–1844)

Herod assumes that his wife's body hides "truth", that is, her desire for So-hemus, and, being unable to draw out her confession of this, he executes her. Nevertheless, although her performance of theatricality is deficient, Cary's heroine ends victorious despite her death. Like Philargus in *Urania*, Herod deeply repents what he has done to his wife, and although, unlike Philargus, he does not die at the end, he becomes half mad, wishing for Mariam's restoration to life. Thus, both Wroth and Cary locate the basis of female construction of selfhood in a woman's acknowledgement of the split existing within herself.

Male authors in the period also deal with the gap between innermost female feelings and female appearance, but in most cases quite differently. They usually represent it as a sign of female duplicity, at the time conventionally regarded as a characteristic feature of femininity. This female duplicity is usually linked with a wife's sexual transgression, and even with the murder of a husband. For instance, Alice in *Arden of Faversham* (1591) is portrayed as being discontented in her married life with Arden, who is an ambitious, wealthy landowner, but as successfully disguising both her discontent and her desire for her lover, Mosby. Arden entertains no suspicion of his wife's betrayal, let alone her intention of murdering him. Thomas Middleton also takes a similar approach in most of his plays. In *Women Beware Women* (1621), Livia is described as an epitome of female duplicity, while Isabella is portrayed as a young woman who comes to adopt duplicity as a strategy in order to continue her affair with her uncle, Hippolito. Bianca, on the other hand, is presented as duplicitous from the very beginning. Though looking like an innocent, obedient, well-bred daughter, she agrees to elope with Leantio, a man of much lower social status. Her duplicity is fully displayed in her attitudes to Leantio as she attempts to hide her desire for the Duke, and female duplicity of this kind is presented as leading to the bizarre, chaotic ending of the play. Thus English Renaissance drama frequently centers on female desire, especially as enacted in a wife's adultery, but most male playwrights present the problem as being caused by duplicity arising from supposedly innate female weakness or the horrible power of female desire, both of which were stereotypically assumed to be common attributes of femininity. The few exceptions to this stereotypical representation of female desire include Webster's *The Duchess of Malfi* (1614) and Shakespeare's *Antony and Cleopatra* (1607),[9] to which I shall return later.

In plays written by men, when male characters notice a gap within a woman's identity, they often inflict physical or psychological violence on her in order to eliminate this gap, thereby attempting to deprive the woman of her autonomous self by means of torture. In particular, in scenes where male characters find it difficult to subjugate the power of selfhood of female characters, male playwrights in the English Renaissance tend to use grotesque elements, in their representations of torture. The monstrous hybridity of the cruelties enacted on the stage, at once ferocious, bizarre, and absurd, has the effect of revealing the male characters' desire to belittle the significance of women's resistance to the demands of male authority. In *The Duchess of Malfi*, for instance, when Ferdinand attempts to break the Duchess's belief in the rightness of her secret marriage with Antonio, he shows her the fake corpses of her husband and son, while presenting a dead man's hand to her in the darkness. The terrible incongruities in this scene create an atmosphere of the grotesque since, however deep the Duchess's grief or shock at observing the corpses of her husband and son, or at being forced to grasp the dead man's hand, the audience's knowledge that her shock is elicited by fake figures renders her feelings somewhat absurd, even though it is equally true that the gap between the authenticity of her feelings and the audience's knowledge of the theatricality of the scene adds to the poignancy of her emotions and of her situation.

A further grotesque aspect of Ferdinand's torture of the Duchess is emphasized in the scene in which he disperses madmen in the house where she is imprisoned. This scene often invites laughter from the audience due to the absurdity of the conversation between the Duchess and the madmen. The audience fully understands the deep sorrow of the Duchess, who is in danger of losing her mental balance because of the psychological cruelty of the torture inflicted by her

---

[9] I use the edition of *Antony and Cleopatra* edited by John Wilders, in The Arden Shakespeare (London and New York: Routledge, 1995).

brothers. However, the scene is also bizarre because of the unnatural combination of grief and ludicrousness. By his choice of a form of torture marked by a monstrous hybridity of comic and tragic elements, Ferdinand tries to imply that the Duchess has displayed a frightful doubleness toward her brothers in her rebellion against both their authority and her own royal position, while simultaneously intending to belittle the Duchess's suffering. In the end, however, Ferdinand's torture fails to break her selfhood, and at no point does she ever regret her marriage. The grotesqueness of his torture only underlines the cruelty of his attempt. Moreover, Webster endorses the Duchess's marriage by making Ferdinand, not the Duchess, lose his sanity as a result of his cruelty.

Another example of grotesque elements in the representation of male violence inflicted upon women may be observed in Shakespeare's *Titus Andronicus* (1594).[10] In his revenge upon Tamora, who incited her two sons to rape and mutilate his daughter, Lavinia, Titus sends Tamora a meat pie made of her sons' flesh. Although Shakespeare draws this episode from his source, the effect of the stage representation of this scene is certainly ridiculous and bizarre — or in other words, grotesque. This incident, while truly appalling for Tamora herself, usually invites laughter from the audience.[11] In punishing the uncontrollably assertive Tamora, whose affair with Aaron shows that she refuses to contain her desire within the domain of her husband, Titus cannot rely on a more ordinary manner of revenge. Thus, as in the case of Webster's *Duchess of Malfi*, the grotesque elements in Titus's revenge function to underscore Tamora's assertive power as well as his efforts to belittle it. Titus, like Ferdinand, realizes that in dealing with such an autonomous woman only grotesque actions can be effective, since these are the actions that are most likely to break her sense of self; these men know that in the case of women like the Duchess or Tamora the force and resilience of their personalities are so great that it is impossible to subjugate them to male authority through ordinary means of torment.

The introduction of grotesqueness in the representation of female assertive power which eludes male authority is not limited to plays written by male writers of the West. A similar method is used to the utmost degree in a well-known ghost play in Kabuki, *Tokaido Yotsuya Kaidan*, written by Tsuruya Nanboku (1755–1829). The play was based on a real murder case which took place in Edo

---

[10] I use the edition of *Titus Andronicus* edited by Jonathan Bate, in The Arden Shakespeare (London and New York: Routledge, 1995).

[11] In the Royal Shakespeare Company's production of the play in 1987, directed by Deborah Warner, the grotesque elements in this scene were particularly emphasized.

(now Tokyo), and was first performed in 1825. The heroine, Oiwa, was once a beautiful woman who had married Iemon because he promised to take revenge on the murderer of her father for her sake. However, Iemon is loved by a daughter of a man of high social rank, and, in order to climb up the hierarchy through marriage with this daughter, he has Oiwa murdered in the most cruel way. While Oiwa was alive, she was a docile, submissive wife, but once she is dead and has become a ghost, she becomes an enormously energetic and defiant figure. Totally ignoring gender ideology, she constantly haunts Iemon and his accomplices, displaying her body, grossly deformed by the effects of the poison they have given her, and expressing the resentment and grief she feels on account of their cruel betrayal and murder of her. In *Yotsuya Kaidan*, both morals in patriarchal society and men in authority are portrayed as totally corrupt. By showing the grotesquely deformed body of Oiwa on the stage, Nanboku asserts the absurdity of the social situation which allows such violence upon the female body.

The evils in patriarchal society embodied by Iemon and his accomplices are described as so horrible that anyone who wants to challenge such malicious energy needs even more tremendous power. For this purpose, Nanboku uses an extremely bizarre image for the damage done to the female body in the appearance of Oiwa's ghost. In Kabuki plays, a male actor's body usually represents female beauty; in contrast, in this play it presents the grotesque deformity of a woman's mutilated body. The grotesqueness in this play, however, unlike the meat pie in *Titus and Andronicus* or the wax corpses in *The Duchess of Malfi*, does not signify a male inability to subjugate female challenges to male authority. It is rather a sign of the unusually powerful energy required to challenge the absurdity and corruption in male-dominated society. At the same time Nanboku also indicates in this way the interior energy concealed in the body of the docile Oiwa, an energy which cannot be contained in contemporary gender ideology, since, being liberated after her death, she takes revenge upon her torturers in the most aggressive manner.

In recent years many important issues relating to the significance of boys playing female roles in English Renaissance drama have been discussed in both social and sexual terms.[12] Little attention, however, has been paid to the problem of male writers' incorporation of grotesque elements in describing female assertiveness through the body of a male actor. In plays both in the English Renaissance and in Kabuki, the audiences' awareness of the fictionalization of actions on the

---

[12] See, for instance, Orgel, *Impersonations*; Shapiro, *Gender in Play on the Shakespearean Stage*; Traub, *Desire and Anxiety*.

stage, that is, their awareness that they were watching a fiction of the female produced through the bodies of men, seemed to create a distance in the audience's sense of reality which allowed outrageously grotesque representations of female power. Although the social implications of plays in the English Renaissance are different from those of the Kabuki play, it must be noted that male writers in both theatres deploy qualities of grotesqueness in expressing the power of a female selfhood which men cannot control.

In contrast, neither Mary Wroth nor Elizabeth Cary depends on grotesqueness in describing the strength of female selfhood. Instead, they deeply investigate the significance of the split women feel between their interior self and the outward appearance they are supposed to maintain. As already mentioned, Wroth presents in *Urania* two kinds of assertive women: those who can perform their theatrical selves well, and those who fail in this performance by being unable to keep the balance between the two aspects of their identity. The best performer in *Urania* is of course Pamphilia. Her identity consists of many faces; she is Queen of Pamphilia, an obedient daughter of the King of Morea, and a woman passionately in love with Amphilanthus, the King of Naples. Because of Amphilanthus's faithlessness, she constantly suffers inner pain, but claims a constant self by maintaining her faithful love for him. She grieves over his repeated betrayal, but in the presence of other people, she feigns happiness, by effectively masking her true feelings with behavior in line with assigned roles. The success of her theatricality allows Pamphilia to preserve her authority, but at the same time, as Heather Weidemann has pointed out ("Theatricality and Female Identity," 201), her theatricality sometimes unsettles her sense of autonomy by placing her in a situation in which she constantly suffers from the gap within herself. Urania once tells Pamphilia to disavow her constancy to Amphilanthus since it is no use her victimizing herself for a faithless lover. Pamphilia, however, insists on the construction of her own selfhood through her insistence on the authenticity of her constancy, regardless of Amphilanthus's inconstancy:

> ... To leave him for being false, would shew my love was not for his sake, but mine owne, that because he loved me, I therefore loved him, but when hee leaves I can doe so to. O no deere Cousen I loved him for himselfe, and would have loved him had hee not loved mee, and will love though hee dispise me; this is true love ... Pamphilia must be of a new composition before she can let such thoughts fall into her constant breast, which is a Sanctuary of zealous affection, and so well hath love instructed me, as I can never leave my master nor his precepts, but still maintaine a vertuous constancy. (Wroth, *Urania*, ed. Roberts, 470)

Thus Wroth locates Pamphilia's individual subjectivity in her maintenance of constancy, underlining her independence both from Amphilanthus's changeable subjectivity and from a world concerned only with conventional female outward appearance.[13] Therefore, although, as Weidemann has argued ("Theatricality and Female Identity," 202–4), Pamphilia's identity is delimited by her theatricality, she demonstrates her agency in constructing her sense of self.

She inscribes the feelings of her inward self in her poems or in her narratives of other women's painful stories which parallel her own experience. Since both literary forms, the sonnet sequence and the romance, were inherited by Wroth from male predecessors, above all from her uncle, Sir Philip Sidney, some critics think that Wroth was unable to establish female identity in any unconventional manner.[14] However, throughout *Urania* she subverts conventional norms of femininity, especially the norms expressed in the contemporary ideology of marriage, by showing Pamphilia as able both to perform her theatrical self successfully and to maintain the integrity of her innermost self underneath her appearance. In other words, she never subjugates her autonomous self to anyone, revealing it only privately in her writings or in her conversations with her close female friends, Urania and Veralinda. Thus, in her portrayal of Pamphilia, Wroth describes a detachment of female selfhood from female appearance, insisting on the plural faces of femininity, which male authority can never wholly manipulate.

Another difference between Wroth's attitude to female selfhood and that of male writers can be observed in relation to the theme of female revenge. An interesting example is seen in a tale told by Veralinda in Book IV of *Urania* (Part I). Her father, the King of Frigia, seduced many women in his kingdom and then deserted them. When Veralinda comes back to her country with her knights, the first scene she encounters is a band of angry women attacking her father, the King.

> [T]hey found the King bound, a great ring of armed men about him, and some six or seven women (for Gentlewomen I cannot call those, used such cruelty) with great rods whipping him, having stripped his upper

---

[13] See also Shaver, "Agency and Marriage," 179–80.

[14] Waller, "Struggling into Discourse," 238–56, for instance, takes this position, one which has been challenged by feminist scholars such as Lewalski, *Writing Women in Jacobean England*, and Miller, "Engendering Discourse: Women's Voices in Wroth's *Urania* and Shakespeare's Plays," in *Reading Mary Wroth*, 154–72, and *Changing the Subject*.

part; he complaining, and pitifully crying, the strips being sore, and painefull to his royall body. (Wroth, *Urania*, ed. Roberts, 562)

The women who have been abused by the King have got together to take revenge upon him. They have become extremely violent, intending "to take their full revenge, or as much as they could" (Wroth, *Urania*, ed. Roberts, 563). Even though the King tries to fight against the women with the help of his subjects, he seems to be losing the battle. Only the arrival of Veralinda's husband, Leonius, a courageous prince of Naples, rescues the King from danger. This episode was almost certainly drawn from the contemporary anonymous, though most probably male-authored, play, *Swetnam the Woman-hater Araigned by Women* (c. 1618). Joseph Swetnam was a well-known misogynist, who had published a best-selling pamphlet attacking women entitled *The Araignment of Lewde, idle, froward and unconstant women* (1615). The play is about Swetnam, on whom women take revenge in the final scene, physically attacking him and finally arraigning him in court. The play, however, takes a grossly satirical view not only of Swetnam but also of the women, the violent but also ludicrous nature of whose revenge undermines their justification for their assertion of female integrity.[15] In contrast, Wroth's description of female revenge includes no comical elements. After the battle between the King and the women, Veralinda even listens attentively to one of the women wronged by the King. Wroth's serious treatment of the women's desire and of their justification for their revenge validates both their assertion of their human integrity and their protest against male exploitation of female desire.

Hence Wroth's ways of describing female assertiveness greatly differ from those of the male writers both in English Renaissance drama and in Kabuki who employ grotesque elements to show the tremendous energy of female assertiveness. These elements certainly underline the power of female energy, but the fact that the assertive heroines in these plays were played by male players diminishes the urgency of the issue, distancing the audience from a sense of the authenticity and reality of the female characters' feelings.

Wroth's *Urania* is different from other romances written in the period in that it depends on the technique of dramatic communication between the characters.[16] And yet, since it was not designed for the stage, she did not have to de-

---

[15] Wayne presents an interesting argument on the ambiguities in the treatment of gender in this play in "The Dearth of the Author," 221–40.

[16] For Wroth's employment of dramatic technique in her romance, see Miller, "Engendering Discourse."

pend on the male body to represent female selfhood. Likewise, since Elizabeth Cary did not write *The Tragedy of Mariam* for actual performance in a theater, she probably did not consider the possibility of her heroine being embodied by men. The fact that these women writers did not have to fictionalize the issue of female selfhood through the male body seemed to enable them to pursue the issue in more realistic ways without using appalling, bizarre images.

II

Among the women in *Urania* who cannot perform their theatrical selves well are Nereana and Antissia. They are both characterized by their inability to enact their assumed roles, instead revealing their private feelings blatantly. Nereana is Princess of Stalamine, and her great pride derives from her identity as a princess, that is, her identity in the public sphere. Privately, though, she is a passionate and sexually assertive woman.

Nereana's problem comes from her failure to separate her public identity from her private self; she insists upon her royal power even in the private sphere of desire. This does not happen in the case of Pamphilia; she never displays her secret love in her public life, always expressing her desire in private spaces, such as in her conversation with her female friends or in her talk with Amphilanthus in her bedroom. Nereana is in love with Steriamus, whom she tenaciously pursues, wrongly assuming that her position as a princess enables her to force him to respond to her desire. Despite Steriamus's repeated refusals, she seeks the fulfillment of her desire, and even visits the kingdom of Morea in order to observe Pamphilia, with whom she wrongly thinks Steriamus is in love. People label her as mad, seeing her strong sexual assertiveness as being improper both with respect to her royal position and in terms of the social image of womanhood. People's definition of Nereana's identity as a mad woman does not deter her from setting out for the woods in order to pursue her desire. In the forest, however, the mad shepherd, Alanius, happens to find her and attacks her, redefining her as a goddess of the wood whom he adores; he dresses her in strange attire and admires her as a goddess. Thus, as Jocelyn Catty has pointed out, in the case of Nereana, male violence is inflicted upon her body, not only in sexual terms, that is, in Alanius's attempt to rape her, but also in psychological terms as well: he violently tries to redefine her sense of self (*Writing Rape, Writing Women*, 197–98).

Eventually, Nereana succeeds in imposing her will on Alanius, asserting the dignity of her royal self in commanding him to leave her. Living alone in a cave and undergoing loneliness and misery, she grows humble. However, when Perissus finds her there and listens to her narrative of her pursuit of Steriamus, she is again defined by him as mad. Left alone by Perissus, she goes back to her country, where she is imprisoned and cured of her "madness". After her mental balance has been restored, she is released from prison and restored to her throne. However, when she regains royal power, her former self, with all its pride and self-assertion, comes back.

Thus, as in the case of Limena, in the representation of Nereana Wroth indicates the uncontrollable quality of female desire, which is considered as madness if a woman fails in her performance of masking it under conventional behavior. Nevertheless, it is important to note that Wroth explores Nereana's assertion of desire from various points of view, not presenting it simply as a threat to the male sense of identity. Male playwrights, on the other hand, typically describe female desire as potentially threatening to men.

Many English Renaissance writers dramatize women who assert their desire as objects of satire, which, though indirectly, suggests a male sense of threat when faced with that desire. In City comedies, particularly those by Middleton and Dekker, wives of London merchants entertain desire for men of gentle class, a complication which constitutes the main comic matter of these plays. Female desire is often treated as related to a fanatic, religious principle, especially that of Puritanism or of the sects, as in Middleton's *The Family of Love* (1602) or *A Mad World, My Masters* (1606). In *The Family of Love*, Mistress Purge's pretensions to religious ardour are depicted as motivated by her interest in the orgies held at the religious meetings of the Family of Love, although Middleton's satire is also directed at her husband, who blindly believes that she is learning wifely obedience and chastity at the meetings. Similarly, in *A Mad World, My Masters*, Mistress Harebrain deceives her husband into thinking that she is learning about the wifely virtues from Frank Gullman (actually a bawd), while in fact enjoying assignations with her lover, Penitent Brothel.

In *The Witch of Edmonton* (1621), female desire is even connected to witchcraft, as may be seen in the episode of the farmer who discovers his wife's adultery and attributes it to the witchcraft which he believes has been perpetrated by Elizabeth Sawyer. These playwrights assume that female identity is constructed in terms of consistency and wholeness, and if a particular woman's identity does not correspond to the conventional notion of femininity, they define that woman either as mad or as being under the influence of an evil spell. Wroth, on the other hand, regards female desire as an essential component of female identity.[17] However, she distinguishes passionate women who can perform their the-

---

[17] For discussion of this issue, see Miller, "Engendering Discourse," and Kusunoki,

atrical self well from those who fail in theatricality, and who consequently are labeled as either mad or bewitched.

The play in this period which most closely shares Wroth's concept of female theatricality in relation to female desire is Shakespeare's *Antony and Cleopatra*. As in *Urania*, in the Egyptian scenes in the play female desire is represented as not entirely unseemly. Cleopatra, like Pamphilia, excellently demonstrates her theatrical self. However, except for the scene where she meets Caesar's messenger after her defeat in order to find out Caesar's true intentions, her purpose in deploying her theatricality is solely to hold Antony's affection for her; her dramatic selfhood is strongly dependent on Antony's subjectivity. In the case of Pamphilia, her theatricality is a means to preserve the authenticity of her female individual subjectivity, which is detached from her performance of assumed conventional female roles. Her innermost self contains a contradiction in that, while it consists of her constancy to Amphilanthus, it is independent of his subjectivity at the same time. Therefore, while Wroth describes Pamphilia's female identity as plural and independent, Cleopatra's "infinite variety" is in fact almost always directed towards Antony.

III

Another woman in *Urania* who fails in her performance of a passive female role and is labeled as mad is Antissia. She is passionately in love with Amphilanthus, who had an affair with her for a while and then deserted her. Publicly declaring her passion, which causes her to be defined by others as mad, she pursues him, and in the course of this pursuit her sexual frustration sometimes brings about a genuine mental instability. This instability is in fact a recurrence of the mental suffering caused by an attempted rape by two men during Antissia's childhood, an experience which traumatized her. In *Urania* Part I, she cannot completely recover from this trauma, while in Part II she sometimes comes close to actual insanity. Wroth presents Antissia's sexual assertiveness as uncontainable in the Jacobean concept of modest womanhood; however, the assertion of her desire, though it troubles Amphilanthus, is not portrayed as threatening to his sense of identity.

In the case of *Women Beware Women* and *The Changeling* (1622), on the other hand, female desire is presented as a power which can bring not only ruin to

---

"Representations of Female Subjectivity in Elizabeth Cary's *The Tragedy of Mariam* and Mary Wroth's *Love's Victory*," 154–60.

men but also social chaos. In these plays, Thomas Middleton presents rape as formative of the female self. Even though Bianca and Beatrice-Joanna are both greatly shocked by their physical subjection to the violence of the Duke and De Flores repectively, they eventually come to love their sexual aggressors. Unlike Wroth, Middleton seems to deny utterly the existence of a consistent female interior self. In these plays, both Bianca and Beatrice-Joanna, who experience self-disjointure as a result of the male violence of rape, are portrayed as indeed "the deed's creature" (*The Changeling*, 3.4. 137).[18] Female desire, which is awakened by rape in these plays, becomes a power which evokes outrageous male desire and eventually leads to social chaos.

IV

The characteristic features of the representations of female desire in English Renaissance plays become even clearer when they are compared to the representation of female desire in the well-known Kabuki piece called *Dojoji*. The story of *Dojoji Temple* is dramatized in both Kabuki and Noh plays.[19] The story itself derives from various sources, mostly texts whose purpose was to disseminate the teachings of Buddhism, dating from the eleventh century onwards. The Kabuki version of the story narrates that a young priest, Anchin, encounters the heroine, Kiyohime, during his pilgrimage to Kumano Shrine in the southern part of the mainland. They are attracted to each other, but since Anchin is on his pilgrimage, he leaves her, pledging that he will come to visit her on his way home. However, realizing that his further commitment to Kiyohime will prevent his pursuit of the truth in Buddhism, he breaks his promise, passing the area where she lives without making contact with her. When she learns that Anchin has failed to fulfil his promise, she runs after him, turning herself into a serpent, and catches up with him when he has reached Dojoji Temple. To escape from her, he hides himself inside the great bell of the temple. Suspecting this, Kiyohime, who is now a serpent in her appearance, destroys the bell with flames which issue from her mouth, in the process burning Anchin to death.

Actually, the Kabuki play starts at the point when, hundreds of years afterwards, a ceremony to inaugurate a new holy bell is about to take place in Dojoji

---

[18] I use Patricia Thomson's edition of *The Changeling*.

[19] On *Dojoji*, see Mae Smethurst, "The Japanese Presence in Ninagawa's *Medea*," in *Medea in Performance 1500–2000*, ed. Edith Hall et al. (Oxford: European Humanities Research Centre, 2000), 191–216, esp. 200–1, 208–9.

Temple. While the priests are praying for the successful installation of the new bell, a female professional dancer enters the site of the ceremony. Since women are prohibited from taking part in such a holy event, particularly since the former bell was destroyed in a tragedy caused by a woman, she is dismissed at first by the priests. Nonetheless, impressed by her ardor, the priests finally admit her to the site on the condition that she will dedicate her sacred dance to the inauguration of the bell. While dancing, she is transformed into a serpent, and thus it is revealed that the dancer is in fact the spirit of Kiyohime. The aesthetic highlights both in the Kabuki play and in the Noh version of the same story occur at the moments when the heroine expresses her hidden vindictiveness and sexual frustration. Kiyohime, transformed into a serpent (this is shown by her silver-colored kimono with a pattern of scales), looks from the top of the bell over the frightened priests, and the transformation from her innocent-looking beauty as a young dancer to the beauty of a frustrated mature woman is considered to be the most enjoyable moment for the audience. Thus, while the sources of the story emphasize the dangers of female desire for men pursuing the truth of Buddhism, the representation of Kiyohime in the Kabuki play places in the foreground the aesthetic aspects of female desire as well.

At the same time, the monstrosity of female desire is also made explicit through the representations of a snake crawling around the bell in the final scene. However, the significance of this is complicated, partly because this scene constitutes the climax of the play, presenting ultimate beauty as combined with monstrosity, and partly because the role of Kiyohime, the heroine, is actually played by a man and the whole narrative of female desire is a fiction. And yet the uncontrollable quality of female desire hidden in a woman is stressed, since the beautiful dancer turns into a fire-breathing serpent, an embodiment of female desire and revenge.

Both English Renaissance plays and Kabuki plays are representatives of theatrical traditions in which female roles are enacted by men and in which, therefore, the female desire represented on the stage is a fiction created with full consciousness of the male gaze; and in both of them female desire is presented as a potential threat to social order or to a male sense of identity. When *Dojoji* was written and first performed, patriarchal power as a social system was too strong for any female power to overturn. Nevertheless, privately, female power was still a threat for men who wanted to dedicate themselves to the pursuit of religious truth. The attraction men continued to feel for female eroticism despite its disruptive power seems to be embodied in the combined form of beauty and grotesque monstrosity in the climactic scene of *Dojoji*. English Renaissance plays, on the other hand, were performed at a time when women had begun to feel that their sense of self was no longer entirely contained by the notion of womanhood as defined in patriarchal society, and when some women, such as those mentioned at the beginning of this essay, even took socially disruptive actions to assert what they felt was their self-identification. Female self-assertiveness, in particular, the assertiveness of the sexual self, could thus be an actual threat to male authority in patriarchal society in seventeenth-century England in a way that was not possible in early nineteenth-century Japan. It is interesting to note, however, that, due to an awareness of the male gaze in the audience, as well as of the audience's sense of distance from the authenticity and reality of the female characters' feelings created by the use of male actors, both English Renaissance plays and some Kabuki plays tend to use grotesque elements to represent female self-assertiveness which cannot be controlled by men, a tactic which has the effect of belittling female assertive power. On the other hand, most of the English plays, with a few exceptions such as *The Duchess of Malfi* or *Antony and Cleopatra*, differ from the works in the Japanese tradition in not emphasizing the aesthetic aspects of their representations of women's assertion of sexual self.

In comparison with these male representations of female desire through the body of men, Mary Wroth is more realistic in her representation of womanhood. She presents female desire as a necessary component of female identity in *Urania* as well as in her pastoral comedy, *Love's Victory*. She explores the ways in which a woman can construct authenticity in her sexual assertiveness without losing her integrity in a patriarchal society which denies female desire. Although, unlike male authors of English Renaissance or Kabuki plays, Wroth does not present its threat to men through the image of grotesqueness, she subverts gender-specific notions of behavior. In contrast with conventional assumptions about male behavior, it is Amphilanthus who displays emotional weakness in weeping when he departs from Pamphilia, while she manages to control her emotions. Mary Wroth in *Urania* differs greatly from the writers who were her contemporaries both in the depth of her exploration of a female sense of identity and in representing female desire as having the potential to be a positive human value. She carries out this investigation in her characteristic way, a way in which she considers female identity in terms of theatricality. This technique probably derived from Wroth's own awareness of the strategies necessary for a woman to survive in a patriarchal society without losing her sense of self.[20] At the same time,

---

[20] It can be said, however, that Wroth herself gave up her performance of theatricality when she published the first part of *Urania*. For details of the public outrage occasioned by its publication, see the Introduction to *The Poems of Lady Mary Wroth*, ed. Roberts, 27–36.

since she was well acquainted with the drama of the period, from court performances to performances at public theaters, her knowledge of theater enabled her
to take an authorial position and to express in terms of theatricality her conflict
with the contemporary ideology of marriage.

As has been argued, male writers both of English Renaissance drama and of
Kabuki plays had a tendency to use unnatural combinations of ludicrous, bizarre
elements in representing the limitations of male violence as a means of attempting to subjugate female assertive power. In the case of the two Kabuki plays
examined briefly in this essay, female assertiveness is not necessarily depicted in
sexual terms; in *Yotsuya Kaidan* the heroine's self-assertiveness is directed towards
the absurd social situation which allows abominable male violence to be perpetrated upon the body of a woman. In the other play, *Dojoji*, even though female
assertiveness is presented in terms of desire, male violence is inflicted not upon
the body but upon the mental state of the heroine, as is also the case in *The
Duchess of Malfi*. Thus these male-authored plays vary in their descriptions of the
nature of female assertiveness and of the ways in which men exercise violence
directed towards women. However, a special theatrical condition both of English
Renaissance drama and of Kabuki, a condition in which a female subject was enacted by male actors, seems to have created a unique mode of representation of
the relation of female selfhood to male violence.

Akiko Kusunoki
Tokyo Woman's Christian University

Works Cited

Arden of Faversham, ed. Martin White. The New Mermaids. London: A. & C.
Black, 1997.

Belsey, Catherine. *The Subject of Tragedy: Identity and Difference in Renaissance
Drama*. London: Routledge, 1985.

Bolam, Robyn. "The Heart of the Labyrinth: Mary Wroth's *Pamphilia to Amphilanthus*." In *A Companion to English Renaissance Literature and Culture*, ed.
Michael Hattaway, 257–66. Oxford: Blackwell, 2000.

Butler, Judith. *Gender Trouble: Feminism and Subversion of Identity*. London:
Routledge, 1990.

Cary, Elizabeth. *The Tragedy of Mariam* (1613), ed. A. C. Dunstan. Malone Society Reprints. Oxford: The Malone Society, 1992.

Catty, Jocelyn. *Writing Rape, Writing Women in Early Modern England: Unbridled Speech*. London: Macmillan, 1999.

Findlay, Alison. "Women and Drama." In *A Companion to English Renaissance Literature and Culture*, ed. Hattaway, 499–512.

Hackett, Helen. "The Torture of Limena: Sex and Violence in Lady Mary Wroth's *Urania*." In *Voicing Women: Gender and Sexuality in Early Modern Writing*, ed. Kate Chedgzoy, Melanie Hansen, and Susan Trill, 93–110. Keele: Keele University Press, 1996.

Hanson, Elizabeth. *Discovering the Subject in Renaissance England*. Cambridge: Cambridge University Press, 1998.

Hodgson-Wright, Stephanie. "Beauty, Chastity and Wit: Feminising the Centre-stage." In *Women and Dramatic Production 1550–1700*, ed. Alison Findlay et al., 42–67. Harlow: Pearson, 2000.

Kusunoki, Akiko. "Representations of Female Subjectivity in Elizabeth Cary's *The Tragedy of Mariam* and Mary Wroth's *Love's Victory*." In *Japanese Studies in Shakespeare and His Contemporaries*, ed. Yoshiko Kawachi, 141–65. Newark, DE: University of Delaware Press, 1998.

Lewalski, Barbara. *Writing Women in Jacobean England*. Cambridge, MA: Harvard University Press, 1993.

Middleton, Thomas. *The Family of Love*. In *The Works of Thomas Middleton*, ed. A. H. Bullen, 3: 1–120. 8 vols. London: Nimno, 1885–1886; repr. New York: AMS Press, 1964.

———. *A Mad World, My Masters*, ed. Standish Henning. Regents Renaissance Drama Series. London: Edward Arnold, 1965.

———. *Women Beware Women*, ed. J. R. Mulryne. The Revels Plays. Manchester: Manchester University Press, 1983.

———, and William Rowley. *The Changeling*, ed. Patricia Thomson. The New Mermaids. London: Ernest Benn, 1977.

Miller, Naomi J. *Changing the Subject: Mary Wroth and Figurations of Gender in Early Modern England*. Lexington: University of Kentucky Press, 1996.

———, and Gary Waller, eds. *Reading Mary Wroth: Representing Alternatives in Early Modern England*. Knoxville: University of Tennessee Press, 1991.

Norsworthy, Laura. *The Lady of Bleeding Heart Yard: Lady Elizabeth Hatton 1578–1646*. London: John Murray, 1938.

Orgel, Stephen. *Impersonations: The Performance of Gender in Shakespeare's England*. Cambridge: Cambridge University Press, 1996.

Rawson, M. S. *Penelope Rich and Her Circle*. London: Hutchinson, 1911.

Rowley, William, Thomas Dekker, and John Ford. *The Witch of Edmonton*. In *Three Jacobean Witchcraft Plays*, ed. Peter Corbin and Douglas Sedge. The Revels Plays. Manchester: Manchester University Press, 1986.

Shakespeare, William. *Antony and Cleopatra*, ed. John Wilders. The Arden

Shakespeare. London and New York: Routledge, 1995.

———. *Titus Andronicus*, ed. Jonathan Bate. The Arden Shakespeare. London and New York: Routledge, 1995.

Shapiro, Michael. *Gender in Play on the Shakespearean Stage: Boy Heroines and Female Pages*. Ann Arbor: University of Michigan Press, 1996.

Shaver, Anne. "Agency and Marriage in the Fictions of Lady Mary Wroth and Margaret Cavendish, Duchess of Newcastle." In *Pilgrimage for Love: Essays in Early Modern Literature in Honor of Josephine A. Roberts*, ed. Sigrid King, 177–90. MRTS 213. Tempe, AZ: Arizona Center for Medieval and Renaissance Studies, 1999.

Smethurst, Mae. "The Japanese Presence in Ninagawa's *Medea*." In *Medea in Performance 1500–2000*, ed. Edith Hall et al., 191–216. Oxford: European Humanities Research Centre, 2000.

Swetnam the Woman-hater: The Controversy and the Play, ed. Coryl Crandall. West Lafayette, IN: Purdue University Press, 1969.

Traub, Valerie. *Desire and Anxiety: Circulations of Sexuality in Shakespearean Drama*. London and New York: Routledge, 1992.

Waller, Gary F. "Struggling into Discourse: The Emergence of Renaissance Women's Writing." In *Silent but for the Word: Tudor Women as Patrons, Translators, and Writers of Religious Works*, ed. Margaret P. Hannay, 238–56. Kent, OH: The Kent State University Press, 1985.

Wayne, Valerie. "The Dearth of the Author: Anonymity's Allies and *Swetnam the Woman-hater*." In *Maids and Mistresses, Cousins and Queens: Women's Alliances in Early Modern England*, ed. Susan Frye and Karen Robertson, 221–40. New York and Oxford: Oxford University Press, 1999.

Weidemann, Heather. "Theatricality and Female Identity in Mary Wroth's *Urania*." In *Reading Mary Wroth*, ed. Miller and Waller, 191–209.

Wroth, Mary. *The First Part of The Countess of Montgomery's Urania by Lady Mary Wroth*, ed. Josephine A. Roberts. MRTS 140. Binghamton, NY: Medieval & Renaissance Texts & Studies, 1995.

———. *The Second Part of The Countess of Montgomery's Urania by Lady Mary Wroth*, ed. Josephine A. Roberts, completed by Suzanne Gossett and Janel Mueller. MRTS 211. Tempe, AZ: Renaissance English Text Society in conjunction with Arizona Center for Medieval and Renaissance Studies, 1999.

———. *Lady Mary Wroth's Love's Victory*, ed. Michael G. Brennan. London: The Roxburghe Club, 1988.

———. *The Poems of Lady Mary Wroth*, ed. Josephine A. Roberts. Baton Rouge and London: Louisiana State University Press, 1983.

Wynne-Davies, Marion. " 'So Much Work': Autobiographical Narratives in the

Work of Lady Mary Wroth." In *Betraying Our Selves: Forms of Self-Represen-tations in Early Modern English Texts*, ed. Henk Dragstra, Sheila Ottway, and Helen Wilcox, 76–93. Basingstoke: Macmillan, 2000.

———. " 'For *Worth*, Not Weakness, Makes in Use but One': Literary Dialogues in an English Renaissance Family." In *"This Double Voice": Gendered Writing in Early Modern England*, ed. Danielle Clarke and Elizabeth Clarke, 164–84. London: Macmillan, 2000.

Invasive Procedures in Webster's
The Duchess of Malfi

I. FIGURATIVE ANATOMIZING

In 1497 Alessandro Benedetti, physician of Verona, offers in his dedication of *Anatomice or The History of the Human Body* to Maximilian Caesar Augustus the promise that in studying this work of anatomical dissection,

> you will come forth from this *intimate contemplation* (as it were) of nature and *from the workshop of this private undertaking* and be venerated more worshipfully for lingering there. . . . If you should wish to see these sights (leaving to surgeons and physicians . . . the distasteful duty of dissection, materials worthy of a theatrical spectacle) and more closely scrutinize the particular force and various effects of each, it will be possible sometime for your majesty to judge at greater length concerning the function of nature.[1]

In fact, the early literature of anatomy and dissection in the Renaissance provides an entry to both figurative and literal dissection and dismemberment on the Jacobean stage. John Webster's *The Duchess of Malfi* is often cited for its numerous references to images of decay and putrefaction. But the attention to ailments and the types of confinement necessitated by these maladies bespeaks a much more pervasive thematic focus. The play presents us not only with a diseased society, but with a slew of voyeuristic investigators who struggle to ferret out the source of that disease. Although Ferdinand initially seems to be the instigator of the invasive procedures that wrest privacy and comfort from the Duchess, Bosola, in

---

[1] Benedetti, *Anatomice or The History of the Human Body*, in *Studies in Pre-Vesalian Anatomy*, ed. Lind, 104: 81.

his role as tombmaker, bellman, and stage manager of the Duchess's torments and eventual murder, unwillingly becomes Ferdinand's instrument, his "hand." Bosola is the surgeon who cuts while the physician instructs from his elevated position in the dissection theater, managing the interrogation, psychological torture, and "anatomizing" of the Duchess that Ferdinand vicariously imagines in his desire to make a sponge "of her bleeding heart" (2.5.21) after he has "hewed her to pieces" (41).[2] Medical treatises, religious inquisitions, and legal interrogations in the Renaissance sought to penetrate the secret interiors of resistant bodies — in order to determine "truth," fix blame, or to probe human nature. Much of the psychological violence performed upon women on the Jacobean stage springs from this desire to wrest knowledge from these recalcitrant witnesses. The more they resist, the greater the impulse to penetrate that reserve. Webster's *Duchess of Malfi* demonstrates the age's desire not only to lend autonomy to the individual, but also to assail that privacy through legal and religious procedures of interrogation. At the same time, literary and artistic works press these examinations to near claustrophobic intensity, to test how identity withstands the violence of this social and psychological pressure.

Attempts, similarly, to pluck out the "heart's mystery" of Hamlet are the work of not only Polonius, but also Claudius, Gertrude, Rosencrantz and Guildenstern, even Ophelia — all who seek "by indirection," but also by invasive forms of investigation, to find direction out. Like the early dissections or vivisections in the surgical amphitheater, however, these methods of discovery find at the core a fundamental resistance that the threat of torture or scalpel cannot penetrate. Even more than in the case of Hamlet, the interrogation of the Duchess of Malfi should be placed within the context of early modern institutions of examination, particularly medical/scientific anatomical examination and religious inquisition. The Duchess's responses to her interrogatories recall a witch's or a martyr's resistance to the tortures of isolation, separation, and fragmentation. Her power resides in keeping her secret, despite the powerful coercion of the church and the state.

And what is the secret that these invasive procedures seek to discover? At the core of the Duchess, as with Hamlet, is not an inviolable concept of self, but of the Other. The Duchess follows the example of such diverse models as Lady Macbeth and Richard III as well as Hamlet, who attempt by speech and written word to establish colloquy with an Other. At the exchange of marriage vows

---

[2] Webster, *The Duchess of Malfi*, ed. Fraser and Rabkin. Citations are given parenthetically in the text.

with Antonio in 1.1, the Duchess marks this union with the claim, "Oh, let me shroud my blushes in your bosom, / Since 'tis the treasury of all my secrets" (1.1.503–504). This exchange of vows, then, requires that each spouse house the other's secrets — a radical alternative to the solitary self's custody of its own counsel. Many recent discussions about subjectivity in the Renaissance postulate the self as socially constructed and as, therefore, not autonomous. Catherine Belsey argues that any evidence of Renaissance plays "exalting human integrity, endorsing truth to the self"[3] is deceptive, that one cannot read *The Duchess of Malfi* or *Hamlet* as "endorsing the unified human subject or affirming a continuous and inviolable interiority as the essence of each person."[4] Although she finds evidence in the Renaissance of "an interiority as the origin of meaning and action, a human subject as agent," she denies that it is fully realized on the Renaissance stage, though it is gradually articulated, she claims, through the development of the soliloquy.[5] By contrast, Katharine Eisaman Maus posits an interiority or "human subjectivity" that derives theologically from "the presence of an omniscient spectator": "Renaissance religious culture thus nurtures habits of mind that encourage conceiving of human inwardness, like other truth as at once privileged and elusive, an absent presence 'interpreted' to observers by ambiguous inklings and tokens."[6] Maus contends that a sense of interiority, privacy, and inwardness in Renaissance texts may not create a fully delineated concept of self as unified or autonomous, but anticipates the notion of the later development of a political, individualized self. Like Francis Barker (*The Tremulous Private Body*) and Patricia Fumerton (*Cultural Aesthetics*), Belsey denies interiority, arguing that the self is constituted by the public or social sphere.[7]

Belsey and others[8] place considerable emphasis on the soliloquy as a location

---

[3] Belsey, *The Subject of Tragedy*, 42.

[4] Belsey, *The Subject of Tragedy*, 40.

[5] Belsey, *The Subject of Tragedy*, 42.

[6] Maus, *Inwardness and Theater in the English Renaissance*, 10.

[7] Maus, *Inwardness and Theater in the English Renaissance*, 212, 2–3.

[8] See Belsey's discussion of soliloquy, *The Subject of Tragedy*, 42–54, especially her claim, "How is the impression of interiority produced? Above all by means of the formal development of the soliloquy. The soliloquy, as Raymond Williams has pointed out, is the condition of the possibility of presenting on the stage a new conception of the free-standing individual. ... the soliloquy makes audible the personal voice and offers access to the presence of the individual speaker" (42). (Belsey cites Raymond Williams, *Culture* [London: Fontana, 1981], 142.) In contrast, very traditional notions of selfhood are espoused in Mousley's assertion that the Duchess "claims to live beyond existing discourses of gender and existing constructions of identity" (*Renaissance Drama and Contemporary Literary Theory*, 174). Mousley suggests "that concepts of self and self-naming are

for the embryonic development of subjectivity, but I believe the Renaissance offers an alternative method: not through soliloquy, but through colloquy or dialogue. In fact, the soliloquy appears often as a mask of artifice and deception, or at best an outward sign constituted by the requirements of the public sphere, not the private. To Maus's argument about inwardness and subjectivity, I would add that inwardness is constituted in relationship with an Other, a "secret sharer" who functions as either a complement or an irritant — in either case, helping to shape subjectivity. Not only Antonio, as the secret husband of the Duchess, but Bosola, as her intimate interrogator and torturer, at various times inhabits this interior space where inwardness and selfhood are constituted. In a play where the protagonist never speaks in soliloquy, Webster experiments with ways in which self must constitute some "society" with the Other in order to constitute and maintain a sense of selfhood. As we shall see, the desire for selfhood constituted by an Other cannot be met through the failed soliloquies of Shakespeare's tragic protagonists, Richard III, Lady Macbeth, and Hamlet. The Duchess rejects the form entirely, confirming her selfhood, as it were, not monologically, but dialogically.

In *The Duchess of Malfi* Webster asserts the importance of the shared holding of secrets as the ground of subjectivity by offering a counter-example late in the play with the adulterous liaison of Julia and the Cardinal. When Julia asks to know the secret of the Cardinal's melancholy, which the murder of Antonio and the Duchess's two children has caused, the Cardinal tricks her by revealing a secret that she must then repay with her life:

> Cardinal: . . . why, imagine I have committed
> Some secret deed which I desire the world
> May never hear of!
> Julia: Therefore may not I know it?
> You have concealed for me as great a sin
> As adultery. Sir, never was occasion
> For perfect trial of my constancy
> Till now.
> . . . .

---

too important and potentially self-liberating to be discarded as part of an outmoded paradigm. To jettison concepts of human autonomy and agency . . . may therefore be a mistake" (182). Rather than heroic independence that Mousley finds, a socially constructed self that Belsey sees, or even the "interiority" that Maus marks as a remnant of Protestant ideology, I would claim the creation of a sense of self is both challenged and sustained through the Duchess's relationship to an Other.

> Cardinal: Be well advised, and think what danger 'tis
>   To receive a prince's secrets. They that do,
>   Had need have their breasts hoop'd with adamant
>   To contain them. I pray thee yet be satisfied,
>   Examine thine own frailty; 'tis more easy
>   To tie knots, than unloose them; 'tis a secret
>   That, like a ling'ring poison, may chance lie
>   Spread in thy veins, and kill thee seven year hence.
>   (5.2.249–264)

In sharing the Cardinal's secret and then threatening to reveal it, Julia seals her own death. Ironically, by admitting the Other, in this case a secret bridegroom, Antonio, the Duchess also precipitates her own death, but Antonio's presence also leaves inviolable her heart's mystery, despite the isolation and psychological torture imposed upon her in confinement. What gives her the courage before such violence done to her spirit? For the witch, heretic, martyr, or saint to avoid torture through self-accusation or recantation is not only to deny that Other, but to deny her own identity. Enduring the pain maintains some sense of autonomy from the sanctioned institutions of church or state. *The Duchess of Malfi* offers the "intimate contemplation" promised in Benedetti's anatomical treatise, with the investigation conducted under relentless scrutiny, the Duchess never being left alone on stage. Without the occasion for soliloquy, the Duchess defines herself under constant scrutiny, and Webster, by giving dialogue a privileged position over soliloquy, confirms the means of her self-construction.

In soliloquy, that displays a character's moments of greatest intimacy and, it is assumed, honesty, we still find the nature of a public performance. Indeed, some critics assert that the self is constituted only by and in the public sphere. Patricia Fumerton, for example, claims that "Elizabethans were in the inverse habit of representing private experience as inescapably public":

> The history of the Elizabethan self, in short, was a history of fragmentation in which the subject lived in public view but always withheld for itself a "secret" room, cabinet, case, or other recess locked away (in full view) in one corner of the house. Or rather there never was any ultimate room, cabinet, or other *apart*ment of privacy that could be locked from the public; only a perpetual regress of apartments.[9]

---

[9] Fumerton, *Cultural Aesthetics*, 69.

Although Katharine Eisaman Maus posits the existence of a "psychological interiority," she finds evidence for this phenomenon not in "those places and genres
in which the idea of privacy would seem, as it were, to find a natural habitat —
the sonnet, the miniature painting, the bedroom, the privy chamber — but rather [within] two emphatically public institutions, the courtroom and the theater."[10] The placement reveals a crucial point about the locus for interiority:
that, ironically, it occurs within the commerce of human connection — more
akin to the dialogic marketplace of Mikhail Bakhtin than to the cloister or the
closet. Neither Fumerton nor Maus discusses the "public" nature of the "private"
soliloquy. But both the overblown theatricality of Hamlet's soliloquies and the
marked absence of the Duchess's soliloquies in Webster's play point to the same
message: that on the Renaissance stage there can be no self, no voice of one crying in the wilderness unless that voice is heard. Soliloquies are the result of failing to find the other with whom one communes; the soliloquy is a failed colloquy, marking what should have been said when the Duchess was alive to hear it.
Bosola's soliloquy over the Duchess's dead body confirms that these words spoken to a lifeless interlocutor can do no good:

> A guilty conscience
> Is a black register, wherein is writ
> All our good deeds and bad; a perspective
> That shows us hell! That we cannot be suffered
> To do good when we have a mind to it!
> ... Where were
> These penitent fountains while she was living?
>
> (4.2.354–363)

At the end of 5.2 in another soliloquy, Bosola resolves to seek out Antonio to
aid his cause, a change of heart brought about in part by Ferdinand's refusal to
reward him for the Duchess's death and the Cardinal's attempts to involve him
in the death of yet another woman, his mistress Julia. But what prompts him
most directly to revenge is the memory of the Duchess: "Still methinks the
Duchess / Haunts me. There, there — 'tis nothing but my melancholy. / O
penitence, let me truly taste thy cup, / That throws men down, only to raise
them up" (5.2.342–345). On the occasions that Bosola speaks alone on stage, the
speech marks the failure of colloquy. Despite his good intentions, Bosola's words
as well as actions isolate, alienate, and eventually destroy himself, as do the

---

[10] Maus, *Inwardness and Theater in the English Renaissance*, 31.

words and actions of the Duchess's brothers, whom Bosola describes as hollow men: your "pair of hearts are hollow graves" (4.2.317). By contrast, even though he functions in colloquy as the Duchess's tormentor, Bosola makes the Duchess's self appear, lets the self take shape.

Pierre Bourdieu defines "habitus" as the space or location where identity is shaped. Bourdieu wishes to establish "an experimental science *of the dialectic of the internalization of externality and the externalization of internality,* or more simply, of incorporation and objectification."[11] The desire to delineate a space where the self is constructed links the work of all the critics mentioned. But whether critics argue that the space is exterior (for Fumerton and some cultural materialists), internal (for Maus), or a mixture of the two (for Bourdieu), they all fail to recognize that the Renaissance offers a critique of "self" and its assumed location or construction. Webster offers his protagonist the famous line "I am Duchess of Malfi still" as a response to Bosola's litany of human decay:

> Thou art a box of worm seed, at best, but a salvatory of green mummy ... Didst thou ever see a lark in a cage? Such is the soul in the body: this world is like her little turf of grass; and the heaven o'er our heads, like her looking glass, only gives us a miserable knowledge of the small compass of our prison. (4.2.124–133)

Readers can accept neither of these answers unequivocally. Webster's play strips the accoutrements of the self away, leaving behind an unassailable interiority that occupies the stage despite its invisibility. That interiority is what the cultural instruments of medical, legal, and religious surveillance and punishment attempt to uncover in the Duchess. Offering an important caveat, Elizabeth Hanson is unwilling to draw a direct correspondence among the more acceptable pursuits of knowledge and the callously inhuman practices of sanctioned violence that dominate Renaissance England or this play:

> The circumstances of the English resort to torture suggest that it may have been conceptually allied to other knowledge-producing practices of the period, such as the anatomy lesson or the voyage of discovery, which

---

[11] Bourdieu, *Outline of a Theory of Practice,* 72. Though his work is hardly simple, Bourdieu does break down the assumptions which critics espousing a "self" as private and interior often wish to assert. But the insistent focus on dichotomy (exterior/interior) remains in Bourdieu's formulation, even as he attempts by paradoxical chiasmus to unmake it.

locate truth in the material world but beyond the limits of common perception. . . . If torture shares an epistemic stance with other more respectable Renaissance projects of discovery, however, it also presents an extremely primitive version of that stance.[12]

As Hanson acknowledges, the practice of extracting information by means of
torture offers parallels with other, more acceptable practices of investigation, such
as dissection or exploration. But can language itself be the site of torture?
According to Jody Enders, both interrogation and the infliction of pain in order
to extract information were, in the late Middle Ages, given the name of torture,
whether verbal or physical.[13]

Confirming this complicity of language in the exercise of torture, Elaine
Scarry suggests that, under torture, "The question, whatever its content, is an act
of wounding; the answer, whatever its content, is a scream."[14] The practices of
discovery in a variety of fields in the Renaissance, especially the anatomizing and
interrogations of science and religion, are conducted in ways strongly reminiscent
of the invasive procedures, primarily verbal, enacted upon Webster's protagonist.

II. THE SECRETARY'S HANDWRITING AND THE
SURGEON'S HAND

Ferdinand's invasion of his sister's chambers in 4.1 is palpable in only one way,
through the presence of his hand, which he presumably stretches out from behind the arras for his sister to recognize and kiss as a sign of reconciliation. This
elaborate ruse, occasioned by his oath that he would never look upon the Duchess, is made grotesque by Ferdinand's offer of not his own hand to kiss, but by
what he claims is the severed hand of her husband, Antonio. Later, we learn that
this hand is merely a replica, part of the "presentations . . . fram'd in wax/ By the
curious Master in that Qualitie, / Vincentio Lauriola," which the Duchess has
mistaken "for true substantial bodies" (4.1.113–116). As if to confirm his sister's
moral blindness, Ferdinand borrows the term "substantial bodies" from contemporary theological discourses on the nature of the eucharist to comment on her

---

[12] Hanson, *Discovering the Subject in Renaissance England*, 25–26.

[13] Enders, *The Medieval Theater of Cruelty*, 41–42. Enders also cites Edward Peters,
Torture (New York: Basil Blackwell, 1986), 28, in her argument that the term "torture"
is used to refer to both interrogatories and to physical infliction of pain.

[14] Scarry, *The Body in Pain*, 46: quoted in Enders, *The Medieval Theater of Cruelty*,
43.

lack of discernment. Moreover, Ferdinand's use of the hand reminds us that the Duchess unconventionally woos her steward Antonio in a scene where he functions as her (secretary's) hand. Summoning Antonio with the words "Take Pen and Incke, and write: are you ready" (1.1.369), the Duchess creates the potentially intimate relationship of master and secretary, as Jonathan Goldberg and Alan Stewart[15] have detailed. The writing of the Duchess's will, Antonio's apparent task, promptly escalates to the wooing scene and concludes with the Duchess's offering of her hand in marriage, but also literally her hand to raise Antonio from his kneeling position before her. Finally, she makes Antonio "Leade your Fortune by the hand / Unto your marriage bed" (496–497).

But what of those who cannot "write" themselves or be carried in written form by their readers, secretaries, and friends? To recognize the importance of the secretary's hand, we must set the handwriting context by looking at two moments when the secretary's hand is absent and, thus, when the written message cannot be delivered because of the distraught condition of the letter-writer. Lady Macbeth's intimacy with her husband is defined by the reception of his letter early in the play. Immediately after Lady Macbeth reads the letter, Macbeth himself arrives at Dunsinane, as if summoned by her giving breath to the words he has written (1.5).[16] Conversely, the sign of Lady Macbeth's undoing late in the play, marked pointedly by her isolation from Macbeth, is revealed by the Gentlewoman's report to the Doctor,

> Since his Majesty went into the field I have seen her rise from her bed, throw her nightgown upon her, unlock her closet, take forth paper, fold it, write up'n it, read it, afterwards seal it, and again return to bed; yet all thus while in a most fast sleep. (5.1.4–8)

The failed attempt to communicate with the absent husband provides the context for the sleepwalking immediately following — an attempt to communicate that marks the growing sense of alienation in Lady Macbeth that will culminate in her death. The severing of this relationship is delivered, then, by the letter written, read, and sealed in her sleep, a letter that cannot be delivered. But not only the bedchamber, but the tent on a battlefield also becomes the setting for

---

[15] Goldberg, *Writing Matter*, and Stewart, "The Early Modern Closet Discovered." Note also Psalm 45:1, "My tongue is the pen of a ready writer," a psalm often recited at the marriage service.

[16] Shakespeare, *Macbeth*, ed. Harbage. Citations appear parenthetically in the text.

a failed desire to communicate what cannot be merely verbalized, as the example of *Richard III* offers.

In a rash of commands as Richard plans to retire before the battle of Bosworth Field, he assembles a virtual battery of accoutrements about him:

> Give me some ink and paper.
> What, is my beaver easier than it was?
> And all my armor laid into my tent?
> ... Send out a pursuivant-at-arms.
> ....
> Fill me a bowl of wine. Give me a watch.
> Saddle white Surrey for the field tomorrow.
> Look that my staves be sound and not too heavy.
> ... Is ink and paper ready? ...
> Bid my watch guard. (5.3.49–75)[17]

Why would the implements of writing be found within this insistent catalogue of armament unless to mark a place for a disclosure, a disarming, through letter-writing? Yet after marshaling forces for the morning and assuring his protection for the night, Richard falls not to writing, but to sleep, where another text entirely is written in his nightmarish version of ghostly apparitions. In his detailed examination of handwriting in the Renaissance, Jonathan Goldberg argues that, paradoxically, the secretary, as "the place of the lord's secret," helps, by his presence, to define the privacy of his lord.[18] But if, as Goldberg suggests, the secretary "is a living pen,"[19] then the very presence of writing implements in Richard's tent suggests the desire to share thoughts with a correspondent, through the medium of pen, paper, and secretarial hand. Being unable to do so demarcates the isolation and alienation that the soliloquy also depicts. He suffers a severed friendship, its absence parodied in the appearance of a ghost who curses, rather than communing with the king. In such a space or habitus, bereft of friend and of the means to express the personal, private thought, no "self" can stand. He goes to his battle as if to his death — and Lady Macbeth awakens from her sleepwalking only to seek her eternal sleep as well.

Not all written documents are destined to miscarry, however. The Duchess offers herself, i.e., her "will," to the hand of her secretary, Antonio. This private

---

[17] Shakespeare, *Richard III*, ed. Harbage. Citations appear parenthetically in the text.
[18] Goldberg, *Writing Matter*, 268.
[19] Goldberg, *Writing Matter*, 265.

scene contains an overtly public expression, both verbal and written. The Duchess most powerfully asserts her identity when she surrenders it, in her willingness to marry, albeit in secret, to Antonio.[20] "The scene of writing and of reading is, like the grave, a private place," claims Francis Barker.[21] Barker's analysis is of Pepys's *Diary*, an auto-writing, rather than the Duchess's will, which engages the hand of her secretary Antonio; nevertheless, each marks a place not so much by the nature or subject matter of the document as in the act of writing itself. Barker claims, "The very writing, which as its epistemological principle grasps the outer world as an accessible transparency, recedes from that world towards an inner location where the soul . . . apparently comes to fill the space of meaning and desire." Barker finds the *Diary* "despite being so richly populated with others and with the furniture of gossip and events, . . . the record of a terrible isolation."[22] The Duchess has both her will and her way in 1.1, winning Antonio's hand in marriage, but this intimate moment conducted over pen and paper (and of course under the surveillance of Cariola) is the only semi-private moment that the play will offer the couple.

Webster delivers a fairly pessimistic view of the written word's power to sustain or protect. And Goldberg's discussion of exemplary handwriting pictured in Renaissance texts confirms this skeptical message. In detaching the body from the hand, "the material production of letters has been moralized, spiritualized, placed . . . within a regime of value that appears to take its source from some transcendent realm." Goldberg concludes that "the mind arises from the hand" rather than from the person grasping the pen.[23] The secretary's "hand," shorthand for the one who writes the master's most secret thoughts, has been crossed and countered in *The Duchess of Malfi* with the image of the severed hand of 4.1, one cut off from the sources of humanity and compassion.[24] Metonymy, anoth-

---

[20] Such willingness to offer oneself in the form of a written document, however, does appear in the desire of John Donne, who confidently assigns his "self" to the public medium of paper. In a passage from Donne's letter to the Duke of Buckingham we find, "I deliver this paper as my Image; and I assist the power of any Conjurer, with this imprecation upon my self, that as he shall teare this paper, this picture of mine, so I may be torn in my future, and in my fame" (Scarry, *The Body in Pain*, 75–76). Willingly, Donne sends himself — and his fame and future as well — through the hands of friend and foe, passing himself around in manuscript as he passes his poems.

[21] Barker, *The Tremulous Private Body*, 2.

[22] Barker, *The Tremulous Private Body*, 7.

[23] See Eaton's discussion of handwriting and severed hands in "A Woman of Letters," 54–74, esp. 59, citing Goldberg's argument.

[24] For a fine discussion of the significance of hands, see Neill, "'Amphitheaters in the Body'," esp. 26–32, a discussion of the importance of hands in medicine, in handwriting,

er form of poetic dismemberment, has appeared earlier in Ferdinand's request, "Send Antonio to me; I want his head in a business ... I stand engaged for your husband, for several debts at Naples: let not that trouble him, I had rather have his heart, than his money" (3.5.27, 33–35). Antonio's hand seems almost entirely powerless before the engines of the Duchess's undoing. On the contrary, Ferdinand's "hand" in the business of torturing and finally executing the Duchess is Bosola's, whose increasingly recalcitrant participation in Ferdinand's plans is evident as he retreats to disguise himself in performing the required actions. The hand offered the Duchess in the dimly lit scene of 4.1 also comments ironically on Antonio's earlier departing line, as he leaves with his eldest son for the supposed safety of Milan: "Since we must part, / Heaven hath a hand in't: but no otherwise, / Than as some curious artist takes in sunder / A clock, or watch, when it is out of frame / To bring't in better order" (3.5.59–63). Antonio, raised, in Bosola's words, "by that curious engine, [the Duchess's] white hand" (3.2.294), preserves the privacy of the secretary's closet for his wife's use. This architectural space, substitute for interior space, is also characterized by Bosola: "His breast was filled with all perfection, / And yet it seemed a private whispering room; / It made so little noise of 't" (3.2.257–259).

This cluster of hand imagery, when combined with an unusual piece of stage business, may even allude to the medical imagery that informs other areas of the play. Ambroise Paré's *Apologie and Treatise* defines surgery in three ways, each with a specific reference to the hand:

> Chyrurgerie is an Art, which teacheth the way by reason, how by the operation of the hand we may cure prevent and mitigate diseases, which accidentally happen unto us. ... [or] it is that part of Physicke which undertaketh the cure of diseases by the sole industry of the hand; as by cutting, burning, sawing off, uniting fractures, restoring dislocations, and performing other workes. ... [or] the quick motion of an intrepid hand joyned with experience: or an artificiall action by the hands used in Physicke, for some convenient intent.[25]

For Paré, the surgeon's hand is the artful undertaker of cures, that effects wholeness by either dissevering the diseased part or uniting stray parts. The play,

---

and in rhetoric. Neill also cites the detailed discussion of hands in the play offered by Randall, "The Rank and Earthy Background of Certain Physical Symbols in *The Duchess of Malfi*," esp. 172–79.

[25] Paré, *Apologie and Treatise*, 91. Paré here offers an extended definition. The Greek *cheirourgia* means "hand-work."

however, focuses on the action of dismemberment and, by extension, the psychic division that provokes madness. The arena for such procedures is described as a confining space, a prison, but with the clear sense of its being as well a theater, a place for voyeuristic observation of a family of corpses, the severed hand of a husband, and the dance of the psychically fragmented lunatics. The visibility of the body in pain, Barker concludes, is "not the issue of an aberrant exhibitionism, but formed across the whole surface of the social as the locus of the desire, the revenge, the power and the misery of this world."[26] Moreover, dismembered limbs, provoking the melancholic sense of loss enunciated by Freud, may also explain why parts of loved ones, even the actual "flesh" of the Duchess, her children, are presented as lifeless fragments before her eyes.[27]

III. THE SURGICAL THEATER

Benedetti comments on the requirements of a dissecting theater built on the model of the Roman amphitheater that should be "of such a size as to accommodate the spectators and prevent them from disturbing the masters of the wounds, who are the dissectors. These must be skillful and such as have dissected frequently."[28] This theater for the Duchess becomes the site of her brother's ghostly visitation, of the gruesomely realistic wax images of her family, and, in 4.2, of the mad folk's visit from the "common hospital" (4.1.127), whose comic antics are supposed to force her to a cure (4.2.43). In fact, images of dissection and cure are consistently conflated in these scenes of confinement, torture, and death.

The theater, of course, is also a prison, a cage, and the site to which Bosola comes in disguise, a visitation that her brothers had promised she would endure if she were to marry: "yet believe't / Your darkest actions — nay, your privat'st thoughts — / Will come to light" (1.1.322–324). The Cardinal adds, "The marriage night / Is the entrance into some prison." "Why might I not marry?" asks the Duchess of her brother Ferdinand. "I have not gone about, in this, to create / Any new world, or custom" (3.2.110–112). But she has, of course, and her punishment is apportioned accordingly in 4.2. Because she dares to marry despite her brothers' objections, her transgressive "masculine" behavior must be con

---

[26] Barker, *The Tremulous Private Body*, 19.

[27] For an application of Freud's "Mourning and Melancholia" to Jacobean drama, see Walworth, " 'To Laugh with Open Throate'," especially 55–60.

[28] Lind, *Pre-Vesalian Anatomy*, 83.

signed to pent-up rooms, subjected to the control of both medicine, in her en-forced "cure" by the visitation of the madmen, and law, through her torture and execution.

In his role as servant of Ferdinand, Bosola also enacts the role taken by the surgeon in the anatomical demonstrations and dissections for students of medi-cine as early as the thirteenth century. While the professor read from a textbook or lectured from a chair overlooking the dissecting table, the surgeon performed the messier tasks of the dissection, while the ostensor pointed out the organs under study.[29] It was common that the physician or the professor of anatomy never sullied his hands with a dissection. The surgeon, a name synonymous with barber until well into the sixteenth century, was the lowly carver, a bloody ser-vant. To this day in England physicians are titled "Dr." while surgeons are "Mr." (because they work with their hands). To this role Bosola is consigned, the in-strument of a crude anatomy performed upon the Duchess's psyche.

In his examination of dissecting theaters, beginning with the frontispiece of Vesalius's *De Humani Corporis Fabrica* (1543), Jonathan Sawday notes that the dissecting theater, often well-stocked with spectators, was a place of ritualized drama, attended by "the careful allocation of seats according to social rank, the playing of music ... the procession which heralded the entrance of the anato-mists, [and] the organization of the lesson."[30] Dissecting theaters were sites of lessons beyond those of anatomy. Vesalius's frontispiece features a number of allegorical reminders to students of anatomy, including unsubtle reminders of the transitoriness of life. Further, as Sawday notes, the image of the dissected female corpse, its exposed womb marking the center of the frontispiece, represents "the structural coherence of the universe itself, whose central component — the prin-ciple of life concealed in the womb — Vesalius is about to open to our gaze."[31] The design of dissecting theaters in basilica-like, domed rooms visually recalled not only public theaters, but also the sacred spaces of the early Christian *mar-tyrium*, a small church constructed on the site of a martyrdom.[32] The body, both centrally located and fixed by the concentric rings of the dissecting amphi-theater, is the noble image of Vitruvian man, ironically pinned and splayed below

---

[29] Cunningham, *The Anatomical Renaissance*, 43–44. More on background can be found in Vivian Nutton, " 'A Diet for Barbarians': Introducing Renaissance Medicine to Tudor England," in *Natural Particulars: Nature and the Disciplines in Renaissance Europe*, ed. Anthony Grafton and Nancy Siraisi (Cambridge, MA: MIT Press, 1999), 275–93.

[30] Sawday, *The Body Emblazoned*, 75.

[31] Sawday, *The Body Emblazoned*, 70.

[32] Sawday, *The Body Emblazoned*, 69.

the rings of spectators rising above. Sawday finds that the Renaissance theaters of anatomy offer lessons on human mortality.

In addition to their function as *memento mori*, these anatomy theaters offer another lesson about control, not only in the practicing upon the defenseless body, but in the surveillance to which the body is subjected. What is celebrated in this image? The glorious complexity of the human body? Or, more specifically, the powers of catalogue and classification to which the body is subjected by the images of medical authority? When it is recalled that the subjects of dissection were often criminals, the link between the instruments of political and medical surveillance become clearer. Another interpreter of the frontispiece of the *Fabrica*, Andrea Carlino, notes that both here and in the portrait of Vesalius that follows the title page, women are the subjects of dissection.[33] Because women were less frequently executed for capital crimes, their cadavers were less readily available. The choice, then, of the female body for the frontispiece is deliberate: its opening and disclosure allowing for control by means of public scrutiny. Sawday notes that the uterus, once seen, "had to be mastered in a complex process of representation" in the anatomy textbooks. Yielding "some of the most beautiful (and disturbing) images of anatomy that have survived from the early modern period," claims Sawday, "the female body could be reconstructed . . . as something both fetishistically adored, and violently suppressed."[34]

Although she is not literally dissected, the pregnancy of the Duchess marks her early in the text as an object of both reverent fascination and disgust by Bosola:

> I observe our Duchess
> Is sick a-days, she pukes, her stomach seethes,
> The fins of her eyelids look most teeming blue,
> She wanes in the cheek and waxes fat in the flank.
> . . . .
> A whirlwind strike off these bawd farthingales,
> For, but for that, and the loose-bodied gown,
> I should have discovered apparently

---

[33] Carlino, *Books of the Body*, 43–53. Incidentally, both the frontispiece and the portrait show paper, inkwell, and pen lying near the body, ready for the anatomist's note-taking.

[34] Sawday, *The Body Emblazoned*, 222.

The young springal cutting a caper in her belly.
$$\text{(2.1.70–73, 156–159)}$$

Bosola's image of stripping the Duchess to reveal her condition reflects a similar anxiety of the brothers over the Duchess's lasciviously "open" nature. The prodigality of the Duchess's womb (she bears three children in the course of the play) defies any attempt at control. Torri L. Thompson has identified in a number of Renaissance texts the "need for mortification or physical discipline of the female body."[35] Key features targeted for containment are woman's "unruly member," her tongue, and woman's impurity after childbirth until she undergoes the ritual of "churching." Citing *Certaine Questions by way of Conference betwixt a Chauncelor and a Kinswoman of his concerning Churching of Women* (1601), Thompson argues,

> The parturient female body signifies in early modern England a marginalizing, yet empowering experience, a marker of inequality, but a sign interpreted by male authority as innately subversive. In order for the Anglican Church to reappropriate reproduction, women are constructed as sinful and in need of redemption from their most obvious signification of their differentiated status.[36]

Yet Webster very early in the play begins to conflate the imagery of confinement due to pregnancy with confinement over the loss or threatened loss of material possessions. First, a bawdy exchange in 2.2 among the servants intimates their knowledge of the Duchess's condition, "There was taken even now a Switzer in the Duchess' bedchamber. ... With a pistol in his great cod-piece" (2.2.36–40). Next, Antonio reports the loss of the Duchess's wealth, but in language that at least glances at the delivery of the treasure she has been bearing in her womb:

> Gentlemen,
> We have lost much plate, you know; and but this evening
> Jewels, to the value of four thousand ducats
> Are missing in the Duchess' cabinet. ...
>   'Tis the Duchess' pleasure
> Each officer be locked into his chamber
> Till sun-rising; and to send the keys

---

[35] Thompson, "Female Bodies Misbehaving," 33.
[36] Thompson, "Female Bodies Misbehaving," 32.

Of all their chests, and of their outward door
Into her bedchamber. (2.2.52–59)

To cover the Duchess's necessary confinement due to childbirth, Antonio directs that the men of the household be confined, their keys to chests and doors being delivered to the bedchamber, a ruse ironically foreshadowing the Duchess's future confinement by her brothers. Moreover, Antonio describes the invasive procedures of childbirth, conducted in the Duchess's chamber, in the language of torture, a procedure that the Duchess will also later endure at the hands of her brothers. Privately to Delio, Antonio admits that the Duchess, in childbirth, is "exposed / Unto the worst of torture, pain, and fear" (65–66). But obviously the Duchess will accept this torture willingly to deliver a son. The torments at her brothers' hands, by contrast, yield no issue, no admission of guilt.

Although her brothers are threatened both psychologically and economically by the Duchess's production of heirs, her own health is threatened, according to Renaissance medical treatises, when the potential for reproduction is restricted. In *A Brief Discourse of a Disease called the Suffocation of the Mother* (1603), Edward Jorden offers a medical explanation for the disease to which the Duchess succumbs in her prison's confinement. Separated from Antonio, she has no recourse to the sexual reproduction that, for Jorden, maintains the psychological and physical health of most women. In chapter six, "Of the Causes of this disease," Jorden warns of the consequences of curtailing normal bodily functions: either sexual reproduction or menstruation. The site of the disease is the womb:

> in this disease the want of due and monethly evacuation, or the want of the benefit of marriage in such as have beene accustomed or are apt thereunto, breeds a congestion of humors about that part, which increasing or corrupting in the place, causeth this disease. And therefore we do observe that maidens and widowes are most subject thereunto. Motion and rest being well ordered do preserve health, but being disordered do breed diseases, especially to[o] much rest and slothfulnesse is a meanes of this griefe, by ingendering crudities and obstructions in womens bodies, by dulling the spirits and cooling naturall heate, &c. So likewise sleepe and watching, the one by benumming, the other by dissipation of the spirits and natural heate, may occasion this griefe.[37]

---

[37] Jorden, *A Brief Discourse*, Sig. G2r. This is taken from Aristotle and Galen: see Michael MacDonald, *Witchcraft and Hysteria in Elizabethan London* (London: Routledge, 1991) for Jorden and his sources. Useful studies on the history of science include Lesley Ann Dean-Jones, *Women's Bodies in Classical Greek Science* (Oxford: Clarendon Press,

Jorden in the next paragraph clarifies that melancholy often causes the "suffocation of the mother": "an affect of the Mother or wombe wherein the principal
parts of the bodie by consent so suffer diversly according to the diversities of the
causes and diseases wherewith the matrix is offended."[38]

> Lastly the perturbations of the minde are oftentimes to blame both for
> this and many other diseases. For seeing we are not maisters of our owne
> affections, wee are like battered Cities without walles, or shippes tossed
> in the Sea, exposed to all maner of assaults and daungers, even to the
> overthrow of our owne bodies.[39]

The body under siege, or torture, nevertheless maintains its unassailable interiority — here, figured as the womb. The brothers can destroy the production of
that womb, her children; they can block Antonio's access to that site. But they
cannot legally or morally penetrate the site themselves. No matter how beleaguered she is physically, the Duchess maintains a psychological integrity. The
sites reserved for husband and children remain inviolate interiors.

"I account this world a tedious theater, / For I do play a part in't 'gainst my
will" (4.1.83–84), asserts the Duchess after she has seen what she assumes are the
dead bodies of her family. "Let Heaven, a little while, cease crowning martyrs /
To punish them [her brothers]. / Go, howl them this: and say I long to bleed.
/ It is some mercy when men kill with speed" (108–111). While the play may be
the theater of God's judgment, it is also the inquisitional theater overseen by torturers and executioners that plague the Duchess not with swift death, but with
its suspension. "The masochistic rites of torture and suffering," claims Gilles
Deleuze, "imply actual physical suspension (the hero is hung up, crucified or suspended)." Moreover, in this form of masochism,

> the subject clings to his [sic] ideal. There is a desire for scientific observa-
> tion, and subsequently a state of mystical contemplation. The masochistic
> process of disavowal is so extensive that it affects sexual pleasure itself;

1994) and Joan Cadden, *Meanings of Sex Difference in the Middle Ages* (Cambridge: Cambridge University Press, 1995).

[38] Jorden, *A Brief Discourse*, Sig. Cr–v. Jorden also lists other terms for "suffocation
of the mother": *passio hysterica, suffocatio, praefocatio, strangulatus uteri, caducus matricis*
(Cr). The diversity of names, causes, and symptoms makes this disease subject to a catch-
all diagnosis: "the varieties of those fits is exceeding great, wherein the principall parts of
the body doe diversly suffer" (Cv). Jorden provides numerous, disparate, and colorful case
study examples.

[39] Jorden, *A Brief Discourse*, Sig. G2r–v.

pleasure is postponed for as long as possible and is thus disavowed. The masochist is therefore able to deny the reality of pleasure at the very point of experiencing it.[40]

It may be easy to place Ferdinand in the role of sadist, one who desires to see the Duchess tortured. But it is the role, rather, of masochist, of the desire for pain brought upon himself, that best characterizes Ferdinand as well as his desire for confining and tormenting the Duchess.[41] While she calls for a martyr's end, he persists, with Bosola joining him in this masochistic intrigue, in prolonging the suffering for both himself and his sister. Deleuze comments that the masochist "postpones pleasure in expectation of the pain that will make gratification possible."[42] Ferdinand's images of masochistic tortures also derive from inquisitorial practice, which are also familiar to us from accounts of early Christian martyrdoms under Nero as well as more contemporary burnings of witches and heretics. He indulges in a fantasy of imagined punishments of the Duchess and her lover in a pseudo-voyeuristic conversation with his brother:

> I would have their bodies
> Burn't in a coal-pit, with the ventage stopped,
> That their cursed smoke might not ascend to Heaven:
> Or dip the sheets they lie in, in pitch or sulphur,
> Wrap them in't, and then light them like a match:
> . . . .
> Till I know who leaps my sister, I'll not stir.
> That known, I'll find scorpions to string my whips,
> And fix her in a general eclipse. (2.5.67–71, 78–80)

Ferdinand strings his whips with pointed biblical allusion (I Kings 12:11, 14; 2 Chronicles 10:11,14), yet he plans to delay these tortures until he can wrest from his sister a confession when he visits her bedchamber in 3.2. Although he comes

---

[40] Deleuze, *Masochism: An Interpretation of Coldness and Cruelty*, 33.

[41] On the relationship of the twins Ferdinand and the Duchess, see Findlay, *A Feminist Perspective on Renaissance Drama*, 100–115. Findlay also recognizes that "Ferdinand's torture chamber is a magnificent palace where he re-creates [the Duchess] as an object indistinguishable from the grotesque mannequins of her husband and children" (104). An extensive discussion on melancholy and the Lacanian analysis of the twin relationship is offered for *The Comedy of Errors* in Enterline, *Tears of Narcissus*. The connections with Webster's twins are striking, particularly in discussion of the issues of self and identity. See Enterline, *Tears of Narcissus*, 191–230.

[42] Deleuze, *Masochism: An Interpretation of Coldness and Cruelty*, 71.

"prepared / To work [Antonio's] discovery" (3.2.93–94), he fears the violent consequences of such a revelation and instead cautions the Duchess to do harm to herself rather than reveal her secret or force him to extract it from her. Offering her a poniard, he recommends suicide; barring that, "If thou do love him, cut out thine own tongue / Lest it betray him" (109–110). Ferdinand recommends glossotomy, a familiar torture for martyrs who too vociferously protest their faith (and a punishment for treason in Byzantium). The silencing also carries in its violent mutilation clear sexual connotations. A woman's transgressive power must be tamed, finally, by torture and death.

Every woman in the play is subjected to this silencing. Yet the Duchess counters this stereotypical image of the woman meeting her death with shrieks of terror by calmly observing, "I would fain put off my last woman's fault, / I'd not be tedious to you" (4.2.226–227). Language and gesture that send just the opposite message, however, attend her apparent subservience. To her executioners the Duchess advises,

> Pull, and pull strongly, for your able strength
> Must pull down heaven upon me;
> Yet stay, heaven gates are not so highly arch'd
> As princes' palaces; they that enter there
> Must go upon their knees. Come violent death,
> Serve for mandragora to make me sleep . . . (4.2.229–235)

The strangulation, to which she chooses to kneel, becomes a moment of womanly transcendence. Not even calling for the drugs that would ease her suffering, the Duchess chooses violent death as her sleeping potion. By taking the sting from Bosola's orchestrated death scene, remaining unmoved by his display of the engines of death and refusing to act the "woman's part" in confronting death, she meets her end all the more nobly.

Ironically, the strangulation of the Duchess, the children, and Cariola affirms the power of speech that must be silenced in the innocent. Unlike her mistress, Cariola vociferously mounts an argument for her life, with her reasons progressing from religious, to social obligations, to political intelligence: "I am not prepared for [death]" (243), "I have not been at confession / This two years" (252–253), "I am contracted / To a young gentleman" (247–248), and "I'll discover / Treason to [Ferdinand's] person" (249–250). Her final excuse, "I am quick with child" (253), which might have temporarily stayed the execution of a witch, immediately provokes her strangulation, the reminder of a woman's reproductive powers threatening the male worlds of Malfi, of Ferdinand's Calabria, and of the Cardinal's Catholic Church. No woman remains intact, either psychologically or physically, not even the Cardinal's mistress Julia, whose speech is also silenced, not by strangulation, but by poisoning. Although she proposes to Bosola that she can determine the source of the Cardinal's melancholy by "wind[ing] my tongue about his [the Cardinal's] heart / Like a skein of silk" (5.2.220–221), Julia's tongue proves no match for the Cardinal's strategy. When he demands her secrecy about his murder of the Duchess and her children, Julia agrees, kissing a poisoned Bible that brings her death (5.2.275–280), but not until she tells the Cardinal that she has betrayed his counsel to Bosola, who has overheard the admission of murder. Although Julia begins the scene by offering to serve as the Cardinal's secretary or confidante who would "remove / This lead from off your bosom" (5.2.229–230), the Cardinal keeps not colloquy, but his own counsel, further isolating himself from human feeling:

> Julia: It is an equal fault,
> To tell one's secrets unto all, or none.
> Cardinal: The first argues folly.
> Julia: But the last tyranny. (246–248)

At the moment when they are deprived of the colloquy of shared speech with the Other, the women use their voice — or their silence — as powerful antidotes against male power.

IV. TORTURE AND CURE

Francis Barker's assessment that "the Jacobean body is at once sacred and profane, tortured and celebrated in the same gesture"[43] accords well with the radically contradictory ways in which women's bodies are presented in the play. The Duchess, Julia, the Cardinal's mistress, and Cariola, the Duchess's servant, are all threatened with interrogation and death. As the Duchess's body undergoes the surveillance of her captors, it is both exalted as an icon of beauty and vessel of fertility and vilified as the repository of lustful contagion that must be contained and eventually silenced. Once she is under lock and key, the testing of the Duchess's mind begins in earnest. The first attempt by Ferdinand to drive his sister to despair is the theatrical presentation of the bodies of Antonio and her children, preceded by the grotesque proffering of a "dead hand" for the Duchess to kiss. A second trial is the visit of the madmen, though the action posits both sinister and compassionate motives. The final testing of the Duchess's mortifi-

---

[43] Barker, *The Tremulous Private Body*, 27.

cation is not Ferdinand's idea at all, but Bosola's. His complicity in the surveillance, discovery, capture, torture, and final execution of the Duchess forces
Bosola to play the role of surgeon-assistant and executioner, but also of the
prompter of the Duchess's meditation on death, even as he serves as her torturer.
As her nemesis, Bosola ironically shares moments of intimacy denied even Antonio at the end of her life.

Edward Peters's *Inquisition* details some of the strategies employed by Richard
Topcliffe, one of Queen Elizabeth's official torturers. The practices range from
infliction of pain to confinement, including the placement of the prisoner in the
Pit, "a subterraneous cave, 20 feet deep, and entirely without light." Other tortures mentioned are the more familiar rack, the iron gauntlet enclosing and
squeezing the prisoner's hand, chains or manacles attached to the prisoner's arms,
and fetters attached to the legs. Two others merit more careful consideration:

> a cell or dungeon, so small as to be incapable of admitting a person in
> erect posture: from its effect on its inmates, it has received the name of
> "Little Ease" ... the [next] I believe, from the inventir, is called "The
> Scavenger's Daughter." It consists of an iron ring, which brings the head,
> feet, and hands together, until they form a circle.[44]

The ironically familiar names given these tortures, "ease" and "daughter," remind
of the way in which the horrible is made familiar for the Duchess through Bosola's gradual revelation of his identity and of her destiny. Yet even when the
actions of Bosola replicate those expected under the formula of torture and execution, his manner and language borrow from the religious tradition of meditation. When Ferdinand ignores Bosola's suggestion to "go no farther in your cruelty — / Send her a penitential garment, to put on, / Next to her delicate skin
and furnish her / With beads and prayerbooks" (4.1.119–121), Bosola subsequently vows, "When you send me next [to the Duchess], / The business shall
be comfort" (136).

Just what "comfort" Bosola may offer is restricted by the kinds of invasive
procedures that Christians may practice on each other. Certain prohibitions govern aspects of the medical profession as well. Careful to make a distinction between the noble profession of the surgeon and the ignoble undertakings of bar-
bers, Benedetti offers us some insight upon Bosola's role as comforter/torturer in
the play:

---

[44] Peters, *Inquisition*, 141.

Tradition holds that kings themselves ... have ... dissected [criminals] alive in order that while breath remained they might search out the secrets of nature. ... But our religion forbids this procedure, since it is most cruel or full of the horror inspired by an executioner, lest those who are about to die amidst such torture should in wretched despair lose the hope of a future life. Let barbarians of a foreign rite do such things.[45]

Benedetti's caveat against torturers who have adapted the procedures of vivisection to extract confession rather than to elicit scientific truth or to effect some cure explains the protracted suffering imposed upon the Duchess in 4.1. Although he claims that "This night / I will force confession from her" (3.1.78–79), Ferdinand's meeting with the Duchess fails to provoke either her admission of guilt or her suicide. Ferdinand's subsequent stratagems abandon the language of religious or legal absolution. Bluntly stated, his purpose in presenting the images of the dead Antonio and children is to "bring her to despair" (4.1.116–117). But if Ferdinand, in Benedetti's equation, is the barbarian, Bosola is more difficult to place.

Bosola claims that Ferdinand "doth present to you this sad spectacle, / That now you know directly they are dead. / Hereafter you may, wisely, cease to grieve / For that which cannot be recovered" (4.1.56–60). Yet the Duchess answers by invoking a litany of tortures that she would gladly endure if they would end the pain of enduring life after the loss of her husband and children:

> Duchess: ... bind me to that lifeless trunk,
> And let me freeze to death.
> Bosola: Come, you must live.
> Duchess: That's the greatest torture souls feel in hell:
> In hell that they must live, and cannot die.
> Portia, I'll new kindle thy coals again,
> And revive the rare and almost dead example
> Of a loving wife.
> . . . .
> The Church enjoins fasting;
> I'll starve myself to death. (4.1.68–75)

---

[45] Lind, *Pre-Vesalian Anatomy*, 82.

When Bosola counters, "Oh, fie! despair? Remember / You are a Christian" (74–75), the Duchess responds with a call for an end to the "comforts" of delay and its exquisitely intensified misery of torture:

> Good comfortable fellow
> Persuade a wretch that's broke upon the wheel
> To have all his bones new set: entreat him live,
> To be executed again. Who must dispatch me? (4.1.79–82)

At the moment of her greatest literal confinement, the Duchess is most free to speak her mind. And the images she uses are certainly as violent as the action that will be taken against her. The references to Portia's swallowing of burning coals, of a faithful wife being bound to the corpse of her husband, of starvation, are all radical forms of suicide — no gentle, "womanly" death. Released from the silence with which she protected her children and saved her husband from the watchful eye of her enemies, the Duchess now breaks every rhetorical rule that binds sisters, wives, and subjects to church and state law. By taunting Bosola with the threat to take her own life, she maintains a wilful desire to choose her own death, rather than submit to the death provided by the men. Even her death scene, unlike the death of Cariola immediately following it, places her in control, not the executioners, much less Bosola. Her heroic stance seems to flout her conventional social roles.

Mary Beth Rose's discussion of the play locates the Duchess as the centerpiece of a Protestant-inspired tribute to marriage, granting "full attention and distinction to the private life."[46] Extending Frank Whigham's claim that the Duchess is "the first fully tragic woman in Renaissance drama,"[47] Rose adds, "it is the full recognition of the importance of the private life ... that makes her tragic stature possible ... the Duchess' heroism helps to define and clarify the heroics of marriage."[48] Undeniably, Rose's survey of Protestant treatises on marriage confirms this characterization. Yet marriage and family exist by 4.2 only in memory and provide little comfort. The sacrifice of the Duchess is not merely a

---

[46] Rose, "The Heroics of Marriage in *Othello* and *The Duchess of Malfi*," 233.

[47] Whigham, "Sexual and Social Mobility in *The Duchess of Malfi*," 174.

[48] Rose emphasizes the heroic image offered in marriage by noting that this heroism is rooted in "stoicism, religious martyrdom, and medieval treatises on the art of dying" ("The Heroics of Marriage," 210–16). Yet she ultimately claims that Antonio defines the Duchess in terms of Protestant moral treatises with "the idealization of marriage and the elevation of the private life, a combination of elements particularly amenable to the construction of female heroism" (228).

death in service to the memory of Antonio, but a statement of her own honor, which can be proven by a courageous confrontation with death and her nemesis, Bosola. With her reference to the Catherine-wheel, a device laden with sharp knives used to mutilate and kill St. Catherine of Alexandria, the Duchess, not Bosola, introduces the explicit language of torture in Act 4. Suddenly, the typical relationship of torturer and tortured suffers a reversal. In her examination of Renaissance forms of torture in England, Elizabeth Hanson notes that a "potential for reversal, for the subject under discovery to be revealed as the discoverer's confrere, arises because ... the will to constitute one's own authority — is ultimately what is also driving the discoverer."[49] This colloquy between the victim and the torturer, then, ironically creates a bond with Bosola as the Duchess approaches her death. When confronted with a mighty will in opposition to her own, the Duchess gains in magnificence — her first occasion to speak out and to speak with authority after her years spent hiding her true nature, whispering her curses. If she cannot have a loyal husband at her side, the Duchess gains even more stature in sparring with a loyal enemy.

Is it possible that a device of torture might be confused with an instrument of healing? Such blurring of these distinctions occurs consistently between the instruments of surgery and those of torture; similarly in the play, the appearance of madmen in the Duchess's chamber claims to cure, although it seems intended rather to exacerbate melancholy. Ferdinand tells Bosola,

> I will send her masques of common courtesans,
> Have her meat served up by bawds and ruffians,
> And, 'cause she'll needs be mad, I am resolved
> To remove forth the common hospital
> All the mad folk, and place them near her lodging;
> There let them practice together, sing, and dance,
> And act their gambols to the full o' th' moon.
> If she can sleep the better for it, let her. (4.2.124–131)

Although Bosola advocates compassion, Ferdinand counters, "Intemperate agues make physicians cruel" (141). His purpose is to drive the Duchess to madness, not to cure her of a melancholy "that seems to be fortified / With a strange disdain" (4.1.11–12). A servant, however, offers an alternative explanation for the visit of madmen:

---

[49] Hanson, *Discovering the Subject in Renaissance England*, 20.

> Your brother hath intended you some sport.
> A great physician when the Pope was sick
> Of a deep melancholy, presented him
> With several sorts of madmen, which wild object,
> Being full of change and sport, forced him to laugh,
> And so th' imposthume broke; the selfsame cure
> The Duke intends on you. (4.2.39–44)

Edward Jorden's treatise on the suffocation of the mother includes a chapter titled "Of the cure of this disease, so much as belongeth to the friends and attendants to performe," which offers a medical basis for the "cure" suggested by Ferdinand:

> Galen boasteth that he did every yeare cure many diseases by this stratagem of moderating the perturbations of the mind by the example of Aesculapius who devised many songs and ridiculous pastimes for that purpose. To which end also other phisitions have used divers sorts of fallacies to encounter the melancholike conceits of their patients.[50]

In the same chapter Jorden adds,

> Another course hath been taken sometimes in these cases, by removing the cause of these afflictions, or by inducing of other perturbations of a diverse nature. Whereby as (experience teacheth us) most grievous diseases have been oftentimes cured beyond expectation.[51]

Without intending it, Ferdinand actually comforts the Duchess with his cruelty:

> Duchess: Indeed I thank him: nothing but noise, and folly
>   Can keep me in my right wits, whereas reason
>   And silence make me stark mad. Sit down,
>   Discourse to me some dismal tragedy.
> Cariola: Oh, 'twill increase your melancholy.
> Duchess: Thou art deceived;
>   To hear of greater grief would lessen mine.
>   . . . .
>   I'll tell thee a miracle,
>   I am not mad yet, to my cause of sorrow.

---

[50] Jorden, *A Brief Discourse*, Sig. [G4r] 24.
[51] Jorden, *A Brief Discourse*, Sig. H.

> Th' heaven o'er my head seems made of molten brass,
> The earth of flaming sulphur, yet I am not mad.
>
> (4.2.5–10, 23–26)

Yet again in the play the instruments of torture, though they be drawn from the nightmarish allusion to Moses's curse upon Israel for its idolatry (Deuteronomy 28:23), paradoxically becomes one of comfort, if not healing, for the Duchess. It is certainly the opposite for Ferdinand.

In 5.2, in contrast to the visit of the madmen, who simply reinforce the Duchess's reason and dignity, the Doctor's medicine is completely discredited by Ferdinand's wily wisdom. After recommending folk cures for physical ailments — a salamander's skin for sunburn and the whites of an egg for sore eyes (60–65) — the Doctor asserts that to cure the diseased mind requires the domination of the mad: "I find by his eye, he stands in awe of me. I'll make him as tame as a dormouse" (71–73). Ferdinand promptly attacks the Doctor and makes his escape, threatening to turn the Doctor into a cadaver suitable for carving in his own dissection theater: "I will stamp him into a cullis; flay off his skin, to cover one of the anatomies this rogue hath set i' th' cold yonder, in Barber-Chirurgeons' Hall" (76–79). Clearly, the man of science is unable to effect a cure of mad Ferdinand, but Webster provides another means of cure through the language and rituals of the religious rites of confession, contrition, and repentance. As with medical treatment, it is only through pain and suffering that this process offers a "cure."

V. MORTIFICATION

It is left to Bosola to exact the process of examination, torture, and execution in 4.2. Calling himself first the tombmaker and then the bellman sent to the condemned on the night before their execution, Bosola suggests that he acts in order "to bring [the Duchess] / By degrees to mortification" (175–176). Yet Bosola's words have neither shamed nor humiliated the Duchess, though she has been reminded, through the presentation of the coffin and the cords of strangulation, of her ultimate mortification, the death or decaying of her living body. "Does not death fright you?" "Yet, methinks, / The manner of your death should much afflict you, / This cord should terrify you?" asks Bosola (211, 213–215).[52] Yet the

---

[52] Greene reads these questions, and the character, of Bosola as highly ambivalent: "In the long torment scenes, the whole of Act IV, he kills the Duchess in a spirit of fascination, almost of scientific inquiry, testing, probing, observing her reactions . . . partly to

language of the rack suggests the application of Jody Enders's "universal aesthetics of cruelty that rhetoric helps to identify because so much of cruelty is indigenous to rhetoric" (*The Medieval Theater of Cruelty*, 232).[53] Her discussion of
mnemonics or the *artes memorandi* argues that the "logical system of places,
spaces, containers, and icons by which means any rhetor could generate and store
words, stylistic devices, topoi, [and] proofs . . . owed its genesis to a cultural need
to answer acts of violence with acts of commemoration, iteration, and regeneration" (64). The *artes memorandi*, however, also informed the practice of religious
meditation. A rich patristic tradition, tinged with the exuberance of affective
piety and mysticism, fed both Protestant and Catholic interest in meditative
modes during the sixteenth and seventeenth centuries. *The Spiritual Exercises*
(1548) of Ignatius Loyola relied upon meditants' ability to imagine vividly, for
example, the setting of Christ's crucifixion and to put themselves imaginatively
at the foot of the cross, bombarded with sensuous details and driven to an emotionally impassioned response. The purpose of meditation in both traditions was
the same: to aid meditants in recalling and regretting their past sins, to stir up
reminders that could form the basis of a deeper faith, and to make the experience sufficiently vivid that it would affect their future lives. In addition to the
mnemonic prompts developed by each individual, meditational tracts regularly
describe the role of a spiritual director. These guides may urge meditants, first,
by means of the sense, then by rejection of mere sense data, to recollection, and
from thence to the restoration of what had been thought irrevocably lost. Bor-
rowing from these opposing traditions, Bosola's role in Act 4 functions in a profoundly ambivalent way for the Duchess.[54] Is Bosola leading the Duchess, by
degrees, to an acceptance of the death that she so heroically approaches? Or is

---

comfort her, partly to bring her to despair, but primarily, to discover what he needs to
know: for her death teaches him to live": "Women on Trial in Shakespeare and Webster,"
16.

[53] Enders, *The Medieval Theater of Cruelty*, 232. Enders suggests that medieval stage-
craft and systems of torture are "conjoined by the influential forensic tradition. . . . The
European Middle Ages inherited a classical rhetorical legacy that characterized torture as
a hermeneutic legal quest for truth, a mode of proof, a form of punishment enacted by
the stronger on the weaker, and a genre of spectacle or entertainment" (3). Enders, that
is, links the practice of torture to the practice of rhetoric. Although the texts she examines are medieval, rather than Jacobean, plays, her argument accounts for the cruelty of
Webster's Act 4. Bosola's careful use of rhetorical strategies renders words as instruments
of psychological torture applied to the Duchess.

[54] The basic outline of the meditational mode that I suggest stands behind the pattern of Bosola's actions in Act 4 may be found in Martz, *The Poetry of Meditation*, and
Lewalski, *Protestant Poetics and the Seventeenth Century*.

he employing the methods of the torturer in forcing her to imagine the grim details of her death?

The pattern of questioning and slow procession to the Duchess's death imitates an interrogation familiar from the *Malleus Maleficarum*. In Part III, Question 14, the questioning of a witch is described:

> the Judge shall use his own persuasions, and those of other honest men ... to induce her to confess the truth voluntarily; and if she will not, let him order the officers to bind her with cords, and apply her to some engine of torture and then let them obey at once, but not joyfully, rather appearing to be disturbed by their duty. ... The next step of the Judge should be that, if after being fittingly tortured she refuses to confess the truth, he should have other engines of torture brought before her, and tell her that she will have to endure these if she does not confess.[55]

The studied reluctance of Bosola in his performance of the Duchess's interrogatory put in the light of the *Malleus Maleficarum* forces us to reckon with even greater evil in the scene. Following a version of this procedure that induces fear in the victim, Bosola shows the Duchess instruments of her impending death as engines of a psychological torture. Rather than revealing the whereabouts of Antonio, however, the Duchess more adamantly calls for her own death, seeking to frustrate any further attempts at intimidation or invasion.

Both the Duchess and Ferdinand, at the hour of their deaths, comment on the insignificance of physical pain in the presence of the psychological fragmentation that they are enduring. Bosola, disguised in 4.2, comments of the Duchess, "A little infant, that breeds its teeth, should it lie with thee, would cry out, as if thou wert the more unquiet bedfellow" (4.2.139–141). Insistently, the Duchess calls for her own death in 4.2, fearing the pain of living far more than the physical pain of strangulation. Similarly, in 5.2, after his scuffle with Bosola in which he wounds his brother the Cardinal and delivers to Bosola his death wound, Ferdinand acknowledges the relative nature of physical pain before that which is far more feared:

---

[55] Kramer and Sprenger, *The Malleus Maleficarum*, 225–26. Displaying the instruments of torture, however, also may derive from the iconographical tradition of angels showing the Christ Child the instruments of his future torture and death. Enders, *Medieval Theater of Cruelty*, 135–142, notes that "pedagogical violence" (141), or the threatened or actual beatings of students in the classroom, was a frequent incentive for learning. Thus, Bosola's role as torturer, confessor, and instructor, borrows from several traditions.

Now you're brave fellows. Caesar's fortune was harder than Pompey's;
Caesar died in the arms of prosperity, Pompey at the feet of disgrace.
You both died in the field, the pain's nothing. Pain many times is taken
away with the apprehension of greater, as the toothache with the sight of
a barber that comes to pull it out. There's philosophy for you. (5.2.57–62)

Wholeness, integrity, for both Antonio and the Duchess, may be found in death,
not in the fragmentation imposed upon the family, the body, and the psyche by
the torture of pain and isolation. Interrogatories, like surgical dissections, seek in
their fragmenting of the external integrity of an individual, to reveal an interior.
As Devon Hodges says of dissection, "The anatomy of a body is an act of destruction and of revelation; but each moment of revelation also fragments the
integrity of things."[56] The "fragmenting methods of an anatomist"[57] cannot
order a world. Nevertheless, the association of science and its attendant capacity
to know, through dissection, and to cure, through medical procedure, is inexorably tied to the action of rooting out heresy, to exposing truth, to overcoming the
interior that will not speak.

VI. EPILOGUE: THE HEART'S MYSTERY

Webster's play, like Shakespeare's *Hamlet*, with its focus on claustrophobic enclosure, insidious pestilence, and false feigning, exposes the perverse pleasures of
those who seek to violate the secrets of the bedchamber, the closet, the womb,
the heart. And we spectators, despite our sympathies, are placed in the inquisi-
tor's camp, attempting to impose meaning from our position of interpreters,
much as the court of Elsinore seeks to know the heart of Ophelia's mystery:

> Her speech is nothing.
> Yet the unshaped use of it doth move
> The hearers to collection. They aim at it,
> And botch the words fit to their own thoughts,
> Which, as her winks and nods and gestures yield them,
> Indeed would make one think there might be thought,
> Though nothing sure, yet much unhappily.
>   (*Hamlet*, 4.5.7–13)[58]

---

[56] Hodges, *Renaissance Fictions of Anatomy*, 70–71.
[57] Hodges, *Renaissance Fictions of Anatomy*, 75.
[58] Shakespeare, *Hamlet*, ed. Harbage. Citations appear parenthetically in the text.

But the invasive procedure of interpretation is certainly not the most insidious. The history of examination and incarceration detailed in Michel Foucault's *Discipline and Punish* and the instances cited in chapter one of Katharine Eisaman Maus's *Inwardness and Theater in the English Renaissance* suggest that the way of knowing the "invisible personal interior" (Maus, *Inwardness and Theater*, 12) is through the study of public institutions of sanctioned violation. Not only religious inquisition, but also scientific investigation is premised on the belief that what is invisible and unknown will yield to the instrument and the institution of study.[59] Yet the opposition to these probings remains just as firm, with the resistance expressed in Hamlet's retort to Rosencrantz and Guildenstern: "You would play upon me; you would seem to know my stops; you would pluck out the heart of my mystery" (3.2.49-51) and his warning to Laertes, "Yet have I in me something dangerous, / Which let thy wisdom fear" (5.1.249-250). Even a character prone to weakness, Cariola, may rise to the occasion and show that she is no hollow center. When Antonio suspects that she has allowed Ferdinand access to the Duchess's chamber and threatens to stab her, Cariola retorts, "Pray, sir, do; and when / That you have cleft my heart, you shall read there / Mine innocence" (3.2.144–145). Exactly what lies within the inward heart, that knowledge forbidden to inquisitors, is shaped in the Renaissance not simply by the "self," but by the construction of the Other. At the center is a welcomed presence. Its familiar colloquy with the host is what constitutes the concept of interiority, that private, inviolable — and shared — space. In medieval hagiographies, a divine presence sustains martyrs through the most excruciating of physical trials. The secular version of that companionship, supplied by a husband, albeit absent, sustains the protagonist who, despite her vulnerability, remains unviolated.

Defined always in relationship to others — as wife, mother, sovereign, sister — the Duchess is alone on stage for no more than ten lines, immediately before she inaugurates her wooing of Antonio (1.1.348–356). She has no privacy even when Antonio and Cariola sneak away in 3.2 to play a trick on her, since Ferdinand immediately enters to hear and answer her musings. When Ferdinand visits his sister in the darkness of 4.1, there is not even a moment when she has the stage to herself. The violation is most graphically portrayed with the invasion of madmen sent by her brother to disturb her peace. Her death offers the only opportunity to escape the company of her ministers of pain:

---

[59] Maus, *Inwardness and Theater in the English Renaissance*, 50.

> any way (for heaven sake)
> So I were out of your whispering: Tell my brothers,
> That I perceive death . . .
> Best gift is, they can give, or I can take. (4.2.222–225)

In this last, most marked isolation, from husband, children, brothers, and servant, the Duchess departs "to meet such excellent company / In th' other world" (212–213), namely Antonio. And with almost the same breath, she offers a final opportunity to her brothers for soliloquy over her body, rather than colloquy with her, "Go tell my brothers, when I am laid out, / They then may feed in quiet" (236–237). On every other occasion, the Duchess chooses to speak in colloquy, whether with servant, husband, or enemy — an interlocutor's presence saving her from madness. Even when that colloquist is Bosola, she is sustained by human contact inherent in dialogue. Hers cannot be the language of soliloquy, which isolates, dissevers, fragments the individual from the only basis of self-knowledge and identity, the Other, whom she continues to hold in ghostly conversation. She remains "Duchess of Malfi still" because she is not, like Hamlet, a solitary voice speaking in the void of Elsinore.

Unlike the Duchess, Hamlet is frequently alone for soliloquies that are regularly explicated as earnest investigations of the soul, the proper method of revealing his true nature and determining appropriate action. Yet the soliloquies are often occasions of posturing, not of serious introspection. Performative, hyperbolic, staged, self-indulgent, they reveal Hamlet's obsessions, note his confusions, but bring us no closer to the "heart's mystery" that he so carefully protects from the investigators of the play. Modern sensibilities have preferred the concept of the soliloquy as a means of self-interrogation or introspection, but Hamlet's soliloquies end with his resolving nothing and offering at least as much bombast and rationalization as they do confession or insight. Would that Horatio were more in his company.

If the soliloquy is, as I suggest, not a moment of personal revelation or introspection, but a failed colloquy that laments the absence of the Other to whom these anxieties and fears can be spoken, then Horatio is the key to protecting the heart's mystery of the Prince.

> Blest are those
> Whose blood and judgment are so well commeddled
> That they are not a pipe for Fortune's finger
> To sound what stop she pleases. Give me that man
> That is not passion's slave, and I will wear him
> In my heart's core, ay, in my heart of heart,
> As I do thee. (*Hamlet*, 3.2.78–84)

"Something too much of this," remarks Hamlet after this astonishing revelation of his trust in a friend who is in every way imaginable his opposite. Having divorced himself from family, friends, and counselors, the better to pursue his secret motive of a father's revenge, Hamlet yet relies on the constancy of Horatio that defines and protects his heart's core from all invasive means of discovery. Hamlet's final appeal is that Horatio forgo the suicide that would join the friends in death so that Horatio, holding Hamlet's secret in his own heart, may speak for his friend:

> If thou didst ever hold me in thy heart,
> Absent thee from felicity awhile,
> And in this harsh world draw thy breath in pain,
> To tell my story. (5.1.340–343)

Yet it is not entirely clear that Hamlet's philosopher friend will be able to reveal Hamlet's truth under the close questioning of Fortinbras and the new police state of Denmark.

The final words of the Duchess and Antonio, while not spoken to each other, nevertheless reassert their colloquy that has been suspended for much of the play. The point of connection, however, is in the references to the shared bond of children. In her last word to Cariola, the Duchess asks, "I pray thee look thou givest my little boy / Some syrup for his cold, and let the girl / Say her prayers ere she sleep" (4.2.203-205). Antonio, wounded mistakenly by Bosola, hears stoically of his family's death

> Bosola: O good Antonio,
>   I'll whisper one thing in thy dying ear,
>   Shall make thy heart break quickly. Thy fair Duchess
>   And two sweet children —
> Antonio: Their very names
>   Kindle a little life in me.
> Bosola: Are murdered!
> Antonio: Some men have wished to die
>   At the hearing of sad tidings: I am glad
>   That I shall do't in sadness. (5.5.54–61)

In farewell, Antonio offers a last word of protection for the remaining child, "let my son fly the courts of princes" (5.5.71). He also commends the friend who has served as colloquist throughout his period of separation from the Duchess: "I do not ask / The process of my death. Only, commend me / To Delio" (5.5.68–70).

A curious ventriloquizing of the colloquy between the Duchess and Antonio is attempted twice in the play — at the moment of, and after the Duchess's

death. In the first, the Duchess revives from her strangulation for a final colloquy
with Bosola. But their topic is the word on which the Duchess revives: her husband's name:

> Bosola: Her eye opes,
> And heaven in it seems to ope, that late was shut,
> To take me up to mercy.
> Duchess: Antonio!
> Bosola: Yes, madam, he is living.
> The dead bodies you saw were but feigned statues;
> He's reconciled to your brothers; the Pope hath wrought
> The atonement.
> Duchess: Mercy. (4.2.345–351)

Although Bosola is only partially truthful, since Antonio lives unreconciled to
the Duchess's brothers, it is enough to garner him heaven's mercy. The Duchess
does not even acknowledge Bosola, as if she were already in the presence of the
Other. Again, this time from beyond the grave, the Duchess renews the colloquy
in 5.3 with the Echo that, stage directions note, arises *"from the [Duchess'] grave."*

> Antonio: It groaned, methought, and gave
> A very deadly accent!
> Echo: *Deadly accent.*
> . . . .
> Antonio: 'Tis very like my wife's voice.
> Echo: *Ay, wife's voice.*
> . . . .
> Antonio: Echo, I will not talk with thee,
> For thou art a dead thing.
> Echo: *Thou art a dead thing.*
> Antonio: My Duchess is asleep now,
> And her little ones, I hope, sweetly. O heaven,
> Shall I never see her more?
> Echo: *Never see her more.*
> Antonio: I marked not one repetition of the echo
> But that, and on the sudden, a clear light
> Presented me a face folded in sorrow. (5.3.19–45)

Antonio's own words return to him in his "wife's voice," a final reminder of the
bond in colloquy that resists the ravages of torture, time, and death itself.

Like Hamlet, Webster's Duchess undergoes rigorous examination by inquisitional figures, relatives, and pawns of institutional powers. Neither protagonist, even in death, reveals the interior knowledge that outsiders seek to know. What constitutes the interior, implied but not revealed by Hamlet's soliloquizing, or by the Duchess' resistance to the temptation of madness and the horrors of threatened torture, is a bond with an absent presence that shapes the interior, repulses the invasive procedures practiced against the prisoner, and keeps madness at bay.

Webster's play offers us a secular image of the martyr, whose definition, Julia Kristeva reminds us, derives from the verb martyreô, meaning " to bear witness." In *Powers of Horror* Kristeva clarifies:

> The avowal of faith is thus from the very start tied to persecution and suffering. This pain, moreover, has wholly permeated the word "martyr," giving it its basic, ordinary meaning of torture rather than testimony. . . . the [speech of] faith addressed to the other is pain; this is what locates the act of *true communication*, the act of avowal, within the register of persecution and victimization. Communication brings my most intimate subjectivity into being for the other; and this act of judgment and supreme freedom, if it authenticates me, also delivers me over to death.[60]

The psychic violence and pain undergone by the Duchess of Malfi ultimately enable her most eloquent form of expression: the colloquy with her heart's mystery that resists the invasive practices of church or state.

Ellen Caldwell
California State University, Fullerton

Works Cited

Barker, Francis. *The Tremulous Private Body*. Ann Arbor: University of Michigan Press, 1995.

Bourdieu, Pierre. *Outline of a Theory of Practice*. Cambridge: Cambridge University Press, 1977.

Cadden, Joan. *Meanings of Sex Difference in the Middle Ages*. Cambridge: Cambridge University Press, 1995.

Carlino, Andrea. *Books of the Body: Anatomical Ritual and Renaissance Learning*, trans. John Tedeschi and Anne C. Tedeschi. Chicago: University of Chicago Press, 1994.

---

[60] Kristeva, *Powers of Horror*, 129.

Comensoli, Viviana, and Anne Russell, eds. *Enacting Gender on the English Renaissance Stage.* Urbana: University of Illinois Press, 1999.

Cunningham, Andrew C. *The Anatomical Renaissance.* Aldershot: Scolar Press, 1997.

Dean-Jones, Lesley Ann. *Women's Bodies in Classical Greek Science.* Oxford: Clarendon Press, 1994.

Deleuze, Gilles. *Masochism: An Interpretation of Coldness and Cruelty.* New York: Zone Books, 1991.

Eaton, Sara. "A Woman of Letters: Lavinia in *Titus Andronicus.*" In *Shakespearean Tragedy and Gender,* ed. Shirley Nelson Garner and Madelon Sprengnether, 54–74. Bloomington: Indiana University Press, 1996.

Enders, Jody. *The Medieval Theater of Cruelty.* Ithaca: Cornell University Press, 1999.

Enterline, Lynn. *Tears of Narcissus: Melancholia and Masculinity in Early Modern Writing.* Stanford: Stanford University Press, 1995.

Findlay, Alison. *A Feminist Perspective on Renaissance Drama.* Malden, MA: Blackwell, 1999.

Fumerton, Patricia. *Cultural Aesthetics: Renaissance Literature and the Practice of Social Ornament.* Chicago: University of Chicago Press, 1993.

Garner, Shirley Nelson, and Madelon Sprengnether, eds. *Shakespearean Tragedy and Gender.* Bloomington: Indiana University Press, 1996.

Goldberg, Jonathan. *Writing Matter: From the Hands of the English Renaissance.* Stanford: Stanford University Press, 1990.

Grafton, Anthony, and Nancy Siraisi, eds. *Natural Particulars: Nature and the Disciplines of Renaissance Europe.* Cambridge, MA: MIT Press, 1999.

Greene, Gayle. "Women on Trial in Shakespeare and Webster: 'The Mettle of [their] Sex'." *Topic 36: The Elizabethan Woman* 36 (1982): 5–19.

Hanson, Elizabeth. *Discovering the Subject in Renaissance England.* Cambridge: Cambridge University Press, 1998.

Hodges, Devon. *Renaissance Fictions of Anatomy.* Amherst: University of Massachusetts Press, 1985.

Jorden, Edward. *A Brief Discourse of a Disease called the Suffocation of the Mother.* London, 1603.

Kramer, Heinrich, and James Sprenger. *The Malleus Maleficarum,* trans. and ed. Montague Sommers. New York: Dover, 1971.

Kristeva, Julia. *Powers of Horror: An Essay on Abjection,* trans. Leon S. Roudiez. New York: Columbia University Press, 1982.

Lewalski, Barbara. *Protestant Poetics and the Seventeenth Century.* Princeton: Princeton University Press, 1970.

Lind, L. R. *Studies in Pre-Vesalian Anatomy.* Philadelphia: American Philosophical Society, 1975.

MacDonald, Michael. *Witchcraft and Hysteria in Elizabethan London.* London: Routledge, 1991.

Martz, Louis L. *The Poetry of Meditation.* New Haven: Yale University Press, 1954.

Maus, Katharine Eisaman. *Inwardness and Theater in the English Renaissance.* Chicago: University of Chicago Press, 1995.

Mousley, Andy. *Renaissance Drama and Contemporary Literary Theory.* New York: St. Martin's Press, 2000.

Neill, Michael. "'Amphitheaters in the Body': Playing with Hands on the Shakespearean Stage." *Shakespeare Survey* 48 (1995): 23–50.

Nutton, Vivian. "'A Diet for Barbarians': Introducing Renaissance Medicine to Tudor England." In *Natural Particulars: Nature and the Disciplines in Renaissance Europe*, ed. Anthony Grafton and Nancy Siraisi. 275–93. Cambridge, MA: MIT Press, 1999.

Paré, Ambroise. *The Apologie and Treatise of Ambroise Paré*, ed. Geoffrey Keynes. Chicago: University of Chicago Press, 1952

Peters, Edward. *Inquisition.* New York: Free Press, 1988.

———. *Torture.* New York: Basil Blackwell, 1986.

Randall, Dale B. J. "The Rank and Earthy Background of Certain Physical Symbols in *The Duchess of Malfi.*"*Renaissance Drama* n.s. 18 (1987): 171–203.

Rose, Mary Beth. "The Heroics of Marriage in *Othello* and *The Duchess of Malfi.*" In *Shakespearean Tragedy and Gender*, ed. Garner and Sprengnether, 210–40.

Sawday, Jonathan. *The Body Emblazoned: Dissection and the Human Body in Renaissance Culture.* New York: Routledge, 1995.

Scarry, Elaine. *The Body in Pain: The Making and Unmaking of the World.* New York: Oxford University Press, 1985.

Shakespeare, William. *Complete Works*, ed. Alfred Harbage. New York: Viking Press, 1979.

Stewart, Alan. "The Early Modern Closet Discovered." *Representations* 50 (1995): 76–100.

Thompson, Torri L. "Female Bodies Misbehaving: Mortification in Early Modern English Domestic Texts." In *Bodily Discursions: Genders, Representations, Technologies*, ed. Deborah S. Wilson and Christine Moneera Laennec, 19–37. New York: State University of New York Press, 1997.

Walworth, Alan. "'To Laugh with Open Throate': Mad Lovers, Theatrical Cures, and Gendered Bodies in Jacobean Drama." In *Enacting Gender on the English Renaissance Stage*, ed. Comensoli and Russell, 53–72.

Webster, John. *The Duchess of Malfi*. In *Drama of the English Renaissance: II. The Jacobean Period*, ed. Russell A. Fraser and Norman Rabkin, 475–515. New York: Macmillan, 1976.

Whigham, Frank. "Sexual and Social Mobility in *The Duchess of Malfi*." *Publications of the Modern Language Association* 100 (1985): 167–86

C.
Violence toward Women
in Shakespeare's
Othello

The "Erring Barbarian"
and the "Maiden Never Bold":
Racist and Sexist Representations in *Othello*

I

A charismatic Blackamoor stands before the senate of Venice and, despite his disclaimer of rude speech, narrates a mesmerizing tale of savage cannibals and malformed monsters. Equally poised and eloquent, a plucky Venetian lady also confronts the senate to defend her love for the exotic warrior for whom she has defied all accepted rubrics of complexion, clime, and degree. Both Othello, the complete man whom passion cannot rule, and Desdemona, the liberated woman who dares to choose her own mate, explode early modern concepts of blacks and women. Yet by the end of the play, traditional categories overwhelm them both, and these magnificent lovers have been reduced to the erring barbarian and submissive wife of conventional ideology. Moreover, this conformity has plunged them into a vortex of violence that culminates in the suicide of Othello and the murder of two wives. The story of their plummet from self-fashioning individuals into racist and sexist clichés forms the tragedy of Othello.

Although the term "racism" was not coined until 1936 and our conception of a "racial identity" is a twentieth-century phenomenon, a number of commentators, including Michael Neill and Emily Bartels, have persuasively argued that as a result of England's confrontation with very different peoples and mores in its emerging imperialist enterprises, something akin to a racial ideology developed during the period that produced the play *Othello*.[1] Moreover, although early modern xenophobia was certainly expansive enough to embrace all levels of cultural difference, historical and cultural events suggest the existence of a

---

[1] See Neill, "Unproper Beds," 394; Bartels, "Making More of the Moor," 433–54.

distinct color prejudice at this period.[2] Similarly, even though the term "sexism" did not enter the English lexicon until 1968, the division of the human race into binary opposites that privilege the male over the female is of venerable origin. And although, as Linda Woodbridge and Valerie Wayne demonstrate, the blatant misogyny so characteristic of the medieval period may have dwindled into a residual discourse by the time of *Othello*'s production, the relationship between the sexes and the role of women in society remained a central area of contestation at this period. This controversy saturates the drama of the time and is chronicled in the formal literary debate of the *querelle des femmes*.[3] Documents from this period thus suggest that racism and sexism, although not yet named ideologies, lurked within the language and mores of the time. However, the lack of specific linguistic terms to categorize these circulating discourses may have resulted in the effacement of issues of race and gender, both in performances of *Othello* and in the criticism written about the play, at least until the latter part of the twentieth century.

During the past decade, however, a series of excellent essays has discovered the intersection of race and gender in the play. Karen Newman denies the traditional readings that polarize Desdemona's fairness against Othello's blackness, positing femininity not as opposed to blackness and monstrosity, as white is to black, but as identified with the monstrous. Ania Loomba and Emily Bartels also find sex and race inseparable in conversations regarding the play, like Newman linking Moor and woman as Other within a white patriarchal society. Finally, David Bevington identifies Othello and Desdemona as victims of both racism and sexism.[4] However, none of these valuable discussions has focused on the

---

[2] For some valuable examinations of color prejudice in early modern England, see Hunter, "*Othello* and the Colour Prejudice"; Jones, *Othello's Countrymen*; Jordon, *White Over Black*; Barthelemy, *Black Face, Maligned Race*; Hall, *Things of Darkness*; Hendricks, "Race: A Renaissance Category?".

[3] See Woodbridge, *Women and the English Renaissance*, 244–68; Wayne, "Historical Differences: Misogyny and *Othello*," 154–55. For a particularly cogent discussion of the *querelle des femmes* controversy, see Woodbridge, *Women and the English Renaissance*, 13–138.

[4] Newman, " 'And wash the Ethiop white'," first published in *Shakespeare Reproduced*, ed. Howard and O'Connor, and Waller, "Academic Tootsie: The Denial of Difference and The Difference It Makes," were two of the first essays to focus centrally on the intersection of race and gender in the play. Other significant studies of this nexus include Loomba, *Gender, Race, Renaissance Drama*; Boebel, "Challenging the Fable: The Powers of Ideology in *Othello*"; Hawkins, "Disrupting Tribal Difference: Critical and Artistic Responses to Shakespeare's Radical Romanticism"; Parker, "Fantasies of 'Race' and 'Gender'"; Park, "The Traffic in Desdemona: Race and Sexual Transgression in *Othello*," and

degree to which Othello and Desdemona, as Moor and woman, not only share the position of alterity within their patriarchal system but also follow parallel progressions in their indoctrination into ideology and their decline from the freedom of self-fashioning individuals into the constriction of ideologically constructed pigeonholes. Expanding previous treatments of the nexus between race and gender in the play, my essay presents this reduction as dynamic, not static. Not only are Desdemona and Othello depicted as mutual victims of the constricting discourses of racism and sexism, but they are shown to be complicit in their own restriction through their recruitments into conventional subject positions that they come to accept as natural. Other commentators have identified an oppressive racist/sexist system operating throughout the play; my essay demonstrates the way in which individuals get drawn into this oppressive system. Ultimately, I argue, the play dramatizes not only the brutal treatment of women — two wives are first humiliated then slain by their husbands — but also the cultural cruelty perpetrated against the racial Other, as Othello and Desdemona become joint victims of societal violence.

In this essay I propose to use the model of human subjectivity developed by Louis Althusser to trace the parallel descents of Othello and Desdemona from the daring, non-conforming individuals that they appear to be in the opening scenes to the conventional erring barbarian and obedient wife to which they are diminished by the final curtain. Althusser describes the liberal humanist self as a subject constructed by ideology, which he defines as "a determinate (religious, ethical, etc.) representation of the world whose imaginary distortion depends on their [individuals'] imaginary relation to their conditions of existence."[5] According to Althusser, ideology as inscribed in the Ideological State Apparatuses or ISAs (the family, church, school, and cultural institutions) recruits or "hails"

Pechter, "Have You Not Read of Some Such Thing? Sex and Sexual Stories in *Othello.*" Bevington comments briefly on Othello and Desdemona as victims respectively of racism and sexism in his introduction to *Othello*, in *The Complete Works of Shakespeare*, 4th ed., 1121. However, among all of these valuable studies, none treats the influence of ideology upon the construction of both Othello and Desdemona.

Singh ("Othello's Identity, Postcolonial Theory, and Contemporary African Rewritings of *Othello*,") offers a contrary reading of the play, warning against what she sees as the tendency in contemporary criticism to collapse the categories of race and gender by assuming a similar history of marginality, whereas, she insists, the victimization suffered by blacks and women is very different. I will try to heed her caveat in this essay by pointing out the very different, although also similar, recruitments into ideology experienced by Othello and Desdemona.

[5] Althusser, "Ideology and Ideological State Apparatuses," 156.

individuals into subject positions sanctioned by a given ideology, positions that they then misrecognize as natural and universal, even as they misconstrue themselves as free agents and the generators rather than the effects of language and meaning. Althusser's term for this subliminal coercion into the subject positions endorsed by the convention ideology is "interpellate."[6] Although no one in the early modern period would have referred to recruitment into subjectivity by ideology, the conflicting claims of nature (biological determinism) and nurture (social constructionism) — nature's livery or fortune's star — were actively debated in both the homiletic and the fictional literature of the time. Moreover, although no one at this time would have construed the issues in Althusser's terms, the act of interpellating individuals into preconstituted societal roles certainly predates Althusser's codification of this phenomenon. In this essay, therefore, I contend that originally both Othello and Desdemona deviate from the societal norms for blacks and women in both Renaissance Venice, in which the play is set, and early modern England, in which it was written. In my reading, Iago, representing not the dominant discourse of Venice but instead the largely repressed xenophobia and misogyny of his society, is determined to coerce these two deviants — the Westernized Moor and the unruly woman — into accepted subject positions within a racist and sexist ideology. My essay details the strategies by which Iago achieves the refashioning and programming of Othello and Desdemona, thereby defending himself against the threat of the racial and sexual Other. I will also seek to demonstrate that Iago's coercive classifications not only inflict enormous torment on his unfortunate recruits but also lead to the most serious kind of violence against women, as Iago transforms Othello into the prototypic abusive husband and Desdemona into the classic battered wife. Iago's manipulations ultimately result in the murder of two wives and the disgrace and suicide of one abusive husband, as well as the presumed torture and death of the other.

In addition to his role in my paradigm as recruiter for society's racist and sexist ideologies, Iago has traditionally been cast by critics in a number of emblematic parts, including medieval Vice and stage Machiavel.[7] However, Iago cannot be reduced to a mere stage emblem, because the character projects a shocking and frightening mimetic authenticity. Unfortunately, we have all met this recognizable human type — the individual deficient in self-esteem who

---

[6] Althusser, "Ideology and Ideological State Apparatuses," 162–73.

[7] For an examination of Iago as a psychological development from the medieval Vice, see Spivack, *Shakespeare and the Allegory of Evil.* For an analysis of Iago as both the morality play Vice and the Machiavellian villain, see Spencer, *Shakespeare and the Nature of Man*, 122–35.

seeks to inflate his self-image by feeling superior to other sexual, ethnic, or racial groups. Virginia Woolf observes that "Women have served all these centuries as looking-glasses possessing the magic and delicious power of reflecting the figure of man at twice its natural size."[8] Similarly, the presumed inferiority of different racial as well as sexual groups has traditionally served as a mirror to magnify the white European male's sense of his own personal worth. My essay posits lowborn Iago as embodying this pervasive need to feel superior to others in a competitive, hierarchical society, and identifies racism and sexism as the solutions that he develops to satisfy this need. Such personal inadequacies make characters like Iago ripe for interpellation into extreme, residual brands of ideology. Thus Iago represents the male chauvinist and white supremacist par excellence,[9] and when strong, virtuous women like Desdemona or eminent, admirable blacks like Othello threaten his valued sense of superiority, he is driven to recruit them into his own racist/sexist ideology.

II

By the time that *Othello* appeared on the London stage in 1604 or 1605,[10] African characters of varying colors, generally referred to as Moors and possessing a constellation of recognizable character traits, had become a familiar part of the London theatrical scene. The early modern society and its corollary stage tradition depicted the Moor as passionate, libidinous, jealous, violent, bestial, treacherous, thieving, and pagan,[11] an image very different from that of the dig-

---

[8] *A Room of One's Own*, 35.

[9] Though Shakespeare would certainly not have been familiar with these terms, and the idea of white supremacy would probably have been assimilated into a more comprehensive xenophobia at this time, I suspect that the character traits represented by this type would have been very familiar in the early modern period, even as they are today. Although the terms are certainly anachronistic, the personality type that they describe probably is not. Viewing Iago from a different although related perspective, Adelman ("Iago's Alter Ego," esp. 127, 128, 133) locates Iago within a Kleinian paradigm, seeing him as representing a type of injured "I" (ego), a man who views himself as chronically slighted and betrayed and who must project onto Othello his own emptiness and fragmentation in an effort to make himself whole.

[10] Knutson identifies 1604–1605 as the date of *Othello*'s debut with the King's Men, *The Repertory of Shakespeare's Company 1594–1613*, 107, 120.

[11] For some valuable discussions of the early modern construction of the Moor, see Jones, *Othello's Countrymen*; Jordan, *White Over Black*; D'Amico, *The Moor in English Renaissance Drama*; and Barthelemy, *Black Face, Maligned Race*. For an interesting recent examination of the early modern association of the Moor with monstrosity, see Aubrey, "Race and the Spectacle of the Monstrous in *Othello*."

nified general whom we encounter at the beginning of the play. The drama enacts the conflict between Othello, who struggles desperately to resist succumbing
to the clichés of his society, and Iago, who schemes indefatigably to catch his
soul and ensnare it in a prison of platitudes.[12]

Iago's attempted ensnaring of Othello opens the play. Significantly, Iago introduces his scenario with a warning to Brabantio against burglary, "Look to
your house, your daughter, and your bags!" (1.1.82).[13] Iago proceeds to degrade
the relationship of Desdemona and Othello to a bestial sexuality as he performs
a charivari — the traditional raucous denunciation of an unnatural or transgressive coupling[14] — under Brabantio's window. In Iago's lurid scenario, Othello
becomes an "old black ram" tupping Brabantio's "white ewe" (1.1.90–91) and a
"Barbary horse" making with Desdemona "the beast with two backs" (1.1.114,
119–120), in short, the libidinous Negro and black rapist of European (and, I
should add, American) fantasy.[15]

Other characters cooperate in demeaning, or, at best, marginalizing Othello.
Roderigo, following Iago's cue, attempts to construct Othello as "a lascivious
Moor" (1.1.129), and Brabantio links him with the forbidden practice of witchcraft. Brabantio and Roderigo also indulge in crude racial jibes such as "thick
lips" and "sooty bosom." Other racist remarks are less overt. As Paul A. Jorgensen points out, "Othello emerges as one of the most respected and capable military executives in Shakespeare"[16]; yet despite the esteem in which he is held by
the senators of Venice, before Othello can be totally accepted, he must be lin-
guistically whitewashed by the Duke: "If virtue no delighted beauty lack, / Your
son-in-law is far more fair than black" (1.3.292–93). Moreover, the Duke also
needs Othello's martial expertise; had Othello not been so valuable a comman-
der, his blackness might not have been so easily discounted.

However, notwithstanding both these covert and overt expressions of racist

---

[12] Barthelemy was one of the first commentators to observe Othello's efforts to escape
the role fated for the Moor onstage, suggesting that "as he moves to free himself of the
confines of the role, he moves inexorably closer to it" (*Black Face, Maligned Race*, 154).
Berry also notes Othello's futile attempts to escape racist categories and to assimilate into
white Venetian society ("Othello's Alienation," 320).

[13] All quotations are from the *Complete Works of Shakespeare*, 4th ed., David
Bevington.

[14] For an examination of the charivari motif as an informing element of the play, see
Bristol, "Charivari and the Comedy of Abjection in *Othello*," 75–97.

[15] On Iago's depiction of Othello as the black rapist, see Boebel, "Challenging the
Fable," 139.

[16] Jorgensen, *Shakespeare's Military World*, 117.

sentiment, many of the characters in the play are not presented as racist. Although some commentators interpret Desdemona's statement, "I saw Othello's visage in his mind" (1.3.255), as a rejection of his physical difference, I see it as an affirmation of her mental union with her soul mate — a kind of "marriage of true minds." I would agree with Bevington that she never gives the slightest indication that she regards her husband as different or foreign because he is black and older; she remains unswervingly fond of him, admiring, and faithful. If she errs, she does so by overvaluing Othello and failing to recognize his fallibility.[17] Similarly, Cassio idealizes his general as he does his general's lady, and makes no reference to racial difference. Moreover, although the horror of the final catastrophe draws from Emilia passionate slurs possibly tinged with racist overtones, throughout the play Emilia seems as oblivious to Othello's racial difference as does her mistress. However, since blackness at this period was associated not only with pigmentation but also with moral soil, Emilia's final accusations, "O, the more angel she, / And you the *blacker* devil!" (5.2.134–135); "She was too fond of her most *filthy* bargain" (164); and "O gull!, O dolt! / As ignorant as *dirt!*" (170–71; emphases mine), might be read as reflecting racial bias. Finally, despite the covert racism revealed in the Duke's attempt to "wash the Ethiop white," the play also stresses the enormous respect that "valiant" Othello evokes from those in authority, not only the Duke and the senators of Venice but also the governor of Cyprus. Arguably, only three individuals fall victim to Iago's racist innuendoes; tragically, one of these is the valiant Othello himself.

However, when Othello first strides onto the stage in the second scene, we are surprised to discover a man who explodes all the clichés of accepted belief initially invoked by Iago. Instead of the passionate Moor, we meet a Stoic whom the full Senate considers "all in all sufficient," a nature "whom passion could not shake" (4.1.270–271). Instead of the libidinous Moor, we confront the Platonic lover who wishes his soul mate to share his warrior camp not to please the palate of his appetite but "to be free and bounteous to her mind" (1.3.263–268). Instead of the black rapist, we find a lover who claims to lack the phallic potency conventionally ascribed to the black male, a man in whom "the young affects" are now "defunct" (1.3.266–267). Instead of the jealous Moor, we espy a most indulgent husband, who fondly protests to Iago, "'Tis not to make me jealous / To say my wife is fair, feeds well, loves company, / Is free of speech, sings, plays, and dances well" (3.3.197–199). Instead of the violent Moor, we detect a general

---

[17] See Bevington's perceptive discussion of Desdemona in his introduction to *Othello*, in *The Complete Works*, 1118.

of magnificent poise who can quell a riot with the simple but eloquent line, "Keep up your bright swords, for the dew will rust them" (1.2.60). Instead of the treacherous Moor, we encounter a man of "free and open nature, / That thinks men honest that but seem to be so" (1.3.400–401), a comrade perhaps too trusting of his fellow soldiers. Finally, instead of the pagan Moor, we meet a devout Christian who rebukes his quarreling subordinates, "Are we turned Turks, and to ourselves do that / Which heaven hath forbid the Ottomites? / For Christian shame, put by this barbarous brawl!" (2.3.164–166). In short, we confront a man who appears to have valiantly resisted indoctrination into racist ideology and has fashioned himself into the very antithesis of the demonized Moor.

How then does Iago so easily destroy Othello's magnificent creation? How does the wily spider snare so great a dragonfly as Othello? Critics have traditionally offered a variety of solutions to this conundrum. Jorgensen sees Othello as the plain soldier, untutored in social interactions, who cannot progress from the casque to the cushion.[18] Other critics have stressed Othello's gullibility. Still others have focused on Othello's lack of self-esteem. This insecurity is manifested in a series of unintentional admissions, as when Othello poignantly reassures himself of the unimportance of physical appearance, "For she had eyes, and chose me" (3.3.203), or when he ironically apologizes for his lack of rhetorical skill, "Rude am I in my speech" (1.3.83), or when he reveals his craving for an audience, "She loved me for the dangers I had passed, / And I loved her that she did pity them" (1.3.169–170). This insecurity surfaces in Othello's oft-quoted soliloquy in the temptation scene, in which, in a return of the repressed, he admits to feelings of inferiority deriving from his race, age, and lack of courtly sophistication:

> Haply, for I am black
> And have not those soft parts of conversation
> That chamberers have, or for I am declined
> Into the vale of years — ... (3.3.279–282)

I find all of these explanations persuasive, but would focus particularly on Othello's feelings of insecurity as the site of his vulnerability, an insecurity resulting from his internalization of society's racism — a racism that he initially resists in a heroic act of self-definition. In destroying the Moor's self-fashioned persona and conscripting him into the subject position of racial Other, Iago, imitating the typical strategies of the colonizer, first recruits Othello into the subject

---

[18] Jorgenson, Shakespeare's *Military World*, 259–65.

position occupied by Brabantio. He then manipulates the Moor to mimic the white patriarch by viewing Desdemona through her father's proprietorial perspective and himself through the patriarchal gaze, echoing not only Brabantio's thoughts but also his words. Through this racist/sexist astigmatism, Othello constructs himself as Alien, Desdemona as disobedient daughter and thus, ineluctably, as disobedient wife, and his miscegenative union with Desdemona as a violation of the laws of clime, complexion, and degree. This misrecognition is revealed in his most fatal admission, "And yet, how nature erring from itself ..." (3.3.243). Later, Othello will be psychically possessed by Iago; thus, the subordinate becomes the master, and Othello becomes the colonized "mimic man."[19]

Significantly, only after Othello comes under the influence of Iago and begins to believe that Desdemona has betrayed him does he start to construct himself as black,[20] as if, in losing Desdemona's love, he has lost the metaphorical whiteness (the freshness of "Dian's visage") that her love has conferred upon him. Similarly, only after Othello is psychically penetrated by Iago, in the "temptation scene" with its climactic conclusion in a parodic marriage, does he begin to associate his blackness with moral turpitude, mimicking Iago's racist idiom as he also echoes the Ensign's bestial imagery. As Doris Adler informs us, at this time both "black" and "white" held multiple meanings, designating a dark or lighter hue or a blond or brunette, identifying a Moor/Negro or a European, denoting soil or cleanliness, or indicating moral filth or purity.[21] As Othello declines from "honorary white" to total Outsider,[22] viewing himself more and more through the white, patriarchal gaze, he moves from accepting his racial pigmentation as a romantic impediment ("Haply, for I am *black*," 3.3.279) to associating his blackness with moral filth ("My name, that was as fresh / As Dian's visage, is now *begrimed* and *black* As mine own face," 3.3.402–404) to linking blackness generally with metaphysical evil ("Arise, *black* vengeance, from the hollow hell!," 3.3.462; emphases mine). Moreover, as Othello becomes more and more convinced of Desdemona's perfidy, a betrayal that he blames on racial

---

[19] For a discussion of the " 'mimic man' who was 'whitewashed' by Western culture, and yet excluded from its full entitlements," see Singh, "Othello's Identity," 292. For a fuller treatment of this topic, see Fontenot and Fanon, *The Wretched of the Earth*.

[20] As far as I am aware, Snow ("Sexual Anxiety and the Male Order of Things in *Othello*," 398–402) is the first commentator to note this important progression.

[21] Adler, "The Rhetoric of Black and White in *Othello*," 248.

[22] I borrow the term "honorary white" from Loomba, *Gender, Race, Renaissance Drama*, 52.

and sexual difference, he first tries compulsively to project his perceived grime onto Desdemona and, imitating Iago, to turn her virtue into pitch. Later, torn with ambivalence, he begins to construct her as white, describing her as "this *fair*" (4.2.73) with "*whiter* skin of hers than snow" (5.2.4) and a complexion as "*pale*" as her "smock" (5.2.282), comparing her to things both white and cold — snow, alabaster, pearls (emphases mine).[23]

In the end, of course, Iago succeeds in recruiting Othello into the subject position[24] of the demonized Moor. Othello, totally relinquishing his torturously fashioned identity, mimes the conventional gestures and postures associated with this role. Passionately rolling his eyes and gnawing his nether lip, he is frenzied in his jealousy, violent in his murder of his helpless wife, bestial in his incoherent fit, and treacherous in his attempted assassination of Cassio. (Although, I should add, from first to last, Iago, not Othello, represents the treacherous manipulator, the thief of jewels, reputations, and human sanity.) Totally integrated into the role of racial Other, Othello denies both his name and his identity, "That's he that was Othello. Here I am" (5.2.292). Finally, Othello equates himself not only with the savage Turk but also with either the false Judean or the ingrate Indian — depending on how one reads this textual crux[25] — and,

---

[23] Critics commenting on Othello's attempts to tar Desdemona with his own blackness include Newman, " 'And wash the Ethiop white'," 151–52; Loomba, *Gender, Race, Renaissance Drama*, 59; Neill, "Unproper Beds," 410; Berry, "Othello's Alienation," 328; Parker, "Fantasies of Race," 95; and Adelman, "Race as Projection," 126 n. 5. Less often remarked is Othello's effort to construct his wife as white, although Boose does discuss Othello's consistent association of Desdemona with "white translucent-shining-pure-cold-virginal image clusters" in "Othello's 'Chrysolite' and the Song of Songs Tradition," 433. Also relevant is Hall's warning against the tendency to naturalize whiteness even as, I would add, the patriarchy has traditionally naturalized maleness. She explains that when we speak of "race," we almost always refer to blackness or Jewishness; we naturalize whiteness and fail to realize that whiteness, like blackness, is a cultural construct, even as gentileness is also a cultural construct. See, Hall, "Reading What Isn't There: 'Black' Studies in Early Modern England," 25.

[24] See Hanson, "Discovering the Subject in Renaissance England," 74–85.

[25] The term "Judean" appears in the Quarto, "Indian" in the Folio. Either term can be used to support my reading of Othello as ultimately rejecting himself as racial Other, since both American Indians and Jews were traditionally linked with Turks as pagan aliens threatening the white Christian hegemony of the period (see Calderwood, *The Properties of Othello*, 7), or simply as the ethically, culturally, and religiously strange (Hall, *Things of Darkness*, 5). The following quotation from *Hic Mulier or the Man Woman* (Facsimile edition [University of Exeter, 1973], B2) exemplifies this nexus, including also a linking of these pagan aliens with the unruly woman. In excoriating the "mannish woman," the pamphleteer rants, "If this be not barbarous, make the rude *Scythian*, the untamed *Moor*, the naked *Indian*, or the wild *Arab*, Lords & Rulers of well governed Cities."

judging himself through the gaze of his white patriarchal community, he condemns and executes the despised Alien.

I would insist, however, that despite his degeneration at the end of the play, Othello never totally alienates our sympathy. Indeed, it is precisely the reduction of this independent, unconventional man into the figure of the conventionalized Moor that evokes both pity and terror. Ultimately, the destruction of Othello's integrity and dignity are far more tragic than his death.

III

In discussing both racism and sexism in early modern England, we should be careful not to totalize conventional ideology and to remember that multiple rather than unitary discourses circulated during this period (as during all historical epochs). Thus, I am not implying that Iago's racist and sexist attitudes represent the only acceptable stance at this time or even the dominant one, although the literature treating xenophobia suggests that Iago's views may offer a hyperbolic example of early modern society's dominant discourse on race. Conversely, I agree with Wayne that the Ensign's violent and vituperative misogyny was, by this time, already a residual rather than a dominant gender discourse.[26] I identify at least three discourses toward woman circulated during the period that produced *Othello*, and locate all three of these ideologies within the play: i.e., first, the residual (yet still operative) misogynist discourse espoused by Iago that inscribes all women as scolds and whores; second, the dominant discourse that presents marriage as both hierarchical and mutual, a discourse originally endorsed by Othello and enthusiastically embraced by Desdemona; third, the emerging feminist discourse that denies the double standard and speaks for equality between the sexes, a discourse expressed by Emilia. Within this template, Othello's tragedy occurs when, under the influence of Iago, the Moor shifts his allegiance from a discourse advocating harmonious complementarity to one affirming dominance and submission, ownership and servitude. Desdemona's tragedy resides in her failure to question the dominant discourse of woman's subservience within marriage, even when this union is stripped of mutuality. In my interpretation, therefore, Iago seeks to interpellate Othello into the clichés of society's racism (a racism perhaps more pervasive in early modern England than in the Renaissance Venice of the play) as well as into a reactionary but still prevalent misogyny.

Several invidious assumptions inherent in the ideology of the early modern

---

[26] Wayne, "Historical Differences: Misogyny and *Othello*," 154-55.

patriarchy undergirded the pervasive sexism of that society. One of these assumptions divided human personality into two contrary genders, masculine and feminine. This schema depicts women as passionate rather than rational, pliant rather than resolute, passive rather than active, helpless rather than competent — in short, as not fully mature and responsible human beings. It follows, therefore, that these irrational, irresponsible creatures must be guided by their more rational and mature mates, hence the valorizing in these immature creatures of the qualities of obedience, piety, patience, chastity, and silence. Like children, they should be ruled, commanded, and even chastised, protected from male predators and guided by Christian precepts, seen and not heard. Helen Carr draws a disturbing parallel between the white patriarchy's construction of the racial and sexual Other:

> Both are seen as part of nature, not culture, and with the same ambivalence: either they are ripe for government, passive, child-like, unsophisticated, needing leadership and guidance, described always in terms of lack — no initiative, no intellectual powers, no perseverance; or, on the other hand, they are outside society, dangerous, treacherous, emotional, inconstant, wild, threatening, fickle, sexually aberrant, irrational, near animal, lascivious, disruptive, evil, unpredictable.[27]

Another equally pernicious dichotomy separated the female sex into two binary opposites. The privileged member of this gender division, whom Marilyn French associates with the "inlaw" virtues, is not a child or a primitive but a superior, supernal being, represented in sacred lore by the Virgin Mary, in secular verse by the Courtly Lady, and in the defenses of the *querelle des femmes* by the ideal wife. However, despite the period's glowing sonnet cycles and polemical encomia, there is little evidence that this reverence was ever more than a literary exercise or that these hardworking wives and mothers ever occupied more than a mythological pedestal. Moreover, if a woman deviated from her elevated ethical status or fell from her lofty moral (and mythological) perch, she was tarred with the outlaw feminine traits. She would then be stigmatized as a temptress (represented by Eve and denigrated in the writings of the early church fathers), a shrew (ridiculed in Western literature from the Middle Ages to the present, and during the Medieval period tortured with ducking stools, stocks, iron bits, and public ridicule), and the whore (the traditional butt of misogynistic writing).

---

[27] Carr, "Woman/Indian: The 'American' and His Others," 50; quoted by Loomba, *Gender, Race, and Renaissance Drama*, 45.

Thus, women were denied the normal fallibility allotted the other half of the human race and, as any object of a vestigial twentieth-century chivalry is fully aware, balancing on a pedestal can be almost as uncomfortable as being pushed into a ditch.[28]

Just as the attitudes toward Othello in the play run the gamut from erasure of racial difference (Desdemona, Cassio) to extreme racial animus (Iago), with a number of gradations in between (Brabantio, the Duke, Emilia), so the perspectives of Desdemona participate in a broad spectrum of essentializing gender representations. From one point of view, *Othello* can be read as anatomizing conventional attitudes toward both race and gender. Moreover, just as in the opening scenes of the play Iago consistently invokes the clichés of accepted belief that Othello consistently contravenes, so the males in the play continually evoke conventional feminine categories that Desdemona continually violates. Throughout the play, the men in Desdemona's life seek to present her as a *tabula rasa* onto which they can inscribe their own fantasies of womanhood, even as Iago seeks to reduce Othello to a text onto which he can write his malignant racist fables.[29] For Desdemona, whether adored or reviled, honored or battered, remains the play's cynosure, and, like the colored glass in a kaleidoscope, her image changes with the shift in perspective from one male observer to another.

Let us consider some of these perspectives. Desdemona's conventional father Brabantio myopically sees Desdemona as the ideal daughter: "A maiden never bold; / Of spirit so still and quiet that her motion / Blushed at herself" (1.3.96–98), while also regarding her as a valuable commodity, a precious "jewel" (1.3.198) to be merchandised as he sees fit. The aristocratic lieutenant Cassio, a firm advocate of the madonna/whore dichotomy, idealizes his general's bride as the incomparable courtly lady, through his poetic idiom transforming Brabantio's "maiden never bold" into the "divine Desdemona," that "paragons description

---

[28] French identifies the "inlaw" feminine principle with the benevolent aspects of nature and such qualities as nutritiveness, compassion, mercy, volitional subordination, and voluntary relinquishment of power-in-the-world; the "outlaw" feminine values are associated with the malevolent aspects of nature, such as darkness, chaos, magic, sexuality (*Shakespeare's Division of Experience*, 13–14, 16–17); Henderson and McManus, in their discussion of the positive and negative images of women circulating during this period, cluster the denigrated "outlaw" traits under three negative stereotypes: the seductress, the shrew, and the vain woman, countered by the positive "inlaw" icons: the chaste, constant woman, the nurturing, self-sacrificing wife, and the pious saint (*Half Humankind: Contexts and Texts of the Controversy About Women in England, 1540–1640*, 47–63).

[29] On Desdemona as a *tabula rasa*, see Callaghan, *Woman and Gender in Renaissance Tragedy*, 78.

and wild fame" (2.1.75, 64). Conversely, Iago, the arch misogynist, slurs Desdemona as the "supersubtle Venetian" and potential whore; while Cassio exalts Desdemona's spirituality, Iago gloats upon her carnality. The repartee between the two soldiers as they stand guard upon the Citadel at Cyprus (2.3.12–26) graphically illustrates Cassio's and Iago's contrasting inscriptions on the fair paper of Desdemona. Yet, however much Iago may fantasize about Desdemona's appetite and sexual pranks, his catholic misogyny embraces not only Desdemona but the entire female sex. Even as he attempts to sully Desdemona as a whore, he also defames his own wife as a strumpet who dallies with both Cassio and Othello, and jibes at Bianca as a "huswife that by selling her desires / Buys herself bread and clothes" (4.1.96–97). The antithetical depictions of Emilia parallel those of Desdemona: Iago typically belittles her as a scold, while Desdemona protests that "she has no speech" (2.1.102–105). Moreover, although Emilia speaks boldly against the gender double standard, throughout much of the play she seeks slavishly to appease her wayward husband. Similarly, since the pathological liar Iago alone labels Bianca as a prostitute, the audience does not know how to evaluate her, and recent critics have begun to question Iago's accusations.[30] Yet, however we may interpret Bianca, or even Emilia, Iago's animosity clearly envelops all females, and he seeks not only to degrade but also to destroy all of the women in the play. Initially, therefore, Iago attempts to inscribe Desdemona, as well as Emilia and Bianca, as a whore. Unable to do this, he recruits Othello into his misogynistic, as well as racist ideology, and Othello, as his factor, successfully conscripts Desdemona into the role of passive, obedient wife.

Othello's more complex responses to his beloved span the spectrum of clichés represented in the European value system that he has internalized and combine the diverse inscriptions of Cassio, Brabantio, and Iago. On the one hand, as Calderwood notes, Othello, like Cassio, idealizes Desdemona as a disembodied Petrarchan divinity[31] — the perfect chrysolite, the fountain from which his current runs. Typically, however, when convinced by Iago that his madonna is tainted, Othello swerves one hundred eighty degrees and, parroting Iago's idiom

---

[30] In "Women and Men in *Othello*," 218–19, Neely seeks to rehabilitate all three of the women in the play, arguing that these three women represent a balance among romanticism, affection, and modesty. For an informative survey of critical opinion on Bianca, see Nina Rulon-Miller, "*Othello*'s Bianca: Climbing Out of the Bed of the Patriarchy."

[31] "Speech and Self in *Othello*," 297–98. In this essay, Calderwood traces Desdemona's descent from the disembodied Petrarchan spirit of Othello's opening address to the dismembered and disarticulated body of his babbling outburst.

and ideas, degrades his goddess to a devil. However, throughout the last two acts of the play, Othello's dialogue remains saturated with the ambivalence between adoration and vilification so characteristic of the madonna/whore obsession. Additionally, like Brabantio, the European patriarch whom he echoes, Othello perceives his wife as property — his purchase, his jewel (chrysolite, pearl).[32] Inviting her to the nuptial bed, he employs the lexicon of commerce: "Come, my dear love, / The purchase made, the fruits are to ensue; / The profit's yet to come 'tween me and you" (2.3.8–10), and later laments his loss in the language of patriarchal possession: "O, curse of marriage, / That we can call these delicate creatures ours, / And not their appetites!" (3.3.284–86). Internalizing the patriarchal values of his social milieu, Othello views Desdemona's unfaithfulness as a defacement of his private property, not only a loss of love but also a loss of male honor. However, Othello extends patriarchal authority far beyond what was legally allowed, either in the Venice of the play or early modern England, when he unquestioningly affirms his prerogative not only to chastise, but even to execute his wife. Othello never questions his right to kill Desdemona if she is unchaste, sanctifying his murder as a sacrifice. Lastly, and most important, I believe, Othello sees Desdemona not as a unique individual but as an idealized reflection of himself, a role that Desdemona enthusiastically accepts, calling herself an "unhandsome warrior" when she fears that somehow she has failed to fulfill her husband's martial ideal (3.4.153). As Carol McGinnis Kay expresses it, "The basis for their love, then, is the grand romantic image of Othello that they both admire and pity, the image of Othello that Desdemona reflects to him."[33] Moreover, as his "*fair* warrior," Desdemona not only serves as a mirror to magnify his heroic identity but also ratifies his honorary whiteness in his adopted society. With his *fair* warrior a presumed deserter, Othello's martial occupation is lost (3.3.361–373; emphasis mine); with his magnifying mirror crazed, Othello declines into the stigma of racial Otherness.

Yet, when Desdemona first appears before the senate of Venice, she defies the shopworn clichés with which the men who love, laud, loathe, and lust after her attempt to incarcerate her. Instead of the "maiden never bold" (1.3.96) her father misconceives her to be, we meet a woman of adventurous spirit, who threw away the book of gender etiquette as she wooed the man of her choice, who risked

---

[32] Snow ("Sexual Anxiety," 386 n. 4) comments on the recurrent theme of women in the play as possessions: Brabantio's sense of his daughter as a jewel; Othello's view of his wife as a pearl; Cassio's reference to Bianca as a bauble. Boose also analyzes the jewel motif in the play in "Othello's 'Chrysolite,'" 427.

[33] Kay, "Othello's Need for Mirrors," 265.

loss of status by eloping with an exotic stranger, and who boldly confronts the senate of Venice to defend her love. Instead of the aloof courtly lady of Cassio's visions, we encounter a woman of frank sensuality, who proudly proclaims the "violence" of her love and passionately asserts, "That I did love the Moor to live with him" (1.3.251). Finally, instead of the subtle Venetian whore that Iago and Othello later construct, we confront a woman of astonishing constancy and devotion, who commits herself unequivocally to her husband. In the early scenes of the play, therefore, Shakespeare has created in Desdemona a woman "who can be both frankly sexual and utterly virtuous, who can moreover combine in herself sexual appetite and maternal nurturance without becoming whorish or overwhelming."[34] In Desdemona, Shakespeare presents an oxymoronic blend of boldness and docility, sophistication and naiveté, sensuality and chastity, a formidable and unconventional woman who challenges all feminine ideals of the period.[35]

As with Othello, we must ask, "What happened?" How can we explain Desdemona's rapid disintegration from the unconventional, confident, articulate young woman in the opening scenes to the dazed and defenseless wife of the denouement? Following Irene Dash, I suggest that, like Othello, Desdemona is never as unconventional as she first appears. Despite her defiance of social mores in choosing her husband and her bold selection of a mate outside of accepted kinship associations, her attitude toward marriage remains thoroughly conventional. From the very beginning of the play, she defines herself in relation to men, as either a wife or daughter but not as an independent individual, and her triple reference to "duty" in her defense before the senate accentuates her acceptance of her subservient female role in the traffic in women:[36]

---

[34] Adelman, *Suffocating Mothers*, 73.

[35] In "Women and Men in *Othello*" (211–12), Neely protests that during the past one hundred years or so critics of *Othello* have divided into two camps: the Othello critics, who view the text through Othello's eyes, not only accepting Othello's high estimate of himself but also idealizing Desdemona as Othello does at the beginning of the play; and the Iago critics, who take their cues from Iago, demeaning both Othello and Desdemona as the Ancient does. Commentators seeking to release Desdemona from the essentialist prison in which she has been incarcerated by patriarchal critics include, in addition to Neely and Adelman, Garner ("Shakespeare's Desdemona"); Greene (" 'This that you call love': Sexual and Social Tragedy in *Othello*"); W. D. Adamson ("Unpinned and Undone? Desdemona's Critics and the Problem of Sexual Innocence"); Ann Jennalie Cook ("The Design of *Othello*: Doubt Raised and Resolved"); Irene Dash (*Wooing, Wedding, Power: Women in Shakespeare's Plays*; and Dreher (*Fathers and Daughters in Shakespeare*, 87–95).

[36] Dash, *Wooing, Wedding, and Power*, 119–20.

> My noble Father,
> I do perceive here a divided *duty*.
> To you I am bound for life and education;
> My life and education both do learn me
> How to respect you. You are the lord of *duty*;
> I am hitherto your daughter. But here's my husband,
> And so much *duty* as my mother showed
> To you, preferring you before her father,
> So much I challenge that I may profess
> Due to the Moor my lord. (1.3.182–191; emphases mine)

As Dash expresses it, the play becomes "the tragedy of a woman, of women, pummeled into shape by the conventions that bind." This view is supported by Edward Snow's assertion that Desdemona's "loss of self-confidence and forthrightness under the pressure of Othello's accusations only emphasizes a process intrinsic to the institution of marriage in a patriarchal society."[37] As I argue above, Othello's unconscious assimilation of his society's racial biases renders him vulnerable to Iago's conditioning. Similarly, Desdemona's acceptance of her society's deleterious subordination of women makes her susceptible to Othello's recruitment. Both Othello and Desdemona incorporate into themselves the cultural clichés of their society and this acceptance destroys them.

Moreover, Desdemona perilously internalizes the socially sanctioned identification of the wife with the husband, as Milton, echoing St. Paul, instructs, "He for God only, she for God in him."[38] Othello also recalls that, during their courtship, Desdemona sighed, wishing "That heaven had made her such a man" (1.3.164). Through this double entendre, Desdemona reveals her desire to escape, if only vicariously, from the claustrophobic confines of the woman's role in the patriarchal system. Once they are married, Othello becomes for Desdemona not only her dearest friend but also the extension of her being, the warrior who fulfills her romantic yearnings. As she explains:

> I saw Othello's visage in his mind,
> And to his honors and his valiant parts
> Did I my soul and fortunes consecrate. (1.3.255–257)

---

[37] Dash, *Wooing, Wedding, and Power*, 104; Snow, "Sexual Anxiety," 408. For a contrary reading that stresses Desdemona's unconventionality in both her selection of her own husband and her "exogamous choice of a racial outsider," see Park, "The Traffic in Desdemona," 1072.

[38] *Paradise Lost*, ed. Hughes, 4. 299, p. 93.

Desdemona's identification with her husband is so complete that when he inexplicably turns on her, she withdraws, cowed into passivity, denial, and helplessness. Refusing to be inscribed as whore, yet coerced into the sexist philosophy dominating the age, she accepts her subordinate subject position. She thus affirms her duty to obey her husband in all things and his right to chastise her — even though she is unaware of her fault — and she never attempts to retaliate against Othello or expose him. Even after he publicly humiliates her, striking her and demeaning her before Lodovico, she takes no steps to escape or even defend herself until the very end of the play when the crazed Othello threatens her with death.[39] Instead, she responds to his brutality with love and forgiveness, "Unkindness may do much, / And his unkindness may defeat my life, / But never taint my love." (4.2.166–168). As expected of the loving, self-denying wife, she seeks excuses for her violent husband, blaming herself:

> Nay, we must think men are not gods,
> Nor of them look for such observancy
> As fits the bridal. Beshrew me much, Emilia,
> I was, unhandsome warrior as I am,
> Arraigning his unkindness with my soul;
> But now I find I had suborned the witness,
> And he's indicted falsely. (3.4.150–156)

Finally, she lies to protect her mate, with her dying breath asserting his innocence and her responsibility in words that also imply that she, like Othello, has been stripped of identity. When Emilia demands, "O, who hath done this deed?" she murmurs, "Nobody; I myself" (5.2.127–128). Ultimately, therefore, Desdemona shrinks her vibrant personality to the Procrustean bed of patriarchal marriage, declining from a dynamic, self-fashioning individual into the classic battered wife.[40]

---

[39] For a provocative contrary reading that depicts Desdemona as much less passive than I do, see Bartels, "Strategies of Submission," 417–33. See also Pechter's essay in this volume.

[40] In an earlier article, I discussed the degree to which the portrait of Desdemona corresponds to that of the battered wife of contemporary clinical literature (Deats, "From Pedestal to Ditch," 87–90). Ruth Vanita in " 'Proper' Men and 'Fallen' Women in Othello," 355, n. 22 also situates Desdemona within contemporary narratives of battered women, associating Desdemona's dying "lie" with the deathbed avowals of Indian battered and murdered wives who seek to exonerate the murderous actions of their husbands and in-laws.

As a number of feminist critics have demonstrated, the role of woman in marriage constituted a major site of contestation within early modern society, and although moralists unanimously proclaimed the subordination of the wife to the husband in the nuclear patriarchal family, the degree of obedience that the wife owed the husband was actively debated. The Puritans of the period loudly affirmed the right, indeed the obligation, of the Christian to place conscience above law and defy even the monarch if necessary to preserve Christian integrity.[41] Logically developing the ubiquitous analogy between father and king, some moralists of the period also affirmed, albeit somewhat reluctantly, that even as the Christian subject should passively (and even sometimes actively) resist the unchristian demands of an ungodly magistrate, so the Christian wife might practice a similar resistance to the unlawful or unchristian demands of a tyrannical husband, with the recommended resistance ranging from passive non-compliance to outright disobedience.[42] Marriage manuals also debated the degree to which chastisement of the wife by the husband should be permitted, with the majority of the Puritan marriage guides, at least, deploring corporal punishment of the wife by the husband. Thus William Whately, in the widely read manual *A Bride-Bush*, while exhorting the husband to "keep his authority" within the family, nevertheless also admonishes him to rule with gentleness, kindness, and diplomacy, not with force and rage. Moreover, Whately implies, without absolutely stating, that the wife may disobey any unlawful commands: "The wife indeed should cast her eye only upon the lawfulness or unlawfulness of the thing, asking none other

---

[41] The attitudes toward obedience to the unjust or ungodly monarch ranged from an unconditional affirmation of absolute obedience and total denial of the doctrine of conscience, to a sanction of conscientious non-compliance coupled with a prohibition against active resistance, to an endorsement of resistance led by lesser magistrates, to a fervent advocacy of resistance, even rebellion, by the people as well as the magistrates. For a lucid discussion of these various different views, see Strier, *Resistant Structure*, 170–77.

[42] For defenses of the doctrine of conscience in the family sphere, see Henry Smith, *A Preparative to Marriage: Of the Lord's Supper; Of Usurie*, facsimile edition (1591, repr. Amsterdam: Theatrum Orbis Terrarum, 1975), 64; Perkins, *Christian Oeconomie* (London: Felix Kyngston, 1609), 103–9, 128; Whately, *A Bride-Bush or Wedding Sermon* (London: 1617), 23, 42; William Gouge, *Of Domesticall Duties*, facsimile edition (1622, repr. Amsterdam: Theatrum Orbis Terrarum, 1976), 326–27. Although the treatises of Whately and Gouge were published several years after the accepted date of *Othello*'s composition, I submit that these texts are relevant as reflections of the ideological climate of the time.

question but whether it offend God, yea or no."[43] William Perkins, in an important treatise published in 1609 — thus roughly contemporaneous with *Othello* — went even further, denying that the husband may chastise his wife, insisting instead that the husband

> hath no power or liberty granted him in this regard ... He may reprove & admonish her in word only, if he seeth her at fault ... But he may not chastise her either with stripes, or strokes. The reason is plain; Wives are their husbands mates, and they two be one flesh. And no man will hate, much less beat his own flesh, but nourisheth and cherisheth it.[44]

Furthermore, although maintaining that the wife should obey the husband in all things not contrary to God's will, Perkins also insists that if the husband is an unbeliever and breaks God's law (striking, threatening, or forsaking the wife), the wife is justified in leaving him. Perkins even goes so far as to affirm that "if the husband threateneth hurt, the believing wife may flee this case."[45] In light of these contemporaneous debates on spousal violence, I suggest that even as *Othello* interrogates the racial tensions of the time, so it also foregrounds these conjugal controversies, critiquing marital violence and challenging the venerated concept of the uncompromising obedience of the wife to the husband.

The play develops this critique through several strategies. First, the scene in which Othello publicly strikes his wife graphically portrays Othello's brutality, Desdemona's defenselessness, and the abuse of power inherent in the doctrine of wifely subservience and unquestioned obedience. Moreover, the play accentuates this focus by the quadruple reiteration of the word "obedient," even as Desdemona's acceptance of the female role in marriage had earlier been established by the triple repetition of the word "duty." After Othello's violent attack upon Desdemona, Lodovico remonstrates, "Truly, an *obedient* lady. / I do beseech your lordship, call her back" (4.1.251–252). Othello complies, gloating:

> Ay, you did wish that I would make her turn.
> Sir, she can turn, and turn, and yet go on
> And turn again; and she can weep, sir, weep;

---

[43] Whately, *A Bride-Bush*, 18, 22–33, esp. 23.

[44] Perkins, *Christian Oeconomie*, 127: the biblical quotation is from Ephesians 5:29, which is quoted in the exhortation read at the communion service after matrimony in the *Book of Common Prayer*, 1559.

[45] Perkins, *Christian Oeconomie*, 107.

And she's *obedient*, as you say, *obedient*,
Very *obedient*. . . . (4.1.257-261; emphases mine)

Secondly, the play dramatizes the perils of unquestioning obedience, since the tragic catastrophe can be directly traced to the excessive compliance of two abused wives: Emilia's demeaning filching of the handkerchief to please her conniving spouse, and Desdemona's failure to defy, expose, or, at the very least, flee from her husband, even when she intuits his murderous intentions. In both cases, total submission leads to violence against women. Lastly, the play offers an alternative female point of view on marriage — the perspective of Emilia.

The play counterpoises two sets of marriages: one, a fresh, young nuptial, full of ardor and promise; the other, a weary, sterile alliance, stuck in the conjugal rut of dissatisfaction and routine abuse. In both cases, the husbands mistreat their wives, whereas the women respond with unflinching devotion to their mates, and, in both cases, the excessive subservience of the wives to their husbands contributes to the tragic catastrophe. However, both Emilia's perspective on marriage and her progression from servilely obedient wife to defiant spouse contrast with Desdemona's contrary perspective and trajectory. In the beginning of the play, Desdemona is unusually articulate and bold, whereas Emilia is very much the browbeaten wife; as Desdemona moves from eloquence to silence, Emilia becomes more and more outspoken. Ultimately, unlike Desdemona, Emilia breaks the cycle of spouse abuse and speaks for dignity and equality between husbands and wives, presenting women not as goddesses or temptresses or whores but as human beings. Emilia's passionate indictment of the gender double standard echoes "Venetian Shylock's plea for human recognition for another victimized group,"[46] reminding the audience, as Desdemona does not, that what is sauce for the goose is also sauce for the gander. Later Emilia defies her husband and delivers an unvarnished narration of events, invoking the doctrine of conscience even as she acknowledges her subordination: " 'Tis proper I obey him, but not now" (5.2.203). Ultimately, female bonding provides Emilia the courage to resist her bullying husband, and although her devotion leads to her death, she offers a standard of value in the play and a foil to Desdemona's submission.[47]

---

[46] Grennan, "The Women's Voices in *Othello*," 283.

[47] Neely argues that Emilia is dramatically and symbolically the fulcrum of the play ("Women and Men in *Othello*," 213). Other critics seeking to rehabilitate Emilia include Grennan ("Women's Voices," 281–85) and Greene ("Sexual and Social Tragedy in *Othello*," 29).

IV

I have argued throughout this essay that, on one level at least, this rich and complex play is centrally concerned with interrogating racial and gender clichés, commenting on the way that this conventional thinking fixes and limits human growth and poisons human relationships. However, there are differences in the interpellations of Desdemona and Othello. Whereas keeping women silent and in their place has always served the purposes of the patriarchy, inciting racial minorities to violence has not, and the programming of Othello to commit anti-social behavior contravenes the conscious goals of the Venetian society, which crucially needs the services of its token black general. Therefore, in conditioning Desdemona into wifely obedience, Iago can be seen as supporting the goals of the white, male hegemony, whereas in recruiting Othello into spousal violence, he appears to be subverting the best interests of his society. Nevertheless, despite these differences, there are still salient similarities in Iago's manipulations of Desdemona and of Othello. As the embodiment of society's male chauvinism and racial intolerance, Iago becomes the conduit through which society enforces its sexist and racist strictures against female filial disobedience and interracial marriage, without seeming to do so. Iago thus conscripts both Desdemona and Othello into subject positions antithetical to those that they occupied at the beginning of the play, and although the extreme positions into which they are both recruited would not have been explicitly endorsed by the patriarchal code of their society — Desdemona is more submissive than required, Othello more violent than authorized — both positions are ratified in sexist and racist discourses. Also, both compulsive operations offer Iago the scapegoats that he needs to reinforce his precarious feelings of white, male superiority even as he becomes the scapegoat for his own society, which punishes him for enforcing its sexist and racist prejudices. Finally, despite their differences, within the logic of the play both recruitments prove destructive and lead to violence against women.

In "The Patriarchal Bard," Kathleen McLuskie cautions feminist critics against dishonestly co-opting Shakespeare for feminist causes.[48] Recalling this prudent caveat, I realize that in this essay I may be accused of appropriating Shakespeare to a materialist feminist agenda. Certainly, the majority of Shakespeare's plays do not appear "feminist" in the contemporary meaning of the word and these plays frequently represent, and perhaps even celebrate, a type of "femininity" that twentieth-century feminists understandably disparage. Nevertheless,

---

[48] McLuskie, "The Patriarchal Bard," 88–108.

I contend that when viewed in the context of the early modern period, some of Shakespeare's plays, and particularly *Othello*, can be seen as actively subverting the dominant ideology of the age. I further insist that by focusing on the issues of race and gender and their intersection in the text, one can read in the play a radical interrogation of the very type of femininity that McLuskie appropriately deplores, as well as a questioning of the racial clichés of the early modern period. Using this approach, the critic may re-experience the radical subversiveness of the play, a subversiveness that had been effaced by almost four hundred years of patriarchal appropriation and has only begun to be rediscovered during the past decade.

Ultimately, therefore, I agree with Newman that by making the black Othello a hero and the initially transgressive Desdemona sympathetic, Shakespeare's play calls into question the hegemonic ideologies of race and gender in early modern England.[49] Moreover, I would develop Newman's argument to insist that by embodying society's white supremacist and male chauvinist ideologies within the character of the diabolical Iago, the play comments trenchantly on the pernicious effects of racism and sexism on the construction of difference within the early modern milieu. Sadly, even after almost four hundred years, this comment still has resonance for society today.

Sara Deats
University of South Florida

Works Cited

Adamson, W. D. "Unpinned or Undone? Desdemona's Critics and the Problem of Sexual Innocence." *Shakespeare Studies* 13 (1980): 169–86.

Adelman, Janet. "Iago's Alter Ego: Race as Projection in *Othello*." *Shakespeare Quarterly* 48 (1997): 125–44.

———. *Suffocating Mothers: Fantasies of Maternal Origin in Shakespeare's Plays, "Hamlet" to "The Tempest."* New York: Routledge, 1992.

Adler, Doris. "The Rhetoric of Black and White in *Othello*." *Shakespeare Quarterly* 25 (1974): 248–57.

---

[49] Newman, " 'And wash the Ethiop white,' " 93. Hawkins agrees with Newman that Shakespeare treats not only Othello and Desdemona, but all of his anti-tribal, interracial, co-starring lovers very sympathetically. In fact, she questions that any other author has written so excellent and sympathetic a part for a black actor as has Shakespeare ("Disrupting Tribal Difference," 115–26, esp. 115, 123–24).

Althusser, Louis. "Ideology and Ideological State Apparatuses." In idem, *Lenin and Philosophy and Other Essays*, trans. Ben Brewster, 129–73. London: New Left Books, 1971.

Aubrey, James R. "Race and the Spectacle of the Monstrous in *Othello*." CLIO, 22 (1993): 221–38.

Bartels, Emily C. "Making More of the Moor: Aaron, Othello, and Renaissance Refashionings of Race." *Shakespeare Quarterly* 41 (1990): 433–54.

———. "Strategies of Submission: Desdemona, the Duchess, and the Assertion of Desire." *Studies in English Literature* 36 (1996): 417–33.

Barthelemy, Anthony Gerard. *Black Face, Maligned Race: The Representation of Blacks in English Drama from Shakespeare to Southerne*. Baton Rouge: Louisiana State University Press, 1987.

Berry, Edward. "Othello's Alienation." *Studies in English Literature* 30 (1990): 315–33.

Bevington, David. Introduction to *Othello*. In *The Complete Works of Shakespeare*, ed. idem, 4th ed., 117–21. New York: HarperCollins, 1992.

Boebel, Dagny. "Challenging the Fable: The Power of Ideology in *Othello*." In *Ideological Approaches to Shakespeare: The Practice of Theory*, ed. Nicholas Ranson, 137–46. Lewiston, NY: Edwin Mellen Press, 1992.

Boose, Lynda. "Othello's 'Chrysolite' and the Song of Songs Tradition." *Philological Quarterly* 60 (1980): 427–37.

Bristol, Michael D. "Charivari and the Comedy of Abjection in *Othello*." In *True Rites and Maimed Rites: Ritual and Anti-Ritual in Shakespeare and His Age*, ed. Linda Woodbridge and Edward Berry, 73–97. Urbana: University of Illinois Press, 1992.

Calderwood, James. *The Properties of "Othello"*. Amherst: University of Massachusetts Press, 1989.

———. "Speech and Self in *Othello*." *Shakespeare Quarterly* 38 (1987): 293–303.

Callaghan, Dympna. *Women and Gender in Renaissance Tragedy: A Study of King Lear, "Othello," "The Duchess of Malfi," and "The White Devil"*. Atlantic Highlands: Humanities Press International, 1989.

Carr, Helen. "Woman/Indian: 'The American' and His Others." In *Europe and Its Others: Proceedings of the Essex Conference on the Sociology of Literature, July 1984*, ed. Francis Barker et al., 2 vols. 2:46–60. Colchester: University of Essex Press, 1985.

Cook, Ann Jennalie. "The Design of *Othello*: Doubt Raised and Resolved." *Shakespeare Studies* 13 (1980): 187–96.

D'Amico, Jack. *The Moor in English Renaissance Drama*. Tampa: University of South Florida Press, 1991.

Dash, Irene G. *Wooing, Wedding, and Power: Women in Shakespeare's Plays*. New York: Columbia University Press, 1981.

Deats, Sara Munson. "From Pedestal to Ditch: Violence Against Women in Shakespeare's *Othello*." In *The Aching Hearth: Family Violence in Life and Literature*, eds. eadem and Lagretta Tallent Lenker, 79–93. New York: Plenum Press, 1991.

Dreher, Diane Elizabeth. *Domination and Defiance: Fathers and Daughters in Shakespeare*. Lexington: University of Kentucky Press, 1986.

Fontenot, Chester J., and Frantz Fanon. *The Wretched of the Earth*. New York: Grove Press, 1963.

French, Marilyn. *Shakespeare's Division of Experience*. New York: Ballantine Books, 1981.

Garner, S. N. "Shakespeare's Desdemona." *Shakespeare Studies* 9 (1976): 233–52.

Gouge, William. *Of Domesticall Duties*. Facsimile of the 1622 edition. Amsterdam: Theatrum Orbis Terrarum, 1976.

Greene, Gayle. " 'This that you call love': Sexual and Social Tragedy in *Othello*." *Journal of Women's Studies in Literature* 1 (1979): 16–32.

Grennan, Eamon. "The Women's Voices in *Othello*: Speech, Song, Silence." *Shakespeare Quarterly* 38 (1987): 275–92.

Hall, Kim F. "Reading What Isn't There: 'Black' Studies in Early Modern England." *Stanford Humanities Review* 3 (1993): 23–33.

———. *Things of Darkness: Economies of Race and Gender in Early Modern England*. Ithaca: Cornell University Press, 1996.

Hanson, Elizabeth. *Discovering the Subject in Renaissance England*. Cambridge: Cambridge University Press, 1998.

Hawkins, Harriett. "Disrupting Tribal Difference: Critical and Artistic Responses to Shakespeare's Radical Romanticism." *Studies in the Literary Imagination* 26 (1993): 115–26.

Henderson, Katherine Usher, and Barbara F. McManus. *Half Humankind: Contexts and Texts of the Controversy About Women in England, 1540–1640*. Urbana: University of Illinois Press, 1985.

Hendricks, Margo. "Race: A Renaissance Category?" In *A Companion to English Renaissance Literature and Culture*, ed. Michael Hattaway, 690–98. Oxford: Blackwell, 2000.

Hic Mulier or the Man Woman. Fascimile of the 1620 edition. University of Exeter, 1973.

Howard, Jean E., and Marion F. O'Connor. *Shakespeare Reproduced: The Text in History and Ideology*. London: Methuen, 1987.

Hunter, G. K. "*Othello* and the Colour Prejudice." *Proceedings of the British Academy* 51 (1967): 139–63.

Jones, Eldred D. *Othello's Countrymen: The African in English Renaissance Drama.* Oxford: Oxford University Press, 1965.

Jordon, Winthrop D. *White Over Black: American Attitudes Toward the Negro, 1550–1812.* Chapel Hill: University of North Carolina Press, 1968.

Jorgensen, Paul A. *Shakespeare's Military World.* Berkeley: University of California Press, 1956.

Kay, Carol McGinnis. "Othello's Need for Mirrors." *Shakespeare Quarterly* 34 (1983): 261–70.

Knutson, Roslyn Lander. *The Repertory of Shakespeare's Company 1594–1613.* Fayetteville: University of Arkansas Press, 1991.

Loomba, Ania. *Gender, Race and Renaissance Drama.* New York: St. Martin's Press, 1989.

McKewin, Carole. "Counsels of Gall and Grace: Intimate Conversations Between Women in Shakespeare's Plays." In *The Woman's Part: Feminist Criticism of Shakespeare,* eds. Carol Ruth Swift Lenz, Gayle Greene, and Carol Thomas Neely, 117–32. Urbana: University of Illinois Press, 1980.

McLuskie, Kathleen. "The Patriarchal Bard: Feminist Criticism and Shakespeare: *King Lear* and *Measure for Measure*." In *Political Shakespeare: New Essays in Cultural Materialism,* eds. Jonathan Dollimore and Alan Sinfield, 88–108. Ithaca: Cornell University Press, 1985.

Milton, John. *Paradise Lost,* ed. Merritt Y. Hughes. New York: Odyssey, 1962.

Neely, Carol Thomas. "Women and Men in *Othello*: 'What should such a fool / do with so good a woman?'" In *The Woman's Part: Feminist Criticism of Shakespeare,* eds. Lenz, Green, and eadem, 211–39. Urbana: University of Illinois Press, 1980.

Neill, Michael. "Unproper Beds: Race, Adultery, and the Hideous in *Othello*." *Shakespeare Quarterly* 40 (1989): 383–412.

Newman, Karen. "'And wash the Ethiop white': Femininity and the Monstrous in *Othello*." *Fashioning Femininity in English Renaissance Drama,* ed. eadem, 71–93. Chicago: University of Chicago Press, 1991.

Park, Hyungji. "The Traffic in Desdemona: Race and Sexual Transgression in *Othello*." *The Journal of English Language and Literature* (Seoul) 41 (1995): 1061–82.

Parker, Patricia. "Fantasies of 'Race' and 'Gender': Africa, *Othello*, and Bringing to Light." In *Women, "Race" and Writing in the Early Modern Period,* eds. Margo Hendricks and eadem, 84–100. London: Routledge, 1994. 84–100.

Pechter, Edward. "'Have You Not Read Some Such Thing?': Sex and Sexual

Stories in *Othello*." *Shakespeare Survey* 49 (1996): 201–16.

Perkins, William. *Christian Oeconomie*. London: Felix Kyngston, 1609.

Rulon-Miller, Nina. "*Othello's* Bianca: Climbing Out of the Bed of Patriarchy." *Upstart Crow* 15 (1995): 99–114.

Singh, Jyotsna. "Othello's Identity, Postcolonial Theory, and Contemporary African Rewritings of *Othello*." In *Women, "Race," and Writing in the Early Modern Period*, eds. Hendricks and Parker, Smith, Henry. *A Preparative to Marriage: Of the Lord's Supper; Of Usurie*. London, 1591.

Snow, Edward A. "Sexual Anxiety and the Male Order of Things in *Othello*." *English Literary Renaissance* 10 (1980): 384–412.

Spencer, Theodore. *Shakespeare and the Nature of Man*. London: Macmillan, 1942.

Spivack, Bernard. *Shakespeare and the Allegory of Evil*. New York: Columbia University Press, 1958.

Strier, Richard. *Resistant Structure: Particularity, Radicalism, and Renaissance Texts*. Berkeley: University of California Press, 1995.

Vanita, Ruth. "'Proper' Men and 'Fallen' Women: The Unprotectedness of Wives in *Othello*." *Studies in English Literature* 43 (1994): 341–56.

Waller, Marguerite. "Academic Tootsie: The Denial of Difference and the Difference It Makes." *Diacritics* 17 (1987): 2–20.

Wayne, Valerie. "Historical Differences: Misogyny and *Othello*." In *The Matter of Difference: Materialist Feminist Criticism of Shakespeare*, ed. eadem, 153–180. Ithaca: Cornell University Press, 1991.

Whately, William. *A Bride-Bush or a Wedding Sermon*. London, 1617.

Woodbridge, Linda. *Women and the English Renaissance: Literature and the Nature of Womankind, 1540–1620*. Urbana: University of Illinois Press, 1986.

Woolf, Virginia. *A Room of One's Own*. 1929. Repr. New York: Harcourt Brace & Co., 1957.

"Too Much Violence":
Murdering Wives in *Othello*

These stage directions make one think rather of the murder of Nancy by Bill Sikes, than of Othello and Desdemona. Even now there is too much violence. Why should Desdemona spring out of bed, to be brutally thrust back into it? ... "Tradition" was right in confining Desdemona to her couch: Mr. Fechter is wrong in hazarding the ludicrous effects of the opposite course.

— Sir Theodore Martin
(quoted in Sprague, *Shakespeare and the Actors*, 214)

It is a truth universally acknowledged that, of all the acts of violence against women represented on the English Renaissance stage with such generous abundance and peculiar gusto, Othello's murder of Desdemona, followed quickly by Iago's murder of Emilia, is the most flagrant. Once we proceed beyond this proposition, however, universal agreement is out of the question, and even a rough consensus may be too much to expect. We cannot be sure what these enactments of violence did to or for their audiences, or what their audiences did with them, or why they continue to fascinate us four centuries later, or whether any substantial connection exists between Renaissance interests in such enactments and our own. In speculating about these matters, I take my lead from Sir Theodore Martin's reaction to Charles Fechter's mid-nineteenth-century prompt book. "Even now," Martin says, "there is too much violence." The introductory phrase serves as a reminder that the normative theatrical practice in Martin's time was to downplay, if not eliminate, Desdemona's resistance at the end; but more striking than its frame of reference, "even now" echoes the effectively originating act of violence in *Othello*, Iago's appalling image (and enactment) of an assault — not only on Brabantio's daughter but on Brabantio himself: "Even now, now, very now, an old black ram / Is tupping your white ewe."[1] The echo is presumably unintentional, but the comment as a whole pulsates with an emphatic anger which renders the issue of conscious control highly problematic. Martin was married to Helena Faucit, one of the premier Desdemonas of the nineteenth-century stage, so his overheated reaction may be taken to reflect a personal investment; but the stage and critical history of *Othello* indicates that the scene of Desdemona's and then Emilia's murder has deeply disturbed audiences across a range of personal and historical experience. From this angle, Martin's peculiar response is also a typical one. Reacting with too much violence to the problem of too much violence, he reproduces a kind of turmoil that extends back in a more or less unbroken line of reception to the earliest evidence we have for this play's effect, Henry Jackson's description of an Oxford audience in 1610, "moved ... to tears" by "the celebrated Desdemona" who, though dead, "entreated the pity of the spectators by her very countenance" (quoted in Evans, *The Riverside Shakespeare*, 1978). If in this respect Martin may be said to embody tradition, tradition is also the substance of his appeal, as the appropriate and even perhaps remedial response to the problem. " 'Tradition,' " he says, "was right." This claim, I want finally to argue, is precisely wrong. Tradition, the nightmare of history registered in the weight of previous theatrical and critical response to *Othello*, does not solve the problem of too much violence: it reproduces and thus perpetuates it.

§

In an essay on "The Women's Voices in *Othello*," Eamon Grennan calls the Willow Song scene (4.3) "one of the most dramatically compelling scenes in Shakespeare."

---

[1] 1.1.87–88. All *Othello* quotations are taken from Honigmann's Arden 3 edition and will henceforth be interpolated parenthetically. The idea that Iago's words assault Brabantio himself is reinforced by the pun on "ewe/you"; see Neill, "Changing Places," 122. There is a similar pun on "yew/you" in Webster's *White Devil* (1.2.239–241), a play saturated with *Othello* echoes. Christina Luckyj, the play's editor in 1996, refers to Webster's pun as "obvious" (21). Iago himself twice echoes his own violent phrase, first to describe the Turkish invasion (1.1.149), subsequently to describe the sudden and inexplicable rage of Cassio and Montano: "friends all, but now, even now, / In quarter and in terms like bride and groom" (2.3.175–176).

To account for the perfection of the sequence one could point to its intimacy, the quotidian familiarity of its action, its unhurried simplicity, its willingness to be ordinary. One might also refer to the atmosphere of private freedom within this protected feminine enclosure[, an] interlude suggesting peace and freedom, within the clamorous procession of violent acts and urgent voices. (277)

Grennan emphasizes the difference of the scene, its felt presence as an interlude closed off from the aggressive anxiety of the male-dominated action on either side. Kenneth Burke understood the scene in much the same way and recognized it as a characteristic performance within the affective economy of Shakespearean tragic practice in general: "*Act IV*: 'The Pity of It.'" Indeed, might we not, even as a rule, call this station of a Shakespearean tragedy the 'pity' act? There can be flashes of pity wherever opportunity offers, but might the fourth act be the one that seeks to say pity-pity-pity repeatedly?" ("*Othello*," 174). Burke gives many examples — Cordelia's reunion with Lear, Ophelia's death, Mariana at the grange — working out of similar material: a quiet lull in the action, women's voices and vulnerabilities, songs, pathos.

In distinguishing between women and men, or between the conventional tragic effects of pity and fear, both Grennan and Burke offer an understanding that seems inevitably to consign Emilia and Desdemona to a secondary or dependent status. Hence for Burke,

when Desdemona says to Othello, who has just struck her, "I have not deserved this," she almost literally repeats the Aristotelian formula for pity (that we pity those who suffer unjustly). ... Desdemona's "willow" song is particularly sad because, in her preparations for Othello's return ... there are strong forebodings (making her rather like a victim going willingly towards sacrifice). She seems doubly frail, in both her body and her perfect forgiveness — an impression that the audience will retain to the end, so that the drama attains maximum poignancy when Othello, hugely, throttles her. ... from this point of view ... the "pity act" might serve to "soften up" the audience so that they would be more thoroughly affected by the butchery still to come. ("*Othello*," 174, 178)

In this version, *Othello* functions as a purgative ritual (albeit a failed one, Burke seems to suggest) in the service of which Desdemona, though she performs an important role, is nonetheless relegated to a status decidedly subordinate to the more compelling energies embodied in the male protagonist's actions.

To a remarkable degree, current critical response continues to operate within a similar affective economy: the violence perpetrated on the female body, in *Othello* and elsewhere on the Renaissance stage, is understood as instrumental, serving personal or cultural needs that are defined in terms of male interests; it either redeems or reinforces the patriarchal order.[2] This continuity may reflect the depth of interpretive tradition. The subordination of female presence is strikingly evident throughout the play's long stage history. The Willow Song itself — "what most moves us … the brief, beautiful pause in the center of action" (Grennan, "The Women's Voices in *Othello*," 277) — is absent in the first Quarto. Perhaps it was added in revision or, more likely, cut when the company lost the boy's voice required to bring it off.[3] The scene as a whole has been consistently eliminated or reduced in performance. Helena Faucit lamented "how sad it is that the exigencies of our stage require the omission of the exquisite scene … so important for the development of [Desdemona's] character, and affording such fine opportunities for the highest powers of pathos in the actress!" (quoted in Carlisle, *Shakespeare from the Greenroom*, 182). Faucit was speaking about the "theatrical exigencies" of a later stage — chiefly (it may be assumed), the extensive script-cutting required to accommodate the elaborate and time-consuming scenic spectacles of nineteenth-century production. Since the scene was not needed for the plot, it must have been a prime candidate for elimination.

---

[2] For Leonard Tennenhouse, "it is ultimately Shakespeare himself who deprives Desdemona of her capacity to speak" or to "exercise patriarchal authority. These political features are returned to the male by way of Othello's vengeance, which operates, then, much as a theater of punishment," produced by "Shakespeare's collaboration with Iago" (*Power on Display*, 125–26). According to Mitchell Greenberg, "Patriarchal ideology, an ideology that finally the tragedy espouses," serves to drive the action in which Othello sacrifices Desdemona: "Venice, Venetian society, can no more tolerate this extravagant, sexual, uneconomical other than can Brabantio. In order to save itself, Venice (England) must rid itself of what it most fears in itself. But before it can afford to do away with its excessive barbarian, it uses him to destroy that other threat to Patriarchy, the willful independent female, whose act of sexual and political 'freethinking' shook the foundations of society" ("Shakespeare's *Othello* and the 'Problem' of Anxiety," 31). Susanne Collier focuses on the stabbed or nearly stabbed heroines of *Cymbeline* and *Philaster*, who are said to illustrate the "attempt to eradicate female powers, both physically and politically" ("Cutting to the Heart of the Matter," 42). For Sara Eaton (" 'Content with art'?: Seeing the Emblematic Woman in *The Second Maiden's Tragedy* and *The Winter's Tale*") the aestheticized bodies of the Lady (*Second Maiden's Tragedy*) and Hermione are framed as monuments in order to deprive them of their capacity to arouse sexual or epistemological anxiety. Celia Daileader's "(Off) Staging the Sacred" also focuses on the Lady and on Webster's Duchess, whose dead bodies, though, she sees as invested with religious feelings of miraculous sacrifice.

[3] See Honigmann's discussions (*Dramatist's Manipulation of Audience Response*, 346–48 and *The Texts of "Othello"*, 39–40).

But more is involved than the material demands of Victorian *mise-en-scène*. The scene was cut from the eighteenth-century stage as well, going back at least to Addison's time. Francis Gentleman, writing in the *Dramatic Censor* (1770), suggests the reasons. "If Desdemona was to chaunt the lamentable ditty, and speak all that Shakespeare has allotted for her in this scene, an audience ... would not know whether to laugh or cry, and Aemilia's quibbling dissertation on cuckold-making, is contemptible to the last degree" (quoted in Carlisle, *Shakespeare from the Greenroom*, 181). Gentleman takes us beyond strictly theatrical exigencies to more broadly cultural determinants. Like Ophelia's songs, which were similarly censured at the time, the Willow Song scene was felt to diminish the dignity of tragedy with domestic female babble, thereby disrupting or contaminating at once the norms of genre and gender. Too much womanly presence interferes with the appropriate effects (laughter instead of tears, pathos instead of fear, chronicles of small beer instead of the history-making of politics and war); it demands restriction ("guardage" [1.2.70]), if not elimination.

How do we explain this felt need? Writing about the exclusions from the First Folio to the Shakespeare canon over the centuries based on the changeable criteria of what "sounded right," Stephen Orgel remarks that the early "texts may, of course, be unauthentic, but they may also be evidence that Shakespeare had a greater range of styles than we care for" ("The Authentic Shakespeare," 3).[4] Diana Henderson expands on the point: "During the nineteenth century, the heyday of gendered ideology of separate public and private spheres, the generic tag *domestic tragedy* developed as a way of acknowledging these classically improper or 'impertinent' plays" ("The Theater and Domestic Culture," 174). Renaissance audiences seemed to think of genres less as fixed and rigorously distinct categories and more as a set of generative possibilities and may have thought of gender and sexual difference in a similarly fluid way (Laqueur, *Making Sex*).

---

[4] Elsewhere Orgel marshals evidence to conclude that Renaissance drama is not "generically pure ... Even the purest of Renaissance tragedies would have appeared *to an audience* to belong to a mixed genre because in performance it would have included *intermezzi* between the acts, or in England, jigs at the end. ... the genres constituted not an idea about the necessary structure of plays, but an idea about the potentialities of theaters to realize the classic forms. And what the models then offered ... was just the opposite of that rigid consistency we find in them: a very fluid set of possibilities" ("Shakespeare Imagines a Theater," 46; Orgel's emphasis). Orgel develops a similar claim in "Shakespeare and the Kinds of Drama." The *locus classicus* remains Johnson's *Preface to Shakespeare*, where it is offered with mixed feelings — at once the transcendence and transgression of generic norms.

When at the end of *Othello* Lodovico exhorts us, with Iago and the others on stage, to "look on the tragic loading of this bed" (5.2.361), he points to the bodies of Othello, Desdemona, and Emilia. That the women share space with the protagonist, not just as adjuncts but as presences who have earned their own place in the story, presumably did not jar on the sensibilities of the original spectators (hence Jackson's absorption in Desdemona at the end), as it did on the nineteenth-century interpreters, theatrical and critical, who labored diligently to erase them from the final picture (Pechter, "*Othello*", 147–50).

The restoration (and even highlighting) in our time of the Willow Song scene, and of a female presence generally in *Othello*, is an extraordinary accomplishment. Whether or not it constitutes a recovery of Shakespearean intentions, it does seem to have opened up more interesting literary and theatrical possibilities than the ones transmitted to us by the interpretive tradition. About Emilia, whom I shall turn to first, this seems to be specially true. But tradition is not always obedient to the reformative will. It is shaped often by irreversible and recalcitrantly material accidents — an adolescent boy actor's voice cracking in the ring, an author's or somebody else's second thoughts, changing theatrical technologies; and by others I will get to: the Victorian star system, for instance. And then there are still others that are unmentionable because, like Althusserian ideology, they cannot be externalized into perception. Some objects poison sight. Even the visible ones are not necessarily changeable as a consequence of critical understanding. The sheer immovable mass of inertia accounts for a lot in history, theatrical and critical and otherwise, and in *Othello*, where inertia is named Iago, the potentially emancipatory and clarifying efforts of innovation are brutally frustrated. From this perspective, we might be skeptical about the new forms of prominence given to the women in *Othello*: are they really so radically discontinuous with the old forms of erasure? Perhaps current attentiveness to the women's voices in the play is, even now, just a subtle way of silencing them yet again.

§

"Alas! she has no speech" (2.1.102), says Desdemona, dismissing Iago's nasty complaints about Emilia's noisiness. Desdemona seems right until the middle of the play. Emilia has no existence apart from her instrumentality to the plot. She passes the handkerchief to Iago, but does not know what she is doing: "what he will / Heaven knows, not I, / I nothing, but to please his fantasy" (3.3.301–303). We need a verb here. Whatever we supply — "do", "know," "am" — seems less consequential than the absence itself. Emilia fills a place in the plot, but the play does not encourage any deeper interest on our part.

In the context of these expectations, her sudden eruption into prominence is remarkable. It begins, perhaps, with her disgusted generalization about men:

'Tis not a year or two shows us a man.
They are all but stomachs, and we all but food:
They eat us hungerly, and when they are full
They belch us. (3.104–107)

The intensity comes out of nowhere, and the lines invite us to look toward a substantial personal history, more than "a year or two," from which it has been produced. (Toward it, but not into it. Presumably, we don't want to fabricate a detailed girlhood for Shakespeare's heroines, like Mary Cowden Clarke[5]; but the sense that it is there is important for the dramatic effect.) This impression of sensibility and intelligence, far exceeding mere plot function, emerges into full prominence by the Willow Song scene. The speech about the double standard is a major part of this, but so is the affectionate wit of her rejoinder to Desdemona's idealism: "I do not think there is any such woman." "Yes, a dozen, and as many to th'vantage as would stock the world they played for" (4.3.83–84). By the final scene, her persistent unwillingness to shut up, like Cleopatra's in the midst of Antony's efforts to achieve the heights of heroic demise, requires Othello to share space with her at the center of our concern. Bradley sensed this in 1904 and saw the pattern of emerging prominence:

> towards few do our feelings change so much within the course of a play. Till close to the end she frequently sets one's teeth on edge; and at the end one is ready to worship her. . . . From the moment of her appearance after the murder to the moment of her death she is transfigured; . . . who has not felt in the last scene how her glorious carelessness of her own life, and her outbursts against Othello . . . lift the overwhelming weight of calamity that oppresses us, and bring us an extraordinary lightening of the heart? (*Shakespearean Tragedy*, 196–98)

Bradley must have been reading his way out of the theatrical tradition; Victorian productions drastically cut her part (they probably recognized and wished to avoid the risk of an upstaged protagonist). But Bradley, though he could not have known it, was also reading his way into future performances through to our

---

[5] Mary Cowden Clarke, *The Girlhood of Shakespeare's Heroines: A Series of Fifteen Tales*. London: Bickers & Son, 1893. A New Edition, Condensed by her sister, Sabilla Novello. Original Edition: 3 vols., 1851–1852.

own time. On the twentieth-century stage, Emilia's enraged refusal to be silent
— "like a bellow from the mouth of Melpomene herself," in Herbert Farjeon's
description of Edith Evans; "I don't believe Mrs Siddons could touch her" —
can "come to dominate the play."[6]

Emilia's most impressive quality in the context of the dramatic action is a
pragmatic common sense. Responding to Desdemona's difficulty in imagining
infidelity, "Wouldst thou do such a deed for all the world?" Emilia insouciantly
points out that "The world's a huge thing: it is a great price / For a small vice.
. . . the wrong is but a wrong i'th'world" (4.3.67–69, 79). Sex is just sex, marital
fidelity is marital fidelity; they aren't the essence and totality of experience. This
is Iago's tone, "the wine she drinks is made of grapes" (2.1.249–250), but without cynicism or malice; the words take us out of the claustrophobic intensity of
the play's world into the larger space of the real world — or maybe just the different space of comedy. As Burke says, "Emilia here utters the basic heresy
against the assumptions on which this play is built" ("*Othello*," 185). Given the
intolerable experience of a beleaguered audience, such apostasy must seem like an
attractive possibility.

Burke's point, though, is that Emilia ultimately serves the purposes of the
tragic engagement she seems to undermine. Since "many average members of the
audience might be secretly inclined to resist" the "*excessive* engrossment" of high
tragedy, it might seem "unwise of the dramatist to let their resistance be expressed on the stage." The effect, however, at least according to Burke, is the reverse: "*her* voicing of our resistance" acts as a lightning rod; by absorbing and redirecting such feelings away from the action, Emilia therefore "protects, rather
than endangers, the tragic engrossment" ("*Othello*," 185; Burke's emphasis). This
shrewd and powerful analysis is particularly applicable to the finale, where Emilia's mockery of Othello's stupidity, by externalizing our own feelings, may seem
designed to write us into a more appreciative response to the Moor's greatness
of heart.[7] But there are no guarantees that performers and theatrical audiences

---

[6] Quoted in Hankey, *Othello*, 321, who gives three other instances of Emilia's domination in twentieth-century productions.

[7] Burke is in good company making this argument about Emilia's function, including
Bradley ("the only person who utters for us the violent common emotions which we feel,
together with those more tragic emotions which she does not comprehend" [*Shakespearean
Tragedy*, 197]); Empson ("the mouthpiece of all the feelings in us which are simply angry
with Othello, but this judgement of him is not meant to keep its prominence for long"
["Honest in *Othello*," 227]); Siemon ("a particularly telling displacement of energy from
the idealized feminine victim onto a domestic 'virago' double" [" 'Nay, that's not next,' "
45]); and McAlindon ("fearless and ferocious condemnation . . . calculated both to vent

will stay within the enclosure of (an assumed) original intent. If writing is an "essential drifting . . . cut off from all absolute responsibility, from *consciousness* as the authority of last analysis, orphaned, and separated at birth from the assistance of its father" (Derrida, *The Margins of Philosophy*, 316), how much more so is theatrical writing, especially centuries after the original productions? Emilia's power at the end can be made to serve the interests of a heroic protagonist, but may also assert her own interests, taking over the place made available by Othello's evacuation. (Hankey's twentieth-century examples focus on Emilia's adding vitality to otherwise dull productions.) Even in the original productions, Emilia may have earned her place in the story as more than a surrogate or foil; her transformation at the end of the play is potentially interesting in its own right.

It is, for all her roaring, a quiet change, taking place under the diversely inflected reiterations of "my husband" (138–150). The play is smart enough not to specify what is going through her mind; audiences can be counted on to endow Emilia with something like their own thoughts, reviewing her actions and their contribution to the catastrophe. Whatever she comes to realize, Emilia commits herself to resistance:

> Othello: Peace, you were best!
> Emilia: Thou hast not half the power to do me harm
> As I have to be hurt. O gull, O dolt,
> As ignorant as dirt! Thou hast done a deed
> [*He threatens her with his sword.*]
> — I care not for thy sword, I'll make thee known
> Though I lost twenty lives. (156–162)

This is thrilling, both as reckless bravado and also as a kind of heroic self-affirmation in the Stoic mode, claiming in the first lines of her speech that "she can endure more than he can inflict (*harm* = hurt)" (Honigmann, *Othello*, 318). But Emilia seems to be claiming a different power for herself, less grand and assertively masculine than self-sufficiency. Aside from the fact that Shakespeare

---

and to dispose of our feelings of moral outrage" [*Shakespeare's Tragic Cosmos*, 144]). The basic claim is a version of Empson's tremendous idea about *Hamlet*, imagined as Shakespeare's reflection: "He thought: 'The only way to shut this hole is to make it big. I shall make Hamlet walk up to the audience and tell them, again and again, "I don't know why I'm delaying any more than you do; the motivation of this play is just as blank to me as it is to you; but I can't help it." What is more, I shall make it impossible for them to blame him. And *then* they daren't laugh'" ("*Hamlet*," 84; Empson's emphasis).

(and other Renaissance writers) treat Stoic claims with skepticism,[8] "harm" does not quite equal "hurt." The difference is unelaborated but arresting; it points to an order of sensibility separate from Othello's murderous rage. To this rage she is totally vulnerable, and it would be self-deluding to assert otherwise. But if he can indeed harm her, he cannot hurt her, because the hurt derives from Desdemona's death. The power she claims then takes the form of the affectionate loyalty she feels for her mistress, which is hers quite independently of the consequences (almost inevitably lethal, to be sure) of expressing it.

This may be more than we, hearing her speech, can know at this point. It is certainly more than Emilia knows; she still hasn't figured out the narrative facts, let alone their meaning. But even before the handkerchief becomes an issue, she seems to intuit the truth:

> Villainy, villainy, villainy!
> I think upon't, I think I smell't, O villainy!
> I thought so then: I'll kill myself for grief!
> O villainy, villainy! (5.2.186–189)

Despite these exclamations, her next speech is suddenly quiet and reflective, as though the quality of her voice has caught up with the inaudible mental processes that have been propelling her forward: "Good gentlemen, let me have leave to speak. / 'Tis proper I obey him — but not now. / Perchance, Iago, I will ne'er go home" (192–194).

The thoughtfulness here is directly opposite to the thoughtlessness — indeed, mindlessness: "I nothing, but to please his fantasy" — at the beginning of her story. Absorbed then into the conventional narrative of wifely obedience, she now seeks to do something Othello himself (and Cassio) could not, find a position of her own outside the space defined by Iago's malignant norms — in her case, literally outside Iago's home. Even now she accepts the conventional story as "proper"; she understands her greater loyalty to Desdemona and to the truth as transcending but not undermining the law. Her deference, requesting the "gentlemen" to let her speak, echoes Desdemona at the beginning, submitting to the Senate's authority. The extraordinarily intimate direct address, "Perchance, Iago, I shall ne'er go home," managed only once earlier in the play (4.2.117),

---

[8] Brutus is the substantial instance in Shakespeare. Honigmann (*Othello*, 318) cites a very close analogue to Emilia's speech from *Henry VIII*, 3.2.387 ff, but the speaker is Wolsey. "To suffer, as to do, / Our strength is equal" (*Paradise Lost*, 2.199–200) is another good analogue which, according to Merritt Hughes's note, echoes Mucius Scaevola thrusting his hand into the fire, but the speaker is Belial.

makes it clear that she is still inside his home. (The effect is like Othello's heart-breaking "uncle" to Gratiano four lines later and at 252: at last he is part of the family [Honigmann, *Shakespeare: Seven Tragedies*, 94].) Emilia is not sure what she is doing or where she is going; she makes it up as she goes along, feeling her way into a new selfhood, or into selfhood at last. Modern audiences will proba-bly see her on the path to Nora's exciting exit from Torvold's home at the end of *A Doll's House*. People sometimes wonder where Nora is going, and it is even less clear where Emilia can go, given the limited possibilities for women in the Renaissance. Before we can begin to consider such possibilities, she is abruptly despatched — as by Frank Finlay, Olivier's Iago, with "a brisk and business-like stab in the back" (Tynan, *"Othello": The National Theatre Production*, 19).

§

Desdemona's is another voyage. Unlike Emilia, Desdemona begins with a pow-erful voice, trumpeting her love for Othello to the world with a self-declared "downright violence" (1.3.250), too much violence for some tastes; but she seems to dwindle away during the course of the play, and "Nobody. I myself" (5.2.122) in her final speech seems to constitute an act of self-erasure, an accession to nul-lity. This quality — or absence of qualities — made her of little interest to eighteenth-century interpreters: "a part of 'unvarying gentleness'" with "'no shining qualifications,'" according to Gentleman, Desdemona "is sufficiently characterized by terms like 'fond' and 'simple'" (Carlisle, *Shakespeare from the Greenroom*, 240, 241). Coleridge's sustained reflection on Desdemona's character-lessness said much the same thing but made a virtue of defect. For him, reces-siveness was precisely the source of her power as a profoundly moving object of desire.

> "Most women have no character at all", said Pope, and meant it for satire. Shakespeare, who knew man and woman much better, saw that it, in fact, was the perfection of woman to be characterless. Everyone wishes a Desdemona or Ophelia for a wife — creatures who, though they may not always understand you, do always feel you, and feel with you. (Foakes, *Coleridge's Criticism of Shakespeare*, 185)

Coleridge's description established the terms for nineteenth-century response. Hazlitt, who brought a different set of critical and political concerns to Shake-speare, nonetheless says of Desdemona that "her whole character consists in hav-ing no will of her own, no prompter but her obedience" (*Characters of Shake-spear's Plays*, 205). Anna Jameson acknowledges a "transient energy, arising from the power of affection" but insists that the "prevailing tone to the character" is "gentleness verging on passiveness — gentleness, which not only cannot resent — but cannot resist" (*Shakespeare's Heroines*, 175). Bradley at the end of this line recognized that Desdemona changes during the course of the action, beginning with "the active assertion of her own soul and will" and "showing a strange freedom and energy, and leading to a most unusual boldness of action" (*Shakespearean Tragedy*, 165–66). But like Coleridge and Hazlitt, Bradley understood the later absence of will as Desdemona's essential quality ("Desdemona is helplessly passive. She can do nothing whatever. She cannot retaliate even in speech; no, not even in silent feeling" [145]), and it was this condition which inspired his own deeply affectionate response: "the 'eternal womanly' in its most lovely and adorable form, simple and innocent as a child" (164) and full of "heavenly sweetness and self-surrender" (165).

Such dissent as there was in the nineteenth century came mostly from the theater. The Booth edition (1881) records Ellen Terry's remark that although "my appearance was right" for Desdemona (that is, "a poor wraith of a thing"), "it took strength to act this weakness and passiveness of Desdemona's. I soon found that like Cordelia, she has plenty of character" (quoted in Siemon, " 'Nay, that's not next,' " 44). Later on, Terry complained that "no character in Shakespeare . . . has suffered from so much misconception," as "a ninny, a pathetic figure"; in fact, Desdemona "is strong, not weak" (Terry, *Four Lectures on Shakespeare*, 128–29). Helena Faucit in 1885 reflected similarly on Desdemona's appeal for her as a young woman growing up early in the century: "I did not know in those days that Desdemona is usually considered a merely amiable, simple, yielding creature, and that she is generally so represented on the stage. This is the last idea that would have entered my mind" (*On Some of Shakespeare's Female Characters*, 246). Both Faucit and Terry could build on a performance tradition dating back to the late eighteenth century (Hankey, *Othello*, 52–53), when "the awesome, majestic" Sarah Siddons "surprised" and "amazed" audiences "at the transition from her erstwhile tragic majesty to sweet tenderness. The part even seemed to change her physically, 'absolutely [lowering] the figure of the lovely being which had been so towering in Euphrasia, or terrific in Lady Macbeth' " (Rosenberg, *The Masks of Othello*, 51). But Siddons's performance did not establish either a norm or an ideal for the part on the nineteenth-century stage. For Elizabeth Inchbald, writing at the beginning of the century, " 'her face can never express artless innocence, such as the true representative of the part requires: her features are too bold, her person too important for the gentle Desdemona.' " As Carlisle wryly comments, "too much tragic majesty remained" (*Shakespeare from the Greenroom*, 241). At the beginning of the next century (1911), William Winter made much the same complaint, describing Siddons's performance as "greatly overweighting a part the predominant and essential characteristic of which is gentleness" (*Shakespeare on the Stage*, 250). Unlike Inchbald, who could well have seen Siddons's performance, Winter was working only with hearsay; but his very willingness to trust report testifies to the established stability of the nineteenth-century consensus.

One way to measure the power of this consensus is to focus on the question of Desdemona's resistance in the murder scene. Othello's "Down, strumpet!" and "Nay, if you strive — " (5.2.78, 80) are textually embedded stage directions that call unambiguously for Desdemona's physical struggle. George Swan understood as much in his advice to Garrick: "he was convinced [that] Desdemona should so effectually resist Othello's efforts to smother her that he would be forced to use the dagger after all. Swan interpreted the text to imply that Desdemona twice struggles from Othello's grasp." But Swan's advice was hypothetical, probably not deriving from theatrical practice and almost certainly not leading to it.[9] In a similar way, a strongly resistant Desdemona on the nineteenth-century stage remained only an un- or under-represented possibility. Though his acting edition called for fierce struggle, "Fechter's performances apparently did not enact" them fully if at all (Siemon, "'Nay, that's not next,'" 43), for reasons already suggested by Martin's evocation of Nancy and Bill Sikes.

Or consider the case of Fanny Kemble. Playing the role for the first time in 1848, she determined to "'make a desperate fight of it ... for I feel horribly at the idea of being murdered in my bed. The Desdemonas that I have seen, on the English stage, have always appeared to me to acquiesce with wonderful equanimity in their assassination. On the Italian stage they run for their lives.'" But she was thwarted on the one hand by an apparently edited script ("'Shakespeare's text,'" she worried, "'gives no hint of any such attempt ...'") and on the other by the material realities of costume and taste: "against that possibility was the 'bedgown' she was wearing" (Sprague, *Shakespeare and the Actors*, 213; Carlisle,

---

[9] Swan played Othello at the Theatre Royal, Dublin, in 1742, but it "is not clear whether his notes reflect the business that he himself had used or whether they were the result of his ruminations after his retirement from the stage." In either event, "The typical stage Desdemona in the eighteenth century probably did not put up the vigorous struggle Swan imagined for her. Nor did she in the nineteenth century." Perhaps George Skillan's advice much later in the French's Acting Edition, that anyone of Desdemona's "'quality and strong spirit' naturally reacts with abhorrence to the sudden threat of violent death and fights for self-preservation," was also probably relegated to the realm of unrealized potential. For this material, see Carlisle, *Shakespeare from the Greenroom*, 258–61.

Shakespeare from the Greenroom, 259). When Kemble revisits the question in 1884, she thinks differently. She

> berates Salvini for failure to follow the stage tradition and the manifest "intention of Shakespeare" ... for a passive Desdemona ... : "The terrified woman cowers down upon her pillow like a poor frightened child. Indeed, the whole scene loses its most pitiful elements by allowing Desdemona to confront Othello standing, instead of uttering the piteous pleadings for mercy in the helpless prostration of her half recumbent position. (quoted in Siemon, " 'Nay, that's not next,' " 43)

Kemble's change of mind probably had something to do with the weight of contemporary opinion against making a fight of it. Siemon quotes an "outraged response" in mid-century "to Brooke's Desdemona [Sarah Anderton] having 'struggled in almost an erect position' as 'out of character' " (43). It probably had something to do as well with the sheer power of the normative tradition — the "unalloyed delight," as Charlotte Vandenhoff's 1851 performance was described, "to see her sad, fearful, yet gentle as a bruised dove bend meekly to the implacable jealousy of the swart Othello, and receive her death, while kissing the hand which gives it" (quoted in Carlisle, *Shakespeare from the Greenroom*, 244). Sustained exposure to this sort of thing must have been very difficult to resist.

   This is not to say that resistant Desdemonas did not appear: Gustavus Brooke's and Salvini's (as well as the other Italians'), as we have seen; Madge Kendal opposite Ira Aldridge; Faucit and Terry as well. But these possibilities too were under-represented. Faucit "fell as a victim to the star system," which required that a leading actor, "whether woman or man, had to shine as the dominant light in a play, not merely contribute to the effect of chiaroscuro." As a consequence, "she rarely acted the role during her touring days, the longer and much the finer part of her career." As for Terry, though "she gave a memorable interpretation, spirited as well as pathetic," her "theatrical fortunes were bound up with" Irving, and when he abandoned Othello after 1881, Terry's "Desdemona was lost to the stage from that time. [Hence] the two actresses who should have been most identified with the role actually performed it for relatively brief periods" (Carlisle, *Shakespeare from the Greenroom*, 249–50). Like the dramatic character, the role itself on the pre-twentieth-century stage is saturated with the pathos of defeated potentiality.

   Maggie Smith, who performed opposite Olivier in the premier production of our time, suggests how far we have come from the nineteenth-century theatrical tradition. Smith of course is not "a poor wraith of a thing," like Ellen Terry; her body type did not predispose her to representing a bruised dove, and she played Desdemona out of her own strength.

The milksop Desdemona has been banished from this stage and a girl of real personality and substance comes into her own. Fighting back, not soppily "hurt", but damned angry, she makes the conjugal battle less one-sided and so more interesting and certainly more exciting. When these two throw the book at each other bodies come hurtling after it; and what a relief it is not to see two high-bred ninnies bleating reproachfully at each other from opposite sides of the stage but actually striking each other to the floor in the grandeur of their agony. (Tynan, *"Othello": The National Theatre Production*, 16)

But in modern criticism, as distinct from theatrical interpretation, the image of Desdemona's self-surrendering sweetness has managed to sustain itself, though at an increasing distance from the veneration of earlier response. Burke's willing victim, "doubly frail, in both her body and her perfect forgiveness," can sound surprisingly soppy, like residual angel-in-the-house sentiment. Burke's locus, to be sure, is ritual enactments rather than gender norms or marital relations. Whether or not every man wants a woman like Desdemona, as Coleridge claimed, every sacrificial plot does, and "the willow song casts her perfectly in the role of one preparing meekly for sacrifice" (Burke, *"Othello,"* 184).

This relocation of affect portends a more radical change in recent criticism: a withdrawal or even reversal of affect. Jane Adamson is struck by "Desdemona's strange passivity in the face of the violence that assails her" (*"Othello" as Tragedy*, 236). Where nineteenth-century audiences delighted in Desdemona's prostrate speechlessness, for Adamson "her peculiar passivity" is "most disturbing" (220): "what we find hardest to bear" in the murder scene is Desdemona's "terrible silence ... She has no strength or will to resist it or even to cry out for help" (257). More recent criticism, motivated by an augmented methodological and ideological self-consciousness, has nonetheless experienced a similar discomfort.[10] Ania Loomba recalls that "as undergraduates at Miranda House, Delhi ... who were 'dissatisfied' with Desdemona's silence in the face of her husband's brutality, we were told that we did not 'understand' her because we had never been 'in love.'" Loomba acknowledges Desdemona's self-assertiveness early in

---

[10] Adamson herself, working in an attenuated Leavis tradition, claimed no systematic grounding for her response, though such claims were being made, particularly in America, by critics subsequently designated "first-wave feminists." According to W. D. Adamson, writing the same year *"Othello" as Tragedy* was published (and perhaps exaggerating), "many of today's younger critics find it hard to write 'innocence' without writing 'life-denying' in front of it. [They] often see [Desdemona's] innocence as a neurotic defense mechanism, or even at one extreme a 'life-destroying' characteristic, the epitome of 'the sexual unreality the race longs for'" ("Unpinned or Undone?", 179).

the play, but laments that "she then betrays it by her submissiveness. Discussions with my own students located such a betrayal as the source of our own uneasiness" (*Gender, Race, Renaissance Drama*, 39).

Whether celebrating or deploring it, the critical tradition has been remarkably consistent for two centuries in describing Desdemona as silent, submissive and in a sense even complicit in her own murder. It is therefore worth noticing on what an unsubstantial foundation this massive interpretive edifice has been constructed. Despite Adamson's "terrible silence" and Loomba's "silence in the face of her husband's brutality," Desdemona vigorously protests her innocence in the murder scene (5.2.58–61, 66–68) and, finally desperate, looks for any expedient to protect herself against Othello's murderous assault: "O, banish me, my lord, but kill me not! . . . Kill me tomorrow, let me live tonight! . . . But half an hour! . . . But while I say one prayer! . . . O Lord! Lord! Lord!" (77–83). This is not merely speech; it seems to be the powerfully sustained eloquence Henry Jackson heard in 1610 ("she pleaded her case very effectively throughout," *optimè semper causam egit*). As Anthony Dawson argues, "Jackson's account . . . puts into question the reading of the victimized, subjected Desdemona that some recent critics have seen as central to the cultural work the play is said to have performed" ("Performance and Participation," 35). To be sure, these lines can be delivered in the manner Kemble recommended, as "piteous pleadings for mercy" (Shakespeare's dramatic writing is infinitely appropriable); but the embedded stage directions, "Down strumpet!" and "Nay, if you strive — " are a different matter. The words nineteenth-century script-doctors cut away, strong twentieth-century interpreters seem to have erased.

Such extraordinary reconstructions of the murder scene cannot have been created out of nothing; but if we look backward over the action of the play it is hard to find the evidence of acquiescent self-surrender on which they would be based. Perhaps the earliest relevant episode shows Desdemona, just before the Temptation Scene, acceding to Othello's request to cease soliciting for Cassio and "to leave me but a little to myself": "Shall I deny you? No, farewell, my lord" (3.3.85–86). But this is hardly a defeated submission. Othello has apparently already informed Desdemona that he intends to reinstate Cassio (3.1.45 ff), and he promises as much here again: "I will deny thee nothing" (84). Moreover, Desdemona's exit speech, "Be as your fancies teach you? / Whate'er you be, I am obedient" (88–89), makes obedience sound like self-affirmation, almost bravado. If we hear an echo of Emilia's "I nothing, but to please his fantasy," this probably registers as contrast. Unlike Emilia, Desdemona manifests a distinct and even freely critical identity, implying perhaps that Othello is caught up in silly obligations of military protocol ("your fancies"), while she at least is holding up her end of the bargain. Indeed, commentators are sometimes irritated by her needling here, although Othello's "Excellent wretch!" just after confirms the context of affectionate delight within which he has understood the exchange.

With the first signs of Othello's madness, Desdemona maintains this tone, meeting his insistence head on with her own ("The handkerchief." "I pray, talk you of Cassio" [3.4.94]) and resistance ("I'faith, you are to blame" [98]). Her first instinctive reaction to the slap is a protest, "I have not deserved this" (4.1.240). After the appalling "rose-lipped cherubin" speech, when Othello accuses her of being a "strumpet," she is again angrily assertive in denying the charge: "By heaven, you do me wrong" (4.2.83). This is not "peculiar" or "strange passivity in the face of violence" — it is not passivity at all; and in the context of the Renaissance theatrical practice, audiences of *Othello* would have much more likely been impressed by Desdemona's self-assertion than by her passivity.[11] Even at the end of the bordello scene, although she is by now almost fully traumatized ("Do not talk to me, Emilia; / I cannot speak, nor answers have I none / But what should go by water" [104–106]), Desdemona nonetheless generates an impressively sarcastic anger: "'Tis meet I should be used so, very meet. / How have I behaved that he might stick / The small'st opinion on my greatest misuse?" (109–111). These lines are delivered on an empty stage, Desdemona's only soliloquy; the play seems to be going out of its way to emphasize resistance in the face of inexplicable hostility — which is just what Henry Jackson heard.

That this resistance seems to diminish in the course of the dramatic action is certainly true, but the question is what we make of its diminution. About her request to Emilia, "Lay on my bed my wedding sheets . . . And call my husband hither" (4.2.107–108), Neill says that "Desdemona shrouds herself here in a narrative of eroticized self-immolation as self-consciously as Othello in his final speech will dress himself in the narrative of heroic self conquest," pointing to "the fashion, increasingly popular amongst aristocratic women in the early seventeenth century, for having one's corpse wound in the sheets from the marriage night" (*Issues of Death*, 165). But Desdemona is not acting with coherently self-

---

[11] The Renaissance stage at this time was rich in examples of the performance of passivity, faithful wives who were astoundingly acquiescent to bizarre husbandly assaults on the model of the protagonist of *Patient Grissil*, a joint venture by Dekker, Haughton, and Chettle produced in 1600, which was evidently quite popular and generated a series of spinoffs and imitations. The passivity of Annabel in *The Fair Maid of Bristow* and of Luce in *The London Prodigal*, both in the King's Men's repertoire at the same time as *Othello*, is especially worth noting (see Pechter, *Patient Grissil*; Knutson, *The Repertory of Shakespeare's Company*, 115–18; and Woodbridge's discussions of the "Patient Grissill figure" in *Women and the English Renaissance*, 125–26, 198–99, 211–17, and 358).

conscious purposivity, and in its immediate context her request seems to be a
hopeful gesture, designed to "win my lord again" (4.2.151), presumably by reminding him of what she remembers about the shared delight in their original
union.

By the Willow Song scene, she has abandoned protest (at least temporarily)
for acquiescence. "We must not now displease him," she tells Emilia (4.3.15), acceding to Othello's request for Emilia's dismissal. We know that the accession
has the effect of facilitating the murder, but what is her intention? One place to
look for an answer is in the long and tortuous speech, addressed to Emilia or
herself or both, with which Desdemona first reflects on the meaning of Othello's
transformation:

> Something sure of state
> Either from Venice, or some unhatched practice
> Made demonstrable here in Cyprus to him,
> Hath puddled his clear spirit, and in such cases
> Men's natures wrangle with inferior things
> Though great ones are their object. 'Tis even so,
> For let our finger ache and it indues
> Our other healthful members even to that sense
> Of pain. Nay, we must think men are not gods
> Nor of them look for such observancy
> As fits the bridal. (3.4.141–151)

Desdemona begins with an attempt to account for Othello's inexplicable harsh-
ness as a displacement of political irritation ("something sure of state"). In effect,
she buys into a distinction between the male public sphere and the female domestic sphere ("inferior things"), thereby abandoning her earlier desire to share
the totality of Othello's life. This distinction between male and female nature is
almost immediately negotiated with a sense of shared bodily existence: "our finger" is not a peculiarly female possession. But then bodily existence seems to
have become gendered female, as in the next lines "we" is clearly limited to
women in contrast to the men as "them." In acknowledging the inevitable abate-
ment of love from "the bridal," Desdemona picks up on Emilia's speech just a
minute or two earlier, "'Tis not a year or two ... / They belch us." She lacks
Emilia's disgusted abhorrence, but moves in that direction — which is to say, toward the origin of such beliefs in Iago's voice. As Othello himself had suc-
cumbed to a generalizing misogyny, "that we can call such delicate creatures
ours," so Desdemona begins apparently to settle into a generalizing misandry, us
and them. She echoes his acquiescence in necessity ("'Tis destiny unshunnable,"

"Nay, we must think"), both of them echoing Iago at the very beginning ("Why there's no remedy. 'Tis the curse of service"). Who can blame her? She has more of a cause, and after all, the wine she drinks *is* made of grapes. Maybe Auden was right to think Iago was right: "given a few more years ... and she might well, one feels, have taken a lover" (269).

This entire process is abruptly reversed, however, in the extremely awkward and complicated set of reconsiderations at the end of Desdemona's speech:

> Beshrew me much, Emilia,
> I was, unhandsome warrior as I am,
> Arraigning his unkindness with my soul,
> But now I find I had suborned the witness
> And he's indicted falsely. (151–155)

Turning on the earlier self who was arraigning Othello's unkindness, she tries to recapture the feelings of their reunion on the beach when Othello had addressed her as "my fair warrior." Her status as an "unhandsome warrior," though, seems still to occupy the present ("as I am"), and it is difficult to sort out the putatively real Desdemona at the end of the speech from a variety of superseded voices earlier on. Can "my soul" be totally recreated into a new "I" that now suborns its own earlier position? The attempt at a wilful self-reconstruction may be qualified by a passive resonance in "find"; from this position, the different beliefs at the end of the passage are not so much affirmed as observed in a way that renders them problematically abstract, maybe even dissociated.

It is possible to understand this speech as "a nervous *refusal* to acknowledge — even to herself — that Othello could possibly be jealous or suspicious" (Adamson, *"Othello" as Tragedy*, 225; Adamson's emphasis). Desdemona is then pathologically self-deluding, deliberately disconnecting herself from the truth of her situation in a way that abandons self-protection. If "Nobody. I myself" constitutes self-cancellation, then this speech seems to be the place from which she embarks on the course that reaches that termination. But is Desdemona refusing the truth of what Othello has become or affirming the reality of what he was when she saw his visage in his mind, and further affirming the value of her continuing response? "Unkindness may do much, / And his unkindness may defeat my life / But never taint my love" (4.2.161–163). Like Emilia at the end, Desdemona asserts her own power here. Othello's unkindness may defeat her life, but it is her choice to love him. Julia Genster is one of several recent commentators who hear in Desdemona's "last words," asking to be commended to her kind lord, "not an act of submission but a challenge" ("Lieutenancy, Standing In, and

Othello," 804–5).[12] From this perspective Othello was right (though he had the wrong word for it) to say "That we can call these delicate creatures ours / And not their appetites" — sensing in Desdemona a powerful energy that he would never fully own, that was Desdemona's own self.

In the beginning of the Willow Song scene, responding to Emilia's "Would you had never seen him!" Desdemona once again reaffirms her choice: "So would not I; my love doth so approve him / That even his stubbornness, his checks, his frowns / — Prithee unpin me — have grace and favour" (16–20). In the way "my love" is represented as acting independently of and in contradiction to the self-preserving "I," Desdemona strikes a note of passivity and self-exposure that may seem to verge on masochism. But the song that follows, for all its plaintive pathos, moves into a stronger and more assertive tonality. According to Joel Fineman,

> The central, we can say the most Shakespearean, fact about this 'Willow song' is that it is *not* by Shakespeare, and would have been recognized as such, i. e., as non-Shakespearean, by the original audience of the play. What is called Desdemona's 'Willow song' is, in fact, a traditional ballad, reproduced in miscellanies, that appear to have captured Shakespeare's aural imagination. ("The Sound," 94; Fineman's emphasis)

But the even more important fact is that ballads in the play are part of the anonymous tradition by which Iago acquires power over people's souls, as in his transformation of Cassio at the end of Act Two. If he performs his cultural work "close to the unstable ground of consciousness itself" (Neill, "Unproper Beds," 395), this is precisely the place from which Desdemona's discourse is generated in the scene. Like Brabantio at the beginning ("Have you not read ... / Of some such thing?"), she is traumatized to the point where anything comes out of her mouth that has found a place in her mind ("Mine eyes do itch, / Doth that bode weeping? ... I have heard it said so" [57–59]), including especially the song: "That song tonight / Will not go from my mind" (28–29).

---

[12] According to Wine, " 'My kind lord' is the Othello whose 'visage' she saw 'in his mind'; her 'Nobody' could be only the 'false', stereotypical Moor as Othello is now. The effect of these words is to remind Othello of what he knew when he addressed the Senate" (*"Othello": Text and Performance*, 34). Calderwood pursues a similar line: "She announces in effect that her acceptance of his authority has derived not from his institutional status as her husband, not from his masculine capacity to do her harm, but from consent freely given, from nothing more forceful than the 'downright violence' of her own love as she declared it before the Senate" (*The Properties of "Othello"*, 36).

In this context, the remarkable thing is that the song does not take possession of Desdemona's soul; she takes possession of it. She substitutes a female singer, and her affection for "Barbary" is clearly a displacement of her affection for Othello. The play goes out of its way to emphasize her transformative power by calling attention to her mistake: "Let nobody blame him, his scorn I approve — / [*Speaks.*] Nay, that's not next" (51–52). The words pick up on her own claim at the beginning of the scene, "My love doth so approve him," now establishing "I" and "my love," problematically disconnected earlier, as an absolute identity. Revising herself, she also revises tradition. The "right" line in the versions that survive is "her scorns I do prove."[13] The original audiences would not have focused on the details but might well have sensed the fundamental difference between the tradition, which emphasized the passive suffering of unrequited love, and Desdemona's version, which proclaims even in the midst of such grief a continuing affirmation of her own power to love. "O, you are well tuned now: but I'll set down / The pegs that make this music, as honest / As I am" (2.1.198–200). Honest Iago keeps his promise for everyone in the play, with the partial exception of Emilia. But Desdemona sings her own song.

When Alan Sinfield declares that "Desdemona has no character of her own" (*Faultlines*, 54), his uncanny echo of Coleridge's claim that "Desdemona has no character at all" is striking evidence for the continuity over the centuries with which we have been replacing Desdemona's voice with silence and transforming her presence into absence. The nineteenth century doted on its own created emptiness, and now we deplore it; but the tenacity with which the basic structure has sustained itself is remarkable — and perplexing. The adorably prostrate Desdemona served the nineteenth century in ways that look either silly to us now (Lillian Gish tied to the railroad tracks) or pornographic. The objectionably prostrate Desdemona of contemporary opinion must also be serving important cultural needs, but it is difficult to be sure what they are. Robert Brustein once said that "the passive, virtuous, all-suffering Desdemona is a part ... difficult to cast in an age of women's liberation" (quoted in Wine, "*Othello*": *Text and Performance*, 67); but current criticism has generally cooperated in maintaining the construction of Desdemona as instrumental and subordinate to male designs larger than any that might be claimed for her own. There is some substantial

---

[13] Honigmann (*Othello*, 340) reproduces from Furness (*A New Variorum Edition of Othello*, 277) the version derived from Percy's *Reliques* (1765), cautioning that we "should not assume, however, that Percy's version gives the ballad verbatim as Shakespeare found it" (339).

basis for this construction. It seems accurate to say that "Desdemona only invokes the right to owe duty to her husband and not her own autonomy"; even
the strongest theatrical Desdemonas have represented the character as fundamen-
tally unwilling and almost unable to imagine selfhood in terms of an exclusively
self-enclosed or self-contained space.[14] But to conclude from this that Desdemona therefore does not serve the interests of "our critique of the silencing of
women in literature and in the classroom" (Loomba, *Gender, Race, Renaissance
Drama*, 40) moves into much more speculative territory. It assumes — unneces-
sarily if not wrongly — that Desdemona's affectionate generosity necessarily constitutes an acquiescence in her own victimization, and perhaps even contributes
to the continuing disempowerment of at least some members of the audience.

Henry Jackson's response — not only moved to tears by the pathos of Desdemona's situation, but impressed with the power of her performed selfhood — is
an intriguing exception to subsequent interpretation. There is no reason to be-

---

[14] Compare Maggie Smith's reaction to the slap: it "is not the usual collapse into
sobs; it is one of deep shame and embarrassment, for Othello's sake as well as her own.
She is outraged, but tries out of loyalty not to show it. . . . 'I have not deserved this' is
not an appeal for sympathy, but a protest quietly and firmly lodged by an extremely
spunky girl" (Tynan, "*Othello: The National Theatre Production*, 10). The sentiment described here is similar to Faucit's, explaining why Desdemona struggles against the murderous Othello: " 'I felt for *him* as well as myself, and therefore I threw into my remon-
strances all the power of passionate appeal I could command. . . . I thought of all his
after-suffering, when he should come to know how he had mistaken me! The agony for
him which filled my heart, as well as the mortal agony of death which I felt in imagination, made my cries and struggles no doubt very vehement and very real' " (quoted in
Carlisle, *Shakespeare from the Greenroom*, 260).

In both these passages, Desdemona's feeling for herself is represented as inextricably
bound up with her feeling for Othello. It may be, though, that the performance is being
thought through as much in terms of theatrical dynamics as character. Faucit's Brabantio
said that her strength "restored the balance of the play by giving [Desdemona's] character
its due weight in the action," and Faucit herself reports that Macready liked her strength:
"I added intensity to the last act by 'being so difficult to kill' " (quoted in Carlisle,
Shakespeare from the Greenroom, 249). This sounds like Tynan's point about Maggie Smith
and the greater theatrical interest and excitement in a "less one-sided" struggle.

Fanny Kemble's explanation of the desirability of struggle is superficially similar but
really going in the opposite direction: it emphasizes Othello's "inefficient clumsiness . . .
his half smothering, his half stabbing her," which in turn reflects on "Othello's agony" in
the deed: "*That* man not to be able to kill *that* woman outright . . . how tortured he must
have been" (quoted in Carlisle, *Shakespeare from the Greenroom*, 259). Here the effect is to
draw the attention away from Desdemona and over to the protagonist's internal struggle,
which was the consistent endeavor of the nineteenth-century stage. This is closer to the
self-erasing false consciousness which contemporary criticism tends to find in the play.

lieve that Jackson was a protofeminist, but as Paul Yachnin points out (*Stage-Wrights*, 26–31), his rhetorical training seems to have predisposed him to an appreciative response to theatrical performance independent of his own particular opinions. Yachnin argues that Renaissance theater negotiated a "powerless" position for itself — meeting the audience in a space outside the normalizing structures of real belief and action (1–24). This is not the space within which most current interpretation wishes to engage with Renaissance drama. We're interested in role models; maybe we have to be.[15] However we explain it, the fact of Desdemona, subdued to the very quality of Othello rather than committed to her own autonomy, is simply an intolerable prospect, not to be endured. It so violates fundamental convictions about the world that it has been rendered invisible. We see instead the passivity and prostration inflicted on us by a perverse interpretive tradition, thereby reinforcing this tradition in a way that, like Desdemona herself as we fabricate her, seems to cooperate with the forces that defeat desire. O, the pity of it.[16]

Edward Pechter
Concordia University and University of Victoria

Works Cited

Adamson, W. D. "Unpinned or Undone? Desdemona's Critics and the Problem of Sexual Innocence." *Shakespeare Studies* 13 (1980): 169–86.

Adamson, Jane. *"Othello" as Tragedy: Some Problems of Judgment and Feeling*. Cambridge: Cambridge University Press, 1980.

---

[15] Role models do not work well with tragedy, where no prudent course of action is available and where every path leads to catastrophe; but current critics are just doing what Coleridge was doing, and Rymer, and (more generally) Sidney and Heywood and other apologists for poetry around the time *Othello* was written: claiming some influential connection between the actions performed on the stage and the beliefs of the spectators. There are always connections between fictional plots and ideological agendas, though we tend to sound foolish when we make them. Empson says that "you ought to be able to appreciate in literature beliefs you don't agree with" but immediately adds that "when these rather subtle points are broadened into a confident dogma they lead I think to bad criticism" ("Honest in *Othello*," 242).

[16] The liberal use of "we" and "our" here and throughout may seem counter-intuitive in denying space for any response uncontaminated by the play's interpretive traditions. For a fuller justification of this claim, see Pechter, *"Othello" and Interpretive Traditions*, from which this essay has been adapted.

Auden, W. H. "The Joker in the Pack." In idem, *The Dyer's Hand and Other Essays*, 246–72. New York: Random House, 1948.

Bradley, A. C., *Shakespearean Tragedy: Lectures on "Hamlet," "Othello," "King Lear," "Macbeth"*. London: Macmillan, 1904; repr. 1964.

Burke, Kenneth. "*Othello*: An Essay to Illustrate a Method." *Hudson Review* 4 (1951): 165–203.

Calderwood, James. *The Properties of "Othello"*. Amherst: University of Massachusetts Press, 1989.

Carlisle, Carol Jones. *Shakespeare from the Greenroom: Actors' Criticisms of Four Major Tragedies*. Chapel Hill: University of North Carolina Press, 1969.

Collier, Susanne. "Cutting to the Heart of the Matter: Stabbing the Woman in *Philaster* and *Cymbeline*." In *Shakespearean Power and Punishment: A Volume of Essays*, ed. Gillian Murray Kendall, 39–58. Newark, DE: University of Delaware Press; London: Associated University Presses, 1998.

Daileader, Celia R. "(Off) Staging the Sacred." In eadem, *Eroticism on the Renaissance Stage: Transcendence, Desire, and the Limits of the Visible*, 79–106. Cambridge Studies in Renaissance Literature and Culture 30. Cambridge: Cambridge University Press, 1998.

Dawson, Anthony B. "Performance and Participation: Desdemona, Foucault, and the Actor's Body." In *Shakespeare, Theory, and Performance*, ed. James C. Bulman, 29–45. London and New York: Routledge, 1996.

Derrida, Jacques. *The Margins of Philosophy*, trans. Alan Bass. Chicago: University of Chicago Press, 1982.

Eaton, Sara. " 'Content with art'?: Seeing the Emblematic Woman in *The Second Maiden's Tragedy* and *The Winter's Tale*." In *Shakespearean Power and Punishment: A Volume of Essays*, ed. Kendall, 59–86.

Empson, William. "*Hamlet*." In idem, *Essays on Shakespeare*, ed. David B. Pirie, 79–136. Cambridge: Cambridge University Press, 1986.

———. "Honest in *Othello*." In idem, *The Structure of Complex Words*, 218–49. London: Chatto and Windus, 1951.

Evans, G. B., et al., ed. *The Riverside Shakespeare*. Boston: Houghton Mifflin, 1997.

Faucit, Helena. *On Some of Shakespeare's Female Characters*. Edinburgh: Blackwoods, 1885; repr. New York: AMS Press, 1970.

Fineman, Joel. "The Sound of O in *Othello*: The Real of the Tragedy of Desire." *October* 45 (1988): 77–96.

Foakes, R. A., ed. *Coleridge's Criticism of Shakespeare: A Selection*. London: Athlone Press, 1989.

Furness, Horace Howard. *A New Variorum Edition of Othello*. 7th ed. Philadelphia: Lippincott, 1886.

Genster, Julia. "Lieutenancy, Standing In, and *Othello.*" *English Literary History* 57 (1990): 785–809.

Greenberg, Mitchell. "Shakespeare's *Othello* and the 'Problem' of Anxiety." In idem, *Canonical States, Canonical Stages: Oedipus, Othering, and Seventeenth-Century Drama*, 1–32. Minneapolis and London: University of Minnesota Press, 1994.

Grennan, Eamon. "The Women's Voices in *Othello*: Speech, Song, Silence." *Shakespeare Quarterly* 38 (1987): 275–92.

Hankey, Julie. *Othello.* Plays in Performance Series. Bristol: Bristol Classical Press, 1987.

Hazlitt, William. *Characters of Shakespear's Plays.* In *The Complete Works of William Hazlitt*, ed. P. P. Howe, 4: 165–361. London and Toronto: J. M. Dent, 1930.

Henderson, Diana E. "The Theater and Domestic Culture." In *A New History of Early English Drama*, ed. John D. Cox and David Scott Kastan, 173–94. New York: Columbia University Press, 1997.

Honigmann, E. A. J. *Shakespeare: Seven Tragedies: The Dramatist's Manipulation of Audience Response.* London: Macmillan, 1976.

———. *The Texts of "Othello" and Shakespearian Revision.* London and New York: Routledge, 1996.

———, ed. *Othello.* Walton-on-Thames: Thomas Nelson, 1997.

Hughes, Merritt Y., ed. *John Milton: Complete Poems and Major Prose.* New York: Odyssey, 1957.

Jameson, Anna B. *Characteristics of Women: Moral, Poetical, and Historical*, 1832; repr. *Shakespeare's Heroines.* London: George Bell & Sons, 1905.

Knutson, Roslyn Lander. *The Repertory of Shakespeare's Company, 1594–1613.* Fayetteville: University of Arkansas Press, 1991.

Laqueur, Thomas. *Making Sex: Body and Gender from the Greeks to Freud.* Cambridge, MA: Harvard University Press, 1990.

Loomba, Ania. *Gender, Race, Renaissance Drama.* Manchester: Manchester University Press, 1989.

McAlindon, T. *Shakespeare's Tragic Cosmos.* Cambridge: Cambridge University Press, 1991.

Neill, Michael. "Changing Places in *Othello.*" *Shakespeare Survey* 37 (1984): 115–31.

———. *Issues of Death: Mortality and Identity in English Renaissance Tragedy.* Oxford: Clarendon Press, 1997.

———. "Unproper Beds: Race, Adultery, and the Hideous in *Othello.*" *Shakespeare Quarterly* 40 (1989): 383–412.

Orgel, Stephen. "The Authentic Shakespeare." *Representations* 21 (1988): 1–25.

———. "Shakespeare and the Kinds of Drama." *Critical Inquiry* 6 (1979): 107–23.

———. "Shakespeare Imagines a Theater." In *Shakespeare, Man of the Theater: Proceedings of the Second Congress of the International Shakespeare Association, 1981*, ed. Kenneth Muir, Jay L. Halio, and D. J. Palmer, 34–46. East Brunswick, NJ, London, and Mississauga: Associated University Presses, 1983.

Pechter, Edward. *"Othello" and Interpretive Traditions.* Iowa City: University of Iowa Press, 1999.

———. *"Patient Grissil* and the Trials of Marriage." *Elizabethan Theatre* 14 (1996): 83–108.

Rosenberg, Marvin. *The Masks of Othello: The Search for the Identity of Othello, Iago, and Desdemona by Three Centuries of Actors and Critics.* Berkeley: University of California Press, 1961.

Siemon, James R. " 'Nay, that's not next': *Othello*, V.ii in Performance, 1760–1900." *Shakespeare Quarterly* 37 (1986): 38–51.

Sinfield, Alan. *Faultlines: Cultural Materialism and the Politics of Dissident Reading.* Berkeley: University of California Press, 1992.

Sprague, Arthur Colby. *Shakespeare and the Actors: The Stage Business in His Plays (1660–1905).* Cambridge, MA: Harvard University Press, 1948.

Tennenhouse, Leonard. *Power on Display: The Politics of Shakespeare's Genres.* New York and London: Methuen, 1986.

Terry, Ellen. *Four Lectures on Shakespeare*, ed. with an intro. Christopher St. John. London: Martin Hopkinson Ltd. 1932.

Tynan, Kenneth, ed. *"Othello": The National Theatre Production.* New York: Stein and Day, 1967.

Webster, John. *The White Devil*, ed. Christina Luckyj. London: A. & C. Black, Ltd., 1996.

Wine, Martin L. *"Othello": Text and Performance.* London: Macmillan, 1984.

Winter, William. *Shakespeare on the Stage.* New York: Moffat, Yard and Co., 1911; repr. New York: Benjamin Blom, 1969.

Woodbridge, Linda. *Women and the English Renaissance: Literature and the Nature of Womankind, 1540–1620.* Urbana and Chicago: University of Illinois Press, 1984.

Yachnin, Paul. *Stage-Wrights: Shakespeare, Jonson, Middleton, and the Making of Theatrical Value.* Philadelphia: University of Pennsylvania Press, 1997.

"Let it Be Hid":
The Pornographic Aesthetic of
Shakespeare's *Othello*

Utter my thoughts? Why, say they are vile and false:
As where's that palace, whereinto foul things
Sometimes intrude not? who has a breast so pure,
But some uncleanly apprehensions
Keep leets and law-days, and in session sit
With meditations lawful? (*Othello* 3.3.140–145)[1]

The final act of *Othello* visually confronts its audience with what is arguably the most unforgettable stage tableau in all of Shakespeare. Before the forces of institutional morality burst in and feebly attempt to assert control over the chaos of the bedroom, the audience has been led into the forbidden space of this hitherto off-stage room — the imagined chamber toward which the play has always pointed, the place which it has repeatedly eroticized, and the space which until now it has kept discreetly hidden, blocked from audience view behind one of a number of fictive doors that we have consented to imagine. In the closing act, when the final door to the play's last bedroom figuratively swings open, we are allowed/compelled to be the only witnesses to the act of erotic violence that we have already been induced to see: Desdemona strangled on her wedding sheets, dying in suggestive paroxysms in the violent embrace of the alien black husband.

---

[1] *Othello*, in the Arden Shakespeare, ed. M. R. Ridley (London: Methuen, 1958; repr. 1960). Unless otherwise noted, all *Othello* quotations are from this edition.

All Shakespearean tragedy ends with control returning to the representative forces of social order. However, in the other tragedies, those forces are not only considerably more successful, but they also conclude the play by paying tribute to, not trying to erase and avoid, the tableau of tragic violence: Hamlet is elevated to the stage like a soldier and given funeral accolades; Lear's endurance receives an awed encomium from the play's survivors; Octavius Caesar grudgingly orders that tribute be paid to Antony and Cleopatra before ordering everyone back to Rome; and even the spiked head of the slaughterous Macbeth is implicitly honored as it is raised up to tower over the victors below. By contrast, the ending of *Othello* provides no eulogy but only what New Cambridge editor Norman Sanders calls "Cassio's lip service remark, 'For [Othello] was great of heart', standing for the final panegyric" (20). Moreover, beyond even the omitted tribute, what this play's concluding spokesman presents as a formula for the reassertion of order is an explicit indictment of not only the tragic loading on the bed but those who watch it — the viewers who are, implicitly, the play's own audience: "The object poisons sight, / Let it be hid" (5.2.365–366). The play then concludes in aversion and avoidance with Lodovico beating a hasty retreat, determined to cover up the picture on the bed and then go "straight aboard, and to the state" (371) avoiding as quickly as possible that condemned sign of a now hidden sign, the bed and its euphemized "loading"(F) or "lodging" (Q1 and 2) that are together said to poison sight.

In the final moments of this play, the "object" of such consternation and that which infects its watchers is ultimately identified as the "work" of Iago, the figure from whom most of the play's ubiquitous commands to "look ... watch ... see" have emanated, the nasty little fellow to whom an audience owes a substantial amount of its own fascination with this particular Shakespeare tragedy. From *Othello*'s opening scene, the audience's ears have been filled with references to "looking", usually spoken by Iago and repeatedly phrased in either the imperative that commands the listener's visual attention or in rhetorical questions that solicit it while simultaneously assuming compliance. The "look" command, since Iago's initial use of it on Brabantio, has been, throughout the play, directed towards an increasingly sexualized image, yet an image that, until the final act, has been available only through the participatory act of imagining it. Only with Lodovico's last use of the ubiquitous injunction — "Look on the tragic loading of this bed" (364–365) — does the command make contact with its at last literal and concrete referent, the sexual scene now elevated in mute display on the play's at last visible bed. But precisely as the fetishized object of aesthetic gratification becomes visually available to its viewers, that same spectacle is suddenly condemned, enclosed, and the watchers of it, rebuked — "the object poisons sight,

/ Let it be hid." And at this moment, the inclusive implication of Iago's earlier rhetorical questions, such as that which I have here used as an epigraph, should likewise become clear. To Othello's increasingly voyeuristic demands to "Make me to see't, or at the least so prove it ..." (3.3.370), where proof becomes merely an afterthought to seeing, and to his pleas for a "satisfaction" that is increasingly bound up with "ocular proof," Iago had responded with a damning question that explicitly implicates the audience in his tawdry pact: "Would you, the supervisor, grossly gape on? / Behold her topped?" (3.3.395–397). By the end of this play, the audience, the ultimate "super-visors"of it — have indeed grossly gaped.[2] Yet in taking the audience through that final fictive door and into the bedroom space to be discovered within the voyeuristic fantasy they came to see, this tragedy fulfills the aesthetic conditions which, again in Iago's voice, it had explicitly laid out:

> What then / How then?
> What shall I say? Where's satisfaction?
> it is impossible you should see this,
> Were they as prime as goats, as hot as monkeys,
> As salt as wolves in pride, and fools as gross
> As Ignorance made drunk. But yet, I say,
> If imputation and strong circumstances,
> Which lead directly to the door of truth,
> Will give you satisfaction, you might have't. (3.3.401–409)

As most academics who teach Shakespeare know, the question the observant student wants to ask is the prurient one that is built into the text of this play: whether Othello and Desdemona did or did not consummate their marriage. The question is unavoidable. It is layered into the dynamics of the drama in a way that it is not, for instance, in *Romeo and Juliet*. Because we know what happened in Juliet's bedroom, the consummation never becomes an issue of obsessive curiosity to the audience. The dramatic construction of *Othello*, however, seduces its readers and watchers into mimicking Iago's first question to Othello:

---

[2] In "Grossly Gaping Viewers and Jonathan Miller's *Othello*," I have earlier discussed the way that placing a mirror into the final bedroom scene and making the television audience have to peer into it in order to see the image of Desdemona lying on her bed draws attention to audience voyeurism. An excellent psychoanalytic study of the voyeuristic dynamic is Freedman, *Staging the Gaze: Postmodernism, Psychoanalysis, and Shakespearean Comedy*. See also Cavanagh's exploration of Spenser in *Wanton Eyes & Chaste Desires: Female Sexuality in "The Faerie Queene."*

"Are you fast married?" (1.2.11) What is important is not any presumed answer to the question, which can probably be argued either way. What is important is the fact that we need to ask it.

If *Hamlet* is, as Stephen Booth has famously said, a play about an audience that can't make up its mind (152), then *Othello* is one about an audience that finds itself aroused by, trapped within, and ultimately castigated for its prurience. And the audience implied by this play and structured into it from its opening scene is definitively masculine in gender: from Iago's arousal of the first male watcher of the play with his injunction to "Look to your house, your daughter, and your bags" (1.1.80), men are the lookers and women are the objects to be looked at, trapped within and constructed by the pornographic images transmitted inside of an increasingly lethal circuitry of male discourse that is constructed by and itself constructs this play's disturbing male bond.

The dynamic linking any play to its audience is no doubt inherently a voyeuristic suture. But *Othello* exploits that linkage more relentlessly than does any other play in the canon. And although images of erotic violence enacted on a bed may be all too familiar by the twenty-first century to make us uneasy with what they invite, my own rough survey of pre-Shakespearean playscripts suggests that *Othello* may have been the first (extant) play of its kind in English drama.[3] Although in pre-*Othello* plays an audience might hear about some salacious act that had occurred offstage, texts and prop records indicate that before *Othello* the bed had, in general, been restricted on stage to its use as a deathbed: as a place for kings like Henry IV to die. *A Woman Killed With Kindness* and the arbor scene in *The Spanish Tragedy* might both be candidates for the first sexually suggestive stagings of the bed with the woman on it. But nothing extant prior to *Othello* approximates its use as a staging area for sexual violence, a kind of drama that collapses the poles of the word "death" and brings to full representation the orgasmic undertones always present in the Elizabethan use of this term.[4] And Shakespeare's apparent transgression of the previously observed limits of stage decorum may itself have served as something of a catalyst to open the way for the sex-and-violence sensationalism that shortly afterwards flooded the Jacobean and later the Restoration stage.

In *Othello*, Shakespeare seems to have been shaping a new kind of dramaturgy.

---

[3] I would welcome any information to the contrary: i.e., prior to *Othello*, do early modern English playscripts exist in which the bed is explicitly used on stage for a place of erotic consummation?

[4] See especially Neill, "Unproper Beds: Race, Adultery, and the Hideous in *Othello*."

Through a dramatic construction that critics from A. C. Bradley on have un-easily recognized as being somehow "different" from that of the other major tragedies,[5] this play holds up a mirror that mercilessly exposes the complicity of the audience's spectatorship. On the first two of the three successive bridal nights of the play's construction, Othello and Desdemona are isolated behind the bedroom door while the audience of watchers is turned over to the control of Iago, positioned as participants in the increasingly violent, masculine anti-epitha-lamion he orchestrates without. The spatial design solicits attention inward. More damningly, however, the voyeuristic desire for *dramatic* satisfaction aroused by the construction of the first two nights compels the action of the climactic third one and implicates the play's watchers in the amorphous "cause" that Oth-ello's lines allude to as he enters the bedroom on the final night, bringing with him not only the violence from the street outside but, at long last, the voyeuristic desires of the audience: "It is the cause, it is the cause" (5.2.1).

It is in the bedroom where this play consummates its union with its audience; and that same space of viewer gratification is where the play likewise dis-covers the audience as its "guilty creatures sitting at a play," left at the end of the fantasy castigated for their voyeurism and, as the forces of moral order exit for Venice, dramatically abandoned within the indicted fantasy. Characteristically, in what one might even call nearly a condition of Shakespearean tragic catharsis, a Shakespeare tragedy always provides, at closure, a viable secondary figure in whom the masculine desires of the audience may find a sufficiently heroic site for transfer and displacement.[6] But in *Othello*, there is no Horatio, no Macduff, no Edgar, no Octavius, nor are there any other mitigatingly heroic rituals availa-ble to absorb the masculine anxieties that this tragedy seems designed to arouse. The figure who occupies the requisite structural position in *Othello* is Cassio, but Cassio's all too apparent character weaknesses, plus the fact that the play leaves him disabled and implicitly rendered impotent by the wound in his thigh, all work to disqualify him as any kind of acceptable model. By refusing to provide any such escape mechanism, the play leaves its audience trapped within a highly problematic identity polarized between Othello and Iago. And it seems likely that this uncomfortable male position is the key gender factor that, along with

---

[5] See Sanders, for instance: "It is the ending of the play that separates it most strik-ingly from the other tragedies. In the first place, there is no emphatic reestablishment of public order ... or even the gesture of picking up the pieces" (*Othello*, New Cambridge edition, 20).

[6] Berger, in "Text Against Performance: The Example of *Macbeth*," discusses the way MacDuff provides such a figure for the masculine desires of the audience.

the racial factor, has worked to give *Othello* a special place in the four hundred years of the Shakespearean cultural legacy.

In performance, *Othello* has been simultaneously one of the most popular of all the plays and one that has also disturbed its audiences in peculiarly noteworthy ways, confronting them as it does with the taboo issues of not only sexual violence but also the ugliness of racism played off against the deepest white racist fears of miscegenation.[7] Yet another factor that no doubt accounts for the peculiar anxieties that have historically attended *Othello* is the way it substantively differs from its counterparts in its refusal to gratify the audience's need for the retributive justice that is an important condition for the dispersal of anxiety and aggression that is in drama called catharsis. Not only do the forces of political order refuse to legitimate the role of *Othello*'s watchers, but they refuse to mete out any genuine retribution to the salacious little villain whose "work" has lured the audience into the space of condemnation. With the exceptions of Aaron the Moor and Iago, all of Shakespeare's tragic villains repent their evil; but Aaron is sentenced to a horrific death, while Iago — as opposed to all other villains in the tragedies — exits the play neither killed on stage nor with any such condign punishment even suggested. What ultimately is most problematic about Iago is the audience's own relation to him — something that might be called, in D. H. Lawrence's phrase, "the fascination of the revulsion."

Despite the fact that from the play's opening scene the audience has been aware of the sordidly vicious, misogynist and racist nature of the vision that this "Ensign" holds up as a standard for all men to rally around, it is nonetheless to this same jocularly obscene, inexplicably attractive force of malignity that all male characters in the text are drawn and to whom an audience owes a large amount of its theatrical pleasure. It is Iago who repeatedly stands at the fictive boundary of the play, talking to the audience, confiding in them, and luring them into a tawdry complicity that depends upon their tacit consent to be given access to

---

[7] It was only in the past decade or so that *Othello* criticism really began to take account of the crucial way that race and racism construct this play and the way that race, gender, and sexuality function as linked discourses within it. Without suggesting that the following is an inclusive list, at least some of these important critiques are: Vaughan, *"Othello": A Contextual History*; Newman, " 'And Wash the Ethiop White';" Hall, *Things of Darkness*; Callaghan, " 'Othello was a white man';" Loomba, *Gender, Race, Renaissance Drama*; Pechter, *"Othello" and Interpretive Traditions*; Barthelemy, *Black Face, Maligned Race*; Cowhig, "Blacks in English Renaissance Drama and the Role of Shakespeare's Othello,"; Singh, "Othello's Identity, Postcolonial Theory, and Contemporary African Rewritings of *Othello*;" and Parker, "Fantasies of 'Race' and 'Gender': Africa, Othello, and Bringing to Light."

what Iago alternately calls his "heavenly shows" and "dangerous conceits [that] are in their natures poisons" (3.3.331). Through such consent, an audience yields to Iago, much as does Othello, the role of leading them inward into the doubly represented space of the play's forbidden, offstage room and the mind's unacknowledgeable fantasies. Iago plays the pander who opens the door to the listener's pornographic imagination. And through the figure of Iago, Shakespeare's play mirrors a specific triad of concerns — political, social, and literary — that had suddenly emerged into cultural consciousness at the end of the sixteenth century as a result of England's recent contact with a type of literature we would today label pornography.[8] Far more than Iago's being a genuine "character" with discernibly coherent motivation, Iago is a role, a strategy within the *Othello* text, and Iago is the strategy that shapes this play's construction.

Pornography in its original literary manifestation is by definition male-authored and male-subscribed — not only authored by a male but subscribed by a culture which deprecates the feminine and invests the masculine with sexual desire accompanied by fear, guilt, and loathing of female sexuality. Although its ideological functions are undoubtedly numerous, the primary job that pornographic literature fulfills in its unacknowledged bond with a culture is providing a medium for reconstituting and circulating the society's norms about male power and male dominance. Its special authority lies in the way that it codes itself inside of transgressive, often violent sexual narratives that only seem to oppose the cultural authority by which they are tacitly enabled. As a medium for reifying masculine dominance, pornography has been, correspondingly, a medium for constructing feminine subservience, often in narrative forms of erotic bondage.

Since pornography as a genre is thus a primary carrier for all the culture's erotic "master plots" and often repeats the very same stories that occur in romance and other institutionally more legitimate forms, pornography has a way of lurking right beneath and tacitly working as pattern for the only erotic fantasies the culture knows how to construct: the kinds of fantasies defined by the gendered polarization of both cultural and physical power that underlie and seep into Desdemona's thrilled desire to be "subdued / Even to the utmost pleasure of my lord" (1.3.246–247), or her determination to be passive, unprotesting, obedient and ever the "gentle Desdemona" even when she is subjected to Othello's physical abuse. What may be valuable about pornography as an excavation

---

[8] I have discussed the intersection of these concerns in greater detail in "The 1599 Bishops' Ban, Elizabethan Pornography, and the Sexualization of the Jacobean Stage," in *Enclosure Acts: Sexuality, Property, and Culture in Early Modern England*, ed. Richard Burt and John Michael Archer (Ithaca: Cornell University Press, 1994), 185–200.

site is that perhaps especially here, where the culture's erotic narratives transgress the legitimate, can we clearly see the shape of things that constitute the legitimate. Desdemona has fallen in love with stories about Othello that are the essence of romance — stories in which he appears as the conquering warrior bearing tales of a world that she, in fulfilling the archetype of her role as "a maiden never bold; / Of spirit so still and quiet that her motion / Blushed at herself" (1.3.94–96), can experience only vicariously, through loving such powerful men. In part, she falls in love with romance itself, as culture has implicitly trained her to do by guaranteeing that heterosexual desire will be circulated and endlessly reconstituted through such stories of male heroism, male power, male conquest. Yet these same tacitly authorized stories about warrior/lovers, daughters eloping at midnight with exotic dark strangers, commanding males who sweep women away into exotic lands to discover erotic delight, are also the groundwork for tales we would recognize as pornographic. In fact, influenced by his loss of territorial control in his presumed loss of Desdemona's body, Othello begins to re-narrate his epic story of martial conquest from the grounds of the pornographic, where the female body becomes a sexual topos to be multiply "occupied" by men and further devalued by sexual congress with "pioners," who belonged to a class of soldier so low that dishonorable discharge was often considered a preferable alternative.[9]

> I had been happy if the general camp,
> Pioners and all, had tasted her sweet body
> So I had nothing known . . .
> Farewell! Othello's occupation's gone. (3.3.346–348; 358)

Moreover, the Othello and Desdemona story of the black male and white woman is itself a primary site for pornographic narration, and one that has, since the lewdly racist images in Iago's scene-one descriptions to Brabantio, already been suggested to the audience as available for just such kind of generic appropriation.

Because of pornography's inherently deflective logic and its defensive fantasy that construes all women as insatiably carnal, pornography as a genre frequently disguises itself as an exposé of women's lust, often structured as a dialogue between two women confessing to one another the "pranks / They dare not show their husbands. Their best conscience / Is not to leav't undone, but keep't un-

---

[9] See the New Cambridge edition notes for 3.3.347. As the ultimate threat against Lucrece's resistance, Tarquin had likewise invoked a similarly literal form of social class de-gradation by threatening to place Lucrece's (dead) body with a household servant's.

known" (3.3.203–205). Within the deflected logic of this formula, the lustful female speakers created by the pornographic author do indeed become the "fair papers" and "goodly books" that were made to write "whore" upon, for "pornography" itself means, literally, a written story of whores. And indeed, this was the form in which pornography first arrived in England in 1584 under the title of Pietro Aretino's *I Ragionimenti*. In Aretino's dialogues, the male fantasy is displaced into the voices of an older and a younger woman debating the merits of becoming a nun, a wife, or a courtesan; the conversation is, of course, merely an excuse to describe and revel in the graphic "porntopia" fictionalized here as the older woman's experiences.

Prior to 1584, Aretino had been known in England only as a political satirist and poet, and had even been compared to Tasso and Petrarch by none other than Gabriel Harvey. Then word began to come from continental sources about Aretino's other productions, in particular, his obscene sonnets on the positions of love written to accompany the erotic drawings of Giulio Romano, which were standardly referred to in Italian treatises as "I Modi," but which are coded in all English references as either "the postures" or "the pictures."[10] And in 1584, the *Dialogues* were published by John Wolfe, none other than Gabriel Harvey's own publisher. Shortly afterwards, Aretino moved from being known as the "divine Aretine" to being the exemplar of the obscene, or, more colorfully put, "an italian ribald, [who] vomits-out the infectious poyson of the world, [so that] an Inglish horrel-lorrel must licke it vp for a restoratiue."[11] The impact of *I Ragionimenti* can perhaps be measured by the fact that the form which pornography took for the next 150 years across Europe was Aretino's dialogue between two

---

[10] See David O. Foxon, *Libertine Literature in England, 1660–1745* (London: New Hyde Park, 1965), 11–12. The most accessible version in English of the text and history of "I Modi" is *I modi: The Sixteen Pleasures: An Erotic Album of the Italian Renaissance: Giulio Romano, Marcantonio Raimundi, Pietro Aretino, and Count Jean Frederic-Maximilien de Waldeck*, ed. and trans. with commentary by Lynne Lawner (Evanston: Northwestern University Press, 1988). For an excellent analysis of erotic texts in the Elizabethan era, see Ian Moulton, *Before Pornography: Erotic Writing in Early Modern England* (Oxford: Oxford University Press, 2000). And for studies of the intersecting concerns over gender and subjectivity underlying the period's attacks on the theater, see especially Laura Levine, *Men in Women's Clothing: Anti-theatricality and Effeminization 1579–1642* (Cambridge: Cambridge University Press, 1994) and Katherine Eisaman Maus, "Horns of Dilemma: Jealousy, Gender, and Spectatorship in English Renaissance Drama," *ELH* 54 (1987): 561–584.

[11] The phrase comes from one of Gabriel Harvey's attacks on Thomas Nashe. See *Pierce's Supererogation* in *The Works of Gabriel Harvey*, ed. A. B. Grosart (London, 1884), II, 91–96.

women, an emulation that has led modern biographers to call Pietro Aretino, appropriately enough, the "father" of modern pornography.

By connecting Shakespeare's conception of Iago to that other Venetian scoundrel, Aretino, I am not implying that Shakespeare necessarily used Aretino as a source for *Othello* nor that Iago should be read as an allusion to him. In Shakespeare's own time Aretino's name had come to be a layered metaphor that not only represented a certain type of salacious text and its aroused reader's response, but also provoked a volley of self-legitimating political responses from various state and social institutions reacting against this newly available form of moral transgression. Shakespeare's play re-presents that mirror. And to enable that representation, the text includes not Arch-imago, the arch image-maker of Spenser's *Faerie Queene* whose dream pictures of a lascivious Una abed with the squire cause Red Crosse Knight to betray his quest, but a dramatically viable character named I-ago, the picture-making Imago whose occupation as "Ensign" locates him as the bearer of signs within the play, and bearer, as well, of a certain ugly cultural standard that rallies its followers into a male bond formed around the time-honored misogyny and racism that the "Ancient" both disseminates and perpetuates.

No doubt because Shakespeare's culture did recognize its own image in what it denounced as an invasion of literary obscenity from Italy, Aretino was not only well known by the 1590s, he was infamous; so much so that David McPherson has argued that the deluge of works in the 1590s depicting Italian diabolism owes its impetus more to England's contact with Aretino than with Machiavelli.[12] Within a decade of Aretino's arrival, suddenly writers like Thomas Nashe and John Marston began experimenting with a type of literature that cannot be defined as generically belonging to either the Elizabethan bawdy or the Ovidian sensual. This new type — works like Nashe's *The Choice of Valentines; or, Nashe, his Dildo*, and both Marston's *Metamorphosis of Pigmalion's Image* and *The Scourge of Villanie* — bear the graphic stamp of Aretino. And it was this newly transgressive literature that provided, as well, a rich opportunity for the moralists, theologians, and satirists like Joseph Hall, Gabriel Harvey and, ironically enough, again John Marston to excoriate in print. Quite probably, what had popularized Aretino as the exemplar of the obscene was the use that had been

---

[12] David McPherson, "Aretino and the Harvey-Nashe Quarrel," *PMLA* 84 (1969): 1551–58; p. 1551, n. 3. See also the excellent work of David O. Frantz in his article, "'Leud Priapians' and Renaissance Pornography," *Studies in English Literature* 12 (1972): 157–72, and his book, *Festum Voluptatis: A Study of Renaissance Erotica* (Columbus: Ohio State University Press, 1989).

made of him in the scurrilous Harvey-Nashe pamphlet wars where Harvey had attacked Nashe's immoral writings by calling him the "English Aretine." Ben Jonson's allusions are those that best illustrate the dual pleasure and outrage that constitute the poles of the English response to Aretino. In *The Alchemist*, Sir Epicure Mammon devises a pleasure palace to excite his moribund sexual fantasies by imagining it will be

> Fill'd with such Pictures as Tiberius took
> From Elephantis, and dull Aretine
> But coldly imitated. (*The Alchemist*, 2.2.43–45)

In *Volpone*, however, Corvino lashes out at

> some young Frenchman, or hot Tuscan blood
> That had read Aretine, conned all his prints,
> Knew every quirk within lusts labyrinth
> And were professed critic in lechery. (*Volpone*, 3.7.59–62)[13]

Running parallel with this newly sexualized literature and the printed attack on it, the last years of Elizabeth's reign were marked by a likewise abrupt increase in censorship designed to halt circulation of these two newly emergent literary forms - forms which, we might add, were becoming frequently indistinguishable from one another. In 1599, the official censors of the press issued orders to ban such works as John Hall's *Virgidimiarum*, Marston's *Pigmalion's Image* and *The Scourge of Villanie*, Marlowe's *Elegies*, Davies's *Epigrams*, the Harvey–Nashe pamphlets, and certain books "against women," apparently a reference to Robert Tofte's *Of Marriage and Wyving* and *The XV Joyes of Marriage*, thought to be an earlier version of *The Batchelars Banquet*, also translated from the French by Tofte.[14] Although the books characterized as being "against women" were actually witty arguments designed to make women so disgusting as to discourage men from marriage and the state's concern to ban them almost certainly reflected its desire to protect not women but rather the patriarchal institution through which they were subordinated, the list nonetheless rather neatly draws together graphic sexuality, verbal invective, and misogyny as the elements the state found it expedient to suppress. They are also the three interests bound together in England's emerging pornography, a pornography that never became original, but

---

[13] Ben Jonson, *Three Comedies: Volpone, the Alchemist, Bartholomew Fair*, ed. Michael Jamieson (Baltimore: Penguin Books, 1966).

[14] For details about the ban, see my article cited above in note 9.

contributed only one new element to the genre: the imprint of scatological revulsion.

By censorship, the state acknowledges the power possessed by the censored object. But it is safe to assume that the reaction of the Elizabethan state was political, not altruistic, and intended to protect its own authority to set limits. One may assume that in suddenly enacting an unexpected ban on certain popular literature, the state was legitimizing its authority by asserting it, reifying its not-to-be-questioned social boundaries by redrawing them. And these political concerns are likewise what Lodovico and the state representatives speak to when they conclude the play by ordering redistribution of property rather than eulogy, and censorship rather than the condign retribution we have come to expect from Shakespearean tragedy. Instead of anything that would ritually mark or affirm some connection between the society and the dead bride and groom whom Lodovico has reduced to the "loading on the bed," the final movement is invested in taking things away, in dissociating the state from the sign of transgressive excess that lies on the bed. Having seized upon and redistributed the house and fortunes of the man who has been depersonalized back to "the Moor," Lodovico turns to address the Iago problem. When he does so, however, it is within a syntax that makes "torture" merely parallel with the logistics of organization and reserves its imperative emphasis for the authority of enforcement.

> To you, lord governor,
> Remains the censure of this hellish villain:
> The time, the place, the torture, O, enforce it! (5.2.363–365)

Not only is the audience's need for retribution left wholly ignored, and Iago's punishment turned over to the questionably capable hands of Cassio, the new "lord governor," but, as Lodovico and company depart abruptly for Venice, the audience ends up left behind, positioned inside the play's inner space, confronting the condemned fantasy object, while Iago exits alive and dangerous and still a part of the highly civilized culture of which he is a subterranean part. In a rhetoric of sound and fury that actually signifies very little, the state pronounces Iago a "hellish villain" and a "Spartan dog." But it is never implied (though a remarkable number of critics have inferred) that the state either can or wants to kill Iago. As the rational structures attempt to reestablish the boundaries that have been violated, it becomes increasingly clear, through all that is *not* being said and done, that the violation the Venetian representatives are most concerned to enclose is the excessive passion of Desdemona and Othello, the sign of which they order hidden. When the officials on stage finally provide the overdue indictment of Iago, the language in which it is framed — which accuses Iago of having created a "work" that is itself an "object" that "poisons sight" and must "be hid" — is both descriptively odd and grossly inadequate to encompass the enormity of his crimes. What Lodovico's phrasing makes Iago sound guilty of is having crafted a piece of unseemly and socially offensive art.

Lodovico's sentence likewise dramatizes precisely what the state has always done with pornography — overtly torture and suppress, but covertly ensure its existence. The state's "cunning cruelty" for Iago will be, as Lodovico says in a rather revealing construction, to "torment him much and hold him long" (5.2.335). But if we have learned anything from this play, we should recognize that as a fantasy content, as the voyeur's aroused imagination, and indeed as a literary genre, pornography is fed, not starved, by prohibition. Like Iago, it must be denied promotion to be aroused to action; its life depends on its suppression.

The writer who seems best to have understood such seeming paradoxes inherent in the demands of the emerging form was John Marston, whose *Metamorphosis of Pigmalion's Image* deliberately experiments with masturbatory strategies of inhibited desire which stimulate the reader's arousal by creating a friction with it. As Marston's poem leads its male reader towards the given object of desire, the centripetal figure of the waiting female body, it alternately arouses him with prurient questions much like Iago's and then prohibits his access by refusing to show what the reader has been led to imagine, a denial technique that, like Iago's "pursed up" thoughts, his "stops" and "close denotements" (3.3.127),[15] only guarantees that the aroused reader will demand the voyeuristic satisfaction of "Make me to see it." At the end of *Pigmalion*, a seeming reversal unexpectedly appears in appended verses entitled "The Authour in prayse of his precedent Poem," where suddenly the poet radically switches his stance and, in the voice of the moralist, scathingly attacks his readers as "lewd Priapians" whose prurience has been "tickled up" by the poem which the author now disclaims as a piece of "chaos indigest" which he "slubbered up" to "fish for fools" - who are, of course, his readers. The poem and its annexed verses together constitute the paradox of pornography's split mentality, the seeming contradiction of Iago's dual stance. By appropriating the voice of the moralist disgusted by what he graphically describes, the strategy neutralizes the guilt of the sexualist and allows the two psychic figures to co-exist in the reader. Only *because of* such a split can the moralist

---

[15] F and Q2 (seconded by Rowe and Theobald) read "dilations" for Q1's "denotements," the reading which Capell chooses. Steevens finally added "delations." For a complex illumination of meanings, see especially Patricia Parker in "Shakespeare and Rhetoric: 'dilation' and 'delation' in *Othello*," in *Shakespeare and the Question of Theory*, ed. Patricia Parker and Geoffrey Hartman (New York and London: Methuen, 1984), 54–74.

revel in what he simultaneously decries, and the voluptuary be whipped for the pleasures that arouse him. The split is most vividly illustrated in *Othello* by Othello's vacillating stances during the bedroom murder. Having erotically murdered the seducing strumpet he sees on the bed, Othello then priggishly aligns himself with Iago as another "honest man ... [who] hates the slime/ That sticks on filthy deeds" (148–149).

Important to understanding the voice in which the pornography of late sixteenth-century English literature speaks is the recognition of how the genre, although originally appropriated from the Italian, nonetheless reflects its own particular origins. As distinct from the pleasure principle of its Italian progenitor, the idiom of English pornography is invested in the language of slime, poison, revulsion, disgust, garbage, vomit, clyster pipes, dung, and animality that emerges in Iago's every mention of sex and eventually displaces the Othello music. Moreover, it is an idiom that English pornography borrowed from the *moralists* who began writing against sexualized literature. It is likewise the language that John Marston, more than any other writer, contributed to English satire in his 1598 work *The Scourge of Villanie*, which purports to be an attack on sexual writing, spoken in the voice of the moralist.[16] In the Juvenalian coarseness of the *Scourge* persona, Marston seems to have opened up new rhetorical strategies for the satirists to explore; moreover, his newly coarsened language of sexual bluntness likewise provided a rich muck-pit for drama to mine and may well have provided a "father tongue" not only for Iago but also for such characters as Thersites, Bosola, and other Jacobean malcontents who — along with Marston's own dramatic scourgers of sexual vice — emerged on the English stage shortly thereafter. The persona-speaker of *The Scourge* is, very much like Iago, a bluntly honest man who hates "the slime of filthy sensuality" which he endlessly describes in snarling ejaculations at

> *Aretine's* filth, or of his wandering whore ...
> of *Ruscus* nastie lothsome brothell rime
> That stinks like Ajax froth, or muck-pit slime
>   (lxi. ll.144, 146–147)

---

[16] John Marston, *The Scourge of Villanie*, in *The Poems of John Marston, 1575?–1634*, ed. Arnold Davenport, Liverpool English Texts and Studies (Liverpool: Liverpool University Press, 1961). Davenport likewise sees Marston as instrumental in the creation of this new language of the Jacobean stage. See his introduction to *Poems*.

> Out on this salt humour, letchers dropsie,
> Fie, it doth soyle my chaster poesie. . . . (lxi. ll.155–156)

Marston's bitter Scourge persona is pornographic, but he fails to lure his readers into complicity. Shakespeare's exuberant Iago makes his watchers have to admire his success, disarming an audience even as he appalls them with his witty images of lewd jocularity, comically memorable pictures like "the old black ram tupping . . ." that are carefully interlarded among his passages of scatological bluntness. And in Iago's prurient descriptions of Desdemona, he does not so befoul the whole image that desire will turn to revulsion; he soils her just enough in the making to render her carnally available to his listening audience's fantasies. From the opening scene of this play, to be a spectator is to be invited into an Iago-orchestrated world of images centered upon the availability of Desdemona's body — the locus where, inexorably, the action of the drama likewise leads.

If contemporary analysis of pornography agrees on anything, it may be the recognition that beneath the overt sexuality and apparent life impetus of the pornographic script, its true objective is not sex but death — and in particular, death experienced as erotic completion. Beneath Iago's salacious script and its "pageant to keep men in false gaze" (1.3.19), the target of the fantasy is the figure whom the script has violently eroticized since its opening moment, the one it eventually succeeds in isolating behind its bedroom door, and the one it finally stifles into silence. She is Iago's target, she becomes Othello's, and she is likewise the voyeuristic object that the language of the play has endlessly invited the audience to "look" at and objectify. Even her identity as the appropriate target has been available to the audience since first hearing her name.

It was, after all, *Des-demon* who first transgressed against the boundaries of patriarchal enclosure, creating a fissure in two of its most sacred texts by self-authorizing her own marriage and then disrupting the state's discourse of sanctioned aggression with a counter-claim that privileged her own "downright violence" and the right to live with the man she married. Her arrival into the Venetian Council in 1.3 visually and verbally represents what her intrusion threatens: to drive wedges into the structures presided over by the masculine paterfamilias who is the carrier of authority and unity. It is thus appropriately through Brabantio, the father, that the culture transmits the warning that becomes a rallying cry. Under the banner that "she has deceiv'd her father, [and] may do thee" (1.3.293), the men of this play repeatedly regroup and bond into a shared identity that progressively isolates the object of desire and resignifies it as an object of mutual threat. Along with Desdemona herself, the watchwords are carried to Cyprus by the Ensign: "She has betrayed her father . . ." The echoed warning in-

forms the strange logic of Othello's conviction that "she must die, else she'll betray more men" (5.1.6); and it reifies itself once more even in the parodically
deflected eulogy that Gratiano speaks when he enters the bedroom and looks at
Desdemona, murdered on her bridal bed. Gazing at the figure of his dead niece
Gratiano, too, aligns himself with the patriarchal text and, instead of eulogizing
the tragedy of this young bride, his text instead condemns Desdemona as the
implicit agent of her father's death: "Poor Desdemona, I am glad thy father's
dead; / Thy match was mortal to him, and pure grief / Shore his old thread at-
wain. . . ." (5.2.205–207).

The pervasive idea of women as the ultimate threat to masculine control and
the male bond finally transforms every performance in the play into the misogynistic violence that utterly overwhelms *Othello*'s concluding act. While Othello
goes from the male violence outside in the street, emblematically bringing it with
him into the bedroom to execute the "fair devil" within, Bianca simultaneously
magnetizes blame for the violence outside when, ignoring her own safety, she
rushes out in the street to save Cassio. It is Iago who directs both forms of aggression. But it is Cassio's silent complicity as he psychologically bonds with his
attackers that confirms Iago's script. And though his injuries are not so severe as
to prevent him from verbally rallying to Roderigo's defense and insisting that
Roderigo be cleared from accusation, Cassio — whose life was actually saved by
Bianca's intervening presence — says nothing in Bianca's behalf as Iago turns
blame for the attack on her. What ultimately happens to Bianca is not explicit
within the text, but the issue is hardly irrelevant in terms of the intense focus
that this play places on the heterosexual bond. Moreover, the text does provide
an inference that is both the logical one for the situation and one which fits the
play's larger pattern of a disturbing parallel among its three women/three men/
three couples. Since Iago is in total command and literally directing this scene,
what happens to Bianca lies wholly within his control. After sending Cassio off
to a surgeon, Iago — with the Venetian authorities as his audience — moves to
solidify his accusations against Bianca by once again invoking the regime of male
looking at a female body and reading it for signs of its presumptive guilt.

> What, look you pale? —
> Stay you, good gentlewoman; look you pale, mistress?
> Do you perceive the gestures of her eye?
> Nay, an you stir, — we shall have more anon:
> Behold her well I pray you, look upon her,
> Do you see, gentlemen? nay, guiltiness
> Will speak, though tongues were out of use. (5.1.103–109)[17]

---

[17] At line 104 Qq read "gentlewoman" and F reads "gentlemen." Either is logical, but

When a remarkably calm Bianca rejects his subsequent reading of her body as a text betraying signs of guilt ("He [Cassio] supp'd at my house, but I therefore shake not"), Iago seizes upon the authoritative language of an arresting officer — "O did he so? I charge you go with me" (119), and concludes the scene by asserting further legal control over her as he orders her to come with him: "Come, mistress, you must tell's another tale." From this reference in conjunction with those above — that "we shall have more anon" and "guiltiness / Will speak, though tongues were out of use" — Iago seems to allude to a confession that the authorities will forcibly extract from Bianca even if she initially refuses to speak it. By inference, Bianca, undefended by Cassio and under a charge from Iago that goes unchallenged by the Venetian authorities, is being hauled off to prison. My inference of such callous treatment seems further justified by the fact that neither Cassio nor the authorities make any move to exonerate or lift the accusation from her in the play's final scene, even after they know of Iago's guilt from the letter found on Roderigo's body. Bianca exits the play under accusation and, is, in fact, never spoken of again.

In this play it is not just Othello who calls the woman he loves a "whore" — it is every male in the drama who has any narrative relationship with a woman. Moreover, it is always Iago's innuendoes, the Ensign's presence and its implicit call for the rallying of the male bond, that prompt each man to do so. Iago labels all three women in the play whores, and by the end of the fourth act Othello has denounced Emilia as a "simple bawd" and "subtle whore" (4.2.20, 21). But in ways that form a disturbing parallel with Othello's willingness to call Desdemona a whore, Cassio, around Iago, sniggeringly characterizes the woman with whom he has sexual relations a "customer," a "monkey," a "bauble" and a "fitchew" (4.1); Roderigo, around Iago, believes that the Desdemona he idealizes is available for sexual purchase had he but jewels and gold enough to buy her; and even her father, influenced by Iago's smutty pictures, is willing publicly to brand his own daughter as a woman who, having "betrayed" his incestuous fantasies by marrying Othello, will now betray her husband and, *ergo*, become a whore. In this tragedy, not only Desdemona but all the women are the "fair papers" on which the men of the play write "whore." And for the women, the consequences of such male inscription are lethal.

Within the *Othello* text the "whore" that all the men imagine and with which

---

if the former, then Iago — perhaps physically — has probably here intercepted Bianca's move to follow Cassio and is addressing her (whom he earlier called "strumpet") with deriding sarcasm. At line 106, Qq reads "an you stirre" and F, "if you stare." Most editors follow the Q reading; Sanders further notes how the "stir" reading here suggests that "Iago has a hold on Bianca, who starts to struggle and is threatened by him."

term they so quickly brand the women they love is a label that, for the women, is so threatening that all three of them circle warily around it, so desperate to extricate themselves from what, in Desdemona's death, is dramatized as its literal stranglehold that they willingly displace the term onto other women as if such displacement would stand as proof of their own purity. In the final night scene between Desdemona and Emilia, as both women nervously try to suppress their half-conscious knowledge of the coming violence that lies heavy in the air, their dialogue compulsively cycles back, again and again, to sexual infidelity. Interestingly enough, as each of the women tries to come to terms with the loathing she feels projected at her by her husband, each seems implicitly to consider the possibility that she might have made — or might make — some other choice. But such a possibility, while discursively acceptable and even consciously accessible as a topic among Shakespearean males,[18] is for the women always already framed within the dangerous cultural binary of virgin and whore. Moreover, that binary clearly acts not only as an external inhibitor but, even more problematically, also as a set of stringent rules that culture has trained all women, even those who represent such widely different social classes as do the three in *Othello*, to inter-

---

[18] Linguistic evidence of such a powerful double standard exists, of course, in the fact that while female infidelity is marked by a number of perjorative, often powerfully punitive terms (such as "whore," "strumpet," etc.), in English and probably most other languages there are no counterterms for naming unfaithful males.

Two Gentlemen of Verona provides a lighthearted example of the kind of license for male infidelity that is stringently denied to women in Renaissance drama. Similarly, the young male lovers in *A Midsummer Night's Dream* are comic in their changeability; while conversely, Helena and Hermia both remain faithful, thus virtuous, and the comedy of the women's roles lies in the way Hermia projects her fury, not at Lysander for his betrayal, but at Helena, the other woman to be despised for having stolen him. In terms of male license within this implicit double standard, *All's Well that Ends Well* offers a much more pointed criticism of the way that Bertram's credit with his peers goes up, not down, when he abandons his wife and is thought to have seduced the virginal Diana; even in the play's final scene where he is chastised for such bad behavior while Diana's revelations of supposed sexual congress threaten her with prison, Bertram's behavior is ultimately always to be forgiven by not only the society but also the betrayed wife herself. The one overall exception to this understood rule about gender and sexual fidelity may perhaps occur in *Antony and Cleopatra*. For while Antony follows the rule that allows males to violate the rule, and thus lives with marital and sexual infidelities himself while raging at Cleopatra as a "triple-turned whore" for the lovers she has enjoyed before him, Cleopatra is in some regards a unique Shakespearean female. While she remains virtuous and does not sexually betray Antony during the course of the play, she alone among Shakespearean heroines is at least allowed to chat happily with other women about her earlier lovers. Despite the exception, however, Cleopatra exists in an emphatically pre-Christian, pagan world, and, as Shakespeare makes clear, this world ends with Egypt's invasion by Octavius Caesar and his "Roman thoughts."

nalize. And thus, in the Desdemona–Emilia exchange, no sooner is the thought of infidelity even partially expressed than it is instantly retracted and quickly displaced onto some imagined other woman, the presumptive "whore" whose existence must be theorized in order to carry the transferred guilt of the speaker's unacknowledgeable fantasies and thereby confirm the position of virtue from which she must always be seen — by herself as well as others — to speak.

The women's scene takes place shortly after Othello, having hit Desdemona and humiliated her in front of the shocked Venetian ambassadors, has ordered her to bed. From the digressive Willow Song in which Desdemona sings forlornly about a woman deserted by her love, her dialogue shifts in jarring transition to the sudden observation that "This Lodovico is a proper man" (4.3.35), to the logically unrelated question she keeps pushing at Emilia about the supposedly unimaginable existence of women so vile as ones who could possibly "abuse their husbands / In such gross kind" (61–62). Its almost Pinteresque construction suggests that the absent connectives that would lend it logical coherence lie in precisely such an interplay of denial, repression and displacement. And Desdemona's sequence is then immediately followed by a similar, though much more conscious one from Emilia. Beginning with an initially candid acknowledgment that "There be some such [women], no question" (62), and the admission that she could even imagine herself doing such a deed, Emilia's dialogue then likewise becomes suggestively entangled with guilt and repression. Retracting her earlier candor she next insists that if she ever did commit adultery, she would "undo't when I had done it" (70–71), and then reconstructs the imagined act as something she might do not for herself but only to better her husband: she might "make her husband a cuckold," but it would be only "to make him a monarch" (74–75). Emilia's attempt to contain her resentment inside the accepted double standard is, however, only partially successful, and thus she concludes this scene with an angry outburst that essentially justifies a woman's adultery by insisting that women, too, have affections, desires for sport, and frailty. And yet, even though she has, in effect, already admitted that sexual infidelity is an entirely thinkable option and one that she could potentially imagine herself committing, in the very next scene, when she hears Iago frame his accusation of Bianca in terms of "this is the fruit of whoring" (5.1.115), Emilia immediately disavows that dangerously liberated space with which she had flirted just moments before and reclaims the position of moral superiority by joining with her husband in denouncing/chastising Bianca with "Fie, fie upon thee, strumpet!" (120) — an appellation which Bianca, too, then instantly displaces by equating herself with Emilia in insisting that she is "of life as honest / As you, that thus abuse me" (121–122).

In this play's darkly pessimistic exploration of sex and gender bonds, such painful ironies abound. While the three women blame problems in their relationships with men on some imagined other woman and simultaneously go either or almost to the death in defense of the men with whom they are bonded, the three men repeatedly affirm the actually lethal male bonds among them and either kill their mates or complicitly allow them to be condemned, potentially to death. Not just Desdemona, but to greater degrees likewise Emilia and Bianca, clearly recognize that some kind of problem exists within their marital/sexual bond. But the condition of the heterosexual bond in this play seems to require that women must locate the problem not within the males with whom they are joined or even within the internal dynamics of the relationship. Instead, the problem must be externalized and projected elsewhere, almost inevitably on another female. Thus Bianca, instead of challenging Cassio's insulting query, "What do you mean by this haunting of me?", transfers her anger into a jealous accusation that the handkerchief he has given her to copy is "some minx's token" or something he has had from some "hobby-horse" (4.1.143; 151–152). The presumptive other woman rather than Cassio receives the opprobrium; and once that site has absorbed the anger, what Cassio receives is Bianca's invitation to supper.

This pattern of gender-conditioned deflection is, moreover, reified by its parallel in the reactions of both Emilia and Desdemona. Desdemona's Willow Song — always understood as a site onto which she transfers her own sense of despair, abandonment, and intuition of her own death[19] — is also a complex site where, having run out of all of the earlier, impersonal excuses through which she has tried to account for the irrational rage being projected at her by her husband, she at last struggles with the issue of blame. Having retracted the line "*Let nobody blame him, his scorn I approve,* — "with the interjection "Nay, that's not next" (4.3.51–52), she replaces it with "*I call'd my love false love; but what said he then? ... If I court moe women, you'll couch with moe men*" (54; 55). Although the accusation occurs only in deflected form inside the fictional voices of a song, Desdemona does here at last, for a moment, replace self-accusation with an accusation of a male/Othello figure. But even her accusation that he is a "false love" is couched in terms of a presumptive infidelity with some implied other woman, and as she elucidates the accusation further by allowing him to respond, even the recognition that his rage is based on a belief in her infidelity is tangled up with his threat to "couch with more women." Not even the outspoken Emilia proves

---

[19] Compare the essay by Pechter in this volume.

capable until the play's final scene of facing the genuine rage she harbors against her husband. That wives may fall is, she vigorously asserts, their husbands' faults. But the fault that she finds — one which seems wide indeed of Iago, whose contempt for women is so strong as to make sexual infidelity the least believable of perhaps any accusation — again implicates the ubiquitous other woman: if men "slack their [sexual] duties" it is because they "pour our treasures into foreign laps." And wives' infidelities are thus justified because husbands have "change[d] us for others" (4.3.87–88; 97). Desdemona's fatal flaw, it has often been argued, is her extreme passivity, her refusal to read Othello's anger and confront it with anger of her own at his abuse. Yet Bianca and Emilia — neither of whom could be accused of passivity — fare no better, and, in ways that echo Desdemona, each of them goes almost to the death in defense of men who routinely treat them with contempt. Bianca's and Desdemona's abjection might be excused by the fact that they are in love. But the fact that Emilia's actions are disappointingly similar argues for a strongly gendered pattern that this play goes to considerable lengths to construct. For despite Emilia's clear dislike of her husband and resentment at his contempt, she nonetheless strives to win his approval by stealing the handkerchief, and even when his villainy is revealed so thoroughly as to make any excuse impossible, her dumbfounded iteration, "My husband . . . my husband . . . my husband?" (5.2.141; 148; 150; 153) exposes the difficulty she has not so much in recognizing his viciousness but in revising her own determined refusal to confront it.

When Emilia does at last break through her own model of the obedient wife and comes into the bedroom to assert the strident truth of her accusations against the world of men, for a brief but critical moment we suddenly have a genuine, awakened "woman reader in this text."[20] But the moment is emphatically short-lived. Clearly, no one on stage wants to hear the brazen, accusing truth of Emilia's revelations; and thus an entire roomful of able-bodied men stands there, dumbly mute, as Iago viciously acts for them all in silencing the only remaining female voice. After threatening his wife and demanding her silence on five different occasions during a fifty-line exchange on stage, when Iago finally draws his sword on her, the only reaction from the men on stage is Gratiano's comment, "Fie, / Your sword upon a woman?" (5.2.225). In Q1 and Q2 the

---

[20] The phrase comes, of course, from Jacobus' "Is There a Woman in This Text?", which was itself a feminist response to Fish, *Is There a Text in This Class?* The first reading to recognize the implicitly feminist position from which Emilia speaks itself appeared in the first feminist collection of essays on Shakespeare: Neely's "Women and Men in *Othello*: 'What should such a fool / do with so good a woman?'."

stage directions (which do not appear in F) indicate that Othello, outraged at Iago's betrayal, "runnes at Iago. Iago kills his wife." But in no text are there directions to indicate that Gratiano, Montano, or Othello make any attempt to protect Emilia, although in almost all *Othello* productions the director adds in a mighty struggle on stage which Iago breaks through, managing to stab his wife despite heroic attempts to stop him. The addition seems unwarranted, not only by the lack of prior language or directions that suggest any kind of struggle to protect Emilia, but also by what follows. As Emilia falls, Gratiano's only response is "The woman falls, sure he has kill'd his wife" and "He's gone, but his wife's kill'd" (237; 239). Moreover, although the bond between the two women receives the powerful affirmation of Emilia's dying request to be laid next to her mistress,[21] since none of the men ever verbally responds to her plea or says another word about her, we have no idea whether it is ever honored or whether her body lies ignored on the floor and the men simply step over it as the scene continues. Even when the Venetian authorities indict Iago, the murder of his wife is glaringly absent from their indictment, apparently an act not deemed criminal enough to warrant inclusion and it thus goes unmentioned, despite the fact that it is Iago's one crime which all of the men on stage actually witnessed. As was likewise true of Bianca, all reference to Emilia simply disappears.

As violence once more erupts in the bedroom and the audience witnesses yet the second murder of a wife by her husband, the room on stage defined by the bed progressively becomes a space of collective misogynist aggression, presided over by the representatives of Venetian culture, orchestrated by the Imago of that society, and venting itself on the now not one but two women who finally lie dead within that space, their bodies trapped in death even as in life inside of the voyeuristic apparatus of cultural meanings. It is usually assumed that Othello's final lines "Killing myself, to die upon a kiss" (5. 2. 360), direct that the final "loading" on the bed and the object that poisons sight must be the tableau of the black man on the bed, on top of the white woman, and thus dying "upon" a kiss. Consequently, most texts include the stage direction *"He falls on the bed and dies."* In actuality, the only authoritative stage directions that have Othello falling on the bed occur much earlier, at line 199, just prior to Emilia's "Nay, lay thee down and roar," and that direction occurs in the two Quartos but not in Folio. At the moment of Othello's suicide at line 360, Q1 directs only *"He dies,"* and

---

[21] It is possible to read Emilia's lines as saying *either* that she wishes to have her body placed on the bed next to Desdemona's *or* that she is asking to be buried next to her mistress.

Folio simply says *"dies."*[22] Given the ambiguities about just which bodies besides Desdemona's constitute the bed's final loading, the staging of this scene actually includes several possibilities: Desdemona's body alone; Othello's and Desdemona's together; a trio of Othello's, Desdemona's, and Emilia's; or the final bed that the play directs its audience to "look" at could even contain just the bodies of the two women. But regardless of which possibility is staged, the signifying presence of the bed carries with it its own "loading" of eroticized cultural meanings. And thus in the tableau to which this play leads, the effect threatens to become the cause; the tragic loading/lodging on the deathbed threatens to transform it back into a bed of sexual desire; and the image of victimization re-eroticizes the script with its indissociable invitation to audience voyeurism. On the one hand, the play's action accuses its audience. By the final act, refracted incidents of misogynistic violence become so repetitious that they collectively constitute a moral demand for the masculine consciousness of the play's targeted audience to look at, see, and confront the image of a collective cultural guilt. But while the action accuses, the picture seduces. What an audience is ultimately left gaping at does emblematically signify the culture's guilt; but it also signs the culture's desire. It demands that its audience "look" at the bed. But the spectacle thus commanded to vision is the very same one that invites voyeuristic transfer. The picture mutely speaks. And the unease its silent tableau so clearly provokes from the men on stage perhaps makes the most expedient solution seem to be enclosure and exit: "Let it be hid."

Through both the ambivalence of the play's closing sign and the talent of the pornographic artist whose "work" this is, the sexualist and the moralist within the watchers are ultimately assured of a coexistence within the text of *Othello*. And it is precisely that ambivalence that Lodovico unconsciously repeats when he orders the watchers of this play to "look" at what "poisons sight." By the play's conclusion its supervisors have most certainly "grossly gaped"; but in doing so, they have further invested Iago's work with the collective power of the culture's own guilt, violence, prurience, desire, and revulsion. Thus there could be, I suspect, no more appropriate a message for the creator of this "work" to offer than the enigmatic hieroglyph with which Iago leaves Othello and *Othello*'s audience:

> Demand me nothing, what you know, you know;
> From this time forth I never will speak word. (304–305)

---

[22] Siemon, in " 'Nay, that's not next'," offers an excellent reprise of the various complexities and multiple possibilities implicit in staging the final scene of *Othello*.

In every unacknowledged and unacknowledgeable way, the audience does "know what it knows," and what it knows is mutely signified by the sign on stage at closure. Yet however much anxiety this play may provoke by its moral indictment of an audience's misogyny and prurience, the audience may nonetheless exit this play with the comfort of its secret intact. For in a way that extends the implications of an audience's pact with Iago far beyond the boundaries of any performance, as he leaves the play the creature who has both solicited and controlled our gaze has, after all, promised his watchers that he will never more speak word.

Lynda Boose
Dartmouth College

Works Cited

Aretino, Pietro. *I Modi: The Sixteen Pleasures: An Erotic Album of the Italian Renaissance: Giulio Romano, Marcantonio Raimundi, Pietro Aretino, and Count Jean-Frédéric-Maximilien de Waldeck*, ed. and trans. Lynne Lawner. Evanston: Northwestern University Press, 1988.

Barthelemy, Anthony. *Black Face, Maligned Race: The Representation of Blacks in English Drama from Shakespeare to Southerne*. Baton Rouge: Louisiana State University Press, 1987.

Berger, Harry, Jr. "Text Against Performance: The Example of *Macbeth*." *Genre: Forms of Discourse and Culture* 15 (1982): 49–79.

Boose, Lynda E. "Grossly Gaping Viewers and Jonathan Miller's *Othello*." In *Shakespeare, the Movie: Popularizing the Plays on Film, TV, and Video*, ed. eadem and Richard Burt, 186–97. London: Routledge, 1997.

———. "The 1599 Bishops' Ban, Elizabethan Pornography, and the Sexualization of the Jacobean Stage." In *Enclosure Acts: Sexuality, Property, and Culture in Early Modern England*, ed. Richard Burt and John Michael Archer, 185–200. Ithaca: Cornell University Press, 1994.

Booth, Stephen. "On the Value of *Hamlet*." In *Reinterpretations of Elizabethan Drama*, ed. Norman Rabkin, 137–76. New York: Columbia University Press, 1969.

Callaghan, Dympna. "'Othello was a white man': Properties of Race on Shakespeare's Stage." In *Alternative Shakespeares*, ed. Terence Hawkes, 2:196–215. London: Routledge, 1996.

Cavanagh, Sheila T. *Wanton Eyes and Chaste Desires: Female Sexuality in "The Faerie Queene."* Bloomington: Indiana University Press, 1994.

Cowhig, Ruth. "Blacks in English Renaissance Drama and the Role of Shakespeare's Othello." In *The Black Presence in English Literature*, ed. David Dabydeen, 1–25. Manchester: Manchester University Press, 1989.

Donaldson, Ian. *The Rapes of Lucretia: A Myth and its Transformations*. Oxford: Clarendon Press, 1982.

Fish, Stanley. *Is There a Text in This Class? The Authority of Interpretive Communities*. Cambridge, MA: Harvard University Press, 1980.

Foxon, David. *Libertine Literature in England, 1660–1745*. London: New Hyde Park, 1965.

Frantz, David O. "'Leud Priapians' and Renaissance Pornography." *Studies in English Literature* 12 (1972): 157–72.

———. *Festum Voluptatis: A Study of Renaissance Erotica*. Columbus: Ohio State University Press, 1989.

Freedman, Barbara. *Staging the Gaze: Postmodernism, Psychoanalysis, and Shakespearean Comedy*. Ithaca: Cornell University Press, 1991.

Hall, Kim F. *Things of Darkness: Economies of Race and Gender in Early Modern England*. Ithaca: Cornell University Press, 1995.

Harvey, Gabriel. *Pierce's Supererogation*. In *The Works of Gabriel Harvey*, ed. A.B. Grosart, 3 vols., 2:91–96. London: privately printed, 1884; repr. New York: AMS Press, 1966.

Jacobus, Mary. "Is There a Woman in This Text?" *New Literary History* 14 (1982): 117–54.

Jones, Ann Rosalind, and Peter Stallybrass. *Renaissance Clothing and the Materials of Memory*. Cambridge: Cambridge University Press, 2000.

Jonson, Ben. *Three Comedies: Volpone, The Alchemist, Bartholomew Fair*, ed. Michael Jamieson. Baltimore: Penguin Books, 1966.

Levine, Laura. *Men in Women's Clothing: Anti-Theatricality and Effeminization 1579–1642*. Cambridge: Cambridge University Press, 1994.

Loomba, Ania. *Gender, Race, Renaissance Drama*. Manchester: Manchester University Press, 1989.

Marston, John. *The Scourge of Villanie*. In *The Poems of John Marston, 1575?–1634*, ed. Arnold Davenport, 93–176. Liverpool English Texts and Studies. Liverpool: Liverpool University Press, 1961.

Maus, Katherine Eisaman. "Horns of Dilemma: Jealousy, Gender, and Spectatorship in English Renaissance Drama." *ELH* 54 (1987): 561–84.

McPherson, David. "Aretino and the Harvey-Nashe Quarrel." *PMLA* 84 (1969): 1551–58.

Moulton, Ian. *Before Pornography: Erotic Writing in Early Modern England*. Oxford: Oxford University Press, 2000.

Neely, Carol Thomas. "Women and Men in *Othello*: 'What should such a fool / do with so good a woman?'" In *The Woman's Part: Feminist Criticism of Shakespeare*, ed. Carolyn Ruth Swift Lenz, Gayle Greene, and eadem, 211–39. Urbana: University of Illinois Press, 1980.

Neill, Michael. "Unproper Beds: Race, Adultery, and the Hideous in *Othello*." *Shakespeare Quarterly* 40 (1989): 383–412.

Newman, Karen. "'And Wash the Ethiop White': Femininity and the Monstrous in *Othello*." In *Shakespeare Reproduced: The Text in History and Ideology*, ed. Jean E. Howard and Marion F. O'Connor, 143–62. New York and London: Routledge, 1987.

Parker, Patricia. "Shakespeare and Rhetoric: 'dilation' and 'delation' in *Othello*." In *Shakespeare and the Question of Theory*, ed. eadem and Geoffrey Hartman, 54–74. New York and London: Methuen, 1984.

———. "Fantasies of 'Race' and 'Gender': Africa, Othello, and Bringing to Light." In *Women, "Race," and Writing in the Early Modern Period*, ed. Margo Hendricks and eadem, 84–100. New York and London: Routledge, 1994.

Pechter, Edward. *"Othello" and Interpretive Traditions*. Iowa City: University of Iowa Press, 1999.

Ridley, M. R., ed. *Othello*. The Arden Shakespeare. London: Methuen, 1958; repr. 1960.

Sanders, Norman, ed. *Othello*. New Cambridge Edition. Cambridge: Cambridge University Press, 1984.

Siemon, Jim. "'Nay, that's not next': *Othello*, V.ii. in Performance, 1760–1900." *Shakespeare Quarterly* 37 (1986): 39–51.

Singh, Jyotsna. "Othello's Identity, Postcolonial Theory, and Contemporary African Rewritings of *Othello*." In *Women, "Race," and Writing in the Early Modern Period*, ed. Hendricks and Parker, 287–99.

Talvacchia, Bette. *Taking Positions: On the Erotic in Renaissance Culture*. Princeton: Princeton University Press, 1999.

Vaughan, Virginia Mason. *"Othello": A Contextual History*. Cambridge: Cambridge University Press, 1994.

PART TWO:

VIOLENCE BY WOMEN

"Women are Wordes, Men are Deedes":
Female Duelists in the Drama

The occasional portrayal of women as duelists in early modern English plays would seem to cast doubt on the simplistic proverb in Howell's *Devises*: "Women are wordes, Men are deedes."[1] Although female duelists were almost entirely unknown in the culture of early modern England, there are several notable female fighters in drama, the best known of which is *The Roaring Girl*'s Moll Cutpurse. To some extent, such characters do disprove the old proverb; more exactly, however, they demonstrate the inadequacy of the dichotomy it presents. Deeds and words are not the simple oppositions that the saying offers: they are in fact two poles on a continuum that might be called "action." The relation of word to deed complicates what is accomplished in the duel. Female characters who duel (or who come close to doing so) may engage in a masculine behavior, but they do so in uniquely feminine — specifically didactic and pacific — ways. Once we acknowledge the duel as the complex and meaning-bearing act that it is (a sort of inverse speech-act), we can recognize that female characters who enacted duels

---

[1] Howell, *Devises*, sig. Dii^r. The accompanying verse goes even farther, suggesting that women who do not conform to the rule are abnormal:

> If nought but wordes in women to be founde,
> Then what are they, men, women, or Monsters,
> That yeelde lyke fruite: or else a hollowe sounde,
> Which substance none, but ayre forth utters.
> By deedes and not by words, men praise obtayne,
> Monsters, no men, whose deedes their words doe stayne.

Though the syntax is muddled, the sense is that the "lyke fruite," or deeds, of women indicates the monstrous nature of those women who perform deeds. Incidentally, a variant of the aphorism is still actually a state motto for one of the mid-Atlantic states of the U.S.A. (!).

were performing a different act than were their male counterparts. Their modification of early modern and theatrical dueling practices is part of a subtle redefinition of what it meant to be a woman at that time.

To understand how the duels of female characters deviated from those commonly enacted by male dramatic characters, it is necessary to recognize the distinction between the judicial duel and the duel of honor. The early modern duel of honor derived largely from the medieval legal procedure of the judicial duel, often called trial by combat. Both kinds of duel were highly ritualistic procedures moving from accusation to appointment and thence to the combat.[2] In the judicial duel, the victor's public accusation led to public proof; his physical mastery over the other man combined a prosecutor's presentation of evidence with an executioner's performance of the law's judgment. His victory proved the truth of his statement, whether it consisted of an accusation or the denial of it. The duel of honor, on the other hand, defended one's reputation rather than the factual value of any given statement; it most frequently resulted from the impugning of a man's honor. Winning a duel effectively refuted insult because honor was conceived in part as the spiritual component of physical strength.[3] In the duel of honor, victory signified not "I've proved you wrong," but "I've proved you less worthy than I." What mattered to the duelist was public opinion, not righteousness nor even (sometimes) fact. Nonetheless, the popular conception of the duel of honor was colored by the ritual's legal antecedent, and the significance of the one often bled into the other.

Almost no duels of honor on record in early modern England were fought by women.[4] When women engaged in physical aggression, the commonest form of

---

[2] For excellent explanations of the various aspects of the judicial duel, see Neilson, *Trial by Combat*; Lea, *The Duel and the Oath*; Brown, "Society and the Supernatural"; and Bartlett, *Trial by Fire and Water: The Medieval Judicial Ordeal*. The laws governing the legal use of the judicial duel may be found in Bracton, *De Legibus et Consuetudinibus Angliae*, ed. Woodbine and trans. Thorne, 2:386–388, 390–392, 399–402.

[3] In "Foreign Country: The Place of Women and Sexuality in Shakespeare's Historical World," Phyllis Rackin distinguishes Renaissance notions of gender from our own by characterizing modern gender ideology as "constructed on the basis of physical difference," whereas during the Renaissance "masculine superiority tended to be mystified in the spirit, feminine oppression justified by the subordinate status of the body" (76).

[4] The qualification in this statement depends on the definition of "duel of honor" as well as that of "on record." *The Life of Long Meg of Westminster* recounts an episode in which Meg's mistress, "who had a great delight to be pleasant," persuaded one of her suitors to challenge a man who had insulted her (B4r). This man was a fabrication created by mistress and maid: the mistress invented the man and the insult, and the maid, Long Meg, agreed to dress in masculine clothing and engage in the combat for the fee

their violence, according to court records, was husband-beating.[5] Though the
sheer volume of antifeminist tracts demonstrates the society's patriarchal bias, almost none of them indicates that women were taking up the sword in large
numbers. In *The Instruction of a Christian Woman*, for example, Vives urges
women to abstain from energetic physical activities such as dancing;[6] sword-
fighting never even enters the picture. Only *Hic Mulier* (1620) alludes to women

---

of a new petticoat. Such stories, particularly when they appear in anonymous pamphlets,
may be taken with more than a grain of salt. However, it is a fact that in medieval Germany, Switzerland, and Bohemia, women were legally permitted to engage in the trial by
combat (though they could substitute a [male] champion if they wished instead). The
procedure was complicated by the need to even the odds. This is Lea's account of different regional laws:

> The chances between such unequal adversaries were adjusted by placing the man
> up to the navel in a pit three feet wide, tying his left hand behind his back, and
> arming him only with a club, while his fair opponent [Lea wrote in 1866] had
> the free use of her limbs and was furnished with a stone as large as the fist, or
> weighing from one to five pounds, fastened in a piece of stuff. A curious regula-
> tion provided the man with three clubs. If in delivering a blow he touched the
> earth with hand or arm he forfeited one of the clubs; if this happened thrice his
> last weapon was gone, he was adjudged defeated, and the woman could order his
> execution. On the other hand, the woman was similarly furnished with three
> weapons. If she struck the man while he was disarmed she forfeited one, and
> with the loss of the third she was at his mercy, and was liable to be buried alive.
> According to the customs of Freisingen these combats were reserved for accusa-
> tions of rape. If the man was vanquished, he was beheaded; if the woman, she
> only lost a hand, for the reason that the chances of the fight were against her.
> (*The Duel and the Oath*, 153)

I should point out that rapier-fighting *would* have been easier than sword-fighting for
women if they had only been trained, since the rapier was so much lighter than swords,
clubs, or rocks above a certain size.

[5] In *A Preparative to Marriage*, Henry Smith reiterates the traditional *res/verba*
division: "Husbands must hold their hands and wives their tongues" (58, cited in Henderson and McManus, "The Contexts," in *Half Humankind: Contexts and Texts of the Controversy about Women in England 1540–1640*, ed. Henderson and McManus, 53). For historical perspectives on violent women, see Underdown, "The Taming of the Scold: The
Enforcement of Patriarchal Authority in Early Modern England," 129–32, and Davis,
Society and Culture in Early Modern France, 140–42.

[6] See Vives, *The Education of a Christian Woman* (1540), ed. Fantazzi and Matheeussen, 1: 148–157. Similarly, neither sword- nor rapier-fighting is mentioned by such commentators on female behavior as Robert Cleaver, *A Godly form of Household Government*
(1598); Thomas Becon, *New Catechism* (1564); Joseph Swetnam, *The Arraignment of
Lewd, Idle, Froward, and Inconstant Women* (1615); Samuel Rowlands, *The Bride* (1617);
John Wing, *The Crowne Conjugall* (1632); Alexander Niccholes, *A Discourse of Marriage
and Wiving* (1620); or Thomas Gataker, *Two Marriage Sermons* (1623).

who exchange "for Needles, Swords."[7] This text decries women who "will be manlike not only from the head to the waist, but to the very foot and in every condition: man in body by attire ... man in nature by aptness to anger, man in action by pursuing revenge, man in wearing weapons, man in using weapons."[8] Yet *Hic Mulier* is more concerned with dress than with behavior; the evident focus of the author's anxiety suggests that this passage greatly exaggerates the frequency of the phenomenon described.

Among aristocratic women, training in appropriate behavior would have discouraged any taste for wielding weapons.[9] Like a number of other aggressive sports, fencing endorses the aggressive penetration of the space of others.[10] For a man, to be permeable is to be shamed; to attack and to penetrate, on the other hand, is to dominate other men physically. In contrast, women's training emphasized containment and restraint.[11] Much of the training of the gentlewoman involved the skills of housewifery; yet certain dicta regarding body language and personal space (referring, essentially, to proxemic assumptions) were imposed upon women in order to ensure that they assumed the proper demeanor.[12] Important traits that women were urged to develop included humility, constancy, temperance, and the fear of public shame, tellingly known as "shamefacedness."[13] Overall, many different aspects of female training taught proxemic as-

---

[7] Anon., "Hic Mulier" and "Haec Vir," in *Half Humankind*, ed. Henderson and Mc-Manus, 268.

[8] "Hic Mulier," 270.

[9] Training in the art of fence was available to any man with ready money, since the only qualification needed to take lessons was the ability to pay for them. However, in *Paradoxes of Defence* (1599), George Silver points out that when the Italian fencing-master Signior Rocco founded his fencing school in London, "[h]e taught none commonly under twentie, fortie, fifty, or an hundred pounds" (64).

[10] These assumptions embody some of the assumptions Paster discusses in *The Body Embarrassed: Drama and the Disciplines of Shame in Early Modern England*. Paster's work examines "the subjective experience of being-in-the-body" (2).

[11] Based on her own examination of women's courtesy manuals, Ruth Kelso has asserted that a woman's modesty was indicated in her "behavior, carriage of the body, use of the eyes, gestures, and the choice and wearing of clothes" (*Doctrine for the Lady of the Renaissance*, 25).

[12] Proxemics is a field of sociological inquiry pioneered by Edward T. Hall, the study of "the spaces that people feel it necessary to set between themselves and others as they vary in different social settings, or between different social groups or cultures" (OED).

[13] Kelso quotes Barnaby Rich, who characterizes shamefacedness as "a restraint to withhold [good and virtuous women] from all those artificial abillimentes that do either smell of vanitie or breed suspect of honesty: for Bashfulnes is it that moderates their thoughts, makes them modest in their speaches, [and] temperate in their actions" (Rich,

sumptions directly opposed to those that men learned from fencing. Men of wealth and status learned to manifest assertiveness through their bodies, while women at the same social level were taught to efface themselves physically.[14] Dueling was generally perceived as inconsistent with feminine modesty, a substantial element of feminine honor; as a result, any woman's attempt to eradicate a stain on her honor by means of the duel would have stained her honor a second time by means of the inappropriate recourse she chose.

Even without cultural proscriptions against feminine aggression, women who used blades would have been unusual because the sword was cumbersome and difficult to wield, while the rapier called for specialized training. Moreover, swords of any kind bore a ritual significance unlikely to be prized by anyone whose violence was directed towards a practical end. Some early modern women — most famously Englishwomen Moll Frith and Long Meg — used the sword, and they may even have been trained in its use. These, however, were cross-dressed women — women in male attire.[15] Literal female-to-male impersona-

---

The Excellency of Good Women, 22; quoted in Kelso, *Doctrine for the Lady of the Renaissance*, 43). The French text entitled "Le Doctrinal des Princesses" urges that "if shame does not preside, / Shame has a place and honor is assaulted / Without good deportment" (in *Le Lexique de Jehan Marot*, ed. Trisolini, 94. [Many thanks to Bridget Cowlishaw for the translation.]). Women were taught to keep their eyes downcast; timidity was encouraged and the blush considered a sign of reverence and maidenly virtue. Richard Brathwait's *The English Gentlewoman* urges women to "[be] *still* from the clamours and turbulent insults of the *World*; *still* from the mutinous motions and innovations of the *flesh*" (49; quoted in Ziegler, "My Lady's Chamber: Female Space, Female Chastity in Shakespeare," 86). The body language of the young girl was firmly governed by those in charge of her; conduct books urged that she be trained to stand composedly with her feet together, avoiding unnecessary body-movement (Kelso, *Doctrine for the Lady of the Renaissance*, 50). Her gait should be a medium stride performed "slowly, but not too slowly, lest she be taken to be loitering for a purpose" (Kelso, *Doctrine*, 50). When she dines, "she should sit erect with feet and knees together, to be known as a virgin and not a prostitute" (Kelso, *Doctrine*, 50). These postures entirely eliminate any self-assertiveness expressed through gesture, making the young woman a still figure, an icon rather than a living human being. Art historian Joaneath Spicer asserts that feminine virtues such as containment had their own body language and, in fact, women painted in assertive poses often connoted negative traits, as in allegories of Pride or Vanity ("The Renaissance Elbow," 100).

[14] Many apparently contradictory instances, when women attempted to gain notice, can be understood as occasions that ultimately redounded to the credit of their husbands or their families — conspicuous consumption in finery, for example.

[15] Reliable evidence about these two women is scanty. It would seem, however, that though they became generally known as cross-dressed women, they successfully disguised themselves as men on many occasions, revealing their sex only at the end of such escapades, if at all. Like the women in Dekker and van de Pol's study, these women used

tion was not common during the period, but it was far from unheard-of. Records are inaccurate, of course, because, if successful, the disguise went undetected. However, Rudolf M. Dekker and Lotte C. van de Pol have found one hundred and nineteen cases mentioned in seventeenth- and eighteenth-century Nether-landish documents, and fifty cases in Great Britain during the same period; they consider these cases "the tip of the iceberg."[16] Significantly, Dekker and van de Pol are able to say with certainty, "practically all our disguised women came from the lower classes."[17] Their economic situations militate against the possibility that these women had the equipment or the specialized knowledge needed for the art of fence.

The link suggested in *Hic Mulier*, then, between crossdressing and violence seems to have an underdetermined relation to historical fact. But the text usefully indicates the source of its author's belief in swashbuckling women: it urges its readers not "to believe every vain Fable which you read or to think you may be attired like Bradamant ... that you may fight like Marfiza and win husbands with conquest; or ride astride like Claridiana and make Giants fall at your stir-rups."[18] Romances — fictions — are the culprit. Such texts softened the impact of cross-dressed and physically aggressive women by placing them in the context of the chivalric romance. In these contexts, combat itself bore a different mean-

---

masculine disguise to gain greater freedom, but they did so only periodically, and on spe-cific occasions.

[16] Dekker and van de Pol, *The Tradition of Female Transvestism in Early Modern Eu-rope*, 1, 3. Dekker and van de Pol's study is a fascinating and valuable account of female transvestism during the period. They record that the tradition of female transvestism existed throughout Europe but was strongest in the cold-weather countries of England, Germany, and the Netherlands (2). It was acceptable for women to wear men's clothing for certain restricted periods, as during festivities, often when they were traveling, and sometimes when they were hunting (8). The commonest professions for documented cross-dressed women were those of soldiers and sailors. Natalie Zemon Davis extrapolates from evidence that "[t]he usual stratagem for women who wanted to join an army or a navy in England, France, and the Netherlands was to hide their identity and cross-dress as a man" ("Women in Politics," 168). The women were probably discovered because the close quarters in which soldiers and sailors lived prevented them from concealing their sex forever. It is difficult to tell whether these careers were popular among cross-dressed women or whether they are the ones in which cross-dressers were most frequently dis-covered (Dekker and van de Pol, *Tradition of Female Transvestism*, 9–10).

[17] *Tradition of Female Transvestism*, 11. Many of the women studied by Dekker and van de Pol found that it was easier to get work commonly allotted to adolescent boys than to men because their feminine appearance made them look much younger than men of their own age (15). Most were single and alone in the world, and they found more and better economic opportunities disguised as men than they did as women (32–35).

[18] "Hic Mulier," 271.

ing and the female knight emblematized purity as an aspect of true nobility. But in social practice, the typical fighting woman would have been perceived in just the opposite way.[19]

Given the drama's emphasis on the spoken word, it is not surprising that many early modern plays granted to the duel of honor the significance of the judicial duel. In these cases, the statement that provokes the challenge to the duel serves as a predictive speech act: I name you and proclaim you as traitor (or oath-breaker, liar, or the like). The challenge is both statement and promise: my hand will prove the truth of my refutation upon your body. In other words, both the challenge and the insult that precedes it propose truth-claims which the combat is supposed to prove. In Middleton and Rowley's *A Fair Quarrel*, for example, Captain Ager challenges the Colonel after the Colonel calls Ager "son of a whore." Ager prepares for the combat but stops short when his mother, fearful for his life, pretends that she has indeed been unchaste. Ager goes to the appointed meeting-place to call off the duel but challenges the Colonel again when, responding to his withdrawal, the Colonel calls Ager a coward. That charge is one that Ager believes he can, in conscience, fight against. In other cases, men in the drama fight for vengeance: for example, Clermont fights to avenge the death of his brother Bussy in the less well-known sequel to *Bussy D'Ambois*, *The Revenge of Bussy D'Ambois*.

By contrast, female characters attempt the duel primarily as a didactic device. Even when they are cross-dressed and carrying weapons, they do not imitate man "in action by pursuing revenge"[20] any more than their real-life counterparts did. Paradoxically, their combats are not initiated by the circumstances that prompt male characters to fight; on the contrary, their motive is frequently the same one that prompted duels for men in real life: perceived disrespect towards

---

[19] Elizabeth was wise enough to take full advantage of romance forms when she portrayed herself as a fighting woman, an androgynous ruler, and a woman wedded to her country; Spenser's Britomart and Belphoebe reflect the trend towards mythologizing the ruler. See, among others, Berry, *Of Chastity and Power: Elizabethan Literature and the Unmarried Queen*; Bowman, " 'She There as Princess Rained': Spenser's Figure of Elizabeth"; Cerasano and Wynne-Davies, eds., *Gloriana's Face: Women, Public and Private, in the English Renaissance*; Doran, "Juno versus Diana: The Treatment of Elizabeth's Marriage in Plays and Entertainments, 1561–1581"; Frye, *Elizabeth I: The Competition for Representation*; Levin, *The Heart and Stomach of a King: Elizabeth I and the Politics of Sex and Power*, eadem, "Power, Politics, and Sexuality: Images of Elizabeth I"; Strong, *The Cult of Elizabeth: Elizabethan Portraiture and Pageantry*; Woods, "Spenser and the Problem of Woman's Rule"; and Yates, *Astraea: The Imperial Theme in the Sixteenth Century*.

[20] "Hic Mulier," 270.

them or theirs. Unlike early modern male duelists, however, these female characters approach the duel as a possibility for rehabilitation rather than as an opportunity for punishment. The insults documented as the impetus to the early modern duel seem to intend to humiliate or penalize the addressee for his bad
behavior. In dramatic duels in which women play a part, the women want their
opponents to learn a lesson about respect for others — primarily, respect for "the
weaker sex." Female characters engage in the duel (if they do so at all) with
much less braggadocio than male characters, often agreeing to keep their combat
unknown. Their purpose is not to punish their opponent but to change his view
of what is due to women. In the plays that I shall discuss — Beaumont and
Fletcher's *The Maid's Tragedy*, Heywood's *The Fair Maid of the West*, Middleton
and Dekker's *The Roaring Girl*, and Beaumont and Fletcher's *Love's Cure, Or
The Martial Maid* — women have many different objects in mind when they
step up to the duel. But none are bloodthirsty, like so many male duelists in
early modern drama, and almost none are egotistical, like the general run of
duelists in England at that time. I shall examine the first three plays briefly and
conclude with a longer analysis of *Love's Cure*, in which Clara's approach to the
duel ultimately enables her both to give and to receive instruction in manners.

To an ironic eye, the tragedy of *The Maid's Tragedy* is the lack of self-determination for women in patriarchal societies. But the intended referent of the
title was probably the death of Aspatia, seemingly a secondary character. As the
play's only virgin, the sword-fighting Aspatia must, perforce, be the title figure,
although she is not the main female character. The play opens in Rhodes with
the wedding of Aspatia's former fiancé, Amintor, and Evadne; the king himself
has made the match, having urged Amintor to break off his engagement with
Aspatia. But as Amintor learns from his scornful bride on his wedding night, the
king has urged this action to cover up his own liaison with Evadne. Humiliated,
Amintor nonetheless feels he may not revenge himself upon the monarch. Eventually, Evadne regains a sense of feminine virtue and kills her royal lover, but
Amintor repudiates both her and her action. Meantime, Aspatia, heartbroken at
Amintor's faithlessness to her, disguises herself as her own brother and forces
Amintor into a duel. Once engaged in fighting, however, she remains passive,
and Amintor gives her her death-wound.[21] As she dies, he discovers her identi-

---

[21] This plot twist, which appears in this 1610–1611 play, also appears in Sir Philip
Sidney's *The New Arcadia* in the story of Parthenia, who disguises herself as the Knight
of the Tomb and goes to seek death at the hand of Amphialus, who has killed her husband Argalus in combat (*The Countess of Pembroke's Arcadia [The New Arcadia]*, ed. Skretkowicz, 395–99).

ty and pledges his love once more; he then commits suicide, hoping to join her in death. Howard B. Norland, editor of the Nebraska edition of the play, reads the plot as an indictment of royal absolutism. Of the suicidal Aspatia, he says, "she represents the tragic implications of the king's abuse of his royal prerogative to serve his selfish ends."[22] But the moral action centers on Amintor, and I find Aspatia's duel central to his reeducation in appropriate values.

On his way to his nuptial bed, Amintor receives doleful congratulations from Aspatia. Alone, he tries to dismiss her grief and rationalize his change of affection: "My guilt is not so great / As mine own conscience, too sensible, / Would make me think; I only brake a promise, / And 'twas the king that forc'd me" (2.1.129–132). Amintor refuses responsibility for his change of heart, though he grants, "[the king] had not my will in keeping" (2.1.127). Amintor remains similarly passive throughout the play. He does not force his wife to break off her affair, nor does he take revenge, resolving instead to live as a cuckold. He unintentionally aids Aspatia in her suicide as, almost despite himself, he finds himself engaged in the duel. Though Amintor characterizes his lack of initiative as submission to the king's overriding authority, his pliability throughout the play contrasts with other characters' decisiveness and reveals his rationale as an excuse for inaction.

Aspatia's behavior teaches Amintor, first of all, how to prosecute his own claims. Norland reads Aspatia's behavior as perverse; he calls it "the diseased picture of unrequited love" and refers to her "morbid, self-indulgent grief."[23] I disagree: this Ophelia-figure becomes the moral linchpin of the play. As the forsaken bride, she is the object of considerable audience sympathy. But she cannot derail her fiancé's wedding, and she is socially proscribed from revenge. Given these limitations, Aspatia pursues her course of self-slaughter by means of an *acceptable revenge*. Posing as her brother (away on a military expedition), she challenges the righteousness of Amintor's behavior. Had her brother, the eldest able-bodied male of her family, been in Rhodes, he would have been almost obligated to challenge Amintor's faithlessness; posing as a male, she gains at least the opportunity to do so. To serve as her own champion is in itself not an inconsiderable assertion of will, since women were generally obliged to depend on male relatives to act on their behalf.

---

[22] Introduction to *The Maid's Tragedy*, ed. Norland, xvii. This is also the edition to which my citations of the text refer.

[23] Introduction to *The Maid's Tragedy*, xvii.

Aspatia's donning of masculine garb, her picking up of the sword, could easily have been interpreted as the immodest behavior of a loose woman, particularly since prostitutes were among the most common transgressors of sartorial gender boundaries in early modern England.[24] But Aspatia's refusal to use the sword (logically, she would not have known how to wield it) ensured that she would retain audience sympathy. Yet, though we may now read her behavior as masochistic, we should not perceive it as a parallel to Amintor's passivity. Certainly, since she strikes wide of him but invites his blows, the duel is no contest. But Aspatia's primary purposes are to meet death and to make Amintor understand the results of his compliance: she has no wish to revenge his desertion of her by killing him. She is implicitly contrasted with Evadne, who enters as Aspatia dies to urge Amintor to love her for killing the king. Evadne's regicide is immodest in its aggression, just like the immodesty of her earlier willingness to enter into the affair. Despite the king's corruption, Evadne's regicide is unforgivable. But because Aspatia has neither the intention nor the ability to win this duel, she retains her status as a modest maiden. Amintor shows how greatly he values that quality when, before he dies, he regrets his wrong to Aspatia more than his rejection of Evadne, though that too has resulted in a woman's suicide.

Aspatia's "death by suicide" makes her a morbid heroine. Her choice is difficult for us to read positively. But for a specifically Renaissance audience, it would have linked her with the heroic female suicides of Rome. For us, her suicide is at least a form of self-determination. Despite the paucity of options available to her, Aspatia has not hesitated to pursue her desires as best she can. Until Amintor's marriage, she has tried to influence public opinion in her favor, hoping to sway Amintor by that means; afterward, she seeks death at his hands.

Aspatia instructs Amintor by making him understand that he cannot abdicate responsibility for his actions. She begins by challenging Amintor to the duel on the grounds of "[t]he baseness of the injuries [he] did her" (5.3.58). Before the fight, Amintor acknowledges the justice of the charge, going so far as to say that he will not fight because his conduct has been indefensible (5.3.83–85). But Aspatia urges him on, first striking and then kicking him. Finally, he accepts her challenge and proceeds to the combat. By forcing Amintor physically to kill her, Aspatia literalizes the plight in which his faithlessness had placed her. For a male courtier, breaking a promise at the ruler's behest may be justifiable. But the engagement between Aspatia and Amintor had been a contract that designated

---

[24] Cf. Howard, "Crossdressing, The Theatre, and Gender Struggle in Early Modern England."

her fate: in dissolving it, Amintor denies Aspatia any future in their society, since such a contract is all too close to a marriage. The broken engagement sharply limits any further possibility of another engagement for Aspatia, since it diminishes her value on the marriage market; more importantly, the engagement is clearly regarded by Aspatia as a marriage, a commitment that defines her future. Without it, Aspatia feels that any possible future she can have is no future at all.

Once Amintor realizes the significance of his past actions and whom he has now killed, he realizes what he must do. With Aspatia's body in his arms, he chides himself: "I wrong / Myself, so long to lose her company. / Must I talk now?" (5.3.242–244). With his love for Aspatia renewed, he sees a way both to withdraw from his dishonorable marriage and to rejoin the woman he loves without committing the sin of adultery. Immediately, he stabs himself to death. The heretofore malleable Amintor finally takes decisive and dramatic action, pursuing a course controversial both in his world and in that of the authors. At the end, Amintor takes an active role in deciding his fate.

Moll Cutpurse and Besse Bridges, heroines of *The Roaring Girl* and *The Fair Maid of the West* respectively, differ greatly from Aspatia. In broad terms, one could say that their dramas are part of the *querelle des femmes* tradition.[25] In *The Roaring Girl*, the duel of honor is a persistent theme throughout the first half as a truth test. Though both plays interrogate women's potential (and even, perhaps, the potential of gender categories), they are also largely concerned with the relation between female reputation and female action. In these plays, men use language as a way to control women, whether directly through commands or indirectly through slander. While in reality unprotected women had little recourse if unrelated men attempted to establish an intimacy through these means, both

---

[25] In *Women and the English Renaissance: Literature and the Nature of Womankind, 1540–1620*, Linda Woodbridge seeks "the impact of the formal [*querelle des femmes*] controversy on other genres" (114) and notes that "[t]he literature exactly contemporary with the height of the controversy over women in male attire ... from about 1610 to 1620 ... rejoices in assertive women" (244), but warns that "the connection between literature and life in the Renaissance was oblique rather than direct" (265). I suggest here a rather classic New Historicist move: that these two heroines appeared in plays written and enjoyed partly because they both present and contain dangerous energies. Other critics have noted that Moll Cutpurse seems rather purer than her real-life counterpart, and Besse, despite considerable ability, is entirely submissive to the patriarchal order. The creation of Besse and Moll seems to me to revise earlier stereotypes of the shew. As Shepherd asserts in *Amazons and Warrior Women: Varieties of Feminism in Seventeenth-Century Drama*, esp. 74–81, the presentation of such characters suggests that assertive women may still be rendered "safe."

Besse and Moll resort to the sword to teach importunate men a lesson. When they fight, however, neither Moll nor Besse attempts to prove her worthiness. One heroine would hesitate to believe that feminine worth could be proven by such means; the other has already passed the point where community opinion affects her. Thus, neither one fights her opponent in a competitive spirit; instead, they fight for a reason that seems derived from that of the trial by combat: to reestablish truth. But neither one fights to disprove an accusation against her in particular, as one opponent in the judicial duel would have. Instead, Besse and Moll fight to combat the problems that result when a man looks down on the female sex in general. As these two women are independent (though not necessarily subversive) figures, their combats, while not the focus of these dramas, are significant parts of them.

Besse Bridges, in *The Fair Maid of the West, Or, A Girle worth gold*, is undoubtedly a male fantasy on the order of patient Griselda. Besse waits faithfully for her Spencer to return from his voyage; when false news of his death reaches her, her only desire is to bring his body home to England. As she waits for Spencer, she establishes a thriving business; once she establishes her plan to find Spencer's body, she purchases a ship, hires old (disappointed) suitors as crew, and sails off to Fiall disguised as a man, fighting sea-battles with Spanish warships along the way. Yet Heywood's drama suggests that the great wonder of Besse is not her remarkable accomplishments but her fidelity to the man she loves. On two occasions, men who meet Besse confuse her with Queen Elizabeth, referred to as "the Virgin Queene" (5.1.101). Alluding to Besse's impending conquest of the King of Fesse's affections, the Chorus predicts,

> He sends for her onshore, how he receives her,
> How she and Spencer meet, must next succeed.
> Sit patient, then, when these are fully told,
> Some may hap say, I, there's a Girle worth gold.
>
> (4.12.16–19)[26]

What renders Besse a prototypically biblical "virtuous woman" (with reference to Proverbs 31:10–31) is not her considerable abilities but her chaste nature and charity towards others.

Besse's greatest challenge throughout the play is not so much to attain her goals as to maintain her reputation. From the first, Besse's status is in question;

---

[26] All quotations from this play are from Heywood, *The Fair Maid of the West*, ed. Pearson.

though two captains describe her as sweet, modest, and honest, the unfortunate Caroll comments incredulously, "Honest, and live there? / What, in a publike Taverne, where's such confluence / Of lusty and brave Gallants?" (1.1.32–34). Directly after she becomes Spencer's fiancée, she is insulted by Caroll, who insinuates to Spencer when he finds the two sitting together, "She would draw [no wine] to us, / Perhaps she keepes a Rundlet for your taste, / Which none but you must pierce" (1.7.26–28). When Spencer tells him to mind his manners and says that Besse is worthy to sit with them, Caroll gives him the lie, leading to a duel in which Caroll is slain. Spencer must flee the country, and Besse feels guilty over the death: "My innocence / Hath beene the cause of blood, and I am now, / Purpled with murder, though not within compasse / Of the Lawes severe censure" (1.11.2–5). Besse's virtue is always clear to us, the audience; it is the male characters whose false assumptions must be repeatedly corrected by Besse's actions.[27]

Besse relocates to an inn in Foy which Spencer has given to her. There, as mistress of the establishment, she still must endure the insults of Roughman, a roarer who tells his friend Forset that he must "know of what burden this vessell is ... and til then, I cannot report her for a woman of good carriage" (2.2.3–6). As he himself says, his domineering words are both a test of Besse and a strategy to subordinate her to him. When Roughman blusters, "I tell thee maid, wife, or what e'er thou beest, / No man may enter here but by my leave. / Come, let's be more familiar" (2.2.75–78), Besse shrewdly suspects that his bluster conceals cowardice. After an encounter in which she repeatedly pacifies his choler, she secretly resolves to challenge him. Dressed as her own (fictional) brother, she puts on a sword and challenges Roughman to a duel late at night: "You are a villain, a Coward, and you lie" (2.7.18). More to our surprise than that of Besse, Roughman submits himself immediately, and at her command, he gives up his sword, ties her shoe, and lets her stride over his prone body. She then agrees to spare his life but warns him not to attempt to domineer in Besse's house or threaten her guests, "Which if I ever shall hereafter heare, / Thou art but a dead

---

[27] As Howard points out, "As long as Bess inhabits the tavern world her chastity remains a subject of wonder and doubt" ("An English Lass amid the Moors: Gender, Race, Sexuality, and National Identity in Heywood's *The Fair Maid of the West*," 103). Besse's difficulty is, in fact, the barmaid's dilemma: to keep her customers, she must make the place pleasant to them. The demands of her job guarantee that men will often try to enforce upon her greater intimacy than she is willing to grant. Besse actually manifests a fair degree of rhetorical skill in her ability to keep most men at a distance while making them feel welcome to the inn, but Heywood's plot places more emphasis on the two over-aggressive men with whom Besse's careful rhetoric fails.

man" (2.7.59–60). Yet, believing the encounter unknown to anyone in Foy, Roughman returns to Besse's household and continues his behavior. Finally, Besse shames him publicly: "You base white-lyver'd slave, it was this shooe / That thou stoopt to untie: untrust these points: And like a beastly coward lay lang / Til I stridd over thee. Speake, was't not so?" (3.5.39–42).

Besse follows up this public humiliation with the threat of further violence. Oddly enough, her threat seems to acknowledge the unfitness of a duel for one in women's garb: "Give me that Rapier: I will make thee sweare, / Thou shalt redeeme this scorne thou hast incurr'd, / Or in this woman shape Ile cudgell thee, / And beate thee through the streets" (3.5.45–48). When Besse treats Roughman in a literally man-to-man fashion, he reveals himself as a coward. So she promises to enact traditionally female violence — man-beating — if he does not redeem his cowardice, not by attempting to bully her, but by finding a truer model of manhood.

Besse thus uses three different disciplinary devices, and, though her aims vary, not one is employed to seek vengeance. The initial challenge to combat is a test; revelation of it is a disciplinary device; and the final threat is a didactic device, a sort of Skinnerian negative reinforcement of cowardice.[28] Besse knows from the first that the mastery Roughman attempts to gain over her servants is an oblique strategy towards controlling Besse herself. She does not want to punish him for it but rather to teach him to give up the attempt. The privilege of masculinity that he assumes does not belong to all men, only to Spencer, the man she regards as her husband. Roughman tries to win Besse by acting as though she is his; to disprove his act, she appears as her own male protector. But when Roughman refuses to admit absent authority as legitimate, Besse humiliates him, actually forcing him to confess to his cowardice so that she may, from then on, dominate him. If Roughman cannot be dissuaded from wooing her, he must be emasculated. But Besse uses the combat itself as a warning, not a castration; only when Roughman refuses to change his ways does she use public shame to control him (and further threats to redeem him). Though she wins the duel before it begins, she needs to follow up with a public recital of it to bring it home to her opponent. Besse even states that her original intention is to correct, not punish:

---

[28] Howard's comment on the incident is very telling. She argues that "as a cross-dresser who knows how to wear and use a sword, Bess *could* be that threatening figure from the masculine imagination: the castrating woman who turns the world upside down" ("An English Lass," 105). My point, of course, is that none of the female duelists I discuss turn out to be the castrating woman at all. Howard further argues that Besse's strategy is enacted "to teach a man to be more manly" (105); on that point I disagree.

as "Besse Bridges brother," she urges, "Roughman thou art blest / This day thy life is sav'd, looke to the rest" (2.7.48–49). This correction of manners eventually is supplemented by her correction of fact, which brings him not only to feel shame but also to recognize the respect owed to the woman he patronized before, as the further threat makes him recognize what his mistaken notions of manliness have deserved.

In Heywood's play the combat is ancillary to other concerns, but in *The Roaring Girl* combat serves both as a plot device and more broadly as a symbolic theme. When his father attempts to manipulate Sebastian by complaining of him to friends, the young man regards the ploy as an oblique attack in a fencing bout: "How finely, like a fencer, / My father fetches his by-blows to hit me! / But if I beat you not at your own weapon / Of subtilty —" (1.1.232–235).[29] Sebastian has a strategy in mind, one even more subtle than his father's. But when Sir Alexander refers to Moll as a "naughty pack," suggesting her sexual promiscuity, the rhetorical combat threatens to become literalized: "I say, that tongue / That dares speak so, but yours, sticks in the throat / Of a rank villain: set yourself aside / . . . Any here else had lied" (1.1.262–266). The code of a gentleman forbids Sebastian to challenge his own father's words, but he comes as close as he can to the threat of it. Perhaps the effect may be lessened, however, by his aside before the outburst: "Now is my cue to bristle" (1.1.256). His father responds more to Sebastian's concealed comment than to his open threat: "I'll pierce you deeper yet" (1.1.268). To conceal his desire for Sebastian to make a mercenary match, Sir Alexander plays the part of the neglected father of an unfilial son; to conceal his more serious interest in gentle Mary Fitzallard, Sebastian pretends to a serious love for the cross-dressed Moll. No combat erupts because neither one is as yet deceived by the other; both play instead to the community opinion of Sir Alexander's dinner guests, drawn from the gentry. Neither Sebastian nor Sir Alexander speaks truth since both wish to affect the opinion of their community, the lever with which each hopes to budge the stance of the other. At that point, the implied challenge fades away, suggesting early on that the regard for truth or for honor in this society is not very great.

Trivial causes for anger erupt in this society. A quarrel is hinted at but is effeminately turned aside:

> Goshawk: Thou hast the cowardliest trick. . . . I could find in my heart
> to make a quarrel in earnest.

---

[29] All quotations from this play are taken from Middleton (and Dekker), *The Roaring Girl*, ed. Bullen.

Laxton: Pox, and thou dost — thou knowest I never use to fight with
            my friends — thou'lt lose thy labor in't. (2.1.96–100)

Into this effete and gossipy society comes Moll, wearing a man's jerkin and a
woman's riding skirt, Haec Vir incarnate. Moll has received a great deal of
critical attention in the last twenty years. Many readers have interpreted her as
subversive of the established social order, based on the estimate of her community, which responds primarily to her adoption of men's clothes and secondarily to
her free speech: "This wench ... strays so from her kind / Nature repents she
made her" (1.1.339–340); "Some will not stick to say she is a man. / And some,
both man and woman" (2.1.216–217); "a monster with two trinkets" (2.2.81);
"that bold masculine ramp" (5.2.15).[30] If we listened solely to the play's citizens,
we would believe that no women in early modern London had ever considered
combining masculine and feminine raiment. But as Deborah Jacobs comments,
"At every point in the play where there is a potential debasing of the social
order, the figure of Moll Cutpurse, as an instrument of the state ... deflates
these challenges. The play may, in fact, be staging some sort of resistance, but it
is not written on Moll's body, and it certainly does not triumph."[31] Aside from
the challenge to received mores accomplished by her clothing choice, Moll enforces rather than subverts traditional society. She plays the part of Plautus's
clever servant, aiding Sebastian and Mary Fitzallard in their thwarting of the
blocking father-figure. She saves a spendthrift from false arrest and forces two
petty criminals to confess their tricks to the gentlemen in her company. As Jean
Howard comments, "it is not always perfectly clear that [Moll] embodies a consistent social philosophy or class-gender position."[32]

But Moll *is* interested in improving the lot of other women. Though she
tosses off a neat couplet on her willingness to aid gentlemen in scrivener's bands

---

[30] See, for example, Comensoli's discussion of Moll's "boldly unconventional nature"
("Play-making, Domestic Conduct, and the Multiple Plot in *The Roaring Girl*"); Rose's
assertion that Moll is "an embodiment of female independence boldly challenging established social and sexual values and, by the fact of her existence, requiring evaluation and
response" ("Women in Men's Clothing: Apparel and Social Stability in *The Roaring Girl*,"
368); Dollimore's argument that "the representation of gender inversion generates an interrogation of both the sexual metaphysic and the social order" ("Subjectivity, Sexuality,
and Transgression: The Jacobean Connection," 65); and Howard's comment that the play
is "traversed by discourses of social protest not found in most of the plays I have so far
examined" ("Crossdressing, the Theatre, and Gender Struggle," 436).

[31] "Critical Imperialism and Renaissance Drama: The Case of *The Roaring Girl*," 78.

[32] "Crossdressing, the Theatre, and Gender Struggle," 438.

(set down for debt), her primary concern is to lessen society's misogyny. On four different occasions, she speaks of the peculiar wrongs of woman in London society, saving her greatest exasperation for male gossips who ruin the reputations of chaste women: "How many are whores in small ruffs and still looks! / How many chaste whose names fill Slander's books! .... a fencer may be called a coward; is he so for that?" (5.1.357–367). Moll's point is that gossip feeds on falsehood.[33] To trust it is to be deceived; to spread it is to be a liar. Gossip is particularly pernicious because it seems not to originate with any single person and therefore cannot be stopped. But Moll warns her acquaintances not to trust gossip, which wrongs more people than it characterizes truly. For women, as she points out, gossip is particularly harmful because rumors of unchastity may ruin a woman's life. Moll herself is another story: "Perhaps for my mad going some reprove me; / I please myself, and care not who love me" (5.1.360–361).

Moll's duel is prompted by the arrogant and sexist assumptions of Laxton, the gallant who, upon making her acquaintance, attempts to buy sex from her. His apparent delicacy enables her to avoid the use of falsehood when she plans to teach him a lesson. He begs, "Let's meet," and Moll accedes: " 'Tis hard but we shall meet, sir" (2.1.297–298). Laxton, however, expects to meet for purposes of fornication; Moll intends to meet for combat. Upon their meeting, Laxton does not recognize her; she is dressed as a man. Moll responds to his amazement with a promise: "I'll swear you did not [know me]; but you shall know me now" (3.1.57). Moll's triple pun plays on Laxton's continued failure to understand Moll's virtuous character. As she agrees that he has not recognized her, he understands her to mean that he shall gain carnal knowledge of her; in fact, her intention is to teach him more about what kind of person she is.[34]

When Moll offers to match Laxton's prostitute's fee in a wager as to who will win their combat, she also explains her intentions: "To teach thy base thoughts manners: thou'rt one of those / That thinks each woman thy fond flexible whore; / If she but cast a liberal eye upon thee" (3.1.72–74). In a lengthy speech, Moll strongly condemns men who assume that a friendly woman is a loose one; she criticizes men who make their reputations by telling other men about fictional conquests of real women. Equally, she condemns those who seduce virtuous women in financial straits, women who feel they cannot afford to deny their se-

---

[33] In his Introduction to *The Roaring Girl* by Middleton and Dekker, Mullholland touches briefly on this point (29–30).

[34] Rose notes the first two of these three meanings ("Women in Men's Clothing," 381).

ducers. She challenges Laxton to justify his assumption that he could buy her favors and tells him, "In thee I defy all men, their worst hates / And their best flatteries" (3.1.93–94). In this play, in which the secondary plot depicts a war of merchant wives and gallants against merchant husbands, Moll's duel brings word and deed together. But though Moll threatens to "write so much / Upon thy breast, 'cause thou shalt bear't in mind . . . I scorn to prostitute myself to a man," she does not actually do so (3.1.109–112). Instead, she uses the duel to teach Laxton a lesson *by means of* her conquest. Upon Laxton's submission, Moll threatens to kill him, forcing him to try various formulae to assuage her wrath:

> "I do repent me; hold!" (3.1.117)
> "I ask thee pardon." (3.1.121)
> "I yield both purse and body." (3.1.122)
> "Spare my life!" (3.1.125)

When Laxton begs for his life, taking Moll as seriously as he would a man, she treats him according to the code between gentlemen.[35] When he appeals to her mercy, on the other hand, she shows none. Moll's intention is to return Laxton to true dealing. Their combat, as she says, gives Laxton a "true" knowledge of her. Indeed, their fight is (for her, at least) a return to the truth, since she brings him to the dueling field through subterfuge.

Unlike Moll, Clara, the heroine of Beaumont and Fletcher's comedy *Love's Cure, or, The Martial Maid*, seems at first not to fit the pattern of the woman who duels with a didactic purpose. Clara approaches fighting with a masculine appetite for the sport; certainly, she gives it up reluctantly. Yet, like Aspatia in *The Maid's Tragedy*, Clara eventually proposes to enact the duel as a means of self-slaughter. Despite (or perhaps because of) these odd plot twists, *Love's Cure* concludes by subverting gender constructions of the period more effectively than even *The Roaring Girl* does. In threatening the enactment of a duel, Clara forces upon the men in the play a new perception of their role as representatives of their families. Of the female duelists I discuss here, Clara is the figure whose action most clearly alters the community's understanding of gender. By bringing together *virtus* and *eros*, Clara suggests the possibility of a more flexible role for both sexes. Cross-dressed from childhood, Clara first appears as a Britomart figure who fights with her suitor rather than searching for him as Britomart does.

---

[35] See Mullholland's brief discussion of this scene and its relation to a parallel incident in the anonymous jest-biography *Long Meg of Westminster* ("Introduction" to *The Roaring Girl*, 15–16).

But Clara becomes most powerful when she changes her trousers for a dress, uniting what the playwrights characterize as masculine force and feminine gentleness.

As the play begins, the noble Clara, raised as a boy in the Spanish camps of the Eighty Years' War, returns with her father (Don Alvarez) to their native Seville. Their presence completes the household of her mother Eugenia and her younger brother Lucio, who has been raised in Seville as a girl in order to protect him from the family's enemies. After a joyful reunion, the parents pledge to restore both children to a proper sense of gender. Comic complications occur when Clara falls in love with the family's enemy, Vitelli, a man both attracted and repelled by her skill at swordsmanship; her brother Lucio eventually becomes infatuated with this man's sister.

Though Don Alvarez and his elder child are mentioned in the play's opening, they do not appear onstage until Scene 3. Clara's entrance at that point is clearly meant to disorient the audience. Wearing male attire, she is addressed by her father: "My loved Clara ... Lucio is a name thou must forget / With Lucio's bold behavior" (1.3.257–259).[36] While Clara has now resumed her female name, she has not yet returned to female clothing. A brawl with Vitelli breaks out before Don Alvarez and his wife have exchanged more than a few words, and Clara and her father both draw their swords to fight. Only when the victory is won does Don Alvarez have the opportunity to present this swordsman to his wife. He reassures Eugenia, saying, "to increase thy comfort, know, this young man ... / Is not what he appears, but such a one / As thou with joy wilt bless — thy daughter Clara" (1.3.395–398). Perplexity among audience members would be understandable, to say the least.

Clara causes gender confusion entirely different from that of Middleton and Dekker's Moll. Though Moll is described as a monster, she is supposed to be easily recognized as a woman character.[37] Moll fashionably combines men's and women's clothing (like the women at whom *Hic Mulier* is aimed). Clara's disguise is meant to be complete: she effectively impersonates a man. Unlike Moll,

---

[36] All quotations from this play are from Beaumont and Fletcher, *Love's Cure Or, The Martial Maid*, ed. Mitchell.

[37] Both Rose ("Women in Men's Clothing," 367) and Howard ("Crossdressing, the Theatre, and Gender Struggle," 436) make much of this aspect of *The Roaring Girl*. While it is true that there are a number of disguised women in early modern drama, the fact that Clara would prefer to continue her life as a man indefinitely suggests to me that the playwrights actually characterize her not even as a man–woman or hermaphrodite but rather as a woman who has *crossed over* into masculinity — a cultural transsexual, if you will. I would argue that this aspect of Clara's identity renders her portrayal even more subversive than Moll's.

Clara has no wish to confuse others by dressing or acting anomalously; with her father's endorsement, she has dressed and acted as a man for sixteen years. Clara accepts the ideology that keeps the sexes separate; she simply wants to continue passing as a man. As the action moves inevitably towards a showdown between Vitelli and a member of the Alvarez family, the play pointedly asks how Clara can return to heterosexual womanhood and still continue to defend her family.

Clara's initial problem with a woman's role is comic: a man's social rank, his bearing and standing in the world, are much more fluid than that of his female counterpart. Raised as a male in a battlecamp, Clara has become a soldier. Despite her one impassioned speech about gentlemen's honor, Clara comprehends her masculine role in a way that was becoming increasingly outdated in Jacobean society.[38] She is bluff, outspoken, distrustful of courtiers, and constantly mindful of the battlefield. Her behavior makes her a fine companion among men but fits her for no corresponding female role. When she reverts to women's costume, she must learn to behave appropriately to her rank. Born not only a woman but a lady, she finds that her soldierly habits translate to a lack of gentility when she aspires to womanhood.

Clara's love for Vitelli enables her to find an appropriate mode of behavior. The use of Petrarchan rhetoric throughout the play serves as an index to the changing merits of *eros* and *virtus*. When Vitelli anticipates the return of Alvarez and his child at the play's opening, he imagines his hatred of the family as a hawk that slept while no male Alvarez lived in Seville:

> But now, since there are quarries worth her sight ...
> I'll boldly cast her off, and gorge her full
> With both their hearts. (1.1. 124–127)

The image mimics the Petrarchan trope of love's quarry. Vitelli literalizes the trope of love as pursuit, turning it into a literal hunt with the intent to wound or kill. The imagery is undercut by parody in the next scene, which opens with the cross-dressed Lucio's domestic concern for the care of his mother's poultry. Yet the violence of Vitelli's appetites cannot be tamed by Lucio's domesticity; in this society, male and female are polarized to such dangerous extremes that Clara

---

[38] Rather amusingly, this element of the plot brings changes on a stage convention commonly used in the depiction of *male* soldiers. In her chapter on the stage misogynist, Woodbridge comments on "a figure from the debate about changing sex roles in peacetime — the soldier who returns to find his martial masculinity inappropriate in a civilian world where women's tastes and values prevail" (*Women and the English Renaissance*, 278–79).

and Lucio may be recognized early on as *pharmakoi* that cure the community. Violence and sex are conjoined in the masculine sphere and need tempering by the feminine.

Clara eventually develops a playful Petrarchism that metaphorizes her former life on the field of battle, and she consciously develops both feminine rhetorical skill and a new concept of honor. But at first she also literalizes Petrarchan tropes, though she regards *eros* as a weakness, something to be treated with contempt. Her evident satisfaction at being the inflicter of wounds is comical, especially when her too literal account of her experiences causes Lucio to remonstrate at her language:

> Clara: [W]ith that [sword], and this well-mounted, skirred
>   A horse troop through and through, like swift desire,
>   And seen poor rogues retire all gore, and gashed
>   Like bleeding shads.
> Lucio: Bless us, sister Clara,
>   How desperately you talk. (2.2.751–755)

Clara conceives herself as being as speedy and overpowering as desire, love's arrow. She effeminizes the enemy, gashing them open to bleed like fish on a hook. Lucio, already feminized, finds these images frightening: they suggest men with a lack, an absence, their power gone.

When Clara first enters the stage, she reveals the contempt of the old military aristocrat for the new man. Alvarez's response indicates the problem that will result: "My loved Clara ... though thy breeding / I' the camp may plead something in the excuse / Of thy rough manners, custom having changed, / Though not thy sex, the softness of thy nature ... Yet now [Fortune] smiles" (1.3.257–267). Though a gentleman may behave boldly, harshly, even roughly without impropriety, a woman who does so is judged unwomanly, and in so doing she loses caste.[39] Social rank is the unspoken concern of the play. Alvarez's wife is named

---

[39] In *Still Harping on Daughters: Women and Drama in the Age of Shakespeare*, 51–57, Jardine points out that the popularity of humanist education for gentry and noblewomen may perhaps be explained by its use in indoctrinating women into the values of obedience, modesty, and chastity. Nearly all scolds who were publicly shamed belonged to small towns and wood-pasture villages (Underdown, "The Taming of the Scold," 134). There is some indication that gentlewomen and noblewomen were more carefully trained in subordination than were women of lower rank, who also had a greater measure of economic independence from men.

Eugenia, from the Greek, meaning "well-born." Until Vitelli's sister, Genevora, is introduced late in the play, the young woman who serves as an implicit contrast to Clara is Malroda, Vitelli's mistress. Malroda repeatedly charges Vitelli with having taken not her virginity but her respectability. Although the axis of gender is placed in the foreground, rank inflects the various representations of gender.

When Clara is still dressed in masculine garb, she shows a confident understanding of social codes. But as a woman, Clara acts in ways that consistently misplace her on the scale of social rank. Dressed in women's attire, she hums a martial air, casually proposes to fence with her brother, complains of her confining skirts, and permits without reproof her servant Bobadilla's crude joke about women's buttocks. When Bobadilla echoes her disdain for overly formal courtiers, we must acknowledge that her socialization seems more in keeping with that of her servant than with her own standing as a gentlewoman. Losing her temper with Bobadilla, she addresses him as "You dogskin-faced rogue, pilcher, you poor John, / Which I will beat to stockfish" (2.2.732–733). These piscatory terms of opprobrium are common in Shakespeare's scenes of servant- and tavern-life; compare them to Malroda's entirely womanly and high-styled rage:

> Leave your betraying smiles,
> And change the tunes of your enticing tongue
> To penitential prayers; for I am great
> In labour even with anger, big with child
> Of woman's rage, bigger than when my womb
> Was pregnant by thee. (3.3.1161–1166)

Malroda's anger, like Clara's, manifests a clear sense of gendered power relations, but her choice of words shows her drawing on a source of woman's strength — the womb — to convey with dignity her elemental anger at the inequity of their positions. Clara's language, on the other hand, is ridiculous without her possession of the phallus (represented by the sword) that is implicitly compared with a lack on the part of the addressee. Malroda rails in a way appropriate to a lady of high rank; Clara, in a way common to men who own nothing beyond the power of the phallus. The contrast indicates that Clara needs, not a phallus, but rather a better understanding of linguistic codes.

When Clara falls in love, she recognizes intuitively that she must play a game both like and unlike that of war: "I begin to find / I am a woman, and must learn to fight / A softer, sweeter battle, than with swords" (2.2.875–877). Vitelli first responds to Clara's swordsmanship with admiration for her as a woman: "Oh you the fairest soldier I e'er saw; / Each of whose eyes, like a bright beamy shield / Conquers without blows, the contentious" (2.2.801–803). As Malroda later explains, Vitelli is an experienced seducer. Clara can hardly win him with threats of force; yet her rhetorical power is insufficient to sway him from his intention to kill her male relatives. Ruefully, Vitelli warns her of his intentions: "[H]e, whose tongue thus gratifies the daughter / And sister of his enemy, wears a sword / To rip the father and the brother up" (2.2.814–816). Clara refuses the traditional women's role to which he would assign her; when he begs for a token to remember her by, she urges their triviality:

> Vitelli: A ribbon or a glove.
> Clara: Nay, those are tokens for a waiting maid
>   To trim the butler with.
> Vitelli: Your feather.
> Clara: Fie; the wenches give them to their serving men.
>   (2.2.839–842)

Clara's gift refigures both Vitelli's Petrarchan rhetoric and his urges to phallic violence. She gives him her much-prized sword, urging him to recognize the implications of receiving this gift as a love-token:

> Oh, this favour I bequeath you, which I tie
> In a love-knot, fast, ne'er to hurt my friends;
> Yet be it fortunate 'gainst all your foes . . .
> As e'er it was to me. I have kept it long,
> And value it, next my virginity. (2.2.860–865)

When Clara realizes what gift would be appropriate, she speaks lovingly but with authority; at this point she combines and redefines *eros* and *virtus*, using Vitelli's desire for a favor to bridge the gulf between them. Rather than hoping to overcome his wish for vengeance with physical or rhetorical force, she takes the opportunity to set up a counter-custom with meanings that must reverse his plan to murder her father. This initial maneuver is successful. Vitelli responds, "I'll not infringe an article of breath / My vow has offered to ye" (2.2.870–871).

In giving Vitelli her sword, Clara both literally and symbolically divests herself of violence and phallic power. Handing over her manhood to Vitelli, Clara transforms it from a killing weapon to a love-token, forcing Vitelli to redefine what he may do as a man if he wants to enact the role of lover. From this point, Clara moves steadily toward revising less the notion of femininity (as she has before) than the notion of masculinity. In so doing, she satisfies society by conforming to accepted notions of womanhood; at the same time, she weakens the link between violence and masculinity derived from the military elite community of late medieval feudalism.

When Clara and Vitelli next meet, Clara has just witnessed the attempted robbery of Vitelli by his mistress and her lover. After chasing them away, Clara speaks with consummate tact: she apologizes "[f]or pressing thus beyond a virgin's bounds / Upon [his] privacies" (4.2.559–560). This done, the two frankly negotiate the question of marriage. Vitelli explains his fear of being mastered by Clara, at which point she gives up more than her sword:

> from this hour
> I here abjure all actions of a man,
> And will esteem it happiness from you
> To suffer like a woman. . . .
> I will show strength in nothing but my duty
> And glad desire to please you. (4.2.1587–1595)

With her pledge of subordination, Vitelli capitulates as well, whimsically sealing their vows with a kiss and a comment on Clara's hermaphroditic qualities: "Madam, though you have / A soldier's arm, your lips appear as if / They were a lady's" (4.2.1601–1603).

Clara's capitulation may seem to contemporary readers an unnecessary lowering of herself. But if we accept the play's presentation of Vitelli as inherently desirable, we must recognize why Clara must renounce her martial skills and masculine ways.[40] Clara unsettles Vitelli's gender assumptions but cannot entirely overturn them. When Malroda loses her temper, curses Vitelli, and threatens to pistol him, he shows none of the admiration that he had for Clara's swordsmanship. Instead, he threatens to have her placed in a house for Magdalens and warns her that his willingness to maintain her financially depends on her docility (3.3.1226–1229). Vitelli places Malroda in a double-bind: he has promised to love her only so long as she remains subordinate to his wishes. For her to complain of his treatment, even with just cause, is to break her bond and forfeit his regard. According to his definition, she has no recourse at all in case of ill-treatment. Though she may make some headway with the grandeur of her angry speech, any threat of real violence from her is unacceptable. Clara is potentially much more dangerous: Malroda's threat of physical violence is laughable, whereas Clara could indeed carry out such a threat. Though Clara's charm for him is in her Amazonian quality, her hermaphroditic blending of masculine

---

[40] In "*Hic Mulier*: The Female Transvestite in Early Modern England," Lucas rightly, I think, suggests that Clara's promise recalls a scene in *The Life and Pranks of Long Meg of Westminster* (1582) when Long Meg submits to her new husband's beating rather than choosing to fight with him. Both scenes "allay . . . the anxieties about the bellicose female transvestite who attacks men" (79).

and feminine, Vitelli fears to take on any role toward her but that of conquering Theseus.

Even after her new vow, however, Clara never perceives herself as a subjugated warrior. Aware that love is a "softer, sweeter battle" than war, she works within her self-imposed constraints to master Vitelli without resorting to the superior swordsmanship that would shame him to acknowledge. The play comes to a climax with the showdown between the noble houses of Alvarez and Vitelli. Now an enemy to bloodshed, Clara must dissuade her father, brother, and lover from killing one another. When the king's proclamation authorizes a duel to settle the two families' feud for good, Clara develops a strategy that seeks to redefine manhood and honor. In this plan, Clara is aided by Genevora, Vitelli's sister, whose traditional femininity has inspired Clara's effeminate brother to discover traditionally masculine traits within himself.

Simon Shepherd has argued that, in contrast to Clara's more serious problems, "Lucio's training in manhood is comic and grotesque."[41] That assertion is, I think, untrue. As Clara has been the avatar of aristocratic manhood at the play's opening, Lucio assumes that mantle by the play's end. Lucio's lust for Genevora, Vitelli's sister, aids him in the development of a sense of masculinity: "My poor womanish soul, which hitherto hath governed / This coward flesh, I feel departing from me; / And in me by [Genevora's] beauty is inspired / A new and masculine one, instructing me / What's fit to do or suffer" (4.4.1798–1802). The result is that he, not Clara, fights a duel. He seeks out Lamorall, Genevora's suitor, who has threatened him and taken Genevora's glove from him, and challenges him for possession of it. In the process of the duel he also wins Lamorall's sword, so symbolic of manhood that Lamorall begs him to take his life as well. In response, Lucio offers his own sword as a token of friendship. He takes only the favor in sign of victory, asking merely to be regarded as an equal.

Genevora's influence over Lucio's masculinity is most salutary in its effect upon his understanding of honor. After winning the duel, Lucio condemns the widespread custom of publicly proclaiming his own victory: "I have no tongue to trumpet mine own praise / To your dishonour: 'tis a bastard courage / That seeks a name out that way, no true born one" (5.1. 1888–1890). By promising not to publicize his own triumph, Lucio trumps Lamorall a second time. His decision creates a new definition of manhood that places private merit above reputation. In doing so, he redefines masculinity according to the model of Castiglione's courtier rather than according to the old military ideal. This very con-

---

[41] Shepherd, *Amazons and Warrior Women*, 88.

sonance with the courtly ideal, however, could be read as a masculine mode already modified by feminine values because of its devaluation of public opinion. Whatever their significance, these new ideals are vanquished as soon as Lucio's father acknowledges him and suggests that they stand together in a public duel. Family allegiance gains priority over newer conceptions of masculine honor.

Surprisingly, the protocols of the duel receive negative comment from most of Alvarez's former comrades-in-arms. His friend Sayavedra perceives the legal duel as lowering men to the level of beasts; he calls it "[b]eyond the bounds of Christianity" (5.3.2046). Clara, too, regards this practice as more bloodthirsty than honorable.

Clara's initial address to the men relocates the issue of social construction by applying it to the tradition of the duel. Who better than Clara could recognize that social practice does not offer universal rules? She urges that if she could discard the male clothing she had grown accustomed to, then Vitelli too could overcome the urgings of custom and lay aside his vendetta for her sake. Arguing that "[c]ustom, that wrought so cunningly on nature / In me, that I forgot my sex . . . You did unweave" (5.3.2097–2100), she implies, as Hic Mulier says, that "[c]ustom is an idiot." Reinforcing Clara's argument, Genevora attempts to recast valor as moral courage: "he is most valiant / That herein yields first" (5.3.2148– 2149). To no avail; the men remain obdurate in their decision to duel.

Finally, the Assistant asks, "Are you men or stone?", to which Alvarez replies, "Men, and we'll prove it with our swords" (5.3.2179–2180). Men, as opposed to stones, have feelings, may respond to reason, and may answer appeals. What aspect of manhood does Alvarez plan to prove? Swordsmanship proves the capacity of men to inflict pain, to conquer, to subdue others. Clearly, to alter the course of events, the women must conquer their menfolk. Yet the method must avoid brute force, despite the fact that Clara may be the best swordsman of either family. Were she physically to subdue the men, she would inspire such unease in Vitelli that she might lose his affections. Her solution must conquer the men without resorting to physical means.

Following Clara's plan, Genevora resorts to their final strategy: she promises, "The first blow given betwixt you, sheaths these swords / In one another's bosoms" (5.3.2184–2185). The two women stand poised, each with a rapier pointed at the other. Their tableau stops the proceedings short. The strategy succeeds, according to Jonathan Dollimore, because it short-circuits the homosocial uses that the men have been making of the women:

> the currents of sexuality and violence, circulating between the men and sustaining sexual difference between male and female, are suddenly

switched off. .... If [the women] die the most necessary spectators and objects of masculine performance disappear. Also ... men become redundant as the women threaten to perform phallic violence on themselves in order to forestall male violence.[42]

I offer a different interpretation: far from making men redundant, the women's pledge to kill one another holds up to the men a mirror of their senseless violence, showing its failure to make good on several of the premises underlying it. First, the men's decision to fight has been based on the assumption that the duel will bring honor to the winners and shame to the losers. In contrast, the women's suicide pact promises that both parties will die, thereby transforming "loss" into honorable martyrdom. Yet the pointlessness of the pact makes it monstrous, just as the pointlessness of the duel makes it barbaric. In forming the pact, the women also criticize the men's desire for honor, recalling Lucio's comment two scenes earlier that " 'tis a bastard courage / That seeks a name out that way" (5.1.1889–1890). The pact undermines the notion that the men can prove their manhood through enacting the duel: as the women demonstrate, the willingness to risk death is not an exclusively male prerogative. If women too die in "combat," how can that combat define or indicate one's masculinity?

Finally, the women's pledge reminds the men of the aspect of honor that they have neglected: protection of the family. The strategy places the men in a domestic rather than a public context once again, and redefines manhood as a regard for one's relatives. If Vitelli causes his sister's death in order to avenge his uncle, what has he gained? The proof of manhood is rooted in defense of the family, on which this vendetta and the proposed duel are based. If the duel results in the destruction of the family, then it no longer serves its intended purpose. Once the family refuses to be defended on these terms, the men must discard the concept of honor that has compelled them to ignore reason, break promises, and discard the appeals of those they love. Though the women's gesture may be called masochistic in that they promise to turn their violence upon themselves rather than on their men, the gesture is never put to the test. It remains rhetorical, a manipulative device whose certain success means that they will never have to perform what they have pledged. After considering their options, the menfolk give up the combat and own themselves beaten by people more resolute than their opponents: in Alvarez's words, "These devilish women

---

[42] Dollimore, "Subjectivity, Sexuality, and Transgression," 74.

/ Can make men friends and enemies when they list" (5.3.2192–2193). Clara's strategy has succeeded, and *eros* has been wedded to *virtus* at last.

In each of the plays I have discussed, the female duelist instructs her antagonist by offering to become his opponent. From our vantage point, of course, the opponent is generally a representative of the larger system to which these women are responding; in fact, such an interpretation may not be altogether anachronistic. Because of its ritual qualities, the duel could never serve merely as a fight on formal terms. It always bore some larger significance, offering a subtle commentary on the character of those who engaged in it. Even in the drama, the women who duel are seldom isolated, aberrant cross-dressers like the independent Moll. Most play a leading part in the heterosexual love-stories that are commonly a focus in their plays. These active and enterprising figures break down the dichotomy offered in the proverb with which I began. Women who duel may use the sword in addition to their tongues but, even if their medium is action, they continue to try to say something through their performance. Perhaps this communicative aspect may be owed to the biases of the male playwrights who created these characters; it is, however, a characterization that grants women a degree of independent agency. By the very lack of innovation in their portrayal of women, these plays do, to a small degree, present the possibility of broader definitions of gender roles. They restructure the negative portrayal of gender fluidity found in *Hic Mulier* and *Haec Vir*, and in doing so they offer an alternative to the extreme polarization of the sexes evident in those and many other popular documents of the period.

Jennifer Low
Florida Atlantic University

Works Cited

Bartlett, Robert. *Trial by Fire and Water: The Medieval Judicial Ordeal*. Oxford: Clarendon Press, 1986.

Bauer, Dale M., and Susan Janet McKinstry, eds. *Feminism, Bakhtin, and the Dialogic*. Albany: State University of New York Press, 1991.

Beaumont, Francis, and John Fletcher. *Love's Cure Or, The Martial Maid*, ed. Marea Mitchell. Nottingham: Nottingham Drama Texts, 1992.

———. *The Maid's Tragedy*, ed. Howard B. Norland. Lincoln, NE: University of Nebraska Press, 1968.

Berry, Philippa. *Of Chastity and Power: Elizabethan Literature and the Unmarried Queen*. London: Routledge, 1989.

Bowman, Mary R. " 'She There as Princess Rained': Spenser's Figure of Elizabeth." *Renaissance Quarterly* 43 (1990): 475–502.

Bracton, Henry de. *De Legibus et Consuetudinibus Angliae*, ed. G. E. Woodbine, trans. S. E. Thorne. 2 vols. Cambridge, MA: Belknap Press, 1968.

Brathwait, Richard. *The English Gentleman*. London: John Haviland, 1630, STC 3563, repr. Amsterdam: Theatrum Orbis Terrarum, 1975.

Bremmer, Jan, and Herman Roodenburg, eds. *A Cultural History of Gesture*. Ithaca, NY: Cornell University Press, 1991.

Brink, Jean R., Allison P. Coudert, and Maryanne C. Horowitz, eds. *The Politics of Gender in Early Modern Europe*. Kirksville, MO: Sixteenth Century Journal Publications, 1989.

Brown, Peter. "Society and the Supernatural: A Medieval Change." *Daedalus* 104 (1975): 133–51; repr. in idem, *Society and the Holy in Late Antiquity*, 302–32. Berkeley: University of California Press, 1982.

Cerasano, S. P., and Marion Wynne-Davies, eds. *Gloriana's Face: Women, Public and Private, in the English Renaissance*. Detroit: Wayne State University Press, 1992.

Comensoli, Viviana. "Play-making, Domestic Conduct, and the Multiple Plot in *The Roaring Girl*." *Studies in English Literature, 1500–1900* 27 (1987): 249–66.

Davis, Natalie Zemon. "Women in Politics." In *A History of Women: Renaissance and Enlightenment Paradoxes*, ed. eadem and Arlette Farge, 167–83. Cambridge, MA: Belknap Press, 1993.

———. *Society and Culture in Early Modern France*. Stanford: Stanford University Press, 1965.

de Certeau, Michel. *The Practice of Everyday Life*, trans. Steven Randall. Berkeley: University of California Press, 1984.

Dekker, Rudolf M., and Lotte van de Pol. *The Tradition of Female Transvestism in Early Modern Europe*. New York: St. Martin's Press, 1989.

De Lauretis, Teresa. "The Violence of Rhetoric: Considerations on Representation and Gender." In eadem, *Technologies of Gender: Essays on Theory, Film, and Fiction*, 31–50. Bloomington: Indiana University Press, 1989.

Dickenson, John. *Greene in Conceit: New Raised from his Grave to Write the Tragic History of Fair Valeria of London*. London: R. Bradocke, 1598. STC 6819.

Dod, John and John Cleaver. *A Godly Forme of Houshold Government*. London, 1630.

Dollimore, Jonathan. "Subjectivity, Sexuality, and Transgression: The Jacobean Connection." *Renaissance Drama* 17 (1986): 53–81.

Doran, Susan. "Juno versus Diana: The Treatment of Elizabeth's Marriage in

Plays and Entertainments, 1561–1581." *Historical Journal* 38 (1995): 257–74.

Fletcher, Antony, and John Stevenson, eds. *Order and Disorder in Early Modern England.* Cambridge: Cambridge University Press, 1985.

Frye, Susan. *Elizabeth I: The Competition for Representation.* New York: Oxford University Press, 1993.

Henderson, Katherine Usher, and Barbara F. McManus, eds. *Half Humankind: Contexts and Texts of the Controversy about Women in England, 1540–1640.* Urbana: University of Illinois Press, 1985.

Hendricks, Margo, and Patricia Parker, eds. *Women, "Race," and Writing in the Early Modern Period.* New York: Routledge, 1994.

Heywood, Thomas. *The Fair Maid of the West, Or, A Girle Worth Gold.* In *The Dramatic Works of Thomas Heywood,* London: G. Pearson, 1874; repr. ed. John Pearson. 6 vols. 2:255–331. New York: Russell and Russell, 1964.

"Hic Mulier" and "Haec Vir." In *Half Humankind: Contexts and Texts of the Controversy about Women in England, 1540–1640,* ed. Katherine Usher Henderson and Barbara F. McManus, 264–76; 277–89. Urbana: University of Illinois Press, 1985.

Howard, Jean E. "Crossdressing, the Theatre, and Gender Struggle in Early Modern England." *Shakespeare Quarterly* 39 (1988): 418–40.

———. "An English Lass amid the Moors: Gender, Race, Sexuality, and National Identity in Heywood's *The Fair Maid of the West.*" In *Women, "Race," and Writing in the Early Modern Period,* ed. Hendricks and Parker, 101–17.

Howell, Thomas. *Devises.* London: H. Jackson, 1581. STC 13875.

Jacobs, Deborah. "Critical Imperialism and Renaissance Drama: The Case of *The Roaring Girl.*" In *Feminism, Bakhtin, and the Dialogic,* ed. Bauer and McKinstry, 73–84.

Jardine, Lisa. *Still Harping on Daughters: Women and Drama in the Age of Shakespeare.* New York: Columbia University Press, 1983.

Jones, Ann Rosalind, and Peter Stallybrass. *Renaissance Clothing and the Materials of Memory.* Cambridge: Cambridge University Press, 2000.

Kelso, Ruth. *Doctrine for the Lady of the Renaissance.* Urbana: University of Illinois Press, 1956.

Lea, Henry Charles. *The Duel and the Oath.* Philadelphia: University of Pennsylvania Press, 1974.

Levin, Carole. *The Heart and Stomach of a King: Elizabeth I and the Politics of Sex and Power.* Philadelphia: University of Pennsylvania Press, 1994.

———. "Power, Politics, and Sexuality: Images of Elizabeth I." In *The Politics of Gender in Early Modern Europe.* ed. Brink, Coudert, and Horowitz, 95–110.

The Life of Long Meg of Westminster. London: Robert Bird, 1635. STC 17783.

Lucas, R. Valerie. "*Hic Mulier*: The Female Transvestite in Early Modern England." *Renaissance and Reformation* 12 (1988): 65–84.

Middleton, Thomas (and Thomas Dekker). *The Roaring Girl*. In *The Works of Thomas Middleton*, ed. A. H. Bullen. 8 vols. 4:1–152. London: J. C. Nimno, 1885–1886; repr. New York: AMS Press, 1964.

Mullholland, Paul. "Introduction." In *The Roaring Girl*, by Thomas Middleton and Thomas Dekker, ed. idem, 1–65. Manchester: Manchester University Press, 1987.

Neilson, George. *Trial by Combat*. Glasgow: William Hodge, 1890.

Norland, Howard B., ed. *The Maid's Tragedy*. Lincoln, NE: University of Nebraska Press, 1968.

Paster, Gail Kern. *The Body Embarrassed: Drama and the Disciplines of Shame in Early Modern England*. Ithaca: Cornell University Press, 1993.

Rackin, Phyllis. "Androgyny, Mimesis, and the Marriage of the Boy Heroine on the English Renaissance Stage." *PMLA* 102 (1987): 29–41.

———. "Foreign Country: The Place of Women and Sexuality in Shakespeare's Historical World." In *Enclosure Acts: Sexuality, Property, and Culture in Early Modern England*, ed. Burt and Archer, 68–95. Repr. of "Historical Difference / Sexual Difference" in *Privileging Gender in Early Modern England*. Ed. Jean R. Brink. Kirksville, MO: Sixteenth-Century Journal Publishers, 1993. Vol. 23 of *Sixteenth-Century Essays and Studies*.

Rich, Barnabe. *The Excellency of Good Women*. London: Thomas Dawson, 1613. STC 20982.

Rose, Mary Beth. "Women in Men's Clothing: Apparel and Social Stability in *The Roaring Girl*." *English Literary Renaissance* 14 (1984): 367–91.

Shepherd, Simon. *Amazons and Warrior Women: Varieties of Feminism in Seventeenth-Century Drama*. New York: St. Martin's Press, 1981.

Sidney, Sir Philip. *The Countess of Pembroke's Arcadia (The New Arcadia)*, ed. Victor Skretkowicz. Oxford: Clarendon Press, 1987.

Silver, George. *Paradoxes of Defence* (1599). London: Shakespeare Association Facsimiles, 1933.

Spicer, Joaneath. "The Renaissance Elbow." In *A Cultural History of Gesture*, ed. Bremmer and Roodenburg, 84–128.

Strong, Roy. *The Cult of Elizabeth: Elizabethan Portraiture and Pageantry*. Berkeley: University of California Press, 1977.

Swetnam, Joseph. *The Arraignment of Lewd, idle, froward, and unconstant women*. London: E. Allde for T. Archer, 1615. (STC 23533.) Repr. in *Half Humankind: Contexts and Texts of the Controversy about Women in England, 1540–1640*, ed. Henderson and McManus, 189–216.

Trisolini, Giovanna, ed. Anon., "Le Doctrinal des Princesses et Nobles Dames faict et deduict en XXIIII Rondeaulx et Premierement. . . ." In *Le Lexique de Jehan Marot dans le doctrinal des princesses et nobles dames*, ed. eadem, 87–101. Ravenna: Longo, 1978.

Underdown, D. E. "The Taming of the Scold: The Enforcement of Patriarchal Authority in Early Modern England." In *Order and Disorder in Early Modern England*, ed. Fletcher and Stevenson, 116–36.

Vives, Juan Luis. *De Institutione Feminae Christianae*, ed. C. Fantazzi and C. Matheeussen, trans. C. Fantazzi. 2 vols. Leiden: Brill, 1996–1998.

———. *The Education of a Christian Woman: A Sixteenth-Century Manual*, trans. Charles Fantazzi. Chicago: University of Chicago Press, 2000.

———. *A very fruteful and pleasant boke callyd the Instruction of a Christen woman*, trans. Richard Hyrde. London: Thomas Berthelet, 1541. STC 24858.

Wing, John. "The Crowne Conjugall, or the Spouse Royall, A Discovery of the true honor and happines of Christian Matrimony." London: John Beale, 1632. STC 25845.

Woodbridge, Linda. *Women and the English Renaissance: Literature and the Nature of Womankind, 1540–1620*. Urbana: University of Illinois Press, 1984.

Woods, Susanne. "Spenser and the Problem of Woman's Rule." *Huntington Library Quarterly* 48 (1985): 141–58.

Yates, Frances A. *Astraea: The Imperial Theme in the Sixteenth Century*. London: Routledge, 1975.

Ziegler, Georgianna. "My Lady's Chamber: Female Space, Female Chastity in Shakespeare." *Textual Practice* 4 (1990): 73–100.

"You make me feel like (un)natural woman":
Reconsidering Murderous Mothers in
English Renaissance Drama

It is wartime. On a stormy heath in first-century Britain, Bonduca, Queen of the Iceni, stands, her two grown daughters by her side. Across from them, a detachment of anxious Roman soldiers holds its collective breath as the women stare back defiantly. "Bring up the swords, and poison," calls Bonduca to a nearby attendant (4.4.85).[1] As the tools of destruction are brought forth, the youngest daughter begins to cry in desperation. Her mother scorns her pleas for mercy. "Behold us, Romanes," Bonduca proclaims (4.4.88). There is no turning back now. The time has come for Bonduca's daughters to die. In horror, Swetonius, the Roman general, gasps: "Woeman. Woeman. / Unnaturall woeman" (4.4.92–93). But Bonduca is not listening as she prepares her children for death. . . .

I begin with this scene from John Fletcher's *The Tragedie of Bonduca* (1611–1614) to highlight a particular critical problem: dramatic representations of child murder by mothers differ significantly from those in court records and popular pamphlets, and more importantly, from actual cases.[2] Most documented incidents of child murder are infanticides, usually perpetrated by lower-class, and

---

[1] All citations are of Fletcher, *Bonduca*, ed. Hoy, in *The Dramatic Works in the Beaumont and Fletcher Canon*, ed. Bowers. I would like to extend my gratitude to Sharon Beehler and especially Linda Woodbridge for their invaluable suggestions as this essay underwent its many incarnations. Thanks also to Kent Cartwright, Jane Donawerth, Susan Lanser, and Charles Rutherford, for their helpful comments on and direction of the project from which this piece issued. A final salute to Gregory Colón Semenza, for his critical guidance and amicable support.

[2] In this essay, the term "child murder" will be used to define cases where parents — specifically, mothers — kill their children. Since the children murdered in most dramatic texts are older, and even adult, I prefer this term over the more common "infanticide."

often single, women. However, a majority of plays portray child murderers as queens who vengefully slay their older, even adult, legitimate issue. How do we account for these differences, and why, if at all, do they matter?

The work of Frances Dolan and Betty Travitsky in particular provides a useful starting point for understanding the problem of child murder representations. Dolan's study of popular seventeenth-century pamphlets depicting child murder concludes that "representations of murderous mothers ... suggest that violence against children is not unnatural or strange, but is, instead, familiar."[3] Child murder often is portrayed problematically as either an act of madness, resulting in the mother's later punishment and/or reformation, or as a tragic act of mercy, saving the offspring from poverty or disgrace. In either case, some realism of the violence and its impact on the community is preserved, suggesting that, while child murder was not by any means condoned, it may have been an accepted part of reality. It was a cultural signifier with implications for constructions of gender and class roles, and even individual identity. Yet Dolan's work only touches on how these meanings may have translated into plays of the time.[4]

Betty Travitsky, however, focuses on how popular and historical representations of child murder translate into dramatic discourse. Her analysis of historical material and seven tragic plays of the Elizabethan and Jacobean monarchies reveals only vague parallels between the everyday and the theatric. Travitsky argues that the "interest of Renaissance male dramatists" excludes realistic representations of child murder in practice.[5] Because early modern women were subordinate to men in the social hierarchy, upper-class "women out of bounds" were particular objects of curiosity, meriting inclusion in the tragic art form. But playwrights clearly elided the realism of the lower-class woman's plight and any corresponding infanticidal acts. Thus child murder representations serve primarily to demonize women and illustrate a cultural anxiety about female transgression.[6]

While these studies contribute significantly to our thinking about child murder portrayals, they problematically ignore other possible meanings for the dis-

---

[3] See Dolan, *Dangerous Familiars: Representations of Domestic Crime in England 1550–1700*, 148–49.

[4] Specifically, she looks at Shakespeare's *The Winter's Tale* as a dramatic example where the cultural fascination with the act is maintained, but the realistic factors are fantastically aestheticized. Dolan notes that while child murder has been associated with mothers, canonical drama seems to preserve the violence enacted by elite fathers, whose abuses "can be forgiven" (*Dangerous Familiars*, 169). Literary tradition thus privileges the most unrealistic portrayals of child murder, neglecting popular and legal perspectives.

[5] See Travitsky, "Child Murder in English Renaissance Life and Drama," 76.

[6] Travitsky, "Child Murder," 77.

crepancies in class and motive of the murderer, as well as the age of the victim. The gap between the real and dramatic representations suggests that the "convention" of murderous *queens* killing their *adult* offspring in monstrous, "unnatural" assaults must carry additional cultural resonances, above and beyond the spectacular element that it obviously provides.

What then is the function of child murder representations? This essay will argue that they are important not only for expressing a misogynistic fear of women and authority, but also for highlighting a specific political concern of the time: succession. Dramatic child murder centrally involves constructions of national identity and anxieties about the future of the monarchy and its subjects. The powerful relationships between mother and child, and ruler and nation, are metaphorically united within these plays, as they were in political rhetoric of the late sixteenth and early seventeenth centuries. This premise will be tested against two dramatic representatives of the child murder motif: Sackville and Norton's *Gorboduc; or Ferrex and Porrex* and John Fletcher's *The Tragedie of Bonduca*. Before doing so, however, I will first sketch the cultural backdrop that informs my discussion.

During the sixteenth and seventeenth centuries, a prevalent metaphorical connection between the nuclear family and the nation proliferated in public discourse. Both Elizabeth and James wrote and spoke repeatedly in terms of their familial governance of the country. Elizabeth pronounced herself wed to England and mother of all its people, and James framed his relations in terms of both husband to the nation and father to his subjects.[7] The nuclear family was understood to represent the nation and the religious state in miniature. Hierarchy therefore defined not only an early modern political ideology, but also what religious and social customs encouraged: ideally, strict adherence to boundaries of position, law, and nature — whether that be within the family, the community, or the nation as a whole.

Children were integral to early modern society, with particular duties and

---

[7] In an effort to withstand political pressures to marry, Elizabeth repeatedly spoke of her "marriage" to the nation and her parenting of its peoples during her speeches. William Camden recounts a 1559 proclamation to Parliament, wherein she states, "Yea, to satisfie you, I have already joyned my self in Marriage to an Husband, namely, the Kingdom of England. ... And do not (saith she) upbraide me with miserable lack of Children: for every one of you, and as many as are English-men, are Children and Kinsmen to me. ..." See Camden, *The History*, ed. MacCaffrey, 29. For details on James's image-fashioning, see especially Hale, *The Body Politic: A Political Metaphor in Renaissance English Literature*, 111; and Perry, *The Making of Jacobean Culture: James I and the Renegotiation of Elizabethan Literary Practice*, 130.

roles. Their positioning in relation to familial and social structures hinged less on the child as an individual, and more on him or her as a future subject of the crown and member of the civil community. The historical work of Keith Wrightson and Lawrence Stone has extensively mapped the relationship and power dynamics between parents and children during this time, suggesting some of the underlying ideology of why child murder therefore was so offensive on various levels.[8]

Very few children were completely raised and educated by their own parents in a static environment. Their upbringing was a group responsibility. Aside from the attentions of their parents and older siblings, most youth were given into the care of other families for fostering, service, and/or schooling (as in the upper classes); for working an apprenticeship (as in the middle classes); or for laboring in the fields or cities (as in the lower classes). Lawrence Stone estimates that "from just before puberty until they married some ten years later, about two out of every three boys and three out of every four girls were living away from home."[9] It is clear that a significant part of children's lives and education was spent under the aegis of other people, rather than in the immediate domestic realm of their parents.

For the most part, it seems that this fostering system succeeded in shaping dutiful subjects. Regimens of appropriate conduct and daily tasks maintained a sense of law and order in children's lives. Additionally, corporal punishment served as a regulating form of discipline, enforcing the strictures that society wished to use in molding its fledgling citizens. These exchange and education practices appear to be relatively universal over class boundaries, suggesting a cultural standard and supporting the parallel between nation and family structure. A primary goal of raising children, then, was to respect a hierarchy that was effectively represented as natural, not only to take pleasure in the creation and support of one's own offspring.

Additionally, Patricia Fumerton suggests that children (particularly of the aristocracy) were critical to the society's symbolic understanding of itself: "Elizabethan aristocratic society created itself in great part by transcending fragmentary experience through an imaginative re-creation of its practice of exchanging trivial

---

[8] Stone, *The Family, Sex, and Marriage In England 1500–1800*; Wrightson, *English Society 1580–1680*. See also Tucker, "The Child as Beginning and End: Fifteenth and Sixteenth Century English Childhood," and Illick, "Child-Rearing in Seventeenth Century England and America," in *The History of Childhood*, ed. deMause.

[9] Stone, *The Family, Sex, and Marriage*, 107.

things (especially children)."[10] In families of the gentry, children received strict social training, acted as servants, learned appropriate court skills, and served as their families' representatives away from the household. Fumerton emphasizes their importance in social advancement as they curried favor with powerful aristocrats and the queen. The noble, "civilizing" experience of circulating children continued to benefit families once their offspring were of marriageable age: they became unifying tokens of social ascendancy, wealth, and dynastic power.

Fumerton argues that this process made the child a "kind of aesthetic artifact ... [which] performed a generative cultural function."[11] Children served as social liaisons between families, signifying the civilized (and civilizing) nature of English society. While fostering may have emotionally distanced young people from their nuclear family, it is this system of exchange that linked the society as a whole. "In freely giving children," she continues, "the English aristocracy generated social bonds that communicated a mystical force seeming to sustain life even in the face of death."[12] Implicitly, grown children represented hopeful, redemptive figures; they continued to survive beyond and in spite of the death and strife in the world around them.[13] Ultimately, they provided cultural links between the generations and embodied society's "self." Their purpose was not only to transmit beliefs and virtues, but to act as symbolic icons of it as well.[14] In training and exchanging, and in raising their children, adults exerted some control over their nation's current and future definition. They delineated, reinforced, and maintained its religious, political, and familial boundaries through shaping the younger generation.

The disorder and power abuses that have been traced in these representations thus appear more severe than originally supposed. Child murder is not just about the murderer and her motives, but about its victims and the implications of their elimination. What, precisely, is at stake when mothers kill their children? It

---

[10] Fumerton, *Cultural Aesthetics: Renaissance Literature and the Practice of Social Ornament*, 31.

[11] Fumerton, *Cultural Aesthetics*, 37.

[12] Fumerton, *Cultural Aesthetics*, 37, 42.

[13] See also Tucker, "The Child as Beginning and End," 231–33.

[14] It is important to note here that valuing children in terms of the symbolic, generative purposes of society is mostly characterized by the middle to upper classes. The most likely "symbolic" value a child might have for a lower-class parent would be that of an extra mouth to feed. Still, children were useful as an extra labor force if nothing else, and thus were accepted as long as they could be financially supported. The mother/child relationship in early modern society thus may differ between the classes, in accordance with the differing values of the offspring.

would seem to be quite a bit more than the already tragic loss of a human life.

Peter Stallybrass, in "Patriarchal Territories," discusses the heavily symbolic nature of the female body during the early modern period. In political, religious, and literary discourse, women function as ideological constructs, often defined and directed by their male guardians. More particularly, he notes the conflicting ideologies of virgin/whore and mother/murderer that permeated public discourse of the time. After 1560, growing popular anxiety about maternal abuses resulted in increasing indictments of mothers (usually single and lower-class) who were thought to have killed their children. In this way, "The ideological formation of the family and the state was staked out across the physical bodies of 'criminalized' women."[15] Importantly, most pamphlets and plays portraying child murder were written during that period — generally between 1560 and the later 1600s. The literature of the time thus may participate in and/or be reflective of this ideological movement.

Literary representations of this widespread concern about women and the abuse of their "natural" office as mother are critically important because they transcend the realms of the personal and moral to figure those of the communal and political. The early modern ideological parallel between the body natural and the body politic makes this appreciable. As noted earlier, Elizabethan and Jacobean societies often constructed the monarch as the land/nation, or in a familial relationship with it and their subjects. The English people thus are the children of the monarch, whom he or she is responsible for nurturing, guarding, and directing. In plays where murderous queens in particular kill their adult offspring, the metaphorical impact is even more horrific than the literal one: child murder is a statement of national sedition.

This political valence should not be disregarded. While I am not suggesting that playwrights merely inserted a scene with child murder whenever they wanted to get their audience's attention, I would like to argue that the motif marks a significant rhetorical point in the drama, where the body natural becomes the body politic, with universal tragic implications. The child murder motif not only describes a world where mothers kill their children, queens misuse power, and women are "unnatural"; the act responds to and/or creates circumstances which bring about the metaphorical and potentially literal death of English civilization.

The list of plays representing child murder is a substantial one, including

---

[15] See Stallybrass, "Patriarchal Territories: The Body Enclosed," in *Rewriting the Renaissance*, ed. Ferguson, Quilligan, and Vickers, 131.

works such as Sackville and Norton's *Gorboduc*, Marlowe's *2 Tamburlaine*, Greville's *Mustapha*, Fletcher's *Bonduca*, and Beaumont and Fletcher's *Tragedy of Thierry and Theodoret*. And there are assuredly more in which the motif makes an appearance.[16] Alfred Harbage's *Annals of English Drama* reveals that, to a large extent, these shocking dramas were crafted for upper-class audiences, either as closet dramas or as private theater productions.[17] While several, such as Marlowe's *2 Tamburlaine*, were played at public theaters like the Rose and the Globe, the two plays I will discuss here seem representative of the majority in their being privately performed and politically-minded in nature.[18] In addition, they provide Elizabethan and Jacobean period examples of common "types" of child murder portrayals.[19] *Gorboduc* was played before Queen Elizabeth in January 1562 at Whitehall by the Gentlemen of the Inner Temple, as part of the Christmas festivities. *The Tragedie of Bonduca*, while acted by the King's Men in 1613, has a more obscure performance history; however, evidence seems to suggest a run at the Blackfriars, another private forum.[20]

---

[16] See also Buchanan, *Jeptha*; R. B., *Apius and Virginia*; Marlowe, *The Jew of Malta*; Shakespeare, *Titus Andronicus*. Many of these plays depict murderous fathers killing their adult children.

[17] According to Harbage's *Annals*, *2 Tamburlaine* was performed at the Rose; *Mustapha* was a closet drama; *Alaham* was a closet drama; *Gorboduc* was performed at the Inner Temple/Whitehall; *Bonduca* was performed at either the Globe or the Blackfriars (see below 20 for preferring Blackfriars); *Thierry and Theodoret* was performed at the Blackfriars. See Harbage, *Annals of English Drama 975–1700*, rev. Schoenbaum.

[18] As noted here, evidence suggests that plays including the child murder motif were performed before audiences of various classes, although the majority do appear to be targeted for the upper ones (for those who could read and have access to printed materials and those who could afford private performances). An aristocratic audience might find the motif's succession threat more immediately threatening and politically harrowing because of its members' proximity to court issues. Nonetheless, I think it is reasonable to suggest that dramatic examples of royal child murder remain culturally significant for all classes. The death of children was a common denominator in society, and assumably most people would recognize a murderous monarch as threatening to national security.

[19] As with the pamphlet literature Dolan discusses, dramatic representations of child murder often fall into two general types: cases where the mother (or father) is considered mad, tyrannical, and/or vindictive, and those in which the parent (usually the mother) kills her child(ren) to protect or sacrifice them for their own good (perceived as a situation of "death before dishonor" or mercy killing). *Gorboduc* and *Bonduca* follow these respective models.

[20] See Harbage, *Annals*, as well as Chambers, *The Elizabethan Stage*, vol. 2; Greg, *A Bibliography of the English Printed Drama to the Restoration*, vol. 2; and Kawachi, *Calendar of English Renaissance Drama*. Most scholars date *Bonduca* to 1611–1614. Chambers argues for the 1613 dating since the actors on the list of players were in employ during the periods 1609–1611 and 1613–1614. The earlier date seems unlikely because of the types

For these playwrights, then, the challenge was to cater to the interests of their audience, tailoring their themes and styles to the issues of the time. Harbage observes that in coterie drama of the late sixteenth and the seventeenth centuries, patrons increasingly desired extreme spectacle in their entertainment. The Blackfriars audience, especially, demanded "bitterness, bawdry, and 'strong lines'."[21] Class interests appear to be definitive of what types of dramas were played before such elite audiences, for, as he continues, certain types of comedy and tragedy are missing from the private theater repertoire: "there are few romantic or folk comedies, no domestic or middle-class tragedies, and no heroical biographies."[22] But more importantly, perhaps, private dramas offered a forum for the expression of political and social issues. It is to the plays themselves that I would now like to draw our attention.

Of the Elizabethan dramas that represent child murder, perhaps none is so rhetorically direct and striking as Sackville and Norton's *Gorboduc; or, Ferrex and Porrex* (1561/1562). Performed for Queen Elizabeth at Whitehall in 1562, the play offers an ominous view of the consequences of uncertain succession, at a time when the queen had neither produced nor designated an heir. *Gorboduc's* theme of political upheaval begins with the king's division of lands between his two sons, spurring sibling rivalry and eventual fratricide. The drama is brought to a climax, however, by the queen mother's murder of her remaining son and heir, crucially illustrating the political impact of the child murder motif. While her performance is not the exclusive or even primary plot action in *Gorboduc*, its violent presence significantly contributes to the gravity and magnitude of the play's message.

The power of the child murder motif lies mostly in the language used to describe the horrific act. In *Gorboduc*, we can see how the familiar, "natural" woman becomes something other — a frightful icon of divine and political force, a monster consuming the nation's future. Her act amplifies the dramatic action while also highlighting the central thematic agenda. For the purposes of my

---

of plays being written then; Fletcher was also increasingly prolific during this later time period. Since it is known that the King's Men put on the play, we can narrow its location to either the Globe or the Blackfriars. Considering the Globe's destruction by fire in June 1613 and its reconstruction in June 1614, along with the increased usage of the Blackfriars by the King's Men as not only a winter stage but indeed year round, it is perhaps more likely that *Bonduca* was acted at the private theater. This supposition would also seem to correlate with Harbage's discussion of the types of dramas that were aimed at the upper-class private audience.

[21] Harbage, *Shakespeare and the Rival Traditions*, 83.

[22] Harbage, *Shakespeare and the Rival Traditions*, 85.

argument, I will focus my discussion on scenes that specifically employ the language of unnaturalness and deal with the act of child murder and its repercussions on the characters and plot. In so doing, we may gain a better sense of the various representative effects of the child murder motif in a dramatic context.

As act 4 scene 1 opens, we witness a process of self-transformation from queen and mother to cold-blooded avenger. Videna mourns her son Ferrex, whom her other son, Porrex, has murdered. Her extensive monologue contains a long stream of epithets uplifting Ferrex's position as a beloved son and denouncing Porrex for his crime:

> Traitor to kin and kind, to sire and me,
> To thine own flesh, and traitor to thyself,
> The gods on thee in hell shall wreak their wrath,
> And here in earth this hand shall take revenge. (4.1.31–34)[23]

Videna not only characterizes the fratricide as a betrayal of family bonds, but also invokes the diction of treason. She divorces herself from the biological tie to her son and calls him to task for the political transgression he has effected. She also declares that the gods will avenge Ferrex, and that she will be their agent of justice on earth. Having just witnessed a dumb-show portraying royal parents who, being moved by the Furies, slay their children, the audience may immediately predict the impending filicidal act. Regardless, the language used here provides grounds for an attribution of guilt to Videna, and a concurrent explanation of her crime in terms of divine and political justice.

Videna ends her speech by disowning her son, Porrex:

> Shall I still think that from this womb thou sprung?
> That I thee bare? Or take thee for my son?
> No, traitor, no; I thee refuse for mine!
> Murderer, I thee renounce; thou art not mine. (4.1.63–66)

In pronouncing sentence on Porrex, she names him "Murderer" and denies that such a traitor could issue from her. Her subsequent description of him as a "changeling," "monster of nature's work," and beast that has a heart made of iron rather than flesh and blood, revokes not only his name as her son, but his humanity as well (69–75). The language aesthetically distances her from him, his act, and all responsibilities she owes him as a mother. It additionally invokes the

---

[23] All citations are made from Sackville and Norton, *Gorboduc; or, Ferrex and Porrex,* in *Drama of the English Renaissance 1: The Tudor Period,* ed. Fraser and Rabkin.

bestiality and body discourses of the world-upside-down that are prevalent in early modern dramas. Thus Videna is able to achieve personal distance from the subject of her crime — a move that might take place to emphasize that no "natural" mother could possibly kill her own child and that Porrex is an inhuman traitor to be cast out of civilization.

Still, in act 4 scene 2, the dramatic impact of Videna's action does not seem any less. She violates the sacred bond between mother and child — not only with her biological offspring, but with her country as well. Once again, the rhetorical impact of the descriptive language serves to indict a character for both natural and political treason — only this time, it is Videna who stands accused. The audience's attention is riveted upon Videna's handmaiden Marcella as she gives a passionate, moralistic account of Porrex's murder. Like Marcella, the audience may feel appalled and fearful about what Videna has done. But it is *how* Marcella's transformative language figures the queen's actions that creates such a powerful rhetorical imprint on the audience's imagination.

Marcella repeatedly employs four images to empower her narrative: the heart, the breast, the hand, and the eye. These fractured body parts may resonate with the audience's knowledge that not only has Porrex been slain, his body "broken," but that the political body also has been torn asunder: there are no more children to inherit the kingdom. More literally, though, these specific parts figure the remains of motherhood: the heart images refer to the intense emotions surrounding what is constructed as "natural" motherhood — pity, compassion, and love; the breast provides a poignant nurturing/sustenance symbol; the hand is a device of action, lending aid, comfort, or opposingly, destruction; and finally, there is the image of the eye, noted for vision, whether physical (watchfulness, clarity) or metaphorical (insight, wisdom).

Notably, these parts are counted as part of the "higher" strata of the body natural and, in figurative terms, the body politic. Such a designation may indicate how these images elevate the role of mother, or at least emphasize its characteristics, in a larger social context. However, Marcella's language draws attention to Videna's *lack* of these bodily qualities, thus producing not only a profoundly shocking statement about Videna's character and her role as mother to her children and country, but also reinforcing the theme of disorder and the delineation of civilized womanhood through its negation.

Marcella begins her speech with a series of questions:

> Oh where is ruth, or where is pity now?
> Whither is gentle heart and mercy fled?

> Are they exiled out of our stony breasts,
> Never to make return? (4.2.166–169)

After addressing a loss of compassion and pity ("ruth"), Marcella presents an image of emotional capitulation (a fleeing "gentle heart" and mercy). She suggests that Videna's act defies any "motherly" emotional consideration, and immediately extrapolates the impact of this act to a larger scale: her questions ask whether compassion exists at all. Marcella continues reinforcing this point by juxtaposing cold, impervious stone with the warm, sustaining quality of the breast. The "stony breast" image further emphasizes that Videna has forsaken the "natural" nurturing qualities of motherhood for something other. Marcella's use of the word "exiled" not only indicates an active rejection of those values, but also resonates with the political theme of the play. The treasonous murder of Ferrex has been answered by a violent witholding of compassion. In killing her son, Videna exiles Porrex from her breast's nurturing source as well as any position of inheritance or other gain.

Marcella's next lines stress the universal impact of the heir's murder:

> ... Is all the world
> Drowned in blood and sunk in cruelty?
> If not in women mercy may be found,
> If not, alas, within the mother's breast
> To her own child, to her own flesh and blood
> ... where should we seek it then? (4.2.169–176)

Marcella expands the image of death that Videna's act has invoked into a national symbol of cruelty and destruction. The handmaiden emphasizes the horror of this betrayal by repeating the word "own" — first in "To her *own* child," and then in "to her *own* flesh and blood" (emphasis mine). The power of blood, the mother/child bond, coupled with the act of murder, exceeds Marcella's capacity for rationalization. Her implication is that if mothers have been driven to kill their own children — and especially if the queen, the *national* mother, does so — then certainly there is no mercy left in the world. Videna's murder of her child, the heir and symbolic hopeful future of the nation, is so extreme that it registers not only on an individual level of nature and morality, but also on a political one. By the end of *Gorboduc*, not only are the two princes dead, but their parents are as well. In response to Videna's act (as least in part), the people of England rise up and slay their rulers, catapulting their country into anarchy. Murdering the successors has murdered succession as an institution. The body politic has been destroyed as its mother abandoned her nurturing duties and leadership responsibilities to wreak bloody justice.

Gorboduc is a play whose language capitalizes upon a common set of metaphors employed in the early modern period. Particularly surrounding Videna's murder of Porrex, we find the images of the nurturing body natural/politic put aside for a more destructive, monstrous representation of murderous queens. Because of the overlap between the natural and political here, and in light of the play's more general theme of the problems of succession, one might ask what rhetorical effects it may have had on its audience. Keeping in mind the cultural significations I discussed earlier, I will now consider what civic issues were in debate during the time of production. Exploring the contextual backdrop may illuminate how child murder was a fitting inclusion for this drama and others.

Greg Walker provides compelling evidence regarding the political forces surrounding *Gorboduc*'s production, particularly for its performance before Queen Elizabeth in 1562. His research in the Yelverton papers in the British Library yields an eyewitness account of the play's performance that winter. Surprisingly, the account refers to details in the presentation which are somewhat different in the later editions. These changes, specifically made to the second dumb-show, seem to suggest that "the play in general [was] read by the audience in the specific context of Dudley's suit to marry the queen and the challenge offered to it by the Swedish mission."[24] Queen Elizabeth's favor to Dudley was well known, and many supposed that since his wife was recently deceased, she would marry him, thereby keeping the English crown within national boundaries. However, not surprisingly, she entertained many other royal suitors, one of which — Eric XIV of Sweden — was pressing his suit strongly at the time. Since *Gorboduc* is especially concerned with issues of succession (and, according to Walker's findings, Elizabeth's potential marriage to an insider versus an outsider), we need to consider whether the child murder scene is at all influenced by or rather influences these issues.

As mentioned earlier, when child murder appears in early modern dramas, it is rarely the centerpiece of the play. In *Gorboduc* too, Videna's bloody act is sidelined, left to lengthy mention in act 4, but not commented on afterwards. It would seem that the motif is simply part of a larger plot scheme, amplifying the problems posed by the play. And yet I would like to argue that, while this event may be marginal in some respects, it is a moment that fully embodies the gravity of the situation and its potential effects. The language of child murder is transformative: it makes humans inhuman, mothers into monsters, queens into criminals. But its power does not merely damn women who dare to take their power

---

[24] See Walker, *The Politics of Performance in Early Renaissance Drama*, 212.

too far; rather, it might have registered with its audience as a symbol of the country's imminent danger if the monarch neglected her responsibility to nurture and protect the people.

With *Gorboduc*, the threat of a murderous queen is absolutely central; for Elizabeth, despite all her efforts to masculinize her role, was a woman in charge of her nation's destiny. With her resistance to appointing an heir or to taking a husband and producing one, she paradoxically replicates Videna's crime: threatening and even killing her "children" by not ensuring the order of succession, the understood safeguard of a peaceful future. Her rhetoric of both nurturing and defending the nation did not seem completely to match her actions when it came to supplying England's next ruler. Would the English royal line die out or fall prey to outside influence?

The possibility of Elizabeth's actions not culminating in a bright future for her subjects and the nation itself caused considerable anxiety in the minds of many. Aristocrats at court worried over whether the queen would marry an Englishman, since there was some fear that a foreign alliance would prove less beneficial and even dangerous to the nation's political and economic interests. While Elizabeth's feelings on the issue were certainly central to the debate, other parties made rumblings about a parliamentary selection process to alleviate political pressures surrounding the issue of succession. As Walker's work shows, "*Gorboduc* was read by its first audience as a direct commentary upon, and intervention in, contemporary political debates: not just in general terms, but in the specific context of the Swedish suit for Elizabeth's hand."[25]

With Gorboduc's division of the realm and Videna's murder of Porrex, *Gorboduc* becomes a stage for these conflicting perspectives. The play dramatically criticizes the overturning of marriage and primogeniture as fatal to the nation's welfare, marking those institutions as the best solutions for preserving England's peace and order. Secondly, however, the play promotes succession based on parliamentary decision through an emphasis on the noble counselors' protection and eventual decision about the governance of the realm.[26] *Gorboduc* thus possesses significant rhetorical power, performing a political allegory across the bodies of the nation's monarch and her unfortunate progeny.

The case I have presented for *Gorboduc* and the role that the child murder motif plays within that rhetorical landscape is rather specific in its scope. Yet I

---

[25] Walker, *The Politics of Performance*, 217.

[26] For a more detailed discussion of the play's political rhetoric, see Walker, *The Politics of Performance*, 210–21.

think that this application opens up another direction of critical exploration for child murder representations that previously has been overlooked. Aimed potentially at an elite audience, and significantly distanced from realistic representations of the act in early modern history (i.e., killing queens and adult children rather than poor mothers and their babies), these dramatic moments register in multiple ways. They may possess similar misogynistic language; however, the use and understanding of the motif is necessarily affected by and dependent on the exigence of the play's production and composition. To highlight further how language and cultural moment may influence interpretation with this particular motif, I take us to the performance of another play that represents a murderous queen mother: John Fletcher's *The Tragedie of Bonduca*.

Like *Gorboduc*, *Bonduca* concerns itself with issues of succession, although the nationalistic implications are far more pronounced. In this play based on events from ancient British history, the queen of the Iceni, Bonduca, leads the British troops against Roman invasion. Cautioned by her general and cousin, Caratach, that the Romans are a well-organized, formidable force to be reckoned with (and even admired), Bonduca persists in leading Britain's fighters into the fray. Her bold proclamations of victory are premature, however, and she is eventually captured along with her two daughters by the Roman general, Swetonius. Rather than subject their bodies and honor to further disgrace, she orders her daughters to commit suicide along with her.[27] During the course of exchanges between

---

[27] One might argue whether the death of Bonduca's daughters may rightfully be called a murder rather than a suicide, as they take their own lives. While they do commit suicide, I would like to suggest that their deaths should *also* be considered as cases of child murder. As Wrightson (*English Society*, 115) and Stone (*The Family, Sex, and Marriage*, 171) both support, early modern definitions of parent/child relations were largely based on the younger generation's honoring and obeying the directives of their elders. Bonduca makes her demands for her children perfectly clear: she wants them dead. And she makes sure they have the appropriate means to effect that result — the swords. Her repeated orders and warnings to her elder daughter and Bonvica, coupled with their final obedience to her, implicate her in a murderous connection to their deaths. Compare this scene in *Bonduca* with one in Marlowe's *2 Tamburlaine*. In act 3 scene 4, Olympia, having witnessed the death of her husband at the hands of Tamburlaine's forces, calls for her son's death and her own suicide: "Come back again, sweet Death, and strike us both! . . . / Tell me, sweet boy, art thou content to die? / These barbarous Scythians, full of cruelty, / And Moors, in whom was never pity found, / Will hew us piecemeal . . . / Therefore die by thy loving mother's hand" (3.4.12, 18–21, 23). Her son accepts his death, understanding the gravity of the situation if they are captured: "Mother, dispatch me, or I'll kill myself. . . . / Give me your knife, good mother, or strike home — / The Scythians shall not tyrannize on me" (3.4.26, 28–29). Olympia murders her son, and he is a passive victim. This situation is representative of the mercy-killing type of child murder, as I mentioned earlier. Also notable is Techelles' comment to Olympia after she has

the Roman soldiers and Bonduca and her daughters, the language of the play moves from now familiar expressions of shock regarding her violent actions to admiration for her "valor." This rhetorical transition marks a significant thematic point for the drama.

At the beginning of the passage describing Bonduca's murders, Swetonius, the Roman general, appears mesmerized by the horrific suggestion of murder/suicide that Bonduca proposes: "Woeman. Woeman. / Unnaturall woeman" (4.4.92–93). Swetonius calls into question the legitimacy of the murderous act, while also defining the unnatural quality of her proposed actions. Importantly, this "unnaturalness" occurs on two levels: that of a female assuming violent power, and that of a mother slaying her children. The next few lines appeal to Bonduca's maternal duties and any merciful feelings she may possess, as her younger daughter begs the Romans to persuade her mother to give up her murderous plans. Swetonius answers her plea, telling Bonduca to "Yield and be a Queene still. / A mother and a friend" (4.4.96–97). Swetonius recalls several of Bonduca's roles, those which are socially acceptable for a woman. Importantly, he does not try to stay her with pleas to remember her responsibility to the British troops or even the people in general. His words suggest that she relinquish power and forget violence to return to a more imaginable and secure position for her sex. Swetonius seeks to contain her not only militarily, but also on a more ideological level. The associated implication is that if she does follow through with her threats, she will break the natural and civil order, giving up her roles within society and becoming "other."

Throughout this scene, Swetonius repeats the word "woman," as if vocalizing the word will somehow drive tender, passive attributes into the determined queen. While that effort proves fruitless, it does repeatedly pound his claim into the audience's sensibilities. However, Bonduca is not to be swayed. Whenever Swetonius raises his voice to speak of mercy or to hail her as "woman," she silences him: "No talking," "Talk not" (4.4.88, 107). Her forbidding of *his* speech turns the power tables, as usually early modern women were the ones ordered to be chaste, silent, and obedient. She insists on maintaining her oft-questioned position of royal authority.

Her plan to lead her daughters into death meets with mixed reactions. The elder daughter supports her suggestion fully and is a vocal advocate of the plan.

---

slain her son and is threatening to kill herself: " 'Twas bravely done, and, like a soldier's wife" (3.4.38). The similarities to the murder-suicide scenes in *Bonduca* are striking. See Marlowe, *Tamburlaine the Great, Part II*, ed. Cunningham.

The younger, on the other hand, is terrified and continually begs the Romans to save her. Bonduca is deaf to her pleas, though, and expresses her disgust with her youngest child: "O gods, / Feare in my family. Doe it [kill yourself] and nobly" (4.4.102–103). She has no patience with her daughter's entreaty and accuses her of being weak and fearful. Ironically, the daughter's feelings seem like common emotions for anyone in such circumstances; and yet Bonduca scornfully brings our attention to the fact that a member of her family, her domain, is weak. The audience feels the same fluctuation of judgment of Bonduca's character as with Videna: is there honor and justice in this murderous act, or is it a crime of monumental tragic proportions? Here, as in the pamphlets that Dolan describes in her work, the drama reinforces the mother–child bond; only in this case Bonduca scorns the blood tie and insists her daughter take on the same "unnatural" qualities that she herself manifests, and die.

In the end, Bonduca's orders and threats, the elder daughter's arguments, and Bonvica's sense of duty win out. With a final "long farewel to this world" the girl runs herself through with a sword (4.4.113). The elder daughter, strong in her convictions, taunts the Romans with zealous speeches, proclaiming her honor and courage greater than even their "Saint Lucrece" (4.4.117). She sees only bravery and virtue in the murder-suicide that her mother has proposed, and stabs the sword home, following her sister into death.

At this point in the drama, the language of the Roman characters appears to change from a discourse of accusation to a discourse of respect and supplication. Bonduca, having driven her children to kill themselves, prepares to kill herself by consuming a poisonous draught. However, the Romans plead for her not to die. The Roman officer Curius hails her as "great ladie" (4.4.138), while Swetonius and Demetrius encourage her to "stay" and to "be any thing" (4.4.139–140). The previous charges of unnaturalness and madness seem to have been extirpated, or at the very least, placed aside in the cause of preserving this one female life. They would rather she live, even as a transgressive "thing," than die. It is not entirely clear whether they speak out of sympathy, or of greed (to take her as a prize of war), or whether they fear that her death will make her a martyr figure and rally the British. Regardless, Bonduca answers their requests with scorn:

> When thou shalt fear, and die like a slave. Ye fools,
> Ye should have ti'd up death first when ye conquer'd,
> Ye sweat for us in vain else: see him here,
> He's ours still, and our friend; laughs at your pities;
> And we command him with as easie reins
> As do our enemies. (4.4.141–143)

Offered a desperate absolution by the officers, she prefers to die rather than to live as a slave. She continues to brandish her power against the Romans and death itself. While Bonduca's murder of her children and her own suicide are in some sense sacrificial, it is her force of will and her provision of both motive and means for lethal action that remain most striking. The drama portrays her violence as a transgressive abuse of authority, both natural and political. She is depicted as vainly and selfishly taking lives to preserve her honor, rather than worrying about the consequences for her country and her children's wishes.

As her body fails under the effects of the poison, Bonduca claims victory over the conquest of her lands and power, and counsels them to "place in your Roman flesh a Brittaine soule" (4.4.153). The queen's dying words lend a defiant, heroic quality to her character and seem to transform her death and those of her daughters into a grand, noble act. Swetonius appears taken by the queen's spirit, ordering his soldiers to "Give her a faire ffunerall / She was trewly noble. And a Queene" (4.4.155–156). Whereas once before her "queenship" relied on *not* committing the murders, now she is viewed as the epitome of royal bravery. Swetonius chooses to recoup Bonduca's disorderly act into a violent, but nonetheless admirable, feat. Her use of violence is more acceptable when viewed through constructed masculine values of honor and militarism. The audience, however, may find it hard to forget that she is a woman, a mother, and a queen, and that before them lie three dead bodies. Bonduca has killed herself and her children.

Instead of enacting violence for the purpose of her people's welfare, Bonduca acts more from a sense of maintaining personal honor and militaristic achievement. Warfare, honor, and aggression were subjects coded "male" by early modern society, and so it is perhaps striking that she appropriates these motivations.[28] Paul Green notes that in the second folio edition of the play, Bonduca is listed in the dramatis personae as "a brave Virago." Depending on who addressed the woman by this title and in what context it was used, the term could be praising or damning.[29] While the play's first audience probably did not have access to this textual detail, it is indicative of how her character later may have resonated in the cultural imagination. Emphasizing Bonduca's transgressive militarism reinforces the rhetorical power of transferring male characteristics into the body of the female. Green additionally points out that the weapons employed to

---

[28] See also Stallybrass's discussion of male honor versus female honor, i.e., chastity, in "Patriarchal Territories," especially 135.

[29] See Green, "Theme and Structure in Fletcher's *Bonduca*," 309.

kill the two daughters were swords: "the notion of death by stabbing [is] not only ... a peculiarly Roman death, but also, in a symbolically equivalent way ... an exclusively masculine death."[30] Bonduca takes on not only the conventional personal qualities of the patriarch, but his weapons of enforcement as well. She assumes a masculine authority to penetrate her daughters with legitimate force.

It is particularly interesting to compare this symbolic penetration by a masculinized female agent with the daughters' earlier rapes by Roman soldiers. As Travitsky comments, the play shows little sympathy for their plight, and even lays blame when the daughters tell Caratach of the act: he replies that they should have kept their legs closed.[31] Blame for the act descends on the women: they are guilty of not protecting their own chastity and perhaps of "asking for it." Even as this scene seems to figure the women as victims and "ruined" political pawns, previous and succeeding ones seem to reclaim their power as spiritual and political heirs to Britain.

For example, after the two daughters are raped and escape, they craft a plan to capture their assailants by professing a romantic attraction to them. Bonvica, the youngest, writes a love letter to Junius and entreats him to come to her. When he and his companions arrive in act 3 scene 5, the two daughters chain them and mock them for their ignorance. They are proud of their clever conquest and are not ashamed to use any means possible to exact revenge for the damages done to their bodies and honor. However, as I noted earlier, their cousin Caratach discovers the plot, releases the Romans for the "dishonor" done to them on the field of battle, and shames the women for their behavior. More incriminating than the violation against their bodies, though, is their "base" means of revenge: Caratach cannot sanction their subversive form of warfare. The play's emphasis then is less on the daughters' "ruined" state and more on their misappropriation of military power, much as we see with the portrayal of Bonduca.

Later in the play, and just prior to her death, the eldest daughter makes clear their critical role in state politics: "We were not born for triumphs, / To follow your gay sports, and fill your slaves / With hoots and acclamations. ... Must we gild ore your Conquest, make your State?" (4.4.59–61, 64). Bonduca and her daughters recognize their import as generative members of the British realm and refuse the eventuality of their roles as mocked prisoners of war. To be conquered

---

[30] Green, "Theme and Structure in Fletcher's *Bonduca*," 314.

[31] Travitsky, "Child Murder," 73.

by Rome and used for its purposes — physically and politically — would dishon-
or and destroy not only these individual women but also the spirit and culture of
the realm they embody. The play is primarily concerned with the women's sexuality in terms of its relationship to national power dynamics.[32] Sullied or not,
marriageable or not, Bonduca's daughters are valuable as the royal heirs to
Britain.

Thus, in their mother Bonduca's case, it is less clear whether or not the pene-
trative act of murder is viewed in an equally disinterested manner as that of the
rapes. While there is a definite difference between actual sexual penetration and
a symbolic one that manifests through murderous force, the issue of masculine
authority is inherent in both instances, and the play's problematic treatment of
Bonduca's appropriation of such power begs further investigation. At first, the
queen is ostracized as an "unnatural woman"; however, later in the plot, her acts
and person take on a noble, valiant cast. By assigning the masculine virtue of
"death before dishonor" to herself and her children, Bonduca carves out a socially
redemptive space for them all. Swetonius's judgment seems to be the final word
on the case, for in the rest of the play we do not hear any further of Bonduca or
the murder of her children.

Both Green and Travitsky tend to view the portrayal of child murder in *Bonduca* almost exclusively as a negative consequence of her transgression in the
patriarchal realms. She is, they argue, unable to negotiate the differences between
her natural and political roles, and is ultimately portrayed as a dangerous, rash
woman, suggesting that females are "inherently unfit instruments for rule."[33]
However, we cannot completely elide the fact that in her transgression, in her

---

[32] Calder makes an important observation that "Whereas masculine identity in the
text resides in sexual conquest and military honor . . . feminine identity resides in the
body" ("Male and Female Experiences of War," 215). While she does not focus on the
body politics at a national level, and sees rape as the primary experience of gendered
political conflict in the play, her point is well taken here. The Romans' accusations of
Bonduca and her daughters are all pointed towards violations of the female body and
feminine "nature." I am less convinced by Calder's later suggestion that "the decision of
Bonduca and her daughters to kill themselves is made not because of any loss of military
honor, but rather in recognition of the rape that would occur were they to be captured"
(217). As the leader of her people and a warrior queen, Bonduca is very much representative of and concerned with honor (military or not). Admittedly she and her daughters are
extremely aware of their sexual peril if captured, but I do not think that is the primary
reason for their deaths. *Bonduca* follows closely the sacrificial "death before dishonor"
model of many child murder representations, and it is for this violent act that the queen
is recognized and later praised by the Romans.

[33] Travitsky, "Child Murder," 73.

ability to take on the weapons and demeanor of traditionally male figures, in her aggressive possession of authority to effect the destruction of her offspring, who are also the natural heirs of England, Bonduca possesses a noticeable degree of power. Her disordering of the hierarchy grants her agency, above and beyond that due her as monarch. And her act, which eliminates any potential Roman conquest of the present and future royal bloodline, is an act of national resistance.

Bonduca's acquisition of masculine authority over violence in this household — not only of the nuclear family but of the nation as a whole — is telling in its grandeur. The violence that Bonduca exercises on her own body, representative of the body politic, makes this scene all the more unbelievable and shocking ... and perhaps not so unfamiliar. The audience of 1613 remembered all too well a woman who constructed herself in terms of masculine and divine authority, possessing the power to rule and to make authoritative decisions on behalf of England's welfare. Her natural body was transformed by rhetoric into a masculine, politically acceptable one; but at the same time she was figured in numerous failed marriage negotiations as a model of female virtue and nurturing. The woman was Queen Elizabeth I.

The connection between Bonduca and Elizabeth warrants consideration. Beyond expressing anxiety about women exercising transgressive power and being outside the bounds of "natural" behavior, what does this play's representation of child murder have to offer? Jodi Mikalachki traces the literary heritage of Boadicea, the Iceni queen on whose story Fletcher's *Bonduca* is based, and concludes that in her many incarnations, Boadicea becomes symbolic of England's efforts to craft a national identity and express its anxiety over female rulership. She is a puzzling figure, embodying both "native patriotism" and inherent danger to the masculine-based hierarchy.[34] Mikalachki continues that, while representations of Elizabeth did not often directly include connections to her ancient precursor, Boadicea remained a symbolically significant marker of "changing English attitudes to women in power."[35]

When James succeeded to the British throne in 1603, he was faced with the monumental task of winning over his new subjects. While Elizabeth's reign was fraught with its own problems, many people remembered her rule fondly (and, increasingly, as a "golden age"). Especially during the beginning of James's reign, when he was both praised and criticized most heavily, the rhetoric of "the cult

---

[34] See Mikalachki, *The Legacy of Boadicea: Gender and Nation in Early Modern England*, 116.

[35] Mikalachki, *The Legacy of Boadicea*, 117.

of Elizabeth" seemed alive and well. With his foreign upbringing and radically different style of rule, he relied on powerful advisors and effective spin-doctors to improve his image. As Curtis Perry observes, "In order to capitalize fully on the propagandistic value of asserting continuity between Elizabeth and James, sharp distinctions between the two rulers had to be finessed."[36] James wanted and needed to establish his own power and individuality as a monarch; and yet he also needed to incorporate the legacy of Elizabeth. A new England had to be imagined, one that allowed for her myth to exist but that glorified a return to masculine political authority.

Bonduca finds itself at the intersection of these social and political concerns, taking them up through its treatment of the murderous queen. While I do not necessarily wish to suggest that Bonduca *is* Elizabeth in the play, the language that describes her and the act of child murder resonates remarkably with the historical tensions I have described. Perry's study argues for a Jacobean England in which representations of Elizabeth and female rulership were manipulated in order to achieve particular rhetorical effects on the populace.[37] When we view the play in this light, Elizabeth's military prowess in handling the uprisings in Ireland and directing the destruction of the Spanish Armada may correlate with the militaristic achievements and British nationalism that Bonduca embodies in the drama. And, as I discussed in the case of *Gorboduc*, it is possible that her refusal and/or inability to produce an heir might be construed as a murderous threat to her "children," the English people and the cultural legacy of the Elizabethan age. Such a parallel would at first seem damning and accusatory of the deceased queen, since Bonduca often comes across as rash, "unnatural," and unfit for governance. However, we should not forget Swetonius's and the other Romans' admiration for such valor and strength of will. By the end of the play, the queen has retained her royal designation, preserved the spirit of Britain, and has been buried respectfully.

The transgressive Iceni queen, while she defies conventions in her military conquests and in her mothering practices (to both kin and nation), is established as part of the country's past: dangerous, but irrefutably noble. The new leadership, persuasively masculine, ordered, and in control, advances to power.[38] Em-

---

[36] Perry, *The Making of Jacobean Culture*, 157.

[37] For a more in-depth discussion of these representations, see Perry, *The Making of Jacobean Culture*, 153–87.

[38] A number of critics have, however, questioned just how smooth and effective this transition really is. Boling, "Fletcher's Satire of Caratach in *Bonduca*," and Hickman, "*Bonduca*'s Two Ignoble Armies," base their conclusions primarily on textual evidence.

ploying the dramatic motif of a militaristic queen who slays her children may thus suggest that, no matter how honorable and brave the female ruler, ultimately it is a strong *male* rule that is supremely beneficent and best for the nation's interests. It is impossible to know whether Fletcher intended such connections for his drama, but we may wonder whether his audience may have understood them just the same. *Bonduca*'s representation of the Iceni queen appears to be implicated in the rhetorical dance of king-making and nation-building prevalent during the early years of James's reign. The play provides a rhetorical transition from Elizabethan to Jacobean ideologies.

That dramatic scenes of murderous mothers almost uniformly include queens and slain children who are adults bespeaks a greater rhetorical function for the motif than simple conventionality. Whether intentional or not, the audience's reaction would be guided by their cultural understanding of various symbolic meanings. To kill the heir to the throne, the effective future of the nation, is an act with extremely serious political ramifications. To map this act across the body of a woman, to invert her creative powers into destructive force, problematizes the boundaries of "natural" versus civilized behavior. To figure the body natural as corrupt and monstrous, and to subsume that problem within a character who represents the body politic, makes the marginal absolutely central. When playwrights weave this motif into plays, what first seems like simple theatricality may indeed register as much more politically volatile.

As Greg Walker cogently states,

> That the plays were performed at court made them more rather than less effective vehicles for political debate. That they staked their claim for an audience primarily on the fact that they addressed issues of personal morality and integrity ensured that they were at the centre rather than the margins of those debates, for ... the language of morality was also the language of politics at the royal courts of the Renaissance.[39]

While the play seems to discredit Bonduca and female rule, it also problematizes any neat construction of male authority — whether British (in the figures of Caratach and Hengo) or Roman. Crawford's work, "Fletcher's *The Tragedie of Bonduca* and the Anxieties of the Masculine Government of James I," links these textual inconsistencies with historical context: once settled into office, James and his court practices were often contrasted to the golden reign of Elizabeth and criticized for their "excess." *Bonduca* may be seen, then, as critical of both reigns.

[39] Walker, *The Politics of Performance*, 224.

While Walker speaks of *Gorboduc* as well as several other civic-minded dramas that do not include representations of child murder, his point has specific applicability to our problem. As I discussed earlier, it would seem that the majority of the plays containing the child murder motif either were meant for private reading or were performed for elite audiences. Many also seem to possess overt political concerns, such as succession, "good counsel," or nation building. Private venues probably did not portray lower-class infanticides because they were not a central consideration for wealthier patrons. These plays sidestep reality and the conventions of domestic tragedy to illustrate the political consequences of a monarch's creative and destructive powers.

In bringing to attention other political and cultural forces present during the production of plays like *Gorboduc* and *Bonduca*, I suggest that child murder representations should not be solely interpreted as misogynistic discourse. It is clear that portrayals of queens who slay their children are negative; that they express a social anxiety about women in power; that they challenge the construction of "natural" motherhood. These observations provide constructive ways of thinking about child murder's dramatic impact. Considering the political importance of this motif, however, produces another rich interpretive bounty and further aids us in understanding some of the relationships between early modern drama and culture. We cannot, must not, elide the powerful differences between representation and reality, nor leave untouched what those differences may suggest.

Catherine E. Thomas
The Pennsylvania State University

Works Cited

B., R. *Apius and Virginia*. In *Tudor Interludes*, ed. Peter Happé, 271–317. New York: Penguin, 1972.

Boling, Ronald J. "Fletcher's Satire of Caratach in *Bonduca*." *Comparative Drama* 33 (1999): 390–406.

Buchanan, George. *Jeptha*. In *George Buchanan Tragedies*, trans. P. G. Walsh, ed. P. Sharratt and idem, 64–94, Edinburgh, Scotland: Scottish Academic Press, 1983.

Calder, Alison. " 'I am unacquainted with that language, Roman': Male and Female Experiences of War in Fletcher's *Bonduca*." *Medieval and Renaissance Drama in England* 8 (1996): 211–26.

Camden, William. *The History of the Most Renowned and Victorious Princess Elizabeth Late Queen of England*, ed. and intro. Wallace T. MacCaffrey. Chicago: University of Chicago Press, 1970.

Chambers, E. K. *The Elizabethan Stage*, vol. 2. Oxford: Clarendon Press, 1923.

Crawford, Julie. "Fletcher's *The Tragedie of Bonduca* and the Anxieties of the Masculine Government of James I." *Studies in English Literature* 39 (1999): 357–81.

Dolan, Frances E. *Dangerous Familiars: Representations of Domestic Crime in England 1550–1700*. Ithaca: Cornell University Press, 1994.

Fletcher, John. *Bonduca*, ed. Cyrus Hoy. In *The Dramatic Works in the Beaumont and Fletcher Canon*, ed. Fredson Bowers, 4:149–259. Cambridge: Cambridge University Press, 1979.

Fumerton, Patricia. *Cultural Aesthetics: Renaissance Literature and the Practice of Social Ornament*. Chicago: University of Chicago Press, 1991.

Green, Paul D. "Theme and Structure in Fletcher's *Bonduca*." *Studies in English Literature* 22 (1982): 305–16.

Greg, W. W. *A Bibliography of the English Printed Drama to the Restoration*, vol. 2. London: Oxford University Press, 1951.

Hale, David George. *The Body Politic: A Political Metaphor in Renaissance English Literature*. The Hague: Mouton, 1971.

Harbage, Alfred. *Annals of English Drama 975–1700*, rev. S. Schoenbaum. London: Methuen, 1964.

———. *Shakespeare and the Rival Traditions*. New York: Macmillan, 1952.

Hickman, Andrew. "*Bonduca*'s Two Ignoble Armies and *The Two Noble Kinsmen*." *Medieval and Renaissance Drama in England* 4 (1989): 143–71.

Illick, Joseph E. "Child-Rearing in Seventeenth Century England and America." In *The History of Childhood*, ed. Lloyd deMause, 303–50. New York: Psychohistory Press, 1974.

Kawachi, Yoshiko. *Calendar of English Renaissance Drama*. New York and London: Garland, 1986.

Marlowe, Christopher. *The Jew of Malta*, ed. N. W. Bawcutt. Manchester: Manchester University Press; Baltimore: Johns Hopkins University Press, 1978.

———. *Tamburlaine the Great*, ed. J. S. Cunningham. Manchester: Manchester University Press; Baltimore: Johns Hopkins University Press, 1981.

Mikalachki, Jodi. *The Legacy of Boadicea: Gender and Nation in Early Modern England*. London and New York: Routledge, 1998.

Perry, Curtis. *The Making of Jacobean Culture: James I and the Renegotiation of Elizabethan Literary Practice*. Cambridge: Cambridge University Press, 1997.

Sackville, Thomas, and Thomas Norton. *Gorboduc; or, Ferrex and Porrex*. In *Drama of the English Renaissance 1: The Tudor Period*, ed. Russell A. Fraser and Norman Rabkin, 81–100. New York: Macmillan, 1976.

Stallybrass, Peter. "Patriarchal Territories: The Body Enclosed." In *Rewriting the

Renaissance: The Discourses of Sexual Difference in Early Modern Europe, ed. Margaret W. Ferguson, Maureen Quilligan, and Nancy J. Vickers, 123–42. Chicago and London: University of Chicago Press, 1986.

Stone, Lawrence. *The Family, Sex, and Marriage in England 1500–1800*. London: Harper and Row, 1977.

Travitsky, Betty S. "Child Murder in English Renaissance Life and Drama." *Medieval and Renaissance Drama in England* 6 (1993): 63–84.

Tucker, M. J. "The Child as Beginning and End: Fifteenth and Sixteenth Century English Childhood." In *The History of Childhood*, ed. deMause, 229–57.

Walker, Greg. *The Politics of Performance in Early Renaissance Drama*. Cambridge: Cambridge University Press, 1998.

Wrightson, Keith. *English Society 1580–1680*. New Brunswick, NJ: Rutgers University Press, 1982.

Blood in the Kitchen:
Violence and Early Modern Domestic Work

In Thomas Heywood's 1633 play *The English Traveller* a servant named Roger narrates for his master and mistress a spectacular domestic riot at a neighbor's house, one that involves mutilation, maiming, and even cannibalism. "As I came along by the door," he says,

> I was call'd up amongst them; Hee-Gallants, and Shee-Gallants, I no sooner look'd out, but saw them out with their Knives, Slashing of Shoulders, Mangling of Legs, and Lanching of Loynes, till there was scarce a whole Limbe left amongst them ... One was hacking to cut off a Necke ... [O]ne was picking the Braines out of a Head, another was Knuckle deepe in a Belly, one was Groping for a Liver, another Searching for the Kidneyes.[1]

Alternately recalling epic battle scenes and the dissections of popular anatomy theaters, Roger describes an orgy of bloodshed in which body parts fly so furiously that actual subjects are hard to identify. Mutating into an array of visceral interiors — brains, kidneys, livers — individual bodies blur into an indistinguishable mass of adulterated and edible flesh: "There was such biting and tearing with their teeths," Roger notes, "that I am sure, I saw some of their poore Carcasses pay for't ... There was no stitching up of those Wounds, where Limbe was pluckt from Limbe" (25).

The humor of this narrative rests in the fact that the scene of violence is, in fact, merely a "Massacre of meat" (26), as one character terms it, simply the daily work of food preparation and consumption. Roger's audience, the Wincotts,

---

[1] Heywood, *The English Traveller*, 25. All references to this play will be cited by page number.

gradually understand the comic nature of their servant's conceit, but only after inquiring about the origins of the battle, the arrival of surgeons, and the fate of the ladies. Roger willingly embellishes his story with graphic descriptions of scarred flesh, a body staked from mouth to anus, and, finally, the tasting of sundry limbs. First "Broacht in the Kitchin" by a "Colloricke" cook, the fight stirred up free-floating passions, for, as Roger says blandly, "one had a Stomacke, and another had a Stomacke" (26, 25). While "having a stomach" could simply imply hunger, this expression also referred more abstractly to affections, dispositions, and cravings, and, more specifically, to feelings of resentment, courage, irritation, haughtiness, or pride.[2] As militant servants spark a battle that spreads to passionate gallants, all members of the food chain become indiscriminately mixed with the flesh they battle. Having stomachs (tantamount to being driven by unspecified longings and resentments) makes household members turn into stomachs. Domesticated bodies, in this servant's imagination, are literally positioned on the food chain as entities caught up in an appetitive world of pleasurable destruction and consumption.

What kind of violence does *The English Traveller* describe? Since it occurs in a play that has retrospectively been labeled a "domestic tragedy," this passage raises questions about how scholars define "domesticity" and "violence" as they analyze early modern representations. Roger's comic narration at first seems so evidently to defamiliarize those ordinary acts that typically defined domestic subjects; that is, his fantasy seems to reinterpret daily life as violence and thus throw into relief the importance of a stable and normative domestic structure. As scholars have noted, the post-Reformation household was seen as modeling and providing the training ground for political order.[3] "The father is head of household as king is head of state" is the ubiquitous message trumpeted in sermons and

---

[2] See *OED* entries for "stomach," 5b, 6a, 7a, 8a, 8b, 8c.

[3] Scholars debate whether conceptions of the family changed significantly in the wake of the Reformation. Stone has famously argued that Catholic idealizations of celibacy gave way to celebrations of the spiritual potential of the companionate conjugal union (*The Family, Sex, and Marriage in England, 1500–1800*; see also Hill, *Society and Puritanism in Pre-Revolutionary England*, 443–81). On the value of Stone's work for literary analyses, see Rose, *The Expense of Spirit: Love and Sexuality in English Renaissance Drama.* For skeptical critiques of Stone, see Sharpe, *Early Modern England: A Social History 1550–1760*; Houlbrooke, *The English Family 1450–1700*; Davies, "The Sacred Condition of Equality — How Original were Puritan Doctrines of Marriage?"; and Newman, *Fashioning Femininity and English Renaissance Drama.* One can appreciate Stone's grasp of the discontinuities in "the family" over time without endorsing all of his conclusions (e.g., the novelty of idealizations of marriage; the growth of affective individualism; the shift from an open lineage family to a restricted nuclear family).

conduct manuals. "Upon this condition of the Family, being the Seminary of all other Societies," writes William Perkins in 1609:

> it followeth that the holy and righteous government thereof is a direct mean for the good ordering both of Church and Commonwealth. . . . For this first society, is, as it were, the School wherein are taught and learned the principles of authority and subjection.[4]

As the "first society" and "seminary," the early modern family bore the tremendous burden of inculcating citizenship in a patriarchal and hierarchical world by structuring the proper dependencies that founded church, state and body politic.

A key disciplinary structure through which early modern people learned to rein in their chaotic impulses, the household, like other institutions, was often represented as an organism composed of carefully hierarchized yet interdependent parts.[5] The Pauline conception of marriage involved the unequal yoking of individuals to form "one flesh," as conduct books endlessly stated. "Everie *Wife* should bee then as *a part* of her *Husband*, as a *limme* of him that hath her," writes Thomas Gataker in *A Good Wife Gods Gift*.[6] In the marital body, that is, the wife serves as a necessary if subordinate part. In *A Health to the Gentlemanly Profession of Serving Men*, I. M. characteristically uses the analogy between body and household/commonwealth to order domestic relations by warning against rebellion: "for all desiring to be Heades, then the body must needes fall for want of Eyes to direct him; and if all Eyes, then it must needes perish for want of a mouth to feede him: But being devided into members, every one using his office, and resting contented with his estate, the body remaynes in perfect health &

---

[4] Perkins, *Christian Oeconomie*, ¶3r. Even orthodox early modern writing on domesticity shows that its financial, ethical, and social dimensions came into conflict. For a discussion of these contradictions, see Orlin, *Private Matters and Public Culture in Post-Reformation England*, 126–30; Amussen, *An Ordered Society: Gender and Class in Early Modern England*, 41–47; and Hutson, *The Usurer's Daughter: Male Friendship and Fictions of Women in Sixteenth-Century England*, 17–51.

[5] The human body provided the quintessential grid in Renaissance cosmic, legal, medical, religious, social, sexual, and domestic ideologies. On the metaphorics of the body, see Barkan, *Nature's Work of Art: The Human Body as Image of the World*; Sawday, *The Body Emblazoned: Dissection and the Human Body in Renaissance Culture*; Stallybrass, "Patriarchal Territories: The Body Enclosed"; Harris, *Foreign Bodies and the Body Politic*; Bynum, *Fragmentation and Redemption: Essays on Gender and the Human Body in Medieval Religion*; *The Body in Parts: Fantasies of Corporeality in Early Modern Europe*, ed. Hillman and Mazzio; and Nutton, " 'A Diet for Barbarians': Introducing Renaissance Medicine to Tudor England."

[6] Gataker, "A Wife Indeed," in *A Good Wife Gods Gift*, 9.

happines."[7] Clearly Roger, as a domestic subordinate, is happy to counter this image of organic harmony by describing a full-scale bodily fragmentation, one that clearly disrupts what Perkins saw as the process of familial and civic "subjection." After all, in Roger's story there are no discrete subjects that might be ordered with precision.

Many representations of domesticity did indeed play into early modern ideologies that slotted social groups and genders into societal norms.[8] Read through this lens, Roger's defamiliarizing of household practice might be said to frame everyday tasks as normative and unremarkable. But what if the "ordinary" were already potentially estranged in the early modern imagination? What if bodies were routinely constituted in ways that exposed their potential divisibility and unmanageability? What if the lived experience of domesticity (as well as its textual elaborations) introduced alternative ways of thinking about the body and relations of dependency? As Patricia Fumerton has remarked, "the everyday practice of another period (as also our own) can be charged with strangeness even to its practitioners."[9] Examining *The English Traveller* in the context of the first printed cookbooks in England, we see that representations of household practice might trouble conventional domestic ideologies, both early modern and perhaps our own; for when embodiment is represented as a fraught domestic experience, then the "proper" early modern subjects constructed in somatic terms become unsettled.

We first should acknowledge that early modern households do not completely accord with modern assumptions about the organization, scope, or even social function of the home. Scholars have helped us to overcome our presentist viewpoint by highlighting precisely those features of the Renaissance household that have become alien to later observers: the lack of hallways and thus private living spaces; the sharing of beds among servants, family members, and guests; the inclusion of what would later become professionalized market production; the normative violence; the lack of boundaries between household and community; and

---

[7] I. M., *A Health to the Gentlemanly Profession of Servingmen*, B2v; adapted from 1 Corinthians 12:14–21.

[8] The best account of how domestic violence functioned in the period is Dolan, *Dangerous Familiars: Representations of Domestic Crime in England, 1550–1700*. On domestic ideology, see Orlin, *Private Matters and Public Culture*; Gowing, *Domestic Dangers: Women, Words and Sex in Early Modern London*, 206–31; and Henderson, "The Theater and Domestic Culture."

[9] Fumerton, "Introduction: A New New Historicism," in *Renaissance Culture and the Everyday*, 6.

the sheer amount of labor required to sustain human life.[10] The household was, after all, the primary unit of production as well as consumption in the period. Sometimes headed up by a single woman, sometimes harboring a working husband, servants of different ranks, apprentices, and children, sometimes taking the form of same-sex academic residences or urban shops — the early modern household included non-blood-related "kin" with diverse labor interests.

As the earliest published domestic advice manuals and cookbooks in England shaped conceptions of domesticity, they made readers self-conscious about the meaning of daily life. Housewifery, first published as a subset of knowledge in sixteenth-century husbandry books, broke off as a separate discourse in the 1570s when English cookbooks appeared in bookstalls. Unlike their French counterparts, which were marketed for men of great households, the first English cookbooks addressed housewives of all ranks, a trend that continued until the 1650s when some guides were addressed to professional elite male chefs. In 1600, however, there were two primary discourses found in English guides, which together form a debate about the scope, nature, and definition of domesticity. First, encyclopedic estate management books tied household labor to agrarian production while lauding the importance of indigenous practices. Gervase Markham's 1615 *English House-wife*, to take one instance, fantasized about recovering days of yore by instantiating a national *oeconomia*, for his housewife exemplified the country frugality that he touts as modeling national character. In his vision, the insulated estate, the bodies inhabiting it, and the nation were seen as structurally similar. Markham's thrifty housewife avoids shopping and embraces homegrown food "esteemed for the familiar acquaintance she hath with it, than for the strangeness and rarity it bringeth from other Countries."[11] Kim Hall has underscored the consequences of this rhetorical sleight of hand, for though these recipes call for imported and foreign ingredients, Markham's housewife is said to guard na-

---

[10] See, for example, Orlin, *Private Matters and Public Culture*; Girouard, *Life in the English Country House: A Social and Architectural History*; Friedman, *House and Household in Elizabethan England: Wollaton Hall and the Willoughby Family*; Erickson, *Women and Property in Early Modern England*; Cahn, *Industry of Devotion: The Transformation of Women's Work in England, 1500–1650*; Underdown, *Revel, Riot, and Rebellion: Popular Politics and Culture in England, 1603–1660*; and Amussen, *An Ordered Society*.

[11] Markham, *The English House-wife*, 4. This text was first published along with a gentlemen's recreational guide called *Countrey Contentments* but subsequently became a stand-alone text. Other estate management books included Fitzherbert, *Boke of Husbandry*; Surflet, *The Country Farme*; and Googe, *The Whole Art and Trade of Husbandry*.

tional- and self-integrity, in short, the "domestic" in its multiple meanings.[12] Estate management books thus emphasized an ideal social and national cohesion emanating from household duties and registered in the maintenance of the body.

A second domestic discourse surfaced in the 1570s texts, which targeted urban readers appreciative of tips on banqueting, cosmetics, and social mobility. Placing in the foreground confectionery and physic, these works conjoin households and bodies in a fantasy about infinite alterability rather than integrity, entities whose civilized boundaries were oddly unsettled in daily practice. Rather than emphasize frugal household management, these manuals highlight the pleasures of inventiveness and the cultivation of proper taste. Hugh Plat's popular 1602 *Delights for Ladies*, for instance, invites readers to create decadent desserts molded in the shape of gloves, keys, heraldic devices, and animals. Rather than working to increase efficiency, the housewife was to take pleasure in creating a simulacrum of the real world and in creating elaborate rituals around the presentation of food. A recipe in the 1598 *Epulario* shows that such "civilizing" entertainments might toy with guests' conception of "the real." Entitled "To make Pies That the Birds May be Alive in Them [so that] they Fly Out When It is Cut up," the recipe notes, "Because [the guests] shall not be altogether mocked," the wife should make a small edible pie to accompany the conceit.[13] The fun of defamiliarizing eating, that is, should not substitute for gustatory pleasure. The production of food hints at the delights of impropriety, with mockery of the fixities of nature or of household members built into the construction of unexpected liveness.

The housewife was also instructed to thwart the march of time by creating durable foodstuffs such as cakes, distilled waters, conserves, and preserves, delicacies that could, as texts repeat obsessively, "keep throughout the year."[14] First heralded as a restorative for the body, sugar, even in its more recognizably decadent dessert forms, was imagined to fortify humankind against the ravages of mortality. Yet the rituals surrounding the consumption of desserts sometimes unexpectedly catered to destructive impulses. Aristocratic meals could conclude with

---

[12] Hall argues that the housewife functioned figuratively to "nationalize" goods by laundering foreign products into home-born forms. By processing foodstuffs (especially sugar) into goods that were then labeled as tried and true national staples, the European wife participated in the international trade system including the emergent slave trade (Hall, "Culinary Spaces, Colonial Spaces: The Gendering of Sugar in the Seventeenth Century").

[13] *Epulario, or The Italian Banquet*, B4r.

[14] Guides that emphasize "keeping" include Plat, *Delightes For Ladies*; *A Closet for Ladies*; Murrell, *A Daily Exercise for Ladies and Gentlewomen*; Dod and Cleaver, *A Godly Forme of Houshold Government*, L3v; and Gouge, *Of Domesticall Duties*, 254.

a highly refined food fight carried out in the "void," or banqueting room designed for after-dinner entertainments.[15] Sixteenth-century cookbooks offer a
citizen's version of such spectacles. "At the ende of the banquet they may eat al,
and breake the platters, dishes, cups, and all thynges: for this paste is delicate,"
assures John Partridge in his 1584 *Good Huswives Closet*.[16] Doubly furnishing
the table — first with real trenchers and then with their cunning edible doubles
— the housewife played on the gap between reality and appearance, creating a
game of deceit resolved through a collective oral assault. Given ubiquitous injunctions for the housewife to "keep," the delight in casually destroying copies of
the material world must have been considerable. Housewifery thus tapped into
desires for durability and whimsical sacrifice, for a world to be mimicked or safeguarded, but one whose ravenous destruction could be performed at will. In
short, it offered what Michel de Certeau has termed an everyday "tactic" that
could recast ideologies about economic and social ordering.[17]

Beyond their practical use, these guides offered contrasting frames through
which readers could experience domesticity. Clinging to old-fashioned methods,
Markham made the household the place in which an English population could
preserve the rhythms of past days and criticize aristocratic disregard for the value
of work. Plat, on the other hand, placed the household at the forefront of a malleable future social order dependent on innovation and eager for the mobility denounced in conduct books. Responding to widespread economic changes ushered
in by the emergence of protocapitalism, these guides interpret housewifery in
different ways: its destructive potential is circumscribed as a game, its economic
value becomes the sign of national character. Yet both types of guides emphasize
the housewife's primary responsibility in managing flesh in all of its incarnations.
In doing so, these manuals, perhaps unwittingly, illuminated one troubling aspect
of domesticity, namely the household member's vulnerability to the housewife's
bodily care.

The housewife was to administer an almost daily regimen of diet and purges,
since she was in charge of orchestrating the intake and output of the precarious
humoral bodily economy.[18] Enacting a thoroughly fused medical and culinary
practice, the wife was to supervise a person's vital balance of spirits by trans-

---

[15] Fumerton discusses aristocratic banqueting in *Cultural Aesthetics: Renaissance Literature and the Practice of Social Ornamentation*, 111–68.

[16] Partridge, *Treasurie of Commodious Conceites*, A4r.

[17] de Certeau, *The Practice of Everyday Life*, trans. Randall, xiii.

[18] On the humoral body, see Paster, *The Body Embarrassed: Drama and the Disciplines
of Shame in Early Modern England*, esp. 7–17.

ferring "essences" from food to people through sometimes painful procedures. Cookbooks boast recipes that involve pouring lemon juice into open sores, lancing boils, and sticking feathers infused with oil deep into a patient's nostrils (in order to cleanse the vapors in the head). Lady Catherine Sedley and the Countess of Kent, for instance, recommend putting plasters "as hot as may be endured to the Fundament," navel, and vagina. Lady Grace Mildmay records subjecting a child to a three-day regimen that alternated fasting, enemas, vomits, and sweating with bouts of drinking acerbic liquids.[19] One particularly ghastly recipe for curing eye infections had the housewife extract lice from a person's hair and affix them to the eyeball, for lice were said to suck out pestilent "webs" or eyesores: "Put them alive into the Eye that is grieved and so close it up, and most assuredly the Lice will suck out the Web in the eye, and will cure it, and come forth without any hurt."[20] The wife here is to subject the ailing person to a nightmare of the flesh, since lice were associated in the cultural imagination with vampirism, predation, filth, and the threat of being devoured alive. The writer's promise, that this will "assuredly" cure the eye "without any hurt," only raises the specter of possible injury. Clearly the domesticated body was one not docilely molded by its repeated placement in a political and social hierarchy, but one subjected to mundane and physical modes of subjection and fashioning. Health, it seems, required the threat of an aggressively unmakable and injured body.

Part and parcel of physic was the transformation of the kitchen into a slaughterhouse strewn liberally with blood and carcasses. In *The English House-wife*, Markham begins one recipe with the following injunction, "Take the blood of a hog whilst it is warm and steep in it a quart ... of great oatmeal grits" (63). While we might pause to imagine the ramifications of having a freshly killed hog draping the workspace, we discover that carnage was simply a kitchen commonplace. Hannah Woolley recommends the following cure for consumption and agues:

> Take a Red Cock, pluck him live, then slit him down the back, and take
> out his Intrals, cut him in quarters, and bruise him in a Mortar, with his

---

[19] Lady Catherine Sedley's manuscript receipt book is excerpted in Sloan, *English Medicine in the Seventeenth Century*, 136. See also *The Choice Manual, or Rare and Select Secrets in Physick and Chirurgery: Collected, practised by the Right Honourable the Countess of Kent, late deceased*, 92. For excerpts of Lady Mildmay's manuscripts, see Pollock, *With Faith and Physic: The Life of a Tudor Gentlewoman, Lady Grace Mildmay, 1552–1620*.

[20] Grey, The Choice Manual, 75.

Head, Legs, Heart, Liver and Gizard; put him into an ordinary Still with a Pottle of Sack.[21]

Having somehow killed the cock, either by slitting it open or simply knowing how to wring its neck, the housewife disembowels the animal, bruises it in a mortar, and stuffs the carcass into a distillation tube. The organs and parts are boiled with milk, currants, raisins, and herbs to make a version of chicken soup. When Woolley revises this recipe in a later guide, she heightens the "liveness" of the dismembered animal: "Take two Running Cocks, pull them alive, then kill them," she begins, "Cut them Cross on the Back, when they are almost cold take their Guts, and . . . break them all to pieces."[22] Emptying bodies when they are "almost cold," breaking tissue "all to pieces," and trafficking in warm blood, the housewife isolated and manipulated the boundary between animation and death. The ailing human, waiting to ingest the remedy, might well have quivered in the face of the housewife, who so evidently had her finger on the pulse of life and death.

The Queens Closet Opened offers a cure for kidney stones that depends on "proper" slaughter, the recycling of animal excretions, and astrological animation:

In the moneth of *May* distill Cow-dung, then take two live Hares, and strangle them in their blood, then take the one of them, and put it into an earthen vessel or pot, and cover it well with a mortar made of horse dung and hay, and bake it in an Oven with houshold bread, and let it still in an Oven two or three dayes, baking a new with any thing, untill the Hare be baked or dried to powder; then beat it well, and keep it for your use. The other Hare you must [flay], and take out the guts onely; then distill all the rest, and keep this water: then take at the new and full of the Moon, or any other time, three mornings together as much of this powder as will lie on six pence, with two spoonfuls of each water; and it will break any stone in the Kidneys.[23]

In fortifying the human bodies under her care, the housewife might routinely work with live animals that had to be properly strangled, left in an oven to rot for days, flayed, and distilled. Crystallized in a potent powder and perhaps activated by a full moon, animal spirits lingered as a highly present substance in the

---

[21] Woolley, *The Queen-like Closet*, 11.
[22] Woolley, *The Compleat Servant Maid*, 174.
[23] W. M., *The Queens Closet Opened*, 7–8.

material ingested by humans. Despite a clear difference in attitude toward animals and humans in some contexts, medical and culinary practice emphasized their *shared* bodily spirits. What people consumed was identifiably transformed flesh; and the act of killing a creature *just so* was critical to the maintenance of a healthy human life.

So perhaps it is not surprising that Lady Elinor Fettiplace could record flaying cats and hedgehogs as well as whipping a cock to death. She writes blithely, "When you kill a sheep, take some of the blood and mince in sweet hearbes."[24] Even for women who did not regularly butcher animals, Renaissance guides confronted unblinkingly the fungibility of human and animal parts. A syrup recipe in *The Widdowes Treasure* highlights this transformation: "This decoction is good to eat / always before and after meat. / For it will make digestion good, / and turn your meat to pure blood."[25] Presenting vivid images of visceral domestic work, cookbooks underscore the importance of flesh mutating into flesh, animal meat turning into human blood. Everywhere hearkening toward dinner's vitality and the precariousness of embodiment, cooking and medical care smacked of licensed violence.

As Markham's instructions for the "ordering of meats to be roasted" indicate, the housewife and cook (in more elite households) became authorities on carnage, as they were to contort, amputate and decapitate bodies. "For in all joints of meat except a shoulder of mutton," writes Markham,

> you shall crush and break the bones well, from pigs and rabbits you shall cut off the feet before you spit them and the heads when you serve them to table, and the pig you shall chine, and divide into two parts. ... Hens, stock-doves, and house-doves, you shall roast with the pinions folded up, and the legs cut off by the knees and thrust into the bodies. ... woodcocks, snipes, and stints shall be toasted with their heads and necks on ... bitterns shall have no necks but their heads only (88).

Markham indulges in a vocabulary that makes cooking seem to repeat prior acts of slaughter. Given the visceral imagery of these guides, Roger's view of servants and dinner guests as enmeshed in severed limbs (as a "Knuckle deepe in a Belly")

---

[24] Spurling, *Elinor Fettiplace's Receipt Book: Elizabethan Country House Cooking*, 42; introduction, 20.

[25] *The Widdows Treasure, Plentifully furnished with sundry precious and approved secrets in Phisicke*, irregular pagination.

begins to resemble actual practice or its popular textual elaborations. As cook-books link medicine to butchery, they invite early modern people to glimpse connections between eating and the anatomist's dissection theater.

Hannah Woolley's paraphrase of the then well-known 1508 *Book of Kerving* offers cues for conceptualizing kitchen practice. "In cutting up small Birds it is proper to say thigh them," writes Woolley, as she renders butchery into a lexicon to be mastered, "as thigh that Woodcock, thigh that Pigeon":

> But as to others say ... wing that Quail ... Allay that Pheasant, untack that Curlew, unjoint that Bittern, disfigure that Peacock, display that Crane, dismember that Hern, unbrace that Mallard ... spoil that Hen ... reer that Goose ... unlace that Cony, break that Deer, leach that Brawn ... splat that Pike ... splay that Bream ... barb that Lobster.[26]

Expected kitchen terms such as "thigh," "mince" and "unjoynt" join with less specifically culinary activities — "disfigure," "dismember," "break," and "spoil" — and with more exotic injunctions to "reer," "splat," "splay," "tusk," and "barb" animals. Making mutilation a rhetorical tutorial, guides construct the decorum of violence; they can be said to partake of what Jonathan Sawday describes as the autoptic vision of early modern culture, the epistemological drive to dissect and master the body.[27] The engaging iteration of imaginatively "disfiguring" re-minds us that "carve" also meant "to take at one's pleasure" (*OED*, 9b). When conduct book writers instructed housewives and workers to remain at home quietly learning subjection, did they have in mind these scenes of indulgent stab-bing and flaying? As these books document negotiations around domestic tasks, they also refract the everyday so as to make it available for a reader's consumption in striking ways.

As if literalizing the merger between healing and butchery in kitchen practice, some recipes recycle even the human body. Elizabeth Grey's 1653 cure for epi-lepsy, for instance, advises the reader to mix gold with pearl, amber, coral, and peony seeds; she continues:

> you must put in some powder of a dead mans Scull that hath been an Anatomy, for a woman, and the pouder of a woman for a man: compound all these together, and make as much of the pouder of all these, as

---

[26] Woolley, *The Compleat Servant Maid*, 35.

[27] Sawday, *The Body Emblazoned*, 1–15.

will lie upon a two-pence, for nine mornings together in Endive water, and drink a good draught of Endive-water after it.[28]

When Woolley presents a version of this remedy in her *The Compleat Servant Maid*, she erases the gender requirement of the human donor but elaborates the practitioner's violation of human remains; her reader doesn't just buy cranial powder but is instructed to pound an actual skull into fine particles: "Take the Skull of a Man or Woman," she advises, "wash it clean, then dry it in your Oven, after your Bread is drawn, beat it to Powder, and boyl it in Posset drink, then let the Party drink thereof Morning and evening, or as oft as need requireth" (151). Lady Grace Mildmay similarly recommends grinding a man's skull with a stone mortar to make an herbal syrup for children suffering from the falling sickness.[29] And Timothy Bright includes in his list of the simplest and most indigenous medical ingredients flowers, honey, roots, and "the scalp of a man."[30] Calling for dung, breastmilk, human urine, umbilical cords, and *mummia* (the liquid or dried substance from an embalmed corpse), guides imply a world of metamorphic and absorbable body parts. In this *memento mori* of everyday practice, the housewife and her staff of servants emerge as almost magical healers who resurrect the dead by paradoxically managing injury; they orchestrate an almost Eucharist-like cycling of life as they stand priest-like over the kitchen dresser.[31]

---

[28] Grey, *The Choice Manual*, 3.

[29] Mildmay's manuscript recipe is reprinted in Pollock, *With Faith and Physic*, 114.

[30] Bright, *A Treatise wherein is declared the sufficiencie of English Medicines*, 37. For recipes that call for mummy, see Grey's *The Choice Manual* and *The Queen's Closet Opened*. Piero Camporesi argues that human cranial powder and mummia had medicinal properties recognized widely by continental intellectuals and physicians. Camporesi's central argument is that early modern people collectively conjured up fantasies of the supernatural, including ones involving the recycling of human bodies and ravaging demons, because they were starved and stimulated by fermented bread, hallucinogens, and mind-altering herbs (*Bread of Dreams: Food and Fantasy in Early Modern Europe*, trans. Gentilcore, 40–55).

[31] According to Sawday, there was a growing corpse economy created to supply anatomists in sixteenth- and seventeenth-century Europe. Although statutes restricted the number of bodies that the Barbers-Surgeons Company or the College of Physicians could dissect, private researchers, guilds (butchers, tailors and wax chandlers), and universities all sought "human material," as it was termed, for experimentation and scientific inquiry. When there weren't enough criminals to satisfy demand, some anatomists took up the practice of grave-robbing and trafficking in stolen corpses, a feat made easy by the dire overcrowding of cemeteries. See Sawday, *The Body Emblazoned*, 54–66; Harding, " 'And one more may be laid there': The Location of Burials in Early Modern London"; Parks, "The Criminal and the Saintly Body: Autopsy and Dissection in Renaissance Italy"; and Cressy, *Birth, Marriage & Death: Ritual, Religion, and the Life-Cycle in Tudor and Stuart England*, 465–67.

The body's fragile mortality thus could have been registered in everyday kitchen work, as cooks, servants, or housewives maneuvered among knives dripping with blood and human products. The prevalent trope of the household as an organic unity was perhaps pressured by the realities of domestic practice or its place in the cultural imagination as a kind of shamanism.

It makes sense, then, that early modern plays joke anxiously that the housewives' restoratives were bound up with mortal costs. In *The Nice Valour*, a Clown complains about being beaten, as he says, to a pulpy "cullis. I am nothing . . . but very pap, / And jelly." "I've no Bones, / My Body's all one Bruise," he laments, "whoever lives to see me / Dead, Gentlemen, shall find me all one Mummy / Good to fill Gallipots, and long dildo Glasses."[32] The Clown's allusion to gallipots, earthen jars used in households to store ointments, and dildo glasses, the cylindrical tubes used in distillation, generates a reverie about violence that revolves around the transformative powers of the housewife and her monumental if ghastly goods. The "cullis" to which the Clown refers (a strong broth in which the strength of animal meat was transferred to a weak patient) could even serve as a verb meaning "to beat." "Quit thy father . . . or Ile cullice thee," threatens Lord Rainebow in Shirley's *The Ball*.[33] In the kitchen, creativity, brutality and performance were business as usual; and human bodies could be put in ominous proximity to the recycling of animal parts. The violence of my title, then, points to practices other than spousal murders and suicides, the typical fare of domestic tragedies. Instead routine tasks could be estranged momentarily, in plays, guides, and perhaps in practice, so that their affinities with conventionally defined violence were made apparent.

Recasting the "normality" of domestic life as it surfaces in our critical work, these recipes might steer us toward moments on the Renaissance stage where the domesticated body was by definition radically out of control, or violently "subjected" as part of daily life. Falstaff in Shakespeare's *Merry Wives of Windsor* would be a case in point, since his humiliation at the hands of the two wives he attempts to seduce takes the form of his worry at being distilled, cooked, bathed, and eaten. Having been baptized with "greasy napkins" by the wives, he cries:

> [T]o be stopp'd in, like a strong distillation with stinking clothes that fretted in their own grease. Think of that — a man of my kidney. Think of that — that am as subject to heat as butter; a man of continual disso-

---

[32] Beaumont and Fletcher, *The Nice Valour, or, The Passionate Madman* in *The Works of Mr. Francis Beaumont and Mr. John Fletcher*, 10: 326.

[33] Shirley, *The Ball*, 4.1.204, 209–10.

lution and thaw. It was a miracle to scape suffocation. And in the height
of this bath (when I was more than half stew'd in grease like a Dutch
dish) to be thrown into the Thames, and cool'd, glowing-hot, in that
surge . . . think of that.[34]

Falstaff's fantasy takes on a decidedly domestic tenor, as he imagines the buck-
basket as a limbeck, dairy cask, bathtub, and finally a cookpot. First thinking of
distilling, the chemical process through which the housewife concocted medicines, perfumes, and waters, Falstaff then converts himself into a consumable
Dutch dish, an English man unmade by becoming liquid and foreign ingredients. In a pre-Cartesian Galenic world where the psychological and the material
had not yet divided, it is not surprising that Falstaff's fear could register as the
threat of corporeal liquefaction, or that his emotions could find a material correlate in the daily processes by which the body was tended. He experiences his
laundering as part of the "culture of dissection" threatening his very constitution
or "kidney." But this feeling of torture easily blends into his usual eroticization
of the wives' household duties, for Falstaff was first attracted to Mistress Ford,
he states, because she "discourses, she carves, she gives the leer of invitation"
(1.3.45–46); and here we might return "carving" to its full early modern resonances: as showing appetite, dismembering, castrating, or displaying courtesy.

Alerting us to struggles in the early modern period organized around the axis
of gender, feminist critics have helped us to recognize that dramatic works participate in cultural debates about the meaning of femininity, domesticity, and
marriage.[35] Marital ideology was transformed in the wake of the Reformation.
Protocapitalism increased professionalization, developed markets, generated
demographic flux, and changed wage labor; and tensions between caregivers and
children shaped battles for autonomy carried out throughout a subject's life.[36]

---

[34] Shakespeare, *The Merry Wives of Windsor*, 3.5.112–121. I use *The Riverside Shakespeare*, ed. Blakemore Evans, 1:286–326.

[35] Critics have seen domestic tragedy in particular as a rich repository for unearthing
the construction and contestation of marital, domestic, and gender ideologies. See Gutier-
rez, "The Irresolution of Melodrama: The Meaning of Adultery in *A Woman Killed with
Kindness*," Bromley, "Domestic Conduct in *A Woman Killed with Kindness*"; McLuskie,
" 'Tis But a Woman's Jar': Family and Kinship in Elizabethan Domestic Drama"; Dolan,
"Gender, Moral Agency, and Dramatic Form in *A Warning for Fair Women*"; Christen-
sen, "Business, Pleasure and the Domestic Economy in Heywood's *A Woman Killed with
Kindness*"; and Orlin, *Private Matters and Public Culture*.

[36] See Clark, *Working Life of Women in the Seventeenth Century*; Ingram, *Church,
Courts, Sex, and Marriage in England, 1570–1640*; Rose, *Expense of Spirit*; Belsey, "Disrupting Sexual Difference: Meaning and Gender in the Comedies"; Newman, *Fashioning*

Scholars marshal these historical factors in order to make sense of key moments on the stage when male household members attempt to manage the emotional fallout surrounding domesticity or to scapegoat women for large-scale cultural changes.

But what if Falstaff's fear registers not just the power of women *per se*, but also the mundane authority of domestic subordinates broadly construed? What if his anxiety about becoming the object of housewifery bespeaks a veiled recognition of the increasingly publicized value of the domestic economy? Fletcher's *The Elder Brother* unfolds this possibility by dramatizing a scene in which Charles, a scholar fresh from the university, questions his servant Andrew about the "earthquake" emanating from the kitchen. When Andrew explains that "the Cookes / Are chopping hearbs and mince meat to make pies, / And breaking Marrow-bones," Charles interrupts: "Can they set them again?" Andrew replies blithely: "Yes, yes, in Brothes and Puddings, and they grow stronger / For th'use of any man." Damaged animal skeletons are "set," or healed, when converted into edible puddings that then strengthen human bones; violated flesh, it seems, is useful. Yet in this economy, animal and human bodies exchange under the auspices of militant workers, as the ensuing dialogue suggests:

> Charles: What squeaking's that? Sure there is a massacre.
> Andrew: Of Pigs and Geese Sir,
>   And Turkeys for the spit. The Cookes are angry Sir
>   And that makes up the medly.[37]

In this kitchen massacre, the cooks' hostility, animal sacrifice, and male fright merge in a "medly" of comic terror. Since at this point in the play Charles is a firm bachelor, and since the flurry of activity to which he objects is a wedding preparation, Charles's fright at the sound of kitchen knives suggests broad anxieties about domesticity's potency. Fears about bodily submission move up and down the food chain from animal to worker to householder, with embodiment freighting the weight of dependency.

Charles's concern about domestic workers and not just wives pushes us to complement a reading of the war of the sexes with attention to how domestic conflicts cut through and across lines of gender. Nightmarish representations of

---

Femininity; Cahn, *Industry of Devotion*; Paster, *The Body Embarrassed*; and Adelman, *Suffocating Mothers: Fantasies of Maternal Origin in Shakespeare's Plays, "Hamlet" to "The Tempest."*

[37] Fletcher, *The Elder Brother*, 9: 3.3.1–14.

domestic combat were not restricted to demonizations of the housewife, but could, as Roger's tale suggests, revolve around the potential violence of everyday service. While *The English Traveller* narrates a conventional story of adultery and death, it builds this plot on the bedrock of an expansive domestic structure, for it locates spousal relations within other social relations (i.e., including servants of different ranks, guests, children, householders, and mistresses). Rather than betraying a fear of housewives out of control, Roger's vision of kitchen carnage shows housewifery to be a set of practices that could be taken up by diverse household residents.

DIET AND DOMESTIC DISORDER

The English Traveller consists of two plots, a prodigal-son city-comedy plot drawn almost wholesale from Plautus's *Mostellaria* (*The Haunted House*) annexed onto a domestic tragic plot about adultery. The domestic tragedy involves a love quadrangle that ensues when a married couple, the Wincotts, invite a beloved neighbor (Geraldine) and his friend (Dalavill) into their home. Geraldine and his childhood sweetheart Mistress Wincott forge a secret but chaste marriage-within-a-marriage by exchanging a vow that they will marry when the elder Mr. Wincott dies. Dalavill upsets this oddly legitimate erotic liaison by engaging in a furtive affair with "the Wife," as she is identified in the play. Geraldine then oddly assumes the role of wronged husband, and, with the help of an informing servant, routs out dishonor in the family. Mistress Wincott promptly dies of shame, Dalavill flees the country, and the husband celebrates his new domestic arrangement by pledging eternal devotion to his new "wife," Geraldine. Domestic chaos takes a different form in the citizen comedy plot where a merchant named Lionnel leaves his house in the hands of his wayward son while traveling abroad to make his fortune. Upon his return, the father is duped by his son's steward, who assumes control of the estate and concocts artful fables to cover the son's financial transgressions. After Lionnel Sr. forgives his penitent son and servant, he brings his family in tow to the Wincotts', where the two plots fold together as mirror images of oddly configured all-male households.

Both plots in *The English Traveller* invoke culinary violence. Initially the play presents food merely as an index of contrasting lifestyles. Roger answers his master's casual question — "what's new?" — with a lively domestic tableau: "Dancing newes sir, / For the meat stands piping hot upon the dresser, / The kitchin's in a heat, and the Cooke hath so bestir'd himselfe, / That hee's in a sweat. The Jacke plaies Musicke, and the Spits / Turne round too't" (13). Roger makes the kitchen into the convivial site of all news, the place where the rhythm of turning spits mutates into a frenzied dance. The sweat of labor blurs, in his account, into a bodily revelry that links the cook to the hot meat he prepares; both stew in a festive but arduous rhythm. After commenting on the cook toiling behind the scenes, Roger then converts sweaty labor into a sign of good householding. Equating moral husbandry with the possession of culinary provisions, he makes work signify status. The Wincotts take definition from their ability to command the dance of labor that twins hot bodies and eaten objects as property.

The Wincotts' moderately festive husbandry is allied with neighbor Lionnel Sr.'s merchandising, and both contrast with the orgiastic banqueting initiated by Lionnel Jr., whose house is described as a "House of Hospitality and a Pallace of Plenty; Where there's Feeding like Horses, and Drinking like Fishes" (25). The difference between acquisitive father and over-consuming son is displayed in terms of their contrasting dinners. Before the father's return from his business ventures, Lionnel's steward Reignald and his country servant Robin (modeled on Plautus's Tranio and Grumio) establish the terms by which the father-son conflict will be expressed. When Robin ventures to the city to denounce Lionnel for surfeiting, Reignald brands him as coarse foodstuff and banishes him roundly to the countryside: "Adue good Cheese and Oynons, stuffe thy guts / With Specke and Barley-pudding for digestion, / Drinke Whieg and sowre Milke, whilest I rince my Throat, with Burdeaux and Canarie" (16). Labeling Robin one of the "hinds of the country that comes prying / To see what dainty fare our kitchin yields," Reignald debates values by reference to contrasting menus. Reignald's transformation of the servant into a "hind" and a cheese not only renders humans and food indistinguishable, but also signals the breakdown of household order. Lionnel is eventually reunited with his father, but only after he promises to be a "thrifty son," which means giving up the compulsion to eat, shop, and consort with harlots. The popular story of prodigality becomes, in this incarnation, the tale of a penitent gourmand, with consumption standing in for a range of sexual and social transgressions.

Lionnel Jr. appropriately concentrates on cataloguing his riches as dinner courses rather than appreciating the "dance" of labor enabling his banqueting. Commanding his steward, Lionnel fantasizes about an endless purchase of entrées:

> Lionnel: Let me have to Supper, Let mee see, a Ducke —
> Reignald: Sweet Rogue.
> Lionnel: A Capon —
> Reignald: Geld the Rascall.
> Lionnel: Then a Turkey —
> Reignald: Now spit him for an Infidell . . . (17).

Filling out his list of what to "have to Supper" with plovers, partridges, larks, pheasants, caviar, sturgeon, anchovies, pickle oysters, and a potato pie, Lionnel luxuriates in imaginatively stocking the house with goods. Yet while his master obsesses on the menu, Reignald playfully makes shopping into violence; that is, he endows each dish with social characteristics ("Rogue," "Infidell," "Rascall") and details their impending injuries (castration, execution). While abundant food signals status and pleasure for Lionnel, it suggests to Reignald an exoticized feast in which "others" are sacrificed to satisfy the collective appetites of servant and master; for the servant redraws the boundaries to include himself in a domestic unit contrasted with infidels and eunuchs. The master's autoerotic compulsions about eating are matched by the servant's equally pleasurable reinterpretation of cooking as sacrificial violence.

Roger's subsequent description of domestic "Massacre" echoes Reignald's animation of dinner, with the result that both complicate a familiar moral fable. For as the Wincotts' servant, Roger is less interested in blaming the "massacre" on excesses in expenditure. Imagining gallants and servants as biting mongrels taking advantage of the weaponry of the kitchen, Roger mockingly hints at numerous phantasmatic inversions in the home. Moral indignation thus doesn't account for Roger's pleasure in frightening the Wincotts with the image of home slaughter waged by subordinates and guests out of control. Instead, both Reignald and Roger present unruly forms of embodiment that underscore the potential disarray of service.

We might not be surprised, given this focus, that the story of prodigal Lionnel turns into the tale of an upstart servant. Banishing Robin to the countryside, Reignald utters a threat that highlights the rebellious component of Roger's fantasy: "I, as the mighty Lord ... Of this great house and castle, banish thee / The very smell ath' kitchin, bee it death, / To appear before the dresser" (14–15). Although Reignald simply means that the garlic-scented servant will be killed if he dares to taint the subtlety of their delicacies, his ambiguous phrase — "bee it death / To appear before the dresser" — opens the door for another meaning: the agent of violence seems to be the cook whose ability to "dress" people recovers the etymological tie between cooking and beating.[38] Appearing before the

---

[38] To "dress" someone is to treat him or her "properly," meaning (ironically) with deserved severity, hence, to give a thrashing, a "dressing down"; to chastise or reprimand (*OED* I.9). "To dress" also means "to prepare for use as food, by making ready to cook" (*OED* II.13.a) Both definitions stem from the meaning "to prepare or set straight" (Old French "dresser," "drecier," or "drescer," deriving from the Latin "directiare").

"dresser," the sideboard in the kitchen on which food was prepared, echoes a juridical appearance before an unacknowledged magistrate.

Reignald's playful allusion to the cook's power, marshaled within his claim to mastery, foreshadows his later usurpation of the household. As steward, itself an intimate and liminal position between householder and other "lower" servants, Reignald easily takes command of his master's house.[39] In the tradition of Terence's slaves or Jonson's Mosca, Reignald becomes household governor, director of action, and exchequer. Using "inventions, Braines, / Wits, Plots, Devices, [and] Stratagems," he locks Lionnel and his drunken acquaintances in a jailed sanctuary and concocts an ingenious story about a haunted house in order to dupe Lionnel Sr. (35). A consummate maker of illusions, he improvises outrageous playlets, including a fiction in which a householder has laid a curse upon the Lionnel property by murdering a household subordinate. Like Roger, Reignald has knives on the brain, for he describes the slain ghost as having a "body gasht, and all ore-stuck with wounds" (40); but Reignald explicitly indicts the *master* of the household as the agent of illegitimate violence (perhaps because he has heard his own master threaten to amputate his guests' tongues). Holding the purse, undertaking violent shopping, governing militant cooks, and fictionalizing bloodthirsty masters, the steward makes domestic routine appear sinister. Hubristically reveling in his mastery, Reignald compares himself to Alexander, Agathocles, and Caesar: "These commanded / Their subjects, and their servants; I my Master" (61). The city comedy plot thus foregrounds master/servant and father/son conflicts rather than heterosexual discord.

The crisis in the Lionnel plot concludes when the father agrees to reconcile with his son on one condition: having forgiven the male citizens who joined Lionnel in mischief, his father demands that all female companions be banished. But the suspense of the scene turns on the father's reconciliation not with his son, but with his rebellious steward. Clearing the house of women might create a gynophobic all-male preserve, but it doesn't pave the way for domestic order, for Old Lionnel hints that the servant/master relationship is an ongoing and vexed one; this resolution occurs, for instance, after he almost beats Reignald.

---

[39] Enjoined to supervise household employees, the early modern steward regulated provisions, kept accounts, and served as a "factor" in business deals. Ranked above other servants as chief officer, he often developed a special intimacy with master and mistress. On service relations, see Burnett, *Masters and Servants in English Renaissance Drama and Culture*, 156–57; Dolan, *Dangerous Familiars*, esp. 66–67; and Kussmaul, *Servants in Husbandry in Early Modern England*.

The hint of the master's barely averted violence lingers, heard clearly by neighboring servant Roger who has already shown himself to be acquainted with blood in the kitchen. The aggressivity of housewifery evidenced in cookbooks becomes the story of domestic crisis in *The English Traveller*.[40]

Although the Wincott plot concerns adultery rather than upstart servants, it shares with the citizen comedy a focus on bodily partition and human food, in part because embodiment becomes a key vocabulary for describing the human bonds formed in the Wincott household. Geraldine sees his integration into Wincott's affections as a form of incorporation: "He studies to engrosse mee to himself," says Geraldine, "And is so wedded to my company, / Hee makes mee stranger to my Father's house" (9). With "engross" meaning "to make the body gross, fat or bulky" as well as "to take possession or absorb," Geraldine's subsumption is imagined in corporeal as well as marital terms. Offering his guest free rein over the household, including his wife's bedchamber, Wincott attempts futilely to install, in effect, a second domestic master to substitute for his lack of a son. His wife complies by furtively lodging Geraldine in her "bosom" alongside her husband (31). The Wincotts incorporate Geraldine, locking him fast in their bosoms, beds, and arms as a brother (33), husband, wife, son (13), and lover (31). Recalling the "choice favours" that he "taste[s] in abundance" at the Wincotts', Geraldine responds in kind by using the language of subsumption (87). The language of the play suggests that Wincott's opening of his body/home sets into motion a passionate and potentially destructive cycle of human absorption that spirals beyond his control.

Dalavill, Geraldine's rival for Mistress Wincott's affections, later brings out the potential brutality of this incorporation when he reports to Geraldine the effects of his absence from the Wincott home:

> ... The House
> Hath all this time seem'd naked without you;
> The good Old Man doth never sit to meat,
> But next his giving Thankes, hee speakes of you;

---

[40] The institution of service was rapidly changing in the early seventeenth century as "gentle" servants became a casualty of the shrinkage of great households and larger estates relied increasingly on mobile, lower-class wage earners. Texts such as Darell's *A Short Discourse of the Life of Serving-men* and I. M.'s *A Health to the Gentlemanly Profession of Serving Men* lament the decay of hospitality caused by the creation of a contract-based system of service. See Burnett, *Masters and Servants*, 4–5; 8–9.

> There's scarce a bit, that he at Table tastes,
> That can digest without a Geraldine,
> You are in his mouth so frequent: Hee and Shee
> Both wondering, what distaste from one, or either,
> So suddenly, should alienate a Guest,
> To them, so dearely welcome (54–55).

Having engrossed Geraldine into the fleshy household body, the Wincotts cannot eat without recalling their companion as present food or the absent object of speech. How can Wincott "digest without a Geraldine" in his mouth? At dinner, the Wincotts speculate on the cause for Geraldine's "distaste" while indulging their own tastes, plaintively demonstrating that he has become a constituent part of their collective digestion and appetite. The strangely visceral phrase that Dalavill uses (Geraldine residing "in" a person's mouth) smacks of the cannibalism evident in Roger's earlier speech. Affection, desire, and love are made to speak the language of ingestion; and mourning is represented as the dinner that fails to satisfy. The intensity of domestic relationships in this plot is conveyed through the vocabulary of orality, taste, and the exchange of body parts.

The English Traveller concludes with the reconstitution of the Wincott household achieved by expelling the adulterous mistress and gentleman-companion and by cementing "true" male alliances. The scapegoat symbolically bearing the weight of the household's corporeal trauma is Mistress Wincott, whose confession and penance are expressed as a bodily disintegration. After Geraldine plays the "Doctor" to purge her sin, she commands, "Swell sicke Heart, / Even till thou burst the ribs that bound thee in; / So there's one string crackt, flow, and flow high / Even till thy blood distill out of mine eyes, / To witnesse my great sorrow" (92). With her "sicke Heart" bursting from her ribs, overflowing as liquid into her eyes, Mistress Wincott literalizes the dissolution of unified flesh that her adultery caused. But her disintegration points not only to her adulterous opening of her body but also implicitly (given the language of the play), to her husband's and her own problematic engrossment of Geraldine. Yet her corporeal breakdown paves the way for Wincott to "marry" Geraldine and thus legitimate a homoerotic dyad. Wincott pauses only a moment over his wife's death before realizing with elation that his true love, Geraldine, will no longer go into exile:

> This meeting that was made
> Onely to take of you a parting leave,
> Shall now be made a Marriage of our Love,
> Which none save onely Death shall separate (94).

To seal the marriage, he names Geraldine heir to his estate.[41] No longer a guest, Geraldine moves into the Wincott household as combined son, mistress, gentleman-companion, and duplicate owner. *The English Traveller* accentuates the eroticized, monetary, and queer nature of its final domestic righting. Feasting and mourning simultaneously in the final scene, very near the body of Mistress Wincott and the letter she wanted to write in blood, the new household is still immersed in consumption and mortality.

When the two households meet in the final scene, neighboring servant Reignald has the audacity to compare Mistress Wincott's death with his own upstart behavior: "Burying of Wives," says Reignald, is "As stale as shifting shirts, or for some servants, / To flout and gull their Masters" (93). Unlike moral fables such as *Volpone* where overreaching servants receive due punishment, *The English Traveller* reinstalls the unruly servant into the very nerve center of domestic life. Geraldine enters into spousal "service" in the Wincott home, and Reignald remains Lionnel's steward. Rather than modeling the ideal hierarchy advocated in guides and conduct books, the play creates non-normative, all-male households whose meaning is governed by powerful servants. The expulsion of the mistress is only a tiny fragment of a larger picture in which male subordinates occupy unstable domestic positions. In the play's discourse, domestic subjects must be continually sacrificed, self-divided, and consumed for the system to work.

I am arguing, in effect, that Roger's invention of a kitchen massacre, replete with detachable limbs and gluttonous passions, not only mocks the appetitive expenditure of Lionnel's house or the triviality of domestic work but also parodies Wincott's household network of consuming desire. Throughout the play, hospitality is imagined as stuffing a friend's guts, shame registers as a heart bursting from a rib cage, and desire as the ingestion of flesh. In a sphere in which people metamorphose so readily into food, daily routine and the service relationships sustaining it take on a sinister edge. Tensions between servant and master, as well as the love expressed as incorporation, cannibalism, and subsumption, find condensed form in the tale of a home massacre where people of all ranks are dissected into dinner. The potential adulteration of the household flesh, hardly restricted to a simple act of sexual betrayal, pervades domestic life.

As *The English Traveller* makes clear, domestic disorder isn't attributable only to unruly wives, but also to prodigal children, ambitious servants, and even

---

[41] On how Wincott's remarriage allows Geraldine to bypass the "dubious undertaking" of marriage to become beneficiary by permission of the father/husband, see McLuskie, *Dekker and Heywood: Professional Dramatists*, 158.

obedient subordinates whose fundamental work in the household could trigger alarm. Just as importantly, solutions to domestic crises include the negotiation of "proper" homoerotic and cross-ranked household bonds. The play also allows us to see how "women's work" could be variously articulated and disarticulated from "service." While English cookbooks hailing the wife as the ultimate manager of flesh endowed her with a vast, almost mystical power, *The English Traveller* transfers that potential to domestic workers and household residents. If we read the play with an eye to constructions of gender, we discover the subordination and erasure of the wife in the domestic sphere, but this reading fails to account fully for the representation of *domestic practice* as wayward, internally conflicted, and highly unstable.[42] The latent aggressivity of everyday routine hints at an overdetermined fantasy available to many: nervous householders who fear insurrection, masters and mistresses who seek masochistic identification with their "lowers," servants and housewives who resent being mastered, household subordinates who jockey for position. Flying in the face of the deep structural logic of the well-running *domus* as a harmoniously ordered and hierarchized organic body, *The English Traveller* vividly portrays the *pleasures* of domestic/bodily fragmentation, partition, and conflict. Rather than making an argument for an idealized cohesion, the play uses the circulation, ingestion, and interpenetration of body parts to underscore the malleability of the domestic arena. The homiletic framework of sin and repentance may have allowed female unruliness to be represented and expelled, but the newly reconstructed household hints of dangers on the horizon; for appetite and labor remain as requisite parts of household life.

The English Traveller may help us to reread violence in the genre retrospectively dubbed domestic tragedy. Dramatic representations of potentially fatal disorders in the non-elite household flourished on the London stage between 1590 and 1610 in plays such as *Arden of Faversham, A Warning for Fair Women, Two Lamentable Tragedies, A Yorkshire Tragedy,* and Heywood's *A Woman Killed with Kindness.*[43] Challenging standard definitions of tragedy, these plays located pro-

---

[42] Orlin writes of *The English Traveller*: "the aim of this text is its arduous reclamation of the domestic sphere from the intrusive female" (*Private Matters and Public Culture,* 252). But Orlin goes on to show how the newly reconfigured all-male household is one that attempts to finesse economic discrepancies between the "old orders of patriarchy and privilege" and the new forces of commodification (267).

[43] For a list of non-extant plays in this tradition, see Clark, "An Annotated List of Lost Domestic Plays, 1578–1624." On domestic tragedy as a category, see Adams, *English Domestic, or Homiletic Tragedy 1575–1642.*

tagonists of the middling sort and comic situations in tragic frameworks.[44] When Heywood lodges a food-obsessed city comedy into domestic tragic form, he invites consideration of the workings of this already hybrid genre, for he enlarges a focus on spousal conflict to encompass an entire network of domestic relations, rituals, and practices. *The English Traveller* locates the story of heterosexual betrayal within a nexus of kinship alliances, servant-master tensions, and what has been termed the "homosocial imaginary."[45] Thus it is not surprising that the most capacious fantasy of violence in the play is conceived by a servant who takes pleasure in describing the household's fragmentation. Roger's story of gallants consuming each other might erase the central labor performed by housewives, but it also exposes the unsettling place of household subordinates and the radically alienating quality of early modern domestic practice.

KNOWING HOME

Even as it reframes violence as the domestic unconscious, *The English Traveller* registers the national discourse evident in some household manuals; for it lavishly stakes a claim to domesticity as the ultimate ground of knowledge. When Geraldine discovers his mistress in bed with Dalavill, he analyzes his "passions" by reassigning affect from persons to place:

> . . . You have made mee
> To hate my very Countrey, because heere bred:
> Neere two such monsters; First I'le leave this House,
> And then my Fathers, Next I'le take my leave,
> Both of this Clime and Nation, Travell till

---

[44] Sidney, *The Defense of Poesie*, E4r–E4v. Sidney's differentiation between "grand" subjects of tragedy and "common" comic subjects was conventional, espoused, for instance, by Diomedes and Donatus. On definitions of domestic tragedy, see Orlin, *Private Matters and Public Culture*, 75; Adams, *English Domestic, or Homiletic Tragedy*; Clark, *Domestic Drama: A Survey of the Origins, Antecedents, and Nature of the Domestic Play in England, 1500–1640*; and Powell, *English Domestic Relations, 1487–1653*.

[45] See Bach, "The Homosocial Imaginary of *A Woman Killed with Kindness*." Refusing to reduce the family to a marital dyad, Bach provocatively suggests that there is no domesticity in domestic tragedies at all if we mean by "domestic" a fairly modern sense of the nuclear family built on a privileged and privatized heterosexual relationship. Instead, as she argues for Heywood's *A Woman Killed with Kindness*, the "homosocial imaginary" structures early modern household life.

> Age snow upon this Head: My passions now,
> Are unexpressable (70).

Moving from the scene of betrayal in the bedroom to the conjoined spaces of home and nation, Geraldine transforms his "divorce" from the Wincotts (89) into a national exile. Why should his disaffection with love and marriage — indeed his bodily disjoining from the household — constitute a renunciation of England? Arguing that his flight implies guilt, Geraldine's father puzzles, "why [do] you desire to steale out of your Countrey, / Like some malefactor?" (86). Geraldine's silent answer, of course, is that the country has absorbed the guilt of the "monsters" it births. Only national disarticulation can save him from becoming heir to a land capable of breeding corruption. Geraldine's logic rests on his easy cognitive leap from nation to domus, as well as his sense of "place" as the ultimate determinant of moral action.

What England "breeds" is in fact precisely the subject that opens *The English Traveller*, since Geraldine's position as the titled figure gives him occasion to compare national tastes and inclinations. Envying Geraldine's cosmopolitanism, his audience translates national knowledge into erotic terms, suggesting that the sum of his travels rests in his ability to compare appetites, foods, beauties, and culturally-distinct sexual proclivities. When pressured to say which country produces the best woman, Geraldine turns the conversation to the issue of food. Since each climate and soil determines men's "stomachs," he argues, men naturally prefer native wives: "what is most pleasing to the man [is] there borne," Geraldine concludes. Climate and nationality, in this logic, determine "appetites" (12). The "stomach" that will later be linked to domestic bloodshed, and "taste" that will later be linked to eroticism, are introduced first as the product of the nation. It is no wonder that Geraldine later reads "monstrous" desire as inherently English or that the play's title frames his social place in national terms.[46] For the first scene suggests that culinary, sexual and national appetites stem from

---

[46] I use the word "queer" advisedly, in order to refer to both homoerotic relationships and the non-normative status of early modern domesticity generally (that is, those parts of household practice and relations that contradicted orthodox views of domestic hierarchy). "Queer domesticity" is one in which subject positions and the desires that accompany those positions are fluid. Geraldine's unruly and eroticized place in the household — as married to both mistress and master — is one such non-normative position. But the play suggests that Geraldine's placement in the household is simply the logical extreme of some orthodoxies, so early modern "proper" domestic roles slide readily into potentially disruptive deviance. On "queerness," see Warner, introduction to *Fear of a Queer Planet: Queer Politics and Social Theory*, vii–xxxi.

a common source. Returning to England only to find domestic disorder, travelers in both plots — Geraldine and Lionnel — make a final decision to "stay at home"; and their re-affiliation marks the terms of domestic redemption.

What Geraldine learns is supposedly the truth of home's monstrosity; that is, heterosexual infidelity precipitates a rupture that bleeds into but then finds reparation in the fantasy of national exile. Geraldine's reconciliation with Wincott in the finale thus constitutes a national reunion as well as a homoerotic marriage. Lover to his surrogate father, Geraldine is engrossed back into a community defined specifically as English. After Wincott pledges a "marriage of [their] love," Geraldine finalizes its terms: "It calls me from all Travell, and from henceforth, / With my Countrey I am friends" (94). With the seeming depravity of England giving way to national faith, the play ends with an authorized, homoeroticized national merger that compensates for the tragedy of unauthorized heterosexual desire. In having Mistress Wincott's death to absorb the potential injury posed broadly by domesticity, the play revises discourses nominating the housewife as guardian of national culture.

§

Alongside prevalent representations of the household as the foundational disciplinary site for shaping bodies and subjects was an early modern counter-discourse located in the material traces of domestic practice and its inscriptions. In this discourse, identity-formation and proper embodiment were vexed in everyday practice. Rather than reading "domestication" simply as a synonym for "being tamed," then, scholars might take seriously the aggressive energies circulating in the domus. When we think of early modern domesticity, that is, might we conjure up the image of Lady Macbeth consulting a Renaissance cookbook while she whipped up a narcotic for Duncan's guards? Or Roger's fantasy of a cadre of servants and guests ravenously wounding each other at the dinner table? *The English Traveller* illuminates how discourses promulgated in cookbooks became refracted in dramatic representation. In revealing how theories of national taste transmute into images of live food, the play converts destructive powers into a final investment in a place called home.

Wendy Wall
Northwestern University

Works Cited

Adams, Henry Hitch. *English Domestic, or Homiletic Tragedy 1575–1642*. New York: Columbia University Press, 1943.

Adelman, Janet. *Suffocating Mothers: Fantasies of Maternal Origin in Shakespeare's Plays, "Hamlet" to "The Tempest"*. New York: Routledge, 1992.

Amussen, Susan. *An Ordered Society: Gender and Class in Early Modern England*. New York: Columbia University Press, 1988.

Bach, Rebecca Ann. "The Homosocial Imaginary of *A Woman Killed with Kindness*." *Textual Practice* 12 (1998): 503–24.

Barkan, Leonard. *Nature's Work of Art: The Human Body as Image of the World*. New Haven: Yale University Press, 1975.

Beaumont, Francis, and John Fletcher. *The Nice Valour, or, The Passionate Madman* in *The Works of Mr. Francis Beaumont and Mr. John Fletcher*. 10 vols. London: J. And R. Tonson and S. Draper, 1750. Vol. 10.

Belsey, Catherine. "Disrupting Sexual Difference: Meaning and Gender in the Comedies." In *Alternative Shakespeares*, ed. John Drakakis, 166–90. New York: Methuen, 1985.

Bright, Timothy. *A Treatise Wherein is declared the Sufficiencie of English Medicines*. London, 1580.

Bromley, Laura. "Domestic Conduct in A Woman Killed with Kindness." *Studies in English Literature* 26 (1986): 259–76.

Burnett, Mark Thornton. *Masters and Servants in English Renaissance Drama and Culture*. London: Macmillan, 1997.

Bynum, Caroline Walker. *Fragmentation and Redemption: Essays on Gender and the Human Body in Medieval Religion*. New York: Zone Books, 1992.

Cahn, Susan. *Industry of Devotion: The Transformation of Women's Work in England, 1500–1650*. New York: Columbia University Press, 1987.

Camporesi, Piero. *Bread of Dreams: Food and Fantasy in Early Modern Europe*, trans. David Gentilcore. Cambridge: Polity Press, 1989.

de Certeau, Michel. *The Practice of Everyday Life*, trans. Steven Randall. Berkeley: University of California Press, 1984.

Christensen, Ann. "Business, Pleasure and the Domestic Economy in Heywood's *A Woman Killed with Kindness*." *Exemplaria* 9 (1997): 315–40.

Clark, Alice. *Working Life of Women in the Seventeenth Century*. New York: E. P. Dutton & Co., 1919; repr. London and New York: Routledge, 1992.

Clark, Andrew. "An Annotated List of Lost Domestic Plays, 1578–1624." *Research Opportunities in Renaissance Drama* 18 (1975): 29–44.

———. *Domestic Drama: A Survey of the Origins, Antecedents, and Nature of the*

Domestic Play in England, 1500–1640. Salzburg: Institut für Englische Sprache und Literatur, Universität Salzburg, 1975.

A Closet for Ladies and Gentlewomen, or, The Art of Preseruing, Conseruing, and Candying. London, 1608; repr. 1635.

Cressy, David. *Birth, Marriage & Death: Ritual, Religion, and the Life-Cycle in Tudor and Stuart England*. Oxford: Oxford University Press, 1997.

Darell, Walter. *A Short Discourse of the Life of Serving-men*. London, 1578.

Davies, Kathleen. "The Sacred Condition of Equality: How Original were Puritan Doctrines of Marriage?" *Social History* 5 (1977): 563–81.

Dod, John and John Cleaver. *A Godly Forme of Houshold Government*. London, 1630.

Dolan, Frances E. *Dangerous Familiars: Representations of Domestic Crime in England, 1550–1700*. Ithaca: Cornell University Press, 1994.

———. "Gender, Moral Agency, and Dramatic Form in A Warning for Fair Women." *Studies in English Literature* 29 (1989): 201–18.

Epulario, or The Italian Banquet. London, 1598.

Erickson, Amy Louise. *Women and Property in Early Modern England*. New York: Routledge, 1993.

Fitzherbert, John. *The Boke of Husbandry*. London, 1523.

Fletcher, John. *The Elder Brother* in *The Works of Mr. Francis Beaumont and Mr. John Fletcher*. 10 vols. London: J. And R. Tonson and S. Draper, 1750. Vol. 9.

Friedman, Alice T. *House and Household in Elizabethan England*: Wollaton Hall and the Willoughby Family. Chicago: University of Chicago Press, 1989.

Fumerton, Patricia. *Cultural Aesthetics: Renaissance Literature and the Practice of Social Ornamentation*. Chicago: University of Chicago Press, 1991.

———. "Introduction: A New New Historicism." In Patricia Fumerton and Simon Hunt, eds. *Renaissance Culture and the Everyday*, 1–17. Philadelphia: University of Pennsylvania Press, 1999.

Gataker, Thomas. *A Good Wife Gods Gift*. London, 1623.

Girouard, Mark. *Life in the English Country House: A Social and Architectural History*. New Haven: Yale University Press, 1978.

Googe, Barnabe. *The Whole Art and Trade of Husbandry*. London, 1614.

Gouge, William. *Of Domesticall Duties*. London, 1622.

Gowing, Laura. *Domestic Dangers: Women, Words and Sex in Early Modern London*. Oxford: Clarendon Press, 1996.

Grey, Elizabeth, Countess of Kent. *A Choice Manual, or Rare and Select Secrets in Physick and Chyrurgery: Collected, and practised by the Right Honourable, the Countess of Kent, late deceased*. London, 1653; repr. 1682.

Gutierrez, Nancy. "The Irresolution of Melodrama: The Meaning of Adultery in *A Woman Killed with Kindness.*" *Exemplaria* 1 (1989): 265–91.

Hall, Kim F. "Culinary Spaces, Colonial Spaces: The Gendering of Sugar in the Seventeenth Century." In *Feminist Readings of Early Modern Culture: Emerging Subjects*, ed. Valerie Traub, M. Lindsay Kaplan, and Dympna Callaghan, 168–90. Cambridge: Cambridge University Press, 1996.

Harding, Vanessa. "'And one more may be laid there': The Location of Burials in Early Modern London." *London Journal* 14 (1989): 112–29.

Harris, Jonathan Gil. *Foreign Bodies and the Body Politic.* Cambridge: Cambridge University Press, 1998.

Henderson, Diana. "The Theater and Domestic Culture." In *A New History of Early English Drama*, ed. John D. Cox and David Scott Kastan, 173–94. New York: Columbia University Press, 1997.

Heywood, Thomas. *The English Traveller* (1633) in *The Dramatic Works of Thomas Heywood*, 4: 6–95. 6 vols. London: John Pearson, 1874.

Hill, Christopher. *Society and Puritanism in Pre-Revolutionary England.* New York: Schocken Books, 1964.

Hillman, David, and Carla Mazzio, eds. *The Body in Parts: Fantasies of Corporeality in Early Modern Europe.* New York: Routledge, 1997.

Houlbrooke, Ralph. *The English Family 1450–1700.* New York: Longman, 1984.

Hutson, Lorna. *The Usurer's Daughter: Male Friendship and Fictions of Women in Sixteenth-Century England.* London: Routledge, 1994.

Ingram, Martin. *Church, Courts, Sex, and Marriage in England, 1570–1640.* Cambridge: Cambridge University Press, 1987.

Kussmaul, Ann. *Servants in Husbandry in Early Modern England.* Cambridge: Cambridge University Press, 1981.

M., I. *A Health to the Gentlemanly Profession of Servingmen.* London, 1598.

M., W. *The Queens Closet Opened.* London, 1655.

Markham, Gervase. *The English House-wife.* London, 1631.

McLuskie, Kathleen. *Dekker and Heywood: Professional Dramatists.* Houndsmill and London: St. Martin's Press, 1994.

———. "'Tis But a Woman's Jar': Family and Kinship in Elizabethan Domestic Drama." *Literature and History* 9 (1983): 228–39.

Murrell, John. *A Daily Exercise for Ladies and Gentlewomen. Whereby they may learne and practise the whole Art of making Pastes, Preserves, Marmalades, Conserves* .... London, 1617.

Newman, Karen. *Fashioning Femininity and English Renaissance Drama.* Chicago: University of Chicago Press, 1991.

Nutton, Vivian. "'A Diet for Barbarians': Introducing Renaissance Medicine to

Tudor England." In *Natural Particulars: Nature and the Disciplines in Renaissance Europe*, ed. Anthony Grafton and Nancy Siraisi, 275–93. Cambridge, MA: MIT Press, 1999.

Orlin, Lena Cowen. *Private Matters and Public Culture in Post-Reformation England*. Ithaca: Cornell University Press, 1994.

Parks, Katherine. "The Criminal and the Saintly Body: Autopsy and Dissection in Renaissance Italy." *Renaissance Quarterly* 42 (1994): 1–33.

Partridge, John. *The Treasurie of Commodious Conceites and hidden Secrets, Commonly called the Good Huswives Closet of Provision*. London, 1627.

Paster, Gail Kern. *The Body Embarrassed: Drama and the Disciplines of Shame in Early Modern England*. Ithaca: Cornell University Press, 1993.

Perkins, William. *Christian Oeconomie: Or, A Short Survey of the Right Manner of Erecting and Ordering a Familie*. London, 1609.

Plat, Hugh. *Delightes for Ladies, to Adorne their Persons, Tables, Closets, and Distillatories: With Beauties, Banquets, Perfumes, & Waters*. London, 1602.

Pollock, Linda. *With Faith and Physic: The Life of a Tudor Gentlewoman, Lady Grace Mildmay, 1552–1620*. London: Collins and Brown, 1993.

Powell, Chilton Latham. *English Domestic Relations, 1487–1653*. New York: Columbia University Press, 1917.

Rose, Mary Beth. *The Expense of Spirit: Love and Sexuality in English Renaissance Drama*. Ithaca: Cornell University Press, 1988.

Sawday, Jonathan. *The Body Emblazoned: Dissection and the Human Body in Renaissance Culture*. New York: Routledge, 1995.

Shakespeare, William. *The Merry Wives of Windsor*. In *The Riverside Shakespeare*, ed. Blakemore Evans, 1:286–326. Boston: Houghton Mifflin Co., 1974.

Sharpe, J. A. *Early Modern England: A Social History 1550–1760*. London: Edward Arnold, 1987.

Shirley, James. *The Ball*. London, 1632.

Sidney, Philip. *The Defense of Poesie*. London, 1595.

Sloan, A. W. *English Medicine in the Seventeenth Century*. Durham: Durham Academic Press, 1996.

Spurling, Hilary. *Elinor Fettiplace's Receipt Book*. London: Viking Salamander, 1986.

Stallybrass, Peter. "Patriarchal Territories: The Body Enclosed." In *Rewriting the Renaissance: Discourses of Sexual Difference in Early Modern Europe*, ed. Margaret W. Ferguson, Maureen Quilligan, and Nancy J. Vickers, 123–42. Chicago: University of Chicago Press, 1986.

Stone, Lawrence. *The Family, Sex, and Marriage in England, 1500–1800*. London: Weidenfeld and Nicolson, 1977.

Surflet, Richard. *The Countrie Farme*. London, 1600.

Underdown, David. *Revel, Riot, and Rebellion: Popular Politics and Culture in England, 1603–1660*. Oxford: Clarendon Press, 1985.

Warner, Michael. *Fear of a Queer Planet: Queer Politics and Social Theory*. Minneapolis: University of Minnesota Press, 1993.

The Widdowes Treasure, Plentifully furnished with sundry precious and approved secrets in Phisicke. London, 1595.

Woolley, Hannah. *The Compleat Servant-Maid, or the Young Maidens Tutor*. London, 1683.

———. *The Queen-like Closet, or Rich Cabinet: Stored with all Manner of Rare Receipts for Preserving, Candying and Cookery*. London, 1675.

"A Woman Dipped in Blood":
The Violent Femmes of
The Maid's Tragedy and *The Changeling*

Today, [Hatshepsut] is again on the list of pharaohs, and Egyptologists discuss only whether she was a good ruler and, if so, what were her merits. She possessed one for sure — if it can be considered a merit when one did not kill when there was an opportunity to do so.

Wislawa Szymborska, "The She-Pharaoh"

Writing about the connection between grief and anger in the Greek city-state and the relation of both to the feminine, Nicole Loraux notes that "the city, as a well-organized collectivity, enacts a series of laws and regulations against the danger of unbridled passion [...]. If we are [...] interested in what the city rejects [...] we should seek what the city fears" (*Mothers in Mourning*, trans. Pache, 9–10). Her subject is the order-toppling power latent in maternal mourning, and how such "unbridled passion" is manifested in both the real life of the city and the dramatic fictions it produces on the stage. A grieving mother constitutes a serious threat to the *polis* because "From that moment when mothers obtain only the horrified sight of the child's corpse to compensate for their loss, mourning that has already been transformed into wrath becomes vengeance in deeds. And mothers kill" (49). The fury of a woman wronged in any significant way has always posed a threat to "the city" sufficient to occasion laws, customs, and rites of circumscription designed to prevent this feminine rage from exploding into the social framework.

The tragedies of Jacobean England are not so culturally distant as we might think from those of fifth-century B.C.E. Athens or their later Senecan counterparts. As Juliet Dusinberre observes:

> When Thomas Newton collected together the Elizabethan translations of
> Seneca's *Tenne Tragedies* he provided Shakespeare and his fellow play-
> wrights with a gallery of women enmeshed in the male world of politics.
> [...] Seneca's women suffer atrocious violence, but they also commit it
> [...]. Seneca [...] made accessible to Shakespeare and his contemporaries
> that astounding array of heroines in Greek classical drama who consis-
> tently contradict male images of female weakness, mental and physical.
> (*Shakespeare and the Nature of Women*, 274–75)

In Greek tragedy, "Murder is a woman's crime and counts as one of the model
feminine crimes: as such, murder is worthy of appearing in the tragic catalogue
of *gunaikeía érga* that choruses recite from time to time" (Loraux, *Mothers in
Mourning*, 58).[1] This "model feminine crime" was an integral component of
what Renaissance English dramatists inherited from Seneca along with his five-
act structures, and through him, from the Greeks. But for reasons having to do
with the absorption and adaptation of Roman cultural and primarily patriarchal
values, as Coppélia Kahn observes (*Roman Shakespeare*, 162–63), the image of
the violent woman was suppressed and nearly effaced from the functional mirror-
ing framework of early modern English drama.

Unlike their ancient Greek and Roman dramatic counterparts, the women of
early modern English tragedy tended to kill, for the most part, only themselves.
Rarely do we find a female "murdering minister" who lifts her hand, or even her
voice, against her abuser. But we do find them. Alison Findlay has recently ad-
vanced a well-supported argument that Renaissance revenge tragedy is a particularly "feminine genre" because, among other reasons, it violates the Law of the
Father, resists the practices of patriarchy, and "promotes insubordination" even
when the avenger is male (*A Feminist Perspective on Renaissance Drama*, 49–86),
although she has serious reservations about what it signifies: "The use of violence
by female revengers [...] is deeply problematic from a feminist point of view
since it often reproduces masculine modes of oppression and possibly even the
dominant values of patriarchy" (72). I would argue that "fighting fire with fire"
challenges patriarchy's viability and discloses its inherent structural weakness in
several ways: no system can thrive when even its avatars fail to live up to its re-

---

[1] In a note to this observation Loraux explains that "A father does not kill his son,
even in tragedy, unless he is seized by a fit of madness like Heracles: see Aristotle's *Poetics*
1453b19–22 for a list of possible crimes" (*Mothers in Mourning*, trans. Pache, 58 n. 3).

quirements, and furthermore, if practices known as patriarchal can be assumed by women, then they are not the exclusive provinces of men. If it takes this kind of gender-bending displacement to expose those practices as vicious, so be it.

In this essay I will argue that this critique of patriarchy is precisely what we find in Beaumont and Fletcher's *The Maid's Tragedy* (c. 1611–1613) and Middleton and Rowley's *The Changeling* (c. 1622). I bring forward, into the dock as it were, two notably violent female representations: Evadne from the earlier play, and Beatrice-Joanna from the later one. Neither is a grieving mother;[2] the motive for murder in each case is not blood-revenge but something perhaps even more personal, and moreover something unprotected by legal structures such as those designed to requite citizens bereaved by homicide. Evadne kills to avenge her shame; Beatrice-Joanna hires a killer to prevent an arranged marriage. If feminine initiatives such as these occurred rarely in life or on the stage, they were obviously not unthinkable, and the wonder is that, like Lorena Bobbitt's notorious amateur surgery in our own time, and as Szymborska reminds us in the epigraph to this essay, they did not occur more frequently than they did.[3]

But perhaps they did occur more frequently than historiography has allowed. As Jodi Mikalachki's account of early Britain richly suggests, the active and often violent model of the emerging "nation" itself followed a Boadicean legacy that was only with great difficulty and over a long period of time "rechanneled" into a Romanized culture of warrior men and passive women. Students of early modern England have tended to accept the misogynist model requiring female chastity, silence, and obedience as if it were an "always-already" component of early

---

[2] A compelling example of the avenging mother in Jacobean tragedy might be Lady Macbeth, whose maternity has been the subject of much famous debate. Whatever we make of it, we cannot ignore her recollection that she has "given suck" (1.7.54), and in the absence of any sign of that baby, we may assume that at some point, at least, she mourned a lost child. Although she does not actually kill anyone in the course of the play, she does in fact, like her husband, "wield the knife" herself: the bloody knives that killed Duncan's grooms leave permanent stains on her hands, the guilt and the madness imprinted on her with the bloodstains.

[3] Readers may think immediately of Alice Arden as an early modern English exemplar in this context. See Belsey, "Alice Arden's Crime," for a summary of notorious real-life and dramatic instances of wives who had their husbands killed. Belsey notes that "the existing historical evidence gives no reason to believe that there was a major outbreak of women murdering their husbands in the sixteenth century. What it does suggest, however, is a widespread belief that they were likely to do so. The Essex county records for the Elizabethan period, for instance, [...] list several cases of frightened husbands seeking the protection of the courts" (89). For statistics of wives charged with murdering their husbands in early modern France and England, see also Hufton, *The Prospect Before Her*, 56–57; 294–95.

modern English culture, against which the behavior of "unruly women" was seen as a violation of divine ordinance; such views have become the commonplace inscription of much feminist theory and literary criticism. One of the most important contributions of Mikalachki's work is its reminder that *early modern England* embedded and attempted to efface an *early Britain* literally spearheaded by a warrior woman known for her violent and often savage ways. Holinshed's "spin" on Boadicea's leadership, says Mikalachki, "superimpos[es] a masculinist gender hierarchy" on the battle for Britain that Rome eventually won (*The Legacy of Boadicea*, 13). But neither Rome's nor Holinshed's victory was an easy one:

> Boadicea's treatment in reconstructions of Roman Britain is the best single example of the intersection of early modern misogyny with anxiety about savage native origins. In their concern to recover a civil period of native antiquity, early modern historians projected ancient British savagery onto Boadicea and other ancient queens. Redefining the national problem of ancient savagery as an issue of female insubordination, they sought to isolate a complementary tradition of native masculine civility. Far from containing their anxieties about ancient Britain, however, their emphasis on the savagery of ancient queens raised the even more disturbing possibility that native origins were to be understood entirely in terms of female excess. Savage, rebellious, and self-destructive, ancient Britain as a whole became analogous in their accounts to early modern constructions of insubordinate womanhood. (12–13)

Images of violent women in early modern English drama, then, may be said to suggest vestiges of early Britain itself: they are reminders, perhaps, of a past no longer deemed "respectable," but one which nevertheless remained latent, like some recessive genetic material, capable of re-emerging at any time to challenge dominant definitions of civilized behavior.

In *The Maid's Tragedy*, Aspatia and Evadne wait in vain and then can wait no longer for a male champion to take up their grievances for them. Aspatia's betrothed Amintor has suddenly and reluctantly married Evadne. Amintor is himself a victim of the tyrant's order that forced him to drop her: the King of Rhodes keeps Evadne as his mistress and, to cover his adultery, orders Amintor to marry her. The king's violations are many: he has not only made a whore of Evadne and broken Aspatia's heart but also makes a bawd of Amintor, ordering him to "winke at this, / And be a meanes that we may meete in secret" (3.1.301– 302).[4] Above all loyal to his king, Amintor assents.

---

[4] Citations from *The Maid's Tragedy* follow the Fountainwell Drama Texts edition by Andrew Gurr.

Throughout most of the play, Aspatia performs the conventional role of the jilted fiancée:

> ... this Lady walkes
> Discontented, with her watrie eyes bent on the earth:
> [. . . . . .]
> She carries with her an infectious griefe,
> That strikes all her beholders, she will sing
> The mournfullest things that ever eare hath heard,
> And sigh, and sing againe, and when the rest
> Of our young Ladyes in their wanton blood,
> Tell mirthfull tales in course that fill the roome
> With laughter, she will with so sad a looke
> Bring forth a storie of the silent death
> Of some forsaken virgin, which her griefe
> Will put in such a phrase, that ere she end
> Shee'le send them weeping one by one away. (1.1.103–121)

Her grief is in one respect socially compliant; to set it aside would be to trivialize the sanctity of the betrothal contract. But in the world of this play such contracts are easily voided by the tyrant's whim, and in this context Aspatia's grief is seen as toxic; it is "infectious," and unsociably contaminates a roomful of "mirthful" young women, spoiling their fun and betraying the fiction of order, harmony, and good government in Rhodes. What sends the women "weeping one by one away" is not Aspatia's personal sorrow but its displacement to a fiction, "a storie of the silent death / Of some forsaken virgin" who represents but is not herself.[5] She is expected to "get over it," to accept with some kind of good grace the ruin of her life. A collective recognition of Aspatia's undeserved rejection and its

---

[5] We are reminded of a similar refusal to validate the grief caused by masculine betrayal in Gertrude's cold "I will not speak with her" (*Hamlet* 4.5.1; quotations from *Hamlet* are to the Riverside edition, ed. G. B. Evans). Ironically, it is the men in this scene who recognize Ophelia's need for sympathy and comfort: a courtier says, "Her mood will needs be pitied" (3), and detects the trace of truth in Ophelia's ravings: she "speaks things in doubt / That carry but half sense" (6–7). That "half sense" of her speech is dangerous: "the unshaped use of it doth move / The hearers to collection; they [. . .] / [. . .] botch the words up to fit their own thoughts," and "Indeed would make one think there might be thought, / Though nothing sure, yet much unhappily" (8–13). Horatio finally persuades the Queen to see Ophelia: "'Twere good she were spoken with, for she may strew / Dangerous conjectures in ill-breeding minds" (14–15). Horatio's warning turns out to be well-placed; Gertrude's aside indicates a guilty conscience and her fear of self-exposure: "To my sick soul, as sin's true nature is, / Each toy seems prologue to some great amiss, / So full of artless jealousy is guilt, / It spills itself in fearing to be spilt" (17–20).

cause would require an acknowledgement that good government and kingly virtue are a sham. The illusion must be preserved; its exposure would be, in Loraux's terms, "what the city fears."

In 5.3, however, Aspatia literally takes matters into her own hands and confronts Amintor. Lacking an avenger, and weak with the starvation and sleeplessness caused by her grief, Aspatia finally resorts to masculine disguise, pretending to be a long-absent brother returned to requite "his sister's" honor, and attacks Amintor in the hope of provoking him to kill her in the fight. She punches and kicks him to little effect, as he points out: "What dost thou meane? thou canst not fight, / The blowes thou makst at me are quite besides, / And those I offer at thee, thou spreadst thine armes / And takst upon thy brest, alas, defencelesse" (5.3.116–119). Her strategy ultimately works, but it takes awhile. Aspatia's masculine disguise is more than an instance of the conventional dramatic transvestism that Linda Woodbridge finds "the one unsatisfying feature of the otherwise stimulating transvestite movement [. . .]: Renaissance women so far accepted the masculine rules of the game that they felt they had to look masculine to be 'free'" (*Women and the English Renaissance*, 145). Aspatia's disguise allows her not to live freely but to die, which is the only "freedom" she wants. Aspatia knows exactly what she is doing; she has tried to die by starvation and sleeplessness, and failed. In attacking Amintor, she commits a Jacobean equivalent of "suicide by cop." In this instance it is not only the case, as Jonathan Dollimore argues, that "the female transvestite of the early seventeenth century positively disrupts the [binarism of gender] by usurping the master side of the opposition" ("Subjectivity, Sexuality, and Transgression," 69);[6] the entire play disrupts the binarism of gender by assigning a consistent passivity to its masculine characters. The play's critique of patriarchy discloses a decidedly decrepit and derelict form, its putative primacy undercut from the outset by a masculine failure to perform its principles, and even those principles are interrogated, if not entirely subverted, by the play's actions. The women are left to fend for themselves as well as for the men, which, of course, they do.[7] Findlay calls this a "monstrous parody of

---

[6] For a more complex and, I think, more provocative discussion of what transvestism signaled on the Renaissance stage, see Orgel, "Nobody's Perfect: Or Why Did the English Stage Take Boys for Women?".

[7] Some critics have found this feminine activism particularly difficult to accept, and have demonized it altogether. Broude, for example, argues throughout his essay that Amintor is "the play's central character" despite its title ("Divine Right and Divine Retribution," 246), but notes that "Amintor must look to others to right the wrongs he as suffered. Only when he has been rescued from the consequences of his fatal choice [to submit to the King's abuses] is Amintor able to regain the moral composure with which

phallic power" by which both women are confined "in a self-destructive patriarchal prison" (*A Feminist Perspective*, 73); what indeed is so great about patriarchal power if all it grants is the power to kill? In the context of disrupted gender binaries, it is particularly interesting to note Melantius's promise to commit suicide at the play's end; he will use Aspatia's device of sleepless starvation: "I vow Amintor I will never eate, / Or drinke, or sleepe, or have to do with that / That may preserve life, this I swear to keepe" (5.3.311–313). In the same moment, Aspatia's doddering and craven father, Calianax, in a move which would be funny if it weren't so disgraceful, promises to "go home and live as long as I can" (5.3.305–306). In this play, women wield weapons and take action while the men lock themselves up in their houses and wait for death. One way or another, all the major figures in *The Maid's Tragedy* adopt a form of transvestism: Melantius summons the strength to confront Evadne by vowing to divest himself of "all weaknesses of nature, / That make men women" (4.1.107–108), as if "all the qualities which degrade a man lodge in women" (Dusinberre, *Shakespeare and the Nature of Women*, 276; see also Smith, *Breaking Boundaries*, 89), and is "transformed from a bluff and bloodthirsty warrior into a Machiavellian whose murder plot will keep his own hands clean" (Shullenberger, "A Reappraisal of *The Maid's Tragedy*, 141). Amintor is the embodiment of passive sufferance, "an emotional cripple" (141). The king meets death in a supine position, tied to the bed and expecting a novel form of sexual play: "What prettie new device is this Evadne? / What, doe you tie me to you by your love? / This is a queint one" (5.1.49–51); he dies at the hands of a woman literally "on top." "The adulterous woman adopts a male role; her femininity no longer stands in the way of physical violence. [...] In some ways the Elizabethan tragedy of adultery is the woman's version of the revenge tragedy [...] in a world where action is strength" (Dusinberre, *Shakespeare and the Nature of Women*, 302–3).

Between Aspatia's attack on Amintor and her death, Evadne enters with bloody hands and a bloody knife. She too lacks a champion to defend her. Her brother Melantius might have been that, but his first loyalty is to the king and

---

bravely to confront his tragedy" (255). Broude acknowledges Evadne's agency in Amintor's "rescue" but dismisses it because she is a character "so lacking in moral substance that it is difficult to attach moral significance to the regicide she commits" (255); he assigns that agency instead to "divine retribution" (247–48), as if "the heavens" killed the king while Evadne hid under the bed. Even the strongly feminist Findlay attaches negative implications to the assumption of "masculine" behaviors by the women in both *The Maid's Tragedy* and *The Changeling* because in each case that assumption leads only to their respective destruction (*A Feminist Perspective*, 73–76; 142–46).

his second is to his friend Amintor. He hates his sister for her part in the king's abuse of his best friend. *She* should kill the king: *her* honor is no longer in question:

> Y'are valiant in his bed, and bold enough
> To be a stale whore, and have your Madams name
> Discourse for grooms and pages, and hereafter
> When his cool Majestie hath laid you by
> To be at pension with some needie Sir
> For meat and coarser cloathes, thus farre you knew no feare,
> Come you shall kill him. (4.1.168–174)

All he can see in the way of wrongdoing is hers to him and his friend: "Thy brother and thy noble husband broken" (4.1.181). Later he refuses to acknowledge even her corpse. His grief is only for his dead friend; Evadne's body is "A thing to laugh at in respect of this; / Here was my Sister, Father, Brother, Sonne, / All that I had" (5.3..286–288).[8] He orders Evadne to "kneele and sweare to helpe me / When I shall call thee to it" (182–183). She is to "helpe" him by killing the king; his part is to commandeer for their escape a fort controlled by Calianax, who has to be manipulated into relinquishing the property, his own daughter's despair proving insufficient motive to involve himself in an act of treason. The priorities of these men are exclusively self-protective. Meanwhile, Evadne is trapped in her life of enforced shame and manipulated into regicide: "Here I sweare it, / And all you spirits of abused Ladies / Helpe me in this performance" (4.1.190–192). She can do it, too, as she tells the king in the critical moment: "I am a Tiger, I am any thing / That knowes not pittie" (5.1.71–72), but in order to be her own avenger, she must first redefine herself. She rejects even her name: "I am not she, nor beare I in this breast / So much cold spirit to be cald a woman" (69–70), and exacts revenge in the name of all

---

[8] Several readers have noticed a "suppressed homosexual desire" in Melantius's extreme devotion to Amintor (McCabe, *Incest, Drama, and Nature's Law*, 245; Dollimore, "Subjectivity, Sexuality, and Transgression," 76; Smith, *Breaking Boundaries*, 84). Cf. Shullenberger's comment that "What is perverse about [Melantius's devotion to Amintor] is not that it is homosexual, since it is the deepest and most constant emotional commitment of the play [. . .]. What is perverse is the way that this emotion becomes so all-consuming that Melantius is indifferent and utterly ruthless to all the other characters, including Amintor himself, finally, whom Melantius does not trouble to warn of his intrigue" ("A Reappraisal of *The Maid's Tragedy*," 151–52). For a different reading of male homosocial, rather than homosexual, bonding in Roman culture as reflected specifically in Shakespearean tragedy, see Kahn, *Roman Shakespeare*, 99.

the "abused Ladies" victimized by "a shamelesse villaine, / A thing out of the overcharge of nature, / Sent like a thicke cloud to disperse a plague / Upon weake catching women, such a tyrant / That for his lust would sell away his subjects" (5.1.100–104).

In the introduction to his edition of the play, Andrew Gurr notes that Aspatia is "the only maid" to whom the play's title could apply (3); he is interested only in the virginal reference of the term "maid," and thus disqualifies Evadne. Further on, he argues not only that this is not really a "maid's" tragedy but that it is not really a tragedy at all "in the usual sense" (4):

> [It] has no single great figure brought low by Fortune's wheel or Aristotle's peripeteia. The starting-point of the play is a moral problem, private and political, presented in terms rather of a situation than of an individual. It involves a construction of attitudes to the King's crime and a pair of alternative resolutions for the problem thus presented. For this purpose only attitudes are needed, not characters. The king himself is *never more than a lustful (and with it a jealous)* monarch. Amintor is an honest youth, Melantius a soldier turned revenger, Evadne *a lustful (and ambitious) woman*, Aspatia a wronged maid. Characterisation need bear no more weight than this. (4; my emphasis)

I find this sense of what constitutes "a tragedy" more than a little baffling, as if a "lustful (and with it a jealous) monarch" were not particularly dangerous elements in either a private or a political context.[9] Evadne, meanwhile, is "a lustful (and ambitious) woman"; not for her the exculpating "never more than." For Gurr, the play fails to meet the Aristotelian criterion for tragedy because it "exists in the situation, the ethical dilemma, not in the characters" (5). But in Aristotle's famous formulation, "Plot [. . .] is the principle and, as it were, the soul of tragedy, while characters are second" (*Poetics* 1450b), and both Evadne and Aspatia do in fact undergo precisely the "peripeteia" Aristotle stipulates: Evadne when she agrees to wield a knife, and Aspatia when she takes on Amintor in a fight. In this play, it is the masculine figures who do not, or can not, "turn around."

Against this masculine stasis, Evadne emerges as the play's primary active principle. She rejects any hint of victimization; she had agreed to be the king's

---

[9] See also Broude: "political questions are eschewed, for the heavens seem to be punishing not a king who is an adulterer but an adulterer who happens to be a king" ("Divine Right and Divine Retribution," 248).

mistress not in obedience to a command but quite simply because it suited her to be the mistress of the king.[10] When the king accuses her of consummating her marriage to Amintor instead of sustaining the marital sham, she reminds him:

> I swore indeede that I would never love
> A man of lower place, but if your fortune
> Should throw you from this hight, I bad you trust
> I would forsake you, and would bend to him
> That won your throne, I love with my ambition,
> Not with my eies [...]. (3.1.194–199)

Ambitious she is, but not, as Gurr has it, "lustful," or, if she lusts after anything, it is the king's power, not his body: "Why, it is in me then, not to love you, which will / More afflict your bodie, then your punishment can mine" (3.1.205–206). William Shullenberger offers a most compelling reading of Evadne as positively heroic. Against the appearance that she is "merely the sacrificial pawn in Melantius's strategy," she emerges as

> the most awesome figure in the play [.] The murder of the king is itself a measure of her power: she commits a crime which the patriarchal warriors of the drama implicitly dread, and in the act of murder, Evadne assumes herself some portion of the mystique which had rendered the king inviolable. [...] Evadne's death must come by her own hand because no one else in the play can approach her.
>
> Yet Evadne's power has been implicit from her first appearance in the play, and it comes from a source independent of the murdered king: she radiates a sexual authority which she refuses to curb or shame. ("A Reappraisal of *The Maid's Tragedy*," 147)

Critical reluctance such as Gurr's (see also Broude, "Divine Right and Divine Retribution") to assign the play's emphasis to either Evadne or Aspatia indicates

---

[10] I disagree with McLuskie's view that Evadne's often-noted line, "A maidenhead Amintor at my yeares!" (2.1.220) "turns out to refer not to her autonomy as a sexually experienced woman, but to the prior claims on her favours held by the king" ("Chastity and Tragicomedy," 94). As the speech quoted next clearly indicates, the king's "prior claims" are held — and withheld — at Evadne's will; thus her "maidenhead" line precisely reflects her sexual autonomy. McLuskie argues that this line "presents a paradigm case of the difficulties in offering a feminist reading" of this play (92); obviously I find it very supportive of such a reading.

a larger problem in reading the play as a tragedy with female protagonists. To what else might the title refer? The first reference to the play in the records of English drama is, as Gurr notes, only implicit in the "oblique" evidence of the license granted by the Master of the Revels on 31 October 1611 to another play manuscript identified as "This second Maydens tragedy (for it hath no name inscribed)" (Gurr, "Introduction," 1). For once, the vagaries (by modern standards) of early modern spelling are helpfully suggestive: neither Buc's note, nor the 28 April 1619 entry in the Stationers' Register, nor the 1619 quarto title page (Gurr "Introduction," 1) indicate where the apostrophe belongs. Conventional practice assumes the singular possessive case: Maiden's. What if it were a plural: Maidens'? Could the Jacobean stage have supported a play that emphasized the tragic stature of not just one but two women? The term "maid" or "maiden" carried a double meaning: both "unmarried" and "virgin" (Woodbridge, *Women and the English Renaissance*, 84). In this sense, the play's title refers to both Evadne and Aspatia; though only the latter is a virgin, neither one can accurately be called anyone's "wife"; the play belongs to both of them.[11]

The masculine characters in this play place the virtue of loyalty to the divinely-hedged king in a privileged position over anything else, even when they recognize the tyrant as evil. The feminine challenge to this code is surely one of the most clearly marked social disruptions in the play.[12] But what it disrupts is corrupt: the world of such masculine values is represented here as cold, selfish, destructive, and sometimes downright ludicrous, as in the cases of Calianax and the pathetic — or bathetic — Amintor who agrees to play the king's bawd. Against the void left by these masculine implosions, Evadne emerges as the nearest approximation offered in this play of the heroic.

If "A maidenhead Amintor at my yeares?" is, as Kathleen McLuskie has called it, the "show-stopping line from *The Maid's Tragedy*" ("Chastity and Tragicome-

---

[11] Shullenberger argues that "*The Maid's Tragedy* is a tragedy of maids in the generic sense, for both the central women characters are destroyed by masculine court intrigues" ("A Reappraisal of *The Maid's Tragedy*," 154).

[12] Gossett observes that the risks of absolute loyalty to the sovereign, however vicious, appear to have been a favorite topos with Fletcher, and cites the example of his play *Valentinian* (c. 1610–1614): the emperor Valentinian rapes Lucina, wife of Maximus, and is killed not by an avenging husband but by a eunuch who served Maximus's best friend. Maximus then proposes marriage to the emperor's widow and prepares to take the throne — at which point *she* kills him (" 'Best Men'," 308–9). The agents of justice in this play are not the masculine characters but a eunuch and a widow respectively; this non-masculine agency too appears to be a topos to which Fletcher turned on more than one occasion.

dy," 92), its corollary in *The Changeling* belongs to De Flores: "A woman dipped in blood and talk of modesty!" (3.4.126). The conflicted and contradictory value systems that produce both of those lines mark an important difference between the two plays, but it is a difference that discloses more about the patriarchal settings of the plays than it does about their respective female protagonists. In certain respects, *The Changeling* reverses the pattern of action in *The Maid's Tragedy*: Beatrice-Joanna assigns a male surrogate to relieve her oppression, whereas Evadne is the surrogate champion of "all [the] spirits of abused Ladies." In the earlier play, patriarchal tyranny and the masculine characters' fear of it are exaggerated so that killing it is clearly the only possible remedy. In the later play, autocratic patriarchy is sanitized to look like perfectly normal applications of fatherly prerogative: Vermandero's choice of Alonzo de Piracquo because "the gentleman's complete" (1.1.216)[13] raises the question of whether Beatrice-Joanna's preference for Alsemero, equally well-born and welcome (1.1.175–182; 3.4.1–2), is less appropriate, and less appropriate than, say, the autonomous choice made by the Duchess of Malfi to whom Beatrice-Joanna has been compared unfavorably (e.g. Henderson, "The Theater and Domestic Culture," 181). Vermandero freely exercises his patriarchal right to choose for his daughter, but oddly dismisses the conventionally patriarchal prize, her virginity: "Tush, tush, there's a toy" (1.1.201). This "toy," not an issue for Evadne by the time her play's action begins, is Beatrice-Joanna's most prized possession, so thoroughly has she absorbed the tenets of patriarchy. When De Flores reminds her that her "modesty," as *she* defines it, can hardly be a priority after Alonzo's murder, she resorts to yet another precept of patriarchy, the immiscibility of social positions: "Think but upon the distance that creation / Set 'twixt thy blood and mine, and keep thee there" (3.4.150–151). But that principle too was undercut by Vermandero's arbitrary choice of his daughter's husband. No visibly compelling logic underpins paternal whimsy, as we can see when Beatrice-Joanna quickly and quietly (in a dumb show at the top of 4.1) is permitted to marry the man of her choice after Alonzo is removed. When patriarchy ignores the rules of its own game, it must assume some responsibility for a chain reaction of consequent social violations. Beatrice-Joanna's criminality begins in her secret desire to marry her choice; it is this desire that leads to her more overtly criminal act of hiring De Flores to kill Alonzo. Perhaps in this regard Beatrice-Joanna's only mistake was to get someone else to kill for her: Juliet Dusinberre has argued that "women who contrive without the power to accomplish tend, like Middleton's Beatrice

---

[13] Quotations from *The Changeling* follow the edition by M. L. Wine.

committing murder through De Flores' agency, to live in a fantasy world immune from the realities of action" (*Shakespeare and the Nature of Women*, 283).

But Beatrice-Joanna is not the only figure in this play cloistered from "the realities of action." Molly Smith has pointed out that Vermandero throughout the play remains "blissfully ignorant" of the crimes that "had occurred within his own castle walls and were orchestrated by his own daughter and trusted servant. The last lines of the play [. . .] suggest that Vermandero's status as patriarch has been permanently destroyed"; at the end of the play, she notes, he is "reduced to silence" (*Breaking Boundaries*, 110). It is important to recognize that Middleton and Rowley distribute the moral culpability of their characters in a relatively even-handed way. Vermandero dismisses his daughter's protection of her virginity and hands off to his servant De Flores the hospitable duty of showing Alonzo around the castle, thereby enabling De Flores to kill him and hide the body; Alsemero, like Alibius in the asylum-plot, distrusts his wife's chastity without knowing of any warrant for his suspicions.

Taken together, the crimes and misdemeanors of the two represented households can only with difficulty be said to represent points on a scale of values. Beatrice-Joanna gets the brunt of critical censure in discussions of the play, as if Vermandero, De Flores, even Alsemero were her innocent victims, although, as she tells Alsemero moments before she dies, she has never actually been unfaithful to him because, in the first instance, her sexual relationship with De Flores preceded her marriage to Alsemero, and in the second, she never actually consummated that marriage (5.3.62, 82). She is "a woman dipped in blood" in several ways: as Vermandero's daughter, she is "that of your blood was taken from you / [. . .] / Let the common sewer take it from distinction" (5.3.150–153). His "blood" put her in the position of being marketed like a commodity. Margot Heinemann's observation that "Murder, to Beatrice, is a commodity, like anything else one buys" (*Puritanism and Theatre*, 175) should be read in the context of the rest of the play's "commodifications," only one of which is, as Heinemann suggests, that of De Flores. Unlike Beatrice-Joanna, De Flores is quite happy to be bought, for the right price. He presents Beatrice-Joanna with Alonzo's severed finger still wearing a diamond ring, but that ring will "hardly buy a capcase for one's conscience" (3.4.44).[14] When Beatrice-Joanna offers him money for the murder, he escalates his fee: his first response to her request is that he would do anything "to be employed / In any act of yours" (2.2.121–122); moments later

---

[14] Marjorie Garber notes of this ring-display that "*The Changeling* is not a play that will hide castration under a bushel" ("The Insincerity of Women," 19).

he accepts money as a down payment (2.2.128 s.d.), but once the deed is done he will accept nothing less than her body, and claims to be offended by her offer of "salary": "Do you place me in the rank of verminous fellows / To destroy things for wages? [. . .] I could ha' hired / A journeyman in murder at this rate, / And mine own conscience might have slept at ease / And have had the work brought home" (3.4.64–71). His protest, as the old joke puts it, is merely a haggling over price. De Flores's prostitution, ironically, is bought by what Beatrice-Joanna's father had earlier dismissed as "a toy."

Given the battering Beatrice-Joanna's behavior has received at the hands of critics, it is interesting to notice that her contract with De Flores is really the reverse of Melantius's manipulation of Evadne in the earlier play, as I have suggested above. Beatrice-Joanna hires De Flores as a hit-man, and, like Macbeth's murderers ("We are men, my liege" [3.1.90 ff]) and Edmund's Captain in *King Lear* (5.3.39) he will "do 't" for the right price; in both Shakespearean antecedents, murder-for-hire is "man's work." It is not so for Melantius, who threatens his sister's life in order to get her to murder:

> Thou shalt not live thus, kneele and sweare to help me
> When I shall call thee to it, or by all
> Holy in heaven and earth thou shalt not live
> To breathe a full houre longer, not a thought.
>
> (*MT* 4.1.182–185)

But Melantius is never blamed, in the critical literature I have read, for turning his sister into a killer; he is blamed only, if at all, for not doing the deed himself. For the same jobbing-out, Beatrice-Joanna is labeled monstrous.

The crucible for critical evaluations of Beatrice-Joanna, as for Alsemero, is the extended scene of the virginity test, from the moment when Beatrice-Joanna discovers Mizaldus's "*Book of Experiment / Called Secrets in Nature*" (4.1.24–25) in her husband's study,[15] through her trial-run of the test on Diaphanta, to her replication of Diaphanta's "symptoms" before Alsemero. It is in this moment that critics decide whether Beatrice-Joanna is the wit-bearing guardian of her own safety ("He cannot but in justice strangle me" [4.1.14]) or a villain made

---

[15] Two fascinating accounts of the historicity or "verisimilitude" of Middleton and Rowley's references to this book are in Randall, "Some Observations on the Theme of Chastity," 358–60 and Boehrer, "Alsemero's Closet," 353–55. Boehrer also supplies a useful summary of critical assessments of this scene that have labeled it comic, debased, or ludicrous ("Alsemero's Closet," 349), but both he and Randall argue persuasively for both its high seriousness and its indispensability to the action of the play.

ridiculous by the imitation of what she has seen her as-yet virginal maid perform. In Diana Henderson's discussion of the scene, for example, "Not only does
the corrupt Beatrice-Joanna successfully counterfeit to pass a bizarre virginity
test, but the common physical actions of the virgin Diaphanta whom she mimics
— sneezing, laughing, and gaping — are thereby made to seem unnatural and
ridiculous, as if all female bodies were inherently grotesque" ("The Theater and
Domestic Culture," 180); Molly Smith finds this scene "simultaneously comic
and tragic" rather than ludicrous or grotesque (*Breaking Boundaries*, 93). Conversely, Dale B. J. Randall finds in Beatrice-Joanna's initiative an admirable
example of a woman working out the best way to save her own life ("Some Observations on the Theme of Chastity," 360). In Marjorie Garber's view, and the
one I find most compelling, the "virginity test" is not a test of virginity at all, but
of its opposite, of sexual and specifically orgasmic experience: "What Beatrice-
Joanna learns in Alsemero's pharmacy, and turns immediately to her own use, is
'what every woman knows': how to fake it. She produces the symptoms, the si-
mulacra of orgasmic response, that delight her husband and confirm his apparent
mastery of her" ("The Insincerity of Women," 27). To this observation I would
add that Alsemero takes on the most passive of all roles: that of voyeur. He en-
joys watching while his wife performs "for him." Beatrice-Joanna knows how to
"act," in both senses of theatrical imitation and of taking action, on her own behalf. She of the hyphenated name (and here I take issue with those critics who
shorten it to "Beatrice") can change her identity without changing her name (unlike Evadne who must first relinquish hers before she can act) because it is already double; it is a name appropriate to a shape-shifter,[16] and consistent with
the changes she undergoes in the course of the play, from the "giddy turning"
(1.1.160) she feels after she meets Alsemero for the first time, to the irreversible
alteration brought about by Alonzo's murder by which she becomes, as De

---

[16] Randall provides a splendid discussion of the dualities implicit in the name Beatrice-Joanna. In Renaissance dictionaries such as John Rider's (1640), under "changeling
child" he finds the definition "Lamia"; under "Lamia" he finds "women or devils in the
shape of women," and in Edward Topsell's *Historie of Four-footed Beastes* (1607), he finds
the explanation that Lamiae are "wonderful desirous of copulation with men" (Randall,
"Some Observations on the Theme of Chastity," 351). His discussion of the paronomastic
references of other names in the play (De Flores = "deflowerer"; Diaphanta is "insubstan-
tially virtuous"; Alibius is "too often in another place") leads him to the double signifi-
cation of Beatrice-Joanna: " 'Beatrice,' meaning she who makes happy or blessed [. . .]
suggests all that Beatrice-Joanna appears to be. 'Beatrice' is the name of the famed human
embodiment of Dante's ideal. 'Joanna,' however, [. . .] had become by the sixteenth century one of the commonest of English names and apparently fallen to the kitchen and the
cottage" (352).

Flores bluntly reminds her in the center of the play, "the deed's creature; by that name / You lost your first condition" (3.4.137–138).[17]

Beatrice-Joanna, the real "changeling" of the play's title despite the *dramatis personae*'s assignment of that designation to Antonio, is Evadne's direct dramatic heir. Garber observes that *The Changeling* is a play "about the pleasure and danger of woman's desire. In the complex dynamics of its heterosexual power relations, the power to withhold becomes the power to control" ("The Insincerity of Women," 27). She could as well have been describing *The Maid's Tragedy*. The "power to control," like the power *of* control, is, of course, the primary goal at which patriarchy (in any of its guises) always aims. This is what is at stake in the radicalized assignment of violent feminine behavior in both of these plays, which return their audiences to the kind of requiting female violence they might have recognized from Newton's/Seneca's *Medea* or *Agamemnon*, not quite as "effaced" from the legacy of Greco-Roman drama or the cultural genetics of early Britain as we might have thought. Any human system of order-sustaining governance (patriarchy included) requires careful maintenance. In *The Maid's Tragedy* and *The Changeling*, the men fail their own culturally inscribed system, the "man's work" noted earlier as identified by Shakespeare's murderers, leaving the women without a contained and authorized structure through which they can address their grievances. Left to their own devices, these "sisters," in the words of The Eurythmics' popular lyric, "are doin' it for themselves."

Naomi C. Liebler
Montclair State University

Works Cited

Aristotle. *Poetics*, trans. Kenneth A. Telford. Chicago: Henry Regnery, 1968.

Belsey, Catherine. "Alice Arden's Crime," *Renaissance Drama* n.s. 13 (1982): 83–102.

Boehrer, Bruce. "Alsemero's Closet: Privacy and Interiority in *The Changeling*," *Journal of English and Germanic Philology* 96 (1997): 349–68.

Broude, Ronald. "Divine Right and Divine Retribution in Beaumont and Fletcher's *The Maid's Tragedy*." In *Shakespeare and Dramatic Tradition: Essays in Honor of S. F. Johnson*, ed. W. R. Elton and William B. Long, 246–63. Newark, DE: University of Delaware Press, 1989.

---

[17] On Beatrice-Joanna's multiple alterations, see Loomba, *Gender, Race, Renaissance Drama*, 75, 100–4.

Dollimore, Jonathan. "Subjectivity, Sexuality, and Transgression: The Jacobean Connection." *Renaissance Drama* n.s. 17 (1986): 53–81.

Dusinberre, Juliet. *Shakespeare and the Nature of Women.* 2nd ed. New York: St. Martin's Press, 1996.

Findlay, Alison. *A Feminist Perspective on Renaissance Drama.* Oxford: Blackwell, 1999.

Garber, Marjorie. "The Insincerity of Women." In *Desire in the Renaissance: Psychoanalysis and Literature*, ed. Valeria Finucci and Regina Schwartz, 19–38. Princeton: Princeton University Press, 1994.

Gossett, Suzanne. " 'Best Men are Molded out of Faults': Marrying the Rapist in Jacobean Drama." *English Literary Renaissance* 14 (1984): 305–27.

Gurr, Andrew. Introduction to *The Maid's Tragedy*, 1–7. Fountainwell Drama Texts. Berkeley and Los Angeles: University of California Press, 1969.

Heinemann, Margot. *Puritanism and Theatre: Thomas Middleton and Opposition Drama under the Early Stuarts.* Cambridge: Cambridge University Press, 1982.

Henderson, Diana. "The Theater and Domestic Culture." In *A New History of Early English Drama*, ed. John D. Cox and David Scott Kastan, 173–94. New York: Columbia University Press, 1997.

Henderson, Katherine Usher, and Barbara F. McManus, eds. *Half Humankind: Contexts and Texts of the Controversy about Women in England, 1540–1640.* Urbana: University of Illinois Press, 1985.

Hufton, Olwen. *The Prospect Before Her: A History of Women in Western Europe 1500–1800.* New York: Vintage-Random, 1995.

Kahn, Coppélia. *Roman Shakespeare: Warriors, Wounds, and Women.* London and New York: Routledge, 1997.

Lennox, Ann, and David Allan Stewart. "Sisters Are Doin' It For Themselves." BMG Songs, 1985.

Loomba, Ania. *Gender, Race, Renaissance Drama.* Delhi: Oxford University Press, 1992.

Loraux, Nicole. *Mothers in Mourning.* Trans. Corinne Pache. Ithaca and London: Cornell University Press, 1998.

McCabe, Richard A. *Incest, Drama and Nature's Law 1550–1700.* Cambridge: Cambridge University Press, 1993.

McLuskie, Kathleen. " 'A Maidenhead, *Amintor*, At My Yeares': Chastity and Tragicomedy in the Fletcher Plays." In *The Politics of Tragicomedy: Shakespeare and After*, ed. Gordon McMullan and Jonathan Hope, 92–121. London and New York: Routledge, 1992.

Middleton, Thomas, and William Rowley. *The Changeling.* In *Drama of the English Renaissance*, ed. M. L. Wine, 601–84. New York: Random House, 1969.

Mikalachki, Jodi. *The Legacy of Boadicea: Gender and Nation in Early Modern England*. London and New York: Routledge, 1998.

Orgel, Stephen. "Nobody's Perfect: Or Why Did the English Stage Take Boys for Women?" *South Atlantic Quarterly* 88 (1989): 7–29.

Randall, Dale B. J. "Some Observations on the Theme of Chastity in *The Changeling*," *English Literary Renaissance* 14 (1984): 347–66.

Shullenberger, William. " 'This For the Most Wrong'd of Women': A Reappraisal of *The Maid's Tragedy*." *Renaissance Drama* n.s. 13 (1982): 131–56.

Smith, Molly. *Breaking Boundaries: Politics and Play in the Drama of Shakespeare and his Contemporaries*. Aldershot, UK, and Brookfield, VT: Ashgate, 1998.

Szymborska, Wislawa. "The She-Pharaoh," trans. Irena Grudzinska Gross. *The New York Review of Books* 46:12 (15 July 1999): 10.

Woodbridge, Linda. *Women and the English Renaissance: Literature and the Nature of Womankind, 1540–1620*. Urbana and Chicago: University of Illinois Press, 1984.

Afterword

When the editors set about choosing a topic for this collection, we found it appropriate to pick a subject that would recall the scholarly pursuits of Paul Jorgensen. We also wanted to involve as many of Paul's former students as possible in the project, so we needed to choose a subject that would fit their scholarly expertise.[1] Although Paul had many interests, we identified one as particularly forward-looking. Because "he was keenly interested in the topic of violence and women,"[2] we made that the focus of the essays gathered here. We realized, too, that whatever topic we chose would have to fit into current critical conversations about the early modern period in England. Fortunately, essays such as those by Susan Dwyer Amussen, Barbara Baines, Nazife Bashar, Lynda Boose, Miranda Chaytor, Suzanne Gossett, Margaret Hunt, Martin Ingram, Leonard Tennenhouse, and David Underdown (all cited in the bibliography) and books by Karen Bamford, Susan Brownmiller, Jocelyn Catty, Frances E. Dolan, Kathryn Gravdal, Stephanie Jed, Guido Ruggiero, and Jonathan Sawday (also cited in the bibliography), as well as earlier books by Paul Jorgensen, have paved the way for a close examination of how violence was represented as entering the lives of English women in the sixteenth and seventeenth centuries. At the 1999 Shakespeare Association of America meeting, a seminar entitled "Reconsidering Rape: Sexual Violence on the Renaissance Stage," led by Karen Bamford and Karen Robert-

---

[1] Paul Jorgensen served as mentor to a large number of graduate students, who (in tribute to his own wide interests) are now engaged in research on an impressive spectrum of topics. Several of his former students were, however, unable to contribute to this collection: scholars including Margaret Loftus Ranald, Elizabeth Pomeroy, Sandra Fischer Ellston, Grace Ioppolo, Marliss Desens, and Susan Wing are simply not working in the area of women and violence. They all, however, have good memories of Paul's teaching and of the fine scholarly example he set for them.

[2] See introduction, p. xliv.

son, attracted several of the contributors to the present collection and intensified the focused conversation that has resulted in the selected essays.

In these essays the authors range over a variety of approaches to the subject of represented violence towards and by women, and in every case violence is regarded primarily as a physical act. Rape, mutilation, kidnapping, and murder all figure in the Part One accounts of female victims from Desdemona to Pocahontas; while in Part Two women are associated with violent acts from dueling to filicide to butchery. However, just as these essays grow out of an intellectual milieu centered on the representation of women and physical violence, so too do they give rise to other areas for investigation. Some of these have been alluded to in the Introduction: the suppression of discourse critical of wife-beating in fiction and drama, the imbalance between male and female domestic violence in mainstream literature, and the fantastic forms of female violence taken in literature; but there are others as well. For instance, while the essays here theorize primarily about the representation of *accomplished* violence, we need to also theorize about non-accomplished violence, such as that referred to by Barbara Mathieson in her study of men who forgo raping a woman who suddenly shows sexual desire. Other instances of thwarted violence can be found in Shakespeare's *Cymbeline*, *Two Gentlemen of Verona*, and *A Midsummer Night's Dream*, in Shirley's *The Cardinal*, and in Jonson's *Volpone*. In these examples, though, there are categories of thwarted violence which can be identified: a disguise and misinformation mislead the villain, the would-be perpetrator has a change of heart, a hero arrives on the scene and saves the intended victim, or the threat of violence is not serious.

In several of these essays there are hints that another form of violence — that which is semantic and psychological rather than physical — also plays a significant role in understanding the representation of brutality in this era. For instance, in Carolyn Sale's discussion of *Titus Andronicus*, "both Lavinia and Tamora's bodies are ritually expunged, and thus co-opted, for the rule of (a new) law." The feeding of Tamora's dead sons to her in a pie followed by its discovery is clearly seen as intending to produce an emotional reaction in the mother, one of horror and pain, that precedes her own ritualistic slaughter. Similarly, in Lynda Boose's consideration of pornography in *Othello*, we are made aware of the "culture's own guilt, violence, prurience, desire, and revulsion," brought about by the mental and emotional effects of *witnessing* staged brutality. Elsewhere, Akiko Kusunoki examines the effects on female selfhood of male violence, demonstrating that, at least for Mary Wroth, woman's inner subjectivity, especially her sexual desire, was represented as physically extracted through aggressive male behavior. And in Wendy Wall's essay we learn that the carving, hacking, and slicing practiced by female cooks and housekeepers was probably an outlet for violent tendencies that could not be carried out safely against human antagonists. In other words, all of these essays indirectly call attention to the period's awareness of violence as both a physical and a psychological phenomenon. The idea that pain and suffering can be imposed through non-physical means was clearly recognized in the early modern period. Most notable among the literary works that represent this idea is Thomas Heywood's *A Woman Killed with Kindness*, in which a husband brings about his wife's death by treating her with kindly acts until her adulterous guilt finally overcomes her.[3] Can we regard this as violent retribution? Certainly Heywood seems to have thought so.

Madelon Gohlke has reminded us that sexual violence and women have long been linked within the paradigms of early modern cultures. In her essay, "Shakespeare's Tragic Paradigms," she observes:

> Images of sexual intercourse as an act of violence committed against a woman run deep in our culture. The depth and persistence of these images, however, may tell us more about the anxieties of a culture in which femininity is conceived as castration and women are perceived paradoxically as a source of maternal power than it does about the actual or possible relations between the sexes. (182)

This understanding of the association between images of sexuality, violence, and power raises questions for us about deep-seated, often invisible anxieties and beliefs that govern a culture, including that of Shakespeare. When we consider Renaissance literary productions in this light, we are forced to acknowledge the implications of violence towards and by women as symptoms rather than or as well as causes of social dysfunction, even in times of prosperity and relative peace.

A literary work of the period which illustrates this aspect of violence against women as a metaphor for social upheaval is Shakespeare's *Cymbeline*, written in 1609–1610. Here the playwright presents a kingdom verging on war, a situation instigated by Cymbeline's queen who, like Lady Macbeth and Tamora, seeks to manipulate male forces into acts of violence. On the other hand, there is the heroine, Imogen, who becomes a metaphor for Britain as she is about to be

---

[3] The expression "to kill a wife with kindness" was a colloquialism for spoiling a woman by over-indulgence; another way to read the title of this play is to see it as referring to a failure on the husband's part to exercise proper control over his wife, leaving her free to indulge in a moral lapse. (Thanks to Linda Woodbridge for pointing this out.)

"raped" figuratively by the Roman Iachimo and actually by her half-brother Cloten. Neither of these threatened acts damages Imogen in the long run, and Britain (in a continuation of the parallel) manages to avoid war. Such a use of violence in literary works positions women as the source of violence as well as the desired victim. Men serve as perpetrators and rescuers; in other words, as responders to female agency. Despite the play's containment of the queen and of Imogen within a strongly male discourse, we cannot fail to appreciate the women's power to motivate action. When the virtuous Imogen regains her proper place at court, the scheming queen is overthrown and peace returns to Britain as Cymbeline restores his dependent role with Rome. Just as Imogen is shown to be dependent upon male rescuers, so Britain, the threatened victim of Roman aggression, proves necessarily reliant upon Rome for peace and prosperity. This brief account of a deeply embedded alignment between female characters and a nation's integrity illustrates a direction for future investigation. The seeds of dissension and of restoration come from within the nation, and both are figured as female: one as corruptor and one as redeemer, one as the instigator of violence and one as the intended victim of violence. The unruly female resents submission to Rome while the virtuous one accepts it. Britain is female; Rome is male.

This paradigm of women and violence as a metaphor for social and cultural chaos probably had significant meaning in a nation ruled by a woman nearing the end of her life. The violence of her death will be felt throughout the nation, and she will be replaced by a non-English male heir. The succession will be peaceful, but not necessarily popular. By not marrying and producing a prince to continue her line, Elizabeth jeopardized England's position of power in the world, or so many people thought. At the same time, however, she was admired for maintaining her independence and for exercising control over those forces which threatened to undermine her authority, that is, figuratively, to "rape" her and by doing so, to "rape" England. Elizabeth's delicate position both as potential perpetrator of violence (as in war and civil punishment) and as potential victim (of scheming advisors and aggressive foreign suitors) gave her a uniquely feminine perspective that allowed her to play aggressors and appeasers off each other. What, then, can we discover about Elizabeth's own views regarding violence against women? Did she staunchly oppose these actions, encourage women to take revenge, ignore husband-bashing, create laws to protect women? How did her own female balancing act as a stateswoman influence her choices and attitudes toward women and violence in her domain? This, too, is an area of unexplored investigation suggested by the essays in this collection.

As soon as we open the study of violence to include non-physical aggression, we enter areas dominated by critics such as Mikhail Bakhtin (violence as the spoken word), Julia Kristeva (violence as the annihilation of the Other), Emmanuel Levinas (violence as the proper functioning of Reason), and Jacques Derrida (violence as inevitable and unavoidable). While these theorists depend upon post-Restoration thought for most of their contributions, and thus are often discounted by critics concerned about imposing contemporary views on events of earlier eras, the questions they raise about subjectivity, about language, and about perception in turn foster questions about the role of violence in sixteenth-century England.

Together, the ideas for future study suggested here and above remind us of the extraordinarily fertile field we plow. As his scholarship and his former students can testify, Paul Jorgensen was acutely aware of this richness and sensed the potential to be found in studies of represented women and violence. Moreover, he also recognized and acknowledged the non-physical as well as physical forms of violence evident in literature, especially Shakespeare's plays, from the English Renaissance. He makes this clear in his previously quoted statement concerning Macbeth that bears repeating:

> ... [Macbeth] takes us upon one of the most profoundly violent, most vividly felt experiences of life that we shall ever know. Through his *tortured mind* and senses we experience a range of sensation extending through the excited inception of shared ambition and hope, through plausible temptation, through reluctant evil, through hopeless labor, through racked nerves and restless fear, to a blasphemous negation of a life robbed of meaning. [emphasis mine][4]

Although this particular statement does not refer specifically to women, it does call attention to Jorgensen's belief that suffering occurs for Macbeth through his "tortured mind." Torture, abuse, annihilation, the inflicting of unbearable suffering, are all forms of violence addressed in this book. That these forms can take non-physical dimensions as well as physical ones permits us to entertain speculations and study that reach through instances of kidnapping, rape, mutilation, and murder against and by women to ways in which language and theater itself exercised similarly aggressive, though non-physical, means of controlling the position of women in early modern England.

Sharon Beehler
Montana State University

---

[4] See Introduction, p. xliii.

Works Cited

Bakhtin, Mikhail. *Problems of Dostoevsky's Poetics*, ed. and trans. Caryl Emerson. Minneapolis: University of Minnesota Press, 1984.

Bamford, Karen. *Sexual Violence on the Jacobean Stage*. New York: St. Martin's Press, 2000.

Derrida, Jacques. *Of Grammatology*, trans. Gayatri Chakravorty Spivak. Baltimore: Johns Hopkins University Press, 1974, repr. 1976.

Gohlke, Madelon. "Shakespeare's Tragic Paradigms." In *Representing Shakespeare: New Psychoanalytic Essays*, ed. Murray M. Schwartz and Coppélia Kahn, 170-187. Baltimore: Johns Hopkins University Press, 1980.

Heywood, Thomas. *A Woman Killed with Kindness*. In English Drama 1580-1642, ed. C. F. Tucker Brooke and Nathaniel Burton Paradise, 295-323. Lexington, MA: D. C. Heath and Company, 1933.

Kristeva, Julia. *Powers of Horror: An Essay on Abjection*, trans. Leon S. Roudiez. New York: Columbia University Press, 1982.

Levinas, Emmanuel. *Basic Philosophical Writings*, ed. Adriaan T. Peperzak, et al. Bloomington: Indiana University Press, 1996.

Bibliography

A. SOURCES

Arden of Faversham, ed. Martin White. The New Mermaids. London: A. and C. Black, 1997.

Aretino, Pietro. *I Modi: The Sixteen Pleasures. An Erotic Album of the Italian Renaissance: Giulio Romano, Marcantonio Raimundi, Pietro Aretino, and Count Jean-Frédéric-Maximilien de Waldeck*, ed. and trans. Lynne Lawner. Evanston: Northwestern University Press, 1988.

Aristophanes. *Lysistrata*, trans. Nicholas Rudal. Chicago: Ivan R. Dee, 1991.

Aristotle. *Poetics*, trans. Kenneth A. Telford. Chicago: Henry Regnery, 1968.

B., R. *Apius and Virginia*. In *Tudor Interludes*, ed. Peter Happé, 271–317. New York: Penguin, 1972.

Baker, J. H., ed. *Reports from the Lost Notebooks of Sir James Dyer*. Vol. 1. London: Selden Society, 1994.

———, and S. E. Thorne, eds. *Readings and Moots at the Inns of Court in the Fifteenth Century, vol. 2: Moots and Readers' Cases*. London: Selden Society, 1990.

Beaumont, Francis, and John Fletcher. *The Captain*, ed. L. A. Beaurline. In *The Dramatic Works in the Beaumont and Fletcher Canon*, ed. Fredson Bowers, 10 vols., 1:541–670. Cambridge: Cambridge University Press, 1966.

———. *Love's Cure, or The Martial Maid*, ed. Marea Mitchell. Nottingham: Nottingham Drama Texts, 1992.

———. *The Maid's Tragedy*, ed. Andrew Gurr. Fountainwell Drama Texts. Berkeley: University of California Press, 1969. — Ed. Howard B. Norland. Lincoln, NE: University of Nebraska Press, 1968.

———. *The Nice Valour, or, The Passionate Madman*. In *The Works of Mr. Francis Beaumont and Mr. John Fletcher*, 10 vols., 10:299–368. London: J. And R. Tonson and S. Draper, 1750.

Beverley, Robert. *History and Present State of Virginia* (1705), ed. Louis B. Wright. Chapel Hill: University of North Carolina Press, 1947.

Bible. See *Geneva Bible*.

Bracton, Henry de (attr.). *De Legibus et Consuetudinibus Angliae*, ed. G. E. Woodbine, trans. S. E. Thorne. 2 vols. Cambridge, MA: Belknap Press, 1968.

Brathwait, Richard. *The English Gentleman*. London, 1630 (STC 3563); repr. Amsterdam: Theatrum Orbis Terrarum, 1975.

Bright, Timothy. *A Treatise Wherein is declared the Sufficiencie of English Medicines*. London, 1580. (STC 3751.)

Buchanan, George. *Jeptha*. In *George Buchanan's Tragedies*, trans. P. G. Walsh, ed. P. Sharratt and idem, 64–94. Edinburgh, Scotland: Scottish Academic Press, 1983.

Camden, William. *The History of the Most Renowned and Victorious Princess Elizabeth Late Queen of England*, ed. Wallace T. MacCaffrey. Chicago: University of Chicago Press, 1970.

Cary, Elizabeth. *The Tragedy of Mariam* (1613), ed. A. C. Dunstan. Malone Society Reprints. Oxford: The Malone Society, 1992.

Castiglione, Baldassare. *The Courtier*, trans. Thomas Hoby 1561; ed. W. E. Henley. London: David Nutt, 1900.

Cervantes Saavedra, Miguel de. *Exemplary Novels*, trans. Walter K. Kelly. London: Bell, 1908.

Chamberlain, John. *Letters of John Chamberlain*, ed. Norman Egbert McClure. 2 vols. Philadelphia: American Philosophical Society, 1939.

Chapman, George. *The Tragedy of Bussy D'Ambois*, ed. Nicholas Brooke. Revels Plays. London: Methuen, 1964.

Chaucer, Geoffrey. *The Works of Geoffrey Chaucer*, ed. F. N. Robinson. 2nd ed. Boston: Houghton Mifflin, 1957.

Clifford, Anne. *The Diaries of Lady Anne Clifford*, ed. D. J. H. Clifford. Stroud, Gloucs: Sutton Publishing, 1990.

A Closet for Ladies and Gentlewomen, or, The Art of Preseruing, Conseruing, and Candying. London, 1608; repr. 1635. (STC 5434.)

Coleridge, Samuel Taylor. *Coleridge's Criticism of Shakespeare: A Selection*, ed. R. A. Foakes. London: Athlone Press, 1989.

Cooke, John. *Greene's Tu Quoque*. Amersham, England: Tudor Facsimile Texts, 1913.

Darell, Walter. *A Short Discourse of the Life of Serving-men*. London, 1578. (STC 6274.)

Dekker, Thomas. *Lantern and Candlelight*. London, 1608. (STC 6485.)

Dick of Devonshire (first acted 1626), ed. J. G. McManaway and M. R. McManaway. Oxford: Oxford University Press, 1955.

Dickenson, John. *Greene in Conceit: New Raised from his Grave to Write the Tragic History of Fair Valeria of London.* London, 1598. (STC 6819.)

"Doctrinal des Princesses et Nobles Dames faict et deduict en XXIIII Rondeaulx et Premierement, Le." In *Le Lexique de Jehan Marot dans le doctrinal des princesses et nobles dames,* ed. Giovanna Trisolini, 87–101. Ravenna: Longo, 1978.

Dod, John and John Cleaver. *A Godly Forme of Houshold Government.* London, 1630. (STC 5388.)

E., T. *The Lawes Resolutions of Womens Rights: or, The Lawes Provision for Woemen.* London, 1632 (STC 7437); repr. Amsterdam: Theatrum Orbis Terrarum; Norwood, NJ: W. J. Johnson, 1979.

The English Reports. Vol. 80. Edinburgh: William Green & Sons, 1907.

Epulario, or The Italian Banquet. London, 1598. (STC 10433.)

Field, Nathan. *Amends for Ladies.* In *The Plays of Nathan Field,* ed. William Peery. Austin: University of Texas Press, 1950. 159–236.

Fitzherbert, John. *The Boke of Husbandry.* London, 1523. (STC 10997.3.)

Fletcher, John. *Bonduca,* ed. Cyrus Hoy. In *The Dramatic Works in the Beaumont and Fletcher Canon,* ed. Fredson Bowers, 10 vols., 4:149–259. Cambridge: Cambridge University Press, 1979.

———. *The Elder Brother.* In *The Works of Mr. Francis Beaumont and Mr. John Fletcher,* 10 vols., 9:97–172. London: J. And R. Tonson and S. Draper, 1750. Vol. 9.

———. *The Faithful Shepherdess,* ed. Cyrus Hoy. In *Dramatic Works,* ed. Bowers, 3:483–583.

———. *The Loyal Subject,* ed. Fredson Bowers. In *Dramatic Works,* ed. Bowers, 5:151–288.

———. *Monsieur Thomas,* ed. Hans Walter Gabler. In *Dramatic Works,* ed. Bowers, 4:415–540.

———. *The Tragedy of Valentinian,* ed. Robert K. Turner, Jr. In *Dramatic Works,* ed. Bowers, 4:261–414.

———, and Francis Beaumont. *The Coxcomb,* ed. Irby B. Cauthen, Jr. In *Dramatic Works,* ed. Bowers, 1:261–366.

———, Nathan Field, and Philip Massinger. *The Queen of Corinth,* ed. Robert Kean Turner. In *Dramatic Works,* ed. Bowers, 8:3–111.

———, and William Rowley. *The Maid in the Mill,* ed. Fredson Bowers. In *The Dramatic Works in the Beaumont and Fletcher Canon,* ed. idem, vol. 9:569–669. Cambridge: Cambridge University Press, 1994.

Ford, John. *'Tis Pity She's A Whore,* ed. Brian Morris. New Mermaids. London: Benn, 1968.

Freud, Sigmund. *Three Contributions to the Theory of Sex.* In *The Basic Writings of Sigmund Freud*, ed. A. A. Brill, 553–629. New York: Random House, 1938.

Gataker, Thomas. *A Good Wife Gods Gift*. London, 1623. (STC 11659.)

Geneva Bible, The: A Facsimile of the 1560 Edition. Madison, Wisc.: University of Wisconsin Press, 1969.

Googe, Barnabe. *The Whole Art and Trade of Husbandry*. [Translation and enlargement of Conrad Heresbach, *Rei Rusticae Libri Quatuor*.] London, 1614. (STC 13201).

Gouge, William. *Of Domesticall Duties*. London, 1622 (STC 12119.2); repr. Amsterdam: Theatrum Orbis Terrarum, 1976.

Greene, Robert, and Thomas Lodge. *A Looking-Glass for London and England*. London, 1594 (STC 15927). Malone Society Reprint, repr. Oxford: Oxford University Press, 1932.

Grey, Elizabeth, Countess of Kent. *A Choice Manual, or Rare and Select Secrets in Physick and Chyrurgery: Collected, and practised by the Right Honourable, the Countess of Kent, late deceased*. London, 1653; repr. 1682. (Wing STC K310A.)

Hamor, Ralph. *A True Discourse of the Present Estate of Virginia and the successe of the affaires there till the 18 of June. 1614*. London, 1615 (STC 12736); repr. Amsterdam: Theatrum Orbis Terrarum, 1971.

Harvey, Gabriel. *Pierce's Supererogation*. In *The Works of Gabriel Harvey*, ed. A. B. Grosart, 3 vols., 2:91–96. London: privately printed, 1884, repr. New York: AMS Press, 1966.

Hawke, Michael. *The Grounds of the Lawes of England*. London, 1657. (Wing STC 1169.)

Hazlitt, W. Carew, ed. *A Select Collection of Old English Plays Originally Published by Robert Dodsley*, 15 vols.. London: Reeves and Turner, 1874.

Heale, William. *An Apology for Women. Or an opposition to Mr. Dr. G. his assertion that it was lawful for husbands to beat their wives*. Oxford: Joseph Barnes, 1609. (STC 13014.)

Henderson, Katherine Usher, and Barbara F. McManus, eds. *Half Humankind: Contexts and Texts of the Controversy about Women in England, 1540–1640*. Urbana: University of Illinois Press, 1985.

Heywood, John (?). *Johan Johan, the Husband, Tyb, His Wife, and Sir Johan, The Priest*. In *Chief Pre-Shakespearean Dramas*, ed. Joseph Quincy Adams, 385–96. Cambridge, MA: Houghton Mifflin, 1924.

Heywood, Thomas. *The English Traveller*. In *The Dramatic Works of Thomas Heywood*, ed. R. H. Shepherd, 6 vols., 4:6–95. London: J. Pearson, 1874.

———. *The Fair Maid of the West, Or, A Girl Worth Gold*. In *The Dramatic Works of Thomas Heywood*, ed. Shepherd, 2:255–331.

———. *The Rape of Lucrece*. In *The Dramatic Works of Thomas Heywood*, ed. Shepherd, 5:161–257.

———. *A Woman Killed with Kindness*. In *English Drama 1580–1642*, ed. C. F. Tucker Brooke and Nathaniel Burton Paradise, 295–323. Lexington, MA: D. C. Heath, 1933.

——— (?). *How a Man May Choose a Good Wife from a Bad*. In *A Select Collection of Old English Plays Originally Published by Robert Dodsley*, ed. W. Carew Hazlitt, 15 vols., 9:5–96. London: Reeves and Turner, 1874.

Hic Mulier or the Man Woman. London, 1620; repr. University of Exeter, 1973.

"Hic Mulier" and "Haec Vir." In *Half Humankind*, ed. Henderson and McManus, 264–76; 277–89.

Hilliard, Nicholas. *A Treatise Concerning the Art of Limning*, ed. R. K. R. Thornton and T. G. S. Cain. Ashington: Carcanet Press, 1981.

Howell, Thomas. *Devises*. London, 1581. (STC 13875.)

Hulton, Paul. *America 1585: The Complete Drawings of John White*. London: British Museum Publications, 1984.

Ingelend, Thomas. *The Disobedient Child*. In *A Select Collection of Old English Plays*, ed. Hazlitt, 2:265–320.

Jonson, Ben. *Epicoene*. First acted in 1609. In *Ben Jonson*, ed. C. H. Herford, Percy Simpson, and Evelyn Simpson, 11 vols., 5:161–272. Oxford: Clarendon Press, 1937.

Jonson, Ben. *Three Comedies: Volpone, The Alchemist, Bartholomew Fair*, ed. Michael Jamieson. Baltimore: Penguin Books, 1966.

Jorden, Edward. *A Brief Discourse of a Disease called the Suffocation of the Mother*. London, 1603. (STC 14790.)

Kingsbury, Susan Myra. *Records of the Virginia Company of London*. 4 vols. Washington, DC: Library of Congress, 1933.

Kramer, Heinrich, and James Sprenger. *The Malleus Maleficarum*, trans. and ed. Montague Sommers. New York: Dover, 1971.

Kyd, Thomas. *The Spanish Tragedy*, ed. Philip Edwards. Revels Plays. London: Methuen, 1959.

The Life of Long Meg of Westminster. London, 1635. (STC 17783.)

Livy. *The Early History of Rome*, trans. Aubrey de Sélincourt. New York: Penguin Classics, 1960.

Lydgate, John. *A Mumming at Hertford*. In *Minor Poems of John Lydgate*, ed. Henry Noble MacCracken and Merriam Sherwood, 2 vols., 2:675–83. London: EETS, 1934, repr. 1961.

M., I. *A Health to the Gentlemanly Profession of Servingmen*. London, 1598. (STC 17140.)

M., W. *The Queens Closet Opened*. London, 1655. (Wing STC M96.)

Markham, Gervase. *The English House-wife*. London, 1631. (STC 17353).

Marlowe, Christopher. *The Jew of Malta*, ed. N. W. Bawcutt. Manchester: Manchester University Press; Baltimore: Johns Hopkins University Press, 1978.

———. *Tamburlaine the Great*, ed. J. S. Cunningham. Manchester: Manchester University Press; Baltimore: Johns Hopkins University Press, 1981.

Marston, John. *The Scourge of Villanie*. In *The Poems of John Marston, 1575?–1634*, ed. Arnold Davenport, 93–176. Liverpool: Liverpool University Press, 1961.

A Merry Jest of a Shrewd and Curst Wife Lapped in Morel's Skin. (Probably written around 1525.) London, 1580 (?). (STC 14521.)

Middleton, Thomas. *All's Lost by Lust*. In *The Spanish Gipsie, and All's Lost By Lust*, ed. Edgar C. Morris. Boston: Heath, 1908. 137–252.

———. *The Family of Love*. In *The Works of Thomas Middleton*, ed. A. H. Bullen, 8 vols., 3:1–120. London: Nimno, 1885–1886; repr. New York: AMS Press, 1964.

———. *A Mad World, My Masters*, ed. Standish Henning. Regents Renaissance Drama Series. London: Edward Arnold, 1965.

———. *Women Beware Women*, ed. J. R. Mulryne. The Revels Plays. Manchester: Manchester University Press, 1983.

———, and Thomas Dekker. *The Roaring Girl*. In *The Works of Thomas Middleton*, ed. Bullen. 4:1–152.

———, and William Rowley. *The Changeling*, ed. Patricia Thomson. The New Mermaids. London: Ernest Benn, 1977. — In *Drama of the English Renaissance*, ed. M. L. Wine, 601–84. New York: Random House, 1969.

———, and William Rowley. *The Spanish Gypsy*. In *The Spanish Gipsie, and All's Lost By Lust*, ed. Edgar C. Morris. Boston: Heath, 1908. 1–126.

Milton, John. *John Milton: Complete Poems and Major Prose*, ed. Merritt Y. Hughes. New York: Odyssey, 1957.

Milton, John. *Paradise Lost*, ed. Merritt Y. Hughes. New York: Odyssey, 1962.

Murrell, John . *A Daily Exercise for Ladies and Gentlewomen. Whereby they may learne and practise the whole Art of making Pastes, Preserves, Marmalades, Conserves* . . . . London, 1617. (STC 18301.)

Ovid. *Ars Amatoria*, trans. J. H. Mozley. Loeb Classical Library. Cambridge, MA: Harvard University Press, 1947.

———. *Fasti*, trans. Betty Rose Nagle. Indianapolis: Indiana University Press, 1995.

———. *Metamorphoses*, trans. Allen Mandelbaum. New York: Harcourt Brace, 1993.

Paré, Ambroise. *Apologie and Treatise of Ambroise Paré.* Ed. Geoffrey Keynes. Chicago: Chicago University Press, 1952.

Partridge, John. *The Treasurie of Commodious Conceites and hidden Secrets, Commonly called the Good Huswives Closet of Provision.* London, 1627. (STC 19431.)

Perkins, William. *Christian Oeconomie: Or, A Short Survey of the Right Manner of Erecting and Ordering a Familie.* London, 1609. (STC 19677.2.)

Pisan, Christine de. *The Book of the City of Ladies,* trans. E. J. Richards. New York: Persea, 1982.

Plat, Hugh. *Delightes for Ladies, to Adorne their Persons, Tables, Closets, and Distillatories: With Beauties, Banquets, Perfumes, & Waters.* London, 1602. (STC 19978.)

Platform for Action at the Fourth World Conference on Women in Beijing. New York: United Nations, 1995.

Purchas, Samuel. *Hakluytus Posthumus or Purchas his Pilgrimes.* 20 vols. Glasgow: J. Maclehose, 1905–1907.

Rich, Barnabe. *The Excellency of Good Women.* London, 1613. (STC 20982.)

Rowley, William. *The Spanish Gipsie, and All's Lost By Lust,* ed. Edgar C. Morris. Boston: Heath, 1908.

———, Thomas Dekker, and John Ford. *The Witch of Edmonton.* In *Three Jacobean Witchcraft Plays,* ed. Peter Corbin and Douglas Sedge, 143–209. The Revels Plays. Manchester: Manchester University Press, 1986.

Sackville, Thomas, and Thomas Norton. *Gorboduc, or Ferrex and Porrex.* In *Drama of the English Renaissance I: The Tudor Period,* ed. Russell A. Fraser and Norman Rabkin, 81–100. New York: Macmillan, 1976.

Shakespeare, William. Modern editions of Shakespeare are cited in individual essays.

———. *The Most Lamentable Romaine Tragedie of Titus Andronicus.* London, 1594. (STC 22328.)

Shirley, James. *The Ball.* London, 1639. (STC 4995.)

Sidney, Sir Philip. *The Countess of Pembroke's Arcadia,* ed. Maurice Evans. Harmondsworth: Penguin, 1977. — Ed. Victor Skretkowicz. Oxford: Clarendon Press, 1987.

———. *The Defense of Poesie (An Apology for Poetry).* London, 1595. (STC 22534); repr. Amsterdam: Theatrum Orbis Terrarum, 1971.

Silver, George. *Paradoxes of Defence.* London, 1599 (STC 22554); repr. London: Shakespeare Association Facsimiles, 1933.

Smith, Henry. *A Preparative to Marriage; Of the Lord's Supper; Of Usurie.* London, 1591. (STC 22687.)

Smith, John. *The Complete Works of Captain John Smith 1580–1631,* ed. Philip Barbour. 3 vols. Chapel Hill: University of North Carolina Press, 1986.

————. *The Generall Historie of Virginia* (1624). In *The Complete Works*, ed. Barbour, 2:225–488.

————. *A True Relation*. In *The Complete Works*, ed. Barbour, 1:3–117.

Spenser, Edmund. *The Faerie Queene*, ed. A. C. Hamilton. London and New York: Longman, 1977.

Spurling, Hilary. *Elinor Fettiplace's Receipt Book*. London: Viking Salamander, 1986.

Strachey, William. *For the Colony in Virginea Britannia: Lawes Divine, Morall and Martiall, etc.* London, 1612. (STC 23350.)

Stubbes, Philip. *Anatomie of Abuses*, ed. Margaret Jane Kidnie. MRTS 245. Tempe, AZ: Renaissance English Text Society in conjunction with Arizona Center for Medieval and Renaissance Studies, 2002.

Surflet, Richard. *The Countrie Farme*. London, 1600. (STC 10547.)

Swetnam, Joseph. *The Arraignment of Lewd, idle, froward, and unconstant women*. London, 1615 (STC 23533); repr. in *Half Humankind*, ed. Henderson and McManus, 189–216.

Tom Tyler and His Wife. London, 1661 (Wing STC T1792; first acted ca. 1560). Malone Society Reprint. London: Chiswick Press, 1910.

Vives, Juan Luis. *De Institutione Feminae Christianae*, ed. C. Fantazzi and C. Matheeussen, trans. C. Fantazzi. 2 vols. Leiden: Brill, 1996–1998.

————. *The Education of a Christian Woman: A Sixteenth-Century Manual*, trans. Charles Fantazzi. Chicago: University of Chicago Press, 2000.

————. *A very fruteful and pleasant boke callyd the Instruction of a Christen woman*, trans. Richard Hyrde. London, 1541. (STC 24858.)

Webster, John. *The Duchess of Malfi*. In *Drama of the English Renaissance: II. The Jacobean Period*, ed. Russell A. Fraser and Norman Rabkin, 475–515. New York: Macmillan, 1976.

————. *The White Devil*, ed. Christina Luckyj. London: A. and C. Black, 1996.

Whately, William. *A Bride-Bush, or a Wedding Sermon (A Direction for Married Persons)*. London, 1616 or 1617; repr. 1623. (STC 25298.)

Whetstone, George. *Promos and Cassandra*. In *Narrative and Dramatic Sources of Shakespeare*, ed. Geoffrey Bullough, 2: 442–513. London: Routledge, 1958.

Whitaker, Alexander. *Good Newes from Virginia*. London, 1613. (STC 25354.)

The Widdowes Treasure, Plentifully furnished with sundry precious and approved secrets in Phisicke. [Probably by John Partridge.] London, 1595. (STC 19434.)

Wing, John. *The Crowne Conjugall, or the Spouse Royall, A Discovery of the true honor and happines of Christian Matrimony*. London, 1632. (STC 25845.)

Woolley, Hannah. *The Compleat Servant-Maid, or the Young Maidens Tutor*. London, 1683. (Wing STC W3273B.)

——. *The Queen-like Closet, or Rich Cabinet: Stored with all Manner of Rare Receipts for Preserving, Candying and Cookery.* London, 1675. (Wing STC W3287.)

Wroth, Mary. *The First Part of the Countess of Montgomery's Urania*, ed. Josephine A. Roberts. MRTS 140. Binghamton, NY: MRTS, 1995.

——. *The Second Part of The Countess of Montgomery's Urania by Lady Mary Wroth*, ed. Josephine A. Roberts, completed by Suzanne Gossett and Janel Mueller. MRTS 211. Tempe, AZ: Renaissance English Text Society in conjunction with Arizona Center for Medieval and Renaissance Studies, 1999.

——. *Lady Mary Wroth's "Love's Victory,"* ed. Michael G. Brennan. London: The Roxburghe Club, 1988.

——. *The Poems of Lady Mary Wroth*, ed. Josephine A. Roberts. Baton Rouge and London: Louisiana State University Press, 1983.

B. STUDIES

Adams, Henry Hitch. *English Domestic, or Homiletic Tragedy 1575–1642.* New York: Columbia University Press, 1943.

Adamson, Jane. *"Othello" as Tragedy: Some Problems of Judgment and Feeling.* Cambridge: Cambridge University Press, 1980.

Adamson, W. D. "Unpinned or Undone? Desdemona's Critics and the Problem of Sexual Innocence." *Shakespeare Studies* 13 (1980): 169–86.

Adelman, Janet."Iago's Alter Ego: Race as Projection in *Othello.*" *Shakespeare Quarterly*: 48 (1997): 125–44.

——. *Suffocating Mothers: Fantasies of Maternal Origin in Shakespeare's Plays, "Hamlet" to "The Tempest."* New York: Routledge, 1992.

Adler, Doris. "The Rhetoric of Black and White in *Othello.*" *Shakespeare Quarterly* 25 (1974): 248–57.

Akrigg, G. V. K. *Jacobean Pageant: or, the Court of King James I.* Cambridge, MA: Harvard University Press, 1962.

Althusser, Louis. "Ideology and Ideological State Apparatuses." In idem, *Lenin and Philosophy and Other Essays*, trans. Ben Brewster, 129–73. London: New Left Books, 1971.

Amiet, Pierre. *Art of the Ancient Near East*, trans. John Shepley and Claude Choquet. New York: Abrams, 1980.

Amussen, Susan Dwyer. " 'Being stirred to much unquietness': Violence and Domestic Violence in Early Modern England." *Journal of Women's History* 6 (1994): 70–89.

———. *An Ordered Society: Gender and Class in Early Modern England*. New York: Columbia University Press, 1988.

Arnold, Janet. *Patterns of Fashion: The Cut and Construction of Clothes for Men and Women c. 1560–1620*. London: Macmillan, 1985.

Atwood, Margaret. *The Handmaid's Tale*. Toronto: McLelland and Stewart, 1985.

Aubrey, James R. "Race and the Spectacle of the Monstrous in *Othello*." CLIO, 22 (1993): 221–38.

Auden, W. H. "The Joker in the Pack." In idem, *The Dyer's Hand and Other Essays*, 246–72. New York: Random House, 1948.

Bach, Rebecca Ann. "The Homosocial Imaginary of *A Woman Killed with Kindness*." *Textual Practice* 12 (1998): 503–24.

Baines, Barbara J. "Effacing Rape in Early Modern Representation." *ELH* 65 (1998): 69–98.

Bakhtin, Mikhail. *Problems of Dostoevsky's Poetics*, ed. and trans. Caryl Emerson. Minneapolis: University of Minnesota Press, 1984.

Bamford, Karen. *Sexual Violence on the Jacobean Stage*. New York: St. Martin's Press, 2000.

Barbour, Philip. *Pocahontas and Her World*. Boston: Houghton Mifflin, 1969.

Barkan, Leonard. *Nature's Work of Art: The Human Body as Image of the World*. New Haven: Yale University Press, 1975.

Barker, Francis. *The Tremulous Private Body*. Ann Arbor: University of Michigan Press, 1995.

Bart, Pauline B., and Patricia H. O'Brien. *Stopping Rape: Successful Survival Strategies*. New York: Pergamon Press, 1985.

Bartels, Emily C. "Making More of the Moor: Aaron, Othello, and Renaissance Refashionings of Race." *Shakespeare Quarterly* 41 (1990): 433–54.

———. "Strategies of Submission: Desdemona, the Duchess, and the Assertion of Desire." *Studies in English Literature, 1500–1900* 36 (1996): 417–33.

Barthelemy, Anthony. *Black Face, Maligned Race: The Representation of Blacks in English Drama from Shakespeare to Southerne*. Baton Rouge: Louisiana State University Press, 1987.

Bartlett, Robert. *Trial by Fire and Water: The Medieval Judicial Ordeal*. Oxford: Clarendon Press, 1986.

Bashar, Nazife. "Rape in England between 1550 and 1700." In *The Sexual Dynamics of History*, 28–42. London: Pluto Press, 1983.

Bauer, Dale M., and Susan Janet McKinstry, eds. *Feminism, Bakhtin, and the Dialogic*. Albany: State University of New York Press, 1991.

Beattie, J. M. *Crime and the Courts in England 1660–1800*. Princeton: Princeton University Press, 1986.

Belsey, Catherine. "Alice Arden's Crime," *Renaissance Drama* n.s. 13 (1982): 83–102.

———. "Disrupting Sexual Difference: Meaning and Gender in the Comedies." In *Alternative Shakespeares*, ed. John Drakakis, 166–90. New York: Methuen, 1985.

———. *The Subject of Tragedy: Identity and Difference in Renaissance Drama*. London: Routledge, 1985.

Bentley, G. E. *The Jacobean and Caroline Stage*. 7 vols. Oxford: Clarendon Press, 1941–1956.

Berger, Harry, Jr. "Text Against Performance: The Example of *Macbeth*." *Genre: Forms of Discourse and Culture* 15 (1982): 49–79.

Berry, Edward. "Othello's Alienation." *Studies in English Literature 1500–1900* 30 (1990): 315–33.

Berry, Philippa. *Of Chastity and Power: Elizabethan Literature and the Unmarried Queen*. London: Routledge, 1989.

Bevington, David. Introduction to *Othello*. In *The Complete Works of Shakespeare*, ed. idem, 4th ed., 117–21. New York: HarperCollins, 1992.

Black-Michaud, Jacob. *Cohesive Force: Feud in the Mediterranean and Middle East*. New York: St.. Martin's Press, 1975.

Boebel, Dagny. "Challenging the Fable: The Power of Ideology in *Othello*." In *Ideological Approaches to Shakespeare: The Practice of Theory*, ed. Nicholas Ranson, 137–46. Lewiston, NY: Edwin Mellen Press, 1992.

Boehrer, Bruce. "Alsemero's Closet: Privacy and Interiority in *The Changeling*." *Journal of English and Germanic Philology* 96 (1997): 349–68.

Bolam, Robyn. "The Heart of the Labyrinth: Mary Wroth's *Pamphilia to Amphilanthus*." In *A Companion to English Renaissance Literature and Culture*, ed. Michael Hattaway, 257–66. Oxford: Blackwell, 2000.

Boling, Ronald J. "Fletcher's Satire of Caratach in *Bonduca*." *Comparative Drama* 33 (1999): 390–406.

Boose, Lynda E. "The 1599 Bishops' Ban, Elizabethan Pornography, and the Sexualization of the Jacobean Stage." In *Enclosure Acts: Sexuality, Property, and Culture in Early Modern England*, ed. Burt and Archer, 185–200.

———. "Grossly Gaping Viewers and Jonathan Miller's *Othello*." In *Shakespeare, the Movie: Popularizing the Plays on Film, TV, and Video*, ed. eadem and Richard Burt, 186–97. London: Routledge, 1997.

———. "Othello's 'Chrysolite' and the Song of Songs Tradition." *Philological Quarterly* 60 (1980): 427–37.

———. "Scolding Brides and Bridling Scolds: Taming the Woman's Unruly Member." *Shakespeare Quarterly* 42 (1991): 179–213.

Booth, Stephen. "On the Value of *Hamlet*." In *Reinterpretations of Elizabethan Drama*, ed. Norman Rabkin, 137–76. New York: Columbia University Press, 1969.

Bourdieu, Pierre. *Outline of a Theory of Practice*. Cambridge: Cambridge University Press, 1977.

Bowen, Barbara. "Aemilia Lanyer and the Invention of White Womanhood." In *Maids and Mistresses, Cousins and Queens: Women's Alliances in Early Modern England*, ed. Frye and Robertson, 274–303.

Bowman, Mary R. " 'She There as Princess Rained': Spenser's Figure of Elizabeth." *Renaissance Quarterly* 43 (1990): 475–502.

Bradley, A. C. *Shakespearean Tragedy: Lectures on "Hamlet," "Othello," "King Lear," "Macbeth."* London: Macmillan, 1904; repr. 1964.

Breitenberg, Mark. *Anxious Masculinity in Early Modern England*. Cambridge: Cambridge University Press, 1996.

Bridenbaugh, Carl. *Jamestown 1544–1699*. New York: Oxford University Press, 1980.

———. *Vexed and Troubled Englishmen*. New York: Oxford University Press, 1968.

Brink, Jean R., Allison P. Coudert, and Maryanne C. Horowitz, eds. *The Politics of Gender in Early Modern Europe*. Kirksville, MO: Sixteenth Century Journal Publications, 1989.

Briscoe, John. "Livy." In *The Oxford Classical Dictionary*, ed. Simon Hornblower and Anthony Spawforth, 878–79. Oxford: Oxford University Press, 1996.

Bristol, Michael D. "Charivari and the Comedy of Abjection in *Othello*." In *True Rites and Maimed Rites: Ritual and Anti-Ritual in Shakespeare and His Age*, ed. Woodbridge and Berry, 73–97. Urbana: University of Illinois Press, 1992.

Brittin, Norma. *Thomas Middleton*. New York: Twayne, 1972.

Bromley, Laura. "Domestic Conduct in *A Woman Killed with Kindness*." *Studies in English Literature 1500–1900* 26 (1986): 259–76.

Broude, Ronald. "Divine Right and Divine Retribution in Beaumont and Fletcher's *The Maid's Tragedy*." In *Shakespeare and Dramatic Tradition: Essays in Honor of S. F. Johnson*, ed. W. R. Elton and William B. Long, 246–63. Newark, DE: University of Delaware Press, 1989.

Brown, Peter. "Society and the Supernatural: A Medieval Change." *Daedalus* 104 (1975): 133–51; repr. in idem, *Society and the Holy in Late Antiquity*, 302–32. Berkeley: University of California Press, 1982.

Brownmiller, Susan. *Against Our Will: Men, Women, and Rape*. New York: Simon and Schuster, 1975.

Burelbach, Frederick M., Jr. "Theme and Structure in *The Spanish Gypsy*." *The Humanities Association Bulletin* 11 (1968): 37–41.

Burke, Kenneth. "*Othello*: An Essay to Illustrate a Method." *Hudson Review* 4 (1951): 165–203.

Burnett, Mark Thornton. *Masters and Servants in English Renaissance Drama and Culture*. London: Macmillan, 1997.

Burns, E. Jane. *Bodytalk: When Women Speak in Old French Literature*. Philadelphia: University of Pennsylvania Press, 1993.

Burt, Richard, and John Michael Archer, eds. *Enclosure Acts: Sexuality, Property, and Culture in Early Modern England*. Ithaca: Cornell University Press, 1994.

Butler, Judith. *Gender Trouble: Feminism and Subversion of Identity*. London: Routledge, 1990.

Bynum, Caroline Walker. *Fragmentation and Redemption: Essays on Gender and the Human Body in Medieval Religion*. New York: Zone Books, 1992.

Cadden, Joan. *Meanings of Sex Difference in the Middle Ages*. Cambridge: Cambridge University Press, 1995.

Cahn, Susan. *Industry of Devotion: The Transformation of Women's Work in England, 1500–1650*. New York: Columbia University Press, 1987.

Calder, Alison. " 'I am unacquainted with that language, Roman': Male and Female Experiences of War in Fletcher's *Bonduca*." *Medieval and Renaissance Drama in England* 8 (1996): 211–26.

Calderwood, James. *The Properties of "Othello"*. Amherst: University of Massachusetts Press, 1989.

———. "Speech and Self in *Othello*." *Shakespeare Quarterly* 38 (1987): 293–303.

Callaghan, Dympna. " 'Othello was a white man': Properties of Race on Shakespeare's Stage." In *Alternative Shakespeares 2*, ed. Terence Hawkes, 196–215. London: Routledge, 1996.

———. *Women and Gender in Renaissance Tragedy: A Study of "King Lear," "Othello," "The Duchess of Malfi," and "The White Devil"*. Atlantic Highlands: Humanities Press International, 1989.

Cameron, Deborah, and Elizabeth Frazer. *The Lust to Kill*. New York: New York University Press, 1987.

Camporesi, Piero. *Bread of Dreams: Food and Fantasy in Early Modern Europe*, trans. David Gentilcore. Cambridge: Polity Press, 1989.

Carlino, Andrea. *Books of the Body: Anatomical Ritual and Renaissance Learning*, trans. John Tedeschi and Anne C. Tedeschi. Chicago: University of Chicago Press, 1994.

Carlisle, Carol Jones. *Shakespeare from the Greenroom: Actors' Criticisms of Four Major Tragedies*. Chapel Hill: University of North Carolina Press, 1969.

Carr, Helen. "Woman/Indian: 'The American' and His Others." In *Europe and Its Others: Proceedings of the Essex Conference on the Sociology of Literature, July*

1984, ed. Francis Barker et al, 2 vols. 2:46–60. Colchester: University of Essex Press, 1985.

Carter, John. *ABC for Book Collectors.* 3rd ed. London: Rupert Hart-Davis, 1961.

Carter, John Marshall. *Rape in Medieval England.* Lanham, MD: University Press of America, 1985.

Cartmill, Matt. *A View to a Death in the Morning: Hunting and Nature Through History.* Cambridge, MA: Harvard University Press, 1993.

Catty, Jocelyn. *Writing Rape, Writing Women in Early Modern England: Unbridled Speech.* London: Macmillan, 1999.

Cavanagh, Sheila T. *Wanton Eyes and Chaste Desires: Female Sexuality in "The Faerie Queene."* Bloomington: Indiana University Press, 1994.

Cerasano, S. P., and Marion Wynne-Davies, eds. *Gloriana's Face: Women, Public and Private, in the English Renaissance.* Detroit: Wayne State University Press, 1992.

de Certeau, Michel. *The Practice of Everyday Life,* trans. Steven Randall. Berkeley: University of California Press, 1984.

Chambers, E.K. *The Elizabethan Stage,* 2 vols. Oxford: Clarendon Press, 1923.

Chaytor, Miranda. "Husband(ry): Narratives of Rape in the Seventeenth Century." *Gender and History* 7 (1995): 378–407.

Christensen, Ann. "Business, Pleasure and the Domestic Economy in Heywood's *A Woman Killed with Kindness.*" *Exemplaria* 9 (1997): 315–40.

Clark, Alice. *Working Life of Women in the Seventeenth Century.* New York: E. P. Dutton and Co., 1919; repr. London and New York: Routledge, 1992.

Clark, Andrew. "An Annotated List of Lost Domestic Plays, 1578–1624." *Research Opportunities in Renaissance Drama* 18 (1975): 29–44.

———. *Domestic Drama: A Survey of the Origins, Antecedents, and Nature of the Domestic Play in England, 1500–1640.* Salzburg: Institut für Englische Sprache und Literatur, Universität Salzburg, 1975.

Clark, Lorenne, and Debra Lewis. *Rape.* Toronto: Women's Press, 1977.

Cockburn, J. S. "The Nature and Incidence of Crime in England 1559–1625: A Preliminary Survey." In *Crime in England,* ed. idem, 49–71. London: Methuen, 1977.

Collier, Susanne. "Cutting to the Heart of the Matter: Stabbing the Woman in *Philaster* and *Cymbeline.*" In *Shakespearean Power and Punishment: A Volume of Essays,* ed. Kendall, 39–58. Newark, DE: University of Delaware Press; London: Associated University Presses, 1998.

Comensoli, Viviana. *Household Business: Domestic Plays of Early Modern England.* Toronto: University of Toronto Press, 1996.

———. "Play-making, Domestic Conduct, and the Multiple Plot in *The Roaring*

Girl." *Studies in English Literature 1500–1900* 27 (1987): 249–66.

Cook, Ann Jennalie. "The Design of *Othello*: Doubt Raised and Resolved." *Shakespeare Studies* 13 (1980): 187–96.

Cousins, A. D. "Subjectivity, Exemplarity, and the Establishing of Characterization in *Lucrece*." *Studies in English Literature 1500–1900* 38 (1998): 45–60.

Cowhig, Ruth. "Blacks in English Renaissance Drama and the Role of Shakespeare's Othello." In *The Black Presence in English Literature*, ed. David Dabydeen, 1–25. Manchester: Manchester University Press, 1989.

Crawford, Julie. "Fletcher's *The Tragedie of Bonduca* and the Anxieties of the Masculine Government of James I." *Studies in English Literature 1500–1900* 39 (1999): 357–81.

Cressy, David. *Birth, Marriage and Death: Ritual, Religion, and the Life-Cycle in Tudor and Stuart England.* Oxford: Oxford University Press, 1997.

Cunningham, Andrew C. *The Anatomical Renaissance.* Aldershot: Scolar Press, 1997.

Daileader, Celia R. "(Off) Staging the Sacred." In eadem, *Eroticism on the Renaissance Stage: Transcendence, Desire, and the Limits of the Visible*, 79–106. Cambridge: Cambridge University Press, 1998.

D'Amico, Jack. *The Moor in English Renaissance Drama.* Tampa: University of South Florida Press, 1991.

Dash, Irene G. *Wooing, Wedding, and Power: Women in Shakespeare's Plays.* New York: Columbia University Press, 1981.

Davies, Kathleen. "The Sacred Condition of Equality: How Original were Puritan Doctrines of Marriage?" *Social History* 5 (1977): 563–81.

Davis, Natalie Zemon. *Society and Culture in Early Modern France.* Stanford: Stanford University Press, 1965.

———. "Women in Politics." In *A History of Women: Renaissance and Enlightenment Paradoxes*, ed. eadem and Arlette Farge, 167–83. Cambridge, MA: Belknap Press, 1993.

Dawson, Anthony B. "Performance and Participation: Desdemona, Foucault, and the Actor's Body." In *Shakespeare, Theory, and Performance*, ed. James C. Bulman, 29–45. London and New York: Routledge, 1996.

Dean-Jones, Lesley Ann. *Women's Bodies in Classical Greek Science.* Oxford: Clarendon Press, 1994.

Deats, Sara Munson. "From Pedestal to Ditch: Violence Against Women in Shakespeare's *Othello*." In *The Aching Hearth: Family Violence in Life and Literature*, ed. eadem and Lagretta Tallent Lenker, 79–93. New York: Plenum Press, 1991.

De Groot, Roger D. "The Crime of Rape *temp*. Richard I and John." *Journal of Legal History* 9 (1988): 324–34.

Dekker, Rudolf M., and Lotte van de Pol. *The Tradition of Female Transvestism in Early Modern Europe*. New York: St. Martin's Press, 1989.

De Lauretis, Teresa. "The Violence of Rhetoric: Considerations on Representation and Gender." In eadem, *Technologies of Gender: Essays on Theory, Film, and Fiction*, 31–50. Bloomington: Indiana University Press, 1989.

Deleuze, Gilles. *Masochism: An Interpretation of Coldness and Cruelty*. New York: Zone Books, 1991.

de Mause, Lloyd, ed. *The History of Childhood*, New York: Psychohistory Press, 1974

Demos, John. *The Unredeemed Captive: A Family Story from Early America*. New York: Knopf, 1994.

Derrida, Jacques. *The Margins of Philosophy*, Trans. Alan Bass. Chicago: University of Chicago Press, 1982.

———. *Of Grammatology*, trans. Gayatri Chakravorty Spivak. Baltimore: Johns Hopkins University Press, 1974, repr. 1976.

Dolan, Frances E. *Dangerous Familiars: Representations of Domestic Crime in England 1550–1700*. Ithaca: Cornell University Press, 1994.

———. "Gender, Moral Agency, and Dramatic Form in *A Warning for Fair Women*." *Studies in English Literature 1500–1900* 29 (1989): 201–18.

———. "Household Chastisements: Gender, Authority, and 'Domestic Violence'." In *Renaissance Culture and the Everyday*, ed. Fumerton and Hunt, 204–25.

———, ed. *William Shakespeare: The Taming of the Shrew, Texts and Contexts*. Boston and New York: St. Martin's Press, 1986.

Dollimore, Jonathan. "Subjectivity, Sexuality, and Transgression: The Jacobean Connection." *Renaissance Drama* n.s. 17 (1986): 53–81.

Donaldson, Ian. *The Rapes of Lucretia: A Myth and its Transformations*. Oxford: Clarendon Press, 1982.

Doran, Susan. "Juno versus Diana: The Treatment of Elizabeth's Marriage in Plays and Entertainments, 1561–1581." *Historical Journal* 38 (1995): 257–74.

Dreher, Diane Elizabeth. *Domination and Defiance: Fathers and Daughters in Shakespeare*. Lexington: University of Kentucky Press, 1986.

Dubrow, Heather. *Captive Victors: Shakespeare's Narrative Poems and Sonnets*. Ithaca, NY: Cornell University Press, 1987.

Dusinberre, Juliet. *Shakespeare and the Nature of Women*. 2nd ed. New York: St. Martin's Press, 1996.

Eaton, Sara. "'Content with art'?: Seeing the Emblematic Woman in *The Second Maiden's Tragedy* and *The Winter's Tale*." In *Shakespearean Power and Punishment: A Volume of Essays*, ed. Kendall, 59–86.

———. "A Woman of Letters: Lavinia in *Titus Andronicus*." In *Shakespearean Tragedy and Gender*, ed. Garner and Sprengnether, 54–74.

Elias, Norbert. *The Civilizing Process*, trans. Edmund Jephcott. Oxford: Blackwell, 1994. (=*Über den Prozess der Zivilisation* [Basel: Haus zum Falken], 1939.)

Empson, William. "*Hamlet*." In *Essays on Shakespeare*, ed. David B. Pirie, 79–136. Cambridge: Cambridge University Press, 1986.

———. "Honest in *Othello*." In idem, *The Structure of Complex Words*, 218–49. London: Chatto and Windus, 1951.

Enders, Jody. *The Medieval Theater of Cruelty*. Ithaca: Cornell University Press, 1999.

Enterline, Lynn. *Tears of Narcissus: Melancholia and Masculinity in Early Modern Writing*. Stanford: Stanford University Press, 1995.

Erickson, Amy Louise. *Women and Property in Early Modern England*. New York: Routledge, 1993.

Estrich, Susan. *Real Rape*. Cambridge, MA: Harvard University Press, 1988.

Faucit, Helena. *On Some of Shakespeare's Female Characters*. Edinburgh: Blackwood, 1885; repr. New York: AMS Press, 1970.

Ferguson, Margaret. "Feathers and Flies: Aphra Behn and the Seventeenth-Century Trade in Exotica." *Subject and Object in Renaissance Culture*, ed. Margreta de Grazia, Maureen Quilligan, and Peter Stallybrass, 235–59. Cambridge: Cambridge University Press, 1996.

Ferril, Arthur. *The Origins of War: From the Stone Age to Alexander the Great*. London: Thames and Hudson, 1985.

Findlay, Alison. *A Feminist Perspective on Renaissance Drama*. Malden, MA: Blackwell, 1999.

———. "Women and Drama." In *A Companion to English Renaissance Literature and Culture*, ed. Hattaway, 499–512.

Fineman, Joel. "Shakespeare's *Will*: The Temporality of Rape." *Representations* 20 (1987): 25–76.

———. "The Sound of O in *Othello*: The Real of the Tragedy of Desire." *October* 45 (1988): 77–96.

Fish, Stanley. *Is There a Text in This Class? The Authority of Interpretive Communities*. Cambridge, MA: Harvard University Press, 1980.

Fletcher, Antony, and John Stevenson, eds. *Order and Disorder in Early Modern England*. Cambridge: Cambridge University Press, 1985.

Fontenot, Chester J., and Frantz Fanon. *The Wretched of the Earth*. New York: Grove Press, 1963.

Foster, Verna A. "Sex Averted or Converted: Sexuality and Tragicomic Genre in the Plays of Fletcher." *Studies in English Literature 1500–1900* 32 (1992): 311–22.

Foxon, David. *Libertine Literature in England 1660–1745*. London: New Hyde Park, 1965.

Frantz, David O. *Festum Voluptatis: A Study of Renaissance Erotica*. Columbus: Ohio State University Press, 1989.

———. "'Leud Priapians' and Renaissance Pornography." *Studies in English Literature 1500–1900* 12 (1972): 157–72.

Freedman, Barbara. *Staging the Gaze: Postmodernism, Psychoanalysis, and Shakespearean Comedy*. Ithaca: Cornell University Press, 1991.

French, Marilyn. *Shakespeare's Division of Experience*. New York: Ballantine Books, 1981.

Friedman, Alice T. *House and Household in Elizabethan England: Wollaton Hall and the Willoughby Family*. Chicago: University of Chicago Press, 1989.

Frye, Susan. *Elizabeth I: The Competition for Representation*. New York: Oxford University Press, 1993.

———, and Karen Robertson, eds. *Maids and Mistresses, Cousins and Queens: Women's Alliances in Early Modern England*. New York: Oxford University Press, 1999.

Fumerton, Patricia. *Cultural Aesthetics: Renaissance Literature and the Practice of Social Ornamentation*. Chicago: University of Chicago Press, 1991.

———. "Introduction: A New New Historicism." In *Renaissance Culture and the Everyday*, ed. eadem and Hunt, 1–17. Philadelphia: University of Pennsylvania Press, 1999.

———, and Simon Hunt, eds. *Renaissance Culture and the Everyday*. Philadelphia: University of Pennsylvania Press, 1999.

Furness, Horace Howard. *A New Variorum Edition of Othello*. 7th ed. Philadelphia: Lippincott, 1886.

Gantz, Timothy. *Early Greek Myth: A Guide to Literary and Artistic Sources*. Baltimore: Johns Hopkins University Press, 1993.

Garber, Marjorie. "The Insincerity of Women." In *Desire in the Renaissance: Psychoanalysis and Literature*, ed. Valeria Finucci and Regina Schwartz, 19–38. Princeton: Princeton University Press, 1994.

Garner, Shirley Nelson, "Shakespeare's Desdemona." *Shakespeare Studies* 9 (1976): 233–52.

———, and Madelon Sprengnether, eds. *Shakespearean Tragedy and Gender*. Bloomington: Indiana University Press, 1996.

Gelles, Richard J. "Male Offenders: Our Understanding from the Data." In *What Causes Men's Violence Against Women?*, ed. Harway and O'Neil, 36–48. Thousand Oaks, CA: Sage, 1999.

Genster, Julia. "Lieutenancy, Standing In, and *Othello.*" *English Literary History* 57 (1990): 785–809.

Girard, René. *Deceit, Desire, and the Novel: Self and Other in Literary Structure*, trans. Yvonne Freccero. Baltimore: Johns Hopkins University Press, 1965.

———. *A Theatre of Envy: William Shakespeare.* New York: Oxford University Press, 1991.

Girouard, Mark. *Life in the English Country House: A Social and Architectural History.* New Haven: Yale University Press, 1978.

Gohlke, Madelon. "Shakespeare's Tragic Paradigms." In *Representing Shakespeare: New Psychoanalytic Essays*, ed. Murray M. Schwartz and Coppélia Kahn, 170–187. Baltimore: Johns Hopkins University Press, 1980.

Goldberg, Jonathan. *Writing Matter: From the Hands of the English Renaissance.* Stanford: Stanford University Press, 1990.

Gossett, Suzanne. " 'Best Men are Molded out of Faults': Marrying the Rapist in Jacobean Drama." *English Literary Renaissance* 14 (1984): 305–27.

———. " 'Man-maid, Begone!': Women in Masques." *English Literary Renaissance* 18 (1988): 96–113.

Gowing, Laura. *Domestic Dangers: Women, Words and Sex in Early Modern London.* Oxford: Clarendon Press, 1996.

Grafton, Anthony, and Nancy Siraisi, eds. *Natural Particulars: Nature and the Disciplines of Renaissance Europe.* Cambridge, MA: MIT Press, 1999.

Gravdal, Kathryn. *Ravishing Maidens: Writing Rape in Medieval French Literature and Law.* Philadelphia: University of Pennsylvania Press, 1991.

Green, Paul D. "Theme and Structure in Fletcher's *Bonduca.*" *Studies in English Literature 1500–1900* 22 (1982): 305–16.

Greenberg, Mitchell. "Shakespeare's *Othello* and the 'Problem' of Anxiety." In idem, *Canonical States, Canonical Stages: Oedipus, Othering, and Seventeenth-Century Drama*, 1–32. Minneapolis and London: University of Minnesota Press, 1994.

Greene, Gayle. " 'This that you call love': Sexual and Social Tragedy in *Othello.*" *Journal of Women's Studies in Literature* 1 (1979): 16–32.

———. "Women on Trial in Shakespeare and Webster: 'The Mettle of [their] Sex'." *Topic 36: The Elizabethan Woman* 36 (1982): 5–19.

Greg, W. W. *A Bibliography of the English Printed Drama to the Restoration*, 2 vols. London: Oxford University Press, 1951.

Grennan, Eamon. "The Women's Voices in *Othello*: Speech, Song, Silence." *Shakespeare Quarterly* 38 (1987): 275–92.

Groth, A. Nicholas. *Men Who Rape: The Psychology of the Offender.* New York: Plenum, 1979.

Gurr, Andrew. Introduction to *The Maid's Tragedy*, 1–7. Fountainwell Drama

Texts. Berkeley and Los Angeles: University of California Press, 1969.

Gutierrez, Nancy. "The Irresolution of Melodrama: The Meaning of Adultery in *A Woman Killed with Kindness.*" *Exemplaria* 1 (1989): 265–91.

Hackett, Helen. "The Torture of Limena: Sex and Violence in Lady Mary Wroth's *Urania.*" In *Voicing Women: Gender and Sexuality in Early Modern Writing*, ed. Kate Chedgzoy, Melanie Hansen, and Susan Trill, 93–110. Keele: Keele University Press, 1996.

Hale, David George. *The Body Politic: A Political Metaphor in Renaissance English Literature.* The Hague: Mouton, 1971.

Hale, John. *The Civilization of Europe in the Renaissance.* New York: Atheneum, 1994.

Hall, Kim F. "Culinary Spaces, Colonial Spaces: The Gendering of Sugar in the Seventeenth Century." In *Feminist Readings of Early Modern Culture: Emerging Subjects*, ed. Valerie Traub, M. Lindsay Kaplan, and Dympna Callaghan, 168–90. Cambridge: Cambridge University Press, 1996.

———. "Reading What Isn't There: 'Black' Studies in Early Modern England." *Stanford Humanities Review* 3 (1993): 23–33.

———. *Things of Darkness: Economies of Race and Gender in Early Modern England.* Ithaca: Cornell University Press, 1996.

Hanawalt, Barbara. *Crime and Conflict in English Communities, 1300–1348.* Cambridge, MA: Harvard University Press, 1979.

Hankey, Julie. *Othello.* Plays in Performance Series. Bristol: Bristol Classical Press, 1987.

Hanson, Elizabeth. *Discovering the Subject in Renaissance England.* Cambridge: Cambridge University Press, 1998.

Harbage, Alfred. *Annals of English Drama 975–1700*, rev. S. Schoenbaum. London: Methuen, 1964.

———. *Shakespeare and the Rival Traditions.* New York: Macmillan, 1952.

Harding, Vanessa. " 'And one more may be laid there': The Location of Burials in Early Modern London." *London Journal* 14 (1989): 112–29.

Harris, Jonathan Gil. *Foreign Bodies and the Body Politic.* Cambridge: Cambridge University Press, 1998.

Hart, Jonathan. "Narratorial Strategies in *The Rape of Lucrece, Studies in English Literature 1500–1900* 32 (1992): 59–77.

Harway, Michèle, and James M. O'Neil, eds. *What Causes Men's Violence Against Women?* Thousand Oaks, CA: Sage, 1999.

Hattaway, Michael, ed. *A Companion to English Renaissance Literature and Culture.* Oxford: Blackwell, 2000.

Hawkins, Harriett. "Disrupting Tribal Difference: Critical and Artistic Responses to Shakespeare's Radical Romanticism." *Studies in the Literary Imagination* 26 (1993): 115–26.

Hazlitt, William. *Characters of Shakespear's Plays.* In *The Complete Works of William Hazlitt*, ed. P. P. Howe, 4: 165–361. London and Toronto: J. M. Dent, 1930.

Heinemann, Margot. *Puritanism and Theatre: Thomas Middleton and Opposition Drama under the Early Stuarts.* Cambridge: Cambridge University Press, 1982.

Helgerson, Richard. *Forms of Nationhood: The Elizabethan Writing of England.* Chicago and London: University of Chicago Press, 1992.

———. *Self-Crowned Laureates: Spenser, Jonson, Milton, and the Literary System.* Berkeley: University of California Press, 1983.

Henderson, Diana. "The Theater and Domestic Culture." In *A New History of Early English Drama*, ed. John D. Cox and David Scott Kastan, 173–94. New York: Columbia University Press, 1997.

Hendricks, Margo. "Race: A Renaissance Category?" In *A Companion to English Renaissance Literature and Culture*, ed. Hattaway, 690–98.

———. and Patricia Parker, eds. *Women, "Race," and Writing in the Early Modern Period.* New York: Routledge, 1994.

Herbert-Brown, Geraldine. *Ovid and the Fasti.* Oxford: Clarendon Press, 1994.

Hickman, Andrew. "*Bonduca*'s Two Ignoble Armies and *The Two Noble Kinsmen.*" *Medieval and Renaissance Drama in England* 4 (1989): 143–71.

Hill, Christopher. *Society and Puritanism in Pre-Revolutionary England.* New York: Schocken, 1964.

Hillman, David, and Carla Mazzio, eds. *The Body in Parts: Fantasies of Corporeality in Early Modern Europe.* New York: Routledge, 1997.

Hodges, Devon. *Renaissance Fictions of Anatomy.* Amherst: University of Massachusetts Press, 1985.

Hodgson-Wright, Stephanie. "Beauty, Chastity and Wit: Feminising the Centre-stage." In *Women and Dramatic Production 1550–1700*, ed. Alison Findlay et al., 42–67. Harlow: Pearson, 2000.

Hoffman, Piotr. *Violence in Modern Philosophy.* Chicago and London: University of Chicago Press, 1989.

Honigmann, E. A. J. *Shakespeare: Seven Tragedies: The Dramatist's Manipulation of Audience Response.* London: Macmillan, 1976.

———. *The Texts of "Othello" and Shakespearian Revision.* London and New York: Routledge, 1996.

Horn, James. *Adapting to a New World: English Society in the Seventeenth-Century Chesapeake.* Chapel Hill: University of North Carolina Press, 1994.

Houlbrooke, Ralph. *The English Family 1450–1700.* New York: Longman, 1984.

Howard, Jean E. "Crossdressing, The Theatre, and Gender Struggle in Early Modern England." *Shakespeare Quarterly* 39 (1988): 418–40.

———. "An English Lass amid the Moors: Gender, Race, Sexuality, and National Identity in Heywood's *The Fair Maid of the West.*" In *Women, "Race," and Writing in the Early Modern Period*, ed. Hendricks and Parker, 101–17.

———. *The Stage and Social Struggle in Early Modern England.* New York: Routledge, 1994.

Hufton, Olwen. *The Prospect Before Her: A History of Women in Western Europe 1500–1800.* New York: Vintage-Random, 1995.

Hull, Suzanne. *Chaste, Silent, and Obedient: English Books for Women 1475–1640.* San Marino, CA: Huntington Library, 1982.

Hulme, Peter. *Colonial Encounters: Europe and the Native Caribbean, 1492–1707.* London: Methuen, 1992.

Hunt, Margaret. "Wife Beating, Domesticity, and Women's Independence in Eighteenth-Century London." *Gender and History* 4 (1992): 10–33.

Hunter, G. K. "*Othello* and the Colour Prejudice." *Proceedings of the British Academy* 51 (1967): 139–63.

Hutson, Lorna. *The Usurer's Daughter: Male Friendship and Fictions of Women in Sixteenth-Century England.* London: Routledge, 1994.

Illick, Joseph E. "Child-Rearing in Seventeenth Century England and America." In *The History of Childhood*, ed. de Mause, 303–50.

Ingram, Martin. *Church, Courts, Sex, and Marriage in England*, 1570–1640. Cambridge: Cambridge University Press, 1987.

———. "Ridings, Rough Music and the 'Reform of Popular Culture' in Early Modern England." *Past and Present* 105 (1984): 79–113.

———. "'Scolding Women Cucked or Washed': A Crisis in Gender Relations in Early Modern England?" In *Women, Crime, and the Courts in Early Modern England*, ed. Jenny Kermode and Garthine Walker, 48–80. London: University College London Press, 1994.

Jacobs, Deborah. "Critical Imperialism and Renaissance Drama: The Case of *The Roaring Girl.*" In *Feminism, Bakhtin, and the Dialogic*, ed. Bauer and McKinstry, 73–84.

Jacobus, Mary. "Is There a Woman in This Text?" *New Literary History* 14 (1982): 117–154.

Jameson, Anna B. *Characteristics of Women–Moral, Poetical, and Historical.* London: G. Bell and Sons, 1832; repr. as *Shakespeare's Heroines: Characteristics of Women*, London: George Bell, 1905; repr. New York: Gordon; Norwood, PA: Norwood Editions, 1978.

Jardine, Lisa. *Still Harping on Daughters: Women and Drama in the Age of Shake-*

speare. New York: Columbia University Press, 1983.

Jed, Stephanie H. *Chaste Thinking: The Rape of Lucretia and the Birth of Humanism*. Bloomington and Indianapolis: Indiana University Press, 1989.

———. "The Scene of Tyranny: Violence and the Humanistic Tradition." In *The Violence of Representation: Literature and the History of Violence*, ed. Nancy Armstrong and Leonard Tennenhouse, 29–44. London and New York: Routledge, 1989.

Jones, Ann Rosalind, and Peter Stallybrass. *Renaissance Clothing and the Materials of Memory*. Cambridge: Cambridge University Press, 2000.

Jones, Eldred D. *Othello's Countrymen: The African in English Renaissance Drama*. Oxford: Oxford University Press, 1965.

Jordon, Winthrop D. *White Over Black: American Attitudes Toward the Negro, 1550–1812*. Chapel Hill: University of North Carolina Press, 1968.

Jorgensen, Paul A. *Lear's Self-Discovery*. Berkeley: University of California Press, 1967.

———. *Our Naked Frailties: Sensational Art and Meaning in "Macbeth."* Berkeley: University of California Press, 1971.

———. *Redeeming Shakespeare's Words*. Berkeley: University of California Press, 1962.

———. *Shakespeare's Military World*. Berkeley, Los Angeles, and London: University of California Press, 1956.

Kahn, Coppélia. "*Lucrece*: The Sexual Politics of Subjectivity." In *Rape and Representation*, ed. Lynn Higgins and Brenda Silver, 141–59. New York: Columbia University Press, 1991.

———. *Man's Estate: Masculine Identity in Shakespeare*. Berkeley: University of California Press, 1981.

———. *Roman Shakespeare: Warriors, Wounds, and Women*. London and New York: Routledge, 1997.

Kappeler, Susanne. *The Pornography of Representation*. Cambridge: Policy Press, 1986.

Kawachi, Yoshiko. *Calendar of English Renaissance Drama*. New York and London: Garland,1986.

Kay, Carol McGinnis. "Othello's Need for Mirrors." *Shakespeare Quarterly* 34 (1983): 261–70.

Keeley, Lawrence H. *War Before Civilization*. New York: Oxford University Press, 1996.

Kelso, Ruth. *Doctrine for the Lady of the Renaissance*. Urbana: University of Illinois Press, 1956.

Kendall, Gillian Murray, ed. *Shakespearean Power and Punishment: A Volume of*

Essays. Newark, DE: University of Delaware Press; London: Associated University Presses, 1998.

Kennedy, Duncan. *Sexy Dressing, Etc.* Cambridge, MA, and London: Harvard University Press, 1993.

Keuls, Eva. *The Reign of the Phallus: Sexual Politics in Ancient Athens*. New York: Harper and Row, 1985.

Kistner, A. L. and M. K. *Middleton's Tragic Themes*. American University Studies, Series 4: English Language and Literature 10. New York: Peter Lang, 1984.

Kittel, Ruth. "Rape in Thirteenth-Century England: A Study of the Common Law Courts." In *Women and the Law*, ed. D. Kelly Weisberg, 2:101–15. Cambridge, MA: Schenkman, 1982.

Knutson, Roslyn Lander. *The Repertory of Shakespeare's Company, 1594–1613*. Fayetteville: University of Arkansas Press, 1991.

Kolodny, Annette. *The Lay of the Land*. Chapel Hill: University of North Carolina Press, 1984.

Kramer, Jerome, and Judith Kaminsky. "'These Contraries Such Unity Do Hold': Structure in *The Rape of Lucrece*." *Mosaic* 10 (1977): 143–55.

Kramer, Samuel Noah. *From the Poetry of Sumer: Creation, Glorification, Adoration*. Berkeley: University of California Press, 1979.

Kristeva, Julia. *Powers of Horror: An Essay on Abjection*, trans. Leon S. Roudiez. New York: Columbia University Press, 1982.

Kupperman, Karen. *Roanoke: The Abandoned Colony*. Totowa, NJ: Rowman and Allanheld, 1984.

Kussmaul, Ann. *Servants in Husbandry in Early Modern England*. Cambridge: Cambridge University Press, 1981.

Kusunoki, Akiko. "Representations of Female Subjectivity in Elizabeth Cary's *The Tragedy of Mariam* and Mary Wroth's *Love's Victory*." In *Japanese Studies in Shakespeare and His Contemporaries*, ed. Yoshiko Kawachi, 141–65. Newark, DE: University of Delaware Press, 1998.

Lake, D. J. *The Canon of Thomas Middleton's Plays*. London: Cambridge University Press, 1975.

Laqueur, Thomas. *Making Sex: Body and Gender from the Greeks to Freud*. Cambridge, MA: Harvard University Press, 1990.

Lea, Henry Charles. *The Duel and the Oath*. Philadelphia: University of Pennsylvania Press, 1974.

Lennox, Ann, and David Allan Stewart. "Sisters Are Doin' It For Themselves." BMG Songs, 1985.

Lenz, Carolyn Ruth Swift, Gayle Greene, and Carol Thomas Neely, eds. *The*

Woman's Part: Feminist Criticism of Shakespeare. Urbana: University of Illinois Press, 1980.

Lerner, Gerda. *The Creation of Patriarchy.* New York: Oxford University Press, 1976.

Levin, Carole. *The Heart and Stomach of a King: Elizabeth I and the Politics of Sex and Power.* Philadelphia: University of Pennsylvania Press, 1994.

———. "Power, Politics, and Sexuality: Images of Elizabeth I." In *The Politics of Gender in Early Modern Europe,* ed. Brink, Coudert, and Horowitz, 95–110.

Levinas, Emmanuel. *Basic Philosophical Writings,* ed. Adriaan T. Peperzak et al. Bloomington: Indiana University Press, 1996.

Levine, Laura. *Men in Women's Clothing: Anti-theatricality and Effeminization 1579–1642.* Cambridge: Cambridge University Press, 1994.

Lewalski, Barbara K. *Protestant Poetics and the Seventeenth Century.* Princeton: Princeton University Press, 1970.

———. *Writing Women in Jacobean England.* Cambridge, MA: Harvard University Press, 1993.

Lind, L. R. *Studies in Pre-Vesalian Anatomy.* Philadelphia: American Philosophical Society, 1975.

Linton, Joan Pong. *The Romance of the New World: Gender and the Literary Formation of English Colonialism.* Cambridge University Press, 1998.

Loomba, Ania. *Gender, Race, Renaissance Drama.* Manchester: Manchester University Press, 1989; Delhi: Oxford University Press, 1992.

Loraux, Nicole. *Mothers in Mourning,* trans. Corinne Pache. Ithaca and London: Cornell University Press, 1998.

Lucas, R. Valerie. "*Hic Mulier*: The Female Transvestite in Early Modern England." *Renaissance and Reformation* 12 (1988): 65–84.

MacDonald, Michael. *Mystical Bedlam.* Cambridge: Cambridge University Press, 1981.

———. *Witchcraft and Hysteria in Elizabethan London.* London: Routledge, 1991.

Marcus, Leah Sinanoglou. "The Milieu of Milton's *Comus*: Judicial Reform at Ludlow and the Problem of Sexual Assault." *Criticism* 25 (1983): 293–327.

Marin, Amy J., and Nancy Felipe Russo. "Feminist Perspectives on Male Violence Against Women: Critiquing O'Neil and Harway's Model." In *What Causes Men's Violence Against Women?,* ed. Harway and O'Neil, 18–35.

Marotti, Arthur F. " 'Love is Not Love': Elizabethan Sonnet Sequences and the Social Order." *ELH* 49 (1982): 396–428.

Martz, Louis L. *The Poetry of Meditation.* New Haven: Yale University Press, 1954.

Masten, Jeffrey. *Textual Intercourse: Collaboration, Authorship, and Sexualities in*

Renaissance Drama. Cambridge: Cambridge University Press, 1997.

Maus, Katherine Eisaman. "Horns of Dilemma: Jealousy, Gender, and Spectatorship in English Renaissance Drama." *ELH* 54 (1987): 561–584.

———. *Inwardness and Theater in the English Renaissance.* Chicago: University of Chicago Press, 1995.

———. "Taking Tropes Seriously: Language and Violence in Shakespeare's *Rape of Lucrece.*" *Shakespeare Quarterly* 37 (1986): 66–82.

McAlindon, T. *Shakespeare's Tragic Cosmos.* Cambridge: Cambridge University Press, 1991.

McCabe, Richard A. *Incest, Drama and Nature's Law 1550–1700.* Cambridge: Cambridge University Press, 1993.

McKewin, Carole. "Counsels of Gall and Grace: Intimate Conversations Between Women in Shakespeare's Plays." In *The Woman's Part: Feminist Criticism of Shakespeare,* ed. Lenz, Greene, and Neely, 117–32.

McLuskie, Kathleen. *Dekker and Heywood: Professional Dramatists.* Houndsmill and London: St. Martin's Press, 1994.

———. " 'A Maidenhead, *Amintor,* At My Yeares': Chastity and Tragicomedy in the Fletcher Plays." In *The Politics of Tragicomedy: Shakespeare and After,* ed. Gordon McMullan and Jonathan Hope, 92–121. London and New York: Routledge, 1992.

———. "The Patriarchal Bard: Feminist Criticism and Shakespeare: *King Lear* and *Measure for Measure.*" In *Political Shakespeare: New Essays in Cultural Materialism,* ed. Jonathan Dollimore and Alan Sinfield, 88–108. Ithaca, NY: Cornell University Press, 1985.

———. *Renaissance Dramatists.* Atlantic Highlands, NJ: Humanities Press, 1989.

———. " 'Tis But a Woman's Jar': Family and Kinship in Elizabethan Domestic Drama." *Literature and History* 9 (1983): 228–39.

McPherson, David. "Aretino and the Harvey-Nashe Quarrel." *PMLA* 84 (1969): 1551–1558.

Mellaart, James. *Çatal Hüyük: A Neolithic Town in Anatolia.* New York: McGraw-Hill, 1967.

Mellars, Paul. "The Upper Palaeolithic Revolution." In *The Oxford Illustrated Prehistory of Europe,* ed. Barry Cunliffe, 70–75. New York: Oxford University Press, 1994.

Mikalachki, Jodi. *The Legacy of Boadicea: Gender and Nation in Early Modern England.* London and New York: Routledge, 1998.

Miller, Naomi J. *Changing the Subject: Mary Wroth and Figurations of Gender in Early Modern England.* Lexington: University of Kentucky Press, 1996.

Montrose, Louis. *The Purpose of Playing: Shakespeare and the Cultural Politics of*

Elizabethan Theatre. Chicago: University of Chicago Press, 1996.

Moulton, Ian. *Before Pornography: Erotic Writing in Early Modern England.* Oxford: Oxford University Press, 2000.

Mousley, Andy. *Renaissance Drama and Contemporary Literary Theory.* New York: St. Martin's Press, 2000.

Mullholland, Paul. Introduction to *The Roaring Girl,* by Thomas Middleton and Thomas Dekker, ed. idem, 1–65. Manchester: Manchester University Press, 1987.

Murray, Mary. *The Law of the Father? Patriarchy in the Transition from Feudalism to Capitalism.* London: Routledge, 1995.

Neely, Carol Thomas. "Women and Men in *Othello*: 'What should such a fool / do with so good a woman?' " In *The Woman's Part: Feminist Criticism of Shakespeare,* ed. Swift, Lenz, Greene, and eadem, 211–39.

Neill, Edward. *History of the Virginia Company of London.* Albany, NY: J. Munsell, 1869; repr. New York: B. Franklin, 1968.

Neill, Michael. " 'Amphitheaters in the Body': Playing with Hands on the Shakespearean Stage." *Shakespeare Survey* 48 (1995): 23–50.

———. "Changing Places in *Othello.*" *Shakespeare Survey* 37 (1984): 115–31.

———. *Issues of Death: Mortality and Identity in English Renaissance Tragedy.* Oxford: Clarendon Press, 1997.

———. "Unproper Beds: Race, Adultery, and the Hideous in *Othello.*" *Shakespeare Quarterly* 40 (1989): 383–412.

Neilson, George. *Trial by Combat.* Glasgow: William Hodge, 1890.

Newman, Jane. " 'And let mild women to him lose their mildness": Philomela, Female Violence, and Shakespeare's *The Rape of Lucrece.*' " *Shakespeare Quarterly* 45 (1994): 304–26.

Newman, Karen. " 'And Wash the Ethiop White': Femininity and the Monstrous in *Othello.*" In *Shakespeare Reproduced: The Text in History and Ideology,* ed. Howard and Marion F. O'Connor, 143–62. New York and London: Routledge, 1987.

———. *Fashioning Femininity and English Renaissance Drama.* Chicago: University of Chicago Press, 1991.

Norsworthy, Laura. *The Lady of Bleeding Heart Yard: Lady Elizabeth Hatton 1578–1646.* London: John Murray, 1938.

Norton, Mary Beth. *Founding Mothers and Fathers: Gendered Power and the Forming of American Society.* New York: Knopf, 1996.

Nutton, Vivian. " 'A Diet for Barbarians': Introducing Renaissance Medicine to Tudor England." In *Natural Particulars: Nature and the Disciplines in Renaissance Europe,* ed. Anthony Grafton and Nancy Siraisi, 275–93. Cambridge, MA: MIT Press, 1999.

Oliphant, E. H. C. *Shakespeare and His Fellow Dramatists*. 2 vols. New York: Prentice Hall, 1929.

Orgel, Stephen. "The Authentic Shakespeare." *Representations* 21 (1988): 1–25.

———. *Impersonations: The Performance of Gender in Shakespeare's England*. Cambridge: Cambridge University Press, 1996.

———. "Nobody's Perfect: Or Why Did the English Stage Take Boys for Women?" *South Atlantic Quarterly* 88 (1989): 7–29.

———. "Shakespeare and the Kinds of Drama." *Critical Inquiry* 6 (1979): 107–23.

———. "Shakespeare Imagines a Theater." In *Shakespeare, Man of the Theater: Proceedings of the Second Congress of the International Shakespeare Association, 1981*, ed. Kenneth Muir, Jay L. Halio, and D. J. Palmer, 34–46. East Brunswick, NJ, London, and Mississauga: Associated University Presses, 1983.

Orlin, Lena Cowen. *Private Matters and Public Culture in Post-Reformation England*. Ithaca: Cornell University Press, 1994.

Park, Hyungji. "The Traffic in Desdemona: Race and Sexual Transgression in *Othello*." *The Journal of English Language and Literature* (Seoul) 41 (1995): 1061–82.

Parker, Patricia. "Fantasies of 'Race' and 'Gender': Africa, *Othello*, and Bringing to Light." In *Women, "Race" and Writing in the Early Modern Period*, ed. Hendricks and eadem, 84–100.

———. "Shakespeare and Rhetoric: 'dilation' and 'delation' in *Othello*." In *Shakespeare and the Question of Theory*, ed. eadem and Geoffrey Hartman, 54–74. New York and London: Methuen, 1984.

———. *Shakespeare from the Margins: Language, Culture, Context*. Chicago and London: University of Chicago Press, 1996.

Parks, Katherine. "The Criminal and the Saintly Body: Autopsy and Dissection in Renaissance Italy." *Renaissance Quarterly* 42 (1994): 1–33.

Paster, Gail Kern. *The Body Embarrassed: Drama and the Disciplines of Shame in Early Modern England*. Ithaca: Cornell University Press, 1993.

Patterson, Annabel. *Reading Between the Lines*. London: Routledge, 1993.

Pearse, Nancy Cotton. *John Fletcher's Chastity Plays: Mirrors of Modesty*. Lewisburg, PA: Bucknell University Press, 1973.

Pechter, Edward. "'Have You Not Read Some Such Thing?': Sex and Sexual Stories in *Othello*." *Shakespeare Survey* 49 (1996): 201–16.

"Othello" and Interpretive Traditions. Iowa City: University of Iowa Press, 1999.

———. "*Patient Grissil* and the Trials of Marriage." *Elizabethan Theatre 14* (1996): 83–108.

Perry, Curtis. *The Making of Jacobean Culture: James I and the Renegotiation of*

Elizabethan Literary Practice. Cambridge: Cambridge University Press, 1997.

Peters, Edward. *Inquisition*. New York: Free Press, 1988.

Plowden, Alison. *The Stuart Princesses*. Stroud, Gloucs: Sutton Publishing, 1997.

Pollock, Linda. *With Faith and Physic: The Life of a Tudor Gentlewoman, Lady Grace Mildmay, 1552–1620*. London: Collins and Brown, 1993.

Powell, Chilton Latham. *English Domestic Relations, 1487–1653*. New York: Columbia University Press, 1917.

Prest, W.R. "Law and Women's Rights in Early Modern England." *Sixteenth Century* [GB] 6 (1991): 169–187.

Rackin, Phyllis. "Foreign Country: The Place of Women and Sexuality in Shakespeare's Historical World." In *Enclosure Acts: Sexuality, Property, and Culture in Early Modern England*, ed. Burt and Archer, 68–95.

Randall, Dale B. J. "The Rank and Earthy Background of Certain Physical Symbols in *The Duchess of Malfi*." *Renaissance Drama* n.s. 18 (1987): 171–203.

———. "Some Observations on the Theme of Chastity in *The Changeling*." *English Literary Renaissance* 14 (1984): 347–66.

Rawson, M. S. *Penelope Rich and Her Circle*. London: Hutchinson, 1911.

Reid, Aileen, and Robert Maniura, eds. *Edward Alleyn: Elizabethan Actor, Jacobean Gentleman*. Dulwich: Dulwich Picture Gallery, 1994.

Relihan, Constance C. *Fashioning Authority: The Development of Elizabethan Novelistic Discourse*. Kent, OH and London: Kent State University Press, 1994.

Robertson, Elizabeth. "Public Bodies and Psychic Domains: Rape, Consent, and Female Subjectivity in Geoffrey Chaucer's *Troilus and Criseyde*." In *Representing Rape in Medieval and Early Modern Literature*, ed. eadem and Christine Rose, 281–310. New York: Palgrave Press, 2001.

Robertson, Karen. "Pocahontas at the Masque." *Signs* 21 (1996): 551–83.

Rose, Mary Beth. *The Expense of Spirit: Love and Sexuality in English Renaissance Drama*. Ithaca: Cornell University Press, 1988.

———. "The Heroics of Marriage in *Othello* and *The Duchess of Malfi*." In *Shakespearean Tragedy and Gender*, ed. Garner and Sprengnether, 210–40.

———. "Women in Men's Clothing: Apparel and Social Stability in *The Roaring Girl*." *English Literary Renaissance* 14 (1984): 367–91.

Rosenberg, Marvin. *The Masks of Othello: The Search for the Identity of Othello, Iago, and Desdemona by Three Centuries of Actors and Critics*. Berkeley: University of California Press, 1961.

Rountree, Helen. *The Powhatan Indians of Virginia*. Norman, OK: University of Oklahoma Press, 1989.

Ruggiero, Guido. "Violence and Sexuality: Rape." In idem, *The Boundaries of*

Eros: Sex Crime and Sexuality in Renaissance Venice, 89–108. New York: Oxford University Press, 1985.

Rulon-Miller, Nina. "*Othello's* Bianca: Climbing Out of the Bed of Patriarchy." *Upstart Crow* 15 (1995): 99–114.

Sawday, Jonathan. *The Body Emblazoned: Dissection and the Human Body in Renaissance Culture*. London and New York: Routledge, 1995.

Scarry, Elaine. *The Body in Pain: The Making and Unmaking of the World*. New York: Oxford University Press, 1985.

Sedgwick, Eve Kosofsky. *Between Men: English Literature and Male Homosocial Desire*. New York: Columbia University Press, 1985; repr. 1992.

Shapiro, Michael. *Gender in Play on the Shakespearean Stage: Boy Heroines and Female Pages*. Ann Arbor: University of Michigan Press, 1996.

Sharpe, J. A. *Crime in Early Modern England 1550–1750*. London: Longman, 1984.

———. *Early Modern England: A Social History 1550–1760*. London: Edward Arnold, 1987.

Shaver, Anne. "Agency and Marriage in the Fictions of Lady Mary Wroth and Margaret Cavendish, Duchess of Newcastle." In *Pilgrimage for Love: Essays in Early Modern Literature in Honor of Josephine A. Roberts*, ed. Sigrid King, 177–90. MRTS 213. Tempe, AZ: MRTS, 1999.

Shepherd, Simon. *Amazons and Warrior Women: Varieties of Feminism in Seventeenth-Century Drama*. New York: St. Martin's Press, 1981.

Shullenberger, William. "'This For the Most Wrong'd of Women': A Reappraisal of *The Maid's Tragedy*." *Renaissance Drama* n.s. 13 (1982): 131–56.

Siemon, James R. "'Nay, that's not next': *Othello*, V.ii in Performance, 1760–1900." *Shakespeare Quarterly* 37 (1986): 38–51.

Sinfield, Alan. *Faultlines: Cultural Materialism and the Politics of Dissident Reading*. Berkeley: University of California Press, 1992.

Singh, Jyotsna. "Othello's Identity, Postcolonial Theory, and Contemporary African Rewritings of *Othello*." In *Women, "Race," and Writing in the Early Modern Period*, ed. Hendricks and Parker, 287–299.

Sloan, A. W. *English Medicine in the Seventeenth Century*. Durham: Durham Academic Press, 1996.

Smethurst, Mae. "The Japanese Presence in Ninagawa's *Medea*." In *Medea in Performance 1500–2000*, ed. Edith Hall et al., 191–216. Oxford: European Humanities Research Centre, 2000.

Smith, Molly. *Breaking Boundaries: Politics and Play in the Drama of Shakespeare and his Contemporaries*. Aldershot, UK and Brookfield, VT: Ashgate, 1998.

Snow, Edward A. "Sexual Anxiety and the Male Order of Things in *Othello*."
    English Literary Renaissance 10 (1980): 384–412.

Spencer, Theodore. *Shakespeare and the Nature of Man*. London: Macmillan, 1942.

Spicer, Joaneath. "The Renaissance Elbow." In *A Cultural History of Gesture*, ed.
    Jan Bremmer and Herman Roodenburg, 84–128. Ithaca: Cornell University
    Press, 1991.

Spivack, Bernard. *Shakespeare and the Allegory of Evil*. New York: Columbia University Press, 1958.

Sprague, Arthur Colby. *Shakespeare and the Actors: The Stage Business in His Plays
    (1660–1905)*. Cambridge, MA: Harvard University Press, 1948.

Squier, Charles L. *John Fletcher*. Boston: Twayne, 1986.

Stallybrass, Peter. "Patriarchal Territories: The Body Enclosed." In *Rewriting the
    Renaissance: Discourses of Sexual Difference in Early Modern Europe*, ed. Margaret W. Ferguson, Maureen Quilligan, and Nancy J. Vickers, 123–42. Chicago: University of Chicago Press, 1986.

Stewart, Alan. "The Early Modern Closet Discovered." *Representations* 50
    (1995): 76–100.

Stone, Lawrence. *The Crisis of the Aristocracy, 1558-1641*. Oxford: Clarendon
    Press, 1965.

———. *The Family, Sex, and Marriage in England, 1500–1800*. London: Weidenfeld and Nicolson, 1977.

Strickland, Agnes. *Lives of the Queens of Scotland and English Princesses Connected
    with the Royal Succession of Great Britain*. 8 vols. Edinburgh: W. Blackwood,
    1850–1859.

Strier, Richard. *Resistant Structure: Particularity, Radicalism, and Renaissance
    Texts*. Berkeley: University of California Press, 1995.

Strong, Roy. *The Cult of Elizabeth: Elizabethan Portraiture and Pageantry*. Berkeley: University of California Press, 1977.

———. *The English Icon: Elizabethan and Jacobean Portraiture*. London: Paul
    Mellon Foundation for British Art, 1969.

Swetnam the Woman-hater: The Controversy and the Play, ed. Coryl Crandall.
    West Lafayette, IN: Purdue University Press, 1969.

Szymborska, Wislawa. "The She-Pharaoh," trans. Irena Grudzinska Gross. *The
    New York Review of Books* 46:12 (15 July 1999): 10.

Talvacchia, Bette. *Taking Positions: On the Erotic in Renaissance Culture*.
    Princeton: Princeton University Press, 1999.

Tennenhouse, Leonard. *Power on Display: The Politics of Shakespeare's Genres*.
    New York and London: Methuen, 1986.

————. "Violence Done to Women on the Renaissance Stage." In *The Violence of Representation: Literature and the History of Violence*, ed. Nancy Armstrong and idem, 77–97.

Terry, Ellen. *Four Lectures on Shakespeare*, ed. Christopher St. John. London: Martin Hopkinson, 1932.

Thompson, Torri L. "Female Bodies Misbehaving: Mortification in Early Modern English Domestic Texts." In *Bodily Discursions: Genders, Representations, Technologies*, ed. Deborah S. Wilson and Christine Moneera Laennec, 19–37. New York: State University of New York Press, 1997.

Tilton, Robert. *Pocahontas: The Evolution of an American Narrative*. Cambridge: Cambridge University Press, 1994.

Tomascelli, Sylvana. "Introduction." In *Rape: An Historical and Social Enquiry*, ed. eadem and Roy Porter, 1–15. New York: Basil Blackwell, 1986.

Toner, Barbara. *The Facts of Rape*. London: Hutchinson, 1977.

Traub, Valerie. *Desire and Anxiety: Circulations of Sexuality in Shakespearean Drama*. London and New York: Routledge, 1992.

Travitsky, Betty S. "Child Murder in English Renaissance Life and Drama." *Medieval and Renaissance Drama in England* 6 (1993): 63–84.

Tucker, M. J. "The Child as Beginning and End: Fifteenth and Sixteenth Century English Childhood." In *The History of Childhood*, ed. de Mause, 229–57.

Tynan, Kenneth, ed. *"Othello": The National Theatre Production*. New York: Stein and Day, 1967.

Underdown, David. *Fire From Heaven*. London: HarperCollins-Fontana, 1993.

————. *Revel, Riot, and Rebellion: Popular Politics and Culture in England, 1603–1660*. Oxford: Clarendon Press, 1985.

————. "The Taming of the Scold: The Enforcement of Patriarchal Authority in Early Modern England." In *Order and Disorder in Early Modern England*, ed. Anthony Fletcher and John Stevenson, 116–36. Cambridge: Cambridge University Press, 1985.

Vanita, Ruth. "'Proper' Men and 'Fallen' Women: The Unprotectedness of Wives in *Othello*." *Studies in English Literature 1500–1900* 43 (1994): 341–56.

Vaughan, Virginia Mason. *"Othello": A Contextual History*. Cambridge: Cambridge University Press, 1994.

Vickers, Brian. *Appropriating Shakespeare: Contemporary Critical Quarrels*. New Haven: Yale University Press, 1993.

Vickers, Nancy. "'The blazon of sweet beauty's best': Shakespeare's *Lucrece*." In *Shakespeare and the Question of Theory*, ed. Patricia Parker and Geoffrey Hartman, 95–115. New York: Methuen, 1985.

Walker, Garthine. "Rereading Rape and Sexual Violence in Early Modern England." *Gender and History* 10 (1998): 1–25.

Walker, Greg. *The Politics of Performance in Early Renaissance Drama*. Cambridge: Cambridge University Press, 1998.

Wall, Wendy. *The Imprint of Gender: Authorship and Publication in the English Renaissance*. Ithaca: Cornell University Press, 1993.

Waller, Gary F. "Struggling into Discourse: The Emergence of Renaissance Women's Writing." In *Silent but for the Word: Tudor Women as Patrons, Translators, and Writers of Religious Works*, ed. Margaret P. Hannay, 238–56. Kent, OH: The Kent State University Press, 1985.

Waller, Marguerite. "Academic Tootsie: The Denial of Difference and the Difference It Makes." *Diacritics* 17 (1987): 2–20.

Walworth, Alan. "'To Laugh with Open Throate': Mad Lovers, Theatrical Cures, and Gendered Bodies in Jacobean Drama." In *Enacting Gender on the English Renaissance Stage*, ed. Viviana Comensoli and Anne Russell, 53–72. Urbana: University of Illinois Press, 1999.

Warner, Michael. *Fear of a Queer Planet: Queer Politics and Social Theory*. Minneapolis: University of Minnesota Press, 1993.

Wayne, Valerie. "The Dearth of the Author: Anonymity's Allies and *Swetnam the Woman-hater*." In *Maids and Mistresses, Cousins and Queens: Women's Alliances in Early Modern England*, ed. Frye and Robertson, 221–40.

———. "Historical Differences: Misogyny and *Othello*." In *The Matter of Difference: Materialist Feminist Criticism of Shakespeare*, ed. eadem, 153–180. Ithaca: Cornell University Press, 1991.

Weidemann, Heather. "Theatricality and Female Identity in Mary Wroth's *Urania*." In *Reading Mary Wroth: Representing Alternatives in Early Modern England*, ed. Naomi J. Miller and Gary Waller, 191–209. Knoxville: University of Tennessee Press, 1991.

Whigham, Frank. "Sexual and Social Mobility in *The Duchess of Malfi*." *PMLA* 100 (1985): 167–86.

Williams, Carolyn D. "'Silence, like a Lucrece knife': Shakespeare and the Meanings of Rape." *Yearbook of English Studies* 23 (1993): 93–109.

Wine, Martin L. "*Othello*": Text and Performance. London: Macmillan, 1984.

Winter, William. *Shakespeare on the Stage*. New York: Moffat, Yard and Co., 1911; repr. New York: Benjamin Blom, 1969.

Wolfthal, Diane. *Images of Rape: The "Heroic" Tradition and its Alternatives*. Cambridge: Cambridge University Press, 1999.

Woodbridge, Linda. "Palisading the Elizabethan Body Politic." *Texas Studies in*

Language and Literature 33 (1991): 327–54.

———. *Women and the English Renaissance: Literature and the Nature of Woman-kind, 1540–1620.* Urbana and Chicago: University of Illinois Press, 1984.

Woods, Susanne. "Spenser and the Problem of Woman's Rule." *Huntington Library Quarterly* 48 (1985): 141–58.

Woolf, Virginia. *A Room of One's Own.* New York: Harcourt Brace, 1929; repr. 1957.

Wrightson, Keith. *English Society 1580–1680.* New Brunswick, NJ: Rutgers University Press, 1982.

Wynne-Davies, Marion. " 'For *Worth*, Not Weakness, Makes in Use but One': Literary Dialogues in an English Renaissance Family." In *"This Double Voice": Gendered Writing in Early Modern England*, ed. Danielle Clarke and Elizabeth Clarke, 164–84. London: Macmillan, 2000.

———. " 'So Much Work': Autobiographical Narratives in the Work of Lady Mary Wroth." In *Betraying Our Selves: Forms of Self-Representations in Early Modern English Texts*, ed. Henk Dragstra, Sheila Ottway, and Helen Wilcox, 76–93. Basingstoke: Macmillan, 2000.

Yachnin, Paul. *Stage-Wrights: Shakespeare, Jonson, Middleton, and the Making of Theatrical Value.* Philadelphia: University of Pennsylvania Press, 1997.

Yates, Frances A. *Astraea: The Imperial Theme in the Sixteenth Century.* London: Routledge, 1975.

Ziegler, Georgianna. "My Lady's Chamber: Female Space, Female Chastity in Shakespeare." *Textual Practice* 4 (1990): 73–100.

Index

Notes on Contributors

Karen Bamford is Associate Professor of English at Mount Allison University in New Brunswick, Canada. She is the author of *Sexual Violence on the Jacobean Stage* (St. Martin's, 2000) and, with Alexander Leggatt, co-editor of *Approaches to Teaching English Renaissance Drama* (MLA, 2002).

Sharon Beehler is Associate Professor of English at Montana State University-Bozeman where she teaches classes in Shakespeare and Renaissance studies. She is the author of *Shakespeare and Higher Education: A Global Perspective*, co-edited with Holger Klein, and of numerous essays on Shakespeare and Shakespeare pedagogy. She is also the editor of *Quidditas*, the journal of the Rocky Mountain Medieval and Renaissance Association.

Lynda E. Boose is Professor of English at Dartmouth College where she also teaches in both Women's Studies and War and Peace Studies. She is co-editor of *Daughters and Fathers* (Johns Hopkins University Press, 1988), *Shakespeare the Movie: Popularizing the Plays on Film, TV and Video* (Routledge, 1997); and *Shakespeare the Movie II: Popularizing the Plays on Film, TV and DVD* (Routledge, 2003). She has published widely on Shakespeare and the English Renaissance, and as an offshoot of her work with international women's peace initiatives in Bosnia, has recently published "Crossing the River Drina: Bosnian Rape Camps, Turkish Impalement, and Serb Cultural Memory" in *Signs* (Winter, 2003).

Ellen M. Caldwell has taught at Vanderbilt University and Kalamazoo College, and is currently at California State University, Fullerton teaching medieval and Renaissance literature. Publications include essays in *ELR* and *American Literature*. Her research interests range from legal and medical practices to issues of female sovereignty in medieval and early modern literature.

Sara Munson Deats, Distinguished Professor of English at the University of South Florida, is former President of the Marlowe Society of America and has published over two dozen essays on Shakespeare, Marlowe, and Renaissance drama, generally in refereed journals and anthologies. She is also author of *Sex, Gender, and Desire in the Plays of Christopher Marlowe* (1997) and co-editor of *Marlowe's Empery: Expanding his Critical Contexts* (2002). As Co-Director of the Center of Applied Humanities at USF, she has co-edited four books relating literature to social issues.

Michael Hall is the Lambuth Clarke Distinguished Professor of English at Virginia Wesleyan College. His work on Shakespeare includes *The Structure of Love: Representational Patterns and Shakespeare's Love Tragedies* (1989), and he also writes on the history of sexuality and romantic love. His current project is a study of the development of parallel male and female versions of courtly love in the twelfth-century courts of William IX of Aquitaine and his granddaughter, Eleanor of Aquitaine.

Akiko Kusunoki is Professor of English at Tokyo Woman's Christian University. She has published *Rebellious Women in Drama and Society in Seventeenth-century England* (Tokyo: Misuzu, 1999), co-edited *The Gordian Knot: The Discourse of Marriage in English Renaissance Drama* (Tokyo: Shohakusha, 2002), and contributed articles on women in English Renaissance drama and society. She is currently writing a book on Shakespeare and Lady Mary Wroth.

Naomi Conn Liebler, Professor of English and University Distinguished Scholar at Montclair State University, is author of *Shakespeare's Festive Tragedy: The Ritual Foundations of Genre* (1995); co-editor of *Tragedy* (a critical anthology; 1998); and editor of *The Female Tragic Hero in English Renaissance Drama* (2002). Her current project is a critical edition of Richard Johnson's prose romance, *The Most Famous History of the Seven Champions of Christendom* (1596/97).

Jennifer A. Low is Associate Professor of English at Florida Atlantic University. Her book, *Manhood and the Duel: Masculinity in Early Modern Drama and Culture*, was published by Palgrave-Macmillan Press in 2003. Her articles have appeared in such journals as *Philological Quarterly* and *Comparative Drama*. Low is currently pursuing a project on spatiality, female sexuality, and the stage-space.

Barbara Mathieson, Associate Professor of English at Southern Oregon University, received a joint Ph.D. from Stanford University in Dramatic Literature and Humanities. Teaching interests include early modern British Literature, World

Literature, and Shakespeare. She has written on Shakespeare, Beaumont & Fletcher, and Toni Morrison, and also has developed an instructional website on scansion for students of traditional verse forms.

Edward Pechter is Adjunct Professor of English at Concordia, Montreal, and the University of Victoria British Columbia. His most recent book is *"Othello" and Interpretive Traditions* (Iowa University Press, 1999); his Norton Critical Edition of *Othello* is scheduled for publication in November 2003.

Karen Robertson teaches English and Women's Studies at Vassar College. She has published essays on Shakespeare, revenge tragedy, and women's letters. Co-editor with Susan Frye of *Maids and Mistresses, Cousins and Queens: Women's Alliances in Early Modern England*, she is finishing a book on Pocahontas among the Jacobeans.

Carolyn Sale is a postdoctoral scholar at Stanford University. Her dissertation, "Contested Acts: Legal Performances and Literary Authority in Early Modern England" investigates the shaping of the early modern author at the intersection between literature and the law. Her current research focuses on representational limits and generic innovation in Renaissance Drama.

Catherine E. Thomas received her B.A. from the University of Maryland, College Park and her M.A. from Penn State University. She is completing her Ph.D. at Penn State, where she teaches classes in composition and Shakespeare. Her dissertation explores the social and political impact of representations of poisoning in English Renaissance literature.

Wendy Wall is Professor of English Literature at Northwestern University, specializing in early modern literature and culture. Author of *The Imprint of Gender: Authorship and Publication in the English Renaissance* (Cornell University Press, 1993), and *Staging Domesticity: Household Work and English Identity in Early Modern Drama* (Cambridge University Press, 2002), she is also co-editor of the journal *Renaissance Drama*.

Linda Woodbridge, Distinguished Professor of English at Pennsylvania State University, is author of *Women and the English Renaissance: Literature and the Nature of Womankind, 1540–1620* (1984); *The Scythe of Saturn: Shakespeare and Magical Thinking* (1994); *Vagrancy, Homelessness, and English Renaissance Literature* (2001); and co-editor of *True Rites and Maimed Rites: Ritual and Anti-*

Ritual in the Age of Shakespeare (1992) and editor of *Money and the Age of Shakespeare: Essays in New Economic Criticism* (forthcoming). She is past president of the Shakespeare Association of America.